North-South Linkages
and Connections in
Continental and Diaspora
African Literatures

North-South Linkages and Connections in Continental and Diaspora African Literatures

Edited by
Edris Makward
Mark L. Lilleleht
Ahmed Saber

African Literature Association Annual Series
Volume 12
Ousseynou B. Traore, General Editor

Africa World Press, Inc.

P.O. Box 1892	P.O. Box 48
Trenton, NJ 08607	Asmara, ERITREA

Africa World Press, Inc.

P.O. Box 1892
Trenton, NJ 08607

P.O. Box 48
Asmara, ERITREA

Cover Design: Roger Dormann

Cataloging-in-Publication Data is available from Library of Congress

ISBN: 1-59221-156-9 (Cloth)
ISBN: 1-59221-157-7 (Paper.)

ISSN: 1093-2976

ANNUAL SELECTED PAPERS OF THE ALA

The 25th ALA Annual Conference was held in Fez, Morroco from March 10-13, 1999.

Series Editor: Ousseynou B. Traore

The ALA is an independent professional society founded in 1974. Membership is open to scholars, teachers and writers from every country. The ALA exists primarily to facilitate the attempts of a worldwide audience to appreciate the creative efforts of African writers and authors. The organization welcomes the participation of all who are interested in and concerned with African literature. While we hope for a constructive interaction between scholars and artists, the ALA as an organization recognizes the primacy of African peoples in shaping the future of African literature.

The ALA publishes the quarterly *ALA Bulletin* for its members. Membership is for the calendar year and available on the following terms (US funds): African students studying in Africa, $5; Income under $15,000, $15; from $15,000 to $35,000, $30; over $35,000, $60 and above $50,000, $80. For membership information, back issues of the *ALA bulletin* and conference papers contact Robert Cancel, ALA Treasurer, Dept. of Lit., 0410, Univ. of Calif. At San Diego, 9500 Gilman Drive, La Jolla CA 92093 (rcancel@ucsd.edu). ALA Headquarters: JoAnne Cornwell, Director, Africana Studies, San Diego State University, 55000 Campanille Drive, San Diego, CA 92182-8132; Tel: 619-594-5305; Fax: 619-594-8006; jcornwel@mail.sdsu.edu.

Contents

Contents

II. "Women Warriors": Women Writers . . .

Contents

Contents

III. Linguistic and Cultural Connections Across the Boundaries

Contents

IV. Literary and Political Developments

Contents

Introduction

Edris Makward
Mark L. Lilleleht
Ahmed Saber

The 25th ALA Annual Conference was held in Fez, Morocco, on March 10-13,1999. This was our third venue on African soil, after Dakar (1989) and Accra (1994). The Fez meeting was equally a landmark in its own right, as it was bringing together, for the first time, a large number of scholars and creative writers and artists from Northern Africa and their counterparts from Sub-Saharan Africa. The stimulating theme of the Conference, *North-South Linkages and Connections in Continental and Diaspora African Literatures*, and the very special location, in the ancient imperial capital city of Fez, attracted some six hundred distinguished participants from North America, Europe, Latin America, the Caribbean and, above all, from many parts of the African continent. There was also a very strong contingent of participants from Morocco and the Maghribi sub-region. After a plenary opening session in the stately Ballroom of the Jnan Palace Hotel attended by over 700 participants and guests, the three-day Conference included some 80 concurrent panels, 5 plenary sessions, 5 round tables and a very stimulating film program professionally and creatively animated by Charles Sugnet showing about 20 highly representative African films of great quality and interest. From all accounts, and from the enormously difficult task of the editors in choosing from a large body of high quality papers, the Fez Conference translated into a highly inspiring and stimulating dialogue between two literary and cultural areas that have often been artificially compartmentalized. The tone and scope of this dialogue were eloquently set from the outset by one of our keynote speakers, former UNESCO

Director-General Amadou Mahtar M'Bow, in his historically sound overview of North-South connections over the centuries through the Sahara desert. His closing remarks continue to ring in our ears, as an accurate reminder of the goals and aspirations of our association which were indeed the central focus of the discussions that led to the founding of our Association at the annual meeting of the ASA (African Studies Association) in Chicago, some 28 years ago:

> The members of the ALA are, to a great extent, the guardians of our literary memory: as creative writers, they enrich it with their works; as educators, they are its broadcasters among the younger generations.

The tone set by Mr. M'Bow was picked up by our other keynote speaker and recipient of the Fonlon-Nichols Prize, the Moroccan poet Abdellatif Laâbi, who shared with us his very personal thoughts about the meaning of writing as "above all, an act of dignity in the face of the human comedy" and his deep love of his city of Fez. Laâbi's two remarkable offerings, "Littérature et éthique" [Literature and Ethics] and "Un continent appelé Fès" [A Continent Called Fez] are included in this selection. Laâbi expressed his candid surprise and joy in receiving the Fonlon-Nichols Prize by reiterating his staunch belief and adherence to the concept of writing that functions above all according to an ethic, transmitting the values of that ethic and insisting that the writer be in harmony with its demands at all levels, including the social and the intellectual.

Another keynote speaker of our memorable Fez Conference was the Senegalese novelist Boubacar Boris Diop, author of an impressive number of critically appraised novels, plays and film scripts in French and who announced the forthcoming appearance of his first novel in his native language, Wolof, *Doomi golo* [Monkey's Child]. Diop revisited in his well attended keynote address, a topic that is well known among ALA members, i.e. the advocacy of writing in one's own native tongue as opposed to writing exclusively in the former colonizer's. Diop added however his own passionate plea for the merits of writing in one's own language by, on the one hand, disclosing all the limitations that confront the Francophone African writer writing in the former colonizer's language, and on the other, stating honestly the apparent greater pleasure and excitement in experimenting in Wolof, his mother tongue:

> At this very moment in my existence, only the Wolof language will allow me to experiment beyond my own limits. I can no longer find elsewhere the happiness that it bestows upon me. When I compare my earlier novels to *Doomi golo* [Monkey's Child], I realize that "the words of France"—in Léon Laleau's words—were helping as much as they were condemning me to keep my mouth shut or to only stutter wretchedly. Like other African writers, I have often had the riling feeling that there is always a little something that refuses to be allowed out in the foreign language. The truth is—and I always seem to have a malicious pleasure in reminding people—that I do not speak French on a daily basis. In the Senegalese society in which I live, it would not make much sense. French is for me a ceremonial language, my Sunday language so to speak.

It goes without saying that this honest statement of Boris Diop did take some of our colleagues in the audience by surprise, to say the least. We do believe, on a second reading, that the language debate is far from closed and that Boris Diop's points presented in his address deserve some additional attention. Christiane Ndiaye's avowed deep and honestly expressed disappointment, in the light of Diop's statements, is, in our view, a clear indication that the debate on language is still topical, and far from over. Indeed, Ndiaye did not mince her words, in her ALA 1999 report which appeared in the Spring 1999 (Vol 25 No 2) *ALA Bulletin* when she summarized them as "frankly heart-breaking" particularly coming from "the author of four novels of delightful creativity":

> What did our ears pick up? That the French language belongs to French culture and that it is not up to Africans who do not master it, to transform it, to "revolutionize it."

One of the cultural highlights of the Fez Conference was, without doubt, the performance on Friday night, March 12, of South African Jane Taylor's highly challenging play *Ubu and the Truth Commission* based on the historic post-Apartheid Truth and Reconciliation Commission. This excellently executed dramatized reading under the highly creative direction and leadership of the author herself was skillfully performed by ALA members who volunteered the very day of the conference opening, on Thursday morning, March 11, and started rehearsing with Jane that morning. The cast included Jane Taylor, Folabo Ajayi-Soyinka, Ada Azodo, Charlie Cantalupo, Jane Hale and others. One other artistic component of the Fez Conference that was highly appreciated by all participants and by our Moroccan hosts and guests, was the presence and performances at various venues of excellent Gambian Griot and Master Kora player, Al-Haji Papa Susso, now a frequent feature of ALA and ASA Conferences. We must also mention here the Preview screening of Moroccan filmmaker Farida Ben Lyazid's latest film, *Keid Ensa* [The Tricks Women Play] presented by the director herself, on Thursday, March 11, and the high quality choice of films from all the regions of Africa selected and shown by Charles Sugnet, throughout the duration of the Conference. Lastly, as a number of poets from Africa and from the Diaspora attended and participated actively in several poetry reading sessions during the Conference. We are including samples of their work at the end of each section of our volume.

As indicated earlier in, there were many high quality papers and presentations among the four-hundred or so programmed at the Fez Conference. This is to say that it was definitely not an easy task to select a reasonable number of papers for this volume, among the sixty or so corrected contributions we received. We therefore wish to apologize whole-heartedly to all those who sent us their papers and whose contributions we were not able to include in this selection, primarily because of limited space. It was not easy either to divide the 36 papers finally retained, into balanced sections, as some of the papers could quite appropriately have been included under more than one heading. We have divided these 36 papers into three sections following the opening section grouping together the keynote addresses.

The first section (II) is entitled "Women Warriors: Women in African and Diaspora Writings" and opens with Elisabeth Bekers' incisive analysis of two incarcerated women characters presented by Egyptian Nawal el Saadawi and Camerounian Calixthe Beyala. This section includes also Janice Spleth's powerful analysis of Driss Chraïbi's *Mother Comes of Age*, a remarkable study of the emancipation of a traditional Maghribi woman, wife and mother who, through her own self-assertion, and the help of her sons, succeeds in resisting authoritative vices in any form. Sally-Ann Murray shows convincingly how Zimbabwean Tsitsi Dangarembga deals with cultural traumas, alienations and neuroses resulting from traditional patriarchy and the encroaching new Western influenced consumerism, and how they lead to a marked shift in people's behaviors and subjectivities. In another sample from this multifaceted chapter, Touria Khannous gives a very sensitive analysis of several recent texts of Algerian writer Assia Djebar including *Vaste est la prison* (1995) and *Le blanc de l'Algérie* (1995), with an emphasis on the importance of remembering the victims of the current Algerian tragedy. Lastly, Fatima Bouzenirh's comparative piece on Leïla Abouzeid's *Year of the Elephant* and Buchi Emecheta's *Destination Biafra* is a very perceptive exploration of the struggle of two African women involved in nation-building in two African contexts that are far apart in many ways, but still have many essential points in common.

The second section (III) or, "Linguistic, Cultural and Historical Connections Across Boundaries," groups together some very challenging and stimulating essays on topics as diverse as linguist and political historian Pathé Diagne's audacious account of the intimate historical, linguistic and intellectual connections and linkages in past centuries, between different parts of the African continent as well as between Africa and the rest of the world and the rigorous analysis of John Miles' Afrikaans text, *Kroniek uit doofpot* [A Deafening Silence] by H.P. van Coller through intertextuality. North-South linguistic and literary linkages are also explored authoritatively by Aidan Southall and Elena Bertoncini. Gudrun Grabher's insightful comparison of Hemingway's short story "The Snows of Kilimanjaro" with a work by a familiar world figure whose name would evoke more readily political or polemical debate rather than literary discussion, namely, Muammar Qaddafi's *Death*, is a journey into the age-old universal philosophical concern with death. Abdelmouneim Bounou's piece on the image of Morocco in 19th and 20th century Spanish travel narratives reveals an initial vision characterized by a highly prejudiced perception of a world of mystery, treachery, nostalgia and pride. Eileen M. Ketchum examines with remarkable insight, *écriture féminine* or feminine writing in the context of 17th century and 20th century Francophone fiction, and concludes that "while the political and geographic situations may change, the need remains for women to discover and express their individuality through a continually evolving model of *écriture féminine*." One final contribution from this section is Christine Drake's very original approach in positing and exploring her contention that there are definite connections between geography and historical and literary developments, in a given country. She chooses Senegal and such writers as Senghor, Mariama Bâ, Ousmane Sembène, Hamidou Kane, Birago Diop and the like to illustrate her point.

The third and last section (IV) or, "Literary and Political Developments and Approaches," opens with Taïeb Belghazi's very informative contribution on "Identity Politics in Morocco" in which the author surveys a variety of objections to the use of "Identity Politics" in the context of Morocco and comes to the conclusion that "Identities are not simple allegiances to a place, or . . . a property, we ought to realize that they are the stake of power struggle." For his part, Jilali El Koudia draws a broad outline of the development of the short story genre in Morocco, starting in the early forties, evolving and shifting its focus from external to internal reality, from object to subject, from traditional harmony to apparent disruption, and a search for a new equilibrium. Bernth Lindfors's statistical account and discussion of the amount of Anglophone African literary criticism leads him to conclude that scholars of African literature in English "need to broaden their cultural horizons by exposing themselves to more give and take with their African colleagues." Claire Griffiths's well researched paper on "Gender, Education and Literary Output in Francophone West Africa" is highly enlightening with regard to the prevailing concern about the issue of educational access and progress. She concludes without any doubt whatsoever that socio-political environment and educational access are highly salient factors for the production of literature by women. She quotes a prominent Senegalese sociologist and advocate of women's rights confirming her own findings: "the key to developing equity in our society is women's participation in education and politics." We close with

Lucy McNeece's analysis of Mohammed Berrada's *Le jeu de l'oubli* [The Game of Forgetting] within the context of post-colonial considerations. McNeece sees Berrada's text as a celebration of narrative fiction and "an experiment in forms that becomes an instrument for the awakening of a genuinely social, historical, and ethical consciousness."

The Cannibal Reading Me

Abdellatif Laâbi
(Translated by *Victor Reinking* and *Edris Makward*)

There is a cannibal reading me
A fiercely intelligent reader
a dream reader
He doesn't let a word go by
without measuring its weight in blood
He even picks up the commas
to find the tasty bits
He knows that the page vibrates
with a splendid breathing
And the excitement that makes the
prey
enticing and submissive
He waits for a sign of fatigue
falling over my face
like a sacrificial mask
He seeks the weak spot
before pouncing:
the unnecessary adjective
the inexcusable repetition
There is a cannibal who reads me
to feed himself.

I. Keynote Addresses

Quelques réflexions relatives aux relations culturelles et littéraires transsahariennes et à ces mêmes relations entre le continent et les diasporas africaines à travers l'Océan Atlantique

Amadou Mahtar M'Bow

Avant de vous livrer, sur la demande des organisateurs, ces "Quelques réflexions relatives aux relations culturelles et littéraires transsahariennes et à ces mêmes relations entre le continent et les diasporas africaines à travers l'Océan Atlantique," je voudrais exprimer mes vifs remerciements à l'African Literature Association, et plus particulièrement à Messieurs Edris Makward et Ahmed Saber, pour l'invitation qu'ils nous ont adressée à participer à son 25ème Congrès annuel. Nous tenons aussi à associer à ces remerciements tous ceux qui nous reçoivent dans cette ville de Fès si chère à nos coeurs. Nul lieu n'était, sans doute, plus indiqué pour tenir ce Congrès que cette cité de l'art, du savoir et de la foi, qui s'enorgueillit d'avoir été un des plus importants carrefours intellectuels, grâce notamment à sa vieille université—la Quaraouyine—dont le rayonnement s'est étendu, des siècles durant, de l'Andalousie musulmane aux confins de la zone sahélo-soudanienne ouestafricaine.

Nous avons été d'autant plus sensibles à votre invitation que le thème de ce Congrès nous touche au plus profond de nous-mêmes, mon spouse et moi. Appartenant l'un à l'Afrique, l'autre à la Diaspora africaine d'outre Atlantique, notre vie commune s'est confondue, d'une part avec celle de l'Afrique dans ses luttes émancipatrices, d'autre part avec celle des communautés africaines, que des circonstances tragiques ont fait naître de l'autre côté de l'Atlantique, dans leur quête de justice. Cette vie commune nous à permis de vérifier, jour après jour, combien sont profondes les racines qui nous unissent, et combien ont été douloureuses les épreuves de l'arrachement qui, durant plus de trois siècles de malheurs, nous ont tenus séparés les uns des autres.

L'histoire de cet arrachement, celle des facteurs qui l'ont déterminé et des conséquences qui en ont résultées, sont autant de fondements de notre commun patrimoine historique; elle est aussi une part non moins importante de la mémoire collective de l'humanité. Aussi, devons nous, qui que nous soyons, d'où que nous venions, entretenir cette mémoire, l'enrichir et la transmettre de génération en génération sans oublier ce qu'elle comporte de douleurs et d'injustices, mais aussi de luttes acharnées pour la liberté, pour la justice et pour le respect de la dignité des individus, qui sont autant d'aspirations naturelles de tout être humain.

Peu de peuples ont, en effet, souffert ce que les nôtres ont souffert sur une si longue durée. Peu d'entre eux ont connu tant d'injustices accumulées; tant d'humiliations sans fin, tant de travail harassant stimulé par le fouet du commandeur et qui n'a d'autre limites que le bon vouloir de celui qui l'ordonne. Il en à été ainsi de l'esclavage comme du travail forcé qui lui à succédé sur le continent pendant l'ère coloniale.

Mais la volonté de survivre à toutes les épreuves a toujours été plus forte. Le besoin vital d'être, et de se perpétuer, comme individu et comme collectivité, à été permanent. Il s'est manifesté notamment, par la mobilisation constante des énergies et des intelligences pour sauver l'esprit, réjouir le corps et enchanter le coeur, à travers des formes d'expression culturelle puisées dans l'héritage africain, afin d'atténuer les effets de la servitude.

Cette faculté de résister aux épreuves, cette volonté de les transcender spirituellement, est assurément une des caractéristiques essentielles des cultures africaines. Le refus du désespoir face aux situations les plus désespérantes est le plus grand hymne que l'on puisse rendre à la vie; et il est une des constantes de toutes les cultures du continent.

La singularité de ces cultures, c'est en effet de partager un fonds commun de valeurs sociales et humaines, de postuler une harmonie de l'homme et de son environnement, dans tout acte de la vie, de donner à l'art et à l'expression artistique des finalités identiques que l'on retrouve à quelques nuances près, un peu partout dans le continent, de même que dans la Diaspora, malgré les turbulences de l'histoire et de la longue et tragique séparation.

Le contexte historique et le cadre géographique dans lesquels ont évolué les sociétés africaines ne sont, sans doute, pas étrangers à l'existence de ces caractéristiques communes.

L'histoire des peuples africains à été, en effet, pendant des siècles, celle de brassages continuels de populations à la faveur des migrations intenes, rendues plus aisées qu'ailleurs par les conditions géographiques. Il n'y a guère de peuple africain dont les traditions ne révèlent cette mobilité. L'espace à été longtemps une donnée transitoire, l'existence du groupe en tant qu'entité autonome étant l'element permanent se manifestant à travers la continuité de la chaîne des générations. C'est sans doute pourquoi notre vision de l'histoire à tendance à être plus généalogique que spatiale. On retrace plus volontiers le passé d'un peuple par l'évocation des générations qui se sont succédées, où qu'elles aient pu vivre, qu'en se référant à l'espace géographique qui lui à servi de cadre de vie.

La première grande migration, qui fut, sans doute, le point de départ des mouvements d'amplitudes diverses, est sans conteste celui que provoqua l'assèchement du Sahara. Les peuples qui vivaient, dans le Sahara humide et qui avaient accompli une des premières grandes révolutions technologiques que connut l'humanité, celle du néolithique, ont dû alors se replier, les uns au Nord, les autres dans la vallée du Nil, à l'Est, d'autres au Sud, dans l'Afrique subsaharienne actuelle, alors que d'autres encore demeuraient dans les oasis où la vie était encore possible, servant ainsi d'indispensables relais dans les relations transsahariennes.

On sait comment est ainsi née la brillante civilisation égyptienne, civilisation authentiquement africaine qui à été l'inspiratrice de la Grèce antique, elle même mère de la civilisation romaine dont se réclame l'Occident.

Dans la partie orientale du continent, l'axe nilotique à toujours été la voie transsaharienne principale qui unira sans solution de continuité le Nord au Sud pendant les différentes périodes de l'histoire. De nouvelles civilisations y prirent naissance parmi lesquelles on peut citer celles de Méroé, de Napata, d'Axoum et, plus au Sud, du Monomotapa et des grandes ruines du Zimbabwe qui gardent encore beaucoup de leurs mystères.

De l'Egypte aux régions nilotiques du Sud semble s'être maintenue sans discontinuité des relations culturelles comme celles qui marquent encore l'époque Byzantine. C'est au Patriarcat d'Alexandrie que se rattachent, en effet, les églises coptes qui naissent en Nubie et en Abyssinie, témoignant ainsi de l'existence d'un même espace religieux et culturel qui fait fi de la barrière désertique.

C'est encore de l'Egypte, à partir du 7ème siècle, que l'islam, relayant le christianisme, et contournant l'Abyssinie, gagne les régions de l'Afrique orientale. A l'apport égyptien s'ajoutent d'autres qui arrivent de la péninsule arabique par la voie côtière, et de l'Asie à travers l'Océan Indien. Les cultures africaines peuvent ainsi s'enrichir de nouveaux éléments: des cités florissantes s'édifient comme celles de Sofala, de Kilwa, de Malindi. La littérature, qu'elle soit orale ou écrite, prend un essor nouveau avec l'utilisation, soit de l'Arabe, soit du Swahili, la langue principale de communication dont quelques uns des Etats issus des indépendances, ont fait leur langue officielle.

A la fin du XVème siècle, l'arrivée des Portugais sur les côtes de l'Afrique orientale après celles de l'Afrique occidentale, bouleverse progressivement les données politiques, économiques et culturelles de la région.

L'institution de la traite des esclaves, à la suite de l'installation des Espagnols et des Portugais sur le continent américain, fait basculer toute l'Afrique dans la tragédie. Le processus normal d'évolution est brutalement interrompu. Le Royaume du Kongo, sur le versant Atlantique de l'Afrique au Sud de l'Equateur, fut une des premières victimes du processus de désintégration des états africains dont certains avaient atteint un stade de développement qui n'avait rien à envier à celui de nombreux pays européens, sauf qu'ils n'avaient pas d'armes à feu pour pouvoir assurer efficacement leur défense contre les déprédateurs venus de l'extérieur.

Par ailleurs, nous savons, par la tradition orale, que les migrations internes se sont poursuivies, quelquefois suscitées par le besoin d'échapper à la chasse à l'homme instituée par les négriers, provoquant ainsi d'autres brassages culturels dont l'ampleur et la portée exacte sont loin d'être élucidées.

Avec le partage du continent et la colonisation à partir du XIXème siècle, les échanges culturels et littéraires sont désormais soumis, dans une très large mesure, aux contraintes imposées par les puissances coloniales qui érigent des frontières, établissent des barrières douanières et des contrôles sur les mouvements des hommes et des idées, ce que l'Afrique n'avait jamais connu auparavant.

Quant aux relations entre le Maghreb et l'Afrique subsaharienne occidentale et centrale, elles paraissent avoir été assurées continûment malgré la désertification du Sahara, avec plus ou moins de régularité selon les époques.

Avec l'islamisation, ces relations s'amplifient. C'est dès la fin du VIIème siècle, à partir du Fezzan, et du VIIIème siécle à partir du Maghreb, que l'islam pénètre en Afrique subsaharienne, non par voie de conquête, mais par adhésion spontanée. C'est avec l'empire du Ghana, né pense t-on, au IVme siècle, et qui, au Xème siècle s'étendait sur la grande partie de la zone sahélo-soudanienne comprise entre le Sahara et les fleuves Sénégal et Niger, que l'islam commence à s'implanter dans cette région par la conversion des élites dirigeantes d'abord, puis, par celle des masses de plus en plus nombreuses. En 1076, sa capitale, Kumbi est détruite par les Al-Morabitin (les Almoravides) de Yahia Ibn Ibrahim et de Abdallah Ibn Yassin.

L'émergence des Almoravides ouvre une ère nouvelle dans les relations entre le Nord et le Sud. En effet, ceux-ci érigent le premier Etat transsaharien connu, s'étendant des rives du Sénégal, au Sud, jusqu'en Andalousie, au Nord, avec pour centre le Maroc et pour capitale Marrakech. Ainsi naît un nouvel espace culturel et religieux qui, même après la disparition des Almoravides, ne cessera de prendre de l'importance, s'affirmant siècle après siècle comme un pôle essentiel de l'islam subsaharien.

Cet espace s'imbrique, au fil du temps, avec l'ensemble islamique qui s'étend de l'Indus à L'Est, à la mer Méditerranée et à l'Océan Atlantique à l'ouest, et de la mer Rouge au Nord à Madagascar au Sud, et de l'Afrique septentrionale aux confins de la zone sahélo-soudanienne de l'Afrique subsaharienne. Dans cet espace ouvert, circulent les hommes, les biens, les idées et le savoir, grâce à l'utilisation d'une langue commune: l'arabe. Chacun peut s'enrichir ainsi des expériences des autres et fortifier sa foi au contact des érudits et des penseurs venus d'horizons les plus divers.

Mais c'est avec l'Empire du Mali (XIIIème-XVIème siècle), des Songhay (XIIème- XVIème siècle), et de ceux du Kanem, du Bornou et de l'hinterland Nigérian que les échanges culturels et littéraires s'amplifient et prennent un caractère quasi permanent.

Contrairement à l'Afrique orientale, le Christianisme n'a pas franchi le Sahara Occidental; seules existeront en Afrique Occidentale les religions africaines traditionnelles jusqu'à la pénétration de l'Islam.

Avec l'Islam les relations intérieures et extérieures se développent; la langue arabe se répand donnant naissance à une littérature riche et abondante; des écoles, des universités se multiplient, favorisées par les dirigeants politiques qui, souvent, ramènent du pèlerinage à la Mecque, des érudits de renom pour y enseigner et y poursuivre leurs recherches. Tombouctou et Djenné se distinguent par la qualité de leurs institutions.

Au Sénégal, par exemple, le foyer intellectuel de Pire au Nord de Dakar, qui subsistera jusqu'à la fin du XIXème siècle, formera de nombreux érudits parmi lesquels figurent les initiateurs de la première revolution islamique qui donna naissance, vers la fin du XVIIIème siècle, à la République Théocratique du Fouta dans la moyenne vallée du fleuve Sénégal avec l'imam Abdel Kader, le premier dirigeant, ainsi que Amadou Hamet Bâ, fondateur de Woro Mahdiyou, sur la vallée du Sénégal, El Haj Omar Tall Foutiyou, etc.

L'âge d'or des relations culturelles et littéraires transsahariennes est marqué par des échanges fructueux et par l'émergence en Afrique Subsaharienne d'érudits dont les oeuvres font autorité dans les pays du Maghreb.

Le plus connu d'entre eux fut incontestablement Ahmed Baba né le 2 octobre 1556 à Tombouctou. Il y possédait une bibliothèque contenant 1600 ouvrages au moment de la prise de la ville en 1591 par l'armée marocaine envoyée par le sultan saadien Moulay Ahmed Mansour surnommé le Doré, et conduite par Djouder.

Cette expédition qui mit fin à l'Empire de Gao à la bataille de Tondibi qui eut lieu, pense-t-on, le 2 avril 1591, permettra au Maroc d'étendre pour un temps sa souveraineté sur la région sahelo-soudanienne, donnant ainsi naissance à un nouvel espace politique transsaharien dont le souvenir subsistera pendant longtemps dans la mémoire des habitants de Tombouctou.

Ahmed Baba, exilé à Marrakech, y occupera une chaire d'enseignement public à la demande des oulémas auprès desquels il jouissait d'une grande estime pour son érudition et pour ses qualités humaines. Après la disparition de Moulay Ahmed Mansour, il revint à Tombouctou où il mourut le 22 avril 1627.

Si l'irruption des Portugais sur les côtes africaines au Sud du Sahara, au milieu du XVème siècle eut pour effet de détoumer une part de plus en plus importante du commerce transsaharien vers les régions côtières, les relations culturelles et littéraires n'en demeurèrent pas moins actives. Peu à peu, la langue arabe s'affirme comme langue écrite. À l'instar de Ahmed Baba d'autres érudits publient leurs oeuvres en langue arabe, ou dans les langues africaines en utilisant les caractères arabes.

Le XIXème siécle, avant comme après le partage colonial et le XXème siécle à la faveur du renouveau islamique, sont riches en ceuvres diverses tant poétiques que religieuses. Mais nombre de ces ceuvres demeurent encore inédites malgré les efforts déployés par diverses institutions pour en assurer la traduction et la diffusion dans les langues européennes. Il faut noter, par ailleurs, que la plupart des traités conclus avec les souverains africains par les puissances européennes étaient rédigés en arabe. La tradition orale, elle aussi, recèle de richesses encore insuffisamment explorées. Cette mémoire irremplaçable du passé africain est doublement menacée, d'une part par la disparition des personnes âgées qui en étaient les détentrices les plus avisées et par le processus de modernisation qui éloigne les jeunes générations des sources vives de la tradition; d'autre part par les distorsions dont elle peut être l'objet. Certains dirigeants actuels ont, en effet, tendance à faire manipuler les traditions anciennes de manière à se donner un prestige familial usurpé pour servir leurs ambitions actuelles.

Avec la conquête coloniale, à la fin du XIX siècle, s'instaurent de nouveaux systèmes éducatifs inspirés de ceux des puissances coloniales, et utilisant les langues des colonisateurs. La scolarisation dans les écoles coloniales fait naître progressivement de nouvelles formes d'expression littéraire dans les langues européennes. Cette littérature, peu abondante pendant la période coloniale, a connu, avec les indépendances, la multiplication des écoles et l'émergence d'une élite intellectuelle formée dans les universités, un développement considerable. Mais elle demeure encore limitée et souffre d'une diffusion insuffisante à cause de l'analphabétisme qui est encore trés répandu et de la pauvreté qui limite l'achat de livres.

Avec les nouvelles technologies de l'information et l'apparition du web une ère nouvelle s'ouvre quant à l'accroissement des possibilités d'échange entre les différentes parties de l'Afrique et entre l'Afrique, prise dans son ensemble et les Diasporas d'outre Atlantique. Toutefois, ces nouveaux instruments ne sont accessibles, pour le moment, qu'à une petite élite.

Les barrières linguistiques constituent un autre obstacle aux échanges littéraires. Les ouvrages publiés dans les langues des auteurs ne sont accessibles généralement, tant à l'intérieur du continent que dans les Diasporas, qu'à ceux qui connaissent ces langues.

En ce qui conceme les relations littéraires et culturelles entre l'Afrique et les diasporas d'outre atlantique, une observation s'impose. Pendant toute la période de l'esclavage, ces relations étaient impensables. Les Africains transportés en Amérique perdaient tout contact avec l'Afrique, par la volonté de leurs bourreaux et du fait de leur condition sociale et juridique. Ils étaient placés dans des situations qui rendaient impossibles tout épanouissement intellectuel et toute possibilité d'entreprendre quelque création que ce soit. Le seul moyen de conserver leur mémoire l'était par la voie orale, que plusieurs d'entre eux ont su utiliser, comme l'atteste notamment Alex Haley dans *Roots* [Racines]. Ceux d'entre eux qui savaient lire et écrire ne pouvaient guère s'exprimer sans risquer les plus graves punitions; certains n'ont pu le faire qu'exceptionnellement, en utilisant essentiellement la langue arabe dans laquelle ont été écrits les premiers textes émanant de la diaspora africaine aux Etats Unis.

Parmi ceux dont les textes ont été connus, je voudrais citer: Job Ibn Salomon Jallow (Diop Ibn Souleymane Diallo) originaire du Bundu dans le Sénégal oriental qui, capturé en Gambie en 1730 et vendu dans le Maryland en 1731, put retourner en Afrique en 1734; Ibrahim Abdel Rahman, d'ethnie Peule (Fulani) originaire de Timbo, dans le Fouta Djallon, en République actuelle de Guinée, qui à été esclave à Natchez, dans le Mississipi de 1800 à 1818 et qui savait écrire en Arabe et en Anglais; Oumar Ibn Said, également Peul (Fulani) originaire du Sénégal, qui, vendu comme esclave en 1807 en Caroline du Sud, s'échappe en 1810 pour vivre en Caroline du Nord. Des exemples de leurs écrits ont été reproduits dans une petite brochure publiée par Nashid Ali Muhammad, sous le titre *Muslims in America—Seven Centuries of History (1312-1998)*.

La riche littérature politique surgie en Haïti pendant la période révolutionnaire (1792-1804), n'a eu aucune diffusion en Afrique au cours du XIXème siécle; frappée d'ostracisme par le système colonial, elle demeure encore peu connue de nos jours.

Toutefois, dans le domaine de la création artistique, et en dépit des contraintes qui leur étaient imposées et des interdits de toutes sortes qui les frappaient, les Africains, soumis à la servitude en Amérique, ont pu faire preuve de capacités exceptionnelles. Ils ont pu recréer de nouvelles communautés culturelles vivantes d'essence africaine. Ainsi, ont-ils pu renouveler certaines formes d'expression artistique, et enrichir celles héritées de l'Afrique, d'éléments essentiels, au point de provoquer une véritable révolution dans les domaines de la musique et de la danse contemporaines. Il n'a y pas dans le monde, un auditorium où n'ait pas retenti une musique d'inspiration africano-américaine, une salle où ne se soient pas produites des danses dont les racines sont africaines-américaines.

Les créateurs de la Diaspora ont pu ainsi influencer les créateurs du continent qui a connu depuis les indépendances, l'explosion de la créativité artistique dans tous les domaines, et en particulier dans celui de la musique, devenue un véritable phénomène culturel.

Sur le plan littéraire, et malgré la censure imposée par les puissances coloniales, et le contrôle strict institué sur la circulation des livres, certaines oeuvres de leaders de la Diaspora d'outre Atlantique, comme W.E.B. DuBois, Marcus Garvey, Booker T.Washington, ont pu être introduites, clandestinement, par des navigateurs, surtout sénégalais dont les bateaux fréquentaient assidûment le port de New York. Ces écrits ont pu influencer, bien avant la seconde guerre mondiale, une partie de l'élite africaine montante, et la gagner aux idées panafricanistes. Après la seconde guerre mondiale, les auteurs de la Diaspora africaine des Etats Unis et des Antilles ont progressivement été à la portée des Africains étudiant en Amérique et en Europe et des africains demeurant dans le continent. Parmi les Antillais les mieux appréciés dans l'aire Francophone furent, après René Maran, Léon Gontran Damas et surtout Aimé Césaire.

Le *Cahier d'un retour au pays natal* de celui-ci a été un des premiers témoignages, et des plus denses, de l'identité commune des peuples de la Diaspora outre-Atlantique et de ceux de l'Afrique.

Dans la diffusion des oeuvres d'Africains et de la Diaspora, et dans le renforcement des relations culturelles et littéraires entre la Diaspora et l'Afrique, une mention spéciale doit être faite de l'initiative prise par feu Alioune Diop de créer au lendemain de la deuxième guerre mondiale la "Société Africaine de culture" et les éditions *Présence Africaine*. Grâce à l'action de Alioune Diop, les intellectuels de part et d'autre de l'Océan Atlantique ont pu s'apprécier mutuellement. Les oeuvres de nombreux écrivains de la Diaspora ont été alors diffusées en Europe et en Afrique, soit dans les langues originales, soit dans des traductions en langue française. Un hommage particulier doit être rendu à sa mémoire et à son oeuvre. Et, je voudrais à présent conclure, en remerciant une fois encore l'ALA de son invitation. Les membres de l'ALA sont dans une large mesure les garants de la conservation de la mémoire: créateurs, ils enrichissent de leurs oeuvres; éducateurs, ils en sont les diffuseurs auprès des jeunes générations. Sans leur action ne pourrait être maintenue la nécessaire continuité entre les générations d'hier, celles d'aujourd'hui et de demain.

Reflections on the Trans-Saharan Cultural and Literary Relations and the Same Relations Between the Continent and the African Diasporas Across the Atlantic Ocean

Amadou Mahtar M'Bow
(Translated by *Edris Makward*)

Before delivering, on request from the organizers, these "Reflections on the Trans-Saharan Cultural and Literary Relations and the Same Relations Between the Continent and the African Diasporas Across the Atlantic Ocean," I would like to express my heart-felt thanks to the African Literature Association, and more specifically to Messrs. Edris Makward and Ahmed Saber, for inviting me to participate in this 25th Annual ALA Conference. I also want to associate in these thanks all those who have welcomed us in this city of Fez so dear to our hearts. No other city, without doubt, was better suited to host this Conference than this city of the Arts, of Learning and of Faith, which is proud of having been one of the most important intellectual cross-roads, thanks in particular to its old University—The Quaraouyine University—whose radiance extended for centuries, from Muslim Andalusia to the confines of Sahelo-Sudanese West Africa.

I have been all the more responsive to your invitation as the theme of this Conference touches us very deeply, my wife and me. As one of us belongs to Africa, and the other to the transatlantic African diaspora, our life together has been marked, on the one hand, with that of Africa in her struggles for emancipation, and on the other, with the lives of African communities that tragic circumstances have caused to be born on the other side of the Atlantic, in their quest for justice. This life together has allowed us to confirm, on a daily basis, the depth of the roots that unify us, and how painful the trials of the uprooting which, for more than three centuries, have kept us separated from one another.

The story of this uprooting, the stories of the factors that brought it about and of the consequences which resulted from it are part of our common historical heritage; it is also a very important part of the collective memory of humanity. Likewise, we must all, regardless of who we are, of where we come from, keep alive this memory, enrich it and transmit it from generation to generation without forgetting the weight of pain and injustice it carries, but also the fierce struggles for liberty, for justice and for the respect of the dignity of the individual which are all natural aspirations of every human being.

Few peoples of this world have indeed suffered what our peoples have suffered for so long. Few of them have known so many accumulated injustices, so many endless humiliations, so much back-breaking toil stimulated by the whip of the overseer, which knows no limit but the whimsical will of the person who gives the order. This was the reality of slavery and of the forced labor which took its place during the colonial era.

But the will to survive all trials has always been stronger. The vital need to be and to endure, as individuals and as a collectivity, has been a permanent element of our societies. This need has been expressed, in particular, through the constant mobilization of energies and intelligences in order to save the spirit, to please the body and enchant the heart, through forms of cultural expression drawn from the African heritage in order to mitigate the effects of servitude.

This capacity to resist the trials, this will to transcend them spiritually is certainly one of the cardinal characteristics of African cultures. The refusal to submit to despair in the face of the most despairing realities is the greatest hymn to life; and it has been a constant element of the fabric of all the cultures of the continent.

The singularity of these cultures is indeed that they share a common stock of social and human values, that they assume a harmony of man and his environment in all acts of life, that they give to art and artistic expression identical finalities that are found with only a few slight differences in different parts of the continent and in the diaspora, despite the turbulence of history and of the long and tragic separation.

The historical context and the geographic environment in which African societies have evolved are, without doubt, part of the reason for the existence of these common characteristics. The history of African peoples has been, as a matter of fact, for centuries, that of continual mixing of populations by means of internal migrations made much easier than elsewhere because of the geographic conditions.

There is no African people whose traditions do not reveal this mobility. Space has been, for a long time, a transitory element, the existence of the group as an autonomous entity being the permanent reality manifesting itself through the continuity of the chain of generations. That is doubtless why our vision of history tends to be more genealogical than spatial. We recount more willingly the past of a people through the evocation of the generations that succeeded one another, regardless of their location, rather than emphasize the geographic space where they had elected to live.

The first great migration which was, without doubt, the point of departure of movements of diverse amplitudes, is unquestionably the one that was brought about by the drying of the Sahara. The peoples that lived in the wet Sahara, and that had accomplished one of the first great technological revolutions of humanity, the Neolithic revolution, had then to withdraw, some of them northwards, others, to the Nile valley, eastwards, others southwards, into what is now sub-Saharan Africa, while others still, remained in the oases where life was still possible, serving as indispensable relays in the trans-Saharan relations.

We know how the brilliant Egyptian civilization was thus born, emerging as an authentically African civilization, inspirer of ancient Greece, herself becoming the mother of Roman civilization with which the Western world claimed kinship. In the Eastern part of the continent, the Nilotic axis has always been the principal trans-Saharan track which will unify without chasm, the North and the South, during different periods of history. New civilizations were born there; among them we can mention those of Meroe, of Napata, of Axum, and further to the South, Monomotapa and the great ruins of Zimbabwe which still retain much of their mystery.

It appears that cultural relations like those that left their mark on the Byzantine age, continued non-stop from Egypt to the Nilotic regions of the South. Indeed, the Coptic churches that emerged in Nubia and in Abyssinia were linked to the Patriarchate of Alexandria, bearing witness thus of the existence of a religious and cultural space that ignored the desert barrier. It is again from Egypt, starting in the 7th century, that Islam, relaying Christianity and going around Abyssinia, reaches the regions of East Africa. To the Egyptian contribution we must add others coming from the Arabian peninsula along the coast, and from Asia through the Indian Ocean.

African cultures can thus be enriched by new elements: flourishing cities such as Sofala, Kilwa, Malindi arise. Literature, be it oral or written, experiences a remarkable new development with the use of Arabic and Swahili, the principal language of communication which has become the official language of several states born of independence.

At the end of the 15th century, the arrival of the Portuguese on the coasts of East Africa after those of West Africa throws progressively into confusion the political, economic and cultural realities in the regions. The institution of the slave trade, following the Spanish and the Portuguese on the American continent, tips the whole of Africa into tragedy. The normal process of evolution is brutally interrupted. The Kingdom of Kongo, on the Atlantic shore, from Southern Africa to the Equator, was one of the first victims of the process of the disintegration of African states, some of which had reached a stage of development that had nothing to envy many a European country, except that they had no fire-arms to ensure more efficiently the defense of their countries against the predators from the outside.

Moreover, we know through oral tradition that the internal migrations took place, sometimes stirred up by the need to escape the man-hunt instituted by the slave-traders, thus bringing about other cultural mixing the breadth and the exact scope of which are far from having been elucidated. With the partition of the continent and colonization starting in the 19th century, the cultural and literary exchanges are hence subjected, in a very large measure, to the constraints imposed by the colonial powers erecting borders and establishing customs barriers and controls on the movement of people and ideas which Africa had never known before.

With regard to relations between the Maghrib and sub-Saharan Africa—West and East—they seem to have continued uninterrupted despite the desertification of the Sahara, with more or less regularity in different times. With Islamization, these relations became more important. As early as the end of the 7th century, starting from the Fezzan, and a century later, from the Maghrib, Islam will penetrate sub-Saharan Africa, not through conquest, but through spontaneous choice to join. It is with the empire of Ghana, born, it is believed, in the 4th century, and which in the 10th century, extended to the major part of the Sahelo-Sudanese zone between the Sahara and the rivers Senegal and Niger, that Islam begins to take root in this region through the conversion of the ruling elites, then followed by the masses in increasingly larger numbers. In 1076 the capital city of Ghana, Kumbi is destroyed by the Al-Morabitun (or Almoravids) heirs of Yahya Ibn Ibrahim and Abdallah Ibn Yassin.

The emergence of the Almoravids opens a new era in the relations between the North and the South. Indeed, the latter will establish the first known trans-Saharan state, extending from the banks of the river Senegal in the south, to Andalusia, in the north, and having as its center Morocco, with Marrakech as its capital. Thus a new cultural and religious space was born, which, even after the disappearance of the Almoravids, will not cease to increase in importance, asserting itself, century after century, as an essential pole of sub-Saharan Islam.

With the passing of time, this space becomes part of the Islamic world which extends from the Indus in the East to the Mediterranean and the Atlantic Ocean in the West, and from the Red Sea in the North to Madagascar in the South, and from Northern Africa to the confines of the Sahelo-Sudanese zone of sub-Saharan Africa. In this open space, men, goods, ideas and knowledge circulate freely thanks to the use of a common language, Arabic. Everyone can thus be enriched from the experiences of others and fortify his faith through the contact with scholars and thinkers coming from the most diverse horizons.

But it is with the Empire of Mali (13th-16th centuries), Songhay (12th-16thcenturies), and the empires of Kanem, Bornu and of the Nigerian hinterland that the cultural and literary exchanges become more important and reach a quasi-permanent character. Contrary to what happened in central Africa, Christianity did not cross into western

Sahara; in western Africa, only the traditional African religions existed until the penetration of Islam. With Islam, internal and external relations spread widely; the Arabic language will spread out and give birth to a rich and abundant literature; schools, universities will multiply, with the encouragement of political rulers who will often bring back from their pilgrimage to Mecca renowned scholars who will settle in their countries to teach and pursue their researches. Timbuktu and Djenne will distinguish themselves by the quality of their institutions.

In Senegal, for instance, the center of learning of Pire, north of Dakar, which will be extant until the end of the 19th century, will be the training ground for many erudites among whom were the initiators of the first Islamic revolution which gave birth, towards the end of the 17th century, to the Theocratic Republic of Futa, in the middle valley of the river Senegal. Some of these scholars were Imam Abdel Qader, the first leader of this Islamic Republic, Amadou Hamet Bâ, founder of Woro Mahdiyou, El Haj Omar Tall Foutiyou, on the Senegal river valley.

The golden age of the trans-Saharan cultural and literary relations is marked by fruitful exchanges and by the emergence in sub-Saharan Africa of scholars whose works were highly regarded throughout the Maghrib. The best known of these learned men was Ahmed Baba born 2 October 1556 in Timbuktu. He owned there a library holding 1,600 works at the time the city was captured in 1591 by the army sent by the Saadian Sultan Moulay Ahmed Mansour nicknamed the Golden One, and commanded by Djouder. This expedition which ended the Empire of Gao at the battle of Tondibi which took place, we believe, on 2 April 1591, enabled Morocco to extend for a time her sovereignty over the Sahelo-Sudanese region, thus giving birth to a trans-Saharan political space which will be remembered for a long time by the inhabitants of Timbuktu. In exile in Marrakech, Ahmed Baba will hold there a teaching position at the request of the Oulamas who had a great esteem for his erudition and human qualities. After the disappearance of Moulay Ahmed Mansour, he returned to Timbuktu where he died on 22 April 1627.

While the irruption of the Portuguese on the African coasts south of the Sahara, in the middle of the 15th century, resulted in diverting an increasingly important part of the trans-Saharan commerce towards the coastal regions, the cultural and literary relations still remained very active. Little by little, the Arabic language asserts itself as the written language of the region. Following the example of Ahmed Baba, other scholars publish their works in the Arabic language and in African languages using Arabic characters.

The 19th century, before and after the colonial partitioning, and the 20th century following the Islamic renewal, are rich in poetic and religious works of diverse inspiration. However, many of these works remain in manuscript form in spite of the efforts of a variety of institutions to insure the translation and the diffusion of these texts. One must note, moreover, that most of the treaties concluded between African rulers and European powers were written in Arabic. Likewise, the oral traditions are replete with still insufficiently explored gems. This irreplaceable memory of the African past is doubly threatened, on the one hand, by the disappearance of the old men and women who were its most informed repositories and by the process of modernization which takes the young generations away from the living sources of tradition; and, on the other hand, by the distortions that it can be subjected to. Some present day leaders have, indeed, developed the tendency to give themselves a usurped family prestige to serve their current ambitions.

With colonial conquest, at the end of the 19th century, new educational systems drawn from those of the colonial powers and using the languages of the colonizers, are introduced. The experience in the colonial schools will give birth progressively to new forms of literary expression in the European languages. This literature, of relatively limited importance quantitatively during the colonial period, has experienced a considerable development with the advent of independence, the multiplication of schools and the emergence of an intellectual elite educated in the universities. But it remains still limited and suffers from a poor distribution system, due to illiteracy, which is still wide-spread in our countries, and also poverty, which limits considerably the sales of books.

With the advent of the new information technologies and the appearance of the Web, a new era is ushered in, in view of the increase of possibilities of exchange between the different parts of Africa, and between Africa itself taken in its entirety and the transatlantic diasporas. Still, these new instruments are accessible, for the moment, to a small elite only. Linguistic barriers constitute another obstacle to literary exchanges. Works published in the languages of the authors are generally accessible, within the continent as well as in the diasporas, only to those who know these languages.

Regarding literary and cultural relations between Africa and the transatlantic diasporas, one compelling observation comes to mind. Throughout the period of transatlantic slavery, these relations were unthinkable. Africans transported to America would lose all contacts with Africa, owing to the will of their tormentors, and to their social and judicial condition. They were placed in conditions which made impossible any true development or any possibility of undertaking a creative activity of any kind. The only way they could preserve their memory was through the spoken word, which some of them had learned to utilize expertly as Alex Haley, among others, who has borne witness so convincingly in his *Roots*. Those among them who knew how to read and write could not express themselves without risking the severest punishments; only a few were able to do so, exceptionally, essentially using the Arabic language, in which the first known texts emanating from the African diaspora in the U.S. were written.

Among those in the diaspora whose texts are known to us, I would like to mention Job Ibn Salomon-Jallow (Diop Souleymane Diallo), a native of Bundu in eastern Senegal, who was captured in the Gambia in 1730 and sold in Maryland in 1731, but was able to return to Africa in 1734; Ibrahim Abdel Rahman, a Peul (or Fulani) who hailed from Timbo, in Futa Djallon, in today's Republic of Guinea, who was brought as a slave in Natchez, Mississippi from 1800 to 1818 and who could write in Arabic and in English; Oumar Ibn Said, also a Peul (or Fulani) who hailed from Senegal, was sold as a slave, brought to South Carolina in 1807, then escaped in 1810 and went to live in North Carolina. Samples of the writings of these remarkable individuals have been reproduced in a small publication put together by Nashid Ali Muhammad, under the title, *Muslims in America—Seven Centuries of History (1312-1998)*.

The wealth of political literature which emerged from Haiti during the Revolutionary period (1792-1804) had no circulation in Africa in the 19th century; ostracized by colonialism, it has remained very little known in our time. However, in the domain of artistic creativity, and in spite of the constraints which were imposed on them and all sorts of restrictions that they had to abide by, the Africans who were subjected to servitude in America have been able to show exceptional qualities. They have been able to recreate new living cultural communities of African essence. Thus, they have been able to renew certain forms of artistic expression and enrich those inherited from Africa with essential elements, to the point of bringing about a true revolution in the domains of contemporary music and dance. There is no place in the world, not an auditorium where the sounds of music of African-American inspiration are not heard, not a dance-hall where dance moves whose roots are authentically African-American are not performed.

The creative artists of the diaspora have thus been able to influence the artists from the continent, which has witnessed since the advent of Independence the explosion of artistic creativity in a variety of domains and, in particular, in music, which has become a genuine cultural phenomenon. In the literary field, and in spite of censorship imposed by the colonial powers and the strict control instituted regarding the circulation of books, some works of leaders in the transatlantic diaspora, like W.E.B. Dubois, Booker T. Washington, and Marcus Garvey, were introduced secretly by seafarers, mostly Senegalese, whose ships would frequently make stops at ports overseas, including New York. These writings may have influenced, much before World War II, some members of the emerging African elite, and thus converted them to the Pan-Africanist ideology. After World War II, the authors of the African diaspora in the U.S. and the West Indies have progressively come into the reach of Africans studying then in America and in Europe, and also to Africans on the continent. Among the most appreciated West Indians in the Francophone area were—after René Maran—Léon Damas and, above all, Aimé Césaire. The latter's *Notebook of a Return to the Native Land* was one of the first and most intense among the testimonies of the common identity of the peoples of the diaspora on the other side of the Atlantic and those of Africa.

In the diffusion of the works by Africans and from the diaspora, and in the strengthening of the literary and cultural relations between the diaspora and Africa, one special mention should be made regarding the initiative taken by the late Alioune Diop to create, immediately after World War II, the *African Society for Culture* and the publishing house *Présence Africaine*. Thanks to the action of Alioune Diop, intellectuals from either side of the Atlantic could appreciate one another mutually.

The works of many writers from the diaspora have been distributed in Europe and in Africa, either in the original languages or in French translations. And now I would like to conclude with my repeated thanks to the ALA for its invitation. The members of ALA are, to a great extent, the guarantors for the conservation of memory; as creative writers and artists, they enrich this memory with their works; as educators they are its broadcasters to the younger generations. Without their action, the necessary continuity between the generations of yesterday and those of today and tomorrow could not be maintained.

Un continent appelé Fès: Keynote Address of the Closing Plenary Session of the African Literature Association's Annual Conference, 13 March 1999

Abdellatif Laâbi

Je voudrais d'abord rendre hommage aux organisateurs de ce colloque pour la perspicaité intellectuelle, l'acuité de la vision et l'élan du coeur qui ont présidé au choix de la ville de Fès afin de débattre d'un thème don't l'originalité aiguise vigoureusement l'appétit de la réflexion et du dialogue.

Je dois vous avouer qu'un Faasi (natif de Fès) comme moi a de la difficulté à contenir son émotion au moment de s'adresser à vous. Et je me dis tant pis, ou tant mieux. Si les colloques ne sont pas là pour que les intervenants donnent libre cours à leurs émotions, le poète que je suis n'est pas obligé de faire taire sa sensibilité pour paraître aussi objectif et imperturbable que les autres. Les lieux qui nous accueillient sont autant de stations d'un itinéraire secret. Ce n'set pas seulement l'Histoire qui parle à travers eux, mais les visages, les pierres, les arbres, l'eau, le vent. Ce sont toutes les amours, toutes les joies et les souffrances qui hantent encore l'air qui les caresse, la lumière qui les inonde, les couleurs élues de l'arc-en-ciel qui s'y déploient, les voix et les gestes humains qui les animent.

Ce sentiment revêt plus de force quand celui qui l'éprouve doit se battre depuis longtemps contre cette ruse de l'Histoire qui a fait de lui un nomade ou un exilé si vous voulez. L'errance qui est la sienne rend pour lui les autres lieux presque interchangeables, à telle enseigne que la notion de lieu devient abstraite et que son territoire commence à s'apparenter au "non-lieu".

C'est pour cela qu'être à Fès, aujourd'hui et en cette occasion quelque peu solennelle me trouble et m'enchante. C'est comme un membre dont vous avez été amputé et que vous ressentez de nouveau vif, vibrant, relié au coeur et à l'esprit. Nos racines résistent donc à toutes les intempéries et au saccage perpétrés par tous les prédateurs. Elles restent miraculeusement accrochées à ce noyau insécable de l'identité humaine.

Mais, au-delà de ce sentiment personnel que je tenais à vous partager, je crois que ce ce qui me séduit dans l'idée du choix porté sur Fès est son audace visionnaire. Nous savons à qui nous la devons. Un homme qui réunit en lui la quintessence de l'universel. Marocain, Africain, Américain, Européen de culture, il est un peu comme cette rose des vents qui ne néglige aucune direction. Il est en outre un homme de mémoire qui considère que rien de ce qui nous a constitués humainement ne doit être perdu, au contraire, qu'il faut le regagner sans cesse si nous ne voulons pas succomber à l'amnésie dont nous menace un nouvel ordre culturel mondial aux prétentions hégémoniques.

Permettez-moi de le remercier ici de nous inciter à réfléchir dans un cadre et un lieu où les repères ne sont pas donnés à l'avance, où les habitudes intellectuelles doivent être d'abord sécouees si nous voulons éclairer de lumières neuves le sujet qui nous réunit.

C'est dans cette perspective qu'il me semble que la ville de Fès pourrait fonctionner pour nous comme un sésame. La caverne à laquelle elle nous a fait accéder recèle certes de richesses mais, contrairement à celle des Milles et Une Nuits, elle n'est pas un espace fermé. Dès qu'on y entre, on se retrouve dans un labyrinthe magique dont l'originalité est justement de ne pas désorienter et perdre le visiteur. Nous y sommes invités à un cheminement initiatique où l'Histoire a décidé, pour une fois, de ne pas être ce rouleau compresseur qui déracine pour planter et détruit pour construire. Non pas que le temps ait été aboli. Nous ne sommes pas dans un site fossile ou dans un musée témoin. La vie, y compris la vie moderne, grouille dans cette ville sans altérer pour autant ce qui l'a fondée depuis les origines. Nous nous retrouvons donc dans un espace où la culture, au lieu de subir les changements au point de voir se diluer sa substance, les intègre et les marque de son empreinte. Or, et c'est ce à quoi je voulais en venir, la culture de Fès est le fruit d'un brassage millénaire. Cette grande dame arabo-andalouse mâcinée de berbérité n'est pas si sédentaire qu'on le croit. Elle a eu très tôt le goût du nomadisme et a attiré en retour divers nomadismes. Ville du nord et presque occidentale, elle a entretenu une relation de fascination réciproque avec le Sud et l'Orient. Nul désert n'a pu constituer un obstacle à ce désir. Au contraire, l'aire saharienne a été pour elle l'élément essentiel d'articulation. Sans le désert, Fès n'aurait jamais été par exemple aussi andalouse qu'elle est. Elle n'aurait jamais été aussi africaine. Cette africanité n'est sûrement pas une vue de l'esprit, une théorie ad hoc concoctée pour les besoins de ce colloque. Elle est inscrite dans une histoire certes conflictuelle et parfois dramatique, comme toutes les histoires, mais elle nous donne une autre clé de ce métissage serein qui est le propre de cette ville où la couleur de la peau n'est pas un facteur de différenciation, a fortiori d'exclusion. N'oublions pas que Fès est un des hauts lieux du mysticisme populaire africain, comme en témoignent le sanctuaire vénéré de Sidi Ahmed Tijani ou la place éminente que la musique gnaoui occupe dans la vie quotidienne des Fassis.

Ayant dit cela, je suis loin d'épuiser les composantes de la personnalité culturelle de cette ville. Si je n'ai pas parlé de son statut de capitale spirituelle du Maroc, et donc du rayonnement particulier qu'elle a assuré à la culture musulmane, c'est pour la simple raison que cela est connu de tous, comme l'est d'ailleurs la part de l'héritage culturel juif que Fès continue à préserver. Voilà de quoi nous mettre en appétit intellectuel, en sachant bien sûr que nous sommes dans une ville où un autre appétit, le gastronomique, est particulièrement choyé. Dans ces conditions, je suis persuadé que notre colloque atteindra ses objectifs. Les voies de l'universel ne sont pas aussi impénétrables qu'on le croit. Il suffit de se mettre sur la bonne orbite, dans une disposition d'esprit rebelle aux frontières que d'aucuns voudraient tracer jusque dans les esprits.

L'Afrique est un continent de cette planète sur laquelle nous vivons et qui est notre bien à tous, notre patrie commune. Fès est aujourd'hui sa capitale provisoire parce que nous l'avons désiré. Que ceux qui ont fait naître ce désir en nous en soient remerciés.

A Continent Called Fez:
Keynote Address
of the Closing Plenary Session
of the African Literature Association's
Annual Conference, 13 March 1999

Abdellatif Laâbi
(Translated by *Kevin Barret*)

I would first like to pay tribute to the organizers of this conference for the intellectual perspicacity, the acuteness of vision, and the élan of heart that guided the choice of the city of Fez, in order to debate a theme whose originality vigorously whets the appetite for reflection and dialogue.

I must confess to you that a Fassi (a native of Fez) like myself finds it difficult to contain his emotion at the moment of addressing you. And I tell myself too bad, or maybe too good. If colloquia do not exist for the purpose of the participants allowing free reign to their emotions, still the poet that I am is not obliged to make his sensibility shut up so as to appear as imperturbably objective as the rest. The places that welcome us are so many stations on a secret itinerary. It is not just History that speaks through them, but the faces, the rocks, the trees, the water, the wind. They are all lovers, all the joys and the sufferings that still haunt the air that caresses them, the light that floods them, the chosen colors of the rainbow that unfold them, the human voices and gestures that animate them.

This sentiment takes on more force when he who feels it must struggle, for a long time, against that ruse of History that has made of him a nomad, or an exile if you wish. The wandering that is his makes other places seem almost interchangeable, so much so that the notion of place becomes abstract and his territory begins to resemble a "no-place."

It is for this reason that to be here in Fez, and on this somewhat solemn occasion, both troubles and enchants me. It is like having a limb which has just been amputated, and which you feel once again to be animated, vibrant, linked up once more to the heart and spirit. And thus our roots resist all the bad weather and pillage perpetrated by all the predators. They miraculously remain, clinging to that indivisible seed of the human identity.

But, beyond this personal feeling which I keenly wish to make you share, I believe that what most charmed me in the idea of selecting Fez was its visionary audacity. We know to whom we owe this. A man who combines within himself the quintessence of the universal. Moroccan, African, American and European in culture, he is a bit like that rose of the winds that neglects no direction. He is, additionally, a man of memory, who believes that nothing that has constituted our humanity should be lost, indeed, that it must be continually regained if we are not to fall victim to the amnesia with which a new world cultural order, in its hegemonic pretensions, menaces us. Allow me to thank him here for prompting us to reflect in a space and a place where the landmarks are not given in advance, where intellectual habits ought to first be shaken if we wish to cast new light on the subject that brings us together.

It is in this perspective that it seems to me that the city of Fez might function for us as a magic password. The cavern to which it has brought us certainly harbors riches, but, unlike the one in *The Thousand and One Nights*, it is not an enclosed space. As soon as one enters, one finds oneself in a magic labyrinth whose originality is precisely not to disorient the visitor and get him lost. We are here invited to an initiatic progression where History has decided, for once, not to be that steamroller that uproots in order to plant, and destroys in order to build. It is not that time has been abolished. We are not in an archeological site or an animated museum. Life, including modern life, teems in this city without changing, for all that, what has been at its foundation since its origins. And so we find ourselves in a space in which culture, instead of undergoing changes to the point of seeing its substance diluted, integrates them and marks them with its imprint. Now, and this is what I was getting at, the culture of Fez is the fruit of a millennium-old mixing and steeping. This Arab-Andalusian grande dame of Berber hybrid tinge is not as sedentary as one might think. She developed a taste for nomadism very early, and in turn attracted various other nomadisms. A northern, almost western city, Fez maintained a relationship of mutual fascination with the South and the East. No desert could form an obstacle to this desire. On the contrary, the Saharan air was for her the essential element of articulation. Without the desert, for example, Fez would never have been so Andalusian. And it never would have been so African. This Africanism is surely not a mere intellectual conceit, an ad hoc theory concocted for the needs of this conference. It is inscribed in a history which is certainly conflict-ridden and sometimes dramatic, like all histories, but this history gives us another key to the serene *métissage* which is special to this city where skin color is not a factor of differentiation, *a fortiori* of exclusion. Let us not forget that Fez is one of the Meccas of popular African mysticism, as witnessed by the venerated sanctuary of Sidi Ahmed Tijani as well as by the eminent place occupied by Gnawi music in the daily life of Fassis.

Having said all this, I am far from having exhaustively listed the components of the cultural personality of this city. If I have not spoken of its status as spiritual capital of Morocco, and thus of the particular influence that it has assumed for Islamic culture, it is for the simple reason that this is so well known, as is the share of Jewish cultural heritage that Fez continues to preserve.

All this is more than enough to stimulate our intellectual appetite, keeping in mind of course that we are in a city where another appetite, the gastronomical one, is particularly pampered. Under such conditions, I am convinced that our conference will attain its objectives. The paths of the universal are not as impenetrable as is generally thought. It is enough to put oneself in the right orbit, in an insurgent frame of mind at the borders that nobody wants to draw all the way to the spirit.

Africa is a continent of this planet on which we live and whose value is our common property, our common homeland. Today, Fez is its provisional capital because we wanted it so. A heartfelt thanks to those who have given birth to this desire in us.

Littérature et éthique:
discours de remerciement pour le prix Fonlon-Nichols, 13 mars 1999

Abdellatif Laâbi

Les événements heureux sont assez rares dans la vie des écrivains africains. Les réalités de leur continent prétendu jeune, plutôt vieilli avant l'âge, sont tellement douloureuses qu'elles ne laissent aucun répit à leur conscience, tourmentée par nature. Aussi permettez-moi, l'espace d'un instant de déguster en toute simplicité cette joie que m'offre L'Association des Littératures Africaines en m'attribuant son prix annuel.

Mais voilà qu'en disant cela je sens que ma joie se fait fugace, et je réalise en même temps que l'honneur dont je suis l'object me met dans une situation de responsabilité morale accrue car il ne s'agit pas d'un de ces prix qui servent à lancer une mode littéraire de saison. Nous sommes loin des feux de la rampe, des saisons de maquillage et de tout ce qui fait tourner la machine du profit.

Si j'ai bien compris les critères définis pour l'attribution du prix Fonlon-Nichols, je dirai que nous sommes au coeur de l'éthique. C'est pour cela que je voudrais consacrer l'essentiel de mon discours à cette notion.

Le mot éthique peut paraître excesif quand on le rapporte à la littérature. Après tout si on jette un regard lucide sur l'histoire de la littérature, on découvre que cette dernière n'est pas, comme on voudrait le croire, le domaine privilégié de la vertu. C'est un champ de l'activité humaine presque comme les autres, où les contradictions et les passions battent leur plein, avec leur cortège d'intérêts, d'enjeux de pouvoir et de séduction, d'amour et de haine, de jalousie et de complicité, de bonté et de bassesse, de vérité et d'erreur, de volonté de puissance et de don magnifique de soi. Et dans ce vaste théâtre de la conscience humaine, l'écrivain n'est pas toujours le roc solide qu'on croit, le vigile ne connaissant pas le sommeil, la conscience aiguë à laquelle rien n'échappe. Il est aussi un être comme vous et moi, avec sa force et sa faiblesse, sa fragilité et ses limites, ses connaisances et ses lacunes, ses dons de vision et ses oreilles, sa folie d'espérance et ses accès de désespoir, son amour de la vie et son désarroi face à l'énigme de la mort, et puis ses besoins les plus simples, les plus universels, d'amour, de paix et pourquoi pas, de bonheur. Mais, une fois que nous avons "humanisé" ainsi le personnage au point de le banaliser, se pose une autre question, celle ayant trait à sa responsabilité particulière à partir du moment où il a choisi l'activité qui est la sienne et non une autre. Après tout, et pour ne donner qu'un exemple, celui qui a opté pour la médecine sait qu'il va devoir prêter le serment d'Hippocrate avant d'exercer. Et c'est la fidelité à ce serment qui va déterminer, en bien ou en mal, le déroulement de son exercice.

On me rétorquera que l'exemple est mal choisi car l'écrivain n'est astreint, lui, à aucun serment, à aucun engagement préalable. L'écriture est un acte libre qui lui permet de s'adresser aux autres et de leur proposer sa lecture de la réalité humaine. Les lecteurs sont à leur tour libres d'accueillir cette proposition ou de s'adresser ailleurs.

L'objection paraît pertinente de prime abord. Mais elle ne résiste pas à l'analyse de ce qui fait la spécificité de la pratique littéraire. Car, s'il y a une éthique de la littérature, elle ne réside certainement pas dans une injonction morale qui viendrait s'imposer à elle de l'extérieur. Non que cette injonction ne se présente pas. On peut même dire qu'elle fut la règle dans une phase rélativement récente de l'histoire littérarire, et plus particulièrement des littératures africaines. L'attitude qui prévalait partait d'une appréciation contradictoire du rôle social de la littérature et du statut de l'écrivain. Ce dernier était perçu comme un porteur de conscience, un guide, voire un prophète. Mais il ne pouvait remplir ces divers offices que dans la mesure où il s'inscrivait dans un projet social dont l'élaboration et la mise en pratique relevaient, elles, des idéologues et des politiciens chevronnés. L'engagement de l'écrivain n'avait de validité que s'il adhérait à la ligne d'un parti, d'un mouvement de masse ou d'un appareil d'état, s'il intégrait dans ce que l'on appelait l'intellectuel collectif.

La plupart des écrivains africains ont traversé cette expérience. Certains y ont laissé une partie de leur âme. D'autres l'ont vécue comme une épreuve de feu qu'il fallait assumer pour partager réellement les souffrances, les aspirations et les combats de leur peuple. Quoi qu'il en soit, la phase historique concernée par notre analyse ne laissait nulle place à la marginalité. Le "je" devait être nécessairement un "nous". La culture était une arme de combat, mais une arme d'appoint. Le primat du politique était incontestable.

Les malentendus qui ont entouré et entourent encore la question de l'engagement viennent assurément de là. Ils traduisent une vraie problématique. Au moment où il écrit, l'écrivain peut-il ou doit-il faire taire en lui le citoyen concerné par les affaires de la Cité? Comment une activité aussi solitaire que l'écriture peut-elle être solidaire? L'adhésion à une cause, quelque généreuse qu'elle soit, ne risque-t-elle pas d'émousser chez l'écrivain l'esprit critique, le sens du relatif et de la dialectique de la contradiction inhérente à toute conviction, toute pratique?

Je pense que ces questions resteront abstraites, ainsi que les réponses qu'on pourrait leur apporter, tant que l'on n'aura pas abordé la maitère vivante, celle qui est au centre de notre réflexion, à savoir l'écriture. Mais il faudra l'aborder de l'intérieur, dans le processus d'élaboration et d'énonciation, dans ce corps à corps insolite que l'écrivain livre au silence têtu des mots. Dès lors, la question de l'éthique se présente sous un angle différent. D'injonction extérieure, elle devient intrinsique à l'oeuvre. Ce qui va la déterminer, c'est l'attitude qui sera adoptée dans et face à l'écriture. Je veux parler du combat que l'écrivain mène sans cesse contre lui-même pour ne pas succomber à la facilité, aux modes, à la routine, et pour rejeter toute idée d'acquis "définitif" s'agissant de son travail. C'est ce niveau d'exigence qui l'amène à se remettre en question dès qu'il sent que son écriture s'assagit, se fige dans un moule, se stabilise dans son rapport à la langue, dans sa capacité à inventer des formes nouvelles.

Une telle attitude est aux antipodes de celle de l'écrivain qui construit un style et qui, dès qu'il croit l'avoir trouvé, s'en satisfait pour développer tranquillement sa carrière. Il se gardera alors de toute rupture pouvant déstabiliser le public qu'il a réussi à "fidéliser," comme on dit en termes marchands.

La première existence d'ordre éthique est donc pour moi cet engagement sans calcul dans l'aventure de l'écriture, ce refus de la facilité, de toute concession aux vogues et au système littéraire dominant. L'acte d'écrire est une insoumission permanente dont le prix est connu: la marginalisation. Mais cette liberté souveraine n'est pas négociable, monnayable. C'est elle qui fonde, à mon avis, une certaine vérité à laquelle peut prétendre la parole.

J'en viens maintenant à un deuxième niveau où se révèle le lien de l'écriture à l'éthique. Si le premier est intrinsèque, le second va plutôt de l'intérieur vers l'extérieur. Il découle donc du premier. Si l'écriture fonctionne pour moi selon une éthique, elle transmet les valeurs de cette dernière et impose à l'écrivain d'être en harmonie avec ses exigences dans l'ensemble de ses pratiques, sociales, intellectuelles, et de vie tout court.

Je sais bien que nous sommes là sur un terrain glissant; il faut être aveugle pour ne pas constater qu'il existe dans de nombreux cas, parfois célèbres, un hiatus considérable entre l'écrivain et son oeuvre. J'ai mis personellement beaucoup de temps à admettre cette réalité et à lire sans préjugés les oeuvres de certains écrivains talentueux mais peu respectables en tant qu'hommes. Si l'invective ne sert à rien dans ces cas-là, cela n'empêche pas de se battre à l'échelle individuelle contre l'hiatus de rechercher non pas l'harmonie totale, mais au moins une cohérence entre les exigences de l'oeuvre et les exigences de vie. Car que vaudrait une oeuvre littéraire qui ne reposerait que sur le paraître au lieu d'expliquer l'être? Elle participerait du mensonge triomphant qui vise à entraîner la culture dans sa spirale et ouvrirait la voie à une nouvelle barbarie.

Finalement, il me semble que l'exigence qui se révèle dans l'écriture est celle qui détermine toutes les autres. C'est en se soumettant à elle que l'écrivain devient plus libre. C'est en acceptant ses rigueurs qu'il se forge la sienne. C'est en allant quotidiennement à son rendez-vous qu'il se rend présent à lui-même et au monde, qu'il reste à l'écoute des voix qui vont emprunter sa voix, qu'il reçoit la vie comme un don et s'empresse d'en restituer l'offrande.

La litérature ne gagne rien à s'éloigner de son credo humaniste. Au contraire, elle s'étiole et perd progressivement les facultés qui lui permettent d'être au coeur de l'aventure humaine, de se battre pour les belles raisons de vivre, d'aimer, d'espérer, et d'en appeler inlassablement au sursaut des consciences. Pour moi, l'écriture est avant tout un acte de dignité face à la comédie et à la tragédie humaines. Elle rend insupportables la bêtise, l'indifférence, la démission et le fanatisme. Ecole d'exigence et de liberté, c'est un des biens les plus précieux de l'homme.

Literature and Ethics: Acceptance Speech for the Fonlon-Nichols Prize, 13 March 1999

Abdellatif Laâbi
(Translated by *Kevin Barrett*)

Happy events are somewhat rare in the lives of African writers. The realities of their so-called young continent, which might more accurately be said to have aged beyond its years, are so saddening that they leave no respite for the writer's conscience, tormented in its very nature. But also allow me, for a moment, to simply savor the joy that the African Literature Association has given me in conferring on me its annual prize.

But already in saying this I feel my joy fleeing, and I realize simultaneously that the honor bestowed upon me puts me in a situation of acute moral responsibility. For this is not a case of one of those prizes that serve to launch a seasonal literary fashion. We are far from the footlights, the makeup parlors, indeed from all that keeps the profit machine churning round.

If I have properly understood the criteria used for awarding the Fonlon-Nichols prize, I would say that we are at the heart of the ethical. This is why I would like to dedicate the basic theme of my talk to that notion.

The word ethics may seem excessive when brought to bear upon literature. After all, if one casts a lucid glance at literary history, one discovers that the field is not, as one might prefer to believe, the privileged domain of virtue. It is a field of human activity more or less like the others, where contradictions and passions are at their height, with their retinue of interests, their stake in power and seduction, love and hate, jealousy and complicity, goodness and baseness, truth and error, the will to power and the magnificent giving of the self. And, in this vast theater of the human conscience, the writer is not always the solid rock we think he is, the watchman who knows not sleep, the needle-sharp conscience from which nothing escapes. He is also a being like you and me, with his strength and his weaknesses, his fragility and his limits, his knowledge and his lacunae, his gifts of vision and his blinders, his mania for hope and his fits of despair, his love of life and his helpless confusion before the enigma of death, and then his most simple, most universal needs for love, peace, and, why not, happiness.

But once we have humanized this character to the point of rendering him banal, a new question arises, that of his particular responsibility from the moment he chooses the activity that is his own and no other. After all, to give a single example, one who chooses a career in medicine knows that he or she will have to swear to the Hippocratic oath before practicing. And it is one's faithfulness to that oath that will determine, for good or ill, the course of one's practice.

It may be objected that the example is poorly chosen, for the writer, unlike the doctor, is not beholden to any oath, to any prior agreement. Writing is a free act that allows the writer to address itself to others and propose to them his reading of human reality. Readers, for their part, are free to welcome that proposition or to direct themselves elsewhere.

The objection at first glance seems pertinent. But it does not stand up to analysis of what constitutes the specificity of the practice of literature. For if there is an ethics of literature, it certainly does not lie in a moral injunction to be imposed from outside. It is not that this injunction does not present itself. One might even say that it was the general rule during a relatively recent phase of literary history, especially in African literature. The prevailing attitude grew out of a contradictory appreciation of the social role of literature and of the status of the writer, who was perceived as a bearer of conscience, a guide, indeed a prophet. But he could not fulfill his various functions except to the extent that he enrolled in a social project whose elaboration and realization would then be handed over to ideologues and veteran politicians. The writer's engagement had no validity unless he adhered to a party line, a mass movement, a state apparatus, and found his place in what was called "the collective intellectual."

The majority of African intellectuals have passed through this experience. Some have left a part of their soul there. Others have lived it like a trial by fire that was necessary to accept in order to truly share the sufferings, the aspirations and the struggles of their people. Be that as it may, the historical phase we are analyzing does not leave any place for marginality. The *I* necessarily had to be a *We*. Culture was a weapon of combat, but a secondary weapon. The primacy of politics was incontrovertible.

The misunderstandings that surrounded and that still surround the question of engagement surely stem from this. They convey a truly problematic question. At the moment he writes, can or must the writer silence within himself the citizen concerned with civic affairs? How can an activity as solitary as writing partake of solidarity? Does not adherence to a cause, however generous, carry the risk of dulling the writer's critical spirit, sense of relativity, and dialectics of contradiction inherent in all conviction, all practice?

I think these questions will remain abstract, like the answers one may bring to them, as long as one has not yet reached the living heart of the matter, that which is at the center of our reflection, which is to say, writing. But it must be reached by way of its interior, in its process of elaboration and expression, in the strange hand-to-hand combat the writer delivers over to the stubborn silence of words. From that moment on, the question of ethics presents itself from a different angle. From exterior injunction, it becomes intrinsic to the work. What will determine it is the attitude to be adopted in the face of the work. I wish to speak of the combat the writer ceaselessly engages in with himself in order to avoid succumbing to the facile, the fashionable, the routine, and in order to reject every pre-established "definitive" idea having to do with his work. It is this level of exacting demands that brings him to call himself into question as soon as he feels his writing growing tame, coagulating in a mold, stabilizing in its relation to language, its capacity to invent new forms.

Such an attitude is at the very antipodes of that of the writer who constructs a style and who, as soon as he believes that he has found it, satisfies himself with it in order to allow his career to develop tranquilly.

He will guard himself against any rupture that might destabilize the public which he has succeeded in "making faithful" to him as we say in commercial parlance. For me, the first ethical demand is therefore this engagement without calculation in the adventure of writing, this refusal of the facile, of any concession to vogues and to the dominant literary system. The act of writing is thus a permanent refusal of submission whose price we know: marginality. But this sovereign liberty cannot be converted into cash; it is non-negotiable. This is what, in my opinion, forms the foundation of a certain truth to which language may pretend. I arrive now at a second level where the link between writing and ethics reveals itself. If the first is intrinsic, the second goes rather from interior to exterior. It thus flows out of the first. If writing functions for me according to an ethic, it transmits the values of that ethic and insists that the writer be in harmony with its demands in the whole of his social and intellectual practices, in short, his practice of life.

I well know that here we are on a slippery slope. One would have to be blind not to notice that there exists in many cases, some of them famous, a notable rupture between the writer and the work. I have myself taken a long time to admit this reality and to read without prejudice the works of certain writers who, though talented, are not exactly respectable as human beings. If invective serves no purpose in these cases, that does not prevent us from struggling at the individual level against this rupture, to seek not perfect harmony, but at least coherence between the demands of the work and the demands of life. For what would a literary work be worth if it rested merely on appearances instead of seeking to elucidate reality? It would participate in the triumphant lie which aims to drag culture in its spiral and open the path to a new barbarism.

In the end, it seems to me that the ethical requirement that manifests itself in writing is that which determines all the others. It is by submitting to it that the writer becomes more free. It is by accepting its rigors that he forges for himself his own. It is by going daily to meet with it that he renders himself present to himself and to the world, that he remains tuned in to voices that will borrow his voice, that he accepts life like a gift and hastens to offer something in return. Literature gains nothing in distancing itself from its humanist credo. On the contrary, it withers and progressively loses the qualities that allow it to be at the heart of the human adventure, to struggle for the very good reasons of living, loving, hoping and calling tirelessly for giving consciences abrupt awakenings. For me, writing is above all an act of dignity in the face of the human comedy, and the human tragedy. It renders stupidity, indifference, withdrawal, and fanaticism intolerable. A school of strictness and of liberty, it is one of humanity's most precious possessions.

Ecris et . . . tais-toi!

Boubacar Boris Diop

Les auteurs africains, surtout francophones, consacrent le plus clair de leur temps à expliquer pourquoi ils écrivent dans une langue étrangère. Cela leur donne souvent la fâcheuse impression d'être piégés dans une discussion stérile. Le poète congolais Tchicaya U'Tamsi a dit un jour à quel point il jugeait agaçante la récurrence de ce débat. On raconte aussi qu'il est arrivé à Mongo Beti de rétorquer, excédé, à une auditrice: "Madame, je déteste la langue française, d'ailleurs moi je n'aime que le grec et le latin!" Depuis des dizaines d'années, les mêmes questions appellent les mêmes réponses: notre public, plus sensible à l'oralité qu'à l'expression écrite, n'a pas non plus les moyens d'acheter ou de comprendre nos livres.

Pourtant, à quelques exceptions près—Ngugi wa Thiong'o du Kenya et Cheikh Aliou Ndao du Sénégal, par exemple—les écrivains africains sont hostiles, même quand ils en ont la possibilité, au recours à leurs langues maternelles. Il serait toutefois plus juste de dire qu'ils considèrent l'anglais ou le français comme un moindre mal. Cette attitude exprime surtout leur crainte légitime de se laisser enfermer dans un ghetto qui les isolerait du reste de l'humanité. De fait, on peut difficilement reprocher à un poète ou à un dramaturge de vouloir étendre son propos au-delà de sa communauté d'origine. Le bon sens veut en effet qu'il s'adresse à tous ses lecteurs potentiels, où qu'ils puissent se trouver sur cette terre. Sony Labou Tansi exprime la même idée à sa façon: "J'écris, dit-il, pour le monde entier et pas seulement pour les Congolais".

Tout en comprenant une telle position, on est frappé par le refus qu'elle implique d'établir la moindre corrélation entre la langue et la culture. Cela est d'autant plus surprenant que dans d'autres parties du globe, la question linguistique a toujours été et reste, parfois de manière sanglante, au cœur de la revendication identitaire. En Afrique, la langue n'indique curieusement aucune ligne de fracture idéologique dans le champ littéraire. Des romanciers que tout oppose par ailleurs, sont en accord total sur ce point. Le fait de délaisser le dioula ou le sereer ne signifie pas pour eux qu'ils renient leur africanité. On a même parfois l'impression que les auteurs les plus engagés dans le combat anti-colonialiste sont les moins gênés par cet état de fait.

Le paradoxe n'est qu'apparent, car le créateur africain a, depuis les origines, un double public. Sa volonté de se faire entendre de l'oppresseur est au moins aussi forte que celle d'améliorer le sort de ses compatriotes. Née sous le signe de la protestation collective, la littérature africaine s'est toujours méfiée de l'art pour l'art. Elle est moins intéressée par la réalisation de belles œuvres individuelles que par l'urgence de résoudre des problèmes sociaux parfois dramatiques. Dans la période de lutte pour la libération nationale, il fallait parer au plus pressé. La langue de l'occupant avait le mérite d'exister. Les intellectuels africains ont su y puiser les mots de passe qui ont assuré leur cohésion face à un ennemi commun.

La situation n'est cependant pas la même dans toutes les anciennes colonies. Dans l'espace anglophone, seule la pugnacité de Ngugi wa Thiong'o donne encore un semblant de réalité au débat linguistique. Au Nigeria, les pièces de Wole Soyinka cohabitent sans difficulté avec des œuvres en yoruba ou en haoussa. A en croire certains analystes, cette attitude plus détendue est due au fait que l'occupation britannique s'est finalement révélée moins destructrice pour les élites africaines. En outre, on croit souvent que la langue anglaise a conquis la planète. Ne devrait-on pas dire plutôt qu'elle a été colonisée par les autres cultures? Il se pourrait bien que Ben Okri et Arundrathi Roy la considèrent, sans la moindre trace de culpabilité, comme leur propriété.

Sa suprématie ne gêne que les Français, qui ont une relation quasi névrotique avec leur langue. Et le fait que celle-ci soit en perte de vitesse n'arrange pas les choses. La francophonie est une façon un peu comique de bomber le torse face à l'éternel rival anglo-saxon. En maintenant dans son giron les écrivains francophones de tous les continents, la France veut surtout montrer le rayonnement international et la vitalité de sa langue. Elle a au moins ainsi l'illusion de "tenir son rang" parmi les grandes nations du monde. Mais cette apparente ouverture souffre d'un paradoxe: tout en poussant au combat les auteurs québecois, libanais, suisses ou ivoiriens, l'institution littéraire française ne peut se résoudre à les traiter comme les égaux de ceux de l'hexagone. Par un étrange glissement sémantique, on est arrivé à la situation où un écrivain français se sentirait discrédité d'être appelé francophone.

Ce n'est pas tout. Québecois, Wallons et Suisses romands peuvent se réclamer d'une culture française qui les renvoie à un passé parfois assez récent. Il n'en est pas de même pour les Africains. Tout devrait les éloigner de l'ensemble francophone: la géographie, un passé douloureux, la situation économique, les modes de vie et même . . . la langue. La place qui leur est assignée dans cette famille fort bigarrée est essentiellement politique. Ils y restent pour deux raisons: on a besoin d'eux pour faire nombre et leurs dirigeants n'osent pas déplaire à Paris.

Le caractère insolite de l'arrimage des Africains à la francophonie est encore plus frappant si on considère l'acte d'écrire du dedans: le Suisse Yves Laplace écrit ses livres dans une langue qu'il parle et entend tous les jours autour de lui. Elle est une part importante de sa culture. Il n'y a en revanche rien de commun entre le bamana que le Malien Moussa Konaté parle en famille et le français de ses romans. Ce déphasage absolu entre l'univers de l'écriture et celui de la parole est sans doute unique dans l'histoire des littératures. Il n'est pas sans effet sur le récit lui-même et sur le rapport de l'auteur africain à son propre imaginaire. De ne pouvoir nommer toute la réalité physique ou certains traits culturels spécifiques, lui donne l'impression que le silence prend parfois le dessus sur son verbe. Le fait que les mots se refusent à lui rend souvent sa démarche maladroite. Parole d'emprunt, donc empruntée, parsemée de trous de mémoire? Ce dernier point est capital: il permet peut-être de comprendre pourquoi nos oeuvres, même quand elles essaient de jouer sur le registre de l'humour, ont bien du mal à ne pas rester graves et sérieuses. On peut se demander si nous ne travaillons pas avec une langue morte qui n'existe plus nulle part tant elle est peu marquée par l'évolution du lexique et de la syntaxe, en particulier en milieu urbain. Il suffit de se promener dans les rues colorées, joyeuses et hurlantes de Yaoundé ou de Kinshassa pour saisir d'emblée le contraste entre la vraie vie et nos œuvres de fiction supposées en rendre compte. Elles se veulent le miroir de notre univers mais l'image qu'elles en donnent ne nous ressemble guère.

Pour gérer cet écart, Masa Makan Diabaté a préconisé de "faire des bâtards à la langue française". De son côté, Ahmadou Kourouma, rejetant des normes grammaticales par trop pesantes, les a adaptées au parler malinké. Sa démarche, bien accueillie par la critique, n'en reste pas moins ambiguë. Cheikh Hamidou Kane a clairement exprimé son hostilité à une telle approche: "Je ne suis pas d'accord avec mon ami Kourouma: quand on utilise le français pour écrire en français, il faut le faire correctement", a-t-il déclaré dans un entretien récent. Tout en reconnaissant l'importance de l'auteur des *Soleils des Indépendances*, nombre de ses confrères ont formulé les mêmes réserves, parfois avec beaucoup moins de délicatesse.

Face à ceux qui s'en tiennent à un style rigoureusement classique, le refus de tous les carcans peut paraître novateur, voire subversif. Il n'en est rien. En fait, le "modèle Kourouma", tout en faisant penser à ces danses folkloriques dont raffolent les touristes, est un aveu d'impuissance. Il revient à dire que le malinké doit mourir à l'intérieur de la langue française, que celle-ci n'est pas seulement un instrument que l'histoire nous a temporairement imposés, mais bel et bien notre unique destin. Pourquoi un auteur ivoirien devrait-il donner à la littérature française la sève qui lui manque, quitte à précipiter la sienne dans le néant? Chaque peuple a assez à faire avec lui-même. Il se peut que la langue de Molière ait en effet besoin d'une petite révolution. Et après? Cela ne nous concerne en aucune façon. C'est plutôt l'affaire des écrivains français, ou peut-être suisses et belges, pas la nôtre.

L'impératif, c'est de placer la question linguistique au cœur de la réflexion sur l'avenir des sociétés africaines. De ce point de vue, il vaut mieux s'inspirer de Cheikh Anta Diop que de Ahmadou Kourouma.

Mais en matière de création littéraire, seules valent, en définitive, les convictions fondées sur un vécu individuel et sur des émotions intimes. A force de se focaliser sur la réception du texte, on en est venu à faire bon marché du simple plaisir d'écrire. Tout auteur a le droit de n'écouter que ses impulsions du moment. Même si de jeunes romanciers—Kossi-Effoui et Daniel Biyaoula entre autres—revendiquent de plus en plus fort leur liberté de créateurs, notre littérature reste tributaire de ses desseins politiques originels. Prompt à s'effacer humblement derrière son public, l'écrivain africain a du mal à s'enfermer dans son "Je". Voilà peut-être pourquoi notre champ littéraire se réduit presque toujours aux seuls textes de fiction. Il est dépourvu de ces "pourtours" que sont, pour les littératures plus anciennes, les correspondances entre écrivains, les journaux intimes, les mémoires et les essais ou confessions. On sait souvent peu de choses sur le rapport du romancier à la réalité, sur sa conception du récit, sur la différence entre le texte qu'il a fini par écrire et celui qu'il portait en lui au départ. Il éprouve rarement le besoin de s'exprimer de façon complète et spontanée sur les mécanismes de sa fiction. Des questions lui sont posées du dehors. Il y répond avec beaucoup de bonne volonté, sans craindre d'ailleurs de se contredire de temps à autre. On peut résumer cette situation en disant que quelqu'un parle toujours à la place de l'auteur africain et lui enjoint avec une hautaine sévérité: "écris et . . . tais-toi!"

S'assumer comme une conscience singulière, ce n'est pas trahir sa communauté mais s'abreuver aux sources mêmes de l'art. La fiction est un acte de rupture. Elle cherche moins à dissimuler les conflits et les faillites du groupe social qu'à les faire éclater au grand jour. L'écrivain est, par définition, un traître. Cela veut dire aussi: un être de pur amour. On me permettra de dire pourquoi, après avoir publié des livres dans une langue étrangère, j'ai décidé d'en écrire aussi désormais en wolof. Pendant ces vingt dernières années, le français ne m'a posé aucun problème. Je suis de ceux qui l'ont toujours considéré comme une solution acceptable. Je n'ai jamais eu le sentiment de m'éloigner de mes racines africaines en adoptant une telle position.

A vrai dire, si je ne m'étais pas intéressé de près au génocide rwandais de 1994, mon attitude serait restée exactement la même. Le principal enseignement que j'ai tiré de la tragédie rwandaise, c'est qu'elle résulte en grande partie de la volonté du gouvernement français de préserver ses zones d'influence en Afrique noire. Des centaines de milliers de personnes sont ainsi mortes au Rwanda parce que la France ne voulait à aucun prix abandonner à son sort un bastion francophone "menacé" par l'ennemi anglo-saxon venu d'Ouganda. En outre, la lecture du génocide rwandais par certains intellectuels et hommes politiques français influents a été, à mon avis, d'une totale infamie. Comment juger autrement Jean d'Ormesson, par exemple, qui n'a vu dans les Cent Jours du Rwanda que "des massacres grandioses dans des paysages sublimes"? D'autres déclarations tout aussi insultantes se sont étalées sans gêne dans la presse occidentale. Le dénigrement s'est d'ailleurs vite étendu à tout le continent africain. On commence en effet à lire ici et là que la colonisation a été, quoi qu'on dise, "une servitude volontaire". Les racistes n'ont vraiment

jamais désarmé, mais il y a seulement quelques années ils se sentaient
tenus à un peu de pudeur. A la faveur de ce qui est arrivé au Rwanda, ils
se sont mis à donner libre cours à leur mépris raciste sans le moindre
complexe. Les innombrables victimes de 1994 comptent pour rien, car
c'étaient des Noirs d'Afrique, un continent voué à tous les désastres. Un
tel constat vous incite forcément à vous regarder plus attentivement dans
le miroir. Après tout, mon pays, le Sénégal, entretient avec la France des
relations dites de coopération—en fait néo-coloniales—identiques à celles
qui ont amené Paris à se compromettre gravement avec les bouchers de
Kigali et d'ailleurs.

Ecrire en wolof est une façon de se mettre à l'abri des mauvais
coups et des crachats, un moyen de sentir sous ses pieds un sol ferme et
rassurant. Dans un sens, le sentiment de vivre dans un monde dangereux
ramène chacun de nous à lui-même. Chercher à conforter le statut
littéraire des langues africaines, ce n'est pas mener une bataille d'arrière-
garde mais, au contraire, c'est se tourner vers l'avenir. On ne le dit peut-
être pas assez: de nos jours, la déconnexion des sphères linguistique et
culturelle met en péril des nations entières en les privant de leurs repères.
Ainsi, l'intégration des jeunes émigrés africains dans les sociétés du Nord
se fait de plus en plus au prix d'un renoncement à leur identité. Après
quarante ans d'indépendance, la fascination de l'ex-colonisé pour
l'Occident et son envie de devenir l'Autre, de se perdre en lui, loin de
s'estomper, sont plus fortes que par le passé. Je ne sais pas ce qu'il en est
ailleurs en Afrique, mais au Sénégal, où l'existence des langues nationales
est heureusement loin d'être menacée, il n'est pas rare de voir des couples
d'intellectuels interdire à leurs enfants de parler une langue autre que le
français. Dans certaines écoles privées, la même interdiction est en
vigueur, exactement comme à l'époque coloniale.

J'ai pu me tourner vers le wolof mais je suis conscient que tous les
écrivains africains n'ont pas cette possibilité. Leurs langues maternelles
n'ont pas été codifiées et ils ne les ont pas non plus étudiées à l'université.
La mienne porte, depuis le dix-neuvième siècle, une littérature en
caractères arabes d'abord puis latins. Le fameux poème de Seriñ Musaa
Ka, *Xarnu bi* [Le siècle]—était déjà entièrement consacré dans les années
vingt aux conséquences de la crise économique de 1929 sur son Baol natal.
Il faut aussi savoir qu'au Sénégal, la production littéraire en pulaar, sereer

ou wolof connaît un tel essor qu'elle est en train de surpasser celle publiée en français.

Quid du faible rayonnement international de nos langues? On commet une grave erreur en appliquant à la création littéraire africaine une grille d'évaluation totalement étrangère à notre histoire et à notre dynamique culturelle. Il est loin d'être prouvé qu'un roman en pulaar ou en swahili n'a pas de public. Les chiffres disponibles prouvent exactement le contraire. Mais même à supposer qu'il en soit ainsi, chacun sait que toute littérature s'enfante dans la douleur et sur la longue durée. Il lui faut souvent des siècles pour s'imposer. Jugée à cette aune, la littérature africaine d'expression française n'est peut-être qu'une brève période de transition dans une trajectoire historique plus complexe. Le simple fait d'écrire dans nos langues ne résoudra certes pas tous les problèmes. Compte tenu du temps perdu, la tâche ne sera pas non plus de tout repos. Pourtant, la désaliénation est à ce prix. L'écrivain joue un rôle non pas en disant aux autres ce qu'ils doivent penser ou faire mais, bien plus modestement, en leur parlant d'eux-mêmes, au besoin à travers ses propres phantasmes. Il ne se sert pas seulement de la langue, il la crée également et agit ainsi sur la manière dont la société se perçoit. En écrivant en wolof, j'ai surtout le sentiment de prendre ma place dans une histoire en train de se faire.

Mon changement de cap linguistique a surpris quelques-uns de mes amis. J'ai pu observer dans leurs réactions, de la compassion, une franche hostilité ou du dépit. Pour eux, un choix aussi absurde fait perdre trop de choses à la fois: du public, le prestige auquel donne droit le maniement du français et même le peu de revenus que l'on peut escompter, sous nos cieux, d'une carrière littéraire. Je n'ai jamais déclaré que je ne publierai plus de romans en français. Toute langue, même apprise par la force, finit par enrichir l'être humain. Il serait donc stupide d'aller en guerre contre qui que ce soit. On ne s'est pas moins gêné de me rappeler les exemples de Ngugi wa Thiong'o, Rachid Boujedra et Raphaël Confiant qui n'auraient pas réussi à tenir leur pari de n'écrire à partir d'un certain moment qu'en kikuyu, en arabe ou en créole. J'ai dû parfois répondre à des questions idiotes ou amusantes mais surtout révélatrices d'un certain état d'esprit. Est-ce qu'il existe des verbes en wolof? L'écrit-on de gauche à droite ou inversement?

Tout cela m'a permis de découvrir que bien peu de gens, en Afrique comme en Occident, croient en la capacité des langues africaines à exprimer de façon appropriée l'univers intérieur de l'être humain. Peut-être ai-je eu moi-même les mêmes doutes sans oser me l'avouer. La plus grande victoire du colonisateur c'est que ses victimes, même paralysées par leurs chaînes, peuvent continuer à se croire libres. Notre aliénation est en vérité si profonde que le retour à soi-même demande du courage et un brin de folie. Mais celui qui ose cette aventure en est largement récompensé car—je le sais à présent—écrire dans sa langue maternelle fait éprouver des sensations absolument inouïes. Je peux dire que mon rapport au réel s'en est trouvé modifié en profondeur. Je ne peux être un passeur d'émotions qu'en affinant ma capacité d'écoute, en sachant prendre aux autres ce qui leur sera restitué par la fiction. La rue est devenue ma bibliothèque, le vivier d'images et d'idées qui informent ma création littéraire. Les textes écrits ailleurs, il y a trois mille ans, n'ont aucun sens par eux-mêmes. Leur vraie lumière est dans ce qui se dit autour de moi et qui vient de très loin. Après avoir écrit pendant la plus grande partie de ma vie des romans en français, je peux dire aujourd'hui que j'ai une plus grande aisance d'expression dans ma langue maternelle. Les gestes banals de tous les jours se laissent dessiner sans réticence par ma plume et je n'ai plus besoin de longs détours pour exprimer des sentiments simples. L'exemple de Cheikh Aliou Ndao est très révélateur de la liberté de ton et de mouvement de celui qui travaille avec sa propre langue. Les textes en français de Ndao ont toujours donné de lui l'image d'un écrivain austère et trop raisonnable. Sa production en wolof, bien plus vigoureuse et d'un humour parfois canaille, nous montre son vrai visage, celui d'un homme solitaire et blessé. Il ne suffit pas, en effet, de quelques règles de grammaire bien apprises pour combler le fossé qui nous sépare de la culture occidentale.

La meilleure raison pour utiliser une langue reste toutefois le plaisir que l'on éprouve à le faire. En ce moment précis de mon existence, seul le wolof me permet d'expérimenter, à travers l'écriture, mes propres limites. Je ne trouve plus ailleurs le bonheur dont il me gratifie. Lorsque je compare mes romans antérieurs à *Doomi golo*, je me rends compte que "les mots de France"—dixit Léon Laleau—m'aidaient à dire autant qu'ils me condamnaient à me taire ou à bégayer pauvrement. J'ai souvent eu, à l'instar des autres écrivains africains, le sentiment rageant qu'un petit quelque chose refuse toujours de se laisser exprimer dans une langue étrangère. C'est que—je prends toujours un malin plaisir à le rappeler—je ne parle jamais français dans la vie quotidienne. Dans la société sénégalaise où je vis, cela n'aurait absolument aucun sens. Le français est pour moi une langue de cérémonie, ma langue du dimanche en quelque sorte.

Je suis en train de découvrir, grâce à ce roman en wolof, qu'en littérature le sens est tout entier dans l'écho, dans la pure résonance des mots. Ceux que j'utilise pour écrire *Doomi golo* ne viennent pas de l'école ou du dictionnaire mais de la vie réelle. A présent les mots, capables enfin de hurler de graves insanités, remontent du passé le plus lointain. Et si leur bruit m'est en même temps si familier et si agréable, c'est que j'appartiens par toutes les fibres de mon être à une culture de l'oralité. Par leur seule force sonore, ils me permettent de mieux exprimer l'obscur, le foisonnant, l'hybride et de rester au contact d'un monde qui me serait autrement inaccessible. J'ai, sans exagérer, l'impression d'être devenu du jour au lendemain le maître de terres vierges et quasi infinies. Il m'est possible de les retourner dans tous les sens et de ramener de leurs entrailles de quoi dire, sans grimace, mes émotions les plus intimes.

Le changement de lectorat qui résulte du recours à sa langue maternelle doit s'entendre doublement: tout en s'adressant à un public capable de saisir toutes les nuances de son récit, l'auteur dialogue au second degré avec ses morts. On écrit peut-être moins pour chambouler ce monde-ci que pour renouer le contact avec l'au-delà. Il est difficile pour le romancier qui n'a jamais été coincé dans la langue du conquérant de comprendre une telle déchirure et l'envie maladive de s'en guérir. C'est sans doute pour cette raison qu'il me paraît si naturel d'évoquer mes années d'enfance dans *Doomi golo*. Il n'est en effet nul besoin de s'affubler de masques pour parler à ceux qui nous connaissent si bien. Puisque tout roman est d'abord une confession, je peux passer aux aveux à mi-voix, en étant sûr d'être compris, de toute façon. Il s'agit, en toute humilité, d'ouvrir les brèches qui permettent au lecteur de se mouvoir entre le présent et le passé. Si ce n'est pas moi, qui donc parle dans le récit? Je n'en sais rien mais à ce qu'il me semble, dans un roman comme peut-être dans la vie, personne ne dit jamais rien. Les mots chantent ou rugissent d'une bouche à l'autre au cours des siècles et il s'agit simplement de les fixer par des signes. Il n'est plus sûre façon de piéger le temps que de tendre l'oreille à ce que murmure un inconnu avant de disparaître à jamais au coin de la rue. Ses paroles sont en vérité toujours si anciennes! Elles sont notre âme même et font une heureuse jonction entre hier et aujourd'hui. J'en viens à me demander parfois si en définitive ce passage à l'acte—le retour résolu au wolof—n'est pas une manœuvre inconsciente pour entendre de nouveau la voix de ma mère morte il y a trois ans ou celles d'autres personnes dont j'avais oublié jusqu'à l'existence. Le fait est que ces voix-là émergent d'obscurs recoins de mon passé. Elles y étaient tapies depuis toujours et attendaient seulement que leur soit enfin donnée une seconde vie, aussi longue que l'éternité.

Write and . . . Keep Your Mouth Shut!

Boubacar Boris Diop
(Translated by *Edris Makward*)

African authors, especially those who write in French, devote most of their time explaining why they write in a foreign language. This gives them often the awkward impression of being trapped in a sterile discussion. The Congolese poet Tchicaya U'Tamsi once said to what extent he felt the recurrence of this debate annoying. It is also said that Mongo Beti once retorted to a member of his audience, his patience visibly overtaxed: "Madam, I hate the French language; actually, for my part, I love only Greek and Latin!" For decades, the same questions have called for the same answers: our audience is more sensitive to orality than to the written word, and does not have the means to buy or understand our books.

However, with a few exceptions—Ngugi wa Thiong'o from Kenya and Cheikh Aliou Ndao from Senegal, for instance—African writers are hostile to reclaiming their mother-tongues, even when they have the possibility to do so. It would yet be fairer to say that they consider English or French as a lesser evil. This attitude reveals above all their legitimate fear of allowing themselves to be locked in a ghetto that would isolate them from the rest of humanity. In fact, one can hardly criticize a poet or a playwright for wanting to expand his utterances beyond his own community. Indeed, common sense would want him or her to address all his potential readers, wherever they may be on this earth. Sony Labou Tansi expresses the same idea in his own way: "I write," he says, "for the whole world and not for the Congolese alone."

While understanding full well such a position, one is struck by the refusal it implies to establish even a minimal correlation between language and culture. This is all the more surprising as in other parts of the globe the linguistic question has always been and still is at the heart of identity claims, and sometimes in a very violent fashion. In Africa, language curiously, does not indicate any line of ideological fracture in the literary field. Novelists who may disagree on almost everything else, could still agree totally on this point. As far as they are concerned, the fact that they would forsake the Dioula or the Sereer language does not mean that they are denying their Africanity. Sometimes, one even has the impression that the writers who are most engaged in the anti-colonial struggle are the least embarrassed by this state of things.

The paradox is, in fact, true only in appearance, for the African creative artist has always had a double audience. His will to be heard by the oppressor is at least as strong as his desire to improve the lot of his compatriots. Born under the sign of collective protestation, African literature has always been wary of art for art's sake. It is less interested by the completion of beautiful individual works than by the urgency of resolving social problems that are sometimes dramatic. During the period of struggle for national liberation, one had to deal with the most urgent first. The language of the occupier had the merit of being there. The African intellectuals have known where to draw the *passwords* that have ensured their cohesion facing a common enemy.

Nevertheless the situation has not been the same in all the ex-colonies. In the Anglophone space, only the combativeness of Ngugi wa Thiong'o gives still a semblance of reality to the linguistic debate. In Nigeria, the plays of Wole Soyinka cohabit comfortably with works in Yoruba or Hausa. If we believe some analysts, this more relaxed attitude is due to the fact that British occupation was in the end less destructive for the African elites. Furthermore, it is often believed that the English language has conquered the planet. Should we not say instead that it has been colonized by other cultures? It is indeed quite possible that Ben Okri and Arundrathi Roy consider it, without any sense of guilt, as their own property.

Its supremacy seems to embarrass only the French who have a quasi neurotic relationship with their language. And the fact that the latter is now stalling does not make things any easier. *Francophonie* is a somewhat comic way of throwing out the Gallic chest against the eternal Anglo-Saxon rival. In maintaining in her lap the Francophone writers of all the continents, France wants above all to show the international radiance and the vitality of her language. Thus she has at least the illusion of "keeping up her position" among the great nations of the world. But this apparent overture suffers from one paradox: while pushing Québecois, Lebanese, Swiss or Ivorian authors into combat, the French literary establishment cannot make up its mind to treating them as the equals of the writers of the Hexagon. Through a strange semantic slip, we are now in a situation where a French writer would feel discredited to be called Francophone.

And that is not all. Québecois, Walloons and French-speaking Swiss may claim French culture as theirs, which will connect them with a past relatively recent in some cases. This is not the same for the Africans. Everything should pull them away from the Francophone ensemble: geography, a painful past, the economic situation, their way of life, and even . . . the language. The place that has been assigned to them in this fairly motley family is essentially political. They stay there for two reasons: we need them for the sake of numbers, and their leaders do not dare be unpleasant in Paris.

The unwonted character of packing away Africans to *francophonie* is still more striking if one considers the act of writing from inside: the Swiss Yves Laplace writes his books in a language that he speaks and hears every day around him. It is an important part of his culture. On the other hand, there is nothing in common between the Bamana spoken by Malian Moussa Konaté in his family and the French used in his novels. This absolute gap between the universe of writing and that of the spoken word is without doubt unique in the history of literatures. It is not without effect on the narrative itself and on the relationship of the African author with his imaginary world. Not to be able to name the whole physical reality or certain specific cultural features gives him the impression that silence at times takes precedence over his word. The fact that words refuse to come to him gives him often an awkward bearing. Borrowed speech, hence self-conscious and strewn with memory gaps? This last point is very important: it allows us perhaps to understand why our works, even when they try to play on the humoristic register, have a hard time moving away from a serious and heavy mode. We may want to ask ourselves whether we are not working with a dead language which exists nowhere, for it is little marked by the evolution of the lexicon and by syntax, in particular in an urban environment. One only has to take a walk in the colorful, blithe and loud streets of Yaoundé or of Kinshasa to catch at once the contrast between real life and our works of fiction that are supposed to depict that life. They seek to be the mirror of our universe but the image that they give of it does not resemble us at all.

To manage this divide, Masa Makan Diabaté has advocated that "we produce French language bastards". For his part, Ahmadou Kourouma, rejecting the grammatical norms he found too dull and weighty, has adapted them to suit Malinké speech. His approach, though well received by critics, remains ambiguous still. Cheikh Hamidou Kane has clearly expressed his disapproval with such an approach: "I do not agree with my friend Kourouma; when we use French to write in French, we must do so correctly," he declared in a recent interview. While recognizing the importance of the author of *Les soleils des Indépendances*, many of his fellow writers have expressed the same reservations, and sometimes not so kindly.

Facing those who are content with a rigorously classical style, the refusal of all the yokes, may appear to be innovating, or even subversive. Not so really. In fact, the "Kourouma model," while bringing to mind those folkloric dances that tourists are so fond of, is a recognition of powerlessness. It amounts to saying that the Malinké language must die within the French language; that the latter is not only an instrument that history has *temporarily* imposed, but truly our destiny, and just that. Why should an Ivorian author give to French literature the vigor that it is missing, at the risk of precipitating his own into obscurity? Every people has its hands full with its own problems. It may be that the language of Molière is indeed in need of a small revolution. So what? That is none of our concern. It is rather a problem for French writers, or perhaps their Swiss and Belgian counterparts, but not ours.

It is imperative to place the linguistic question at the heart of the reflection on the future of African societies. From that point of view, we should be looking up to Cheikh Anta Diop rather than Ahmadou Kourouma.

But in the area of literary creativity, in the final analysis, only the convictions that are founded on one's own experience and on one's intimate emotions are the ones that count. Through too much focus on the reception of the text, we have come to a point where the sheer pleasure of writing has been completely lost. Authors have the right to listen only to their own impulse at any given time. But if young novelists–Kossi-Effoui and Daniel Biyaoula among others–are claiming with an increasing insistence, their freedom as creative writers, our literature is still bound to its political goals. Always ready to humbly disappear behind his audience, the African writer has a hard time enclosing himself within his *"I."* This is why our literary field is almost always limited exclusively to texts of fiction. It is wanting in those peripheral genres that include, in older literatures, correspondence among writers, personal diaries, memoirs and essays or confessions. We often know very little about the relationship between the novelist and reality, on his thoughts about narrative, on the difference between the text that he has just finished writing and the one that he had in him when he started. He rarely feels the need to express himself in a complete and spontaneous fashion on the workings of his writing. Questions come his way from the outside. He answers them with a great deal of goodwill, without fear of contradicting himself at times. One can summarize this situation by saying that is always someone who speaks in the place of the African writer and who enjoins him with a haughty and stern posture: *"write and . . . keep your mouth shut!"*

To accept oneself as singular conscience is not to betray one's community but to drink deep at the sources of art. Fiction is an act of rupture. It seeks less to dissimulate the conflicts and the failures of the group than to make them glitter in broad daylight. The writer is, by definition, a traitor. That also means that he is a being of untainted love. Please allow me to say why, after having published books in a foreign language, I decided to write some also in Wolof, from now on. During the last twenty years, the French language has not been a problem for me. I am of those who have always considered it as an acceptable solution. I have never had the sentiment that I was moving away from my roots by adopting this position.

As a matter of fact, if I had not become closely interested in the Rwandan genocide of 1994, my attitude would have remained exactly the same. The principal lesson I got out of the Rwandese tragedy, was that it resulted, to a large part, from the will of the French government to preserve its zones of influence in Black Africa. Hundreds of thousands of people have thus died because they did not want to abandon, at any cost, a Francophone bastion "threatened" by the Anglo-Saxon enemy from Uganda. Furthermore, the reading of the Rwandan genocide by some French politicians and intellectuals of influence has been, in my mind, a total infamy. How else can one judge, for instance, Jean d'Ormesson who saw in *Les cent jours du Rwanda* [The Hundred Days of Rwanda] nothing but "grandiose massacres in sublime landscapes"? Other declarations just as insulting were flaunted in the Western press without any restraint whatsoever. In fact, the disparagement was quickly extended to the whole African continent. One has indeed begun to read here and there that colonization has been, after all, a "voluntary servitude." The racists have really never disarmed, but just a few years ago they felt a little bit of modesty. In view of what happened in Rwanda, they went on to display openly their racist contempt with no restraint. The innumerable victims of 1994 count for nothing, for they were blacks from Africa, a continent plagued with all sorts of disasters. Such an assessment prompts you necessarily to look at yourself in the mirror. After all, my country, Senegal, maintains with France relations that are called "relations of cooperation"—in fact, neo-colonial relations—identical to those that have led Paris to compromise herself seriously with the butchers of Kigali and of elsewhere.

To write in French is a way of keeping away from bad times and from being spat at, a way of feeling under one's feet a firm and reassuring ground. In a sense, the feeling of living in a dangerous world brings back each one of us to himself. To seek to strengthen the literary status of African languages is not to carry out a rear-guard battle, but on the contrary, to look towards the future. It is perhaps not said often enough: in our time, the disconnection of the linguistic and cultural spheres imperils entire nations by depriving them of their landmarks. Thus the integration of young African immigrants in the societies of the North is achieved more and more at the cost of renouncing their identity. After forty years of independence, the fascination of the ex-colonized for the West and his wish to become the Other, of losing himself in him, far from fading away, are stronger than in the past. I do not know how it is elsewhere in Africa, but in Senegal where the existence of national languages is, fortunately, far from being threatened, it is not unusual to see intellectual couples forbidding their children to speak any language but French. In some private schools the same interdiction is the rule, exactly as during colonial times.

I have been able to turn to Wolof but I am aware of the fact that all African writers do not have this possibility. Their mother-tongues were not codified and they did not study them at the University. Mine carries since the 19th century a literature in Arabic characters first, then in Latin characters. The famous poem by Seriñ Musaa Ka, *Xamu bi* [The Century], was already entirely devoted in the 1920's to the consequences of the economic crisis of 1929 on his native Baol. It must also be noted that in Senegal, the literary production in Pulaar, Sereer or Wolof is experiencing such a development that it is now surpassing its counterpart in the French language.

And so what say we about the weak international impact of our languages? It is a serious error to apply to African literary creativity an evaluation grid that is totally foreign to our history and to our cultural dynamic. It has not been proven that a novel in Pulaar or in Swahili has no readership. The figures now available show exactly the contrary. But even if that were the case, everyone knows that literature is always born in pain and not overnight. It sometimes takes centuries to compel recognition. Judged by this yard-stick, African literature of French expression is perhaps only a brief period of transition in a more complex historic trajectory. The mere fact of writing in our languages will certainly not solve all the problems. Taking into consideration the time already lost, the task will not be easy either. However, that is the price for reversing alienation. The writer plays a role not by telling others what they should think or do, but, with much more modesty, by speaking to them about themselves, and if need be, through his own phantasms. He does not use only language for this, but he creates it also and thus plays upon society's own perception of itself. In writing in Wolof, I feel above all that I am taking my place in a history that is in the making.

My change of linguistic direction has taken by surprise many of my friends. I have been able to observe in their reactions both compassion and clear hostility or spite. In their view, such an absurd choice generates the loss of too many things at once: one's audience, the prestige gained through the use of the French language and even the limited revenue that one can expect from a literary career, in our climes. I never said that I would not write novels in French any more. Any language, even those learnt by force, will ultimately enrich the learner. It would thus be silly to go to war against anyone on this. However, this did not stop people from reminding me of the examples of Ngugi wa Thiong'o, Rachid Boujedra and Raphaël Confiant who did not keep their wager to write hence, only in Kikuyu, Arabic or Creole. I sometimes have had to answer some absurd or funny questions but above all revealing of a certain state of mind: Are there verbs in Wolof? Is it written from left to right, or the other way round?

All this allowed me to discover that very few people, in Africa as well as in the West, believe in the capacity of African languages to express adequately the internal universe of the human being. I may have had the same doubts without daring to admit it to myself. The greatest victory of the colonizer is that his victims, even while paralyzed by their shackles, could still believe themselves free. Our alienation is in reality so profound that the return to oneself requires courage and a touch of madness. But he who dares to embark on this adventure, will be greatly rewarded, for—and I know it now—to write in one's mother-tongue brings sensations that are absolutely unparalleled. I can say that my relationship with reality has been modified in depth by this experience. I can only be a ferryman of emotions by sharpening my capacity to listen, knowing how to borrow from others what will be restored though fiction. The street has become my library, the breeding-ground teeming with images and ideas that inform my literary endeavors. Texts written elsewhere, three thousand years ago, carry no meaning in themselves. Their real light is in what is said around me and that comes from very far away. After having written novels in French for the greater part of my life, I can say today that I have a greater ease in expressing myself in my mother-tongue. Commonplace everyday gestures can now be outlined with docility by my pen and I do not need long detours to express very simple feelings. The example of Cheikh Aliou Ndao is very revealing of the freedom of tone and of movement of the writer working with his own language. Ndao's French texts have always given of him the image of an austere and, possibly, too reasonable a writer. His writings in Wolof are more vigorous and display a sometimes rascally humor; they show his true personality, that of a man solitary and hurt. Indeed, a few well learnt grammatical rules are not sufficient to fill in the gap that separates us from Western culture.

The best reason for using a language remains, however, the pleasure that one experiences in doing it. At this particular time in my life, only the Wolof language makes it possible for me to experiment with my own limits through writing. I cannot find anymore, elsewhere, the joy that I derive from it. When I compare my earlier novels to *Doomi golo*, I realize that "the words of France"—in Léon Laleau's often quoted words—helped me to say as much as they condemn me to remain silent or to stammer poorly. I have often had, like other African writers, the frustrating feeling that a little something was refusing to come out in the foreign language. It is a fact that—I always take a sly pleasure in reminding people of this—I never speak French in my everyday life. In the Senegalese society in which I live, that would not make any sense. French is for me a ceremonial language, my Sunday language, so to speak.

I am in the process of discovering, thanks to this novel in Wolof, that in literature the meaning is entirely in the echo, in the pure resonance of the words. The ones that I use in writing *Doomi golo* do not come from school or from the dictionary but from real life. Now the words, capable at last to roar grave insanities, flow from the remotest past. And if the sound they make is at the same time so familiar and so pleasant to me, it is that I belong, through all the fibres of my being, to an oral culture. Solely through their high-sounding force, they enable me to express better the shadowy, the festering, the hybrid and to remain in contact with a world which would otherwise be inaccessible to me. Without exaggeration, I have the impression of having become overnight the master of virgin and quasi-infinite lands. It is possible for me to turn them around in all directions and to bring back from their entrails the means to put in words my most intimate emotions, without putting on airs.

The change of readership which results from this return to one's mother tongue must be understood doubly: while addressing an audience capable of grasping all the nuances of his narrative, the author converses in the second degree with his dead ones. One writes perhaps less to turn this world topsy-turvy than to reconnect with the other world. It is difficult for the novelist who has never been stuck in the language of the conqueror, to understand such a dilemma and the morbid desire to cure oneself of this ailment. It is no doubt for this reason that I found it so natural to conjure up the years of my childhood in *Doomi golo*. As a matter of fact, there is no need to rig oneself out with masks to speak to those who know us so well. Since a novel is above all a confession, I can move on to opening up to my reader in undertones, being sure that I will be understood in any case. Most humbly, we have got to open the breaches that enable the reader to move freely between the present and the past. If it is not I, then who is it who speaks in the narrative? I do not know really, but it seems to me that in a novel, just as perhaps in real life, nobody ever says anything. Words sing or roar from one mouth to the next through the centuries, and we must simply set them down through signs. There is no safer way to trap time than to listen carefully to what is whispered by a stranger before he disappears forever at a street corner. His words are in truth always so ancient! They are our true soul and they are a happy link between yesterday and today. This leads me to ask myself sometimes if ultimately this passage to action—the deliberate return to the Wolof language—is not an unconscious tactical exercise to hear one more time the voice of my mother who died three years ago, or to hear the voices of other people whom I had completely forgotten about. The fact is that those voices emerge from obscure corners of my past. They were hidden there forever, and were only waiting for a second life; a life as long as eternity.

Galloping in the Gallows

Nduka Otiono

You should sing with Pablo,
My country people,
He sees you
Fermenting
Under the skin
Of my love;
He sees you
Sulking
Like dust
Before the rain . . .

And you say
You don't love me
Galloping away in the gallows,
Cherishing my presences
Hugging me in your dreams
Like the ferns
Encircling
A palm tree in the botanical gardens.

Sing with Neruda, sane folks,
For every moment
You see me,
Every moment
You think of me,
Your heart sings,
Your mind fractures into
Tiny pearls of envy for my freedom,
I, madman, citizen of the rainbow.

From *Voices in the Rainbow* (Lagos: Oracle Books Limited, 1997).

II. "Women Warriors": Women Writers

Captive/ating Women Warriors: Nawal El Saadawi's Firdaus and Calixthe Beyala's Tanga

Elisabeth Bekers

In 1978 the Senegalese feminist Awa Thiam opened her *La Parole Aux Négresses*, translated into English as *Black Sisters, Speak Out* (1986), with the powerful and empowering statement that "[African] [w]omen must assume their own voices—speak out for themselves," while cautiously adding, "It will not be easy . . . " (12). This article focuses on two African women, the Egyptian Nawal el Saadawi and the Cameroon-born Calixthe Beyala, who have clearly manifested themselves as speaking subjects, not in the least by distinguishing themselves as novelists in the initially predominantly androcentric field of African literature with their clear emphases on women's experiences. Although Thiam's warning that women's self-manifestation is not achieved without effort has at times painfully rung true for Saadawi and Calixthe Beyala,[1] both authors have persisted in their powerful articulation of the plight of African women. In their creative writing, Saadawi and Beyala have given African women a voice, figuratively but also quite literally. Their female characters are often more than just the narrative focus and frequently appear as narrators of their own life-histories, as in the two novels under review: Saadawi's *Firdaus* (1973, translated from the Arabic as *Woman at Point Zero* in 1983) and Beyala's *Tu t'appelleras Tanga* (1988, translated in 1996 as *Your Name Shall Be Tanga*).

Notwithstanding the vast desert of cultural differences that stretches between the Arab world of Saadawi and the sub-Saharan roots of Beyala, the two novels are remarkably similar.[2] Each work describes an African woman's struggle to speak out against her oppression; each is presented as a first-person narrative, with the female protagonist recounting her own life-story to the reader as well as to a female confidant within the novel itself. It is my intention to examine the significance of the narrative frame to the voicing process described in *Woman at Point Zero* and *Your Name Shall Be Tanga*, but also to the revolutionary potential of both novels. As I will argue, it enables women's voices to be born and heard and gives female characters the opportunity to connect, in spite of their different social and/or racial backgrounds, and it provides Saadawi and Beyala the means to draw the reader·into the telling.

Saadawi and Beyala both present a fictional autobiography of a lower-class African woman rebelling against patriarchal oppression. The Egyptian Firdaus and the West-African Tanga look back on their lives when their deaths are imminent, presenting their histories either by means of one long, retrospective monologue in the case of Firdaus or through a series of interrupted flashbacks for Tanga. Before exploring this analogous narrative frame and its significance, I compare the stories of Firdaus and Tanga, who present their lives as a concatenation of suffering and phallocratic violence, perpetrated by men and women alike, and whose growing awareness of their own and of other women's oppression eventually prompts them to speak out against it.

Although orphaned as a young child, Firdaus, whose Arabic name quite ironically translates as "Paradise," is firmly subjected to patriarchal control and passed from one man to another like an object, from her father to her uncle to her husband. As the English title *Woman at Point Zero* suggests, Firdaus as a woman occupies the lowest position in society, one that offers no rights but demands total submission to phallocratic power. Similarly, the teenage prostitute Tanga feels that her womanhood is reduced to an anonymous collection of body parts which only benefit her male clients: "A thigh, breasts, buttocks. A mass of flesh poured out by the gods to announce the coming of woman, a swelling of flesh that will not be named" (Beyala 16). Quite significantly, to both women, their suffering commences with the clitoridectomy they undergo as children, a ritual genital operation traditionally used to mark a girl's cultural transition into womanhood. This corporeal "chastity belt," as Saadawi labels it elsewhere,[3] is designed to ensure a woman's value in patriarchal societies in which virgin brides are exchanged for dowries (as Firdaus's father intends to do) and women's sexuality serves the satisfaction of men (something Tanga's mother is counting on). The girls counter their parents' practical outlook on their newly-gained womanhood with their own experiences of its painfully repressive implications, of being, as Tanga sarcastically remarks, "fulfilled at the hands of the clitoris snatcher" (Beyala 12).[4] Firdaus bitterly remembers no longer being allowed to happily roam the fields but being forced to stay at home to perform women's work instead. Similarly, while Tanga's mother is exultantly "crying out to every god: 'She has become a woman, she has become a woman,'" the same realization leaves Tanga mute and empty: "I didn't say a thing. I fell heir to the blood between my legs. To a hole between my thighs. All that I was left with was the law of oblivion" (Beyala 12).

        Yet, Tanga is unable to forget and desperately clings on to her lost childhood, as her repeated use of the binary self-descriptive term "girlchild-woman" (Beyala 16) testifies. Also Firdaus is haunted by a sense of deprivation after her clitoridectomy. The loss of that "strong sensation of pleasure" (Saadawi 15) mixes with other experiences of loss, such as the death of her mother and her forced parting from her favorite teacher Iqbal after graduation. Saadawi emphasizes how this psychological agony adds to the physical and sexual abuse her protagonist suffers by the same men who control her life: her uncle, her husband, her lover. While Firdaus gradually learns to guard herself against bodily harm, men's verbal aggression appears just as destructive to Firdaus, turning her into "a dead body with no life in at all, like a piece of wood, or an empty sock, or a shoe" (Saadawi 50). Later, she reveals how her friend's accusation, "'You are not respectable' [. . .] penetrated into my brain like the sharp tip of a plunging dagger" (Saadawi 70). By articulating the destructiveness of non-physical violence in extremely physical terms, Saadawi clearly equates both kinds of misogynist brutality. However, Firdaus's suggested strategy to deal with male (verbal) aggression by means of an operative procedure that echoes her genital excision—"Was there anything that could uproot it from my head the way they extract a bullet, or excise a tumour of the brain?" (Saadawi 71-2)—merely amounts to an act of self-mutilation.

Womanhood is no less trying for Tanga in *Tu t'appelleras Tanga*. At the age of eleven she is raped and impregnated by her own father (Beyala 30), only to be forced into prostitution by her mother in order to feed the family when her father dies. The first time Tanga prostitutes herself, her sexual exploitation serves as a reminder of the patriarchal conditions that were inscribed in her body through excision: "Woman's existence comes to me now. I hadn't known it, yet I recognise it. A memory engraved in the darkness of time" (Beyala 19). Abruptly torn from her childhood and a play-toy tossed from man to man, Tanga gradually loses her grip on herself, becoming "the shadow of a life that's lost its way[,] the body that's wilted from too much suffering" (Beyala 108). Just like Firdaus's, Tanga's body is paralyzed into passivity and inertia through the continuous acts of phallocratic violence. Tanga reproaches her patriarchal government for authorizing women only one activity, reducing their entire existence to their reproductive capacity. At the same time she lashes out against women, including her own mother, for bearing children they are unable to feed. She accuses them of allowing themselves to be lulled into a silent acceptance of their situation by the Governor and his awards for women with large families, and bitterly derides the pride they take in acting as patriarchy's "laying hens [. . .]. As proud as geese in a market-place. Muzzled women. Happy to be heroines. Thanks to the acts of every-day life." The women's participation in their own and their children's victimization fills Tanga with so much disgust that she is briefly tempted to mutilate the very parts of her body which in a patriarchal society constitute her womanhood, "to cut off my breasts, to gather up my buttocks and cut the Gordian knots" (Beyala 58). As with Firdaus, the first thing that comes to Tanga's mind is to take her anger against the phallocratic repression of women out on her own body. On second thought, however, she chooses a less self-destructive solution, firmly resolving not "to multiply myself [and not to] lend my womb to the unfurling of a life. So many children already loiter in the street! I despise feeding the statistics" (Beyala 120).

As their awareness of the predicament of women in phallocratic societies grows, Firdaus and Tanga begin to speak out and act against their condition. By rebelling, both women begin to construct a new identity for themselves or, as Therese Saliba states, their "fighting back is part of the process of claiming a 'self'" (Saliba 142), a "self" that refuses to self-mutilate any longer. Tanga demonstrates against hunger in the streets of Iningué and refuses to continue working as a prostitute, but is consequently accused by her extended family of depriving her mother of an income. They order Tanga's mother to curb her daughter's freedom and "clip her [daughter's] wings before she goes flying off" (Beyala 107), their suggested mutilation reminiscent of the repressive effect of Firdaus's and Tanga's genital excision. Tanga finally runs away from home, trying to relieve some of the misery around her by adopting the handicapped boy Mala, nicknamed "Foot-wreck" in order to "give him his stolen childhood" (Beyala 51). In turn, she is grateful to Mala for having, as she puts it, "closed my genitals with his raw tenderness" (Beyala 131) and for enabling her to withdraw from the phallocratic adult world centered around male sexual pleasure and female reproduction. For a while, caring for the boy brings both of them some degree of domestic bliss, until the day Mala dies at the hospital entrance because they cannot afford the treatment. Like her mother, Tanga comes to realize the significance of money for survival, that "[only] money protects her from decay and holds death at bay (Beyala 23). Yet, instead of prostituting herself or forcing other women to sell themselves as her mother had done, Tanga refuses to participate in women's (self-)destruction and joins a group of counterfeiters, thus effectively stepping out of the cycle of women's victimization.

   Similarly, Firdaus in *Woman at Point Zero* takes action against her oppression. Like Tanga, she runs away, first from her husband when he starts beating her, then from her lover when he allows his friends to abuse her sexually. She finally takes control over herself by making men pay for her sexual services. In contrast with Tanga, who is constantly dreaming of "a house with blue windows, a bed, the same man's voice to wake me every morning" (Beyala16), Firdaus prefers being a prostitute to being an unrespected female employee perpetually living in fear of losing her job or becoming "an enslaved wife" (Saadawi 89). To Firdaus, "the least deluded of all [women] was the prostitute" (Saadawi 86-87), for she can exploit men's oppressive treatment of women. But as a high-class prostitute she is harassed by procurers who tell her that she, as a woman, "cannot do without protection, otherwise the profession exercised by husbands and pimps would die out" (Saadawi 89).[5] In her eyes, precisely this so-called male protection is "the real danger: it was an assault on her reality, the usurpation of her will and of her very existence" (Saadawi 103). She takes her rebellion one step further than Tanga when she reverses the patriarchal abuse of women's bodies by stabbing a male aggressor to death. Her mutilating assault on his body is reminiscent of her own excision, the repeated thrusts of her knife mimicking the countless unwanted penetrations she has suffered in her life: "I raised the knife and buried it deep in his neck, pulled it out of his neck and then thrust it deep into his chest, pulled it out and plunged it deep into his belly. I stuck the knife into almost every part of his body" (Saadawi 95). Although Firdaus's recourse to the principle of "an-eye-for-an-eye" may appear as quite an ambiguous resolution to the patriarchal violence to which she has been exposed throughout her life, it is precisely this reversal that inspires in men a deep fear of Firdaus and thus empowers her where before she had not dared to act: "I realized that I had been afraid, and that the fear had been with me all the time, until the fleeting moment when I read fear in his eyes" (Saadawi 96).

By reacting against their personal oppression Tanga and Firdaus have become "savage and dangerous" (Saadawi 100), "subversive and uncontrollable element[s]" (Beyala 6) in their society's patriarchal structures. The patriarchal forces of control respond to the resistance of these two women warriors by isolating them from society for fear their rebellion might encourage other women to react too: Tanga is thrown in jail for forgery and Firdaus ends up on death row for the murder she has committed. Saadawi and Beyala show that, paradoxically enough, it is precisely in the confinement of their prison cells, with death at a mere arm's length, that these women turn out to be at their most powerful and captivating. It is here they complete their control over their own lives by taking it on themselves to tell their own life-histories.

Though initially reluctant, Firdaus and Tanga are both encouraged by a sympathetic female listener to pass on their stories: Firdaus by the unnamed psychiatrist who is doing research in prison and who had repeatedly begged for an interview, intrigued by the woman's resignation and silence, and Tanga by her cellmate, the French-Jewish woman Anne-Claude who had appealed to her to "[k]ill the emptiness of silence" (Beyala 7). Once resolved to break their silences, both Firdaus and Tanga are eager for their listeners to hear their stories. "Let me speak. Do not interrupt me," Firdaus suddenly commands the medical doctor on the eve of her execution (Saadawi 11). Equally unexpectedly, the seventeen-year-old Tanga, who had been too resolved to "leave this life without disturbing the sleep of men" (Beyala 2), confides her story to her white cellmate, reciprocating Anne-Claude's story with her own portion of madness and suffering. Not knowing how she could possibly talk about her excision, "the bloody slashing of a mutilated childhood" (Beyala 19) and afraid to reveal her devastation and desperation—"for there's nothing left to connect with; nothing left to stride across to get back to my roots"—she had remained "engulfed in silence" (Beyala 108), until, locked in a prison cell with Anne-Claude, she is able to reconnect to her past, thanks to her cellmate.

By constructing a rather elaborate narrative frame around the life-stories of Tanga and Firdaus respectively, Beyala and Saadawi are doing more than just giving African women the opportunity to "speak out for themselves" and assert their identity. They are also able to scrutinize the process and, in particular, the effect of women's coming to make their voices heard, thematically as well as on the level of their novels' narrative structure. Tanga's and Firdaus's connection with Anne-Claude and the psychiatrist respectively, surpasses an ordinary interactive link between (an active) narrator and (a passive) listener. Although the listeners initially appear as outsiders, whether this is because they are white and French-Jewish like Tanga's cellmate or because they belong to a different (higher) social class and are at liberty to leave the prison as is Firdaus's doctor, Anne-Claude and the psychiatrist become important allies to Tanga and Firdaus. Having instigated communication, they now become, as Fedwa Malti-Douglas terms it, important "mediator[s] of discourse" (Malti-Douglas 131).

The narrative frame embracing Firdaus's monologue is exclusively narrated by the psychiatrist who opens the novel by introducing herself and Firdaus and ends it by describing how Firdaus's autobiographical narrative deeply affected her. Firdaus's words continue to resound in the doctor's head, the woman's gaze and courage have become imprinted in her mind. The psychiatrist respectfully concludes her commentary on Firdaus's narrative by emphasizing the rebellious power of Firdaus's voice and pointing out that in a repressive regime a dissident's voice is as lethal as the most dangerous weapon:

But her voice continued to echo in my ears, vibrating in my head, in the cell, in the prison, in the streets, in the whole world, shaking everything, spreading fear wherever it went, the fear of the truth which kills, the power of truth, as savage, and as simple, and as awesome as death, yet as simple and as gentle as the child that has not yet learnt to lie. (Saadawi 108)

Whereas Firdaus refuses to interact with the doctor, the conversations between Tanga and Anne-Claude frequently interrupt Tanga's retrospection. After Tanga's initial hesitation, the tables are turned completely, with Tanga begging Anne-Claude to listen to her story. She even commands Anne-Claude to take on her (Tanga's) identity, an instruction repeated in the novel's title, so that Tanga's story becomes Anne-Claude's own (Beyala 8). Firdaus never explains her motivations for telling her story to the doctor nor asks her to do anything with it— she is actually taken away to be executed as soon as her story is finished. Tanga, on the other hand, clearly begs Anne-Claude to disseminate her (Tanga's) story, insisting that the spreading of her story will benefit the future well-being of women:

You'll tell my story ten times and nobody will believe you. You'll persist, and the eleventh time it will be fine. My story will be the bread dough that must be kneaded in order to survive. Let me free it up so as to build the future. (Beyala 22)

Listening to Tanga in order to pass on her story, Anne-Claude merges with Tanga, exchanging her high-brow philosophical talk for Tanga's ordinary speech, so that she is "a long way from using the kind of pseudo-intellectual speech in which terms ending in *ism* are tossed about, all those chopping block terms that divide people and remove them from life. . ." (Beyala 22). Anne-Claude also acknowledges the critical significance of her identification with Tanga, stating that "I am telling your tale, to perpetuate your life." (Beyala 33). As Firdaus survives in the doctor's mind long after Firdaus has finished telling her story, Tanga's prison death does not prevent her from living on through Anne-

Claude. This female mode of (spiritual) survival through the narrative is in stark contrast with Tanga's male friend's more material need for a son to perpetuate his story (Beyala 120). Although Anne-Claude could be (and has been by some critics) perceived as a rather questionable mediator to pass Tanga's story—after all Anne-Claude herself is imprisoned and emotionally unstable, unlike Firdaus's doctor—through the example of Tanga and Firdaus Beyala and Saadawi have convincingly demonstrated that the power of women deemed misfits by society is not to be underestimated.

Despite the obvious geographical, linguistic and socio-cultural differences between Saadawi and Beyala, both authors are bridging the African continent with their shared efforts to improve their own as well as their fictional and real sisters' fate. This united struggle is, as Beyala writes, the "common vertebral column" to African women writers (Matateyou 614), the unanimity of their messages connecting and strengthening their voices. In *Woman at Point Zero* and *Tu t'appeleras Tanga* this empowering unity between women is even more striking because women's coming to voice is underpinned by the novels' narrative structure. With their fictional autobiographies Saadawi and Beyala have given a voice to women who are speaking about their coming to voice. More importantly, they have also given them an audience, both in and outside the fictional realm. By means of Firdaus's and Tanga's first-person narrative, not only the fictional listener but also the reader is addressed directly, drawing him/her into the telling in more than one sense: i.e. into the women's story as well as into the act of speaking out against the repression of women. The voices of Firdaus and Tanga echo also in the readers' ears, their stories evoking also in the reader an intense "need to challenge and to overcome those forces that deprive human beings of their right to live, to love and to real freedom" (Saadawi iv). With this remark, taken from the preface to *Woman at Point Zero*, Saadawi is referring to the effect that one such narrative had on herself. In this preface, which is original to the English translation, Saadawi reveals that the psychiatrist is her fictional alter-ego and that the story of a female prisoner whom she met while conducting research on women and neurosis at Qanatir Prison encouraged her to write *Woman at Point Zero*. The fact that Saadawi wrote her novel in response to the woman's story is itself a clear illustration of the fact that narratives like Firdaus's and

Tanga's do not only affect their audience in novels such as *Woman at Point Zero* and *Tu t'appelleras Tanga* but that they also have a transformative potential in real life. This implicit appeal to the real world in the novels under review adds to the narrative power of Tanga and Firdaus and enables them to reach not only across the line between fiction and reality, but also across social, national and racial borders. This sweeping narrative force of Firdaus and Tanga is positively the revolutionary force of Saadawi's *Woman at Point Zero* and Beyala's *Tu t'appelleras Tanga*.

Notes

1. Saadawi, who has expressed her concern with the situation of Arab women both in and outside her creative writing, has met with serious opposition from those in power. Not only have her books and articles been blacklisted and censored, she has also been banned from public broadcasting. In the early seventies she lost her job in the Ministry of Health in Cairo; under Sadat she was imprisoned for a few months, together with other Egyptian intellectuals including the female author Alifa Rifaat; as recently as 1991 the Arab Women's Solidarity Association in Cairo, founded by Saadawi, was closed down and its magazine, *Noon*, banned. The outspokenness of the younger Beyala has not always been appreciated either. Her harsh criticism of the inertia of Africa's ruling classes, her outspoken feminist views, her "féminitude" as she prefers to term it, as well as her rather provocative language has in particular shocked certain African readers. Beyala, however, sees herself merely as an "observer of [her] times" and refuses to embellish contemporary Africa in her fiction. She is nevertheless very appreciative of the fact that it is her exiled status which allows her to speak out, which, as she states, "offers me the freedom that is denied to me [in her native Cameroon], my exile offers me the voice that is denied to me, my exile is my survival (Matateyou 612-613, my translation). In this context, Beyala also interprets the recurring accusations of plagiarism with which she has to contend as attempts at silencing her, as "a manoeuvre, a ploy, a desire to hurt. They would like to prevent me from writing" (Mataillet 73, my translation). Although in this paper I do not wish to assess Beyala's alleged plagiarism nor the intention behind these accusations, the

76 *Elisabeth Bekers*

commotion around "The Beyala Case" would have intimidated anyone less vocal than Beyala.

2. The thematic and structural similarities between Beyala's *Your Name Shall Be Tanga* and Saadawi's *Woman at Point Zero* struck me as I was preparing a paper on Saadawi's literary denunciations of female genital excision for the Second Women from Africa and the African Diaspora conference on *Health and Human Rights* held at Indiana University/Purdue University in Indianapolis, 23-27 October 1998. Ideas developed in that paper, in particular on the effect of the narrative strategies used in *Woman at Point Zero*, are drawn upon and elaborated in my present comparison of Saadawi's novel with Beyala's more recent work *Your Name Shall Be Tanga*.

3. By using this term the narrator in Saadawi's novel *The Circling Song* (1976) explicitly refers to the ritual's purpose of reducing a woman's wantonness (Saadawi 1989, 67).

4. The narrators of *Woman at Point Zero* and *Your Name Shall Be Tanga* emphasize the repressive implications of their clitoridectomies rather than the (immediate or long-term) physical pain caused by the operation itself. Much harsher descriptions of the actual excision ritual can be found in other works by Saadawi, namely in her two novels *Two Women in One* and *The Circling Song*, as well as in her autobiographical account in *The Hidden Face of Eve*.

5. Even the successful madam for whom Firdaus briefly worked ultimately suffers defeat by a man, illustrating that only men are to benefit from women's exploitation in a phallocratic society.

Works Cited

Beyala, Calixthe. *Your Name Shall be Tanga*. 1988. Oxford: Heinemann, 1996.

Malti-Douglas, Fedwa. *Men, Women, and God(s): Nawal El Saadawi and Arab Feminist Poetics*. Berkeley: University of California Press, 1995.

Mataillet, Dominique. "Le Cas Beyala." *Jeune Afrique* 1876-1877 (1996): 70-7.

Matateyou, Emmanuel. "Entre le Terroir et l'Exil. Interview Avec Calixthe Beyala." *The French Review* 69.4 (March 1996): 605-15.

Saadawi, Nawal El. *Woman at Point Zero.* 1973. London and New Jersey: Zed Books, 1983.

____. *The Circling Song.* 1976. London and New Jersey: Zed Books, 1989.

Saliba, Therese. "On the Bodies of Third World Women: Cultural Impurity, Prostitution, and Other Nervous Conditions." *Collegiate Literature* 22 (1995): 131-46.

Thiam, Awa. *Black Sisters Speak Out.* Feminism and Oppression in Black Africa. 1978. London: Pluto Press, 1986.

Resisting Dominant Discourses in Driss Chraïbi's *Mother Comes of Age*

Janice Spleth

In his Moroccan fable of self-realization, *Mother Comes of Age*, Driss Chraïbi offers perceptive criticism both of traditional culture in the Arab world and of colonialism and its aftermath. On the one hand, the title character struggles to affirm her identity against the centuries-old custom of sequestering women and relegating them to relatively passive roles within the public sphere of their own communities. On the other, she shares in the efforts of a people fighting for a voice in its own destiny in the colonial and postcolonial era. Mother thus finds herself constructed by a variety of discourses, each of which seeks to form her as a docile subject compatible with its own agenda. The paternalism she encounters as a woman in a Muslim society is often mirrored by the condescension of the colonial powers towards the colonized and eventually by the elitist attitudes of post-colonial politicians in relating to the masses. On occasion, it is possible to read the social as metaphorical for the political and vice-versa. Repeated juxtaposition of the different discourses strengthens the author's case against all abuses of power and targets multiple readerships in different ways. I would like to offer an analysis of two discourses as presented in the text itself, the Arab-Islamic discourse of gender and the Western discourse of the colonized other, in order to show how they intertwine and reinforce each other and how Mother's efforts to assert her humanity as a woman speak directly or indirectly to her various political situations.

Chraïbi introduces us to Mother as a thirty-five-year-old woman who has been in seclusion since her marriage at the age of thirteen to Father, a prosperous Moroccan businessman. Through the efforts of her sons, Junior and Nagib, Mother is brought to defy tradition and leave the house, an act that opens up her horizons and sets her off on a quest for knowledge and selfhood. Chraïbi's representation of Mother's situation is studded with criticism of religious tradition but remains vague in terms of just how this discourse is being disseminated. Indeed, cloistering is not in and of itself mandated by the Koran and even the custom of veiling varies from country to country in Islamic societies. In her study, *The Veil and the Male Elite*, the Moroccan writer Fatima Mernissi attributes the authority for veiling to scholarly interpretations of the words of the prophet. But Mother is illiterate and has no scholarly training in Islamic law. Junior tells us, in fact, that "No one had ever taught her anything" (16). Unlike the specific textual references that reveal the inequities and stereotypes ingrained in the Western discourses cited in Chraïbi's narrative, the traditional discourse that mandates cloistering and veiling is rather taken for granted, although the cause of what Junior refers to as Mother's entombment and imprisonment is explicitly identified: "she had been strangled by the law and by her duty" (48). If the patriarchy has a medium at the beginning of the story, it is Father, whose traditional views will not be passed on intact by his sons. It is he who specifically evokes the general tendencies of religion to privilege men. "In every religion," he says, "you will find only males. Not a prophetess or a single woman sent by God. We have lived for centuries with this order of things and we men have not had any reason to complain" (115). Junior describes him as follows:

> The man, pickled in the brine of his times, in its morality and sense of honor, had done nothing more than apply the letter of the law. Religiously. He had closed her up in the house from the day of their marriage until the afternoon we had made her come outside. She had never crossed the threshold. She had never thought of it. (48)

As this passage demonstrates, the influence of traditional discourse is so strong that it does not appear to require a precise textual source to enforce subjugation. It thus provides an apt illustration of the nature of power as theorized by Foucault: "When I think of the mechanics of power, I think of its capillary form of existence, of the extent to which power seeps into the very grain of individuals, reaches right into their bodies, permeates their gestures, their posture, what they say, how they learn to live and work with other people" (qtd. in Martin 6). Responding to the pervasiveness of religious authority, Mother had accepted her situation apparently without question.

But once she experiences the sights and sounds of the outside world, Mother's thirst for freedom is unquenchable. The park, a dance, a fair—all of these new stimuli awaken Mother's senses. Junior teaches her to read, expanding her view of the world—in time through history and in space through geography. He constantly encourages her "to call her own past into question" (62) and explicitly strives to develop her capacity for critical thinking. He describes his pedagogical approach: "What I kept tenaciously in my sights were the layers of ignorance, of conditioned thinking and of false values which held her prisoner inside herself" (62). Mother is gradually and irreversibly changed by her experience. She even exhibits a certain existential angst in her awareness that the reassuring universe of the past can never return. She tells Junior that "Freedom is a bitter thing. . . . It brings suffering in its wake" (66). As her well-educated son prepares to go off to France to further his studies, she ponders the implications of his having opened the gates of her prison, knowing that she must continue to return to the house every night as before. She tells him: "When I went into our house I was still a child. Living with that man I was afraid of . . . I didn't ask any questions. I didn't know who I was. But now! Now!" (69). Now in fact she has learned to question, and this facility will serve Mother well on several levels.

She eventually confronts her husband and proclaims her personhood, burying her past in a pit over which she plants an orange tree as a symbol of rebirth. With the other cherished objects of her childhood, she also inters her religion. At least, she tells us, "the tree will give some fruit some day that can be eaten with pleasure" (119). The rest of the novel shows her energetically pursuing knowledge and freedom, for herself and others. As she studies depictions of her society in the works of Arab writers, she asks pointedly: "why in the devil is our society so sick? Why did it cloister women like beasts? Why did it veil our faces and clip our wings as no other society?" (103). She sets up classes for other women with whom she shares her enlightenment. She passes her exams, she gets a driver's license, she bobs her hair, and in the final pages of the novel, she boards a ship for France in order to see the West for herself and to further broaden her horizons. Under her influence even Father repudiates a tradition that fails to develop the human capital that is woman. By the closing pages, he thus ceases to be the medium of expression for the discourse of gender in Arabic-Islamic tradition, which loses its voice and its power over Mother in the narrative.

This triumph over the constraints of tradition has an innate appeal for the Western reader who must instinctively see Mother's victory as a product of modernization, a variation on the feminist theme of women's liberation. Houaria Kadra-Hadjadi cites a critic who credits Chraïbi's work with doing as much for the emancipation of the North African woman as any sociological treatise on the subject (164). Danielle Marx-Scoras sees *Mother Comes of Age* as a sequel to Chraïbi's *Un ami viendra vous voir* (1967), a work that was "criticized for being about the alienation of women in a consumer society that was specifically Western" (139). She draws our attention to Chraïbi's interest in the writing of Betty Friedan in *The Feminine Mystique* and to an interview with Chraïbi in which he depicts women as "the last colonized of the earth" (140). While it is unquestionably legitimate to read the novel as a commentary on women's changing roles, it is important not to overlook the implications of Mother's newfound skills in critical thinking for the other discourses that would subjugate and construct her, the discourses of colonialism, racism, Orientalism, and even Marxism. In the post-independence era, Mother will also focus her defiance on the national bourgeoisie. To have been sheltered for decades from the vision of the world taught in French schools, dramatized in motion pictures, and perpetrated by French books puts Mother in a privileged position. By the time she encounters these products of a dominant and hostile ideology, she has already learned to question authority, and has become nearly immune to the accepted doctrines to which even her sons adhere; she takes the same convictions that were born in her rejection of her traditional status as a woman in a conservative Muslim society and levels them forcefully against those other discourses that would constrain her as cultural other or colonial subject. Her ability to resist the one gives her insights into how to resist the other, and this drama is also an important part of her story.

Mother makes her discovery of a nation under colonial rule through the various media by which the dominant political force sustains and propagates itself. Isolated as she has been from the cultural developments around her, she confronts the messages of these media as a naive but prescient observer at a point where, thanks to her own battles and ultimately to Junior's teaching, she has already come to question such pretensions and is unwilling to accept their teachings for the truth they purport to be. Her encounters repeatedly foreground the ethnocentric assumptions of the dominant voices while at the same time illustrating Mother's ability to defend herself from all comers. On a visit to the cinema, for example, Mother views a silent film entitled *Son of Scheherazade*, with Douglas Fairbanks, Jr., or Errol Flynn and a cast of Texans playing Arabs in an outrageous melodrama that Mother appropriates and reinterprets creatively during the intermission, "inverting some scenes and eliminating others that she hadn't liked, extrapolating and transforming Hollywood reality into a dream" (56). Refusing the movie's Orientalist narrative, she replaces it with her own. She evaluates every author she encounters from the standpoint of her personal experience of veracity, throwing out any whose perspective fails her test and thus creating her own regime of truth. She finds Pierre Loti especially disappointing: "You got many honors and made a lot of money with your books, but the Oriental world isn't that at all, not at all" (103). Mother and Junior laugh together over a pedantic passage from *Aziyadé* that claims with scholarly seriousness that "Mohammedans have their heads shaved except for a median fringe. . . . This is due to their firm belief that after death the Prophet Mohammed will grasp them by this tuft of hair to lift them to Paradise" (102). Such references, using academic language to frame spurious generalizations, confirm Homi Bhabha's contention that "colonial discourse produces the colonized as social reality which is at once an 'other' and yet entirely knowable and visible" (70-1). Similarly, it illustrates the polarity of Said's Orientalism which is "on the one hand, a topic of learning discovery, practice; on the other it is the site of dreams, images, fantasies, myths, obsessions and requirements" (Bhabha 71). The French educational system, that finely tuned engine of the colonial policy of assimilation that had told Junior Vercingetorix was his Gallic ancestor, cringes before Mother's impossible questions and her uncanny ability to spot contradictions in the lesson. The teacher complains to Nagib: "You understand, Monsieur, that every time I see her walk into the classroom and sit down in the front row, I'm terror-stricken that she'll open her mouth. Yes, I'm terrified that she will ask me questions" (106). Lucidly, Mother confronts the Western gaze as it is transmitted through its films, writers, and institutions, and stares it down.

One of Mother's best scenes and one of Chraïbi's most creative moments takes place when Mother decides to challenge General Charles de Gaulle who is conveniently meeting with the allied leaders in Casablanca. Again, she rallies her supporters precisely over the issue of truth: "None of us here on earth can go on living a lie. That's principle number one. Second principle: we've had to do too much, far too much. I know armies of civilians and neutrals who feel exactly the way that I do. Let the combatants know that we can give them no more as fact or credence or belief" (73). More to the point, de Gaulle has chosen to wage this war without consulting her, without consulting the women and children, the poor, the weak, or the animals. Should we read "colonial subjects" here as well? In the message she confides to a soldier for the general, her first premise is that liberty belongs to everyone. Her second is a bid to re-appropriate the world after the war and rebuild it in her own terms:

> Those who have suffered the horrors of this war should be in the forefront of the builders of the world of tomorrow. And we don't want any more intermediaries or people who think for us and act for us. We want a world of purity, goodness, beauty, and joy. Men have always made mistakes and committed errors and have always built peace on the ruins of war. We don't want that world anymore. (83)

The pronouncement could easily be both a feminist manifesto and a Moroccan declaration of independence. Especially interesting is the insistence on being able to act without help, Morocco being not a colony of France but a protectorate, a term that carries the connotation of a custodial or parental relationship and facilitated charges of paternalism against the French. Chraïbi is setting up a parallel here between Mother's situation as a cloistered wife and her status as colonial subject, a parallel that is strikingly confirmed when de Gaulle at last appears, and Mother is surprised to note that he looks exactly like Father.

Mother's confrontation with Charles de Gaulle is followed immediately by a chapter in which Mother at long last confronts Father himself. From a feminist perspective, the episode is dramatically necessary. It allows Mother to articulate the flaws of patriarchy and above all to make a case against Father's benevolent paternalism. A careful reading of the chapter, especially on the heels of the one pitting Mother against the French general, suggests that it could be interpreted on two or even three levels as a refusal to conform to the role dictated to her by traditional discourses regarding women's place, the colonial discourses justifying the protectorate, and perhaps even the revolutionary or Marxist discourses that offer yet another form of guidance to emerging peoples. Mother acknowledges Father's material support but challenges his motives, to which he responds: "I've brought you up. You had no past, but I've made a respectable woman out of you. I've made life easy for you. I've solved your problems" (88). Father is in character here as the head of the family extolling his own virtues, but it is also tempting to read his remarks as a reference to one of the major assumptions of the French colonial policy of assimilation, that the colonial subject was tabula rasa and had no history, that colonialism nobly bore the responsibility of the civilizing mission that would make subject peoples equals.

Father's claim to have brought Mother up is also consistent with the interpretation of this passage as a confrontation between colonizer and colonized and prepares her further tirades against his paternalism. While she has matured physically under his "protective custody," her soul has failed to develop, and she has been kept in such ignorance of reality that she tells us she knows nothing "except the nourishment you stuff me with, the orders and the instructions you constantly mete out to me, the morality you grease me with, the reins you bridle me with and the blinkers you blind me with" (89). She goes on to say that she knows "Not a thing about the people among whom I was born . . . about my own culture or my own origins or my own language or my own religion" (89). This last quote also articulates the Moroccan intellectual's criticism of French colonial policy which, as David Gordon shows, limited the teaching of Arabic and Moroccan history in preference for education in French on subjects identical to those being studied in Paris. All the while, Mother admits to being well fed and cared for rather like an animal in a barn. In other passages she is compared to a child, a horse, and a mule.

At this point, Nagib is accused of having taught Mother to be "a Bolshevik rebel" (90). But Mother denies this and claims to have carried the seeds of revolution within herself. Nagib only provided ammunition. Nagib himself enters the fray, and when Father tries to escort him out, the son turns the tables and physically ejects the father, locking the door behind him. Mother responds by throwing things at her defender and dressing him down: "I don't need any help.... Not from you or anyone else. I am conscious now and entirely responsible for my own life. Do you understand that? I haven't just freed myself from the custody of your father in order to come asking for your protection, no matter how big you are" (93). The reader rejoices in Mother's self-affirmation, her refusal of protection from either husband or son, an important and necessary development given that her emancipation was guided first by Junior, then by Nagib. She herself has finally recognized that she cannot be truly independent if she continues to rely on someone else. The terms "custody" and "protection" in her argument again seem to evoke Morocco's political status, and Mother's plea for independence from her husband on the grounds that she is not a child applies as well to her role as colonized subject. There is thus a double satisfaction in Nagib's ejection of Father, the paternalistic husband who looks so much like General de Gaulle. But Mother's rejection of Nagib's help seems to me to be more complex. Nagib, with his refusal of the French educational system and his cultivation of working-class friends, has complemented Junior's formal education of Mother with a dose of popular culture. In rejecting his aid as well as Father's, is Mother showing us a Morocco free not only from traditional practices and colonial rule, but also from affiliation with International Socialism as well? Is it coincidence that the Russians are depicted in their function as allies to the great colonial powers during World War II rather than as an ideological alternative? Mother's declaration of independence is thus comprehensive and reflects the spirit of the nation, a statement of complete autonomy and a willingness to face the responsibilities of the future without outside support.

While recognizing that the novel is far more complex than can be presented here, my illustrations serve to demonstrate to an extent Chraïbi's double criticism of both tradition and colonialism and something of the way in which the two are inextricably related in the narrative. Not only does Mother's questioning of her prescribed social role prepare her to defend herself against colonial and ethnocentric discourses, but repeatedly throughout the text, Chraïbi invites us to read one form of oppression in terms of the other, constantly making us aware of the similarities between them even when this indiscrete juxtaposition challenges accepted realities. The adroit textual melding of these dominant discourses and Mother's reactions to them has ultimately meant that this is a tale that may be read differently by different readers depending on their own cultural background and bias. Western interpreters of the work have generally chosen to highlight its feminist themes at the expense of other dimensions. Interestingly, the title of the English translation chosen by Harter, *Mother Comes of Age*, seems to enhance the importance of Mother's emancipation and obscure the emphasis on civilization in the original French title: *La Civilisation, ma Mère!* . . . Hédi Bouraoui, in his study of the cultural ambivalences of the text, approaches it from an entirely different vantage point and chooses instead to underscore Chraïbi's questioning of Western culture, specifically his criticism of modernism and industrialism. These various perspectives eventually arrive at similar conclusions, however, and succeed in developing what is the unifying element of the work, Mother's self-assertion and her victorious resistance to authoritative voices in any form. Chraïbi's ingenious paralleling of sexism and colonialism thus succeeds in appealing effectively to different audiences by dramatizing Mother's virtues through the part of her struggle that each reader is culturally best prepared to see.

Works Cited

Bhabha, Homi K. *The Location of Culture*. London: Routledge, 1994.

Bouraoui, Hédi. "Ambivalence structuro-culturelle dans *La Civilisation ma Mère!...*" *Modern Language Studies* 10 (1980): 56-69.

Chraïbi, Driss. *La Civilisation, ma Mère!...* Ed. G. Robert McConnell. Toronto: Aquila, 1972.

____. *Mother Comes of Age*. 1972. Trans. and introduction by Hugh Harter. Washington, DC: Three Continents Press, 1994.

Gordon, David C. *North Africa's French Legacy 1954-1962*. Cambridge, MA: Harvard University Press, 1962.

Kadra-Hadjadji, Houaria. *Contestation et révolte dans l'oeuvre de Driss Chraïbi*. Algiers: ENAL, 1986.

Martin, Biddy. "Feminism, Criticism, and Foucault." *Feminism and Foucault: Reflections on Resistance*. Ed. Irene Diamond and Lee Quinby. Boston: Northeastern University Press, 1988. 3-19.

Marx-Scouras, Danielle. "A Literature of Departure: The Cross-Cultural Writing of Driss Chraïbi." *Research in African Literatures* 23.2 (1992): 131-44.

Mernissi, Fatima. *The Veil and the Male Elite: A Feminist Interpretation of Women's Rights in Islam*. 1987. Trans. Mary Jo Lakeland. Reading, MA: Addison-Wesley, 1991.

Said, Edward. *Orientalism*. London: Routledge, 1978.

The Sanctuary and the Prison: Women's Rites/Rights/Writing and Political Activism

Pushpa N. Parekh

The role of North African women in the struggle for independence and their continuing resistance to post-independence conditions of neo-colonialism as well as fundamental nationalism is of increasing interest to scholars as well as activists. I will examine selected literary expressions by women as they map out the geo-political, socio-economic, as well as cultural spaces within colonial, nationalist and post-colonial discourses in the context of Arabo-Islamic traditions, debates and feminism. Leïla Abouzeid from Morocco and Nawal El Saadawi from Egypt revisit, re-negotiate and rewrite these realities through a complex and often symbolic ritual of reconfiguring time and space in order to transform and transcend concepts of linear history and geo-political boundaries.

Abouzeid in *Year of the Elephant* and Saadawi in *Memoirs from the Women's Prison* address issues of women's participation, roles and struggles in nation formation, as well as foreground their critique of patriarchal, fundamental, colonial, neo-colonial, and imperial containment of the definitions of national identity as it relates to women. The two authors also examine the specific forms of state institutions and patriarchally-defined ideology that structure the diverse socio-political dimensions of a nation in terms of monolithic, hierarchical, and oppressive paradigms, whether extremist, fundamental or West-oriented. In her narrative, the Moroccan and Egyptian woman respectively, enacts multiple ways of writing/righting the nation. The act of writing (putting words to paper) is also an act of righting (reconstructing and re-envisioning) the wrongs of nation-making. My theoretical approach to as well as critical analysis of the two narratives underscores the consistent and often compelling interplay of women's creativity, activism and spirituality. Writing the nation for Abouzeid and Saadawi involves defining as well as redefining and claiming women's rights through identifying and signaling the patriarchal dimensions of the nation's historical processes. While male-centered narratives of nation delineate an individual or communal hero's quest, the women's narratives provide an alternative mapping of the terrain. If this terrain is the nation at various stages of its formation, fragmentation, and evolution in the post-independent times, women's alternative mapping involves envisioning woman's journey as a rite of passage—one focused not on seeking something outside (as implied by "quest"), but one which involves a transformative vision. This transformative vision, in turn, allows for alternative rationalization of the nation-state and re-examination of colonial and patriarchal formulations and definitions.

In their narratives, Abouzeid and Saadawi recount the moments of history through intercepting the official versions of historical events and figures. Zahra in *Year of the Elephant* and Saadawi in *Memoirs from the Women's Prison* are the "native informants" who reveal the fluid, evolving process of subject constitution for women as they engage in the daily round of private and public activities during specific phases of their nation's colonial and post-colonial history. Zahra is one of several participants in the guerilla warfare, fighting in Morocco's liberation struggle since 1912; she is one of many who witness the moment of independence in 1956, and the return of the Sultan from exile; she who hid weapons, burnt shops and raised donations for the war effort, is also among the women who, in post-independence times, found themselves spurned and rejected by their husbands as well as fellow activists who gained positions of power. Her inner state of anger, frustration and cynicism regarding the brusque and brutal ways in which a woman can be divorced by a man and left with only "whatever the law provides" is a strong indictment of patriarchal interpretations of Islamic law in order to subjugate women: "'Whatever the law provides!' And what is that? Expenses for a hundred days? That shows the extent of the law's regard for women. Throw them out on the streets with a hundred days of expenses" (Abouzeid 10-1). Ironically, she finds herself divorced for the very reasons that she, her husband and others had fought the war for. While her adherence to her cultural practices and religious beliefs was encouraged and utilized by national forces during the fight, in post-independence times the same Zahra is considered too traditional by her husband. Zahra's journey hence traverses the complex, conflicting and often contradictory impulses and forces of post-colonial nationhood.

Written in prison, Saadawi's *Memoirs from the Women's Prison* recounts her imprisonment along with thirteen other women activists for alleged "crimes against the state," during Anwar Sadat's term of Presidency in 1981. Not released until after his assassination, Saadawi continued to be threatened; armed guards were stationed outside her house until she left the country to be a visiting professor at universities in North America. The *Memoirs* is an expression of a woman's experience of political oppression. This experience becomes the driving force for exposing the mechanisms of dictatorship that violate the rights of women from diverse classes and religious backgrounds. Through the testimonial genre and through acts of transgression, Saadawi participates in a counter-hegemonic and anti-authoritarian project. She appropriates the power to rename historical events and its narration through memory and writing. She celebrates the role of Egyptian women in national liberation struggles through the remembrance of their participation in the nationalist demonstrations of 1919 to end British occupation of Egypt, in student protests of 1946 demanding the renegotiation of Anglo-Egyptian Treaty of 1936 and withdrawal of British troops, to the present instances of political activism. These include protests against Anwar Sadat's foreign policies, Camp David of 1979 among them, as well as internal policies of instituting the Internal Security Police and oppressive martial laws such as the Emergency Law and the "Law No. 95 for the Protection of Values from Shame," which aimed at perpetuating the myth of the Islamic woman's domestic and submissive role. Saadawi, like Abouzeid, unveils the contradictions of "new colonialism" and "imperialism." Confronting the despotism of Egypt's ruling system, critiquing the hegemony of American imperial agendas in supporting such dictatorial systems, and exposing the mystification of events by the Western media, Saadawi further unveils the shackles that imprison people today, "north and south, east and west": "the technology of false consciousness, the

technology of holding truths behind amiable humanistic slogans"
(Saadawi 202).

Abouzeid and Saadawi's narratives are specific to the socio-
political conditions of women at specific geographical spaces and
historical moments; therefore, they differ in their artistic focus, political
agendas, and cultural affiliation. Yet their narratives share a certain
consciousness that we can justifiably term feminist, womanist or
emancipatory, as they identify not only the specific nature of the
subjugation and oppression of North African Arab women but also the
specific resources available for women within their cultural, social and
political systems. Their writings are grounded on certain principles and
ideologies that have shaped Arab feminist poetics and discourses but also
shift our perception of these discourses in crucial ways. In the
"Introduction" to *Year of the Elephant*, Elizabeth Fernea argues for the
differing models of feminism:

> Certainly most people, whatever their cultural and
> religious background, would agree on certain basic
> requirements for emancipation: equal rights under the
> law, for example; equal access to economic wealth and
> health; protection from various forms of human
> oppression such as prison, murder, slavery, physical
> abuse. But within these general grounds, each culture,
> each woman, surely has the right of choice, the right to
> form her own "feminist" program using elements from
> her own and other cultural traditions to fulfil new needs.
> The final model or ideal of feminism, then, may differ in
> emphasis, in the pace of implementation, but the goals of
> justice would be the same. (xxiii)

Abouzeid weaves the tale of a collective struggle for national
independence and a personal struggle for a woman's independence after
divorce. These struggles identify certain problems within the
colonial/patriarchal structures. By questioning the viability of certain
family laws, especially those governing divorce, Abouzeid mounts an
important challenge to the patriarchal practice of the *sharia* or the Islamic
law. Based on the Koran and the *hadiths* (customs or practices of Prophet

Mohammad), these laws have been interpreted to meet the needs of certain social conditions. In the chapter titled "Women in Islamic Law, in the Koran and in Tradition," Wiebke Walther examines the complex relationship between Muslim women and the Islamic law:

> If the *hadiths*, such as those which reflect attitudes toward women, are examined closely, it soon becomes apparent that they contain a very wide range of views, some of which are contradictory. In one place, Muhammed is reported to have said: "I have left behind no temptation more harmful to my community than that which women represent for men." (82, V, 200) In another, the following saying is also attributed to him: "The whole world is delightful, but the most delightful thing in it is a virtuous woman." (82, II, 168). . . . It may therefore be assumed that this literature does indeed include the *Sunna* ("custom" or "example") of the Prophet, but reflects to a greater extent the various trends and opinions within the Muslim community in the first two centuries after Muhammed. The representatives of different views and factions wanted to stabilize a social structure made up of the most diverse elements. They hoped to arrive at a standard of general validity by attributing to the Prophet Muhammed values and modes of behavior which they considered religiously and ethically appropriate. (48-9)

Zahra's narrative argues for the reform of laws that violate the rights of women within the context of structural and ideological shifts defining the modern nation of Morocco. It is this challenge that embarks her on a spiritual journey, a journey in which she defines her own rite of passage. She recognizes and retains the values, derived from her religious and cultural traditions, such as the recognition of women's right to property, as attested to in the Koran the wisdom of retaining women's traditional skills, such as spinning wool, a skill that connects the younger generation to their grandmothers and elders, as well as reverence for the sheikh who symbolizes the intrinsic values of Islam, and guides her to experience the spiritual dimensions of life, suffering, work and faith. Zahra, in her search for independence, does not reject all her traditions simply because some need modification and reform. She stands up to implement those changes in her own life; she does not submit to the custom of passively becoming a burden for her sister and her family, after her divorce, nor does she blame herself for not having borne any children during the years of her marriage. She creates a new sanctuary for her beliefs. While the sheikh and the mosque provide her religious security and consolation, Zahra realizes her need to create an economic place for herself in the women's workforce of Casablanca. It is in the last few pages of the novella, that Zahra finds resources for her strength in her spiritual beliefs, and an understanding of women's collective suffering and spirit to survive and forge a future for themselves. Ultimately, Zahra's sanctuary is the inner peace she gains, a peace that allows her to continue the struggle for achieving various levels of autonomy:

> Work, faith, and other things that aren't so important.
> The important thing is I remember God and concentrate
> on the idea of mine that we are only passing through this
> life to build a road to the next one. (Abouzeid 68)

Saadawi's entry into the debates central to Arabo-Islamic traditions is more radical and she clearly mounts her critique of the patriarchal and neo-colonial politics of Egypt through a whole corpus of writings that include novels, memoirs, a play, as well as a travel text. Well-known as a leading Egyptian feminist, sociologist, medical doctor, and writer, Saadawi was dismissed from her post as director-general of health education in the Ministry of Health in Cairo in 1972 for her political writing and activities. Later, in 1991, the Egyptian government shut down her organization, the Arab Women's Solidarity Association, and she went into exile in the United States. Since then, she has been able to go back to Egypt. Saadawi who was one of the speakers at the 1996 ALA Conference at Stony Brook, New York, clearly revealed that she is still actively involved at the grass-roots level, in fighting patriarchy, authoritarianism, imperialism and fundamentalism.

In this context *Memoirs from the Women's Prison* addresses two specific concepts central to Arabo-Islamic cultures, that of woman's sexuality and its control, imprisonment and exploitation in the existing structures of Egyptian society. Fedwa Malti-Douglas in *Men, Women, and God(s): Nawal El Saadawi and Arab Feminist Poetics* argues for the specific ways in which Saadawi's consciousness—artistic, social and political—delineates an Arab Feminist poetics that inform her writing. In narrating the autobiographical account of her journey from her home where she is arbitrarily arrested by Anwar Sadat's Security Police (who could summon, interrogate and imprison at will any person who expressed or revealed the true state of affairs in Egypt), to *Barrages*, the women's prison, and finally her release and exile, Saadawi identifies "prison" as a space of contesting and competing ideologies and powers, a space where threats of "national unity" and fear of "sectarian rift" ironically foster divisiveness and dehumanization. But, as Malti-Douglas points out, prison is also "an important rite of passage" for Saadawi (160). This rite involves an encounter and struggle with the multiple but ultimately irrational mechanisms of control and violation exercised by Sadat's regime. Saadawi, early on, as a female medical doctor had challenged the gendered categorization of professional roles, and by stepping into the prison, she continues her acts of transgression. She forges solidarity among the diverse women, the middle-class intellectuals, the prostitutes, the religious conservatives, as well as murderers, and displaces the tools of destruction with those of creation. The crucial weapon in this transformative act is the collective resistance of the women, however they may be armed, with or without the veil, with a pen or a hoe. Malti-Douglas refers to Saadawi's displacement of the male-homosocial bonding with the female "homosocial family unit" (167), where even the prison guard (*shawisha*) participates in helping the prisoners. From demanding and getting cleaner bread and decent toilets, from securing a secret radio to exercising, the women organize to change abusive situations and keep themselves fit for further revolutionary acts. While the prison space is thus reconfigured, the women also reverse the effect of imprisonment. Facing the Precautionary Detention Officers, the women assume the stance of an impenetrable wall and physically confront them. By using their rigid bodies (whose movements have adapted to the restricted prison space) as instruments of resistance, they reverse a condition of subordination to one of confrontation. The prison becomes a space for not only defying the oppressor but also a site for spiritual healing through a unity that defies "bars or steel partition" (97). Following the death of Sadat, and the end of the ordeal of investigation, Saadawi is finally released from all charges. However, she remembers her cell-mates and continues to help them in every way possible, effecting their transfer from the *Barrages* prison to a hospital and finally their release.

Abouzeid and Saadawi, in their respective narratives, raise certain important issues in the context of women writing the nation. Some of these are: women's movements, organizations and strategies seen in a historical perspective; women's awareness of and struggle for human rights and remedial measures; coalitions in achieving transformation; women's migration, displacement and mobilization; women's engagement in modes of participatory development; women's education and work; women's economic development in rural and urban sectors; women's survival strategies; women's autonomy (organizational, theoretical and personal).

In writing the nation through women's struggles for their rights, in the context of both personal and collective rites of passage, Abouzeid and Saadawi address the complex reality of women who confront a variety of patriarchal structures, in the form of state interventions and in the process of effecting change. They explore women's power to change their given conditions through understanding and challenging the interactive ways in which the legal, economic, and political structures of their nations oppress or devalue women. This power, the authors suggest, can transform the prison of nation space to a sanctuary.

Works Cited

Abouzeid, Leïla. *Year of the Elephant.* Trans. Barbara Parmenter. Austin: Center for Middle Eastern Studies, The University of Texas at Austin, 1989.

Fernea, Elizabeth. "Introduction." *Year of the Elephant.* Leïla Abouzeid. Austin: Center for Middle Eastern Studies, The University of Texas at Austin, 1989. xi-xxvi.

Malti-Douglas, Fedwa. *Men, Women, and God(s): Nawal El Saadawi and*

Arab Feminist Poetics. Berkeley: University of California Press, 1995.

Saadawi, Nawal El. *Memoirs from the Women's Prison*. Trans. Marilyn Booth. Berkeley: University of California Press, 1994.

Walther, Wiebke. *Women in Islam: From Medieval to Modern Times*. Trans. C.S. Salt. Princeton, NJ: Markus Wienar, 1993.

Some Very *Nervous Conditions*: Culture and Commodity in Tsitsi Dangarembga's Novel

Sally-Ann Murray

Tsitsi Dangarembga's *Nervous Conditions*, first published in 1988, is a retrospective narrative of female coming-to-consciousness in colonial Rhodesia during the mid 1960s to early 1970s. Many critics have argued that the story, conveyed through the insightful presence of the mature narrator, guides us to conclude that patriarchy is Tambu's "primary incentive" in learning to mold her own life, since "everywhere around her she perceives the injustice intrinsic to the position of woman" (Veit-Wild 332). Yet patriarchy, viewed in isolation from other powerful cultural claims made upon the characters, cannot adequately account for the stories of five women and their men contained in the novel. My purpose is not to sweep aside either the authorial or critical interest in exploring patriarchal oppression as an influential experiential logic in the novel – this would be foolish. Yet I have found myself probing beyond the obvious in an attempt to understand the cultural dynamics of Dangarembga's story, and picking up on those small moments where critics suggest that Dangarembga in fact deals with extremely volatile cultural exchanges. Some critics acknowledge this volatility rather paradoxically, by granting Dangarembga complete authorial *control* over the nervous energy of her characters (Veit-Wild 332). Others, like Chapman, argue that whatever Dangarembga's manifest focus in *Nervous Conditions*, her narrative "remains jittery about its own attempts to transfer African issues, contexts and values to Western-style dialogues, and vice versa" (308). Such recognitions imply that patriarchy is part of a more elusive cultural mix: one which, I argue in this paper, includes the ambiguous role of commodity culture in the identity formation of Dangarembga's characters.

Here, Burke is helpful with historical-sociological detail. His volume reminds us that in the time-period in which Dangarembga locates her story, commodification was emerging as an important social dynamic in many African societies, Rhodesian among them. After World War II, Rhodesia saw the proliferation of "capitalist functionaries and state officials whose interest in penetrating what they called the 'African market' necessarily demanded that they try to change the nature of African selfhood" (11). While this emergent "African market" is not consistently represented in the novel, I hope to show that the pressures and possibilities which it entailed, both economic and symbolic, contribute to the characters' nervous conditions. Commodities were being experienced as excitingly "new" entities through which self could be shaped and announced through consumption. Given the attractions of such novelty (despite its being limited to comparatively privileged social classes), readers might find it in themselves to assess humanely, rather than judgmentally, a character's infatuation with commodity novelty as an emblem of status, say, or to assess with understanding rather than dogmatic critique another character's frenzied attempt to delineate her rebellions through commodified youth cultures such as mini skirts and secret smoking. This is to read the novel with a degree of sympathy that the older, narrating consciousness does not always work to encourage. The mature consciousness retains something of the moralizing self-righteousness which characterizes the young girl who is given to harsh judgement of her "westernized" cousin, Nyasha.

Despite the reservations of the older Tambu, it seems to me that Dangarembga assumes, in developing the conceptual setting of her narrative, that readers will understand that the novel's action occurs within the context of commodity capitalism associated with modernity. As Chapman has remarked, for instance, the "African specificity" of the novel "is sufficiently muted" to allow the culturally particular to encompass also a more generalized cultural domain. The educated, mission-inflected version of Shona patriarchy on which the novel focuses also reaches beyond the immediate social and historical context in order "to operate as an analogue of the general topic of patriarchy" (307). This uneasy shifting gives us characters who are trying to locate meaningful identities at the interface of cultural repertoires such as "Shonaness" and "Africanness", capitalist modernity and patriarchal tradition, community and individualism. Although she does not find these cultural intersections untroubled, Dangarembga herself has commented on the likelihood that the cultures which make up Zimbabwean life will increasingly be obliged to accommodate the styles, designs and beliefs of the influential West (Chapman 307).

Many of the characters have a contradictory relation to capitalist modernity, given their status as members of an emergent black elite. We find them being culturally assimilated, forfeiting what some would see as their "authentic" Shona culture, but we also see their moving and sometimes innovative attempts to devise newly-meaningful cultural strategies. It is to the ensuing contradictions—which are variously *en*abling and *dis*abling—rather than simply to neuroses provoked by colonialism, that their "nervous conditions" may be attributed. Such attention to volatile cultural repertoires helps the critic to hypothesize that a nervous condition may entail not only neurotic, debilitating anxiety but also a curiously energizing strength. In addressing Dangarembga's uneven representation of cultures such as the popular, the commodified, the modern and so on, the point is not to dismiss her for *failing* to be thorough or coherent. It is more interesting to admit from the start that the culture of modernity, especially in the guise of the commodity, is inherently a slippery customer.

Taking this further, we could argue that such ambiguity is itself a perplexing feature of commodification: the consumption of goods may entail both an alienating manipulation of the self by capitalism, and the pleasurable, self-satisfying agency of choice, novelty and expanded cultural horizons. We could recollect, here, Marx's observations on the enigmatic character of the commodity: "At the first glance, a commodity seems a commonplace sort of thing. Analysis shows, however, that it is a very queer thing indeed, full of metaphysical subtleties and theological niceties" (43-44). For Marx, the commodity is at once grotesque and wonderful, capable of standing with its feet on ordinary ground, and of a perverse, fantastical recasting of everyday materiality. The consumption of commodities, in other words, may yet entail the *production* of imaginative human identities. It is not to be theorized merely as a culture from which degradation, destruction and manipulation ensue. Or, using Burke to return us to the Rhodesian context of Dangarembga's novel, we need to understand that the interface of traditional with commodity cultures was not always characterized by the mechanical manipulation of black people by self-serving colonial-commercial powers. It "was also shaped by individual acts of will and imagination, [and] engagement" (10).

Let me begin to explore the curious cultural (dis)connections which make up *Nervous Conditions* by turning to the opening pages of the novel. An alert reader will notice how Tambu reconstructs her girlhood experience and environment as having been shaped by practices drawn from several cultural sources. Some of these are nostalgically presented as part of a lost Shona "tradition"—gender and age as influential criteria in the use of the river for washing and bathing, for example. Other activities are presented more ambiguously as part of the market-related cultures of a modernity which entails both opportunity and limitation, especially for black people in a colonial context. Tambu explains, for instance, that while the building of the Government's District Council Houses "to enable the administration of our area" (3) fundamentally altered the domestic-social routines of the surrounding homesteads, not all of these changes caused abjection and alienation. A subsistence economy where people grew their own food stuffs co-existed with new forms of commercial exchange: the "entrepreneurial among us ... built their little tuckshops which sold the groceries we needed—bread, tea, sugar, jam, salt, cooking oil, matches, candles, paraffin and soap" (3). Some even began to extend this commerce into forms of popular cultural expression that were simultaneously pleasurable and political. They set up a gramophone "where the youth could entertain themselves with music and dancing. They played the new rumba that, as popular music will, pointed unsystematic fingers at the conditions of the times" (4). Here, Dangarembga seems to be granting the capacity of people to wrest meaningful kinds of identity and collectivity from even compromised commercial exchange: she refers to a "solidarity," a "stamping of feet to the pulse of these social facts." The narrating voice is clearly critical when it recounts that the authorities, alarmed by such bonding, curtailed it through duplicitous measures: by erecting a beer-hall, where people could buy cheap mass-manufactured beer and be lulled into cultural acquiescence; where they could be steered away from any independent entrepreneurial—or political—action.

If the forms of inventiveness which mark the popular cultural moments in this passage are obviously to be valued as a nascent political populism, it is also true that pointed observations about the intersection of ideology and commerce are scarce in the novel, whether we consider these observations to emanate from the narrating consciousness or from the author. Instead, the novel rather haphazardly refracts the popular into forms of commercialized culture of the 1960s—whether youth culture, mass culture or middle class culture—and this hybrid cultural space becomes the informing context for a narrative of female empowerment. The dominant culture of the novel is not popular in the proper sense, that is as cultural practices developed by "the people" for their own satisfaction. Instead, the most visible, powerful culture of the novel is modern education, represented as a congruence of the official cultural technologies sanctioned by modern colonialism. These are most overtly embodied in the novel as the masculinist morality of the mission household. Nevertheless, the modes of authoritative pedagogy through which appropriate "modern" subjectivities are produced is also inflected through the persuasive codes of consumption which comprise the other face of a modern sensibility. Readers need only glance at the passages which deal with Tambu's arrival at the mission household in order to understand this: Tambu's education begins not with official book learning, but with a felt sense that the design and decor of the "Babamukuru" home distinguish it as worth knowing more about. I discuss this section in detail later in the paper.

If Dangarembga's most explicit engagement in the novel is with the formation of a young girl's identity under colonial education, it is the knowledge associated with consumption that must bear the weight of her ambivalence: such knowledge is compromised, implicated as it is in attempts to control people's experience; elite in being a marker of social distinction; and yet also subject to creative reworking by individuals in their efforts to fashion meaningful identities. Dangarembga suggests that if commercial popular culture can disable young women like Nyasha and Tambu, offering them insubstantial role models, commodification is also a persuasive, even inevitable constituent in the formation of black subjectivity in Rhodesia in the 1960s and 1970s.

Let me pursue the matter of Dangarembga's ambivalent authorial attitude to modern consumer culture in *Nervous Conditions*. At times, she seems to think that modernity and its associated consumerism are western cultural fetishes which betray the African through hyperbolic promises of freedom, enlightenment, fulfilment which never quite materialize—or which materially alter Africans' lives mainly by delivering them into the hands of false gods who demand from them the uncritical worship of God, goods and the good life. Within this scenario, one drawn by many African writers and theorists, consumer culture appears as but a form of continuing colonialism through which otherwise independent indigenous people are unequally reconciled to western capitalism. Pertinent here is Zimbabwean Dambudzo Marechera's scathing ridicule, in *The House of Hunger*, of the way in which "the Modern African Family" was produced through the consumption of both western commodities like "Fanta Orange Tastes So Good" and of Christian religion (151).

At other times, though, Dangarembga's position is slightly different: rather than simply critiquing consumption, she struggles to represent the complex role played by modern commodity culture in the lives of her characters, and to demonstrate that this culture entails paradoxical restrictions and expansions. Significantly, for example, the movement of Tambu from the homestead to the mission (and beyond and back) is not only to be read as a shift deeper into racist capitalism. Rather, she is presented by Dangarembga as a character who must learn, using a welter of cultural resources, to negotiate her "self". Think of the event which enables Tambu to continue her education at the Rutivi school near the homestead. It is not difficult to read this event through negative theories of commodification. By selling her mielies (maize) on the market in Umtali, Tambu begins her experience of the commercial knowledge of commodities. Her mielies become commodities in that for "them"—in actuality for them plus the added-value of Mr Matimba's fanciful embellishments concerning Tambu as but one child among many in a destitute African family—she acquires a hitherto unimaginable sum of money. The use-value of this money, in turn, further locates her within the market economy of modernity. For the critic of commodification, then, it could thus be said that from the outset of her story of economic and educational "progress" we have embodied in the sale of the mielies a scenario in which the child (dis)associates earnings from labor. Her one morning's work—and this is precisely what her standing near the bus rank disclaiming "nice mielies" is *not*—effects an as if magical transformation. It has the mysterious capacity to transform lives. There is no intrinsic "ten pound" exchange—value attached to the mielies, and Tambu's lesson is that the most ordinary object—corn, in this case—may have attributed to it an enigmatic, supramaterial worth through which it becomes something "other" than "itself". As Marx might put it, the money "is the metamorphosed shape of all [the] other commodities" (88) through which Tambu's life will be altered. Fair enough.

Yet I am also inclined to argue that these transactions invite more than just a cynical reading, connected as they are to the young girl's deeply felt longings and desires. It is not money, per se, which is the final object of her desires. By acquiring money through her creative agency she believes she might then be enabled—through hard work as much as fantastical hopes—to enjoy a degree of freedom from the life which has been planned for her as a poor, subservient rural black girl. It is true that Tambu's educational aspirations, on leaving the homestead for schooling at the mission, are inflected with her wish to shed her dull-skinned peasant self for the shininess, freshness and novelty—dare I say glamour—of what she thinks will be her modern body and identity. Admittedly, too, the novel goes on to reveal the limitations of dreams: entrenched racism renders Tambu's entry into Sacred Heart not as wonderful or liberating as she had imagined it would be. Still, by the end of the narrative she has become a conscious agent of her own life. Associated with her projected longings for new ways of knowing and producing her "self" is not only the formality of book knowledge and an educational mission that is approved of by her mission educators, but more informal, popularized forms of conduct and expectation as are embodied in broadly modern, middle-class codes such as internal plumbing, dining and privacy. In part, the reader might feel uncomfortable that Tambu seeks a metamorphosis into some other body or form, something different from her "previous" self. The dominant metaphors fetishize newness and the as-if magical exchange of one thing for another. Yet despite such reification, another part of the reader might respond sympathetically, for Tambu's projected image of herself and her life at the mission are also humanizing. Away from the abased authority of her father Jeremiah, the complex stoicism and hopelessness of her mother Ma'Shingayi and, perhaps most importantly, the hard labor which is the lot of the indigent rural female, she believes she will become a "real" person with a stimulated mind and an interior life for the first time in her existence. She is not completely wrong.

As I am arguing, Dangarembga is unsure about whether commodities have meliorative or malevolent capacities; whether they can affect her characters' life histories for the better, or for the worse. As I have already said, perhaps it is not surprising that Dangarembga cannot speak with certainty. Her erratic treatment of the role of the commodity in the formation of a black Rhodesian middle class may be linked to the very trickiness of the commodity as an entity. Sometimes it can be actively used by the individual in the negotiation of emergent identities, class positions and imagined status distinction; sometimes it can verge on a form of neo-colonialism which trashes valuable (indigenous) cultures and seduces individuals into apparently privileged patterns of leisure and consumption that actually serve the abstracted economic imperatives of colonial capital's need to manufacture a wider market for goods. Accordingly, there are tensions in Dangarembga's representations of the new forms of market production which influence the identity formation of characters such as Tambu and her brother Nhamo. On the one hand, Dangarembga is critical of the fact that this production pivots on the visible consumption of a range of generic product types like soap, toothpaste and Vaseline petroleum jelly. The use of these commodities (and the bodily display of difference which such use entails) confers an elite status on several characters, separating them from traditional cultural conventions and destabilizing customary hierarchies.

Yet on the other hand, she also seems to understand that this is not a simple process of self-aggrandizement through consumption. It is connected to the uneven imagining of new selves in which one's perceptions of self intersect with the symbolic value of otherwise ordinary goods. The basic "groceries" that could be purchased from the "little tuckshops" (Dangarembga 3) beside the Council Houses and the bus terminus, items which the local people have come to "need", also become symbolically invested with desire, associated with the exchange of an old self for something thought to be better, improved. As Burke has said, from at least the early 1940s in Rhodesia, commercial agents such as advertisers and market researchers had been laboring to produce the black person as "market" and "consumer": products as diverse as "pens, clothing, beer, education, automobile supplies, and especially toiletries of all kinds . . . were . . . pitched to African consumers as the definitional essence of glamor and 'smart' living—commercial codewords for the African elite" (155-156). Toiletries were associated with complex ideological-symbolic codes: hygienic imagery which connected them to Christian morality, an ethic of hard work and responsible domesticity, as well as to civilized manners (and bodies) supposedly the epitome of modernity (Burke 156). Interestingly, though, the changed lives represented in *Nervous Conditions* could be taken to suggest that "exchange" is never merely a metaphor. It is never only the easy figurative transfer of one set of meanings for a different entity. Whatever their fantasies, Nhamo and Tambu, for instance, cannot simply forgo their peasant selves for sophisticated urban identities. If the youthful Nhamo returns to the homestead with soap, toothpaste and sugar, items which he then reserves, arrogantly, for his private use as a defining mark of his own new status as an African versed in the cultures of the modern world, this does not automatically enable him to be produced as a modern person who is remote from rural poverty and labor. He must still on occasions work in the fields, physically negotiating various cultural claims upon his selfhood; he must still sometimes travel by bus; he must still labor to present "another" self which is capable of succeeding at the mission school.

Consider also where Tambu, having just arrived at her uncle and aunt's home, revels in her new possessions. (See the passage "'These are your things, Sisi Tambu, your clothes and your washing things,'. . . the toothbrush, here the vaseline and the flannel and a comb" [76.]) These things—uniforms, underwear, toiletries, "smart casual dresses"—represent for the youthful narrator her imminent possession of a new sense of self and indeed of self-*importance*. As the critically-astute adult Tambu might want us to recognize, of course, these commodities are implicated in the bodily surveillance into which mission education, as a curious vector of modern consumer capitalism, encouraged African people. Yet there are also complicated forms of longing and desire which infuse the young Tambu's identification with the goods, and I find myself unable to read this merely skeptically as a sign of the adolescent's as-yet-unqualified awe for her generous and successful uncle. Dangarembga's own sympathies seem to me to be mobile: to what extent does she wish us to read through and beyond Tambu's childish infatuations with upward mobility, and to what degree may we legitimately form emotional sympathies with her, despite sensing that she is being lined up for a fall? Considered diagnostically, the very syntax of the passage undermines any attempt to read it either critically or empathetically: the indexing of items through adjectives and common nouns, for instance, is at once meant to "describe" the goods which are being heaped upon the young Tambu, and to imply that they defy description even for the adult narrator who is crafting the story. How defy? Not so much because they represent undue excess, I would argue, but because Dangarembga, through her narrator, is struggling to acknowledge that the dreams, aspirations and realities of young black women such as Tambu were being shaped by new and difficult relations to goods. In such a conceptual context, the repeated hyphenation and proliferation of nouns to which Dangarembga must resort signifies her own uncertain response to the situation she describes. She is left searching for words, ways, means . . . something to allow her to know how to conceptualize and convey the place of the commodity in Tambu's changing sense of self.

   Dangarembga most consciously and dramatically expresses the curious power of the commodity and the place of things in social practice in those passages which detail the older Tambu's recollections of her arrival at the mission, and her awed progress up the ironically-named "glamour gradient" of the kitchen, to the dining rooms and living rooms. Here, we have Dangarembga representing a domestic variant of commodity culture in great detail because the description bears upon her criticism of the self-inflated middle class lifestyle of Babamukuru, a member of the first African Christian elite. Dangarembga makes clear the power of commodities to "seduce" the African person who is un-used to their plenty: even the young Tambu is shown to know enough about cultural alienation to use her crafty "thinking strategy" in order to avoid being taken in by the symbolic power of the lifestyle which eroded the cultural identity of her brother Nhamo. In her detailed account of the domestic trappings of the mission household, Dangarembga conjures Baba's hubristic status. Bookcases holding encyclopedia, walls painted in fashionably shaded contrasts, a whole room given over to dining, a fragile flowered tea set that is in daily use, an elaborate display cabinet holding fine china. . . . Yet a dulled sink that has been scoured rather than caressed by modern cleaning material, and a hopeless toil, given the proximity of the bus station, against the dust which might taint the outward, "illusory" signs of middle class "civilization" (71). Dangarembga has the narrator pointedly recollect, for instance, that while her uncle's home was tastefully decorated, the limits of taste and style were always financial, and these in turn were prescribed by the racist determinants of a colonial economy geared towards white advancement and black impoverishment (69). Although the novel does not spell this out, Broughton explains that Babamukuru and others were members of a specifically *African* middle class: their status was provisional rather than secure in that it depended upon the colonial state's determination to create a buffer zone between marginally acceptable black people such as teachers and doctors, and a mass of black people which, it was envisaged, would remain mere units of labor. Despite Baba's hard work (and, we are to discover, that of his wife), his salary cannot buy freedom from racist colonial hierarchies. Here, Dangarembga gives the lie to consumerism as equal opportunity, and to capitalism as freedom of choice. Yet Dangarembga's criticisms are also by no means straightforward. The pages describing Tambu's arrival at the mission house are themselves marked by authorial uneasiness rather than constant censure.

Let's take as an example the studied comments concerning the use or not of harsh scourers:

> the kitchen sink gleamed greyly. This lack of brilliance was due, I discovered years later when television came to the mission, to the use of scouring powders which, though they sterilised 99 per cent of a household, were harsh and scratched fine surfaces. When I found this out, I realised that Maiguru, who had watched television in England, must have known about the dulling effects of these scourers and about the brilliance that could be achieved by using the more gentle alternatives. By that time I knew something about budgets as well, notably their inelasticity. It dawned on me then that Maiguru's

> dull sink was not a consequence of slovenliness, as the advertisers would have us believe, but a necessity. (67-8)

In her review-article on the novel, Broughton cleverly refers to this passage as contributing to the "sociology of detergent" (5): she understands that supposedly trivial household commodities are cathected into status and identity. But the matter of Dangarembga's authorial stance remains difficult to pin down. Yes, Dangarembga has Tambu come to a realization about commodities that is independent of the commercial drives of advertisers: how you manage your household depends on your financial resources, and not simply on "laziness"—that familiar colonial characterization of black people—or even on the extent to which mass mediated advertising has successfully manipulated you into becoming a voracious consumer. Yet in working through this passage I cannot easily separate Dangarembga's authorial voice (and credibility) from precisely the advertising jargon from which she seems to want to distance Tambu: in the passage, notwithstanding her adult self-reflexivity, Tambu sounds rather like a talking head in a detergent ad, and television is both debunked *and* treated as a familiar, even popularly reliable, source of knowledge. It is through television, after all, that she comes to reassess her earlier moral judgements against Maiguru's domestic management. Further, the time-line of Tambu's "discovery" about kitchen commodities and her consequent extending of understanding, rather than criticism to her aunt, is blurred: "I discovered years later"; "By that time". The passage at once exonerates Maiguru for her dull sink and implies that she ought to have known better! These tensions are intensified when we remember that in a novel where the mission house is often referred to as Babamukuru's, the kitchen sink in this passage is, without overt authorial intervention in the *adult* Tambu's account, designated Maiguru's. (We might want to ask where Anna fits into this "sociology of detergent", given that she is the woman generally responsible for the washing up.)

It is also productive to think a little about the culture of the commodity in relation to patriarchy. It is very clear, in the novel, that Dangarembga takes issue with hegemonic patriarchal culture, whether it is manifest as racist colonialism, traditional indigenous hierarchy, or as the gender inequality that persists even under modernity. Given the use of "patriarchy" as an umbrella term, Dangarembga can attribute Nyasha's failure to negotiate a sustaining selfhood to something fairly vague: the difficulty of discovering a role for the educated modern young (black) woman of the 1960s in Rhodesia. Yet it seems to have been difficult for Dangarembga to find an appropriate voice in which to address the evidence, which she herself incorporates into the novel, of the burgeoning capitalist market economy and consumer culture that inform the stories which Tambu tells. Why this difficulty? Because to admit commodity relations into the story as a major plot dynamic would have been greatly to problematize the nature of the "choices" which the protagonists make? For instance: what does it mean to be a modern woman in colonial Rhodesia? How is this subject position inflected through consumption and constrained by racist policy? To what extent is commercial culture in the colonial context yet another form of "patriarchy"?

There is not space to deal with these questions comprehensively. Here are merely a few observations. In Rhodesia in the late 1960s and early 1970s, the rise of a consumer culture and the availability of commercial toiletries and beauty aids intensified many African men's fears about women's independent sexuality. African "women were often depicted as sexually powerful, able to marshall commodities like clothing and toiletries to control men through desire" (Burke 158). Whatever the limited nature of the personal freedoms promised by the consumption of goods and the participation in fashionable trends—they do not after all, provide Nyasha with a finally sustaining sense of self, and she herself is critical of consumption as a means to emancipation—they nevertheless provide outlets that enable Nyasha to explore her identity beyond the designation of dutiful Shona daughter. It is hardly surprising, then, that Babamukuru wishes to marshall his daughter's access to the commodified signifiers of liberated womanhood, be these tampons, minis, sexy novels or unchaperoned leisure. It is through this control that he seeks to manage her nascent sexuality away from impropriety towards respectability and respect. He considers this to be his responsible, fatherly concern, but reading through the discourses of commodity and patriarchy, we can analyze his actions as an anxious attempt, when faced with the cultural challenges represented by consumption, to retain traditional cultural propriety and authority over female behavior. He cannot see that Nyasha's relation to commodities, as to received notions of "Shonaness", is questioning, critical. Nyasha is no passive consumer. While she experiments with the subjectivities that modern market relations make available to her—straightening Tambu's hair, painting her nails, dressing up, smoking—Nyasha also "questions the whole process of assimilation and makes it clear to Tambudzai that real emancipation means more than education and better economic standing" (Veit-Wild 333). Perhaps this is Baba's dilemma: he does not really understand his daughter's cultural experimentation yet he *does* sense that her version of modernity reflects badly on the class privilege which he has garnered through being inculcated into missionised forms of modernity. But he sees enough to make him fear that his daughter's probing relation to the modernity which has produced commodity capitalism, commodity feminism and commodified black people will inevitably prompt her to question her role in a traditional Shona hierarchy and thereby wrest from him the last vestiges of male control over her.

There's much more, of course, to be remarked about Nyasha. Part of her trauma is that she is obliged to displace her desire for social good—her hostility at the injustices of racism and patriarchy—into a daily relation with the supposed satisfactions of consumer goods, colonial education and a middle class lifestyle whose unspoken limit is race. Nyasha's actions and criticisms uncover the occlusions of the Babamukuru-Maiguru household: the inequalities premised on gender, as well as the tenuousness of what the parents project, by means of possessions, style, food, and the organization of space, as their "arrived" status. Despite her voracious appetite for novelty, she is also driven by an anarchic will to refuse the cultures of consumption—she sees these as linking education with goods—which give a black middle class under colonial rule its comparatively privileged place. When she dismisses her father's success as being merely that of a "good munt", when she urges the servant Anna to stop kneeling in her presence and, most dramatically, when she shreds the history text between her teeth, we understand that she is refusing not only the consumption of tainted things associated with her family's class position, but the very ideas which inform this status. In terms of narrative strategy, though, where can all this lead? Are the wages of this ideological "sin", as it were, her necessary death in the novel, since colonial capitalism cannot permit constant critique by those whom it construes as subjects? Compare this with the more promising future which the plot reserves for Tambu. She learns to criticize, yes, but also pragmatically to make the material best of a bad ideological situation. She thereby accommodates herself to the status quo even as she secures for herself a higher position in the hierarchy. I am not eager to derive a moral here, but it's difficult to ignore the awkward possibility that Tambu's survival as the main protagonist occurs precisely because she is marked (by both the author and the historical conventions of the novel) as the more desirable, or durable, or manageable modern subject. She survives and Nyasha fades away because commodified modernity is willing to sacrifice its potentially better, more critical self in order to perpetuate its structures. I am not altogether happy with these flighty speculations, but they ought to be allowed space if we're interested in relating *Nervous Conditions* to the powerful contemporary discourses of modernity and consumption. In comparison with her parents' attempts to fix boundaries so as to exclude the improper and bolster what they perceive to be their proper social status, Nyasha's search for meaning rapaciously crosses cultural divides: she devours (and spits out) varieties of European book learning, acquires superficial competence in traditional Shona practices such as appropriate greetings and clay pot making, and experiments with the rituals of female knowledge popular among her contemporaries: cake-baking, fashion, nail-painting, hair-straightening, the use of tampons. She struggles, unsuccessfully, to shape cultural hybridity into a "whole woman" that she can recognize as herself, Nyasha. Perversely, the hybridity of modernity both gives her wider cultural horizons and makes it difficult for her to set limits to what she chooses in her exploration of self. When she does try to "stop" herself, it is by refusing to conform to conventional eating patterns. Why? Because she has found no cultural belief system that will sustain her—not Shona culture, or colonialism, or liberated femininity or consumption. Her own inquiries have repeatedly revealed the limitations of each of these cultural discourses. Chapman remarks scathingly that Nyasha's supposedly enlightened Western education "has little coherence of idea, action or consequence. Its minor teenage rebellions and freedoms . . . hardly equip the Western teenager for matters of social or political choice let alone the doubly-displaced Nyasha: the African girl caught up in the complex condition of African/colonial dependencies" (308). Is Nyasha's unwillingness to hold on to what she has consumed, despite being attributed by her to forces of patriarchy, also implicated in the very mode of consumerism through which she is expected, as a middle class African, to negotiate her subjectivity? By some critics, Nyasha's "nervous condition", her inability to consume, may be taken to illustrate the fact that consumer needs are in principle unlimited and insatiable, and hence destructive. Work through the conceptual contortions this way: consumer culture is the dominant, even privileged medium for negotiating identity within a post-traditional society; the Rhodesia of which Dangarembga writes is moving conflictingly within both the traditional and the modern, therefore consumption is likely to be emerging as a persuasive subject position for young African women such as Nyasha and Tambu. Yet since commodity culture is premised on infinite consumption, the self is never something at which you arrive, never an achieved entity with which you are able to feel satisfied. While a romantic strand of modernity urges individuals to fashion themselves into "better people" through hard work, study and the acquiring of self-reliance, Nyasha discovers that "the self", especially for a young black woman in her time and place, is in fact an exhaustingly infinite project, one which she finds impossible to sustain.

Yet it remains the case that Nyasha's own turbulent attempts to fashion a meaningful subjectivity occur as much *through* consumption as against it. Interestingly, too, this also holds for *Nervous Conditions*, the novel. For the very mode of address which has made *Nervous Conditions* a successful (widely-read? much-prescribed) work of fiction intersects with the registers through which women's popular culture presents the spectacle of individual lives. Whether we're considering magazines, radio dramas or soap operas, these "women's genres" are characterized by confessional logics, intimate testimonies, and serial self-explorations that are not dissimilar from the techniques which Dangarembga uses to portray the youthful female experiences of Tambu and Nyasha. The adolescent femaleness of these two constitutes a body-centeredness which readers are likely to recognize as much from the true stories and advice columns of women's magazines, as from the narratives of women's struggles for independence contained in the more academically-flavored genre of the bourgeois novel.

Although I have perhaps pushed speculation about characterization and commodity to its limits in the preceding discussion of Nyasha, this "incremental logic" should also have helped to emphasize the fundamental premise of my paper: that critical readings of *Nervous Conditions* need to address the ambivalence towards commodification which marks Dangarembga's text. I have tried to demonstrate something of Dangarembga's nuanced attitude to commodification and goods as these relate to her characters' negotiation of emergent cultural identities. Reading both in and through Dangarembga's own authorial interests, it becomes possible to see *Nervous Conditions* as a novel which grapples with the fact that the curious life of the commodity and the associated cultures of consumption play an important, if not self-evident, role in the fears and aspirations, the desires and delusions of the Sigauke family, as its members learn to conceptualize and to express their modern African identities. They contribute to the skeins of ill-defined nervous condition running through the narrative. Whatever the actual derivation from Sartre's preface to Fanon's *The Wretched of the Earth* (1961), the "nervous conditions" of the title, then, are ambiguous. They do not necessarily designate only the cultural traumas, alienations and neuroses which result from patriarchy or consumer culture; they may also signify powerful forms of agency that provoke a character to shift beyond culturally-entrenched behaviors and assumptions in order to negotiate new subjectivities.

Works Cited

Broughton, Treva. "Adolescent in Zimbabwe." *Southern African Review of Books* 2.1 (October/November 1988): 5-6.

Burke, Timothy. *Lifebuoy Men, Lux Women: Commodification, Consumption, & Cleanliness in Modern Zimbabwe*. London: Leicester University Press, 1997.

Chapman, Michael. *Southern African Literatures*. London/New York: Longman, 1996.

Dangarembga, Tsitsi. *Nervous Conditions*. London: The Women's Press, 1988.

Fanon, Frantz. *The Wretched of the Earth*. Trans. Constance Farrington. Intro. Jean Paul Sartre. Harmondsworth: Penguin, 1961.

Marechera, Dambudzo. *The House of Hunger*. London: Heinemann, 1978.

Marx, Karl. *Capital*. Trans. Eden & Cedar Paul. London: William Dent, 1930.

Veit-Wild, Flora. *Teachers, Preachers, Non-Believers: A Social History of Zimbabwean Literature*. London: Hans Zell, 1992.

Desire and Dissent in the Works of Assia Djebar

John Erickson

In Assia Djebar's works, the motifs of love/desire and dissent are entwined with and coalesce around the notion of Algerian nationhood. In this essay I shall look primarily at the first volume of Djebar's "Algerian Quartet," *L'Amour, la fantasia* (1985), which is a collage of the motifs iterated and developed by Djebar in her subsequent works, to which I shall also refer: *Ombre sultane* (1987) and *Vaste est la prison* (1995), the second and third volumes of her quartet, the work of non-fiction *Le Blanc de l'Algérie* (1995), and *Oran, langue morte* (1997).

Love (*amour*), as it appears in the title of *L'Amour, la fantasia*, evokes both the modern usage denoting human sentiment in regard to one or more individuals, as well as the metonym current in the seventeenth century, *les amours*, denoting love of one's country (*Le Grand Robert*). The other term of the entwining motifs, dissent (from the Latin *dissentire* < *dis-* + *sentire*, to feel), denotes withholding assent, disapproving, or disagreeing (a synonym of "dissidence," whose etymology also denotes being separated or set off from, being in disagreement with, holding a differing opinion—*Le Grand Robert* and *Webster's Third International Dictionary*).

In sum, one side of the equation love or desire/dissent signifies the act of being drawn to or towards, the other to stand apart from. This tension I see as important to an understanding of the *enjeu* of Djebar's work. These abstracted meanings conjoin several motifs, such as writing and language, physical and spiritual exile or distancing, and the articulation of the Algerian nation.

The brief introductory passages of Part One of *L'Amour, la fantasia* provide us with the full vocabulary of desire and dissent that will inform Djebar's work to come. The narrator describes her first experience of love at the age of 17 when she receives a love letter from a strange boy at the *lycée*. Her father, furious, tears up the letter, which she pieces back together. The seemingly harmless wording in French she interprets as swollen with a "désir imprévu, hyperbolique. [. . .] Les mois, les années suivantes, je me suis engloutie dans l'histoire de l'amour, ou plutôt dans l'interdiction d'amour" (16). She enters into a secret correspondence in French. "A l'instar d'une héroïne de roman occidental, le défi juvénile m'a libérée du cercle que des chuchottements d'aïeules invisibles ont tracé autour de moi et en moi... Puis l'amour s'est transmué dans le tunnel du plaisir, argile conjugale" (16). She speaks of the "ritualistic purification" (*lustration* from the Latin *lustratio* < *lustrum*) of the sounds of childhood memory, a purification:

> [qui] nous enveloppe jusqu'à la découverte de la sensualité dont la submersion peu à peu nous éblouit... Silencieuse, coupée des mots de ma mère par une mutilation de la mémoire, j'ai parcouru les eaux sombres du corridor en miraculée, sans en deviner les murailles. Choc des premiers mots révélés: la vérité a surgi d'une fracture de ma parole balbutiante. De quelle roche nocturne du plaisir suis-je parvenue à l'arracher? (16)

She speaks finally of blowing the space within her to pieces, a lost space of voiceless cries, frozen for ages in a "prehistory of love" and of cutting herself adrift once she has discovered the meaning of the first words of love blurted out. She then imagines setting off at dawn, "Ma fillette me tenant la main" (17)—an allusion to the opening sentence of Part One proper that describes her father setting off with her, hand in hand, to bring her to school for the first time, where she will learn the French language in which she will cast the love and desire as well as the pain she has experienced.

The vocabulary of desire and dissent to be found in her later works announces itself in these first passages: love, prohibition, and defiance; enclosure and confinement, breaking out, aphasia and voicing;

a prehistory of love, separation, liberation and exile. Perhaps the primal image is that of the cocoon formed around her in childhood being broken by the discovery of love and sensuality and of her becoming aware for the first time of the "desperate voiceless cries" (*Fantasia* 4) of her women ancestresses. Now liberated by her discovery and the meaning of the first words of love, she will return to her childhood that has been purged and purified, look on it through the eyes of a mature woman in search of the past—not only hers but that of her silenced sisters who have been denied a voice.

The antiphonal presentation that will link love and dissent, personal experience, and the history of the nation throughout Djebar's work appears at the outset of *L'Amour*. The narrative proper of Part One, entitled "La Prise de la ville ou l'Amour s'écrit," alternates between the taking of Algiers by the French in 1830 and the story of the three cloistered girls who secretly correspond with male pen-pals throughout the Arab world (22ff). This part closes with the premonition of the narrator, as a childhood friend of the sisters, that, "derrière la torpeur du hameau, se préparait, insoupçonné, un étrange combat de femmes" (27).

Part One recounts the narrator's early initiation into love, desire, and sensuality. From the very beginning of her childhood, love or desire and dissent are linked, for, in learning to write the French language, she runs up against the conventions that set up prohibitions against the free expression, movement, and acts of the Algerian women. She repeats the phrase "vaste est la prison" several times in her novel by that name—*Meqqwer l'hebs*—a verse taken from a Berber song that links prison to claustration. The elder sequestered women (*séquestrées*) who observe the thirteen-year old narrator's freedom of dress and movement as she dances, and her freedom to cross the threshold leading to the outer world as she goes off to French school, comment: "elle comprendra jamais car elle ne sera jamais de nos maisons, de nos prisons, elle sera épargnée de la claustration" (*Vaste* 279). In *Vaste est la prison*, the prison is a metaphor for the sequestered women, as well as for the resisters during the War of Liberation who undergo incarceration and torture at the hands of the French occupiers.

In *Ombre sultane* the desire of incarcerated women is manifest in their envy of the males' freedom: "Vous vous présentez au monde, vous les bienheureux! Chaque matin de chaque jour, vous transportez votre corps dans l'étincellement de la lumière, chaque jour qu'Allah crée!" (17). Little girls peer out towards the sea, where boys can go but which is forbidden to them. "Ah, imaginer les bains de mer[!]" (110). The boys return, bright-eyed, and hang up their clothes to dry. "Traces d'un paradis proche, qui pourrait nous y introduire?" (110). The boys bring back shells, tease them, and describe the taste of the sea-urchin, a delicacy taboo to females. "Comme si ce garçon se mettait à rêver aux sexe de sa mère et que par bravade il en dévoilait, pour moi et pour lui-même, la nostalgie incestueuse" (110). The desire of the boys to possess the mother will translate into that of the narrator to possess her female ancestresses.

The narrator as a young girl in *Ombre*, upon seeing the Berber dancers/hetaera, expresses the desire of the female child to be free to move about and act:

> Dans le sillage de ces réprouvées dont la vulgarité se gonflait de morgue, je réentendais la scansion bédouine; j'entendais revenir le nay [a melody played on a flute] derrière les collines, et ce, malgré la rumeur du bain surpeuplé. Pour moi, d'emblée, en princesses païennes elles se métamorphosaient. (115)

But, as she will learn, the freedom she aspires to as a liberated woman will also lead to a state of social outcast and to the pain of exile.

Love letters or letters signifying desire and sensuality play an important role in Djebar's novel. As Dorothy Blair says, "[t]he theme of the love-letters is one of the links between the historical and the autobiographical dimensions of the novel as well as a basic part of its structure" (Introduction, *Fantasia*). Aside from the letters exchanged by her three cloistered girl friends and their male pen-pals, the narrator introduces letters of the French during the siege of Algiers in 1830, and that of her own father who "dares" to write directly to her mother, tantamount in Islamic society to an unconventional open declaration of love between a man and his wife (38). The theme of love and its cognates—desire and sensuality—is a dominant theme in Djebar's *Amour*.

The narrator describes at one point receiving a letter from her absent lover-husband who recalls details of her body. She is disturbed because it is "[d]ésir proféré en termes d'écorchures, d'un lieu lointain, et sans le timbre de la voix qui caresse." Suddenly, she says, "ces feuilles se mettent à exhaler un pouvoir étrange." She awakens to the loveless existence of the sequestered women of the past and present, as the pages start to act like a mediator:

> Une intercession [qui] s'opère: je me dis que cette touffe de râles suspendus s'adresse, pourquoi pas, à toutes les autres femmes que nulle parole n'a atteintes. Celles qui, des générations avant moi, m'ont légué les lieux de leur réclusion, elles qui n'ont jamais rien reçu: aucune voix tendue ainsi en courbe de désir, aucun message que traverserait quelque supplication. Elles ne se libéraient que par la psalmodie de leur chant obsidional.
>
> La lettre que je rangeai m'est devenue première lettre: pour les attentes anonymes qui m'ont précédée et que je portais sans le savoir. (77)

The adjective *obsidional*, first appearing in French in the 16th century, derived from the Latin *obsidionalis < absidio* ["siege"]. *Le Grand Robert* characterizes it as a didactic term, "Relatif, propre aux sièges, aux villes assiégées." The word used to describe the song of the women ancestresses is particularly well chosen, for it signifies not only the attempt of women to break through the barriers of male-dominated discourse but the siege of Algiers by the French, who sought to break through the barriers of sovereignty of the Algerian nation.

The love letter from her absent husband thus serves as an interceding or mediating device that calls upon the narrator to become the "bearer" of the voices, words, and story of her silent ancestresses. For the first time she hears their voices and weeps. This is the prelude to what will develop as her sense of engagement in becoming the voice, the *amanuensis*, for her mute sisters. In giving voice to their desires, her writing is animated by her own desires.

The sub-title of the first part of this work, "L'Amour s'écrit" (i.e., *qui est écrit*—that which is written) can also be read as "L'Amour ses cris" (i.e., *ses appels*—the cries of love), readings that suggest love that is written, the cries of her ancestresses, and, as well, the pain and joy of the physical love act. Djebar comments on this pun near the end of the novel: "ma main qui écrit établit le jeu de mots français sur les amours qui s'exhalent; mon corps qui, lui, simplement s'avance, mais dénudé, lorsqu'il retrouve le hululement des aïeules sur les champs de bataille d'autrefois, devient lui-même enjeu: il ne s'agit plus d'écrire que pour survivre" (*Amour* 244).

In speaking about writing of love, the narrator recognizes her irrevocable involvement in transcribing through her own voice the silenced cries of her sisters of the past. She speaks of her wish to write of love but is also aware of the risk involved:

> L'amour, si je parvenais à l'écrire, s'approcherait d'un point nodal: là gît le risque d'exhumer des cris, ceux d'hier comme ceux du siècle dernier. Mais je n'aspire qu'à une écriture de transhumance, tandis que, voyageuse, je remplis mes outres d'un silence inépuisable. (80)

The allusion to "buried cries" relates to a macabre historical event recounted by Djebar in her narrative. In June 1845, some 1500 Berber tribespeople—men, women and children—sought refuge with their animals from the invading French forces in a cave beneath the plateau of el-Kantara. The commanding officer, Colonel Pélissier, ordered his men to set fires at the mouth of the cave to smoke out the resisters. Nearly everyone died of asphyxiation. The motifs of "buried cries" and asphyxiation contained in the accounts of the aggressors are refigured by Djebar to give to Algerian women the possibility of reclaiming their buried past and to give sound to voices of the asphyxiated. The shepherd metaphor Djebar employs, in saying she aspires to writing that is "transhumance" (in French meaning to move flocks from one pasture to another), and replenishing her water skins "with an inexhaustible silence," is ambiguous. "Transhumance" etymologically signifies movement beyond the earth (from the Latin *trans-*, "beyond," and *humus*, "earth") and would seem to imply that she would indeed exhume the cries of her buried sisters of the recent as well as the distant past, and the "inexhaustible silence" with which she would replenish her water skins suggests that, as a *voyageuse*, she would carry them with her (through her writing)—from which one might conclude that she alludes to the act of giving voice to those buried ones.

When later the narrator speaks of the rape of women by the French soldiers during the War of Liberation she again alludes to stifled voices. "Vingt ans après, puis-je prétendre habiter ces voix d'asphyxie? Ne vais-je pas trouver tout au plus de l'eau évaporée? Quels fantômes réveiller, alors que, dans le désert de l'expression d'amour (amour reçu, "amour" imposé), me sont renvoyées ma propre aridité et mon aphasie" (231). In the absence of love freely given, there is aphasia. But writing allows her to express the unforced love that exists between her and her ancestresses. To express love (by word, in writing) breaks the silence. "Ecrire ne tue pas la voix, mais la réveille, surtout pour ressusciter tant de **soeurs** disparues" (233). In *Oran, langue morte* Djebar refers to the many *femmes-victimes* in present day Algeria. What is necessary, she says, is "[l]e récit, non le silence, ni la soumission tourbe noire; les paroles, en dépit de tout, posent jalon, avec le rage, la peine amère, et la goutte de lumière à recueillir dans l'encre de l'effroi. Par instants la mort dévoile sa face: son rictus se déchire d'un coup" (371). Words are necessary as place markers to mark the states of oppression of Algerian women and to preserve memory of them against death. In *Oran* the narrator also describes the many women going about their business, some veiled, some not, who live until the fatal blow comes—to their son, brother, or themselves.

> Je me dis parfois: "Tu les saisis de loin, écris-les en te glissant au plus près de leur corps, de leur **coeur**! . . ." A quoi bon les inscrire, peu leur importe, elles—celle qui va mourir, celle qui va s'abriter, se recroqueviller ou celle qui se tait, yeux baissés, pour survivre?
>
> Après tout, quelle que soit l'approche tentée pour les écrire frémissantes, le sang—leur sang—ne sèche pas dans la langue, quelle que soit cette langue, ou le rythme, ou les mots finalement choisis. (372)

Their blood will remain fresh in the language that writes them. Memory will persist.

Love, then, makes of her the *amanuensis*, the voice of her *aïeules*, her sisters of the past, as well as her sisters of the present. Out of love is born the desire to transmit to future generations the silenced voices and sufferings of her sisters. Transmission becomes an important leit-motif that often reappears. In the short piece, "Fugitive et ne le sachant pas" (rpt. in *Vaste*), Djebar speaks of acts of transmission, often transmission of the past from mother to daughter. That transmission from one generation to another usually centers around an object, such as the *cahiers de musique* of the narrator's mother, or the silver heirloom jam spoon given to the son by his mother in *Vaste est la prison*, which she describes as an "emblème héraldique" (200), or the gift of jewelry and a silk shawl to the narrator by a close woman elder, or the two *plaques d'identité* in *Oran* retrieved from the necks of her murdered parents (27). In regard to her mother's *cahiers de musique*, the narrator speaks of her sadness over their destruction by French soldiers: "Je sentais pourtant à mon tour mon coeur étreint à cause de la navigation de cette écriture venue de si loin, d'au-delà des siècles et des rivages, transmise de femmes à femmes, les unes en fuite, les autres enfermées" (*Vaste* 171).

In the same work, she speaks of her daughter who follows in her footsteps, a liberated woman who will also be cut off:

> Passeuses désormais, elle et moi: de quel message furtif, de quel silencieux désir?
> - Désir de liberté, diriez-vous tout naturellement.
> - On non, répondrais-je. La liberté est un mot trop vaste!
> Soyons plus modestes, et désireuses d'une respiration à l'air libre. (*Vaste* 320)

However, in becoming the voice of her silenced sisters, she finds herself set apart, exiled by her use of the French language, and becomes conscious of the difficulty and dangers that will beset her. In the prologue of *Ombre*, entitled "Luth," she asks what will become of those women (including herself) who are freed from the past—liberty is about to break out, she says. Laughter has faded and their dances have degenerated into confused movement. "[Q]uel soleil ou quel amour nous stabilisera? [. . .] J'ai peur que toutes [. . .] nous nous retrouvions entravées là, dans "cet occident de l'Orient", ce lieu de la terre où si lentement l'aurore a brillé pour nous que déjà, de toutes parts, le crépuscule vient nous cerner" (171-2).

In *L'Amour*, Djebar remarks on the act of writing by the emancipated woman: "Viendra l'heure pour elle où l'amour qui s'écrit est plus dangereux que l'amour séquestré" (15). As we observe in her works to follow, love of country committed to paper will also hold danger, as witnessed by the numerous assassinations of journalists and writers described in *Le Blanc de l'Algérie*. In her later work, notably in *Le Blanc*, from *amanuensis* for her voiceless sisters, she will become the *amanuensis* for the dead and fallen in national conflict in and since the War of Liberation, those who died supporting the cause of a more just and progressive nation.

In describing in *Amour* the letters of the French captains who wrote home Djebar emphasizes the link between love and desire, on the one hand, and the Algerian nation, on the other. At the beginning of the novel, the narrator visualizes the French fleet coming upon the "Impregnable City" of Algiers just before its fall to the French in 1830. The city appears to them as an "Oriental Woman" who sheds her veil before them. But, between the lines, the letters of the captains

> parlent [. . .] d'une Algérie-femme impossible à apprivoiser [. . .]. Ces guerriers qui paradent me deviennent, au milieu des cris que leur style élégant ne peut atténuer, les amants funèbres de mon Algérie [. . .]. Ce monde étranger, qu'ils pénétraient quasiment sur le mode sexuel [. . .] ces croisées du siècle colonial [. . .] y pénètrent comme en une défloration. L'Afrique est prise malgré le refus qu'elle ne peut étouffer. (73-4)

Such conflicts of the past, with the nation torn between warring factions, will be replaced by the present-day fratricide taking place between the militant *intégristes* and the government. In the conflict of the past Djebar foreshadows, at the end of *Vaste*, the conflict informing the elegiacal *Le Blanc*:

> Les morts qu'on croit absents se muent en témoins qui, à travers nous, désirent écrire.
> Ecrire comment?
> Non en quelle langue, ni en quel alphabet—celui, double, de Dougga ou celui des pierres de Césarée, celui

de mes amulettes d'enfant ou celui de mes poètes français
et allemands familiers?

Ni avec litanies pieuses, ni avec chants
patriotiques, ni même dans l'encerclement des vibratos
du *tzarlrit*!

Ecrire, les morts d'aujourd'hui désirent écrire; or,
avec le sang, comment écrire?

Sur quelle planche coranique, avec quel roseau
qui renâcle à nager dans la couleur vermeille?

Les morts, eux seules, désirent écrire, et dans
l'urgence comme on a coutume de dire! (*Vaste* 346)

As I have noted, from being the *amanuensis* of her sisters, living
and dead, Djebar will become the *amanuensis* for the writers and
journalists who died for their country in the War of Liberation and in the
events transpiring since. The narrative of *Le Blanc*, adumbrated in *Vaste*,
is an elegiac discourse of the dead and disappeared. As an epigraph, Djebar
cites the words of Camus: "Si j'avais le pouvoir de donner une voix à la
solitude et à l'angoisse de chacun d'entre nous, c'est avec cette voix que
je m'adresserais à vous." Her narrative gives voice to the solitude and
anguish of the dead and disappeared, to her three close friends who were
assassinated in 1993, but also to numerous dead poets, novelists,
playwrights, and journalists, and an unnamed "directrice de collège"—all
of whom died in a grievous accident or illness or at the hands of assassins
between the years 1960 and 1994. Their names comprise a litany for well-
known and well-loved writers, poets and journalists: Albert Camus,
Frantz Fanon, Mouloud Feroun, Jean Amrouche, Jean Sénac, Malek
Haddad, Mouloud Mammeri, Kateb Yacine, Anna Gréki, Taos
Amrouche, Josie Fanon, Bachir Hadj Ali, Tahar Djaout, Youssef Sebti,
and Saïd Mekbel. They all, like her three friends, were integrally involved
with the cultural life and recent history of Algeria, and their writings and
tireless efforts towards reform and the realization of nationhood tell the
story of post-liberation Algeria (11).

Love relates closely to death in Djebar's works. In *Le Blanc* she
seeks to write a litany, a narrative of spiritual communion with the dead,
that will tell their story. In *Oran*, Ali makes love violently after telling
Isma of seeing, at the age of six, the bodies of his parents, tortured and

shot (96). And death in turn is linked to silence, unutterable words. The last words of the short story "Oran, langue morte" are those of the woman narrator Isma (one sense of the word in Arabic, "name," lends a certain universality to the telling) who tells Olivia that she is leaving Oran because she wishes to see no more violence, to say nothing else, but only to write, "seulement écrire. Ecrire Oran en creux dans une langue muette, rendu enfin au silence. / Ecrire Oran ma langue morte" (48).

In *Le Blanc,* Djebar speaks of how, around the body of the slain writer lying buried "s'entrecroisent et s'esquissent plusieurs Algéries" (12). In honoring these individual writers, she honors the nation—"Une nation cherchant son cérémonial, sous diverse formes, mais de cimetière en cimetière, parce que en premier, l'écrivain a été obscurément offert en victime propitiatoire" (12). She leaves us to infer that these writers through their deaths offer themselves as objects of atonement and expiation for the nation. Djebar calls her four friends who have been assassinated,

> quatres annonciateurs—j'allais dire les *abtals* [heroes] de l'écriture inachevée—, je les tire à moi aujourd'hui, je les installe, eux mes confrères exemplaires, sur les bords de la fondrière: scrutons au fond de la fosse, questionnons ensemble d'autres absents, tant d'ombres dérangeantes!

Together, she says, even if it is 30 years late, "ramenons les asphyxiés, les suicidés et les assassinés dans les langes de leur histoire obscure, au creux de la tragédie" (122-3).

She links the theme of absence to the need to question those dead ones who so disturb the living, to bring them back, wrapped in the winding cloth of their forgotten stories, back to the hollows of tragedy. With her dead writer friends, she would recover the lost stories of the Algerian dead, and thus restore their memory among the living.

She says that no longer is it merely a question of women being exploited and silenced, but that half the land "vient d'être saisie par des ténèbres mouvantes, effrayantes et parfois hideuses" (259). She closes her elegy by linking the events in Algeria with the difficulty of writing about them, of testifying to the horrors that have taken place:

> Le blanc de l'écriture, dans une Algérie non traduite?
> Pour l'instant, l'Algérie de la douleur, sans écriture; pour
> l'instant, une Algérie sang-écriture, hélas!
>
> Comment dès lors porter le deuil de nos amis, de
> nos confrères, sans auparavant avoir cherché à
> comprendre le pourquoi des funérailles d'hier, celles de
> l'utopie algérienne?
>
> Blanc d'une aube qui fut souillée. (275)

The verb *traduire* carries special sense (from the Latin *traducere* [i.e., *faire passer*]); as its first (abstract) meaning it gives: "Faire que ce qui était énoncé dans une langue le soit dans une autre" (*Le Grand Robert*). The third usage of the verb carries a sense of *déchiffrer* and *expliquer*. There is also a concrete sense: "Citer, déférer. V. *Passer (faire). traduire quelqu'un en justice.*"

Djebar thus seeks to understand the reason for the deaths of her friends whose burial was also the burial of the shattered dreams of a utopic nation, a just and pluralistic society that was to rise from the ashes of the War of Liberation. She seeks to forge a new language to give voice to the nation and its dead.

> Dans la brillance de ce désert-là, dans le retrait de
> l'écriture en quête d'une langue hors des langues, en
> s'appliquant à effacer ardemment en soi toutes les fureurs
> de l'autodévoration collective, retrouver un "dedans de la
> parole" qui, seul, demeure notre patrie féconde. (275-6)

To conclude, the motifs of love and desire, on the one hand, and dissent, on the other, are, as I proposed at the outset, entwined with and coalesce around the notion of Algerian nationhood ("notre patrie féconde"). Love and desire inflect the personal relationships of the narrator as well as the solidarity she feels with her sisters past and present, whose silent cries she voices. Love and desire inflect also her relationship with her dead friends of both sexes, whose own stories and desires to bring forth the birthchild of the War of Liberation, the ideal Algeria, lead Djebar to become not only their voice but a voice for nationhood.

Both engagements, that of becoming the voice of her sisters and of the nation, involve her irrevocably in a dissenting mode—against the prohibitions laid on the women of her country and against the forces that have plunged the nation into self-devouring conflict. While love and desire lead her towards positive engagement, dissent separates her, and sets her off not only from the object of her dissent (patriarchal domination, the *intégristes,* the government), but also from the very object of her love (her sisters). Liberation has as its other side imprisonment—in the cell of her emancipation, in the cell of her written French. She becomes an exile, a woman whose life is marked by flight and endless wandering. "Fugitive donc, et ne le sachant pas," she says, "Car de trop le savoir, je me tairais et l'encre de mon écriture, trop vite, sècherait" ("Fugitive et ne le sachant pas" 133). The adverb *trop* betrays her willing self-deception. For one cannot not know and not know too much simultaneously. She must thus avert her mind from the reality of her state of exile, for full consciousness of that state would dry up the ink in her pen. She must remain prisoner of a feigned ignorance. For, as she has said, writing is necessary, "les paroles, en dépit de tout, posent jalon, avec le rage, la peine amère, et la goutte de lumière à recueillir dans l'encre de l'effroi" (*Oran* 372).

Such tensions mark Assia Djebar's work, but, far from taking away from it, they give to it a richness, a fulsomeness, and a vibrancy found in few other authors.

Works Cited

Djebar, Assia. *L'Amour, la fantasia.* Paris: J. C. Lattès, 1985.

_____ . *Le Blanc de l'Algérie.* Paris: Albin Michel, 1995.

_____ . *Fantasia: An Algerian Calvacade.* Trans. Dorothy S. Blair. Portsmouth, NH: Heinemann, 1993.

_____ . "Fugitive et ne le sachant pas." *L'Esprit créateur* 33.2 (1993): 129-33.

_____ . *Ombre sultane.* Paris: J. C. Lattès, 1987.

_____ . *Oran, langue morte.* Mayenne: Actes Sud, 1997.

_____ . *Vaste est la prison.* Paris: Albin Michel, 1995.

Le Grand Robert. Dictionnaire alphabétique et analogique de la langue française. Paris: Societé du Nouveau Littré, 1981.

Webster's Third New International Dictionary. Unabridged. Springfield, MA: G. & C. Merriam Company, Publishers, 1968.

Fatima Mernissi's *Dreams of Trespass*: Self Representation or Confinement Within the Discourse of Otherness

Hasna Lebbady

As a well-known Moroccan sociologist and feminist, Fatima Mernissi has written extensively about Moroccan society and more particularly about the position of women within it. *Dreams of Trespass* is Mernissi's autobiography in which she presents a primarily Western readership with an image of her own supposedly Oriental childhood, pointing particular attention to the lives of the women in her family. Much of the book is devoted to describing different aspects of Moroccan traditions and these women's ambivalent relationship with them. This is the type of material that Mernissi would appear to be best suited to deal with; it is a picture of her own life about which someone like myself can have little to say. Yet although an autobiography claims to present the reader with a real person narrating her actual story, it has now become evident that there is a difference between real experience and the textual representation of that experience. Autobiographies, it follows, fall under the same laws of representation as other narratives, so that what we have here is not so much a real person but a textually constructed one. What I find particularly contradictory about Mernissi's narrative is her use of an orientalist discourse which compels her to represent herself in terms that serve to conceptualize her as the Other.

Dreams of Trespass is an account that takes us back to a colonial situation which it narrates from a postcolonial space. However, Mernissi's narrative does not form part of the discourse one has come to associate with postcolonial writing in which, according to *The Empire Writes Back*, "assumptions about the universal features of language, epistemologies and value systems are all radically questioned" (Ashcroft, et al. 11). The discourse Mernissi uses conforms with the notion of the Orient which Edward Said reveals in his *Orientalism* to be a construct of the European mind. Similarly, it appears to conform with the patriarchal view of woman as Other which has been contested by feminist discourse ever since Simone de Beauvoir's seminal thesis that one is not born a woman but becomes one. In fact, although Mernissi attempts to present a specifically feminist perspective of Morocco, she does not appear to critique either imperialist or patriarchal discourses, but rather to accept their norms without question, making her position appear to be rather ambiguous.

Mernissi begins her book by claiming: "I was born in a *harem* in 1940 in Fez" (1, my emphasis). By making such a claim, she touches upon what appears to me to be the issue of central controversy in the book: her use of the term "harem," which also appears in the subtitle of the book, *Tales of a Harem Childhood*. If she was born in a "harem," then one is led to conclude that "it" must exist. Despite her inclusion of the term "tales," Mernissi acts as if she were simply representing a given and incontestable reality. This raises questions about the extent to which her narrative can really represent her "actual" life story. Her book raises questions similar to those raised by the film *In Search of My Wife's Husband*, which to my mind at best presents a nostalgic construction of a certain way of life. Furthermore, the term "harem," which connotes a lascivious Arab way of life, is closely associated with how the West, particularly those in it whom Said defines as "Orientalists," conceives of the East. Orientalists, including sociologists, normally perceive the Orient as the exotic Other. By making use of the term, Mernissi is accepting a way of viewing the world that is inherent to Orientalist discourse, so that what it enables her to represent is an Orientalist construct of the Morroco.

Upon further reading, it becomes evident that the term "harem" does not remain as unquestioned as that initial statement would lead one to assume. In fact, the writer does not hesitate to use footnotes to distinguish between what she calls "imperial harems" and "domestic harems" (34). However, this distinction does not—to use Homi Bhabha's words—"rethink the terms in which we conceive of community, citizenship, nationality, and the ethics of social affiliation" (Bhabha 174). Rather, by insisting on the use of the term "harem," Mernissi appears to stress the connection between modern Morocco and the Arab past, even while she claims that "The harem kept by the Abbasid Caliph Harun al-Rashid in ninth-century Baghdad had nothing to do with our own" (154). And yet Mernissi is quite aware of the controversial nature of words about which the young Fatima tells us: "People, I discovered, often did not mean the same thing by the same word" (212). This applies to Mernissi's own use of the term "harem" which belongs to an Orientalist discourse and is not how extended households are normally referred to in Morocco.

A considerable amount of space is devoted to the young Fatima's attempts to come to terms with the word, which continues throughout the book.: "'What exactly is a harem?' was not the kind of question grownups volunteered to answer" (39). One wonders if it is a question children ever asked, since children usually accept their situation as normal. The precocious child, Fatima, claims that "whenever I tried to find out more about the word harem, bitter arguments ensued," leading her to conclude that "if words in general were dangerous, then "harem" in particular was explosive" (40). A little later she muses: "A harem had to do with men and women—that was one fact. It also had to do with a house, walls, and the streets—that was another fact" (46). This, paradoxically, only leads her to further mystification on the next page: "The problem was that the walls and everything worked for our harem in Fez, but did not work at all for the harem on the farm" (47). In an effort to explicate the term, and to insist on its connection with the Arabic, Mernissi breaks it down to its root: "The word 'harem' . . . was a slight variation of the word *haram*, the forbidden, the proscribed. It was the opposite of *halal*, the permissible" (61). She goes on to present less concrete manifestations of the term: "Once you knew what was forbidden, you carried the harem within. You had it in your head" (61). This is the case of the peasant whom Fatima and her maternal grandmother discuss on the farm. "He knew that the women on the farm belonged to Grandfather Tazi and that he had no right to look at them" (62). Questions about the "harem" continue even towards the end of the book: "Is a harem a house in which a man lives with many wives?"(150), and "Did you need to have slaves to have a harem?" (155). The fact that Mernissi takes up so much space questioning and attempting to come to terms with the word "harem" suggests that its use *is* problematic and that it is not to be taken for granted in the manner suggested by that opening sentence. However, whereas one would expect Mernissi to be undermining this Orientalist discourse, what one perceives is that she ambiguously flaunts her position within it.

I return to the opening words of the book where Mernissi tells us:

> I was born in a harem in 1940 in Fez, a ninth-century Moroccan city some five thousand kilometers west of Mecca, and one thousand kilometers south of Madrid, one of the dangerous capitals of the Christians. The problems with the Christians start, said father, as with the women, when the *hudud*, or sacred frontier, is not respected. (1)

This narrative begins by being grounded not only in an Orientalist, but also very much in a patriarchal discourse as it is the father's perspective that we get here. It is he who associates women with the aggressive Christians: one form of the Other. The masculinist perspective is what we get elsewhere in the narrative, as in the following explanation:

> Harem was the place where *a man* sheltered his family, his wife or wives, and children and relatives. (61, my emphasis)

Man is central to the notion of the so-called "harem" and women become confined not only within such predominantly patriarchal spaces, but also within the narrative itself in which the subject is male and which is to such a large extent presented from a masculinist point of view. The fact that women are trapped within patriarchal modes of representation is foregrounded here.

Patriarchal discourse is associated not only with the men but even with the women themselves, particularly the older women, such as Fatima's paternal grandmother, Lalla Mani. She is the patriarchal wife and mother who upholds the status quo as is evident in her comment to Fatima's mother:

> You know dear . . . you are lucky to have married such
> an easygoing man as my son. Others would have cast out
> a wife who disobeyed them and insisted on putting
> henna in her hair when they begged her not to. Besides,
> don't forget that Allah has given men the right to have
> four wives. (234)

Such women can only conceive of themselves as patriarchy conceives of them, even when they begin to perceive how unfair this can be, as Yasmin—Fatima's more independent maternal grandmother—does when she claims that "most of the time, the *qa'ida* [invisible rule] is against women" (62). Comments of this kind, however, do not lead such women to actually transgress the rules.

For the women in Fatima's household, transgression is revealed to consist simply of the fact that they "dreamed of trespassing all the time" (1-2), which is the idea that we encounter in the title itself. Numerous references to dreaming occur in the book, and we are given some intimations of what those dreams consist of when we are told, for example, that "[i]mprisoned behind walls, women walked around dreaming of frontierless horizons" (179). This indicates the extent to which the women resent those sacred frontiers referred to by the father, but gives no indication of the means by which such frontiers can be transgressed, apart from the possibility of dreaming. Even when the young Fatima presents us with her own mother's views, these too appear to conform to such a patriarchal perspective. We are told that her mother: "hated communal harem life and dreamt of an eternal tête-à-tête with Father" (6). The question this raises is whether dreaming constitutes a viable form of trespass or whether it simply constitutes another form of confinement within yet another myth—that of romantic love. Romance simply enables women to endure their different forms of confinement. To this extent, dreams are very much in conformity with what patriarchy thinks women should be or do, as dreaming remains a perfectly ineffective form of trespass. What begins to be evident is that the narrative in *Dreams of Trespass* conforms predominantly with patriarchal norms whether it foregrounds the perspective of the man at the center of the enunciation or that of the women who interiorize that perspective, for even when they are presented as attempting to trespass the norm, all that these women have recourse to are myths such as those of romance.

The concern with romance on the part of the women in the household of Fatima Mernissi's childhood is foregrounded by their preference for the singer Asmahan over Oum Kelthoum (104). Those women whom we are told "walked around dreaming of frontierless horizons" (179), ironically, identified with Asmahan who was

> oblivious of Arab culture, past and present, and totally absorbed by her own fatally tragic quest for happiness. She couldn't have cared less about what happened on the planet. All she wanted was to dress up, put flowers in her hair, look dreamy, sing and dance away in the arms of a loving man . . . . Arab women, forced to dance alone in closed-off courtyards, admired *Asmahan for realizing their dreams.* (105, my emphasis)

Such dreams are revealed to be simply romantic fantasies which serve to trap women within the myth of romance. The young Fatima conforms to the patriarchal view of women when she claims: "if I ever led a battle for women's liberation, I definitely would *not forget about sensuality*" (133, my emphasis). Although this can be read as a claim for women to have some rights over their own bodies, by such an insistence on feelings, Mernissi also appears to be conforming to the male view of woman as Other, and to the binary logic which conceives of her as inordinately emotional and romantic.

Some modes of representation available to the women in the household include embroidery and theatrical performances. Embroidery is a traditional woman's craft similar to quilt making in the States, which has only recently come to be valorized as an art. It is through embroidery that some of the women in Fatima's household are able to represent their dreams of escape. We are told that this action on their part constitutes "[r]ebellion in the form of modern embroidery" (210). Such rebellion includes embroidering: "[b]ig birds stretching out their aggressive wings" which, we are told, "meant its creator had flight and escape on her mind" (153). As for the theatrical performances, these are private ones which the women produce and perform themselves. This is how one of the performances affects the young Fatima:

> As I watched Chama perform, I vowed to myself that when I became a grownup woman as tall as she, I definitely would be affiliated with a theatre of some sort. I would dazzle Arab crowds, neatly seated in rows and looking at me, and tell them about how it felt to be a woman intoxicated with dreams. (110)

Although Mernissi goes to some pains to depict such performances as requiring and even developing talent on the part of the performers, there is also much in the text to indicate that Chama's performance makes Fatima wish to become an actress herself in order to dazzle the crowds with her beauty. Paradoxically, by wishing to transgress the norms that serve to confine women, Fatima succeeds only in aspiring to a different ideal of femininity which is no less confining. What she wishes to transgress is the injunction on good Muslim girls against becoming actresses, but her dream is very much in accordance with the patriarchal norms of what a woman should be. Here theater is not presented as a form of self-expression but more as an occasion for the woman to masquerade as a desirable object. It is questionable whether modes such as embroidery and private play acting enable women to transgress the boundaries imposed on them both by the structures of extended households, and by the patriarchal construct of femininity, to which they resort as if it constituted a viable form of escape.

The other mode of representation that is available to the women in Fatima's household is that of story-telling—of narrativity itself. The telling of tales is closely associated with women, particularly those who live in extended households such as the one described by Mernissi. It is not surprising then that Mernissi refers to Sheherazade, the archetypal story-teller, early in the book. Mernissi's involvement with Sheherazade is evident in the numerous references to *The One Thousand and One Nights* in a number of her texts. Her *Tales of a Harem Childhood* can be read as an instance of intertextuality. And there is, of course, much of a positive nature that can be said about the association between these two women's tales. The point of central importance to my argument, though, revolves around the idea that Sheherazade is compelled to narrate her stories to the king under the threat of death. If she does not please the king—the archetypal male in authority—Sheherazade runs the risk of having her head chopped off. A similar concern with the audience appears to be central to Mernissi herself who makes so many concessions to imperialist and patriarchal cultures. As Aunt Habiba, the other story-teller in the household, reminds Fatima: "You had to treat the audience well, if you wanted them to stick around" (109). In this way, writing becomes a form of giving the reader what one thinks he or she wants. Instead of positioning the reader to conform to one's view, writing here becomes a matter of positioning oneself to conform to the reader's view. One can go even further and claim that such writing becomes a matter of allowing the reader to enter the so-called "harem" and enabling him—or her—to see what happens inside it, parading the women for the satisfaction of the reader's curiosity, so to speak.

In a sense, this is what Sheherazade is compelled to do in order to be allowed to survive. Such predominantly patriarchal narrativity, which imposes itself on women, raises interesting questions about what it means to be a woman. In Mernissi's narrative, we are meant to believe that "a woman can fool society by posing as a man" (137), and that this is the only viable means of obtaining power for her. Mernissi refers to such historical figures as Shajarat al-Durr who "had acceded to the throne of Egypt after the death of her husband, Sultan al-Salih" (32). Apart from posing as men, it would seem, women must act like men by adopting their perspectives. Thus even such a woman as Sheherazade only manages to stay alive by shaping her tales to satisfy, even to cure, the king. Her aim is obviously not to come to terms with herself, but to appease the ego of the mighty being so that he would grant her permission to stay alive. To some extent, this is synonymous with saying that women can only *be* according to the norms of patriarchy.

The problem is compounded for Mernissi by the very language she uses which becomes closely associated with the audience she addresses. As Gayatri Spivak has pointed out:

> Those of us from formerly colonized countries are able
> to communicate with each other and with the
> metropolis, to exchange and to establish sociality and

transnationality, because we have had access to the
culture of imperialism. (Spivak 280)

Does this, however, mean that we must come to see ourselves as that
culture sees us? Mernissi's concern with the power of language is revealed
early in the book when Fatima is told by her mother: "to chew [her]
words before letting them out" (10). However, such care for words is
meant simply, as is the case with Sheherazade, to enable women to cope
with their restricted circumstances. Women within patriarchal culture
resort to narrativity to reinforce that culture which is the only way they
can survive within it. This is certainly the case of Aunt Habiba, a
divorced woman and therefore one of the least powerful in the Mernissi
household. Unlike Fatima's mother, whose married status confers on her
the right to partake in rebellious acts such as wearing men's *djellabas*,
Aunt Habiba is obliged to refrain from such acts. We are told that:
"upstairs was also the place to go for story telling. . . . That was the place
where Aunt Habiba had her room, small and quite empty" (17). This
could be read as a room of her own; if so, all it enables her to do is
reinforce the difference involved in being a woman. Her tales are
transgressive only in the sense that they allow for flights of fantasy on the
part of her hearers, whom we perceive: "riding on her words . . .
travel[ing] past Sind and Hind" (19). She claims that "anyone could
develop wings. It was only a matter of concentration" (204). She is
"certain that we all had magic inside, woven into our dreams" (114). Such
discourse, however, dominated as it is by fantasies of flight and magic,
only confirms the views of women that patriarchy upholds. Furthermore,
the claims that Habiba makes do not enable her to escape the confines of
the household in which she is reduced to one of the less prestigious and
more confining positions.

     Although Aunt Habiba's tales lead Fatima to conclude "I could
make frontiers vanish too—that was the message I got, sitting on my
cushions, up on the terrace" (114), what actually becomes evident is that
the tales associated with dreams and magic are not anywhere as
empowering as male discourse. In the novel this becomes associated not
only with the discourse of the father and uncles, but even with that of the
male cousins, and particularly that of Samir who was born the same day
as Fatima. Thus she tells us at one point:

> I still dream of that wonderful day when I will stage a
> theatrical revolt "Samir style," with screams and kicking
> of feet. (117)

Discourse of this kind is more performative, enabling the person involved
to go beyond the state of dreaming, and to actually get things done. The
difference between Samir and Fatima becomes particularly evident at
puberty when he starts reminding her of her status as a woman. It is at
this stage that Fatima is often reduced to silence by his comments. Thus
at one point we are told:

> There was nothing I could say because I realized that for
> the first time in our children's games, all that Samir had
> said was right, and that whatever I said did not matter
> that much. Suddenly, it all seemed so strange and
> complicated, and beyond my grasp. I could feel that I was
> crossing a frontier, stepping over a threshold, but I could
> not figure out what kind of new space I was stepping
> into. (241)

The space that she is stepping into is obviously that of femininity where
a woman knows her place in relation to that of a man—even when that
man is a child her own age. Although the young girl and the more mature
woman writing may feel some regret at this state of affairs, the discourse
Mernissi uses seems to offer little viable means of transgressing them.

What becomes evident is that the textually constructed self
Mernissi presents here conforms to both an Orientalist and patriarchal
discourse. She conforms to an Orientalist view of herself by insisting on
the use of the term "harem" and by doing so she appears to be concerned
with satisfying the Western reader's desire for the exotic, even, one may
hazard to say, the voyeuristic. In this way she colludes with the
Orientalist perception of herself as the Other, the purpose of which is to
keep the Other "in the margins of power, of 'authenticity' and even of
reality itself" (Ashcroft, et al. 77). Such an attempt at self-representation
also compels Mernissi to make use of basically patriarchal modes of
narration which serve to both define and confine women. One wonders
if there is no other mode of being—or of narrativity—which can be

devised by Moroccan women such as Mernissi that would enable them to transgress the constructs imposed on them by the discourse of otherness.

Works Cited

Ashcroft, Bill, Gareth Griffiths, and Helen Tiffin. *The Empire Writes Back: Theory and Practice in Post-Colonial Literature*. London: Routledge, 1989.

Beauvoir, Simone de. 1949. *The Second Sex*. London: Pan Books Ltd., 1988.

Bhabha, Homi, K. *The Location of Culture*. London and New York: Routledge, 1994.

Mernissi, Fatima. *Dreams of Trespass: Tales of a Harem Girlhood*. New York and Ontario: Addison-Wesley Inc., 1994.

Said, Edward. *Orientalism*. New York: Pantheon, 1978.

Spivak, Gayatri Chakravorty. *Outside in the Teaching Machine*. London and New York: Routledge, 1993.

Emerging Womanism in the Works of Tsitsi Dangarembga, Barbara Mahkalisa, and J. Nozipo Maraire

Linda Strong-Leek

Traditionally, Western feminist critiques have failed to address the multidimensional cultural and societal aspects of women of color often living in developing or "underdeveloped" countries. However, women in the diaspora have developed their own theories of feminism, more often referred to as "Womanism," which tends to embrace traditional "African" cultural aesthetics—i.e., the family and community—with a primary focus not on individual, but communal needs. Building on the works of foremothers Anna Julia Cooper and Maria W. Stewart in the 19th century, Alice Walker, in *In Search of Our Mothers' Gardens,* coins the term "womanist" as she states that "a womanist is to a feminist as purple is to lavender" (xi). A womanist, then, is another "shade" of a feminist, literally, ideologically, and figuratively. The agenda of the woman as "second class citizen" is of critical import, but the needs of the entirety of community are the central foci of her struggle. For women of the diaspora, race and gender are inextricably linked. The woman of color is not only a member of the "second sex," but also a member of an often undervalued, formerly colonized, disenfranchised people.

Subsequently, African, African-American and Caribbean women have further developed Walker's treatise as well as their own notions of womanism which are inclusive of their communities' needs. Notably, Chikwenye Okonjo Ogunyemi writes:

I arrived at the term "womanism" independently and was
pleasantly surprised to discover that my notions of its
meaning overlaps with Alice Walker's. Black womanism
is a philosophy that celebrates black roots, the ideals of
black life, while giving a balanced presentation of black
womandom. It concerns itself with the black sexual
power tussle as with the world power structure that
subjugates blacks. Its ideal is for black unity where every
black person has a modicum of power and so can be a
"brother" or a "sister" or a "father" or a "mother" to the
other. (240)

Moreover, in the Introduction to *Ngambika: Studies of Women in
African Literature*, Carole Boyce Davies explicates:

The only formulation of a feminist theory for African
women, however, comes from Filomena Steady
who...defines an African feminism. . . . She posits that
this African brand of feminism includes female
autonomy and cooperation, an emphasis on nature over
culture: the centrality of children, multiple mothering
and kinship; the use of ridicule in African woman's
world view. [She concludes] that the African woman is in
practice much more a feminist than her European
counterpart. "True feminism is an abnegation of male
protection and determination to be resourceful and
reliant. The majority of Black women in Africa and the
Diaspora have developed these characteristics, though
not always by choice." (6-7)

Boyce Davies continues by positing several positions of a "genuine
African Feminism" as follows: "Firstly, it recognizes a common struggle
with African men for the removal of the yokes of foreign domination and
European/American exploitation." It is not, therefore, "antagonistic to
African men," but "challenges them" to acknowledge that many "aspects
of women's subjugations" are different from the "oppression of all
African peoples." Thus, the African collective is maintained and not the

feminist "ideal" of "individuality." Next, it "recognizes that [there were] certain inequities in traditional societies" and that colonialism reinforced "many of these while introducing its own." Although it acknowledges certain "affinities with international feminism," it constructs a "specific African feminism" with different goals because of the realities of women's lives in Africa. "Thirdly, it recognizes that African societies are ancient societies," and so, African women, long ago, "addressed the problems of women's position in society." "Fourthly, African feminism" wishes to maintain "institutions which are of value to women" while rejecting those which seek to disempower them. African feminism, then, does not merely "import Western women's agendas." "Fifthly, it respects African women's self reliance" while acknowledging that "African women are seldom financially dependent." Furthermore, it must "look objectively at women's situation in societies which have undergone a war of national liberation and socialist reconstruction." And finally, it "looks at traditional and contemporary avenues of choice for women." (8-10).

Thus, whether one calls it womanism, African feminism, or "Africana Womanism", these ideological frames identify the complex positions of women of color. They posit themselves within a womanism that is not only woman-centered, but also centered in a world of ancient traditions, cultures, and a multiplicity of ethos vastly dissimilar from their Western counterparts. Race and sex are forever bound, and as the womanist defines and realigns her world view, she must articulate in her own voice the import of her varied world. Pauline Ada Uwakweh states that "[v]oicing is self-defining, liberational and cathartic. It proclaims an individual conscious being capable of independent thought and action" (74). Thus, women of the African Diaspora must locate their own voices, separate from Western feminist agendas.

Hence, Zimbabwean women like Tsitsi Dangarembga, Yvonne Vera, J. Nozipo Maraire, Barbara Makhalisa, Vivienne Ndlovu, and poets like Freedom T.V. Nyamubaya or Bertha Msora, have emerged with "other" voices articulating the experiences of women in Zimbabwe before, during and after the war for independence. These women bring a variety of multi-faceted and yet unheard voices to the womanist/African feminist dialogue. Flora Veit-Wild notes that:

Protracted colonial rule and isolation from the rest of Africa brought about a specific quality in Zimbabwean literature. The typical pattern in the development of African literature—a phase of cultural nationalism and anti-colonial protest followed by a phase of post-colonial disillusionment—shifted in the case of Zimbabwe. Here post-colonial disenchantment and criticism of African leadership emerged even before independence was achieved; a residual cultural nationalism co-existed with a modernist existential perspective. (Veit-Wild, *Teachers* 1)

Thus, the writings of women in Zimbabwe have emerged along this vein—and the woman's voice articulates the disenchantment with not only pre- and post-colonial rule but also patriarchal norms. This work will focus on the novels of two of these authors, Dangarembga's *Nervous Conditions* and Maraire's *Zenzele: A Letter for My Daughter*, and Makhalisa's collection of short stories, *Eva's Song*.

Dangarembga's *Nervous Conditions* is set in colonial Rhodesia in the late 1960's—on the very brink of civil war. Three of her female characters, the main protagonist Tambudzai, her elite cousin Nyasha, and Tambudzai's maternal tete/aunt Lucia, voice the queries of women torn between an alliance to the preservation of traditional values, and the desire to re-evaluate the roles of women. Interestingly, it is the "uneducated" Lucia who triumphs in her ability to query the system which attempts to degrade her, exhibiting more control over her life than either the worldly Nyasha, or the studious Tambudzai.

In *Zenzele: A Letter for My Daughter*, Maraire returns her audience to the midst of the war, relating the oft-omitted stories of women who fought alongside the men as spies, co-conspirators, leaders and soldiers. The narrator recounts, in vivid detail, the experiences of her sister and cousin, risking their lives daily in varied capacities in the movement. Though her account may represent a romanticized version of women fighting for liberation, it at least brings to light these often untold stories. And finally, Mahkalisa escorts her readers into post-independence Zimbabwe. In *Eva's Song*, she presents contradictory and complex images of women in the modern era. The economic issues remain the same, such as the devaluation of the female child in "Flying High," while "new" social issues, such as the woman's "proper" place in the workplace are analyzed in "Big Nuisance." She further explicates the position of women outside the home, delving into the difficulty of sexual harassment in "Ways of the Rod."

Each author articulates the ideal of the womanist ideology—the struggle for respect of woman, a maintenance of traditions which uphold the status of women, and the desire to maintain community. And each author brings with her "external" womanism elements unique to a Zimbabwean world identity. Veit-Wild continues by stating that though "one cannot speak of a clear-cut, distinctly Zimbabwean identity, there are certain common themes—the war of liberation in retrospect has been one major preoccupation of the 1980s—but approaches, styles and outlooks differ greatly, as do the ways in which writers try to come to terms with their past and present. . . . Yet, while one cannot speak of a national literature of Zimbabwe, there are common experiences, there is a legacy, there is a specific national history of literature" (2). And the works of these three women represent those "common themes" while maintaining the experiences of women as paramount in their analyses.

Dangarembga's *Nervous Conditions*, heretofore the most widely read novel by a Zimbabwean woman, challenges societal and traditional values which place the education of male children at a higher premium than their female counterparts. Although women in the West must also meet resistance to intellectual pursuits, no female child is denied access to education based on gender; however, this is a major issue facing women in developing countries. Early in the text, the voice of young Tambudzai articulates the resistance to female autonomy:

> I think my mother admired my tenacity, and so felt sorry for me because of it. She began to prepare me for disappointment long before I would have been forced to face up to it. To prepare me she began to discourage me. "And do you think you are so different, so much better than the rest of us? Accept your lot and enjoy what you can of it. There is nothing else to be done. (20)

Later her brother continues in a similar vein. Christine Sizemore argues that "In Tambu's Shona family, patriarchy is enforced even by boys. Tambu is literally silenced by her brother"; however, she continues, "[i]n spite of her brother's and father's efforts to drive her into silence, Tambu has enough support from the women in her family to maintain her belief in her ability to achieve" (71). Thus, Tambudzai learns from her mother and brother that girls and boys are afforded a different status in Shona society. This also illustrates the extent to which women participate in their own subjugation. Gay Wilentz discusses this reality in, *Binding Cultures*:

> Revealingly, the voice of the community that demands adherence to strict social codes for its women often comes from the women themselves. The paradox of this system, adding to the complexity of linguistic meaning in the novel, is that women often uphold traditions that limit their choices and rights as women. (6)

Although Wilentz is analyzing another novel here—Flora Nwapa's *Efuru*—the statement is true for Tambudzai's mother, Maiguru, and other women in Dangarembga's text. Women are often supporters of traditions that disempower them, but usually for very complex reasons. Tambudzai's mother's voice is among those who discourage her. But after living a life of degradation and abject poverty, she can see no other recourse for women except to accept their respective "lots." However, Tambudzai never allows this to dissuade her. Unlike her mother and even the Western-educated Maiguru, she silently questions and later openly challenges patriarchal authority. If there is no money to send her to school, she will grow mealies (corn) to pay her own fees. Tambudzai remains unabashed in her desire to obtain an education and finds another route to continue until fate and Babamukura intercede on her behalf.

Unlike the initially unquestioning Tambudzai, Nyasha, her cousin who spent her formative years in England, questions every aspect of her life, her mother's life, and the lives of both men and women in colonial Rhodesia. Returning to her homeland after five years, Nyasha can no longer speak her native Shona, nor can she understand or perform the traditional rituals; but most important of all, she cannot acquiesce to the total subservience required by her father and other family members. Moreover, instead of questioning her parents about her language loss, everyone simply decides that Nyasha has rejected her culture. No one wonders how she could lose her native tongue if it was being spoken in her home. The responsibility for the loss of language and culture is shifted, then, from the parents to the child.

At the same time, Nyasha is critical of that very Western presence she knows has corrupted her and the entire society in which she lives. She is most critical of the colonial presence, recognizing the tyranny of minority rule. Patriarchy itself is not her major issue, but the larger frame. The creation of her father as "Lord and master" has its roots in European colonization.

Furthermore, Nyasha's attempts to connect with Tambudzai, other girls at school, and even with her own mother ultimately fail. She is able to voice her opinions, but there is no one to connect with this dissident voice. Sizemore notes that "[v]oice alone without connections can be as dangerous as silence" (72), and this is most certain in Nyasha's case. Although her mother attempts to protect her from her father's wrath, she is never able to enter into a conversation with Nyasha about the way to negotiate with patriarchy without giving oneself to its ideals. Instead, Maiguru utilizes adolescent "baby talk" to appease her husband, rather than confronting him as his intellectual equal. And Nyasha can find no comfort in Tambu, because although she attempts to understand her cousin, she is initially so happy to leave the homestead that she views Babamukuru as her "saviour." Tambudzai eventually recognizes the tyranny of her uncle, rebelling in her own way against the farce of a "wedding" he devises to "appease the soul" of his deceased mother.

Later, Nyasha cries for help in her letters to Tambu; however, Tambu is so enraptured by her new life, she ignores her cries. Nyasha is no longer able to locate a safe space for herself within her father's world of finite rules and regulations. It is then, only Lucia, Tambudzai's maternal aunt/tete, who is able to create a comfortable space for herself within tradition, but outside the realm of marriage.

Lucia is unwilling to acquiesce to the role of wife, but at the same time does not reject motherhood. Instead, she creates a place for herself and her child, using Babamukuru's ego as a weapon to secure a job. But although Babamukuru is responsible for her employment status, she does not allow his power to remain unchecked when he unfairly punishes Tambudzai for refusing to attend her parents "wedding":

> "Well, Babamukuru," said Lucia, preparing to leave, "maybe when you marry a woman, she is obliged to obey you. But some of us aren't married, so we don't know how to do it. That is why I have been able to tell you frankly what is in my heart. I don't go behind your back and say the first thing that comes into my head." Babamukuru applauded Lucia in her absence. "That one," he chuckled to Maiguru, "she is like a man herself." (171)

It is problematic that Babamukuru will admire only in Lucia what he deems "masculine" behaviour. But it is also evident that all the men, including Babamukuru, recognize Lucia as a force to be reckoned with. Anthony Chennels argues that "Lucia announces on her own authority that she is present despite Babamukuru's attempts to discredit her through silence. [Here Chennels is referring to Lucia's entrance into a family discussion from which she was purposely omitted.] Nor is Babamukuru in any way the necessitating agent for her existence. Articulated in Lucia's presence is the economy of the reserves which are almost invariably abreast in Babamukuru's speeches about the family's problems" (67). Outside the bonds of marriage, Lucia is able to voice her opinions without direct repercussions for her actions. Unlike her sister, she has not been broken by years of childbearing, rearing and thankless labour in the fields with a worthless husband. She asserts herself, and defends Tambu, and Babamukuru secretly admires Lucia for her spunk and "unfeminine" behavior. Lucia is the voice of the uneducated though not uneducable woman who knows that in the changing world, a woman must speak on her own behalf.

Also unlike Maiguru, who is tied to the patriarchy and her position as Babamukuru's wife, Lucia creates her own boundaries and utilizes her independent thought to eke out a space for herself and her child in her community. Chennels continues: "Frequently in the novel it is as if the hope for the development of the modern Zimbabwean woman seems to be lodged in Lucia. She is free in her own terms" (70).

And Lucia is the most successful female character in the text as we find
her not locked in an asylum at the end like Nyasha, nor struggling to find
herself in the Roman Catholic girls school like Tambu. Instead, she
defines herself in terms she creates. Lucia never allows any man to
control her. She uses Takesure for the fulfilment of her sensual desires,
and in the same way, uses Babamukuru's ego/status to gain access to his
world. She utilizes what Molara Ogundipe-Leslie deems "male fantasies"
to accomplish her agenda and ultimately gain an independence which will
not require the generosity of any man.

   Transferring the reader from Dangarembga's colonial Rhodesia,
J. Nozipo Maraire's work, *Zenzele: A Letter for My Daughter*, plunges the
reader into the midst of the revolution in Rhodesia, Zimbabwe's struggle
for independence. The story is related from the point of view of the
mother, in the form of a letter to her daughter. In an attempt to pass on
her unique brand of knowledge, the mother pens a letter to the daughter
before her departure for study in the United States. Two of the most
powerful portraits in the text are of the mother's younger sister Linda—a
school teacher by day—and a guerilla fighter by night, and a cousin,
Tinamo, who masquerades as a maid for a high-ranking official in the
Rhodesian army, but in reality is a spy. Maraire's views are no doubt
romaticized versions of the realities of women fighting in the liberation
war, but her voice is important as it is one of the first to articulate the
physical participation of women in the war.

   We first see Tinamo, who had disappeared years earlier after
crossing the border into Mozambique for military training. Upon her
return, her cousin is surprised to find her in a maid's uniform, caring for
the child of a white Rhodesian. But it is all part of a ploy. Later, at a
secret meeting, Tinamo reveals her true position, and at the same time
describes the way Africans utilize colonial ideas of inferiority to gain
access to their secrets:

> "Sisi, we were just talking about the Europeans. You
> know, they are really wonderful! They honestly believe
> that we come from monkeys and they come from God
> ... and they think we are so stupid," added Tinamo
> .... "You see, Sisi, our greatest weapon in the struggle
> has been our presumed stupidity. The Europeans do not

believe that we have brains of any evolutionary
significance. So as far as they are concerned, our capacity
for rational thought is, should we say, ahh, limited."
(139)

Thus, Tinamo utilizes European stereotypes to gather intelligence from
the highest level of the Rhodesian forces, aiding the freedom fighters.
This masking, "playing the role," is a classic tactic in the tradition of
African Diaspora peoples. Tinamo "wears the mask," becoming the docile
servant most unexpectedly because she is a woman. She is like her
counterparts in the United States—the mammy figure who bathed and
"loved" the white children, while putting ground glass in the food, or
small amounts of poison, and continually providing assistance and secrets
to the "enemy." This ability to mask has assisted in the development of
Africana womanhood as women of color have utilized their perceived
inferiority to discover the very hearts of their "masters" without revealing
their true intentions. Tinamo's role, then, is as important as that of her
male counterparts in the physical battles.

The sister, Linda, also in the forefront of the struggle, represents
another dimension of the developing Zimbabwean womanist. Fighting
on the front lines with the men, these women sacrificed as much as their
male comrades, yet are given little attention in historical and fictive war
narratives. This remains true not only of the Zimbabwean struggle, but
most struggles for independence. Nonetheless, Maraire paints a startling
portrait of Linda as warrior:

> Those were the days when Linda grew thin, like a stick.
> She ate, breathed, lived for the struggle. It was her life. I
> saw her sometimes when she came into the company of
> other comrades in fatigues and dark glasses to consult
> with your father, drop off pamphlets, or use the
> telephone. Sometimes she would just come to "crash."
> We tried to feed and protect her as best we could on
> those occasions, but as soon as her strength returned, she
> donned her beret and fled back to a world that I only saw
> in fragments and whispers. (168)

Maraire continues with an overall depiction of the "mjiba," the colloquial term applied to these young women:

> They were women of a new generation who wore trousers like men and could aim just as steady. They were women who killed. There were fit and strong, running through the bush and brandishing AK 47's and machine guns. These were women who crept into the village . . . on their backs, they carried not runny-nosed babies but the hope of a different generation. . . . They were as foreign to our traditional image of women as Eskimos. (168)

Though Maraire may be correct in asserting that these women were "foreign," they also represented the spirit of the traditional grandmother of the Zimbabwean revolution, Mbuya Nehanda, who died resisting the colonial onslaught. Notably, Terrance Ranger notes that "[Nehanda] was behind the rebellion right from the start. Her great injunction was that the African people should touch nothing that belonged to the white man. The defeat of the Africans was the result of the violation of this great order" (210). And in *Spirits of Protest*, Peter Fry states that "Nehanda went to the scaffold refusing baptism" (49), maintaining the traditional religion of her ancestors. Thus, although the idea of woman as warrior may be "foreign," it is apparent from historical accounts that Zimbabwean women have been active in the struggle for independence.

Finally, Mahkalisa's short story collection, *Eva's Story*, presents the various worlds of women in post-colonial Zimbabwe. Makhalisa's issues are undoubtedly contemporary: AIDS, anorexia, women in the workplace, and women in positions of power previously held by men. However, she also questions the value of the education of females, and her analysis presents a community of elder women maintaining traditional beliefs, sometimes at the expense of their own daughters. Her protagonists are faced with an array of choices, such as the choice between European medicines and traditional healers. In one such story, "Flying High," the debate surrounds the young daughter who is "flying high" academically, but who, at the grandmother's insistence, must be given to the traditional healer who promises to cure her father of a prolonged illness. However, the younger brother and mother are adamantly opposed to this concession:

> When she was out of earshot, her uncle said to her father, "I implore you to think very seriously about this matter, my brother. You cannot give our beautiful daughter to that greedy crank! . . ." In the kitchen, the women also continued the debate. . . . "You say it used to be done, mother. Yes, it did. But it was during those days. And I continue to say, if the worst comes to the worst, we should get rid of all our cattle." (27-8)

The argument continues as the debate over the value of a daughter, the value of a father and son, the value of cattle and of traditional medicine over Western medicine escalates. The mother decides she will secretly send her daughter away before allowing her to be traded for medicine that may not work. In the end, though, the daughter is kept, the Western doctor consulted, and the father remorseful for the mistake he almost made. This critique of traditional medicine is not meant to indict all traditional healers, as Western medicine has been forced to acknowledge that there are legitimate sources of traditional medicine, but to question a system that places a limited premium on the lives of its female progeny. Mahkalisa also queries unscrupulous medicine men who utilize their positions and the suffering of people to take advantage of the innocent.

In "Big Nuisance," the title addresses the inequities that remain for women in the workplace not only in Zimbabwe, but also throughout the world. When a new executive position becomes available, the management must decide whether to promote the best person for the job, an "agitating, aggressive womanist," or a man who will fill the position without murmuring for "equal rights":

> "But sir, don't you realize how dangerous that woman is," Cheza persisted. "I don't think she should be allowed to become part of this management committee. We'll have no peace. Already she's been poisoning women's

minds here. For example, women have been happy
enough to go on one month's paid maternity leave
before. That has forced most of them to come back to
work sooner, reducing loss of productivity.... Consider
the loss which the company now makes due to
Mhlanga's advocating for the so-called women's rights!
Such a big nuisance, really." (98-9)

Thus a woman, although an obvious asset to the company, remains a
"nuisance" as she advocates for the rights of women. In the end, the
committee decides that it must carefully consider the male applicants
before making a decision. "We shall interview the two men on the
shortlist just in case" (101).

Similarly in "Ways of the Rod," Makhalisa addresses the problems
of the workplace, but this time the focus is the sexual harassment women
face each day. This issue is complicated in Zimbabwean society by
familial and societal expectations. If a woman gives in to these advances,
then she is branded a "whore", but if she does not, she may lose her job
and ability to care for her family. Although there is presently a
"Women's Bureau" in the country, there is little recourse for women who
are sexually harassed, except to acquiesce or resign their respective
positions.

In "Creating a New Society: Women's Writing in Zimbabwe,"
Veit-Wild writes that:

In Zimbabwe today many young girls leave their rural
homes to live in town, where their illusions and hopes
are too often quickly shattered. In their professional life
... they are often exposed to a very sexist environment.
... To put it bluntly, woman is regarded as a sexual
object. Professional promotion, more often than not,
hinges on not repulsing advances. (176)

Also, a September 28, 1998 article on sexual harassment in Zimbabwe's
The Herald, reports that:

> Sexual harassment at the workplace might soon be dealt with by an independent tribunal if the draft of a sexual harassment bill, still being examined, is allowed to go through Parliament. If approved, the Bill–which is yet to be discussed by the Law Development Commission–will call for the setting up of the tribunal that will informally deal with all cases of sexual harassment at workplaces. ("Tribunal" 1)

The article notes that "cases of sexual harassment are reportedly on the increase in Zimbabwe and only a small fraction of women have taken legal action against perpetrators." Thus, there is much work to do in Zimbabwe and worldwide if sexual harassment is to be afforded appropriate attention.

Mahkalisa begins her story with Linda, having been "properly educated" by her family, recalling the moment she was admonished to retain her dignity and thus, the family pride: "We have given you an education so that you are marketable in the work force. Right?" "We don't expect to hear that you are marketing your dignity in exchange for money." "'That would kill us,' her mother butted in" (36). She is further instructed by her grandmother to "hold the rod," meaning never to acquiesce to unwanted advances. But Linda must soon face this dilemma. After a co-worker, Nina, begins to compromise her integrity by taking "weekend trips" with the boss, Linda's position is threatened. When confronted with the same "opportunity," she declines, and this has a dramatic effect on her job performance:

> She began to be loaded with work, her own and some of Nina's work. When she failed to complete the extra work, she was accused of refusing to do tasks delegated to her. When she failed to complete hers, she was blamed for incompetence. Life became unbearable as there was a new charge each week. (37)

Hence, Veit-Wild's and *The Herald*'s discussions highlight the problems faced by women like Makhalisa's fictional Linda—a life of limited choices and extreme consequences. But all hope is not lost, for Makhalisa allows "fate" to intervene on behalf of the virtuous woman.

Linda does not acquiesce to the advances of her boss and, after her ancestors intervene, she is able to enhance her education and ultimately, her corporate viability. She triumphs against odds meant to demean her and gains access to the corporate world with dignity:

> One Monday morning, Nina was not at work. At about nine that morning, Linda was summoned to the general manager's office. . . . "Congratulations, Ms. Ndlovu, for attaining the scholarship to further your studies in Manchester. Your line manager will explain the rest of the details."(41)

Makhalisa is most aware, however, that women need other avenues to ward off unwanted sexual advances.

Makhalisa's arguments may seem more feminist than womanist. But in this instance, and others, Makhalisa turns to tradition—the ancestral spirits, the "rod" of the grandmother—to bring hope to her protagonist. Thus, she does not simply adopt Western women's agendas or reject the African ideal of intercession on behalf of the ancestors. Here, in the womanist frame, she celebrates that tradition as a solution to a difficult problem.

Thus, women writers in Zimbabwe are developing their own, unique womanism. It acknowledges a particularly Zimbabwean/ developing world cultural and societal view. The issues are concrete and not just philosophical or ideological. Veit-Wild writes that "[a] common characteristic of the various literary attempts of women in Zimbabwe is that their writings closely reflect reality, and in a very immediate and direct way women react to the social situations around them" ("Creating" 171). From the devaluation of the female child, to her denied access to education, her debasement in the workplace, and her attempt to find a comfortable space in traditions which do not demean, the Zimbabwean woman writer brings to the fore her unique voice in the collective voices of women in the Diaspora.

Thus, whether she names herself a womanist, an African feminist, or an Africana feminist, the Zimbabwean woman writer addresses issues of race, class, gender, and culture in her position and within her world. Zimbabwean women writers have entered the debate, and further evolutions into this particularly Zimbabwean womanism continues.

Works Cited

Chennels, Anthony. "Authorizing Women, Women's Authorizing." *New Writing From Southern Africa.* Ed. Emmanuel Ngara. Harare: Baobab Books, 1996. 59-75.

Dangarembga, Tsitsi. *Nervous Conditions.* Harare: Zimbabwe Publishing House, 1988.

Fry, Peter. *Spirits of Protest: Spirit-mediums and the Articulation of Consensus Among the Zezuru of Southern Rhodesia (Zimbabwe).* Cambridge: Cambridge University Press, 1976.

Makhalisa, Barbara. *Eva's Song: A Collection of Short Stories.* Harare: Harper Collins Publishers (Zimbabwe), 1996.

Maraire, J. Nozipo. *Zenzele: A Letter for My Daughter.* New York: Crown Publishers, 1996.

Ogundipe-Leslie, Molara. *Recreating Ourselves: African Women and Critical Transformations.* Trenton, NJ: Africa World Press, 1994.

Ogunyemi, Chikwenye Okonjo. "Womanism: The Dynamics of the Contemporary Black Female Novel in English." *Revising the Word and the World: Essays in Feminist Literary Criticism.* Eds. VeVe A. Clark, Ruth-Ellen B. Joeres and Madolen Sprengnether. Chicago: The University of Chicago Press, 1993.

Ranger, T.O. *Revolt in Southern Rhodesia 1896-7: A Study in African Resistance.* London: Heinemann, 1967.

Sizemore, Christine W. "Negotiating Between Ideologies: In Search of Identity in Tsitsi Dangarembga's *Nervous Conditions* and Margaret Atwood's *Cat's Eye.*" *Women's Studies Quarterly* 25.3/4 (Fall/Winter 1997): 68-82.

Umakweh, Pauline Adu. "Debunking Patriarchy: The Liberational Quality of Voicing in Tsitsi Dangarembga's *Nervous Conditions.*" *Research in African Literatures* 26.1 (Spring 1995): 75-84.

Veit-Wild, Flora. "Creating a New Society: Women's Writing in Zimbabwe." *The Journal of Commomwealth Literature* 22.1 (1987): 171-8.

_____. *Teachers, Preachers, Non-believers: A Social History of Zimbabwean Literature*. Harare: Baobab Books, 1993.

"Tribunal may soon deal with sexual harassment cases." *The Herald* (Harare). September 28, 1998. N. Pag.

Walker, Alice. *In Search of Our Mothers' Gardens: Womanist Prose*. New York: Harcourt, Brace, Jovanovich, 1993.

Wilentz, Gay. *Binding Cultures: Black Women Writers in Africa and the Diaspora*. Bloomington: Indiana University Press, 1992.

The Roles of Women in Hausa Folktales

Anita Mooijman

African cultures are primarily oral cultures, meaning that in African societies, the culture depends on the oral tradition for survival. Thus, the information we gather from oral literature gives us insight into a culture's values, worldview and ideas. In this presentation, I examine the roles of women in Hausa folktales, *tatsuniyoyi*, from an Africa-centered and womanist perspective. In order to examine this topic, I will briefly touch upon some aspects of Hausa history and society, especially women's roles and positions in them, to construct a picture of Hausa life that is used as a basis for comparison with the tales. Then I will discuss the roles of women in *tatsuniyoyi* and to what extent they conform to or diverge from those of Hausa women in real life.

My study takes a culturally centered approach, which also means using the culture's *categories* of oral literature. As Ben-Amos states, "the principles underlying indigenous categorizations are rooted in cultural thought, language and experience. The differences in names of genres, in classes of verbal behavior, and in their symbolic meaning reflect essential cultural concepts" (3). Thus, I use the categories the Hausa use as definitions of genres. The Hausa divide oral prose narratives into two genres: the folktale, *tatsuniya*, and the legend, *tarihi*. These categories were confirmed by the women storytellers whom I interviewed.

Since all existing collections of *tatsuniyoyi* were collected by men from mostly male storytellers between 1885 and 1930 (those dating from the 1960s and '70s are translations of the older collections), even though the genre is usually told by women, I wanted to collect from women storytellers. Fortunately, a Dissertation Completion Grant from Temple University enabled me to collect some 400 *tatsuniyoyi* in 1996 from women in the Maradi area of Niger.

Until recently, the lives and roles of Hausa women have often been ignored or misunderstood by scholars. These misinterpretations stemmed largely from the imposition of Western male standards and values as measures. For instance, Hausa women's economic contributions have long gone undocumented and underestimated because many women work from their homes because of the system of seclusion imposed under Islam.[1] Since Western scholars measured participation in the formal economy, Hausa women's work has often been "invisible." Nonetheless, many Hausa women combine domestic work with a trade of some type. The same holds true in the realm of politics. However, a closer look at Hausa women, historically and currently, shows that the situation is not that simple.

The present position of and restrictions on Hausa women were largely introduced into Hausa society by Islam, especially after the Sokoto jihad of 1804-12. In a short time, women's positions were stripped of power and eliminated until women's public power seriously dwindled. This situation was only made worse by European colonization. Going back in time, though, one can see that before the jihad, Hausa women did indeed have public power and positions of great influence, just like African women in many other parts of the continent. In the Maradi area, where "the Jihad was unsuccessful, women play, or played until recently, a much more significant political role" (Pittin 467).

"According to legend, royal women once led armies and ruled much of Hausaland.... In northern Nigeria, historical traditions include accounts of queens and women warriors of the sixteenth century who are still remembered for their feats," including, among others, Queen Amina and her sister Zaria, after whom a town was named. These women-warriors' "continued popularity in contemporary historical accounts" is significant (Mack, "Royal Wives" 110). For instance, Queen Daura is said to have been succeeded by eight more queens. After a man became ruler, women's influence continued in the "constitutional doctrine that the Magajiya could countermand the orders of the chief and might, if necessary, act to depose him" (Mack, "Royal Wives" 112; M.G. Smith 57). Furthermore, the mother of the emir or a paternal aunt or elder sister of the emir held the title of *Iya*, whose main function was to intercede between the emir and his lesser chiefs (Mack "Royal Wives" 111-2). These positions of royal women are very similar to those in other ancient and traditional African societies such as Kemet (ancient Egypt) and ancient Ethiopia, where the queen-mother (or *Kentake*) was responsible for choosing a king and could depose him if the king was not a just ruler. Similarly, in present-day traditional Asante society, the queen-mother is an important person, who rules together with the king.

Connie Stephens wrote a very interesting and important article on Hausa women's oral art. As she explains,

> Women are most often portrayed in traditional roles as cook and mother. But far from playing dependent wives, many of these heroines consistently challenge and best their husbands. Moreover, oppositions recur, aligning female antagonists with natural and supernatural powers against husbands who represent worldly, political authority. Conflicts occur between these counterforces and are mediated by women with supernatural abilities to nurture and produce life. If anyone must acknowledge dependency, it is a husband, whose political power is no match for his wife's supernatural power and whose cultural role is sustained by her culinary and reproductive abilities. In these tales women are separate and superior; they are highly esteemed in their traditional domain. (Stephens, "Marriage" 223)

Because the women are portrayed as powerful and in power, Stephens asserts that the women who perform *tatsuniyoyi* "argue in a feminist [womanist] vein" (222).

Interestingly, in the interviews I did with storytellers, when asked which character(s) in tales they liked best, several women chose a girl or woman character who had shown intelligence and/or courage; they said that they admired those characters for that. As the following discussion of Hausa tales shows, quite a few courageous and smart female characters, from young girls to mature women, can be found in the tales. Thus, there are some young girls who dare to take great risk for love in tales. In doing so, they show strong determination and willingness to overstep social boundaries such as restrictions based on gender. I can only discuss a few examples of tales here.

An example of a woman going beyond the boundaries set by society is "The woman who traveled as a prostitute" (Tale 38).[2] She has no relatives and sets out traveling and engages in prostitution. After many years of living like that, she is blessed with a son and eventually grand and great-grandchildren. So she goes from having no one to having a big family. In recognition of her achievements, she asks the chief for, and is given, land to start her own town. Significantly, in this tale, the woman never marries, yet is esteemed by her descendants and even by the chief. This confirms what Pittin asserts about prostitution in Hausa society (*karuwanci*), namely that it holds very little stigma, and that women are able to move in and out of it with relative ease, and furthermore, that many prostitutes prefer this lifestyle and choose to remain independent rather than marry. Although the motivations of the woman in the tale are not verbalized, the fact that she never marries, either before or after having her child, and never laments that she was not married, whereas she repeatedly laments the fact that she did not have any relatives and thanks God for her child and subsequent offspring, leads me to infer that this must have been a choice on her part.

"The daughter born of a man" (Tale 17) is very interesting. It tells the story of a girl whose father gave birth to her. The father is killed in a war when she is little, and when she grows up she goes to take revenge and kills the king who killed her father. While she is at it, she kills many kings and becomes very rich and powerful. A particular king is told about this girl, he finds her and asks to marry her. She refuses, but offers to share the town (kingdom) with him as her first minister. He refuses and challenges her. She beats his army, he surrenders and says he will serve her, but she kills him. She then chooses a husband and settles down with him. This tale clearly speaks of a powerful woman. The male-chauvinist king, typically, refuses to share the queen's town and be her first minister, which was really a very generous offer by the queen to someone who is a stranger to her. Although the position of first minister is presumably the highest in the kingdom, he speaks of not wanting to be a *servant* to a woman. Thus, while the girl talks in terms of sharing of power, the man is too biased to be able to think in such terms. He arrogantly claims he will defeat the queen and take her town by force. She defeats him, and when he begs to be her servant, kills him because she could not trust him.

However, the "happy ending" of the tale is not found in the death of any of the kings the girl killed, but in peace and a marriage blessed with many children. Although this may seem an ending that conservatively reaffirms the role of women as wives and mothers, one should not jump to conclusions, for it is clearly stated that the girl went and chose her own husband. She also gives her town (this may refer to the entire kingdom) to her husband. Again, one should not be too quick to say that that confirms the idea of men in power. To some extent, it does, for she might have given the town to a female relative. However, it is obvious from the way she has defeated one king after another that both her marriage and her giving her town to her husband are *deliberate choices* on the part of the girl/queen. One can imagine that after so many years of warfare, she simply wants to devote her time to other, more peaceful ends. The fact that the "happy end" is found in peace and a presumably harmonious marriage clearly reflects the ancient Egyptian philosophical concept of *ma'at* (truth, harmony, balance, justice).

The above story is reminiscent of historical, powerful Hausa women such as Queen Amina. In talking of courageous women as in the tale above, *tatsuniyoyi* do three things at the same time. First, they reflect previous times when Hausa women had more official independence. Secondly, they reflect those Hausa women today who refuse to let social rules deny them opportunities, whether for trade or for happiness. Thirdly, by reflecting both past times and defiant women today, the tales are rebellious in speaking of women or girls who step outside the boundaries set by the male-dominated culture, and thus encourage girls to do the same. Moreover, in showing many girls or women who at first glance seem to be just ordinary people, the tales imply that ordinary girls and women can do extraordinary things, even within a conventional setting. Furthermore, through the examples of these female characters, these tales have a clear message about women taking responsibility for their own lives (with the necessary help from God or supernatural powers at times).

This does not mean that there are no tales which encourage obedience; yet, significantly, the obedience is to women or perhaps male relatives, not to husbands. Thus, there are tales in which girls are rewarded for being obedient to their mother, an old woman, a bird or another kind of non-human messenger/advisor. For instance, in "Girls go to get figs" (tale 2), Daudawa, the girl who is despised by her friends, has to go to great lengths to obey her mother and gather figs so her mother will give her clothes to go to the youth meeting. Then, on her way there, she obeys an old woman by helping her wash, who gives her the name of a young man, which all the other girls are unsuccessful at guessing. So her obeying her mother and the old woman is rewarded by winning the young man all the girls are trying to get.

In general, obedience is only rewarded and appreciated in tales when it involves doing "the right thing." For example, there is a tale about a husband telling his two wives not to untie his dogs, threatening a beating if they do. One day, he is in danger and calls for his dogs. The dogs hear him and start barking. One wife decides to let them go, and they rescue the man. Naturally, the wife is rewarded instead of punished (Tremearne, *Hausa Superstitions* 298). So in tales like these, children are clearly taught to form their own judgement of a situation rather than to simply "do as they are told." Even mature characters in the tales lose out if they disregard sound advice or don't use their own common sense, intelligence or sound judgement, more so than if they do wrong, although serious wrong is usually found out and punished, either by people or by God or other supernatural forces.

Among the Hausa, women are generally known to have more supernatural power than men. All of the women interviewed agreed on this issue. This is especially true of older women. The tales abound with examples of old women (*tsohuwa*) who use their supernatural power, usually to help people. There are many tales in which a girl is asked to help an old woman wash, and if she complies, she is rewarded in some magical way (tales 2, 18 and 27). Another common theme is the old woman who finds discarded babies and adopts them; the babies having been thrown out by a jealous co-wife of their mother. The old woman often has to restore them to life, usually with the help of God (tale 6). In "The snake-son" (tale 26), it is an old woman who advises the tenth girl how to make the snake-son transform into a young man so he won't eat her like he did her nine predecessors.

Women use supernatural power for good or for evil. The tales are full of examples of a co-wife who uses a charm to turn her step-daughter into a bird or needles to kill her step-daughter's boyfriend (tales 7 and 13). On the other hand, there are also many tales of a mother warning her son from the grave to avoid being killed by the step-mother, her co-wife, who tries to poison him (tales 19 and 32). When asked about women's supernatural power, many of the women I interviewed asserted that women use supernatural power mostly to protect themselves from their co-wives. Mariama, a 100 year-old woman in a non-Muslim village, went further in asserting:

> Now, women's supernatural power is stronger than men's. You see, if women do not use power, they will never control men. Allah gave them that power in order to help them. Allah helped women. This is the reason why they dominate men as far as the use of supernatural power is concerned. (Personal interview, 12 July 1996)

This observation certainly is confirmed by tales about marriage.

The importance of marriage in Hausa culture has long been documented and still holds true today. It is a marker of adulthood and status. There are clear influences of social factors on marriage and vice versa. For example, there is a clear link between marriage and women's economic activities to the extent that Pittin speaks of "career strategies" when discussing women's choices regarding marriage, remarriage, non-marriage and prostitution (karuwanci). All of the most successful traders among the women in Barbara Cooper's study "had at one time or another settled into a marriage which was mutually satisfying. These marriages often come late in a woman's income earning career, when her independence has earned her the ability to negotiate the terms of her marriage to her own benefit" (Cooper 251; see also Echard 210 and Coles 191).

In general, a Hausa girl's first marriage is arranged by her parents. Sometimes the girl has a say in the partner chosen, often she does not. The majority of these marriages fail, often within the first year. Hausa women's second, third and later marriages are usually to men closer in age to themselves; they also usually have more say in choosing the husband themselves and, depending on the circumstances, can sometimes make demands about living arrangements, opportunities for economic activity, etc. Nonetheless, divorce rates may not be significantly lower for later marriages (Cooper 375).

Although male domination in Hausa marriage is undeniable, one should try to look beyond the obvious. Baba of Karo sheds some light on this subject. Her first marriage was to a cousin, Duma, and she agreed to the marriage to please her parents. However, before she married this cousin, she promised one of her suitors whom she liked a lot, Maigari, that she would come to him later, which she did after she divorced her cousin. Baba explains that her cousin had done nothing wrong; she just did not like him and she wanted to be with the man she loved. Her father's sister Rabi supported her decision, and that was important in winning her case before her relatives and the *Sarki* (Mary Smith 107-8). However, Aunt Rabi had wanted Baba to marry someone else and it took her four years to accept Baba's choice. Baba clearly states that she and Maigari loved one another (111, 118). It is clear from Baba of Karo's accounts that in marriage men may have official power on their side, but women know how to manipulate men and their rules to get the man or marriage they want. A husband not providing for or mistreating his wife is not nearly the only the reason for a woman to leave a marriage; she may simply not like him or love somebody else. The accounts of several women in Barbara Cooper's study confirm this. Women have much control of marriage, not only as girls—either by refusing to marry someone they don't like or by running away shortly after the wedding—but also as mothers, as mothers-in-law and even as aunts in bringing marriages about or keeping them together, as well as in breaking them up.

Furthermore, there is great similarity between women's views of marriage which are markedly different from men's. This is brought out when a marriage is considered to have been concluded. For men, the payment of the *sadaki* (bride wealth) denotes the moment that the marriage has been contracted. They essentially see marriage as a contract which can be entered into and undone just as any contract. For women, however, marriage is "essentially organic and must be nurtured and watched, but it can unaccountably expire for reasons beyond the control of the couple involved" (Cooper 508). This organic view of marriage is reflected in the language used; women say marriage:

"takes" (*arme ya kama*), rather like a dye, a seedling, a fire, or a pregnancy. . . . When a marriage "refuses to take" (*rme ya kiya*) there is nothing anyone can do to save it—it will eventually 'die' . . . . And a marriage which is perfectly healthy can be 'killed' by others who want to sabotage it with gossip, ill-will, and cruelty. Women see the wedding ceremony as a process as well, something to be watched over, and the various ceremonies are rituals to promote growth, stages of that growth, and evidence that the marriage has "taken." (Cooper 508-9)[3]

Thus women do not consider the marriage to have been concluded until the giving of the *kayan daki* (things for the room) and the *gara* (gift of bride's mother to groom, which can be considerable) at least a week after the bride has moved into her husband's house. Those first days are seen as a test period.

In line with these differing views of marriage between men and women, women also still insist upon traditional rituals which men have been abandoning, such as the washing of the bride. This washing is only done for a first marriage and involves an actual washing by a younger sister of the bride's mother on the day of the wedding as well as decorating the bride with henna several days prior (Mary Smith 88-92). Traditionally, men were also washed and had henna put on for their first marriage, but this practice is diminishing. Traditionally, bride price (*sadaki*) payments were made in cowries. Cowries were symbolic of the feminine:

[the] cowry was likened to the female genitals, and was associated with pregnancy because of its rounded shape. It was also called an "eye," through which one could read the future. . . . Thus cowries were commonly associated with female sexuality and fertility, fate and luck, wealth built in small increments, beauty, affection and the supernatural . . . . With the shift from cowries to French coins in the *sadaki* payment, the associations which came with the cash component, such as colonial taxes, were less positive, and the payment lost many of the symbolic associations of the cowries. (Cooper 488)

Obviously, in "the time of cowries" the above associations were part of the culture and therefore held by men as well as women. Under the influence of Islam, men's notions have changed to seeing marriage as a contract. Yet, just because men's contractual notions of marriage have gained prominence and dominance in present-day culture does not mean women have given up their own organic notion of marriage, and women often refuse to submit to men's notions.

Non-married women and *karuwai* (prostitutes) in Katsina city, Nigeria, often find their lifestyles preferable to marriage (Pittin 52, 93, 293). Although marriage offers women a certain degree of protection and financial security, it is no guarantee of these since men can unilaterally divorce women; women often lose their children in case of divorce; and secluded marriage, which is the norm, places severe restrictions on women's mobility and economic opportunities. In addition, *karuwanci* has relatively little social stigma attached to it, which enables women to move in and out of *karuwanci* with ease. Many *karuwai* remarry, even if they eventually divorce and return to *karuwanci* again, and sometimes they do so more than once (Pittin 213, 348).

In Niger, there are also women who are redefining the roles and status of unmarried women. For instance, many of the women who work for the government prefer to remain single if marrying means giving up their job. They usually have been married once but have divorced and choose not to remarry. Titles like *Madame* or *Hajiya* often protect such single women from being regarded as *karuwai*. By being single yet not *karuwai*, these women carve out new ways for women and redefine women's roles, creating options outside marriage (see Cooper).

Thus, a Hausa woman's success and happiness in life depend on many interrelated factors such as kin, marriage, children, economic activity, social ties and religion, which are all interconnected. The above discussion has attempted to give an indication of the complexity of the situations, positions and roles of Hausa women and of the lives of Hausa women with all their intricacies, complexities and ambiguities. Let us now examine if and how those are reflected in *tatsuniyoyi*, an oral art form of Hausa women.

In some 50% out of the approximatively 400 tales I collected, marriage or its consequences (e.g. co-wives) play a role in some way or another. So marriage is obviously a major theme in the oral tradition of *tatsuniyoyi* and an important issue to the women who perform and create the tales. In view of the fact that Hausa women often depend on their husband for financial support for themselves and their children, that marriage confers adult status in society, that divorce and polygamy are common in Hausa society, and that even a Hausa woman's success in business often depends on the marriage she has entered into (or on not being married at all), it is not surprising that many tales deal with this topic. In this respect, the tales reflect women's concern with marriage and its consequences such as children and co-wives. I examine several tales with regard to statements about or portrayals of marriage and marriage partners to see to what extent the tales and reality converge or diverge.

The discussion of marriage in Hausa society above brought out differences between men's and women's views of marriage. Hausa women tend to view marriage in an organic way, as a *process* that takes time rather than as a simple contractual agreement, as the men mostly see it. Almost always in tales, some sort of process is mentioned: exchange of gifts, decorating the bride with henna, taking the bride to the groom's house, etc. (examples can be found in tales 7, 8, 12, 13, 15, 26 and 38.) The idea of marriage as an organic thing which has to be maintained to stay alive is expressed in the last line of tale 34 (which I used for the title): "The marriage died." The tale mentions the father dividing and passing out cola nuts and the bride being washed and decorated with henna as part of the wedding rituals, as well as the bringing of the brideprice by the groom. After she has been married one year, the girl wants to go home for a visit. This is customary. Her husband refuses to let her make *fura*, telling her to make *tuwo* [4] instead. She makes four batches, plus one for him. Then he refuses to let her take four batches home, and she leaves with three. Her father finds her crying and asks her what is the matter. The girl explains that her husband had been about to beat her earlier and then refused to let her take proper food home. The father tells his daughter to stay home. When the husband comes looking for her, the father tells the husband to take his three batches of *tuwo* back home with him. He tells the chief what he told the husband: "I gave you my daughter, I can take her back." By asserting his right to give away and take back his daughter, the father seems to reflect that idea of marriage as a contract which had been broken by the husband's behavior. However, the tale as a whole reflects the women's view of marriage; since the marriage was not nurtured and maintained, it "died."

Mistreatment is not the only reason for a woman to leave a marriage. For instance, a woman or girl may leave a marriage if she simply does not like the husband or loves somebody else. There are several tales among the ones I collected which clearly evidence love. In "The co-wife's daughter and the prince of Egypt"[5] (tale 7), the unloved daughter whose mother died asks her father to buy her the prince of Egypt when he goes to the market. The father's asking around for him in the market prompts the prince of Egypt to come and visit the girl on Friday. When the prince asks the girl what she wants with the prince of Egypt, the girl answers in no uncertain terms: "I will love him. . . . I'll only love him. . . . just want to love him." He gives her silver and gold and comes back every Friday until the jealous step-mother places needles for him and he falls ill. The girl disguises herself as a beggar boy and goes in search of the prince, and, with the help of some birds, finds and cures him. When the prince visits the girl again and finds out that it was she who cured him, he tells her father that he wants to marry that girl: "I love her." The father tries to push his other (loved) daughter on the prince, but he is adamant. They are married, and the parents go crazy. A variant of this tale is "The co-wife's daughter and the prince" (tale 13). The girl in this tale clearly knows what and who she wants, and her rescue mission shows not only love but also great determination to do all she can to get the man she wants. And the prince also refuses to let the father change his mind about marrying the girl he loves. The tale does not mention either the prince or the girl being very beautiful, so the tale is not concerned with sheer physical attraction.

Even Tremearne has to admit that when it comes to marriages, "there is no denying that an adult girl has a good deal to say in the matter. . . . [Nowadays, the girl's] consent is usually sought." He goes on to explain this by asserting that getting the girl's consent "is solely for the reason that if she objects to the husband provided for her, she will almost certainly be unfaithful; it is not due to any consideration for the happiness of the girl herself" (*Hausa Superstitions* 76). This may be true from the parents' or husband's point of view, but the reason for the girl not to be faithful and thus to undermine the forced marriage has a lot to do with the girl's happiness and her own efforts to achieve it, social or familial pressures notwithstanding.

Tremearne wrote an article entitled "Marital Relations of the Hausas as Shown in Their Folklore," which consists of a one-paragraph introduction and 8 tales. He asserts that the first tale explains why Hausa women are so likely to commit adultery. The tale starts with an argument between a *malam*, who claims that women commit adultery because they learn it when growing up in their mothers' rooms and suckling at their mother's breasts, and another man, who claims it is because they are born in deceit. The rest of the tale is supposed to give the answer to this argument. The argument that women are born deceitful is an old and familiar one, not just in Hausa culture, and is supposedly validated by the tale. However, if one looks closely at the tale, and other tales as well, neither one of the arguments is validated.

The tale continues as follows. The *malam* marries a girl the moment she is born and takes her to his compound where she is fed goat milk in order to prove his point: it is the fact that a girl grows up in her mother's room and suckles at her mother's breasts that causes her to commit adultery. (It is highly unusual for a child not to be with her or his mother until s/he is weaned.) When she has grown up, a prince sees it as his challenge to commit adultery with this girl who has been locked inside the *malam*'s compound all her life. Needless to say, she helps him succeed and get away with it. She tells the *malam* that the (prince's) horse in his compound was a gift from the *Sarki*. When the *malam* goes to thank the *Sarki*, the prince leaves. When some courtiers come back with the *malam* to verify the story, the horse is gone, and they think he is crazy. When summoned, the girl explains to the *Sarki* that she did it on purpose to prove that women are born deceitful, contrary to the *malam*'s theory. The *malam* has to apologize (24-26).

From a man's point of view, and on the surface, this tale seems to prove that women are born deceitful. However, one can argue that, on a deeper level, the tale is about the power struggle between men and women, and confirms that no matter how hard men may try to dominate women and dictate their lives, women will always find ways to outsmart men and do what they want to do anyway. Thus, this tale indirectly makes a case against seclusion. From a women's point of view, the significance of the woman committing adultery lies not in the sexual act, as men might typically see it, but in the resistance of the girl against the domination of the *malam*. Furthermore, since it is the young, possibly uneducated girl who comes up with a trick to fool the much older, educated *malam* and to let the prince escape, who is at a loss and afraid when the *malam* returns, the tale clearly makes a case for the intellectual superiority of women. Thus, the so-called deceit women are born with really is rather cleverness (*dubara*), which they have to call upon in order to resist male domination of their lives.

Tremearne gives several similar tales, all of which seem to assert that a woman can, and will, always outsmart men, including her husband. Thus, the tales are rebellious in the open defiance of husbands by their wives (two of the wives challenge their husbands forthrightly) and assert the incapability of a husband to imprison a wife. It becomes clear that fidelity is up to the woman and is not something she can be forced into. The husband depends on the wife's willingness and cooperation; she is definitely in charge of her own sexuality. The storyteller clearly sides with the wife. Condemnation of possessiveness and male domination are strongly voiced in the tale above, and the adultery on the wife's part is justified as an act of rebellion against the *malam* and his wrongful acts.

One of the tales I collected that deals with adultery has a different story line. Two co-wives go to a celebration together and the husband follows them secretly. At the celebration, it turns out to be the loved wife who is cheating. The husband is very upset and tells her to leave his house (tale 33). In this case, the woman is punished, unlike in the tales collected by Tremearne. This confirms the analysis I gave of the tales above as justifying the act of adultery as an act of rebellion against the oppressive husband. For this tale does not mention any oppressive behavior on the husband's part. The fact that in this case adultery on the wife's part is not condoned makes it all the more clear that in the other tales, the act of adultery was indeed seen as an act of rebellion against a possessive husband, and justified as such.

Thus, in examining the roles of women and girls in Hausa tales, we find that the tales, of course, reflect Hausa culture and society, as in the setting, actions and daily activities of many of the characters. So, we find women in seclusion, women pounding and cooking, as they do in real life. However, the tales also often portray women as independent agents, whose actions speak of their determination to take responsibility for their own lives and happiness. For instance, in the tales about marriage, there are many young girls who are willing to disguise themselves and travel into the unknown to find and rescue their beloved. Similarly, we have seen how adultery is often an act of rebellion against male domination, seclusion and possessiveness on the part of the husband. In these tales about marriage and love, women and girls are often portrayed as smart, courageous characters who take life into their own hands.

Given the social context of the telling of *tatsuniyoyi* by grown and older women to children, these tales send important messages to the little girls and boys listening about male-female relations and proper behavior for men and women. As the discussion has shown, the tales do not uphold ideas about male domination, whether these are sanctioned by Islam or not, but rather voice a strong disapproval of them, either directly or indirectly, while at the same time maintaining pre-Islamic, traditional or womanist notions about women as independent agents in control of their own lives and responsible for their own happiness, and by extension for that of the community.

It is clear from the tales that women have been endowed with plenty of cleverness and supernatural power, and most women and girls in the tales know how to use these gifts or to ask the help of a woman who has supernatural power in order to overcome difficult situations or to get what they want. The tales show in no uncertain terms that between their *dubara* (cleverness) and their *asiri* (supernatural power), women truly are no match for men.

Notes

1. "Islam" in this article is used as referring to Islam as *practiced* in Hausa society. Whether or not these practices are in agreement with Muslim doctrines is beyond the scope of this study.

2. The numbers in brackets refer to the numbers of the tales in the appendix of the dissertation on which this article is based.

3. Baba of Karo uses the same word "taken." Her use indicates that the bride and groom have had sex together for the first time, which was two weeks after the transfer of the *sadaki* in her days (Smith 99).

4. *Fura* is a drink made with millet and water and/or milk. *Tuwo* is a paste made of millet or corn.

5. Tremearne has an almost identical variant of this tale, in which *"Ba-Komi"* takes the place of the prince of Egypt (280-82). Another variant can be found in Connie Stephens' dissertation: performance 402 featuring the prince of Agadez (196).

Works Cited

Ben-Amos, Dan. "Introduction: Folklore in African Society." *Forms of Folklore in Africa: Narrative, Poetic, Gomic, Damatic.* Ed. Bernth Lindfors. Austin: University of Texas Press, 1977. 1-36.

Coles, Catherine. "Hausa Women's Work in a Declining Urban Economy: Kaduna, Nigeria, 1980-1985." *Hausa Women in the Twentieth Century.* Ed. Catherine Coles and Beverly Mack. Madison: University of Wisconsin Press, 1991. 163-91.

Coles, Catherine and Beverly Mack, eds. *Hausa Women in the Twentieth Century.* Madison: The University of Wisconsin Press, 1991.

Cooper, Barbara MacGowan. *The Women of Maradi: A History of the Maradi Region of Niger From the "time of cowries" to the "time of searching for money," 1900-1989.* 2 vols. Ann Arbor, MI: University Microfilms International, 1992.

Echard, Nicole. "Gender Relationships and Religion: Women in the Hausa *Bori* of Ader, Niger." *Hausa Women in the Twentieth Century.* Ed. Catherine Coles and Beverly Mack. Madison: University of Wisconsin Press, 1991. 207-20.

Mack, Beverly. "Royal Wives in Kano." *Hausa Women in the Twentieth Century.* Ed. Catherine Coles and Beverly Mack. Madison: University of Wisconsin Press, 1991. 109-29.

Pittin, Renee I. *Marriage and Alternative Strategies: Career Patterns of Hausa Women in Katsina City.* Diss. University of London, 1979.

Smith, Mary. *Baba of Karo: A Woman of the Moslem Hausa.* 1954. 2nd ed. New Haven, CT: Yale University Press, 1981.

Smith, Michael G. "The Social Functions and Meaning of Hausa Praise-Singing." *Africa: Journal of the International African Institute* 27.1 (1957): 26-43.

Stephens, Connie L. *The Relationship of Social Symbols and Narrative*

Metaphor: A Study of Fantasy and Disguise in the Hausa Tatsuniya of Niger. 2 vols. Ann Arbor, MI: University Microfilms International, 1981.

_____. "Marriage in the Hausa *Tatsuniya* Tradition: A Cultural and Cosmic Balance." *Hausa Women in the Twentieth Century.* Ed. Catherine Coles and Beverly Mack. Madison: University of Wisconsin Press, 1991. 221-31.

Tremearne, Arthur N.J. "Marital Relations of the Hausas as Shown in Their Folklore." *Man* 14 (1914): 23-26, 137-139, 148-156.

_____. *Hausa Superstitions and Customs: An Introduction to the Folklore and the Folk.* 1913. London: Frank Cass & Co. Ltd, 1970.

T'Shaka, Oba. *Return of the African Mother Principle of Male and Female Equality.* Vol. 1. Oakland, CA: Pan Afrikan Publishers and Distributors, 1995.

Reading Fantasia:
Assia Djebar, Frantz Fanon and the
Politics of Representation

Touria Khannous

The publicity given in the French media to the violence in today's Algeria forces the pressing question: "What are writers in exile to make of all this death?" Media accounts of the violence going on since 1991 are a mixture of spectacle and narrative that both horrifies and inures. In its efforts to make sense of the urgency of the situation, the media accords women due attention as equal victims in a state of senseless violence. Allusions to the presence of women in the current conflict could hardly go unnoticed, for practically every Algerian man who is killed, there is a woman who suffers the reverberating consequences. Within the context of France, media reports also serve to stereotype Algerian women and homogenize them with respect to Islam.[1]

My paper explores Assia Djebar's representations of the Algerian woman within the context established by Frantz Fanon, the first intellectual of color to challenge and problematize the representation of the Algerian woman in colonial and nationalist discourses. Djebar's novel *Fantasia* is made more urgent because of a history of misrepresentations of the Algerian woman. Djebar knows Fanon's ideas about the veil and his theories of decolonization, for she worked closely with him during his stay in Algeria, and even contributed articles to his revolutionary newspaper *El-Moujahid*. In her memoir *Le Blanc de L'Algérie*, Djebar pays homage to Fanon, relates her friendship with him and his wife Josie Fanon, and praises his commitment to the Algerian struggle. Djebar's remembrance of Fanon testifies to her admiration of his work on the

Algerian woman. While the rhetoric of Algerian nationalist leaders and French colonial officials created a system that did not include the Algerian woman as an active agent in the national movement,[2] Fanon has, at least, made room for the Algerian woman's contributions to Algerian national history. If the rhetoric of colonialism as well as official nationalism ignores and silences women, Fanon's project attempts to make those silences speak a language of feminist and anti-imperialist resistance. To understand Djebar's representation of Algerian women with respect to their national history, it is necessary, therefore, to first examine Fanon's pioneering exploration of the dynamics of women's roles in the nationalist struggle.

The most coherent rendering of Fanon's ideas about women's roles during the struggle for independence comes in two essays found in his collection, *A Dying Colonialism*: "Algeria Unveiled" and "The Algerian Family." Throughout the former Fanon is very doubtful of the colonialist discourse about the Algerian woman's oppression within indigenous traditions, which is represented by the French in a racially prejudiced way. Thus Fanon chooses to represent the Algerian woman as an agent and as an actor in the anti-colonial struggle, to displace the common stereotypical construction of her as someone incapable of agency. Fanon describes the representation of the Algerian woman in colonial discourse thus: "To begin with, there is the well-known status of the Algerian woman—her alleged confinement, her inconsequence, her humility, her silent existence bordering on quasi-absence. And 'Moslem society' which has made no place for her, amputating her personality, allowing her neither development nor maturity, maintaining her in a perpetual infantilism" (*A Dying Colonialism* 65). Such a representation shows that the French administration endeavored to dominate Algerians by holding their traditions as static and unchangeable.[3] Fanon is suspicious of such a human rights agenda on the part of the French, since he believes that it is ironic and contradictory to have Algerians classified as backward by the same colonial force that has hindered their progress.

Fanon's problematizing of this kind of representation in order to expose its colonialist and "racist arguments," leads him to want to "speak for" the Algerian woman in a language of images and words more representative of her:

The Algerian woman's ardent love of the home is not a
limitation imposed by the universe. It is not hatred of the
sun or the streets or spectacles. It is not a flight from the
world. What is true is that under normal conditions, an
interaction must exist between the family and society at
large. The home is the foundation of social truth, but
society authenticates and legitimizes the family. The
colonial structure is the very negation of this reciprocal
justification. The Algerian woman, in imposing such a
restriction on herself, in choosing a form of existence
limited in scope, was deepening her consciousness of
struggle and preparing for combat. (66)

Here, the Algerian home is a privileged place and a natural manifestation
of Algerian women's position as nurturers of their families. Given his
need to respond to "racist arguments" (40) about the inferior status of the
Algerian woman, Fanon praises the position of the Algerian woman
inside. This "inside" is presumably inaccessible to the French, who see the
Algerian home as the locus of traditional values, and thus an obstacle to
their colonial strategy of assimilation.[3]

Unlike the French, Fanon seems also to understand the true
reasons behind the Algerian woman's confinement. Fanon would
undoubtedly have agreed with Algerian feminist Doria Cherabti
Merabtine who contends that such confinement "expressed, to an extent,
the will of a society that was deprived of everything and wanted to
survive" (42). Merabtine further explains that it was because of the
economic marginalization of Algerians that:

society took refuge in tradition and custom. . . In this
function of biological and symbolic reproduction
assumed by women, it is the whole community's survival
which is perpetuated. It is on women's side that one can
find the identity of these deprived people. To this end,
the Islamic order is jealously preserved in a spatial
dichotomy that perpetuates the role of division—private
space is relegated to the sacred whereas public space is
considered illicit for women. These two spaces are

mutually exclusive. They channel different—if not
conflicting—realities. (42)

Merabtine's main argument is that in colonial Algeria the social control
of women's behavior and bodies is, first and foremost, to be attributed to
Algerian people's grim social reality under colonialism, and is therefore
achieved through women's consent rather than through force.
Furthermore, women's confinement is created through discourses of
nationalism and not, as French accounts of Algeria would have it,
through Algerian patriarchy. Unlike Merabtine, however, Fanon seems
to be aware of the instrumental positioning of Algerian women within
national discourses that used them to symbolize the progressive
aspirations of the secular elite, on the one hand, and the cultural
authenticity endorsed by the Islamists, on the other.

Fanon is in fact very interested in the "instrumentalization of the
veil" in his analysis of women's involvement in the war. He describes the
"young girl, who was wearing a veil only yesterday, going through a
European town swarming with policemen, paratroopers and militia-men"
(41). He portrays veiled women carrying guns and bombs in their bags or
beneath their veils and passing them to male fighters. He also depicts
young Algerian women passing as European women, and being able to
pass through the controlled borders that separate the European city from
the "Casbah." Contrary to common representations of the Algerian
woman's veil as a fixed and stable cultural signifier—"The woman seen in
her white veil unifies the perception that one has of Algerian feminine
society. What we are dealing with here is quite obviously a uniform
which tolerates no modification, no variation" (36)—Fanon shows the veil
as a shifting and changing signifier, which can be an empowering means
of articulating a multiplicity of positions for the Algerian woman. In his
comments on the passage quoted above, David Macey mistakenly assumes
that Fanon's words are revealing of his own negative perception of the
veil:

> Fanon was not looking as an Algerian would look. And
> although he refers in phenomenological terms to the
> Algerian woman's lived experience and even her 'lived
> body' (corps vécu), he makes no attempt to understand

what wearing a veil might mean for her or what its
symbolism might be. (407)

What Macey fails to realize however is that Fanon is referring
here to the foreign tourist in Algeria and not to himself. Fanon is
undoubtedly projecting in this passage the European, orientalist view that
homogenizes veiled Algerian women. He has, after all, rejected European
perceptions of the veiled Algerian women as "a romantic exoticism,
strongly tinged with sensuality" (25). Fanon's view of the veil portrays
the complexity of the Algerian woman's identity against such
homogenizing and stereotypical views. In her essay "The True Lie of the
Nation," Madhu Dubey argues that Fanon's view of the veil in "Algeria
Unveiled" undermines the colonial association between modernization
and liberation, on the one hand, and tradition and repression, on the
other.

In his more complex interpretations, Fanon shows that veiling is
what enables Algerian women's mobility during the anti-colonial
struggle, since she now wears the veil in different contexts to articulate
many positions. Restrictions on women's mobility prior to the
revolution have of necessity been lifted. Their hidden confrontation with
the occupier testifies to the fluidity of assigned spaces in the "inside,"
upon women's crossing over to the European quarters. Not only have
women now entered the French colonial public space but they also
confront directly the double oppression to which they are subjected as
women and Algerians. Fanon is convinced that the Algerian woman's
entry into public space heralds her emancipation once and for all from
Algerian patriarchy.

Critics have commented on how Fanon has seen in such
moments of revolutionary action the Algerian woman's chance to liberate
herself from the veil and to embrace modernity. At this point, Fanon is
so thrilled about women's revolutionary agency that he risks replicating
in his analysis the nationalist fetishistic rhetoric that often links the
decolonized nation to the figure of woman. Fanon is convinced that "the
liberation of the Algerian people was identical with the liberation of
women, and with their entry into history. The destruction of
colonization is the birth of a new woman" (83). According to Sekyi Uto,
Fanon evokes the revolutionary Algerian woman

> in a language that prefigures his description of
> decolonization in the opening paragraphs of *The
> Wretched of the Earth*. Just as decolonization, according to
> 'Concerning Violence,' abruptly and 'without transition'
> transfigures a dehumanized people into 'privileged
> actors,' so the appearance of women upon the public
> stage of revolutionary deeds is nothing less than an
> authentic birth in a pure state, without preliminary
> instruction. (225)

Woman and Algeria, that is, are in a state of resurgence; woman and
colonized Algeria become one, and because both are determined by the
experience of colonialism, both are related to the experience of
decolonization. It is through such a process of decolonization that the
Algerian woman, according to Fanon "ceased to be a complement for
man. *She literally forged a new place for herself by her sheer strength*" (109).
Fanon obviously mistook the temporary mobility of the Algerian woman
for her permanent liberation. He was naïve in his optimism for the
Algerian woman, because as a foreigner, he did not know enough about
the subtle codes of Algerian patriarchy.

Denean Whiting is to be credited for her defense of Fanon against
the allegations of feminists who claim that he has denied Algerian women
their agency in his account of the revolution. She notes with unhidden
anger:

> As of late, Fanon has been put into a lurch of sorts, the
> clichéd 'damned if you do, damned if you don't.' In
> writing about Algerian women, he has been accused of
> reinscribing silence, male privilege, and ventriloquism. If,
> in 1959, he had written of the Algerian revolution
> without a word on the women, he would have been
> accused of sexism; as he has written of the subject, he
> now stands accused of mythmaking with a
> sexist/conservative subtext. (74)

Whiting has in mind Anne McClintock, who argues that Fanon has
assigned no agency to Algerian women; in his account of the revolution,

women mainly carry out orders for Algerian men. Fanon's reading of the Algerian woman, for her, merely links women's agency to "male designation" (366). McClintock's reading of Fanon does not, however, acknowledge his daunting and unprecedented representation of the Algerian woman.

Deanan Whiting is not alone in critiquing such feminist stances against Fanon. Madhu Dubey questions Diana Fuss's and Joan Mowitt's allegations that Fanon "casts woman as a symbolic and epistemological ground rather than as a historical subject of the Algerian nation" (15). Dubey discounts such critiques, insisting instead on the feminist politics that underline Fanon's two texts *The Wretched of the Earth* and *A Dying Colonialism*. If anything, Dubey argues, Fanon's critique of nationalism shares some similarities with feminist critiques of nationalisms, since unlike nationalisms which often place woman in a paradoxical location within their discourses of the modern and the traditional, Fanon refuses to resolve the contradiction between tradition and modernity in his account of women and the Algerian revolution. Fanon's oscillation between tradition and modernity in his discourse on the Algerian woman and the nation, Dubey concludes, might be a calculated strategy.

Fanon's feminism is clear in his representation of the Algerian woman's political activism as a prerequisite for her feminist consciousness, but his reductive identification between woman and nation remains a major blind spot in his account of such activism. Winifred Woodhull, for one, points out that since "Algeria is personified as one woman" (3) in "Algeria Unveiled," Fanon's analysis "obscure(s) tensions that have always existed between nationalism and feminism in Algeria" (22-3). One can almost argue that Fanon's association of the Algerian woman with the colonization and decolonization of Algeria risks confusing the woman question with the question of the nation.

The Algerian woman, whom Fanon identifies with the Algerian nation, did unite with the Algerian man behind a common goal for national independence, but did not experience the liberation Fanon anticipated for her. Fanon's linking of woman and nation, that is, did not let him foresee later exclusions of women within nationalist discourse. His hasty invocation of modernity in the figure of the Algerian woman, in the aftermath of independence, was indeed very misleading. The conflation of independence with Algerian women's liberation, according to Neil Lazarus, is the product of "a utopian conceptualization of the national liberation struggle" (*Resistance* 5). In his essay "Disavowing Decolonization: Fanon, Nationalism, and the Problematic of Representation in Current Theories of Colonial Discourse," Lazarus points out that Fanon "renders himself incapable of understanding exactly what is at stake for the subaltern classes in their involvement in anticolonialism" (91). Lazarus further argues that Fanon's own claims that the Algerian masses have achieved their goal of liberation need to be weighed against the "demobilization" and "disenfranchisement" of the people soon after independence was achieved in 1962" (92).

The question now is: what types of feminist discourses emerge after the moment of independence? What reconstructions of female subjectivity does the subsequent disillusionment produced by independence necessitate? How did women as historical agents in Algeria respond to Fanon's equating of the modern, unveiled woman with the independent Algerian nation? In her essay "Bound and Gagged by the Family Code," Algerian feminist and activist Marie-Aimée Hélie-Lucas makes trenchant critiques of Algerian post-war nationalism, insisting that Algerian women have been silenced and subordinated by the Algerian nationalists in the aftermath of independence. She writes:

> We [Algerian women] cannot organize inside our own countries, nor even speak without facing heavy repression, we are also made to feel that we should not speak outside, that we should hide, in the name of national loyalty, the crimes committed against women and against other oppressed sectors of the people. We are thus made to identify with "the nation", "the people", conceptualized as an undifferentiated mass, without conflicting interests, without classes, and without history —in fact, we are made to identify with the State and the ruling class as legitimate representatives of "the people" . . . . In Algeria, many of us, including myself, kept silent for ten years after Independence, not to give fuel to the enemies of the glorious Algerian revolution. . . . Our rightist forces exploit our silence. (13-4)

Marie-Aimée Hélie-Lucas also makes reference to the family code that was instated in 1984. The code highlights the ambiguous nature of Algeria's dominant ideology, and its own brand of nationalist socialism. In the new socialist rhetoric, which emphasizes secularization, nationalism, and modernization, women are relegated to a marginal status in the legislation of the Family Code, which imposes more restrictions on Algerian women.[4] For Hélie-Lucas, the code aligns women with tradition, against a masculine sphere of modernity:

> One of the earliest slogans of nationalism in Algeria was promoted by the *ulama*. "Arabic is our language. Islam is our religion. Algeria is our country." Women were supposed to raise sons in the faith and preserve traditional moral standards and to teach the language of the forefathers.
>
> Women should be bound by tradition, while men had some access to modernity. Yet, it is now a commonplace that tradition serves the purpose of those in power. Tradition is seen as ahistorical and immutable, modernity draws from the wealthy West–whatever that means. ("Women, Nationalism and Religion" 108)

Hélie-Lucas draws here upon the familiar argument that both nationalism and authoritarian socialism used women's revolutionary labor and returned her to the patriarchal household structure, after they won independence. Along the same lines, Radhakrishnan argues that such "gendered schizophrenia" enables newly emerging nations to "assimilate" the West "selectively," while preserving an essential, "inner" identity in the figure of woman ("Women" 84-85).

Doria Cherifati Merabtine, on the other hand, chooses not to blame the nationalists, who were confronted, she argues, with an Islamic trend to legislate women's status within the family on the basis of Islamic law (Shari'a). The FLN's recognition of women's participation in the war did not translate therefore into the legislation of women's emancipated status in the family:

[T]he legistator was faced with two antagonistic representations of women: the first based on tradition, the second on modernity. This contradiction led eventually to a Family Code that established women's secular tasks and set man-woman relationships in a patriarchal mode. (52)

The family code exemplifies the tension between tradition and modernity in the aftermath of independence. Clearly Algerian society remains male-dominated, from conceptions of nationhood to family relationships.

Asia Djebar's novel, *Fantasia: An African Cavalcade* illustrates her continuing engagement with the problematic representation of the Algerian woman under both colonialism and Algerian nationalism. Djebar's critique of anti-colonial nationalism and women's imprisonment in postcolonial Algeria can be read in the context of Fanon's false hopes for women's liberation in "Algeria Unveiled." Djebar's novel is in a constant dialogue with Fanon. Published in 1985, *Fantasia* explores the interrelations between Algerian women, French colonialism and Algerian nationalism. The novel offers no full narrative account of the French conquest of Algeria in 1830, no linear history of the brutal repressions of a resistant Algerian nationalist movement led by Amir Abdel Kader, and no linear narratives of the Algerian liberation war of the 1950s. Rather, *Fantasia* juxtaposes a series of episodes, including an account of the French conquest of Algeria, a period of Algerian resistance during the occupation, a description of the adult narrator's displaced situation as an educated woman, and an orchestration of three Algerian women's oral accounts in French about their participation during the war of liberation.

The novel's unconventional postmodernist narrative techniques resonate with its critique of the official historical accounts, whose premises it deconstructs. In its first two sections, the novel alternates between historical representations of the French conquest of Algeria that began in 1830 and the author's autobiography. The third and final sections include translated accounts of three Algerian women who participated in the war of liberation that ended in 1962, with the death of one million Algerians. The autobiographical parts of the novel allow Djebar to establish continuing links between Algerian women at the times of the French conquest and the colonial period, as well as women such as herself in postcolonial Algeria. Djebar, however, has admitted her unease with self-representation in *Fantasia*:

> J'y ai intégré un tel apport autobiographique que cela m'a gênée comme femme arabe. [I had included autobiography, which embarrassed me as an Arab woman.] ("Dossier" 75)

In the first section of *Fantasia*, the narrator addresses herself in the third person, and it is only in the last pages of the novel that she is able to finally take on fully her subjectivity by returning to the first person. In the sections entitled "Voice," the first person narrator is in the foreground, and voices of Algerian women evoke figures of female rebellion and storytellers.

Djebar's unease with self-representation is also apparent in her choice of the pen name "Assia Djebar," upon the publication of her first autobiographical novel *La Soif*. In addition to her pen name, Djebar adopts exile strategically as an alternative mode of representation, and as a subversive tool for the construction of an Algerian feminist solidarity. In the final pages of *Fantasia*, the narrator-protagonist positions herself as an exile, physically outside Algeria, while inside the boundaries of France—and the spaces outside of those boundaries for Algerian women like her in the diaspora. For her to become a link between Algerian women back home and France predicates a reclaiming of Algeria through a voyage into a collective past. As the narrator takes it upon herself to mediate the difference between Algeria and France, her vulnerability becomes apparent, for she is "only floundering in a murky bog."

Djebar's acts of self-representation and representation are made possible by her exile. Exile is what gives her the freedom to write and speak from outside Algerian patriarchy and from outside the violence in today's Algeria. In his essay "The Vanished Mediators: On the Nature of Violence in Algeria," Reda Bensmaia reflects on the effects of violence on Algeria's intellectuals. He argues that the ties between Algeria and its intellectuals have been severed by the current crisis. Those same intellectuals who might have performed the function of "intermediaries," "translators," and "interpreters" in the aftermath of independence, have

become, because of either assassination, imprisonment or exile, what
Bensmaia terms

> *phantom* mediators. They have vanished even before
> having the chance to exercise the role that generally falls
> to them in democratic societies. In the period of crisis
> that is gripping Algeria, they may return only as specters
> who (in the best of cases) will haunt the bad conscience
> of those who govern, or for those who believe them to
> be complicit with a shameful state or see them as traitors
> to their nation. (2)

While Bensmaia emphasizes the negative effects of exile on
Algeria's intellectuals, Edward Said argues that "exile" is not a strictly
negative experience:

> [W]hile it is true to say that exile is the condition that
> characterizes the intellectual as someone who stands as a
> marginal figure outside the comforts of privilege, power,
> being-at-homeness (so to speak), it is also very important
> to stress that that condition carries with it certain
> rewards and, yes, even privileges. (59)

Said also points out that a state of exile is a state of being in-between:

> The exile . . . exists in a median state, neither completely
> at one with the new setting nor fully disencumbered of
> the old, beset with half-involvements and half-
> detachments, nostalgic and sentimental on one level, an
> adept mimic or a secret outcast on another. (49)

Speaking specifically about the intellectual as exile he states:

> [The] condition of exile [is] the state of never fully being
> adjusted, always feeling outside the chatty, familiar world
> inhabited by natives, so to speak, tending to avoid and
> even dislike the trappings of accommodation and

national well-being. Exile for the intellectual in this
metaphysical sense is restlessness, movement, constantly
being un-settled, and unsettling others. You cannot go
back to some earlier and perhaps more stable condition
of being at home; and alas, you never fully arrive, be at
one with your new home or situation. (53)

Djebar's condition of exile resonates with Said's idea of exile as
a condition of the mind, which necessitates a critical distance and a
restless opposition to all orthodoxies—both of the colonizer and of the
colonized. In some of his earlier work on exile, Said argues that exile
requires detaching oneself from all belonging and identity, and adopting
what Wallace Stevens called "a mind of winter." Similarly Djebar adopts
exile as a strategy of "distanciation," which can be deployed to
problematize politics of representation, for exile is related not only to the
experience of physical displacement but also to the problematic of
representation.

Critics tend to read Djebar's *Fantasia* as the representation of a
historical truth that both colonial and nationalist discourses overlook.
Djebar's work, in their reading, becomes responsible for the preservation
of the truth of Algerian women's history beyond the falsities of national
and colonial politics.[5] In my reading, however, Djebar's novel is not a
substitute for political truth but rather a venue for granting a voice to the
Algerian woman subaltern whom the language of politics excludes or
attempts to exclude. My analysis also locates Djebar's novel within a
tradition of Algerian women's oral stories, which dates back to the pre-
colonial period. In drawing upon a body of communal stories (legends,
myths, and stories) and rewriting these oral narratives into written text,
Fantasia challenges us to read it as a text in which the oral tradition
figures as significantly as the language in which it is written.

In re-narrating the political history of Algeria through the voices
of Algerian women, Djebar's novel re-visits colonial and national
narratives as well as Fanon's essays on Algerian women. In that sense, the
novel represents a stage in Algerian narratives of decolonization from the
perspective of the Algerian woman. Its alternative representations of the
Algerian woman mark a new stage, therefore, in the representation of
decolonization and post-coloniality. In *The Wretched of the Earth*, Fanon

defines decolonization as a process of thorough social transformation that
alters the organization of society beyond the emancipation of the state
from the colonizer. Decolonization, in Fanon's argument, signifies a
project of resistance that goes on for long after the end of colonialism. It
is interesting to note that Fanon defines decolonization as a third
alternative to colonialism's official representation, as well as to the
national representation of the state. We can therefore read Djebar's
Fantasia as emerging out of decolonization in this sense.

At the heart of Djebar's novel is an affirmation of woman's voice.
Oral narrative as it disrupts linear colonialist discourse provides a venue
for exploring the repressions and exclusions in the official history. The
novel, as it deconstructs the representational project of colonialism,
critiques the sterile rhetoric of the crowds of "interpreters, geographers,
ethnographers, linguists, various doctors and professional writers" (56)
who had come to Algeria upon its conquest by the French. Djebar's
novel moves through and out of the discursive validity of such colonial
rhetoric and toward a reinstatement of women's voices. The novel
constructs the narrative of the French conquest through a collection of
letters, reports, and accounts written by French generals, reporters,
interpreters and artists. The narrator points out that "thirty-seven
witnesses, possibly more, will relate the events of this month of July
1830, some fresh from their experiences, some shortly afterwards. Thirty-
seven descriptions will be published, of which only three are from the
viewpoint of the besieged" (44). Amable Matterer, the "lookout man,"
writes of the first confrontation between France and Algeria: "I was the
first to catch sight of the city of Algiers, a tiny triangle on a mountain
slope" (6). The "war artist Major Langlois will pause to draw dead Turks"
(17). T.J. Merle, who runs the Porte-Saint-Martin theater in Paris, records
the fall of Algiers on July, 1830 thus:

> At ten in the morning of the 4th, we heard a mighty
> explosion, following upon ceaseless shelling since
> daybreak . . . . At the same instant, the horizon was
> covered in dense black smoke, which rose to a prodigious
> height; the wind blowing from the East carried the smell
> of gunpowder, dust and scorched wool, which left us in
> no doubt that Fort Emperor has been blown up, either

by a mine or from its powder magazines catching fire.
(29)

Similarly, the narrator recounts the events of the Berber Ouled
Riah insurrection of 1845 by drawing upon the account of Pelissier, the
colonel in charge of putting down the rebellion. The narrator emphasizes
not only the difference between the French official accounts and her
own, but also the great span of time which separates her own account
from theirs: "Nearly one and a half centuries after Pelissier and Saint-
Arnaud, I am practicing a very special kind of speleology, since in my
descent into those dark caverns my only hand-holds are words in the
French language-reports, accounts, evidence from the past" (77-8). She
writes:

> Thanks to his "too realistic" description, Pélissier
> suddenly resurrects, before my eyes, those Ouled Riah
> who died in their caves on the night of 19 to 20 June
> 1845. The dead woman found lying beneath the body of
> the man who was protecting her from the bellowing ox.
> Because of his remorse, Pélissier keeps this corpse from
> drying in the sun, and these Islamic dead, deprived of the
> ritual ceremonies, are preserved from oblivion by the
> words of his routine report. A century of silence has
> frozen them. The asphyxiated victims of the Dahra that
> words expose, that memory disinters. . . . Pélissier,
> speaking on behalf of this long drawn-out agony, on
> behalf of fifteen hundred corpses buried beneath El-
> Kantara, with their flocks unceasingly bleating at death,
> hands me his report and I accept this palimpsest on
> which I now inscribe the charred passion of my
> ancestors. (79)

In this passage, the narrator's voice consistently disrupts
Pelissier's report. In this account, which depicts the asphyxiated bodies
of the victims of the Dahra, death becomes the ground of representation.
Death is not merely the representation of violence but the index of the
violence of historical representation itself. Djebar's challenge to such

representation signals the need for an alternative project that would require the rewriting of the marginal histories of the Algerian subalterns.

Djebar's main concern in *Fantasia* is to show women's involvement in Algerian resistance and the role they played in disrupting such official representational discourses. This requires her to abandon binary notions of "public" and "private," common in nationalist and colonialist discourses on the Algerian woman, for the latter's participation in the war traverses these divisions so as to render them untenable. Here, women's voices in the novel are also aligned with a subtle and cumulative interrogation of Algerian nationalism. By reclaiming the Algerian woman's oral stories, the novel incorporates a political voice that allows the author to interrogate the segregation of the public and private spheres on which masculinist national narratives are founded. Frederic Jameson has argued that whereas

> capitalist culture, that is, the culture of the western realist and modernist novel, [suffers] a radical split between the private and the public, between the poetic and the political. . . . Third-world texts . . . necessarily project a political dimension in the form of the national allegory: *the story of the private individual's destiny is always an allegory of the embattled situation of the public third-world culture and society.* (69)

In claiming this, however, Jameson seems unaware of the gender dynamics of nationalism in the Third-World, and of its repressions of the private story of woman in its political narratives of the nation. Aijaz Ahmed has, for his part, criticized Jameson's "proposition that the 'third-world' is a singular formation, possessing its own unique, unitary form of determination in the sphere of ideology (nationalism) and cultural production (the national allegory)" (22).

Prior to investigating women's position within Algerian nationalism, Djebar first examines their representation in French official accounts of the war. The author's comments situate racism powerfully in colonial representational discourses. In describing French official accounts, the narrator shows how dominant subjects subordinate others, with the Algerian woman's position at the bottom of the hierarchy. The operation of racism is connected to naturalized surveillance, where dominant subjects wield the power to scrutinize and classify others. Djebar draws upon the report of the Count of Castellane who writes for the *Revue des Deux Mondes* in Paris. In this report, the Count remarks that the Algerian women prisoners who were compelled to march in French victory parades would veil their faces with mud or their own blood in order to protect themselves from the French male's gaze. In Djebar's interpretation of the Count's observations, the latter's remarks betray his racism, since he interprets these women's acts as signs of their ignorance.

Djebar's meticulous interrogation of racism indicates her preoccupation with the complexities of power and the situation of all subjects in discourse. Here she also highlights the Orientalist nature of French colonial reports. Edward Said has pointed out that a very significant feature of Orientalist scholarship is its political motivation, since it was instigated by the colonial administrations, which required Orientalists to be legitimators of their colonial project. What Said calls Orientalism is the accumulated product of centuries of textual evidence through which Europe could assume postures of superiority with regard to the Orient. In Djebar's novel, Algeria is identified with "Woman" in the French official accounts about the conquest of 1830 and the Algerian war of liberation. From the very first encounter, the narrator states that the "impregnable City confronts them with its many invisible eyes" (7). While these men record the incidents from their points of view, Algeria, like Woman, remains invisible to them. Generally, Algeria and the Algerian woman's meaning in French reports is silence and absence, since they both appear to have no presence beyond the myths and perceptions of the French generals and officers.

Because the novel is centered on the feminine collective, it does not risk reproducing the univocal category "Algerian Woman," whom the French occupiers have equated with nation, or whom Fanon identifies with the national cause of revolution. It is such reductive patterns of identifying the woman's body with the Algerian nation that account, in Radhakrishnan's terms, for the "historical failure to coordinate the political or the ontological with the epistemological" (85). Radhakrishnan has pointed out that the nationalists' allegorization of the female body as the national body is what prevents their access to "historical knowledge" about the indigenous woman. Speaking from within the context of Indian nationalism, he states:

> The locus of the true self, the inner/traditional/spiritual sense of place, is exiled from processes of history, while the locus of historical knowledge fails to speak for the true identity of the nationalist subject. The result is a fundamental rupture, a form of basic cognitive dissidence, a radical collapse of representation. (85)

Djebar's novel recovers and represents the knowledge about women that has been subdued in nationalist and colonial narratives.

The final and third section of the novel is divided into five movements alluding to Beethoven's symphony, Fantasia. Each movement consists of a sub-section entitled either "Voice" or "Widow's Voice." Algerian women interviewed by the narrator in this section of the novel are portrayed as heroines who have fought for the liberation of the Algerian nation through the body. Cherifa, Lala Zohra, and Jennet, the peasant women of the mountains, recount the roles they played, and the experiences they endured through the years of fighting for independence from France. Here, the novel evokes Fanon's account of stories of women's resistance during the war of liberation. While peasant women such as Lala Zohra and Cherifa are freer in their resistance, the "city ladies . . . are trapped in the web of impossible revolt" (155). As in Fanon's "Algeria Unveiled," for the city ladies "a bomb" or a "stolen weapon" is whispered about in "hushed voices"(155). Contrary to Fanon's prophecy, Djebar represents the public male realm and the private female space as segregated spaces, even in the aftermath of the revolution. The rural illiterate woman, who participated in the anti-colonial struggle, now embodies the cultural code of seclusion, and the educated narrator who is able to write and read in French gains a degree of freedom otherwise forbidden to the women she seeks to represent. The Algerian woman whom Fanon assumed has liberated herself by participating in the struggle is relegated to the same patriarchal imprisonment that existed prior to the revolution.

The novel underscores the Algerian nationalists' argument about the need to fight for the eradication of the inferior status of women through their access to education when it depicts the narrator's father escorting his young daughter to the French school, against the Islamic tradition which ordained otherwise at the time. The narrator escapes the fate of her veiled female friends only because of her father's desire that she be educated in French. A nationalist, the narrator's father endorses women's liberation; he stands in the novel for the group of nationalists who tried to initiate women's entry into the public sphere. Here, Djebar stresses the nationalists' decision (influenced by the French educational system) to open schooling to girls. Merabtine argues that during the 1940s, nationalist parties encouraged women joining their political parties and initiated their entry into the political arena (44-6). Women's entry into the public domain was developed in "non-conflictual terms vis-à-vis the representation of the traditional woman" (51). Such a change in the representation of the Algerian woman was justifiable, since the new modern Algerian woman was also deployed "in opposition to the colonizer" (51). Merabtine further points out that women who now belong to the Islamist trend have turned away from the model of the modern Algerian woman who is now often associated with "the hawks of neo-colonialism" (52). Djebar's novel reiterates such a pessimistic view of Algerian women, whose historical role in the resistance has been depreciated in the post-colonial period.

As Djebar relates the stories of women who participated in the Franco-Algerian struggle, she also attempts to link their stories to the setting of her own story. The story of Cherifa, whose cries for her brother's dead body symbolize the suffering of all voiceless Algerian women, is threaded into Djebar's narrative of a woman in the contemporary post-independence period; the woman whom the author describes walking along the Rue Richelieu in Paris at night, could be Djebar herself. As the woman walks alone in the street, she experiences a similar experience as that of Cherifa:

> The space is blank, the long empty road is mine alone. I walk at ease . . . suddenly the voice bursts off. It drains off all the scoriae of the past. What voice? Is it my own voice, scarcely recognizable? . . . The mixture of impurities is flushed from my mouth in a harsh deep-throated cry which seems to go before me. (115)

By associating Algerian women who reside in Paris with those who live in Algeria, those who lived in the nineteenth century with those who live in the twentieth century, the novel breaks down temporal and spatial boundaries between Algerian women. By weaving the individual voices of Cherifa with those of the women in Paris, Djebar unifies the struggle of the Algerian woman over time and space.

Towards the end of *Fantasia*, Djebar reflects back on her project and self-consciously questions the representational mode in which it is written. The same issues Djebar has with self-representation arise this time in relation to language, since language also operates within hierarchies of power. The author's questioning of her representational project testifies to her awareness of the colonial dynamics of French which has often served as the linguistic vehicle for the projection of colonial power. Post-colonial critics and writers have reacted against the hegemonic deployment of European languages. In *The Rhetoric of Empire*, David Spurr argues that the colonized are denied language in a double sense; first they are not allowed to speak, and second, they are recognized as incapable of speech. Ngugi wa Thiong'o has also challenged African writers to write in African rather than in European languages. In her reading of Djebar's novel, Gayatri Spivak points out that:

> One of the major motifs of *Fantasia* is a meditation upon the possibility that to achieve autobiography in the double bind of the practice of the conqueror's writing is . . . to learn to be taken seriously by the gendered subaltern, the woman in radical disenfranchisement, who has not had the chance to master that practice. (197)

Spivak further contends that Djebar's position is problematic, especially because of her attempt to express the subjectivity of Algerian women in a colonial language that has denied the specificity of their female experience. Djebar's anxiety over representation calls attention to the inadequacy and incompleteness of all texts, which claim to speak for the Algerian woman, including those of Fanon. After Djebar's project, neither the colonial text nor the masculinist nationalist text, or even Fanon's, can adequately represent the Algerian woman's experience faithfully.

Notes

1. In her essay "Masculin/féminin: les Algériens et le mouvement des femmes," Fatma Oussedik argues that current images of Algerian women in French media indicate that we are now far away from the odalisques, Algerian women of the artist Delacroix who are often presented as a dream: "The page of this orientalism is now well turned" (117, my translation).

2. In her book, *The Eloquence of Silence*, Marnia Lazreg cites the feminist erasures within the rhetoric of the post-independence Algerian governments as follows: "Ben Bella's populist style hid the fact that the socialist doctrine he promoted stumbled on the issue of women. His successor, Houari Boumedienne, advocate of an "Islamic" form of socialism, rationalized the doctrine, no matter how ill-devised it was, without any fundamental change, leaving the conceptual and empirical roles of women in the new state in abeyance" (146).

3. For a detailed discussion of Fanon's critique of the French liberal ideal and its ambiguous project to liberate the Algerian woman, see Eddy Souffrant's "To Conquer the Veil: Woman as Critique of Liberalism."

4. The preface to the Code stipulates that: marriage should occur at an early age so that society is preserved from depravation, it is mainly geared to the procreation of a progeny useful to society; it is based on equality between husband and wife except in legal responsibility, and familial authority, a natural prerogative of the husband; polygamy remains the only valid solution to serious familial discord; divorce is the exclusive right of the husband, for he is the breadwinner; guardianship (hadhana) reflects the concern of Islamic legislation for the protection of incapacitated members of society; divorce takes place by the will of the husband, and at the request of the wife; a wife has to obey her husband as head of the family, breastfeed his offspring and show respect for his parents and kin (Lazreg 151-5).

5. I am referring here in particular to Mary Green Jean's excellent essay "Dismantling the Colonizing Text: Anne Hebert's *Kamouraska* and Assia Djebar's *L'Amour, la fantasia*."

Works Cited

Ahmed, Aijaz. "Jameson's Rhetoric of Otherness and the 'National Allegory'." *Social Text* 17 (Fall 1987): 3-25.

Bensmaia, Reda. "The Vanished Mediators: On the Nature of Violence in Algeria." *Parallax* 4.2 (April-June 1998): 3-16.

Djebar, Assia. *Le blanc de l'Algérie*. Paris: Albin Michel, 1996.

____. *Fantasia: An Algerian Cavalcade*. Trans. Dorothy Blair. London: Quartet, 1987.

"Dossier: Assia Djebar at Heidelberg." *Cahier d'études maghrébines* 2 (1990): 65-70.

Dubey, Madhu. "The 'True Lie' of the Nation: Fanon and Feminism." *Differences* 10.2 (Summer 1998): 1-29.

Fanon, Frantz. *A Dying Colonialism*. Trans. Haakon Chevalier. New York: Grove Weidenfeld, 1965.

Hélie-Lucas, Marie Aimée. "Bound and Gagged by the Family Code." *Third World-Second Sex*, 2. Ed. Miranda Davies. London and New Jersey: Zed Books, 1987. 3-15.

____. "Women, Nationalism and Religion in the Algerian liberation Struggle." *Opening the Gates: A Century of Arab Feminist Writing*. Eds. Margot Badran and Miriam Cooke. London: Virago Press, 1990. 105-14.

Jameson, Fredric. "Third World Literature in the Era of Multinational Capitalism." *Social Text* 15 (1986): 65-88.

Jean, Mary Green. "Dismantling the Colonizing Text: Anne Hebert's *Kamouraska* and Assia Djebar's *L'amour, la fantasia*." *The French Review* 66.6 (1993): 956-66.

Lazarus, Neil. "Disavowing Decolonization: Fanon, Nationalism, and the Problematic of Representation in Current Theories of Colonial Discourse." *Research in African Literatures* 24.4 (Winter 1993): 69-98.

____. *Resistance in Postcolonial African Fiction*. New Haven and London: Yale University Press, 1993.

Lazreg, Marnia. *The Eloquence of Silence: Algerian Women in Question*. Routledge: New York, 1994.

Macey, David. *Frantz Fanon: A Life*. London: Granta, 2000.

McClintock, Anne. *Imperial Leather: Race, Gender, and Sexuality in Colonial Contest.* New York: Routledge, 1995.

Merabtine, Doria Cherifati. "Algeria at a Crossroads: National Liberation, Islamization and Women," *Gender and National Identity: Womenand Politics in Muslim Societies.* Ed. Valentine M. Moghadam. London: Oxford University Press, 1994. 40-62.

Oussedik, Fatma. "Masculin/féminin: les Algériens et le mouvement des femmes." *Pouvoirs* 86 (1998): 117-28.

Radhakrishnan, R. "Nationalism, Gender, and the Narrative of Identity." *Nationalisms and Sexualities.* Ed. Andrew Parker, et. al. New York: Routledge, 1992. 77-95.

Said, Edward. *Representations of the Intellectual.* New York: Pantheon Books, 1994.

Souffrant, Eddy. "To Conquer the Veil: Woman as Critique of Liberalism." *Fanon: A Critical Reader.* Ed. Lewis Gordon, et. al. Blackwell Publishers: Oxford, 1996. 170-8.

Spivak, Gayatri. "Teaching for the Times." *The Decolonization of Imagination: Culture, Knowledge and Power.* Ed. Jan Nederveen Pieterse and Bhikhu Parekh. London and New Jersey: The Zed Press Ltd., 1995. 177-202.

Spurr, David. *The Rhetoric of Empire: Colonial Discourse in Journalism, Travel Writing, and Imperial Administration.* Durham, NC: Duke University Press, 1993.

Uto, Sekyi Ato. *Fanon's Dialectic of Experience.* Cambridge, MA and London: Harvard University Press, 1996.

Whiting, Denean. *Frantz Fanon: Conflicts and Feminisms.* Lanham, MD: Rowman & Littlefield Publishers, Inc., 1998.

Woodhull, Winifred. *Transfigurations of the Maghreb: Feminism, Decolonization and Literatures.* Minneapolis: University of Minnesota Press, 1993.

Political Involvement in Leïla Abouzeid's *Year of the Elephant* and Bucchi Emecheta's *Destination Biafra*

Fatima Bouzenirh

African women's writing, as a relative newcomer to the African literary scene has—in general—provoked the dissatisfaction of male criticism of the canon literary tradition. The reason behind such a reaction is the adoption of a "feminist" orientation which has been qualified as "cultural bastardization" (Stratton 135). A major criticism, however, is the assumption of the absence of a historical dimension in these writings. Historical events, not only provide the framework of Leïla Abouzeid's *Year of the Elephant* and Buchi Emecheta's *Destination Biafra*, but are also at the core of heroines' concerns and predicaments. It is through the exploitation of this dimension that the two writers achieve a re-appropriation of the political space which has been for a long time a male preserve. In fact, this point has been raised not only in the field of literary criticism but also, and more recently, by anthropological scholarship which has shown how women in certain nationalist contexts "are not recognized as reliable reporters or interpreters of history" (Baker 3).

Across geographical borders and cultural areas on the African continent, writers, themes, and concerns can converge and be related in more than one way. This paper argues that both Abouzeid (Morocco) and Emecheta (Nigeria), despite their distinct geographical locations, make—through their heroines' political involvement and therefore, through a gendered perspective—far-reaching comments on issues of nationhood, national identity, colonialism and neo-colonialism.

In *Year of the Elephant,* Abouzeid relates the story of a middle-aged traditional woman, Zahra, who, having been repudiated, comes back to her native village after an absence of forty years. Through a series of flash-backs, the reader is introduced to Zahra's traditional social context: her upbringing by conservative grandparents, her marriage to a teacher—a man she had never met before—and then her moving to the urban center of Casablanca, which saves her from condemnatory attitudes of the mother-in-law because of presumed childlessness. During this period, Zahra's awareness of and struggle against restrictive traditional attitudes are made clear. Although her childhood reveals indifference towards her mother, she nevertheless concedes that "my poor mother lived in a nest of snakes" (13-4). Later, the stigma of childlessness makes her experience and voice a feeling of injustice: "in the face of their [her in-laws] unceasing reproaches, I became convinced that I was indeed the guilty party . . . I am not so sure now that it was my fault." Social criticism on this issue comes in a biting way: "barrenness provides sufficient grounds in a society uninterested in the true causes of such things" (18). Such an indictment implies the extent of the oppression exercised by patriarchal ideology over that women. Zahra is a victim with very little room for resistance in a system that not only victimizes these women but also forces traditional women of the older generation into self-victimization and internal oppression, as is the case for the mother-in-law: "when they announced that he [Zahra's husband] was transferred to Casablanca, she struck her face, tore her dress, and accused him of disloyalty and contempt towards his mother" (19). The pride of traditional women in "giving birth to sons" is yet another indictment of the unequal treatment that takes place in the household.

The journey to Casablanca heralds Zahra's way towards emancipation and transformation. The initial image of entrapment and seclusion is replaced by that of a woman breaking loose from her prison. The imagery of the prison is an important symbol which is skillfully used to make an important comment at the private level. Zahra's feeling of freedom is heart-felt: "I felt intoxicated by my emancipation" (19).

In the course of the first ten years she spends in Casablanca, Zahra becomes a different woman "with both feet on the ground and [her] head held high. But still [she] had not learned to say no, until misfortune struck" (21). With the advent of the nationalist struggle, Zahra joins in as a resistance fighter. At the same time she takes advantage of the literacy classes organized by the nationalists. Zahra, then, achieves emancipation within the limits of her socio-cultural context.

When misfortune strikes her, it is crystallized in the repudiation, which gives more prominence to the gender conflict and makes social the criticism more forceful at the private level: "your papers will be sent to you along with whatever the law provides—how worthless a woman is if she can be returned with a paper receipt like some store-bought object" (1). The repudiation acts as a psychological prod probing Zahra's consciousness about the reductive attitude and representation of woman in a male-dominated society. The realization of such an injustice as a result of an unjustified decision taken by her husband—a teacher to boot—comes to Zahra as a shock. "Where had she gone wrong?" She has benefitted from a sound education at the hand of her grandparents and has stood by her husband as a good traditional wife, obeying orders in the fields of resistance as well.

In this predicament, Zahra manages to pluck up enough courage to fend for herself and survive through carpet-making and small jobs at the French Cultural center. At this level, betrayal is personal and has to do with the construct of woman as an object to be discarded at the husband's leisure.

Destination Biafra, although set in the framework of the civil war in Nigeria, also makes a comment on gender through the political involvement of the heroine, Debbie. As opposed to the heroine of *Year of the Elephant*, Debbie stands for the "New Nigerian woman" who aspires to play a useful and constructive role in her country.

Debbie's story is depicted through a non-linear technique where important historical events are clarified in subsequent episodes in a centrifugal way. Against this background, and, on a private level, Debbie is portrayed as the modern, Oxford-educated *been-to*, whose major trait of personality is an extreme individuality and independence. This makes her stand against any attempt at confinement. She is at first seen as the pride of her parents thanks to her successful western education: "that was what most fathers wanted: a daughter who not only was a *been-to* but who could talk and behave like a European." Debbie, however, refuses the conventional roles cut out for her by her family. She reflects: "if her parents thought they could advertise her like a fattened cow they had another thing coming . . . she did not want to live a version of their life" (44). Subscribing to their type of marriage would mean "to submerge every impulse that made her a full human being" (45). It is in this frame of mind that she shatters their hopes by joining the army, "not as a cook or nurse, but as a true officer." Thus Debbie challenges the conventional roles for women to which most of her entourage subscribe.

This aspect in Debbie's political involvement opens on to the gender issue in the novel, and engages the reader in the gendered conflict against stereotypical representations of women under patriarchal ideology. By choosing to be an army officer, Debbie is cast in an exclusively male role, which makes the comment on male-dominated attitudes more salient. Thus, criticism is directed at the various attempts to push her back into a stereotypical sex role. As Zahra, on a personal level, she experiences a deep sense of betrayal after the emancipation gained through her education.

The criticism underlying the conventional views on women is made evident during Debbie's actual journey to the East of the country as a peace ambassador. Beside the fact that her patriotic motives are misunderstood, her new role is devalued and met with derision in the immediate circles of her fellow officers and "enlightened" politicians. This is the case with Onyemere who advises: "if she can be a useful tool I don't see why we should not use her and others like her" (69-70). The same attitude characterizes the Military Governor. During the visit to his place, she is to use her sexuality to seduce Abosi—a fellow officer—into giving up the idea of secession. For the Military Governor, her being a woman should not be a handicap for the mission she is assigned: "it might help: (she) can use (her) feminine charms to break (Abosi's) icy reserve" (123). Her meeting with Salihu, an officer from the North, shows more violently the rejection of the new role adopted by Debbie. She is "only a woman," and "a plaything exploited by the colonizer" (125). The last insult refers to the fact that Debbie has a white foreign boyfriend, and shows Salihu as the embodiment of extreme intolerance as regards inter-racial relations.

Debbie's mission to the Eastern region of the country to calm down the ambitious Abosi is shattered by violent guerilla incidents, the most significant of which—at the personal level—is the series of rapes she is subjected to, together with other women, including her own mother.

Her rape by marauding soldiers, then by her fellow officer, Salihu, are attempts to make her revert to point zero of her identity as she is perceived in the function of a pure sexual object. The rape, like the repudiation in *Year of the Elephant*, seems to function as a stigma to stop the heroine's journey towards self-identity and fulfillment. Debbie experiences a deep feeling of guilt because "with all her education, she could not lift a finger to help her own mother. . . . They humiliated her and left her to die slowly" (134). Alan Grey, her British boyfriend is, as the other male characters in her immediate circle, far from being the expected progressive young man. He is part of the gender antagonism, as he, too, subscribes to stereotypical roles for women.

As with Zahra in *Year of the Elephant*, Debbie experiences a sense of betrayal as all her attempts to reach a respectable social status through her education are of no avail. If Zahra has found some peace in economic activities and through her friendship with Roukia, Debbie gets determination through the supportive circle of her mother, Babs—her close friend—and Uzoma, a widowed woman in the guerilla struggle. It is worth noting that these characters function as Debbie's doubles. Florence Stratton has singled out the convention of paired or multiple female characters as a feature of African women's fiction, which serves as an "integral part" of the works, and which constitutes an important element of the message.[1] In the context of *Destination Biafra*, these characters reinforce the comments on gender.

In the case of the relationship between Debbie and her mother, the initial conflict caused by conservatism, on one side, and extreme emancipation, on the other, develops into a meaningful and constructive one. Debbie first perceives her mother as a limited woman because of her superficiality; a woman only thinking of her wardrobe (Emecheta 110), but gradually she discovers behind the veil of superficiality, submissiveness and dependence a strong woman who has led a fierce fight for survival, showing astounding courage in the face of the soldiers' insensitivity and bestiality. What she teaches Debbie is the value of life (135). The way in which she confronts her humiliation sheds light on the resilience of traditional women. Through Debbie's reflections, the reader is made to perceive the importance of the strength of these women who have accepted male domination passively only in order to survive. Thus, Debbie discovers that her mother is

> A woman who for years pretended to be so frail and
> dependent that tying her own head scarf was a big
> task—All that show of dependence just to keep alive her
> marriage and to feed her husband's ego, and to think she
> has played that charade for twenty-five years! (157)

Oppression towards women in a patriarchal society takes various forms, and is turned against the older generation as well as the modern one as is made evident in another advice given by the mother: after her humiliation, Debbie should get married for protection, "as an unmarried woman is never respected" (159). The supportive attitude of these women, especially the mother and Uzoma, Debbie's companion in her flight from the assault of soldiers of all sorts, shows a clear intention to uphold the role of the traditional woman in building a new society, a new nation with strong values. The same idea also pervades Abouzeid's novel with the heroine coming out as a dignified woman, able to fend for herself.

The first level in both narratives shows the authors' preoccupation with gender relationships in patriarchal societies. Also, universalization of the gender issue appears towards the end of Abouzeid's novel with the analogous experience of a foreign woman (69). Both writers use gender to criticize the limitations of particular social systems.

Both *Year of the Elephant* and *Destination Biafra* exploit the political involvement of their heroines to make a far-reaching comment which covers nationhood, national identity, colonial and neo-colonial issues as social realities that define people's fate in Africa. In so doing the authors address aspects that a certain type of criticism has denied African women's writing. Chandra Mohanty, in her analysis of negative effects of western feminist criticism on Third World literature by women, has listed "the denial of social and historical agency to women of other cultures, the obliteration of cultural and historical differences and monolithic representation of women" (198). It is in this respect that Stratton mentions "the suppression of anti-colonial discourse" (109). Other scholars have warned against "old stereotypes of the Middle-Eastern woman as a slave or odalisque" (Fernea, "Ways of Seeing" 64). The issue of the colonial discourse in African women's fiction is clarified by Molara Ogundipe-Leslie in her discussion of the female writer's commitment in African literature. The concerns of the woman writer are summarized thus:

> Being aware of oneself as a Third World person implies
> being politically conscious, offering readers perspectives
> on and perceptions of colonialism imperialism and neo-
> colonialism as they affect and shape our lives and
> historical destinies. (9)

Abouzeid's *Year of the Elephant* and Emecheta's *Destination Biafra* do provide these perspectives by grounding their heroines' experience and actions in the thick of political strife, and by besieging the public space of politics which has been declared men's preserve. Thus, these novels are moving away from limiting and limited domestic concerns and "gendered romances."

The link between the personal/private level and the collective/public level has been raised in Barbara Harlow:

> Autobiographies of liberation differ from western
> feminist texts in their insistence on an organic link
> between the problem of personal freedom as women and
> the collective freedom of society as a whole. (qtd. in Hall
> 73)

This "organic link" is an aspect which is relevant to the two narratives under study. In fact, the heroines' political involvement superimposes the personal/private and the national/public levels of meaning in a skillful way. At the center of the public level is a deep concern for the notion of nationhood and independence in an African country.

In *Year of the Elephant* the repudiation acts as a mirror device allowing Zahra to look at her present self while, through well-controlled flash-backs conjuring up the historical past and present of the Moroccan struggle for independence. The resistance struggle and the post-independence period make up the public level in the novel and enlarge the scope of these texts, an aspect which has been hailed by male readership and critics (Boutayeb 74-5).

Zahra's experience as a guerilla fighter starts when she moves to the urban center of Casablanca. At the outbreak of the struggle against colonial occupation, she is in charge of hiding partisans and passing them to the northern borders, smuggling arms, and firebombing collaborators' shops. Other women, Roukia and Safia, are also part of the resistance struggle. It is through this political activism that progress towards personal independence occurs. Although they only carry out orders issued by male nationalists, they are nevertheless full of conviction and sincerity in their patriotism. The gender roles in the Moroccan resistance against foreign occupation has been well-documented in Alison Baker's *Voices of Resistance*. Baker notes that women's roles were considered as "different and complementary to the roles men played, an extension of traditional female responsibilities. . . . Political leadership seemed to have been largely reserved for men . . . [and] only men actually used arms" (9). Despite this situation, for the women in the novel the period of resistance is the time for celebration and the coming to awareness which were part of the construction of national identity. Safia's statement describes this excitement: "all these events frighten me. Its seems as if we're living our entire lives in these days. Yet, despite that, I feel like my soul is blooming" (Abouzeid 49). In this way, *Year of the Elephant* presents an evolution towards a double independence, the personal one closely patterned on the political one which is brought about by the women's activism in part. This is the "small Jihad."

The mirror effect of the repudiation juxtaposes another historical period: the post-independence with its bitter aftermath. In this period, Zahra functions as an observer exploring, through her consciousness, the stage of disillusionment. This dimension is problematized in the conversations with the Sheikh, a symbol of spirituality, moral rectitude and cultural authenticity. The procedure used by the religious man is close to maieutics, exorcising Zahra's psychological ills while, at the same time, diagnosing social and political sores, and thus achieving criticism: "this is what independence has led to" (8). Zahra counters at one point. Indictment is here directed to the public betrayal, embodied in her husband's dismissal of her contributions to the national cause. "Everyone forgets. The nation itself forgets" (8). Zahra's bitterness is part of the pervading criticism. As a guerilla fighter who has managed to carve for herself a national identity, and has reached a state of freedom through resistance, she is unexpectedly let down for no other reason than that of being a traditional woman, and not subscribing to her husband's brand of modernity: "you don't like me eating with my fingers? It does not please you that I sit with the servants? We fought colonialism in their name and now you think like the colonizers!" (54). The private comment shades off into the public one where violent attack is directed at the new bourgeoisie and shallow elite for the sham values they have adopted after putting up such a fierce struggle to rid the country of the colonial powers. The failings in the new image of nationalists are castigated in these terms: "we are waiting for reform to come from the likes of these! You're more dangerous than the colonizers!" (55).

Nationalistic principles are flouted by most of Zahra's resistance companions. Faquih and Rahhal, intoxicated by the newly-gained independence, fall prey to political opportunism. Even Safia helps herself to donations intended for the fiddayyine's families. An exception is Hajj Ali, the blacksmith, who, as a model of integrity, returns, to his shop from which he has served the national cause and educated his children (67). Zahra's thought that "independence has played tricks with their heads" (63) is a clear indictment of the change brought about by the new political atmosphere. Thus *Year of the Elephant* questions the concept and meaning of national independence for the actors in the resistance struggle as well as for the generations after. As the heroine reflects, perhaps too much was expected of it:

> In the beginning of the resistance, we believed the struggle would wash away all spite and malice, just as we thought independence would relieve our cares and heal our sores. . . . In fact, we loaded independence down with a burden it could not bear. (67)

Thanks to the mirror effect created by the repudiation, Zahra's betrayal as a woman and a wife echoes the greater betrayal at the national level. In this context, the two periods of nationhood are significantly divided, not to say "divorced." This device has enlarged the scope of the novel in terms of themes. The political ideals and solidarity of the first period which could pave the way for the "great Jihad" are negated in the second period.

These are the "paradoxes" commented on by Boutayeb (74-5). The irony in Zahra's fate is that when forsaken and destitute, she finds work at the French Cultural center, and comes "face to face with the basic fact that we can't do without the French after all" (Abouzeid 67). The real "regression" that has taken place is in the achievement of nationhood.

Emecheta's *Destination Biafra* also problematizes the notion of nationhood, national independence and national identity through Debbie's political involvement. While in *Year of the Elephant* political resistance is directed against the foreign powers in the struggle for independence, in *Destination Biafra*, the political activism led by the heroine has a double aspect: it bears on the confrontation with the various warring factions in the Nigerian Civil War, but, at the same time, it is centrifugal as it unwinds a vast historical fresco, including the periods of colonialism, independence and the establishment of neo-colonialism and its expansion in the political map of the country. These stages are given through a multidimensional symbolism embodied by the heroine's experience. According to Stratton, *Destination Biafra* has two main ideological functions: "to bring to consciousness women's experience of the war and to challenge conventional constructions of nationalism and heroism" (127). These two functions are achieved through Debbie's political involvement.

The heroine appears on the scene at the end of the first part of the novel which serves as an introduction to the various actors and important events leading to the civil war. Debbie is set in the thick of political strife when she is sent on a peace mission to convince Abosi not to endanger the country's unity. From the beginning, the insistence on her neutrality sets her off as a symbol of national unity. "What was her position in all this mess? She was neither Ibo nor Yoruba, nor was she a Hausa, but a Nigerian" (Emecheta 126). Her commitment was to a unified army and her loyalty was to a unified country. During her struggle to achieve national unity, she encounters several obstacles which finally lead her to experience a deep sense of betrayal.

As the daughter of a corrupt bourgeois family whose values she subverts in the end of the narrative, she realizes, not without biting irony, what the general meaning of Nigerian independence is: "people drank champagne like water—Nigeria was an independent nation at last" (39). The sarcasm present in this statement sets the framework for a more violent indictment directed at the foreign hegemony, "the external involvement in the war" (Stratton 121).

Debbie's friendship with Alan Grey, the ex-Governor's son, enables her to bare the imperialistic intents of the foreign intrusion in the country's political affairs. Indeed, Alan, in his role as a military expert, engages in several "immoral" double-dealings, first with the warring tribes and then with the two rival officers in the Biafran war. Thus, with the new Governor McDonald, they influence the campaign to name the first Nigerian Prime Minister, which creates political disturbances with serious consequences for the country's unity. Alan's motives in such an interference is to secure and protect British economic interests by ensuring their share of the oil riches of the East. Alan's dubious role is also revealed in amplifying the conflict between the two enemy officers—Momoh and Abosi—through selling arms to each camp secretly and providing them with mercenaries.

Debbie's insight into political matters, echoed by Barbara's (Babs), reveals Alan's hegemonic game: "I've always wondered how a tiny place like Britain came to rule so many people. Now I can guess: divide and rule. Is that why you are here? What part are you playing, Alan?" (Emecheta 113). Other characters reinforce the comment on the hegemonic practices in the situation of political instability. Debbie's double, Babs, satirizes the foreign interference which has created a situation of "sham independence" whereby "foreign vultures" hover over the country's resources and in which the ex-colonies have no say as to the choices imposed (117). The phrase "foreign vultures" ironically sends the reader back to the first part of the novel where foreign alliances are made, which likens the whole episode to "the scramble for Africa". Condemnation of this form of neo-colonialism comes at first from the initially progressive officer, Abosi, when he hopes to create an ideal nation: "I would rather say our destination is 'Biafra', since as far as I am concerned we're not yet independent. We sent away one set of masters, without realizing that they had left their stooges behind" (60). At this level, indictment is clearly directed to the fact of keeping the country in a state of dependency.

In *Destination Biafra*, Debbie's political involvement is used to comment on external as well as internal failings in the attainment of nationhood. Thus, alongside the perpetuation of a state of economic dependence, the cultural aspect of neo-colonialism—the Fanonian type—is also the target of social criticism (Fanon 311). This is uncovered through the insightful Babs: "Momoh will listen to anyone whose skin is white and who can flatter him enough" (Emecheta 118). The same concern is reiterated by the bank clerk, Ugoji: "when the Europeans ruled us, few people died; now we rule ourselves, we butcher each other like meat–sellers slaughtering cows" (89).

Several limitations of army politicians and traditional politicians are also part of the public comment made by this historical allegory. Men in the political arena are characterized by greed for power, selfishness, and nepotism. Momoh and Abosi are objects of such an indictment. The novel is also punctuated with male leadership's lack of conviction and blindness to the real needs of their country. The horrifying scenes of aggression and killing reveal the soldiers' insensitivity in a war situation. Destruction and self-destruction is the reality in men's war. Absence of integrity is evident in several comments such as those included in the chapter dealing with "the sons of the rich" who are conveniently sent abroad when their country needs them, while the parents defect to the "safest" side. This is an aspect which Uzoma castigates in her comment: "since he is alive and still has money, he can deny anything. Politicians are good at denying what they said yesterday. . . . It is too late for those whose lives have been lost" (235). It is in this framework that the action of Debbie and her female companions takes on its full meaning. Although women's involvement in war is perceived as a retribution for having ventured in an exclusively male space, the part they play in this war is depicted in a positive way, and stands against the betrayal of national ideals in men's war. The major characteristics of women's political involvement are self-sacrifice, altruism, solidarity and determination. Both Momoh's and Abosi's missions to save the country gutter into political failure. Ironically, the role of leadership is taken up by a woman, Debbie, who becomes a pathfinder and symbolizes national unity. As in *Year of the Elephant*, there is a double journey at this stage. Debbie's mission to the eastern region as a peace ambassador also symbolizes the journey towards the achievement of nationhood. In this perspective, the mission is first seen as an attempt to right the situation created by deficient male leadership. Indeed, in the middle of atrocities, the women form a militia under the leadership of Debbie and Uzoma to protect themselves and the orphaned children (230). The idea of redress is ironically present in Debbie's statement: "You men make all this mess and then call on us women to clear it up" (175).

In the course of this mission, Debbie and her companions are aggressed in the most bestial manner. Beyond the immediate implications for the indictment of male domination and the reduction of female role in war, the wider implication, through the symbolic level, is related to the construct of nationhood. The image of the motherland is here necessary to construe these aggressions on women as an act of defiling the nation by its own sons. Old women like Debbie's mother and the octogenarian nun have also been raped. Through the rape symbolism, "motherland," the favored trope in male canon texts is now ironically desecrated by its very sons, which makes the comment on male political involvement more condemnatory.

The level of symbolism also helps, it seems, to interpret the incidents related to birth. If Abosi's wife's miscarriage can be seen as foreshadowing the failure of hope for the unification of the country, which is made obvious by the officer's "intentions to break away if Aburi talks fail" (88-9), "the baby who is killed in its mother's womb" can point to the negation of the birth of a new nation. The same implication can be given to the death of the orphan child, "Biafra," Debbie carries on her back.

It is also through the level of symbolism that Momoh's monster-child can be part of this general meaning (203). The monster-child stands for unnaturalness in the process of achieving nationhood; unnaturalness refers in the text to the mass slaughtering of civilians by Momoh. Gratuitous bloodshed is, indeed, a curse to be stamped out in situations of conflict on the continent. However, with Momoh's redemption as the leader of the unified army, death paradoxically shades off into hope for a new life.

Debbie's last mission to convince Abosi to surrender is a self-imposed crusade where she double crosses both Alan's and the politicians' intention to provide more weapons to the warring camps. When she finally manages to meet Abosi, his greed for power has changed him beyond recognition. Her mission is dismissed simply on the grounds of her sexuality. As Debbie's shock at discovering corruption even in the ideal Biafra sinks in, she meditates on the "uselessness of the whole charade." At this point of the narrative, Debbie's political involvement uncovers the betrayal that hampers the journey towards nationhood, an aspect which the Sheikh in Zahra's narrative refers to as the problem of "fragile principles."

During the eastward journey, Debbie and the other women are represented as sacrificial figures at the service of a united nation through their determination for survival and life ("life" is the very last word of the novel). In fact, the women militia with the help of the old generation of women put up a ferocious fight through their fearlessness and solidarity. It is thus made clear that the subversive role of Debbie as a national hero, wrenching action from Abosi in a way reveals the shortcomings of male leadership. Self-sacrifice and solidarity with civilians in distress is what it lacks.

Symbolism shows yet another level of meaning through the representative role of Debbie. Her first appearance with Alan, of pure colonial stock, can be construed as the colonial encounter between the colonial power and Africa. Their adventure spells the various facets of foreign interference and the devices used to achieve imperialistic aims. This adventure ends with a separation in terms of geographical location. The losses, however, are great in the cultural, human, and political domains. Debbie's role is nevertheless still apparent as she has the last word in "repudiating" the exploitative Alan Grey (Stratton 109).

By bringing together the private and the public levels in the narratives, *Year of the Elephant* and *Destination Biafra* make insightful comments that bear on several vital issues for emerging nations. Both works achieve this aim by subverting gender-roles through Zahra's and Debbie's political involvement. Although the final impression is that of disillusionment, both heroines manage to voice women's involvement in the struggle for national freedom and nationhood, a reality established scholarly criticism in African Literature has "usefully" relegated to silence. This reality has also been "suppressed in the dominant versions of the war(s)" (Stratton 121). Debbie's war memoirs have just that purpose, and answer the query which is on her mind: "when the history of the civil war was written, would the part played by her and women like Babs, Uzoma and the nuns in Biafra be mentioned at all?" (Emecheta 195).

The attraction of a narrative technique which intertwines both the private and the public levels resides in the fact that it yields a double significance to women's political involvement. Thus, both texts speak of the struggle for nationhood as a dignified and secure "motherland" with due recognition given to the parts by men and women alike. They also speak of the struggle for womanhood through the recognition of a dignified status for women, away from restrictive traditional representations. It is this double awareness that both Zahra and Debbie achieve. Both heroines emerge as strong women and individuals whose resilience has brought into relief the greater dimension of their countries' destinies in critical historical moments. It is through this force that the two women convey the wider meaning of their political involvement at both the private and the public levels. While *Destination Biafra* achieves its aim through a young woman's extreme independence, *Year of the Elephant* exploits faith in religion and fair principles for a return to a just society for women who have experienced the same predicament as Zahra.

Both *Year of the Elephant* and *Destination Biafra* exploit the theme of war resistance and its implication for national identity and leadership, the idea of nationhood and the reality of neo-colonialism. Abouzeid and Emecheta, through a well-controlled narrative technique use two insightful heroines, Zahra and Debbie, to make constructive comments on these issues. As rightly noted by Fernea in her introduction to Abouzeid's work, credit is given to the part played by "ordinary people" in the struggle for Moroccan independence (xvii). In the same way, the heroine of *Destination Biafra* voices the part of "ordinary" women in the Biafran war. As a last comment, it seems that in these two novels the comment on the implications of foreign interference in the affairs of emerging nations in Africa is more forceful than the comment on gender inequality in restrictive societies. The scope of criticism has been tremendously enlarged by the two heroines' political involvement.

Note

1. See the second section, titled "Room for Women," where the author discusses the works of four women writers—Grace Ogot, Flora Nwapa,

Buchi Emecheta and Mariama Bâ—and brings out two features of African women's literature: namely intertextuality and the use of paired and multiple women characters.

Works Cited

Abouzeid, Leïla. *Year of the Elephant: A Woman's Journey Towards Independence.* Trans. Barbara Parmenter. Intro. Elizabeth Fernea. Austin: University of Texas Press, 1989.

Baker, Alison. *Voices of Resistance: Oral Histories of Moroccan Women.* Albany: State University of New York Press, 1998.

Boutayeb, Abdelali. "*Year of the Elephant*: A Novel of Moroccan Paradoxes." *Women and Writing, Conference Proceedings.* Ed. Driss Ouaouicha. Meknes, Morocco: Publications of the Faculty of Letters, 1996. N.p.

Fernea, Elizabeth. Introduction. *Year of the Elephant: A Woman's Journey Towards Independence.* By Leïla Abouzeid. Austin: University of Texas Press, 1989. xi-xxvi.

____. "Ways of Seeing Middle Eastern Women." *Women: A Cultural Review,* 6.1 (1995): 60-6.

Hall, Michael. "Leïla Abouzeid's *Year of the Elephant*: A Post-Colonial Reading." *Women: A Cultural Review* 6.1 (1995): 67-84.

Mohanty, Chandra. "Under Western Eyes: Feminist Scholarship and Colonial Discourse." *Colonial Discourse and Post-Colonial Theory: A Reader.* Eds. Patrick Williams and Laura Chrisman. New York: Columbia University Press, 1994. 196-220.

Ogundipe-Leslie, Molara. "The Female Writer and Her Commitment." *African Literature Today* 15 (1987): 5-13.

Stratton, Florence. *Contemporary African Literature and the Politics of Gender.* London: Routledge, 1994.

Gender, Identity, and the Liminal Self: The Emerging Woman in Buchi Emecheta's *The Bride Price* and Maya Angelou's *I Know Why the Caged Bird Sings*

Maxine Sample

> If growing up is painful for the Southern Black girl,
> being aware of her displacement is the rust on the razor
> that threatens the throat. It is an unnecessary insult.
>
> –Maya Angelou, *I Know Why the Caged Bird Sings*

The term "liminal" was popularized in the 1960s when noted anthropologist Victor Turner proposed that all societies contain rituals that involve the transition from one state to another.[1] Writing in "Betwixt and Between: The Liminal Period in Rites of Passage," Turner asserted that "if our basic model of society is that of a 'structure of positions,' we must regard the period of margin or 'liminality' as an interstructural situation" (4). This liminal phase denotes the middle phase of three such phases Belgian folklorist Arnold van Gennep uses to characterize *rites de passage* marking the transition from one social status to another in ritual time and space: separation, margin (limen), and re-aggregation. The first phase begins with the person's separation and detachment from his or her earlier state or condition. In the final phase the person is reintegrated into society or community with a new identity and the responsibility of conforming to established norms and standards of behavior. These three phases of *rites of passage* were important to

Turner because he regarded them as a process of becoming, of transformation (Turner, "Betwixt" 4).

Liminality thus embodies the experience of being on the margin or on the threshold, "betwixt and between" major statuses like childhood and adulthood or lower and higher social positions. Because Turner hypothesized that liminality designates not just transitional states but sometimes-permanent differentiated social categories, this concept is often appropriated to describe the marginal experience of individuals assigned to the peripheries of the larger social groups to which they belong.

Writing in "Symbolic Geography and Psychic Landscapes: A Conversation with Maya Angelou," Joanne Braxton notes that "women, particularly black women, speak as 'others'. . . from a position of marginality" (44). Of particular interest is the manner in which black women writers of Africa and the Diaspora have addressed women's marginalization in their own cultures and communities. For example, in "Double Liminality and the Black Woman Writer," an essay appearing in *American Behavioral Scientist*, the authors contend that in their fiction, women writers "employ devices associated with liminality" because doing so enables them to conceive of ways to move beyond the fixed position generally assigned to them, and instead of merely highlighting women's limitations, these writers.

> call up the positive and liberating possibilities that accompany the liminal position "releas[ing] the elements of culture and society from their customary configurations, allowing a reconception of structural stereotypes. Because liminality affords the opportunity for reordering reality, it provides a critique of women's structural roles and holds open the possibility for change in these roles." (Mascia-Lees, et al. 106)

The result is a bonding and sharing among women in positive ways that enhance their ability to be something other than what others have determined they must become. In other words, "liminality creates an image of women not fixed in otherness, not fixed in the images created for them rather than by them, but changing, potential, awesome, and surprising, capable of making choices and creating new meanings" (Mascia-Lees, et al.106 110-11).

This paper looks at two different kinds of literary texts by black women writers, one a novel of development and the other an autobiography, to examine how their authors employ devices associated with liminality to articulate issues of female empowerment and self-actualization. Particular attention is given to patterns of trauma and enclosure that shape the female adolescent's quest for selfhood and initiation into womanhood. Nigerian writer Buchi Emecheta has written a number of novels that deal with the gender implications of the strong communal environments in which she places her heroines. *The Bride Price*, one of Emecheta's novels of development, and Maya Angelou's *I Know Why the Caged Bird Sings* utilize tropes of confinement to show the hostile, threatening environment in which the heroine comes of age as a woman. This coming of age experience of both female heroines can be viewed in the context of Victor Turner's concept of liminality used to explain the sociocultural processes involved in rites of passage or "threshold" experiences. In Emecheta's novel, the family is depicted as an enclave of enclosure that serves to stifle the growth and development of females in ways that their male counterparts are not. In Angelou's autobiography, gender, race, and class come together to shape a cage of marginalized existence designated for the maturing adolescent. The extent to which the young heroines accept their "minor" status or subvert efforts to assign them to the periphery of their cultures as they cross the threshold into womanhood is the focus of this paper.

The *Bildungsroman*, or novel of development, charts the individual's growth from childhood innocence to adult maturation, covering stages of rebellion, separation, self-education, alienation, and the quest for a vocation and a "working philosophy" of life (Buckley 17-18). This quest is often characterized by the protagonist's spatial movement in the novel from country to city. Acknowledging that the *Bildungsroman* was initially defined in terms of males' experiences (young women tend not to strike out from home on quests for self-hood), recent critics in their search for significant similarities between novels of male development and novels of female development have discovered interesting differences between the two.[2] One significant difference is the movement of the protagonists: the male journeys away from home while the female remains close to home, her development taking place "in or on the periphery of marriage" (Hoffman 335). Additionally, one certainly cannot ignore the gender dimension of adulthood or maturation since in most societies the socialization process by which boys and girls become women and men is not the same. Annis Pratt addresses this issue when she notes, "In the *bildungsroman* proper, with its expectation that the hero is learning to be an adult, there is the hidden agenda of gender norms, where 'adult' means [for the female] learning to be dependent, submissive, or 'nonadult'" (16). It is not surprising, then, to find that novels focusing on female adolescence appear to groom the heroine for marriage and submission, offering what Pratt designates as "models for 'growing down' rather than for 'growing up'"(14).

Adolescence is characteristically a conflict-ridden period involving the adolescent's proverbial search for identity. In fiction, this initiation into the adult community can be readily found among the Western literary canon. However, as Patricia Meyer Spacks notes in *The Female Imagination*, while numerous novels offer a portrait of this early phase in women's lives, few such novels actually celebrate female adolescence; instead, many tend toward dramatizations of what the adolescent's life will become and sympathetic portraits of rebellion and heroic suffering (158). In women's novels of development, the theme of adolescence is particularly significant because of the disappointment that young women tend to encounter. Their efforts at independence often clash with the expectations and dictates of the societies around them. For the female youth, along with the growth and maturation which accompanies her transition from adolescence to adulthood come lessons about gender barriers. Living in societies that tend to define one's existence in terms of gender designated spheres, the heroine learns that socially sanctioned alternatives are elusive.

Women's novels of development reveal the woman writer's commentary on socially designated women's spheres in cultures where the literary artists themselves have had to confront socially imposed gender boundaries. Cross-culturally, woman writers have been engaged in the process of not only negotiating such boundaries themselves but also communicating such struggles in their works. Sandra Gilbert and Susan Gubar assert in *The Madwoman in the Attic* that like other women, the woman writer "experiences her gender as a painful obstacle, or even a debilitating inadequacy" (50). Thus, as a creative artist, she "searches for a female model not because she wants dutifully to comply with male definitions of her 'femininity' but because she must legitimize her own rebellious endeavors" (Gilbert and Gubar 50). These efforts manifest themselves in identifiable narrative structures (see Pratt) and themes in literature "strongly marked not only by an obsessive interest in [women's] limited options but also by obsessive imagery of confinement that reveals the ways in which female artists feel trapped and sickened both by suffocating alternatives and by the culture that created them" (Gilbert and Gubar 64).

    Through her examination of structural continuities in women's novels, Annis Pratt delineates certain narrative patterns used by women writers of novels of development. Pratt notes that regardless of the time in which the work is written or of the cultural background of the writer, the work seems to reveal that "at each phase [of development] the orderly pattern of development is disrupted by social norms dictating powerlessness for women" (168). The motif of enclosure particularly appears in the novel of social protest and the novel of marriage. Emecheta's two novels of adolescence, *The Bride Price* and *The Slave Girl* display similarities to the narrative patterns Pratt identifies in the woman's novel of social protest. Both novels reflect images of enclosure and escape as the author chronicles the heroines' passage from childhood to adulthood, signaled by their eligibility for and subsequent consent to marriage. Images of enclosure dominate the social space that the protagonists will occupy as adults. In this type of novel, according to Pratt, such authors "treat the family and marriage as enclaves within a wider enclosure, as individual prisons bounded by the walls of a larger community" (59). While Emecheta's heroines may display varying degrees of rebellion, the women are not really outsiders because they are so deeply entrenched in the social forces that enclose them. Although the author may be critical of such social institutions as marriage, the protagonists may not completely or consciously reject these institutions. This pattern of conflict resolution in Emecheta's work is consistent with Pratt's conclusion that in novels of social protest and of marriage, despite the criticism directed against that society and the heroine's rebellion, society triumphs in the end (168).

Unlike some writers who in their criticism of social barriers to women's self-actualization offer alternative space, Emecheta does not create what Pratt refers to as "apatriarchal space." Her women, particularly those in *The Slave Girl* and *The Bride Price* do not escape the enclosures but instead move from one enclosure to another; we see what Pratt calls "archetypal enclosure in marriage," a situation in which women are enclosed within the marital circle and deprived of personal space. This pattern of trauma and enclosure characterizes the novel of marriage and appears in *The Bride Price* and *The Slave Girl*. Anthropologist Jeanne K. Henn notes in "women in the Rural Economy: Past, Present and Future" that while "marriage was the beginning of a man's social and economic emancipation . . . for women marriage marked the transfer of dependence from father to husband" (5). Emecheta's portrait of marriage as a social prison in which women are muted and become the wards of their husbands pervades much of her work. Her focus on enclosure and entrapment is again reminiscent of her own experience of gender as conveyed in her autobiographical novels and seems to bear out Gilbert and Gubar's hypothesis that women writers for whom such experiences are painful obstacles tend to reflect images and themes focusing on women's limited options in the culture from which these women emerged.

Emecheta's representation of the socially designated gender sphere as a socially enclosed prison that limits women's choices and movement appears in *The Bride Price*, another novel of adolescence, where the clash between the West and traditional Africa heightens the sense of frustration that the protagonist experiences as she attempts to maneuver the restricted space assigned to women. This novel offers a portrait of a society in which socially imposed gender boundaries as well as tradition serve to frustrate young Aku-nna's efforts to shape her own future. The adolescent rebellion against the constraints of tradition succumbs inevitably to failure but serves nevertheless as a means by which Emecheta can dramatize the marginalization associated with women's social space.

The Bride Price covers a rather short period of time in the life of the protagonist; Aku-nna is thirteen (child) when the novel begins and sixteen, married and pregnant (woman) as the novel ends with her death. We again see the spatial movement of the protagonist away from the community of her birth to a community where she undergoes a period of initiation to the kind of life she will experience as an adult; finally there is the movement back to the original community once the adolescent has crossed the threshold into adulthood. In a kind of experiential rites of passage the heroine moves through the phases of separation, margin (limen) and re-aggregation. Aku-nna's period of adolescence occurs, for the most part, on the periphery, a quasi-outcast in terms of her position in her new extended family. When her father dies, life in Lagos is traded for life in rural Ibuza when Aku-nna, her brothers, and her mother customarily become a part of the family of the father's senior brother. This loss of a parent is a traumatic event that precipitates Aku-nna's separation or detachment from life in the city. Stripped from her previous life, Aku-nna perceives herself an orphan, as represented by the status which children occupy as a result of the father's death. According to the rationale embraced by the community, "When you have lost your father, you have lost your parents. Your mother is only a woman. . . . A fatherless family is . . . a family without parents, in fact, a non-existing family"(28). The sense of outsideness which Aku-nna experiences once back in the village is further aggravated by being stripped of those comforts of life in Lagos and forced to adhere to village traditions. Though, Aku-nna's western education plays a significant role in creating an enthusiastic and hopeful attitude about her plans for the future, plans which will move her beyond the traditional position of farmer/trader, it also exacerbates the contrast between her hopes and dreams and the stark realities of village life. Images of enclosure appear as Aku-nna's situation becomes more drastic. Emecheta writes, "She and her brother were like helpless fish caught in a net; they could not as it were go back into the sea, for they were trapped fast, and yet they were still alive because the fisherman was busy debating within himself whether it was worth killing them to take home, seeing as they were such small fry" (82). For Aku-nna, time spent in the village is a period of initiation into the traditional ways of her people, one type of education juxtaposed against her western education. Part of this new education is recognizing the boundaries established for her gender. Confronted with such enclosure, Aku-nna expresses a preference for death instead, and until her tragic demise at the end of the novel, she experiences a symbolic death through ostracism. The message is clear: cross the boundaries and cease to exist.

Aku-nna is kidnaped by a suitor and forced into a marriage against her will. We see the ultimate state of imprisonment and powerlessness symbolized by this abduction sanctioned by tradition and unchallenged by Aku-nna's family. Acting on her own resolve to be free, Aku-nna escapes the clutches of her kidnapper by inviting the public humiliation of declaring herself already "disvirgined." Before the marriage can be consummated and her claims challenged, she slips away to her chosen love, Chike, and they flee to Lagos and marry. Total ostracism results when her uncle refuses to accept payment of the bride price from Chike's family, for Aku-nna has broken a most sacred taboo against marrying a descendent of a slave. The uncle curses Aku-nna, who in accordance with traditional superstition, dies during childbirth, the bride price having never been paid. The reader is left with the idea that the story of Aku-nna's life and death will serve as a cautionary tale for the young women who come after her.

Structurally, the novel reveals the kind of unfavorable ending which Pratt associates with women's novels of development: the conflict between the adolescent heroine's goals and societal dictates and expectations. Characteristically, the adolescent heroine learns adult lessons about gender barriers, for "attempts to develop independence are met with limitations and immurement, training in domestic tasks, restrictions of the intellect" (Pratt 29). Aku-nna's initiation from youthful innocence to adult awareness ends with her having learned very painful lessons about gender barriers and the power of tradition.

Thus, the enclosure/escape dichotomy which we see in Emecheta's novels of adolescence is reinforced by the structuring of the works around identifiable and representative stages of female development. Emecheta's novels reveal spatial movement from protective, nurturing social environment as a child, to a somewhat hostile, threatening environment in which the protagonist comes of age as a woman; and the escape to a secure environment under the protective wing of a loving man. The escape does not really offer freedom from enclosure, but the protagonists are too young to be any more self-conscious of the extent to which traditions erect boundaries around the self. As Patricia Spacks remarks about novels containing adolescent heroines, "Marriage, obviously, is the 'normal' conclusion, the orthodox way for a girl to declare herself as an adult" (114). Unfortunately, the protagonist is not a self-probing and self-conscious older woman who is secure in her rebellion against social mores or in her challenge of tradition, who long muted and powerless, has finally found her voice. The absence of this kind of heroine in *The Bride Price* is not a result of Emecheta's inability to take a "feminist stand" but rather the author's realization that a yet dependent teenager—although married—is powerless to challenge generations-old traditions, particularly when her apprenticeship during adolescence has not prepared her for alternatives.

Like *The Bride Price*, Maya Angelou's *I Know Why the Caged Bird Sings* recounts the journey of the young child from her early years across the threshold of womanhood, ending with a teenaged Maya giving birth to a child. In this first of several autobiographies that chronicle stages of her life, Angelou uses the trope of the cage in narrating the life of a black female growing up in America, a member of a community caged by segregation, racial violence, and economic oppression. The marginalization is probably most clearly reflected in the lines of demarcation between the black and white communities of Stamps, Arkansas, in a racial etiquette that reinforces the subordinate place that young Maya and other blacks are to occupy, and in the repeated indignities that blacks are expected to suffer. This narrative is also a story of the politics of race and gender as well as a story of the strength of a family that empowers, and of communities of women that offer hope. The narrator must learn which, if any, of the behaviors associated with the liminal group are appropriate and effective responses to the racial hostilities and indignities that blacks in her community encounter on a regular basis: passive and humble demeanor, acceptance of arbitrary punishment without complaint, or resistance. Angelou writes early in the text, "Momma intended to teach Bailey and me to use the paths of life that she and her generation and all the Negroes gone before had found, and found to be safe ones" (47). Such lessons included learning that blacks did not have the liberty to speak freely, for to talk to whites at all was to risk one's life. A young Angelou struggles to comprehend her status as "other" in the segregated world of the American South and to adopt strategies to avoid being fixed in otherness. The work speaks collectively of the experience of a Southern black girl often overwhelmed and mystified by the specter of whiteness that exerts a tremendous force over the direction of her life and the lives of other black Americans. She recounts, "They [whites] were different, to be dreaded, and in that dread was included the hostility of the powerless against the powerful, the poor against the rich, the worker against the worked for and the ragged against the well dressed" (25).

Caged Bird shares elements of the traditional bildungsroman with its often biographical depiction of a protagonist's quest for self-definition amidst values in conflict. This autobiography depicts a protagonist "relegated to second-class citizenship during her early years" in an autobiographical text that, as Pierre Walker writes in *College Literature*, shapes Angelou's life "much as a bildungsroman would, as a progressive process of affirming identity, learning about words, and resisting racism" (2). Structured around narrated lessons in navigating the boundaries of her race and gender, the autobiography, reads much like the western novel of development. The separation and return motifs figure prominently in the harsh realities that shape the education of the youthful Maya and facilitate her initiation into adulthood. However, as Susan Gilbert notes, "while readers expect to see a lonely, self-conscious youth struggling to escape the oppressive weight of his family, the kind of detachment and rejection that we associate with the bildungsroman or apprenticeship novel usually does not occur in black autobiography, which instead depicts 'total or unconscious absorption in the group'" (106). Certainly, the collective voice is reflected in Angelou's statement that "if growing up is painful for the Southern Black girl, being aware of her displacement is the rust on the razor that threatens the throat. It is an unnecessary insult" (4). Thus Angelou speaks not only as an individual but also as a member of a group.

How does one respond to racism, affirm oneself, and deal with hopeless situations without succumbing to despair? Young Maya learns these lessons from a community of women: a teacher, a mother, and a grandmother who nurture and groom the narrator, guiding the female child through the trauma of segregation, lynching, rape, and childbirth. As in Emecheta's text, patterns of trauma and enclosure shape the narrator's quest for selfhood and initiation into womanhood. Maya's early education takes place in the "school" of her grandmother's store from which she observes the harshness of black southern life. Dignity, subtle resistance, and faith chart a path to transcendence. From Mrs. Flowers, Maya learns the magic ability of books to transport one beyond the ugly realism of her circumstances, and from her mother, Maya learns a fierce joy of life, self-acceptance, and a toughness that will serve the adult Maya well.

Maya's month-long stay at a junkyard while she was a runaway living in a Golding-esque community of other runaway or abandoned youth might be viewed as a characteristically liminal separation period during which reflection and self-assessment occur. Her experience in this multicultural community makes possible Angelou's maturation. She writes, "After a month my thinking processes had so changed that I was hardly recognizable to myself. . . . I was never again to sense myself so solidly outside the pale of the human race. The lack of criticism evidenced by our ad hoc community influenced me, and set a tone of tolerance for my life" (254). As she heads to a new life with her mother she is armed with a positive sense of self and is eager to embrace life's challenges, no longer caged by a negative sense of self imposed by the double marginalization of race and gender.

From the margins of their individual cultures, Buchi Emecheta and Maya Angelou challenge the socially constructed barriers to black women's self-actualization. Angelou's life story subverts the model of female girls "growing down" rather than growing up, offering alternatives to the fixed position that others have determined she—black, female, and poor—must occupy. Emecheta's novel of development questions the legitimacy of social traditions that erect boundaries around the self, revealing the travesty of human potential thwarted by imposed gender norms.

Notes

1. For a more involved discussion of liminality see Victor Turner, "Variations on a Theme of Liminality" in Sally F. Moore and Barbara G. Myerhoff, eds., *Secular Ritual* (Amsterdam: Van Gorcum, 1977), 36-52.
2. A few significant studies worth mentioning are Elizabeth Abel, Marianne Hirsch, and Elizabeth Langland, eds., *The Voyage in: Fictions of Female Development* (Hanover, NH: UP of New England, 1983); Annis Pratt, *Archetypal Patterns in Women's Fiction* (Bloomington: Indiana UP,

1981); Elaine Hoffman, "The Feminine Bildungsroman: Education through Marriage," *The Massachusetts Review* 22 (Summer 1981): 335-57; Charlotte Goodman, "The Lost Brother, the Twin: Women Novelists and the Male-Female Double Bildungsroman," *Novel* 17.1 (Fall 1983): 28-43.

Works Cited

Angelou, Maya. *I Know Why the Caged Bird Sings*. 1970. New York: Bantam, 1993.

Buckley, Jerome Hamilton. *Seasons of Youth: The Bildungsroman from Dickens to Golding*. Cambridge, MA: Harvard UP, 1974.

Braxton, Joanne M. *Black Women Writing Autobiography: A Tradition within a Tradition*. Philadelphia: Temple UP, 1989.

____. "Symbolic Geography and Psychic Landscapes: A Conversation with Maya Angelou." *Maya Angelou's* I Know Why the Caged Bird Sings: *A Casebook*. Ed. Joanne M. Braxton. New York: Oxford UP, 1999. 3-20.

Emecheta, Buchi. *The Bride Price*. New York: George Braziller, 1976.

Fox-Genovese, Elizabeth. "To Write My Self: The Autobiographies of Afro-American Women." *Feminist Issues in Literary Scholarship*. Ed. Shari Benstock. Bloomington: Indiana UP, 1987. 161-180.

Gilbert, Sandra, and Susan Gubar. *The Madwoman in the Attic*. New Haven: Yale UP, 1979.

Gilbert, Susan. "Paths to Escape." *Black Women Writing Autobiography: A Tradition Within a Tradition*. Ed. Joanne M. Braxton. Philadelphia: Temple UP, 1989. 99-110.

Henn, Jeanne K. "Women in the Rural Economy: Past, Present and Future." *African Women South of the Sahara*. Ed. Margaret Jean Hay and Sharon Stichter. London: Longman, 1984. 1-18.

Hoffman, Elaine. "The Feminine *Bildungsroman*: Education through Marriage." *The Massachusetts Review* 22 (Summer 1981): 335-57.

Turner, Victor. "Betwixt and Between: The Liminal Period in Rites of Passage." *Betwixt and Between: Patterns of Masculine and Feminine Initiation*. Ed. Louise Carus Mahdi, Steven Foster and Meredith Little. LaSalle, IL: Open Court, 1987. 3-19.

____. *Dramas, Fields, and Metaphors: Symbolic Action in Human Society.* Ithaca: Cornell UP, 1974.

____. *The Ritual Process: Structure and Anti-Structure.* Chicago: Aldine, 1969.

____. "Variations on a Theme of Liminality." *Secular Ritual.* Ed. Sally F. Moore and Barbara G. Myerhoff. Assen, The Netherlands: Van Gorcum, 1977. 36-52.

Mascia-Lees, Frances E., Patricia Sharpe, and Colleen B. Cohen. "Double Liminality and the Black Women Writer." *American Behavioral Scientist* 31.1 (September/October 1987): 101-14.

Pratt, Annis. *Archetypal Patterns in Women's Fiction.* Bloomington: Indiana UP, 1981.

Spacks, Patricia Meyer. *The Female Imagination.* New York: Alfred A. Knopf, 1975.

Walker, Pierre A. "Racial Protest, Identity, Words, and Form in Maya Angelou's *I Know Why the Caged Bird Sings.*" *College Literature* 22.3 (October 1995): 91-108.

In Search of a New Self

Sharifa Saa-Atma Ma'at

When looking at contemporary writers of African descent, one discovers how the African, Caribbean, and African American experiences in the western world are excruciatingly similar. Many contemporary African continental writers and contemporary diasporic writers use their craft to explore marginalization and dehumanization. To capture the scope of the complex issues involved, writers use diverse, intriguing strategies. What is noteworthy, however, is that quite often within the very texts that reveal the ordeals with the western world, the methods by which marginalization and dehumanization may be overcome are included. Alasan Mansaray's new novel, *The Haunting Heritage: An African Saga in America*, and Loretta Ngcobo's *Let It Be Told* are examples of texts which include many of the issues and responses to them. Whether expressing themselves through character voice, autobiographical sketches, or poetry, Mansaray and Ngcobo offer insight from intimate perspectives.

Mansaray's *The Haunting Heritage*, with its use of allegory and parables, reminds one of Achebe's *Things Fall Apart*, but the former brings its protagonist into the contemporary arena in his encounters with western society. *A Haunting Heritage* could easily be the saga of any contemporary African's experience in America, the so-called "land of milk and honey." The novel, like *Things Fall Apart*, is filled with the myths, legends, beliefs and parables of the fictitious country Manika Kunda, which is really Sierra Leone, West Africa, and the birthplace of the author. The protagonist, Yaya LaTale, who has been trained in traditional ways and in the neocolonial government system (for more than fifteen years), is Mandinka. Gradually the reader learns that Yaya

LaTale, must journey through two levels of understanding—the spiritual and the real—to bridge the abyss between the New and Old World systems. His struggle is allegoric in its commonness; it is painfully and insightfully typical of the new African immigrant's experiences in America.

Mansaray uses a stream of consciousness technique as he attempts to make the reader understand the connection between alienation and dehumanization that will force Yaya, every-African-man, to find his voice in the American experience. Each time Yaya must make a life-changing decision at home or in America, the reader is required to understand the tremendous strain among the spiritual forces at work within his cultural and traditional beliefs, his desperate need to leave home, and Yaya's desire to maintain his cultural ties even as he attempts to remove himself geographically from his peoples' myths and beliefs. The struggle to come to terms with the voice of home and the siren call of America, continues throughout the novel in deliberate passages that are set aside by Mansaray in italics to further emphasize their importance in understanding Yaya's saga. For example, to see Yaya's turmoil, one must understand his relationship with his Grandma Fatu; the reader must be given their history, their relationship, and their language. Grandma has selected Yaya to inherit her knowledge as a bone healer. She does not openly teach Yaya her trade; she comes to him in dreams and finally says to him:

> Yaya, you are now sacred and must know the [sic] scared [sacred] secret for your life will henceforth be by the dictates of the kind spirits of your ancestors. You will communicate with the spirit world, and until you are permitted, no man that is different from you should know what transpires. (161)

Yaya does not wish to accept this calling, and so Mansaray italicizes Yaya's dream response:

> *"No, Grandma, no! Please let me go! I don't need this gift or any bond! I love my ancestors and that's enough! Now can't you see, this is not for me?"* (161)

However, Grandma Fatu has made up her mind, and so Yaya must escape, first from his own village to another place in his country and then to a land across the sea:

> *Well, Grandma Fatu, I thought you loved me. Evidently you didn't love me enough. Not at all. You shattered my world, hounding me. But I'm now far away. I had to leave for my sanity. Maybe now, you will rest. And please, select somebody else to follow in your footsteps. For I'm in a totally different world now, where my mind will be free and I will live a happier life—like these guys! Thank God! Wonderful America! You bastion of freedom—take me to your bosom—where everything is possible! And as for you my people, I won't forget you. I'll be back. Meantime, as always, I will help from here, whenever possible. But as for this sacred secret, I shall mention nothing of it to a soul, not especially to these guys, for as they seem—they will only laugh at me!* (47)

The reader is made aware that even in his struggle to "put away" the past, Yaya finds he cannot forget where he came from or the people he left behind.

Yaya's primary struggle comes from his mental/spiritual battles with his Grandma Fatu, who is his blood; thus, her voice seems to blend with Yaya's inner voice. However, Yaya struggles not only with his own voices, but with the voice memories in every encounter with his transplanted countrymen in America. The cultural importance of these encounters is also presented in italics to help the reader enter into Yaya's psychic growing process.

To illustrate these points, first, the reader sees how Grandma Fatu's voice blends with Yaya's inner voice. Yaya remembers the incidents when his Grandma Fatu sought to seek a

> new carved bond with the ancestors who passed down this gift to us. And then I'll leave you [Yaya] in the hands of their spirits for companions'. . . . *Not quite yet, Grandma Fatu!* He tried to get up, to run and free

himself. But he felt glued and had no control over his body, even as his mind kept telling him: *"Run, run, run, Yaya!"* (Mansaray 161)

As Yaya continues to remember this ordeal he closes his eyes thinking yet hearing Grandma:

"Snake . . ., snake . . ., snake and heritage!"

The memory came back like he did a fast rewind on a video cassette. Two years ago, on a visit to Grandma Fatu, she was sitting on a rattan stool in her room, and him on a bench next to her. She had the leaf in his face and was looking into his eyes, as she said:

Behold for this is your heritage. It is like a snake and you are its skin. A snake never dies because it has shed its skin. It lives on, vibrant and alert with the fresh gleaming skin. For it is only when the snake dies, that the skin dies with it and rots. Yaya, you are just such a skin. . . . When it is time for you to pass it on you will know. . . . And you cannot transfer it but to whom that is chosen. For to do so is to kill the snake.

"Oh, Grandma Fatu, can you ever understand?" Yaya cried out aloud and felt stunned by the echo of his own voice in the stillness of the night. (164)

These messages and parables from Grandma Fatu exacerbate Yaya's emotional and spiritual difficulties in finding a clear unobstructed new life in at home or in America. His Grandma Fatu cannot leave Yaya, and Yaya cannot leave Grandma Fatu, for they are the snake and the skin. When he leaves his village, then his grandma, and then his motherland, Yaya brings disorder into his world. Alienation from his own and his desperation to come to America set the stage for Yaya's face-to-face encounters with the dehumanization process that is America.

When he comes to America, Yaya believes that his opportunities and successes will be immediate. Yaya, however, finds himself totally dependent on his cousin Sidi, who does not replace Grandma Fatu's voice, but adds a new dimension to Yaya's dilemma. Of course, Yaya wishes to work immediately after arriving in America. But his documents are not suitable and he is warned that he cannot seek employment because if he presents his "Social Security Card to employers some might not only refuse to hire him, but might also trap him to be picked up by immigration for deportation" (184). Yaya does not know that in America Blacks also have a history with pieces of paper that free or enslave. Similarly, pieces of paper are problems for contemporary African arrivals since they can mean deportation—a method of controlling an unwanted population. And so:

> Incapacitated in America by a new set of constraints, Yaya depended solely on Sidi for everything, from toothpaste to snacks at bed time. Like a blind man, Sidi was his eyes, his cane and his way into the society. Consequently, if he were to work at all, he looked up to Sidi for a way to his first job; so he pressured him. Sidi never minded.
>
> With the understanding of one who had been through Yaya's route like any newcomer in America, and as one who lived as an illegal alien for many years [coming first legally as a tourist], Sidi was patient and constantly informative, when not consoling. Sensing Yaya's disillusionments . . . Sidi felt compelled to put things in perspective. (184)

Sidi reminds Yaya that "behind the opulent facade lay a unaccustomed dehumanization in stock for the average African. . . . Looking at Yaya's heavy eyes, bowed head and broken shoulders, Sidi could have said, 'I tried to tell you [not to come to America], but you wouldn't listen'" (196). Sidi regularly tells Yaya, "that the experience he was going through was not peculiar, but a rite of passage for the average African when new in the U.S." (197) This is the cultural shock experience for the new

African in America, and though different from the enslaved African who came before him, is no less dehumanizing and debilitating.

Yaya's encounters with his relocated countrymen should have been a vehicle for his comfortable transition in America. It is with these encounters that Mansaray can shatter the conspiracy of silence about the bumpy migration from first to third class status, from protected to unprotected, from knowing to ignorance. For example, there is Yaya's countryman Ahmed Karankay who

> was a grandson, great-grandson, and great-great-grandson of cobblers. In Manika Kunda, before the onslaught of alien civilization and confusion, society was such that principal occupations were carried out by particular families. . . . [Ahmed] has lived in the U.S. for eight years. . . . attended Howard University. . . . A chubby six-footer. . . . A determined Ahmed, however, [after the death of his American wife] moved to Philadelphia a year ago still searching, but now drove a cab, sticking a resume in the hands of every passenger he picked up that had on a tie or a suit. (113-5)

Yaya learns that nothing comes easy in America, especially for people like him, and that his countrymen are in no great positions to assist him. Even under his cousin's care, Yaya finds his condition in America grows worse and he is lured to Houston, Texas, by the tempting promise of an old schoolmate. It is in Houston that Yaya has to come to terms with his past and his present, for he can no longer simply physically run away to anything; he must accept the realities bestowed by both America and Grandma Fatu, who spiritually makes the trip with him. Like Okonkwo in *Things Fall Apart*, Yaya must weigh the past and present to decide if he will become a defeated African in the dehumanization process of America, a traitor to his heritage and legacy, or an African who is able to resolve his cultural and intellectual conflicts. In the end, he will be aware of the connections between the dehumanization of America and his alienation from it.

As readers turn from the male to the female encounters with alienation, marginalization and dehumanization, readers might expect the use of different writing strategies as well as different responses. *Let It Be Told*, edited by Lauretta Ngcobo of South Africa, provides both. First, the writers Ngcobo has selected, provide readers with a British scenario for training grounds in the western world. Second, the experiences are not fictionalized but personal experiences with both the ordeals and the responses. Ngcobo writes of Black women and Black women writers in Britain that:

> As a group we suffer the self-perpetuating psychological mutilation of oppression: battered self-image, which has undermined our confidence; diminished possibilities for self-expression, linked with poor educational opportunities; internalized images of ourselves as depicted by others; and countless self-inflicted wounds. (1)

Later she says of Blacks in general,

> The whole fibre of Black life has been permeated and poisoned by white values and oppression in such a way that many Black people cannot live comfortably with themselves. They have a devouring sense of alienation within. They judge themselves by white standards even while they fight for Black identity. (28)

In *Let It Be Told*, Ngcobo and selected writers speak of their encounters with alienation and dehumanization and what they have done as writers to overcome marginalization as black female writers: "From now on we exist. Where we had no collective considered viewpoint, now we have. In books such as this, we are carving for all Blackwomen a niche in British society" (34).

First to carve a niche is Marsha Prescod, a Black woman who came to England as a small child with her Black pioneering family during the 1950s. It is said that "she tries in her writing to analyze our situation, as Africans in the Diaspora, and her aim is to play whatever part she can in improving that situation, and to encourage others to do so too" (106). Prescod speaks of the influences of her life and how she is finding new influences everyday. She has a Baldwinian aesthetic: the idea that the black writer must not beg for his or her humanity (Davis, Redding, and Joyce 8). She says, "It may seem that I'm suggesting that Black writers or women writers must write from a particular perspective. But not really. I'm saying that when we write, we'll find certain experiences shaping our writing whether we like it or not. The intelligent thing is to understand that and work with it, not try to deny it" (108). She continues, "At times I've been asked if I feel most besieged as a woman or as a Black. Some of the greatest tests of my skill in survival have come from living in a white racist country" (109). So in her writing and in her lectures, Prescod speaks of the dehumanizing of Black people in general and Black women in particular. She finds her voice by facing the influences head on; and in that head-on collision she is forced to action, the action of writing. Her poetry uses the same strategies other Black women have used—"humor, as a tool of survival, to deal with horrors of our loss, and to pass on our skills and strategies . . . . to tell and re-define our experience in our own words" (qtd. in Ngcobo 109) which are summed up in the following poem:

> For us to be free
> we have to know we
> don't let any "ethnicize" us,
> into them marginal categories,
>
> Our positive self cannot be,
> through negative definition,
> saying, "Well, we're not them"
> to work [sic] out[r] own position.
>
> Don't look to *his*-story,
> to discover our existence.
> Don't hide in another's ideasology,
> to develop our own resistance.
> For us to be free,
> *we* have to know we.
> Our own truth
> our own strength,

And our
Black,
black,
black,
black

creativity! (Prescod 120)

Like many writers before her, Prescod has chosen poetry as her response
arena. She has taken ordeals and turned them into weapons to develop
mental strength, not only for herself but also for her readers.

Another writer to carve a niche in British society is Amryl
Johnson, a native Trinidadian and British educated. When it came time
for her to publish her first novel, she found the doors closed. She says, "I
am writing about a period when, in the main, either Black writers in this
country were not taken seriously or else publishers were afraid of what
we had to say. There was no place for us on their lists" (36). She was
writing at a time when she was full of anger from being rejected time after
time after time. Her first novel took years to write because she was in
conflict:

> struggling with some decision as to whether I was first of
> all an individual and then a Black female or if the colour
> of my skin should influence every waking decision. I was
> in danger of loss of identity, struggling to emerge as a
> person beyond any bars or fetters which would hold me
> back. (37)

These were her early years. She did not even know she was in cultural or
personal exile until a Trinidadian friend told her to go home (37). She
went home and celebrated the rediscovery of her own culture. Her trip
helped her to discover her real voice as a writer. She says, "Writing has
become the most important thing in my life. No matter how marvelous
the current man happens to be, if I cannot spend a little time every day
developing my creative strands, I am frustrated" (42). Traveling to and
living in the Caribbean has inspired her collection of poems, *Long Road
to Nowhere* (1985).

Critics have said that readers of Johnson can "see these immediate struggles placed in the context of an overarching desire for historical reconstruction, for re-establishing the continuities of a twice-dispossessed people. Amryl Johnson's work makes an important contribution to this process of rebuilding the shattered fragments" (46). In "Circle of Thorns" she says that:

> There is a ring of rusty iron
> which grates along concrete
> until your blood crawls. (46)

which is "simply" a way of describing the actual experiences of Black people. She also writes of the walls erected to prevent self realization. Her ordeal reminds the reader of Yaya in *The Haunting Heritage*; she must return to her roots to find her voice. In her journey to self-knowledge, Johnson finds:

> New found courage to turn from the power of
> its glare habit of obedience and look at
> yourself without feeling shame you start
>   coming to face the mirror
> still   coming
>   coming. (47)

Johnson, like others between two lands, experiences the paradox of being in two dimensions. There is a severe contrast between the self of the Caribbean and the self of the Briton. There is humor, delight and rhythm in the Caribbean self:

> Yuh mango ripe?
>
> Gran'ma, stop feelin' and squeezin' up meh fruit!
> Yuh ehn playin' in no ban'. Meh mango ehno concertina
>
> Ah tell yuh dis mango hard just like yuh face. ("Granny in de Market Place" 49)

But in her earlier space of anger and alienation in England, she writes
"Midnight Without Pity" (1977):

> Judas
>   Take my hand
> let us go from here
> down into the valley
> Keep your hood tight
> about your neck
> I do not want to see
> your face
> and if you still remember
> the bitter taste
> to know
> you never stood a chance
>   or had a choice
> against a destiny
>   which held you
>   rejected you
> then teach me
> teach me
> teach me
> teach me how
> to count the silver
> and forget the cost
> for I am
> Black
> And I am
> Angry
>
> my name
> is
> Midnight
> Without
> Pity (36)

The three writers, Alasan Mansaray, Marsha Prescod, and Amryl Johnson create a literature of power. All write of reactions to the clashing of cultures or the clashing of races. While the reader is most aware of Mansaray's protagonist's struggle to achieve selfhood, a close reading of the novel shows that even lesser characters are involved in the same process, and it is this intermingling of struggles that further intensifies the isolation, marginalization, and internal strife. Prescod and Johnson make the reader painfully aware that women also have a multi-faceted struggle. To find their voices, women have had to deal with colonization, racism, alienation, dehumanization, and *woman*-selfhood. Even when they come to terms with being women, there are still trials to be faced. These are the things that seem to intensify the "female" and "racial" themes and force writers to develop strategies and techniques to demonstrate their value in the very societies that seek to deny their significance.

Mansaray's novel is destined to become a handbook for multicultural understanding. Mansaray has included the many facets of isolation and dehumanization plus the struggles to reconcile the cultural and intellectual selves. Many immigrants from non-African cultures will be able to sympathize with Yaya's dilemma. Ironically, the story of one African is the story of many Africans and still the story of African Americans who feel like immigrants in the country of their birth. Likewise, Ngcobo's collection lets the reader know the profundity of adding gender to isolation and dehumanization. Many of the British women writers also help, through their diverse, intriguing responses, to illuminate the scope of the complex issues involved in discussing the similar African diasporic experiences with the western world.

Works Cited

Davis, Arthur P., J. Saunders Redding, and Joyce Ann Joyce, eds. "Introduction." *The New Cavalcade*. Vol. 2. Washington: Howard University, 1992. 2 vols.

Johnson, Amryl. "Amryl Johnson." *Let It Be Told: Black Women Writers in Britain*. Ed. Lauretta Ngcobo. London: Pluto Press, 1987. 35-52.

Mansaray, Alasan. *A Haunting Heritage: An African Saga in America*. Dallas: Sahara Publishing, 1995.

Ngcobo, Lauretta, ed. *Let It Be Told: Black Women Writers in Britain*. London: Pluto Press, 1987.

Prescod, Marsha. "Marsha Prescod." *Let It Be Told: Black Women Writers in Britain*. Ed. Lauretta Ngcobo. London: Pluto Press, 1987. 106-20.

"Poetry"

Odia Ofeimun

a trope of wishes, a homecoming
for those whose journeys will never end

whose beginnings were already journeys
speaking for the present and the next

journey to a moon that hides wisdom
in the crook of a face and openness of the heart

a journey that every homeland makes
wishing for eyes that fetch remembered futures

eyes roving from the presentiments of birds
breeding, wave on wave, in seasonal flights

from familiar hurts to other skies, other lands,
yielded to a new dress by affectionate folklore

a journey of wishes to the humid geographies
of children, exiles in a sad country of exiles

those, to whom we return– the good
and fitting death of those who must be reborn

in a country without anthems or boundaries
a native land where homelessness is bliss

bodying the mosques, churches and shrines
with pride stolen from banished kingdoms

banished futures waylaying the homecomer
with new beginnings that are ancient journeys

From *Dreams at Work and Other Poems* (Lagos: Hornbill House, 2000).

III. Linguistic and Cultural Connections

Désir "volé":
Creating a Female Discourse in Seventeenth-Century French and Twentieth-Century Francophone Novels[1]

Eileen M. Ketchum

In her well-known essay "Le Rire de la Méduse," Hélène Cixous declares that "*Voler*, c'est le geste de la femme" [*Voler* is the gesture of the woman][2]—a statement that perhaps fully grasps the depth of the female writer's experience as she struggles to find her own voice within a predominantly male literary tradition. "Voler," an ambiguous term meaning *to steal* and *to fly*, implies the need for the female writer to steal the words from the pre-established male discourse and simultaneously create her own means of expression. By subverting the passages previously forged by male writers, "brouiller l'ordre de l'espace . . . le désorienter" [muddle up the order of the space . . . disorient it] in the words of Cixous, the woman author can thereby "fly" into her own writing domain, creating her own *écriture féminine*. Such a phenomenon can be found in the works of many women in French literary history, from the middle ages to the present.

The notion of *écriture féminine*, or feminine writing, has been widely discussed in French literature since the seventeenth century and may be originally attributed to Guez de Balzac's *Lettres familières de Monsieur de Balzac à Monsieur Chapelain* (1638).[3] In this text, Balzac clearly attempts to describe the essence of feminine writing as opposed to male writing, a discussion that follows throughout the century and which is furthermore illustrated in La Bruyere's *Les caractères* (1688). From the male point of view, women's writing is associated mostly with sentiment and intimate emotions, "il n'appartient qu'à elles de faire lire dans un seul mot tout en sentiment, et de rendre délicatement une pensée qui est délicate" [only women can make one read a single word entirely with sentiment and make a delicate thought delicate] (La Bruyère 37), rather than intellectual and philosophical thought. Moreover, women's writing at this time is considered first and foremost a consequence of biology instead of style.

Twentieth-century feminine theorists have furthered the notion of *écriture féminine*, led particularly by Hélène Cixous, Luce Irigaray, and Julia Kristeva. Rather than simply consider feminine writing in opposition to male writing, as constituting all that male writing is not, the twentieth-century notion of *écriture féminine* has been perceived instead as a feminine *être* or being in itself.[4] As Karen Holme and Helen Wussow discuss feminine writing, "it is a way of assessing not only our voices as women but our whole way of acting in a world that is at once our own and someone else's" (xiii), in other words, a world of literature that has been originally formed by men but which women must make their own by diverting their voices in a new manner. These women writers incarnate both the male traditions that have preceded them and also hold their own, a veritable "métissage" of perspectives that come through in their writing.

Hence, a comparison of seventeenth-century French and twentieth-century Francophone literature may no longer appear surprising, given that these two moments in literary history have witnessed significant developments regarding the notion of *écriture féminine*. According to Joan DeJean, French women's writing truly began in the mid-seventeenth century, encouraging discussion of many new feminist ideas presented in women's novels. In fact, DeJean characterizes women's novels during this period as "tender geographies," in that the "affairs of the heart are portrayed as indissociable from affairs of state" (4). The private domains of love and desire depicted within these novels often insinuate a political undercurrent calling for an amelioration of the female condition in a patriarchal society. One can find similar trends in the recent novels of Francophone women, centuries and continents apart from these earlier women writers. During an era of political and literary change, Francophone women writers have had to struggle against both white and black male domination. The *négritude* movement of the 1930s, which fought to re-establish pride in the black race, failed to recognize the black woman's specific condition or sexual difference within the political and color-coded issues of "blackness." It is not until the 1970s and 80s that the female voice of *négritude* began to emerge strongly in women's novels, simultaneously following and transforming the prototype established by their male predecessors. As Irène Assiba d'Almeida describes this "coming to writing" on the part of African women, the female writers gain a new status as speaking subjects, rather than objects of mythic or symbolic value as in traditional male Francophone literature. "A partir du moment où les femmes se mettent à écrire, elles ne sont plus perçues, ni même étudiées de façon mythique ou symbolique mais comme de vrais êtres humains de chair et d'os, des êtres à part entière" [Following the moment when women begin to write, they are no longer perceived or studied in a mythical or symbolic fashion but as true human beings of flesh and bone, as beings entirely set apart] ("La 'Prise d'Ecriture'" 136).

In order to assert their new identity, women writers from both seventeenth-century France and twentieth-century Francophone countries cleverly undermine the traditional male discourse, particularly the manner in which desire is expressed. No longer content to remain an object of male desire, the female characters in a select group of these novels assert themselves as desiring subjects, thereby implying a new social order and status for women. I will begin by examining two Francophone novels, Mariama Bâ's *Une si longue lettre* and Angèle Rawiri's *Fureurs et cris de femmes*. A less well known novel from the seventeenth century, *Histoire des amours de Cléante et Bélise* from Anne Ferrand, will serve as a prime example of similar literary transformations from an earlier era. It is precisely through their textual subversion of a male expression of desire, that is to say *désir volé*, that these women writers affirm a new model of *écriture féminine*.

Mariama Bâ has certainly influenced the evolution of black women's writing with her epistolary novel *Une si longue lettre*, published in 1980. By structuring this novel in the form of a letter, Mariama Bâ gives the impression that her main character, Ramatoulaye, is writing to all African women who suffer similar experiences. It is significant that the novel begins at the death of Ramatoulaye's husband, an end that truly marks a new beginning for Ramatoulaye. Through her letter to Aïssatou, the reader learns of the history of Ramatoulaye's relationship with her husband and that of Aïssatou with her own husband. Although the two women have similar experiences in their earlier years—they attended the same girls school which encouraged women's emancipation, they met and chose their husbands against the will of their parents, their husbands married another woman during the course of their marriage—their lives diverge according to the decisions each woman makes. I would argue that Mariama Bâ uses these two characters to illustrate the consequences of following tradition versus forging a new path for the modern African woman.

Initially, Ramatoulaye rejects traditional constraints by refusing the husband her mother had selected and choosing to marry the man she loves. She also has a job as a teacher, a lifestyle of which her husband's sisters disapprove because they believe that the woman should remain at home and concentrate solely on her family. Nonetheless, Ramatoulaye acts according to her own volition, disregarding the traditional role of a submissive woman. However, when her husband takes a new wife (who happens to be the childhood friend of her daughter), Ramatoulaye follows convention and remains with her husband. "Je suis de celles qui ne peuvent se réaliser et s'épanouir que dans le couple" [I am one of those who can realize themselves fully and bloom only when they form part of a couple] (82). She seems to have lost her sense of independence and relies on Modou for her identity as his wife. Abandoned by Modou who moves in with his new spouse, Ramatoulaye dedicates her life to her children and finds value in her role as a mother.

Aïssatou has a different reaction when confronted with the prospect of a second wife in her home. Rather than suffer the secondary position as Mawdo's first wife, Aïssatou courageously decides to leave Mawdo and establish life on her own. In a letter to her husband, she writes, "Je me dépouille de ton amour, de ton nom. Vêtue du seul habit valable de la dignité, je poursuis ma route" [I am stripping myself of your love, your name. Clothed in my dignity, the only worthy garment, I go my way] (50). Unlike Ramatoulaye, Aïssatou has chosen to assume her own identity without the support of her husband, follow her own desires and defy the societal practice of polygamy. She moves to France to become an interpreter and ultimately succeeds in becoming the Senegalese Ambassador in the United States. Aïssatou represents perhaps the extreme end of modernity, encouraging women to break free of conventional rules and test their true capabilities in an unending range of possibilities.

It appears at the end of the novel that Mariama Bâ remains torn between her two characters, between tradition and modernity. She seems to value both Ramatoulaye's dedication to her marriage and children, as well as Aïssatou's initiative and courage for challenging societal expectations. Irène d'Almeida points out that this novel is one of choice, that each woman has elected to follow the life she leads. According to d'Almeida, "[c]hoice allows Ramatoulaye and Aïssatou to arrive at self-realization" (*Francophone Women Writers* 118). In other words, each woman acts according to her own desire, whether it be to adhere to traditional values or to pursue alternative avenues. Ramatoulaye remarks this threshold of choice as characteristic of the post-independence era: "Privilège de notre génération, charnière entre deux périodes historiques, l'une de domination, l'autre d'indépendance" [It was the privilege of our generation to be the link between two periods in our history, one of domination, the other of independence] (40). Women writers experience a similar conflict of interests, torn between the desire to maintain tradition, while at the same time protesting those forces that suppress their individuality as women. Mariama Bâ seems to suggest that the decision between tradition and modernity remains up to the individual.

Angèle Rawiri illustrates a similar transformation of a traditional female character into an emerging modern woman in her novel *Fureurs et cris de femmes* (1989). In the beginning of the novel, the main character Emilienne reveals her sole ambition: "Il lui faut, quel que soit le prix qu'elle devra payer, reconquérir son mari qui lui échappe" [She must, no matter what the price that she will have to pay, get back her husband who is escaping from her] (10). For Emilienne, as for Ramatoulaye, her life only retains meaning as the wife of Joseph, and she will therefore do whatever is necessary to regain his love. However, the juxtaposition of Emilienne's somewhat conventional desires with her successful career in a well-paid administrative position represents a rather intriguing contrast of character. One could argue that Emilienne represents the new generation of African women on the threshold of modernity yet constrained by traditional values.

Although their marriage was originally based on mutual love and understanding, conflicts arise when Emilienne begins having trouble with her pregnancies. Unable to fulfill her maternal role and bear Joseph a son, Emilienne loses his respect and desire to another woman who can satisfy this need. The fact that Emilienne makes more money than Joseph only adds to his perception of her as undesirable because he cannot perform his conventional role of providing for his wife and family. Emilienne is convinced that if she can somehow carry a pregnancy to term and give Joseph a son, she will regain his desire.

The situation at home throughout the course of their marriage is certainly less than ideal, considering that Emilienne's mother-in-law lives with her as well as Joseph's niece and nephew. Although Joseph's mother enjoys the luxurious lifestyle that Emilienne provides for her, she disapproves of her modern career and inability to have children. Emilienne loses all sense of individuality in a household where she must submit to her husband and his family before her own needs. "[E]lle ne savait plus . . . où commençait et où finissait sa liberté d'agir dans sa propre maison; elle ne savait plus si elle devait faire passer le bonheur évident de son mari avant ses propres intérêts. Fallait-il pour faire plaisir à tous qu'elle perde sa liberté?" [She no longer knew . . . here her liberty to act in her own house began and where it finished; she no longer knew if she should put her husband's happiness before her own interests. Was it necessary that she give up all her freedom in order to please everyone?] (39). Emilienne has become a silent partner in the destruction of her own freedom of choice.

The true crux of the problem, and perhaps the real instigator for change within Emilienne, develops when their only daughter, Rékia, is found beaten to death. Having lost this final link, Emilienne and Joseph drift apart as Emilienne continues her efforts to please him through seduction, cooking, attempts at becoming pregnant—whatever it takes to have Joseph find her desirable again. When all fails, Emilienne decides to search elsewhere for the love and personal satisfaction missing in her marriage. Her rejection of conventional desire leads her to explore a homosexual relationship with her secretary Dominique. Having finally proclaimed her own desire for another woman, clearly putting her own interests in front of her husband and the rest of her household, Emilienne realizes her authority to force Joseph and his family to leave her home. This entry into a new domain of desire finally frees her from all the binding forces of tradition and marriage which have silenced her into submission.

Although she eventually ends her relationship with Dominique, Emilienne experiences a new social order in which the woman no longer adheres to traditional values. Unlike Mariama Bâ who leaves her heroine in conflict between tradition and modernity, Angèle Rawiri makes her preference clear at the end of her novel. Pregnant once again, Emilienne returns to an empty home, ready to begin life on her own. It would seem that Angèle Rawiri offers a new hope for women, a challenge to reject patriarchal custom and discover one's own desires.

A few centuries earlier, a group of women writers in France were causing a stir among the literary salons of aristocratic and bourgeois society. With the rise of classicism during the second half of the seventeenth century, the literary world of the salons gained notable importance in French society. Indeed, women writers began to acquire greater status for themselves and women in general by subverting traditional representations of literary discourse into acts of defiance against societal convention.

Although very prolific for her time, Anne Ferrand is less known today than her contemporaries such as Mme de Lafayette and Mlle de Scudéry. One of her most famous works, *Histoire des amours de Cléante et Bélise*, published in 1689, depicts the alleged autobiographical story of a woman's revolt against the family order. What is perhaps most interesting about this novel is that it completely reverses the traditional male discourse of desire. In his preface to the 1979 edition, René Godenne remarks that the *coup de foudre* which instigates the love story "perd pour une bonne part de sa valeur habituelle de cliché puisqu'il se produit à sens unique" [loses a good portion of its usual value as a cliché since it occurs in only one direction] (viii). Not only is the *coup de foudre* in one direction, but it falls upon a woman rather than a man: certainly against the grain of traditional discourse of desire. *Histoire des amours de Cléante et Bélise* recounts therefore the desire of a woman for a man and the methods she uses to possess him.

The story focuses on the main character, Bélise, as she relates the story of her love for Cléante to her friend Zélonide. Once Bélise discovers that Cléante is secretly married and does not reciprocate these feelings for her, she decides to win his affections through her intellect. Although Mme Ferrand has borrowed the traditional love quest in her novel, she has altered it to become one based on the intellectual merit of the woman, rather than on her beauty. In addition, she has reversed the direction of the chase.

To her dismay, Bélise is forced to marry a man out of obligation to her parents who have promised her in marriage. One might argue that Anne Ferrand is challenging the rule of prearranged marriages by illustrating the injustice of forcing such arrangements upon a woman, often at the cost of her own happiness. Although Bélise would rather spend her life in a convent where she could continue to freely love Cléante, she chooses to follow her societal duty. "[L]a vertu . . . me fit résoudre à m'attacher malgré moi-même au devoir qu'une Loi injuste m'avait imposée" [Virtue made me resolve in spite of myself to stick to a duty that an unfair Law had imposed upon me] (28-9). Nonetheless, she uses this situation to her advantage, as many men continue to court her in an effort to become her lover. By manipulating these men and learning how to control their desire, Bélise hopes to acquire the skills to please Cléante.

When Cléante's wife falls ill and dies, Bélise takes this opportunity to declare openly her love for him, an action extremely uncommon for women in seventeenth-century French literature. With each letter that she writes him, Bélise becomes increasingly daring in exposing her desire. Eventually, Cléante begins to love her out of pity, flattered at having inspired such an intense and persistent passion in a woman. At this point in the story, when Bélise has finally won the man's desire, the story shifts to Cléante's perspective. Through his point of view, the reader can perceive the manner in which Bélise controls Cléante's desire and eventually abandons him.

Histoire des amours de Cléante et Bélise is ultimately a mirror image of the typical love quest by a man for a woman. Cléante becomes dependent on Bélise and begs her not to leave him at the moment when he loves her the most. After several reconciliations, Bélise eventually responds with coldness to his supplications and takes a new lover, confident in having conquered the man she desired. Unlike traditional love stories where the man abandons his lover once his desire has been satisfied, this novel of Anne Ferrand alters the position of power from the man to the woman. Bélise uses her own ruse to manipulate Cléante, deserting him when she has finally attained his love. Anne Ferrand effectively demonstrates that women do not have to remain simple objects of male adoration, but rather can choose their individual destiny through the realization of their own desire.

The preceding three novels by women from different eras and different countries illustrate a common motif for women's writing across the ages: the transformation of traditional discourse of desire to create a feminine expression of individual choice. For lack of time and space, I have only considered one novelist from the seventeenth century who clearly represents this tendency to bestow women with a new power as desiring subjects. Three hundred years later, Francophone women's novels continue to shape the development of women's writing through a frequently-occurring motif of female characters who must choose between submission to traditional values and following their own individual choices. Furthermore, the decision to maintain tradition or pursue personal desires is not always clear or simple in women's novels across the ages. The rejection of societal conventions by a woman often places her on the margins, a powerful yet lonely position. It is evident that going against the grain to express a *désir volé* has long been an influential tool for women writers, yet societies continue to enforce patriarchal customs. Although the political and geographic situations may change, the need remains for women to discover and express their individuality through a continually evolving model of *écriture féminine*.

Notes

1. Throughout this discussion, I use the term "Francophone" to refer to writers of French literature outside of France. My focus will remain particularly on women writers from French-speaking sub-Saharan Africa.
2. Translations throughout this piece are mine.
3. Joan DeJean makes this claim for Balzac in her article "Sexe, genre et nom d'auteur," in which she describes the characteristics attributed to feminine writing in the seventeenth century.

4. For further discussion of the feminine être, see Karen Hohne's and Helen Wussow's introduction to *A Dialogue of Voices: Feminist Literary Theory and Bakhtin* (1994).

Works Cited

D'Almeida, Irène Assiba. *Francophone African Women Writers: Destroying the Emptiness of Silence*. Gainesville: University Press of Florida, 1994.

___. "La 'Prise d'Ecriture' des Femmes Francophones d'Afrique Noire." *Moving Beyond Boundaries: Black Women's Diasporas*. Ed. Carol Boyce Davies. Vol. 2. New York: New York University Press, 1995. 136-53. 2 vols.

Bâ, Mariama. *Une si longue lettre*. Dakar: Nouvelles Editions Africaines, 1980.

Cixous, Hélène. "Le Rire de la Méduse." *L'Arc* 61 (1975): 39-54.

DeJean, Joan. "L'écriture feminine : sexe, genre et nom d'auteur au XVIIè siècle." *Littératures Classiques* 28 (1996): 137-46.

___. *Tender Geographies: Women and the Origins of the Novel in France*. New York: Columbia University Press, 1991.

Ferrand, Anne Bellinzani. *Histoire des amours de Cléante et Bélise*. 1691. Genève: Slatkine Reprints, 1979.

Hohne, Karen and Helen Wussow, eds. *A Dialogue of Voices: Feminist Literary Theory and Bakhtin*. Minneapolis: University of Minnesota Press, 1994.

La Bruyère. *Les Caractères*. 1688. Paris: Garnier, 1962.

Rawiri, Angèle. *Fureurs et cris de femmes*. Paris: L'Harmattan, 1989.

"It's not everything you can talk, but . . .": Francophone Women's *fin-de-siècle* Narratives

Florence Martin

The new narratives woven by Francophone women writers from the African diaspora at the end of this century across the Atlantic seem to echo one another with similar concerns. What I want to discuss here is not so much the notion of a diasporic female narrative itself, as the writing of a silence around which contemporary novelists seem to hover, pen in hand, ears alert. That breed of silence is completely different from the one they broke when they started to write an age-old silence so eloquently described by Irène Assiba d'Alméïda. It is a haunting silence that seems to come from holding a lasting secret, one which cannot be articulated. As a result, these novels sometimes read like vocal scores whose musical rests would point to an enigma handed down to the narrator. That secret usually originates in a past whose spirit the narrators might have inherited, not knowing exactly how or why. And although this idiosyncratic type of literary haunting takes various shapes from one novelist to the next, it nevertheless always stubbornly endures, like a constant nagging hard to dismiss.

Francophone women novelists respond to it in various ways on both sides of the Atlantic, sometimes in a fashion similar to their contemporary African-American counterparts, also engaged in writing around silence, and whose theories might shed new light on our Francophone texts.

I have chosen to look at a diversified sample of African and diasporic Francophone women's texts which greatly differ from one

another: a *beur* novel, *Georgette!* by Farida Belghoul, *Moi, Tituba, sorcière
... noire de Salem* by Guadeloupe author Maryse Condé, *Les Chemins de
Loco-Miroir* by Haïtian author Lilas Desquiron, and *Le jujubier du
patriarche* by Senegalese novelist Aminata Sow Fall. I propose to read
these texts in light of two female, diasporic, anglophone critical texts,
written by African-American and Caribbean authors Toni Morrison and
Carol Boyce Davies.

The most striking feature shared by all these texts is,
paradoxically enough, what the text does not say, its blanks which
conceal/reveal the presence of the unspeakable. In African diasporic
novels, the unsaid can originate in either the narrator's or her people's
individual past, or the inheritance of a distant, weighty past. In the New
World, this particular brand of silence points to the impossibility to speak
of slavery. Toni Morrison explains this reticence by the fact that the
descendents inherited from their enslaved ancestors their forced muteness,
under

> ... *the bit*. This thing was put in the mouth of slaves to
> punish them and shut them up without preventing them
> from working. .... There's a passage in which Paul D.
> says to Sethe, "I've never told anyone about it, I've sung
> about it sometimes." He tries to tell her what wearing the
> bit was like, but he ends up talking about a rooster that
> he swears smiled at him when he wore it—he felt
> cheapened and lessened and that he would never be
> worth as much as a rooster sitting on a tub in the
> sunlight. (Schappell 103-4)

Going up the stream of history to the initial repression of discourse
induced by the slave's bit both takes into account factual history (it
situates the ancestor's silence in history) and introduces the notion of
linguistic detour necessary to hint at the unspeakable or, here, write
around the unwritable. The rooster is evoked to both avoid shame and
signal the presence of shame. The bit is not fingered, but its profoundly
dehumanizing effect, its smothering, its silencing is described via a
metonymy, rather than its physical reality and torture. Writing will
become an enterprise in establishing a series of *équivalences* in the

cinematic sense of the term.[1] The new system of *équivalences* simultaneously recognizes, honors and surrounds the initial silence. The signified moves on from one image to the next, each new signifier allowing the signifying to be all the more potent.

Although the reference to the bit is an African-American one, our four exemplary Francophone texts do contain instances of silencing handed down from the past to contemporary protagonists. The characters' muteness usually derives from some type of repression (although not the bit) which varies from one novel to the next, yet maintains the female protagonist in a state of powerlessness from which it is difficult to extricate herself.

In *Georgette!* the eponymous protagonist remains mute at school, haunted by the double voice of authority: her Maghribi father's at home, and the schoolmistress' at the French school. Both voices contradict each other to such a point that they leave the little girl speechless. Her schoolmistress interprets her silence as a sign of childish stubbornness:

> Alors, tu as un secret! Tu as peur de le dévoiler en parlant. C'est pas bête comme méthode. Tu vois que tu n'es pas idiote! Seulement, le monde n'a plus de secret de nos jours. Ça veut dire que tes cachotteries sont inutiles. . . . (122)

> [So you have a secret! You are afraid of betraying it by speaking. Not a bad method at all. See, you are not an idiot! But the world harbors no more secrets these days. Which means that your little secrets are useless.] (My translation)

The ability to speak has been taken out of Violaine, one of the two *marassas*[2] in *Les Chemins de Loco-Miroir*. Her ensuing muteness signals a haunting in the strongest sense of the term, since she has been zombified after having broken the social rules she was supposed to follow. Her silence corresponds to the repression which smothers her own rebellion. In the "good" creole society of Haïti, threatening the social order and tradition means being exposed to such treatment: once a zombie, she can no longer rebel, no longer voice out her own revolt.

When her old nanny gives her back her *Bon Ange*[3] and feeds her a salted dish, Violaine wakes up from her zombie state. But the sorrowful nanny realizes:

> Ses doigts effleurent mon visage, se promènent sur mes joues. Elle me sourit, un sourire tout triste. Elle ne peut pas me répondre. Voici qu'elle ne parle pas! Ils ont volé les mots de sa bouche. Elle ne parle pas! (193)

> Her fingers wander over my face, exploring the features of my cheeks. She smiles, but it's a very sad smile. She is unable to answer me. And so, there we have it. She can't speak at all! They've stolen the words from her mouth. She can't speak! (Desquiron, *Reflections* 147)

The woman who used to "despeak" (*déparlait*) like her lover, revolutionary Alexandre, is now walled in silence. The Haïtian social repression has managed to smother the revolution started by Violaine and Alexandre: he is killed and she is mute.

Maryse Condé's Tituba, transplanted from her native Barbados to Salem, New England, and accused of witchcraft, is seen throughout the novel as a talkative, strong character. After her trial, she is thrown in jail for seventeen months. That form of repression muzzles her. Only her freedom will succeed in giving her back her ability to speak to this great talker (who can speak to humans as well as to the Invisible, the spirits who guide her in her trade and talent as a healer). Hence, when she is freed from jail, when finally her chains are broken, she breaks out of her silence:

> Je hurlais et ce hurlement, tel celui d'un nouveau-né terrifié, salua mon retour dans le monde. Je dus réapprendre à marcher. Privée de mes chaînes, je ne parvenais pas à trouver mon équilibre et chancelais comme une femme prise d'alcool mauvais. Je dus réapprendre à parler, à communiquer avec mes semblables, à ne plus me contenter de rares monosyllabes. Je dus réapprendre à regarder mes

interlocuteurs dans les yeux. . . .

Peu d'individus ont cette déveine: naître par deux fois. (190-1)

I screamed, and this scream, the terrified cry of a newborn baby, heralded my return to this world. I had to learn how to walk again. Deprived of my shackles, I was unable to find my balance and I tottered like a woman drunk on cheap liquor. I had to learn how to speak again, how to communicate with my fellow creatures, and no longer be content with a word here and there. I had to learn how to look into their eyes again
. . . .

Few people have the misfortune to be born twice. (Condé, *I, Tituba* 122)

It is telling that Tituba's silence is only perceived as the absence of voice which has isolated her from fellow human beings. Her inner voice—the voice with which she continues to address her dear Invisible spirits, Man Yaya, Yao, or Abena, her mother—has never been squelched. But prison, as the site of repression *par excellence*, has effectively silenced her outer voice. Beneath it all, she is still haunted by her benevolent spirits and has inner dialogues with them, unbeknownst to almost all other prisoners. Only one other prisoner knows Tituba well: Hester Prynn, who, having escaped the pages of *The Scartlet Letter*, is seen entering Condé's pages, sharing a cell with Tituba, becoming her soul mate and after she dies, one of Tituba's faithful invisible spirits.

On the opposite shore of the Atlantic, Naarou, the Senegalese protagonist of *Le jujubier du patriarche* (The Patriarch's Jujuba Tree), cannot remain quiet. As a child, she already used to ask a thousand questions to Naani the griot, from whom she has learned the epic of Yelli's dynasty. Yet a specific form of silence reigns in this epic as soon as her own dynasty is evoked. She belongs to a dynasty of slaves that has been linked to the Yellimané dynasty for as long as the memory can trace. Both dynasties' fates have long been entwined and in some ways interdependent. The wordlessness which weighs down on Naarou reflects the missing chapters in the noble dynasty's traditional oral epic poem that has ignored her own history. "L'usage ne prévoyait pas de retenir l'épopée des esclaves" (30) [It was not customary to include the slaves' epic]. Hence the silence is not repressive *stricto sensu* but results from a voluntary omission with repressive side-effects.

Although the quality of muteness within and around Georgette, Violaine, and Naarou varies from one protagonist to the next, it nonetheless implies the existence, in each novel, of a secret. The latter can be either known and guarded by the protagonist, or carefully hidden from her: some kind of confidential information to which she does not have access, and which, nonetheless, succeeds in haunting her.

Each work depicts an idiosyncratic form of haunting: Georgette is haunted by voices, Tituba by her spirits, Violaine by her African "soul", and Naarou by an epic poem.

Georgette wants to maintain her father's voice out of her schoolmistress's earshot. In her head, these two voices contrast sharply: one is feminine, distant and scholarly, educated in the Western sense of the term; the other, beautiful and intimate, is male and talks about God and the house (in its original sense of *Heim*, the familiar, the intimate):

> La sécheresse de la voix, c'est une vie que mon père connaît pas. La sienne est aussi belle qu'un cheval qui monte au ciel. Il fait ce qu'il veut avec: il chante à Dieu, ou bien il parle aux hommes, ou bien il se tait en silence. Moi, j'ai jamais le choix. Je suis toujours muette. Et si par hasard j'ouvre ma bouche: je dis n'importe quoi. Je casse ma voix dans l'eau à force de marcher dedans. (108)

> The dryness of voice is a life my father has not known. His is as beautiful as a horse riding up to heaven. He does whatever he wants with it: he sings for God, or he talks to men, or he keeps quiet in silence. Me, I have no choice. I am always mute. And if by chance I open my mouth: I say anything. I have waddled for so long in the water that I break my voice in it. (My translation)

Writing can be read as Georgette's attempt to find a substitute to the father's voice which she admires without yielding to her teacher's voice.

But how can one write? Her school note-book contains two types of writing: the paternal, Arabic writing of the Qur'an verses at one end of the copy book; and the writing of the French school *"homework"* (a misnomer if ever there was one!) at the other end. The former reads from right to left, while the latter reads from left to right. In the middle of the copy-book: the white pages of emptiness, of undecided writing, of silence. Two views of the world are clashing, two manners of recording events are contradictory, two sets of interpretations are invading the little girl's note-book and reducing her to aphasia. The novel, which describes Georgette's interior monologue, warns us in its very first sentence of the danger of a constant possibility of sign inversion, of code switching: *"La sonne cloche. . . . Non, la cloche sonne"* (9) [The ring bells. . . . No. The bell rings]. The reader immediately knows that something is off, something "rings" off tune. The little *Beur* girl needs to find her own voice in order to be able to speak out her identity which is now stretched between the house and the school, and find out what her own desired identity might be.

For Tituba, silence has another dimension: imprisoned in a puritan country busy hunting down witches, she cannot talk to others about her invisible spirits:

> Dans la promiscuité de la prison, parmi mes compagnes d'infortune, privée de tout élément de nature à m'aider, je n'avais pu communiquer avec mes invisibles autrement qu'en rêve. Hester me visitait régulièrement. Man Yaya, Abena ma mère et Yao, plus rarement. (195)

> In the promiscuous conditions of the prison, among my companions in ill fortune, and deprived of any natural element to help me, I had never been able to communicate with my invisible spirits other than in a dream. Hester used to come and visit me regularly. Mama Yaya, Abena, my mother, and Yao, less often. (125)

Man Yaya, Yao, Abena are the spirits who have always faithfully helped her. It is their presence and supernatural discourses and power which haunt *and* help her. But she cannot share her haunting with anyone. Her healing powers must remain confidential at a time when revealing her inner voice would lead her to a sure death.

In Desquiron's novel, the *houngan* (or Voodoo priest) has reduced Violaine to silence because of her behavior as he explains to Baron Samedi (the *lwa* or spirit of death):

> Elle ne t'appartient pas encore, ô Baron. Baron ô, la Femme Violaine est à nous. Ce sont nos lois qu'elle a transgressées, c'est à nous de la châtier, de la laver bien propre avant de la mettre entre tes mains. O Papa Baron, sa mère qui l'a mise au monde *nous a confié ce travail. Pitié pour elle.* (178)

> She does not belong to you, yet, O Bawon. The Woman Violaine now belongs to us. She transgressed our laws, and as such, it's up to us to punish her, to wash her clean before placing her once again in your hands. O Papa Bawon, her mother, who brought her into the world, has entrusted us with this task. Have mercy on her. (136)

Violaine is haunted by her "African soul": "je suis née écartelée. Mon âme d'Afrique est mal dans mon corps trop pâle, mal dans ma famille transfuge, et ils sont tous à vouloir que je choisisse mon camp. Je refuse" (83) ["I was born feeling as if I'd been torn in two. My African soul suffers in a body that's too pale for it; it also suffers as a result of my turncoat family, and, needless to say, all of them want me to choose a side, but I refuse" (63)]. Her soul turns her into a rebel, eager to break the laws of her Creole parents' high society, to fall in love with dark-skinned revolutionary Alexandre. Violaine is haunted by her love for him, his child she carries and then loses, her revolt against the prejudice of her cast which rules over her family life and the life of the high society of Jérémie, Haïti. She has been zombified in order to fall into line. Silent, the shadow of herself at the gates of Baron Samedi's kingdom, Violaine survives, a tongueless being, haunted by her forbidden love for Alexandre and her "African roots" which her family is trying so hard to sever.

Naarou, in *Le jujubier du patriarche*, is obsessed with the epic she has learned from Naani:

> Il fallait comptabiliser une évidence: Naarou était une possédée du poème. A treize ans, elle pouvait déclamer sans trébucher un millier de vers, ce qui, vu son âge, était une performance d'autant plus étonnante qu'elle portait la marque du génie. . . . Le chant, alors, s'emparait d'elle et, maître absolu de tout son corps, distillait la séduction comme un air de sirène. (69-70)

> One thing had to be taken into account: Naarou was possessed by the poem. When she was thirteen, she could recite a thousand lines without stumbling on words once, which, at her age, was a surprising performance bearing the mark of genius. . . . The song would then take hold of her and, having become the absolute master of her body, would exude charm like a siren's song. (My translation)

Naarou is thus literally haunted by the song. However, if the song possesses Naarou, she too, in turn, starts to possess the song: she contains it in her, and completes it. Within its main narrative, she places, in prominent places, her ancestors Biti and Warèle, slave women who contributed to the feats of Yellimané, the hero. Until then, their story had appeared only in a fragmentary fashion in the noble male epic. Present in it as mere appendages to the (male) hero, these secondary characters were not full-fledged. Naarou revises and magnifies the traditional representation of her foremothers.

Hence all our protagonists seem to fall prey to some degree of obsession or possession: Georgette is petrified, squeezed between two powerful haunting voices; Tituba is inhabited by her Invisibles' voices and spirits; Violaine is now a zombie; Naarou is possessed by the oral epic poem.

Why all these haunted figures? Why write about women possessed in the literal or figurative sense of the term? The texts seem to correct or skirt a silence inherited from the past. Writing around that weighty silence which has been carried around for so long, like Sisyphus' stone, is an arduous task. Once the presence of silence is recognized, the novelist still has to conduct the delicate play of a multi-dimensional voice able to express the silence itself, the secret it contains and conceals, and a narrator's discourse.

Such a formidable task, Toni Morrison tells us, can be achieved through the creation of a narrative voice, with holes in it meant to be filled by intense moments of silence, a narrative voice which creates a space between the words awaiting the reader's response:

> The difficulty for me in writing—*among* the difficulties—is to write the language that can work quietly on a page for a reader who doesn't hear anything. Now for that one has to work very carefully with what is *in between* the words. What is not said. Which is measure, which is rhythm and so on. So, it is what you don't write that frequently gives what you do write its power. (Schappell 89-90)

She thereby invites her reader to enter in the cracks of her text, to listen for the resonance of the words in the silence which follows them, to adopt the oscillatory rhythm of the said and the unsaid. The author invites us to join in an active reading, along a call-and-response pattern between a sometimes seemingly evasive narrative voice and an attentive reader's inner voice which fills in the narrator's text holes. Morrison treats us to a game, to a sharing of a book as one would to a jazz jam session—as her novel *Jazz* so clearly illustrates.[4]

Belghoul adopts a sort of perforated writing scheme close to Morrison's "holy" textual practice in order to express her narrator's interior monologue. Georgette is seen gradually losing her grip on reality, whether reality be her father's, her teacher's, or her classmates'. Haunted by her own dread of disappointing her father, she imagines a terrifying scene in which her reproachful father accuses her of madness, failure, and curses her:

> Je t'envoye à l'école pour sortir intelligente, instruite. A
> la finale, tu sors plus bête! Ta tête, elle est retournée. Et
> quand j'te parle, tu m'répondes à l'envers. Tu m'dis: la
> sonne cloche. Exprès pour qu'j'comprends pas! Si c'est
> comme ça, tu reste tordue toute ta vie comme un arbre
> mort! (133)

> I send you to school so you can come out of it intelligent
> and educated. In the end, you come out more stupid!
> Your head, it's completely turned around. And when I
> talk to you, you answer in reverse. You tell me: the ring
> bells. On purpose, so I don't understand! If that's the
> case, you'll remain twisted your whole life like a dead
> tree! (My translation)

In this passage, Georgette finally attempts to resolve, or at least further
explain, the initial paradox of the novel. In doing so, she makes clear that
her voice functions "in reverse", that her own discourse will both be
antithetical to her teacher's, and diverge from her father's lines. She also
shows that it is in the very silence, which separates the booming voices
of two contradictory authoritarian systems, that one might find a
meaning, a direction; and that this meaning will not appear
spontaneously on the surface of the text. In fact it is the attentive reader's
task to coax it, to patiently uncover it in the blanks of the text, against
the grain of a traditional reading process.

In this sense, the Caribbean feminine formula of Carol Boyce
Davies— "It's not everything you can talk, but . . ."—with its dangling
musical rest, can apply to our literary corpus:

> A certain kind of opposition and reopening is
> represented in the conjunction "but" and the elliptical
> space that signals the speech outside of the closure
> suggested by **"It's not everything you can talk."** It is
> this "excess," the "supplement," the "left-over" that is
> always there that I want to activate in my understanding
> of "other tongues." (Boyce Davies 153)

Two thoughts come to mind: as a reader, I need to look for the "supplement," the "but," that is written to suggest what the silence contains; and, in order to read the Other's, the narrator's "supplement" I need to pay close attention to her language, her intimate mode of communication, idiosyncratic codes. I need to learn and understand that precise tongue of the Other (just like Condé has understood Tituba). What can we do, then, when the tongue or language of the other has been cut off from that other, as in Violaine's case, for instance? Reading Desquiron's text with Carol Boyce Davies in mind, means focusing on the "but" that surrounds Violaine's silence. Fortunately, she has a *marassa* sister, Cocotte, who forms with her a whole being. Once Violaine has become a zombie, Cocotte feels amputated because of her *marassa* sister's silence. She confides in Sor Mélie who understands her new plight:

> Elle savait, elle, que je pleurais mon âme jumelle envolée, mon autre moi. Elle savait qu'à tout jamais j'avais perdu mon étincelle, que désormais je devrais vivre amputée de la partie lumineuse de moi, que j'allais devoir apprendre à vivre comme ça, comme un oiseau sans ailes. (216)

> She knew I was crying for my departed twin soul, my other self. She knew that from now to the end of time I had lost that spark essential to my being, that henceforth I would have to live as if amputated from the luminous part of myself. I was going to have to learn to live like that, like a bird without wings. (167)

In *Les Chemins de Loco-Miroir*, the narrative voice circulates from one character to the next, each chapter spoken or headed by a different one; yet the novel mostly lets Cocotte and Violaine speak. At the end of the novel, only Cocotte's voice resonates. It does not cover Violaine's silence, but rather, circles around it, and translates it. Cocotte now speaks the language (the "tongue" in the mystic sense of the term) of the now muted Other. By the same token, the reader is now listening to a unique voice, which contains both the language and the silence of a zombie woman, a voice whose tongue is able to express that precise silence.

Condé's Tituba, too, is both silent and talkative. Towards the end of the novel, we learn that the narrative "I" who has been addressing us for the past 300 pages or so, is dead: "Je fus la dernière à être conduite à la potence. Autour de moi, d'étranges arbres se hérissaient d'étranges fruits"(262) ["I was the last to be taken to the gallows. All around me strange trees were bristling with strange fruit"(172)]. Blank page. Then "I" starts its monologue over for a few ultimate pages: "Voilà l'histoire de ma vie. Amère. Si amère" (267) ["And that's the story of my life. Such a bitter, bitter story" (175)].

Who is talking to whom? Condé has become a medium, a clairvoyant who has noted down her Caribbean sister's, Tituba's, words. After having carefully listened to Tituba, Condé has ushered us into the supernatural kingdom of Tituba's death whose language she has mastered. In doing so, she has filled in the blanks of the trial procedures of the Salem witch hunt, which only contained a brief mention of Tituba's fate, and given Tituba a resounding voice, reaching us across time and space.

A similar phenomenon takes place in *Le jujubier du patriarche*. Naarou wants to fill in the spots left empty by griots before her. Since the epic poem is so long, one can never recite the whole work at one sitting, and therefore needs to choose its entry point, its initial snatch of narrative from which to take off with a section of the epic. Such an entry point is, appropriately, called a "gate":

> - Tante Naarou, de grâce, le début.
> - Quel début?
> - Le début de la douzième porte du chant, je dormais. . ..
> - Écoute, Ciré, pas aujourd'hui. A une autre occasion, ou l'année prochaine, ici, pourquoi pas? (125)

> - Aunt Naarou, please, the beginning.
> - Which beginning?
> - The beginning of the twelfth gate to the song. I was asleep . . . .
> - Listen, Ciré, not today. At some other occasion, or next year, here. Why not? (My translation)

Naarou, following in the footsteps of griot Naani, chooses her own points of entry into the epic. This precise gate opens the story of Dioumana's flight. Dioumana is not a woman men necessarily want to hear about. She fled away from her husband—hence broke the rules of the patriarchal order—and took refuge in Tarou the Whale's stomach.[5] Haunted by the silence woven around women and her own genealogy, Naarou succeeds in complementing the original traditional oral historical discourse, generally male,[6] with episodes of her foremothers' history—or her story. Meanwhile, the novel espouses the structure of an oral literature performance, narrates fragments of the main narrative, stitches together pieces of text, leaving blanks which the reader will never be able to thoroughly read through. Sow Fall, as a "writing woman, who lends her voice to all her mute sisters" as Alméïda and Hamou have noted (43), respects Naarou's wishes, when her chatty protagonist opts to remain quiet and not reveal other pieces of the epic poem. Thus, both the narrator and the author remind us that even an avid, curious reader/listener cannot have access to complete knowledge.

The resulting texts—be they African or from the African diaspora—thus stage silence as much as *parole*. As we have seen, the latter may either break the former or encircle it in discursive arabesques. In either case, the inherited muteness, which has haunted the Francophone *fin-de-siècle* narrators, demands a form of writing which uses detours, or even contortions. Georgette/Farida writes an inner monologue around the discourse of authority; Violaine/Cocotte's narrative voice is a twin voice, essentially double, a reflection of the writer's and her fictitious sister's shared voice; Tituba, whose slave voice had been originally silenced (by masters now long forgotten), speaks out now through Condé's writing. Naarou finds in her sister Aminata Sow Fall a fellow griotte who succeeds in both making the oral tradition enter the realm of the written one, and in making Naarou's very resonate in a written book. It is in this precise space, between the original haunting silence and the release of female speech, that these authors are writing, unconsciously echoing the texts of their Caribbean sisters:

> It is this tension between articulation and aphasia, between the limitations of spoken language and the possibility of expression, between space for certain forms

of talk, and lack of space for Black Women's speech, the
location between the public and the private, that some
Black women writers address. (Boyce Davies 153)

In other terms, the *fin-de-siècle* novelist addresses and transcribes her
protagonist's silence. Her written text bridges the public sphere (of the
author) and the private one (of the mute character). However, the author
does not betray her fictitious sister's home secret.[7] Rather, she writes in
the left-over space around silence, in its margins, in the "but" in "It's not
everything you can talk, *but...*" In doing so, she invites her attentive
readers throughout the world to appreciate and respect the private
silence[8] of her quiet heroine.

Notes

1. Truffaut discusses Aurenche and Bost's film adaptations of novels via
the notion of "équivalences". Instead of suppressing scenes which were
impossible to shoot, the film-maker needs to substitute different scenes
to the original literary ones, while transposing the same flavor or idea
into the film (see Truffaut's "Une certaine tendance du cinéma français").
2. *Marassas* or *marasa* are twins or soul twins (but not biologically so).
"The *Marasa* are also *lwa*, with their own feast day. The *Marasa* are
especially revered in the realm of Vodou. They have mystical powers in
rituals and are protected by Loko Miwa" (cf. Robin Orr Bodkin's
glossary in Lilas Desquiron, *Reflections of Loko-Miwa* 189).
3. Her *Bon Ange* is her individual spirit which can only be revived or
awakened from a zombie state through reconnecting to the world via
senses—e.g. eating salt, breathing perfume.
4. For a more thorough analysis of *Jazz* along these lines, see Florence
Martin, "Toni Morrison fait du jazz."
5. "[L]à où Gueladio fait ses adieux à la chasse après que Dioumana se fut
enfuie dans le ventre de Tarou la Baleine,"(95) ["When Gueladio bids
farewell to hunting, after Dioumana fled into Tarou the Whale's
stomach." (My translation)].
6. Griottes usually deal with poems, praise songs rather than historical
texts. See d'Almeïda (5-6); Hale, "Griottes" and *Griots and Griottes*.

7. The Francophone *fin-de-siècle* women authors thus go against the grain of previous male authors, such as Laye Camara, for instance, who made private initiation rites public in *L'Enfant noir*.
8. Here this notion is very distinct from women's public mutism which women authors had to first break by publishing from the 1970s onwards in Africa and elsewhere.

Works Cited

d'Alméïda, Irène Assiba. *Francophone Women Writers: Destroying the Emptiness of Silence*. Gainesville: University Press of Florida, 1994.

d'Alméïda, Irène Assiba and Sion Hamou. "L'écriture féminine francophone en Afrique noire francophone: le temps du miroir." *Études littéraires* 24.2 (Fall 1991): 41-50.

Belghoul, Farida. *Georgette!* Paris: Barrault, 1986.

Boyce Davies, Carol. *Black Women, Writing and Identity: Migrations of the Subject*. London & New York: Routledge, 1994.

Camara, Laye. *L'enfant noir*. Paris: Plon, 1953.

Condé, Maryse. *Moi, Tituba, sorcière . . . noire de Salem*. Paris: Mercure de France, 1986.

_____. *I, Tituba, Black Witch of Salem*. Translated by Richard Wilcox. New York: Ballantine, 1992.

Desquiron, Lilas. *Reflections of Loko Miwa*. Translated by Robin Orr Bodkin. Charlottesville & London: University of Virginia Press, 1998.

Desquiron, Lilas. *Les Chemins de Loco-Miroir*. Paris: Stock, 1990.

Hale, Thomas. *Griots and Griottes: Masters of Words and Music*. Bloomington & Indianapolis: Indiana University Press, 1998.

_____. "Griottes: Female Voices from West Africa." *Research in African Literatures* 25.3 (Fall 1993): 71-91.

Martin, Florence. "Toni Morrison fait du jazz." *Jazz et littérature, Europe* 820-821 (August-September 1997): 95-103.

Morrison, Toni, *Jazz*. New York: Knopf, 1992.

Schappell, Elisa. "Toni Morrison: The Art of Fiction CXXXIV" *Paris Review* 128 (1993): 83-125.

Sow Fall, Aminata. *Le jujubier du patriarche*. Dakar: Éditions Khoudia, 1993.

Truffaut, François. "Une certaine tendance du cinéma français." *Les cahiers du cinéma* 31 (January 1954): 15-29.

The Value of Studying Literature in its Geographical Context: Examples from Senegal

Christine Drake

The literature of any country becomes more alive and vibrant when it is set in its geographical context. Thus novels, short stories, poems, and plays of the Senegalese authors take on a richer meaning and gain both depth and perspective when the reader understands more about the physical, cultural, and economic environments in which they were written.

This paper sets out to examine different dimensions of the geographical environments of such Senegalese authors as Léopold Sédar Senghor, Aminata Sow Fall, Mariama Bâ, Ousmane Sembène, Hamidou Kane, Ken Bugul, Cheikh Aliou Ndao, Birago Diop, and Boubacar Boris Diop. It focuses on some of the pivotal physical, cultural, and economic aspects of the geographical environment and their relevance to the literature.

One has to ask first why Senegal has such a rich literature? Are there geographical influences that have had an impact? I would argue that geography has indeed had a role and has been very important in affecting the country's historical development, from early times, through French colonialism, to the present. The country's location on the westernmost part of Africa was a major reason that the French focused their attention on Senegal. The French settled first, in 1658, on an island at the mouth of the Senegal River, naming it St. Louis, after Louis XIV. By 1669, St. Louis was a trading fort, dealing mostly in slaves and gum arabic. It was not until much later, in 1857, that Dakar was developed as the administrative capital of the whole of French West Africa (*Afrique Occidentale Française*). It was especially in Senegal that the French sought to implement their declared *mission civilatrice*—their attempt to bring French civilization to black Africa. Yet within Senegal only the inhabitants of the four communes of St. Louis, Gorée, Dakar, and Rufisque were granted French citizenship. This early contact with the French led to the development of an educated elite, who not only spoke French but were schooled in the literature and social mores of the western world. In turn, they wrote down stories from the oral tradition, examined and interpreted local conditions, developed characters in their geographical context, and created some of the great literature that is a characteristic and part of the heritage of Senegal. Perhaps no other Francophone country in West Africa has as many gifted authors as Senegal. Senghor, for example, was not just the first president of independent Senegal but a fine literary figure as well who even attained coveted membership in l'Académie Française, as all Senegalese are quick to note. This writer and poet makes frequent references to the environment in which he lived.

It is instructive to examine the key geographical characteristics of Senegal that have influenced the authors. Three aspects of the geographical environment stand out in the literature of West Africa: the physical environment, the cultural environment and the economic environment.

First, in terms of the physical environment, Senegal's topography is unexceptional, consisting mainly of broad, sweeping plains with hills rising to greater altitudes especially in the east and southeast. In the north of the country northeast- to southwest-trending sand dunes exist. Three major rivers, all rising in the Fouta Djallon highlands of Guinea, flow through or border the country—the Senegal River in the north, the Gambia River in the center, which flows partly through Senegal before continuing its course to the Atlantic through the country of The Gambia, and the Casamance River in the south. None has a prominent position by name in the literature but many authors refer to the river in a generic sense—going to the river, living by the river, etc. The river plays a vital role in the economy of the country and the livelihoods of the people. Women wash clothes and dishes, people bathe, fish, and use the rivers to water animals and crops, and for a host of other purposes. Striking, also, is the coastline, with its beauty—its bays and headlands, its breakers with their endless march of waves, its fish that supply protein to the local populations, its backdrop for colorful sunsets, and its other opportunities for people to tap the resources of the sea. Mangroves grow intermittently along the shore, used by people for tannin and as a source of shell fish.

Senegal is a Sahelian country—much of it with a hot and arid climate. The Sahel means "shore," in this case the shore of the desert, not the sea. The searing heat of summer contrasts with the refreshing, delightful winters (except when the winds blow sandstorms out of the Sahara). Such contrasts are caused by the movement of the earth relative to the overhead sun. As the sun appears to move from the Tropic of Cancer at the summer solstice in June to the Tropic of Capricorn at the winter solstice in December, the decreasing angle of the sun's rays and the associated shifting of pressure and wind patterns explain the changing temperatures and weather patterns. Rainfall occurs unreliably during the roughly two to four-month long rainy season in the summer and increases in both amount and reliability from north to south. Indeed, the Casamance area, that area south of The Gambia, is relatively well-watered, with more luxuriant vegetation, able to produce some of the country's demand for rice. By contrast, the north of the country, especially inland, is bleak and barren, its sand or thin soil punctuated with semi-desert scrub. Here the overwhelming colors are brown and gold. Between the more well-watered south and the desert inland north is Sahel savannah—grassland dotted with trees, a savannah "shimmering under the caress of the eastern wind," as Senghor expressed it (comparing it to the beauty of a black woman).

In this savannah the baobab tree flourishes, the national symbol of Senegal. The tree embodies a myth that the gods were angry and so plucked up the baobab and stuck its branches in the ground. Hence its unusual appearance. Many are the stories in Senegal connected with the baobab. *Le baobab fou* is even the title of one novel. Ken Bugul, its author, tells the story of a young woman, alien to both her own land and her adopted land in Europe, and torn apart by patriarchy and colonization, and by western and African values, who undertakes an extensive circular journey, leading from Senegal to Europe and back again in search of her roots in her ancestral village, symbolized by the eternal baobab tree. How fascinating it is to learn more about the baobab, that member of the

Bombacaceae family. Its extremely thick trunk can store tens of thousands of gallons of water. Its very small branches, leafless in the winter months, are covered in the summer with palm-shaped glossy leaves and large single white flowers that open at night. Baobabs can live to over 100 years and maybe very much longer. Trees such as the baobab and the fromagier have served as a focus for village communities over the centuries and serve as the mystic burial places for the local *griots*.

Several of the authors use aspects of the physical geography to illustrate their thoughts or express people's moods and perceptions. Birago Diop, for example, in "Souffles," talks about the wind; he compares the breath of the ancestors to the wind and to the trees that rustle by the river. Several writers make reference to the fact that water is often scarce, unreliable, and precious. Charles Cheikh Sow, in *Cycle de Sécheresse*, talks about the problem of lack of water, and the reaction of animals as they approach, and can smell, the presence of water-only to find that water encased in a cement canal reserved for human use in the city (of St. Louis). He thus laments that water which belongs to everyone, water of the earth that runs beneath one's feet, is available only to those who can get it out of a faucet and who will use it even to water flowers and wash cars while the poor and animals die of thirst. Rainfall in Senegal is unpredictable; drought is common, especially in the north of the country. Here livestock are raised and herded to make maximum use of the sporadic, localized rainfall. Further south in the savannah zone, the seasonal summer rainfall is used for growing the typical Sahel savannah crops of sorghum and millet, as well as cash crops, especially of groundnuts/peanuts. In this middle region of the country crops depend almost entirely on rainfall for their survival and growth. In the more well-watered south of the country, rice and other crops can be grown.

On this unique physical environment the cultural environment has developed.

Second, in terms of the cultural environment, Senegal, as so many countries in Africa, has a great diversity of peoples within its boundaries. At least twenty ethnic groups exist, none with an overall majority, although the Wolof make up the largest group. The boundaries of the country, as with other African countries, were drawn with scant, if any, attention to the wishes of the local inhabitants. At the Berlin Conference in 1884-1885 not a single African was present. Consequently some ethnic groups are split by these artificially imposed boundaries while in other places mutually hostile ethnic groups were included within the same country. The clash of ethnic groups and their perceived stereotypes play a major role in the plot of *La princesse de Thiali*, while the mosaic of very different and warring ethnic groups is also dealt with in Birago Diop's *Contes d'Amadou Koumba*.

Religion is a vital and influential part of culture. In Senegal, over the centuries, people's religions have changed. Respect for the ancestors and the spirits, and what had been called the pantheism of fetishism are still prevalent, though overlain in most of the country today by Islam. Indeed, ninety percent of the population is currently classified as Muslim, although one is reminded of a saying of the late Houphouët-Boigny, former president of Côte d'Ivoire: "Scratch a Christian, scratch a Muslim and you will find an animist underneath." In Senegal, Muslim brotherhoods exert considerable power—not just spiritual, but political and economic as well. The Mouride Brotherhood, for example, founded in 1887 by Amadou Bamba, with its center at Touba, has wielded power for many decades, as has the older Tijaniya Brotherhood especially in northeast Senegal among the Tukulur. The religious leaders, or *marabouts*, feature in some of the literature. Children may be given by their parents to these religious leaders to become their disciples; children who, dressed in tattered clothing, beg from daybreak to dusk. Mosques reflect this part of Senegalese culture on the landscape—mosques with an enormous variety of building styles, architecture, and materials. Religion and its impact feature in a number of ways in the literature. Birago Diop, for example, in "L'Os," collected in *Les Contes d'Amadou Koumba*, refers to the *marabouts*, "inch allah," saying prayers, and so on.

Beggars, who, in Islam, provide a worthy object of charity, have an influence and role in society which may even become the focus of novels. Aminata Sow Fall's *La grève des bàttu* is a satire of what happens when beggars go on strike and the problems that are caused when these recipients of charity are no longer easily accessible. Religion—in this case Islam—is also relevant in understanding polygyny and the conflicts and difficulties it causes. Mariama Bâ's *Une si longue lettre* illustrates the tensions and suffering that occur when a man takes a second wife. Given the role and position of women in Islam, as well as the hard physical labor required of women in the countryside, one can understand more easily why a young girl would be attracted to and want to marry an old man in the city, even to become his second wife. Life in a comparatively rich man's house in Dakar can certainly be appealing when compared with life in the countryside. Ousmane Sembène, in *Ses trois jours*, recognizes and attacks polygamy for being at the basis of most domestic disputes. Indeed, Islam underlies so much of the culture that most of the literature can be understood only in its context.

Islam has greater adherence in the northern and central parts of Senegal. But in the south and in the cities, Christianity is also part of the cultural milieu and is represented in the landscape. Some ethnic groups resisted the spread of Islam and converted to Christianity during the French period. Others, during the period of early French encroachment, used Islam as a weapon to oppose the increasing French power. The first president of Senegal was a Roman Catholic, Léopold Sédar Senghor, a Serer. His writing reflects some of his Christian heritage. Churches and even cathedrals exist in the towns and cities and in the Christian areas of the country.

In terms of the cultural environment, one strong and lasting influence has been that of the French. In so many ways their impact was profound. Colonialism brought with it both advantages and disadvantages. Use of a global lingua franca, improved hygiene and medicine, technology, education, development of infrastructure including railroads, roads, electricity and running water, and the growth of towns and cities, may be considered some of the positive effects of the French. However, even these relatively positive factors have had their downside. Use of the French language undermined the development of local indigenous languages and created bilingual dualism. Writing reduced the power of the oral tradition, though it also enabled its preservation, as in Birago Diop's *Contes et lavanes* and his *Contes d'Amadou Koumba*. The irony is that had there been no French language, these stories would have been almost entirely inaccessible to the West.

The arrival of western medicine and hygiene upset the equilibrium between people and their environment, leading in the years after independence especially to a huge population explosion, which in turn created stress on the natural resources and the environment. Senegal's population has risen from an estimated 3.2 million at independence in 1960 to almost 10 million today. The development of infrastructure led to the ability of the French to increase exports of some of Senegal's resources. It also led to greater inequalities among people, particularly between traditional rural dwellers and people living in the burgeoning cities. This gap continues to increase. Population distribution was also affected: rural to urban migration has led to an over-concentration of people in the western part of the country, especially in Dakar, which is now home to more than twenty percent of the entire country's population.

On the more distinctly negative side can be seen the disruption of traditional ways of life caused by colonialism, and cultural conflict that is described in *L'appel des arènes* by Aminata Sow Fall. Here the protagonist's family struggles with the difference between traditional African and European values. It is only through a return to traditional African values as symbolized by the wrestling match, that the character can feel complete. Another of Mariama Bâ's novels, *Un chant écarlate*, also deals with the inevitable clash of culture, of attitudes, customs, and practices, symbolized in the marriage of a French woman to a Senegalese man.

European power struggles led not only to the imposition of unnatural boundaries, which, for example, cut off the Casamance from the main body of the country, but also brought feelings of inferiority to the Senegalese in many ways, both overt and more subtle. Cultural values transcend language and use of a language is so much more than just words. Ambivalence about the French and a love-hate relationship that developed permeates much of the literature. Senghor's *Hosties noires* and *Chants d'ombre* deal with the revolt of people who have learned to be proud of their "négritude" and their roots, and to regard them as superior to those of whites. Stories of how people have to leave their old familiar ways and environments, maybe for education as in the case of Camara Laye's *L'Enfant noir* (a novel set in Guinea), or for other reasons, as illustrated in *Le Baobab fou*, reflect something of the pain resulting from the colonial period and its aftermath. Senghor's *Joal* speaks of his feelings about his home town. The conflicts that arise from two very different outlooks on life—tradition and modernity—are well illustrated in Hamidou Kane's *L'Aventure ambiguë*. The conflict can also take on religious overtones. Is one tempted to accept a "new" religion (e.g.

Christianity) in order to have greater progress and develop a different attitude toward the environment?

Third, in terms of the economic environment, there is much that affects both the Senegalese authors and their writings. One of the major challenges facing Senegal is poverty. Reference has already been made to the beggars in the city. It is also in the cities where the contrasts between rich and poor are so visible. Senegal has an average annual per capita gross national income of just $1480 (using Purchasing Power Parity), which places it in the lower group of developing countries in the world. The poverty is reflected not only in the country's low per capita GNI and lack of economic development but also in its low human development. Senegal ranks 154th out of 173 countries according to the 2002 United Nations *Human Development Report*. According to that report, literacy, for example, is a low 37 percent (47 percent for men but only 28 percent for women). Certainly there is a small educated middle class, found primarily in the cities, but there is profound poverty in both villages and the urban areas, where hundreds of thousands live in impoverished *bidonvilles* (squatter settlements) and slums.

Part of the root of poverty may be attributed to traditional beliefs and practices, especially where these conflict with westernized ideas of progress and the more productive and efficient use of resources and the environment. Part is the result of endemic slavery, and the removal of tens of thousands of peoples from their homelands to the western hemisphere. However, much of the root of poverty of Senegal lies in the country's colonial history. To help pay for their military campaigns and the cost of administering the areas it conquered, the French demanded that people grow peanuts as a cash crop. From the 1840s onward, peanuts have been exported to France, and to this day 40 percent of the cultivated land is devoted to peanut cultivation. Peanuts quickly degrade the quality of the soil and in places have pushed out the growing of food crops. Colonialists also cut down forests to make room and provide materials for the railroad, as Senghor points out. Industry, small though it is, has caused pollution of air, water, and land.

Not only do the present difficult economic conditions directly affect the authors, who have to contend with inadequate electricity, water supplies, and other necessities. They also affect the literary works themselves. The impact of colonialism in economic terms is vividly reflected in the literature of Senegal. The fact that the French colonialists lived so much above the economic levels of the vast majority of the population, and the treatment meted out by the French to the indigenous population led to tensions that burst out in a number of different ways. Ousmane Sembène sets his novel, *Les Bouts de bois de Dieu,* in Thiès in the 1947-48 railway strike provoked by the racially unequal pay, the poor conditions the railway workers suffered, the shacks in which they were forced to live, the struggles they had to make ends meet, etc., in contrast to the nice colonial homes and lifestyles of the French. That first railroad in West Africa to link the two main French-built cities of Dakar and St. Louis, constructed in 1885 (which also gave peanut farmers along its route a boost), and later between Dakar and Bamako, present capital of neighboring Mali, cost a lot both financially and in human lives. Its purpose was to enlarge French control of the area and make it easier to bring out resources.

Nowhere is the colonial heritage more visible or powerful than in the cities. Dakar, for example, was laid out by the French after 1857, with wide boulevards, squares ("places"), and French-style buildings, both public and private. The port was dredged and developed by the French to serve as a naval base and also to improve trade and commerce.

From having a very small percentage of its people living in towns and cities in the early twentieth century, Senegal has become increasingly urbanized—32 percent at independence in 1960 and 43 percent today. The urban environment is particularly relevant to the study of the literature, both because the authors themselves live in the cities, especially Dakar, and because it provides the context for many of their plays and novels. Sembène illustrates the plight of poor country dwellers who migrate to Dakar to face city life that contrasts so greatly with their traditional culture of the village. Socé, in *Karim, roman sénégalais,* uses the cities of St. Louis and Dakar as examples of "western civilization"—the clothing, customs, and ways of thinking which he refers to as "Europeanization." Karim, as other characters, is torn between the two cultures, valuing and holding onto ancestral traditions, but also very attracted by western practical modernism, loving traditional music and dance but lured also by western music, poetry, dance, logic, etc.

Yet part of the lack of development in Senegal is the result of post-colonial policies and practices. Aminata Sow Fall's *Le Jujubier du patriarche* explores why and how post-colonial politics are so corrupt.

In conclusion, understanding more of the geographical environment in which the literature is written, therefore, is essential for an appreciation of the plots and stories told, the poetry penned, and the plays written and enacted. Indeed, it is impossible to fully understand the literature without it. Geographers ask why people are currently living in their present conditions and to what extent these are the products of the natural or cultural conditions and their interaction. It considers to what extent they are the results of history and to what extent a function of economic development or lack thereof. An interdisciplinary approach thus contributes enormously to an appreciation of the literature.

Works Cited

Bâ, Mariama. *Une si longue lettre*. Dakar: Nouvelles Editions Africaines, 1986.

____. *Un Chant écarlate*. Dakar: Nouvelles Editions Africaines, 1981.

Bugul, Ken. *Le Baobab fou*. Dakar: Nouvelles Editions Africaines, 1984.

Chevrier, Jacques, ed. *Littérature africaíne: histoire et grands thèmes*. Paris: Hatier, 1990.

____. *Littérature nègre*. Paris: Armand Colin, 1984.

Diop, Birago. *Les Contes d'Amadou Koumba*. Paris: Présence Africaine, 1947.

____. *Les Nouveaux contes d'Amadou Koumba*. Préface de Léopold Sédar Senghor. Paris: Présence Africaine, 1967.

Diop, Boubacar Boris. *Thiaroye Terre rouge. Le Temps de Tamango; suivi de Thiaroye Terre Rouge*. Paris : L'Harmattan, 1981.

____. *Le Temps de Tamango. Le Temps de Tamango; suivi de Thiaroye Terre Rouge*. Paris: L'Harmattan, 1981.

Joubert, Jean-Louis. *Littératures francophones d'Afrique de l'Ouest*. Paris: Éditions Nathan, 1994.

Kane, Cheikh Hamidou. *L'Aventure ambiguë*. Paris: Julliard, 1961.

Laye, Camara. *L'Enfant noir*. Paris: Librairie Plon, 1953.

Ndao, Cheikh Alioune. *Du sang pour un trône*. Paris: L'Harmattan, 1983.

Pélissier, Paul. *Atlas du Sénégal*. Paris: Éditions J.A., 1980.

Sembène, Ousmane. *Les Bouts de bois de Dieu*. Paris: Le livre contemporain, 1960.

____. *Xala*. Paris: Présence Africaine, 1973.

Senghor, Léopold Sédar, ed. *Anthologie de la nouvelle poésie nègre et malgache de langue française*. Paris: Presses Universitaires de France, 1945.

____. *Chants d'ombre*. Paris: Éditions du Seuil, 1945.

____. *Hosties noires*. Paris: Éditions du Seuil, 1948.

Socé, Ousmane. *Karim, roman sénégalais*. Paris: Nouvelles éditions Latines, 1935.

Sow Fall, Aminata. *La Grève des battù, ou, les déchets humains*. Dakar: Nouvelles Editions Africains, 1979.

____. *L'Appel des arènes*. Dakar: Nouvelles Editions Africaines, 1982.

____. *Le Jujubier du patriarche*. Dakar: Editions Khoudia: Centre Africain d'Animation et d' Exchanges Culturels, 1993.

Sow, Charles Cheikh. *Cycle de Sécheresse*. Paris: Hatier, 1983.

United Nations Development Programme. *Human Development Report 2002*. New York: Oxford University Press, 2002.

L'image du Maroc dans le récit de voyage Ibérique XIX-XX siècle

Abdelmouneim Bounou

La recherche sur l'image est une orientation récente dans la littérature comparée. L'image est une représentation individuelle et collective où entrent plusieurs éléments aussi bien intellectuels qu'affectifs, aussi objectifs que subjectifs. Dans ce sens, les récits de voyage renseignent beaucoup sur les structures mentales et psychologiques de ceux qui les rédigent et renvoient souvent à des présupposés d'une représentation collective de l'étranger qu'il convient de décrypter.

Il est intéressant d'étudier l'image que les intellectuels espagnols et portugais perçoivent du Maroc à partir de leur expérience personnelle, leurs relations et leurs lectures quand ces auteurs sont réellement représentatifs et quand ils exercent une influence sur l'opinion publique de leur pays.

L'objectif de cette recherche consiste à analyser certaines œuvres espagnoles et portugaises dans le cadre des récits de voyage que nous considérons assez représentatifs sur le Maroc. Mais avant d'aborder l'étude de ces ouvrages écrits par des voyageurs espagnols et portugais du début du XX siècle sur le Maroc, il serait intéressant de voir les motifs ou les raisons qui ont poussé ces derniers à s'aventurer au coeur du Royaume Chérifien.

En effet on peut trouver deux groupes de voyageurs: des intellectuels assoiffés d'apprendre et de contempler la réalité du pays, de voir et d'étudier les caractéristiques des différentes ethnies, les coutumes des habitants (ethnographie et folklore), d'enregistrer des événements, d'approfondir des histoires, des légendes et des superstitions, d'admirer les anciennes et magnifiques architectures. Ces voyages volontaires et involontaires ont une littérature abondante de choses vues, entendues et racontées qui ont fécondé l'imagination des auteurs. Nous pouvons signaler à titre d'exemples: Herlander Ribeiro, *Uma semana em Marrocos*; A. Myrielles Souto, *Portugal e Marrocos*; et Laudelino Miranda de Melo, *Viagen de Portugal à Espanha e Marrocos e volta*.

La découverte du Maroc par les aventuriers portugais propose à la littérature occidentale des thèmes essentiels. D'autres voyageurs entrent dans le cadre d'une mission officielle, c'est le cas des politiciens, des journalistes et des missionnaires. Dans ce deuxième groupe on compte le médecin et grand écrivain Ricardo Jorge auteur de plusieurs oeuvres aussi bien littéraires que médicales. R. Jorge est invité par le docteur Colombani à voyager pour observer l'action sanitaire engagée par la médecine française notamment contre la peste et étudier les possibilités d'intervenir dans ce domaine au profit du protectorat français.

L'écrivain José de Esaguy est chancelier de la légation à Tanger depuis 1934 et auteur de plusieurs ouvrages historiques, sociologiques sur le Maroc; le journaliste Oldemiro Cesar est auteur de *Terras de misterio*. Il est envoyé par le journal *Diario de noticias* pour enquêter sur la guerre des années vingt qui opposa le Maroc à l'Espagne; l'écrivain et journaliste Antonio de Rocha Junior a fait partie d'une mission d'étude au protectorat espagnol. L'auteur est convié par les autorités espagnoles aux fêtes de Ceuta en 1923, ce qui lui a inspiré la publication de *Terras mouras*.

L'écrivain Urbano Rodrigues père du célèbre professeur Urbano Tavares Rodrigues est envoyé aussi par le journal *Diario de noticias* pour faire une reconnaissance des faits locaux et examiner la possibilité pour le Portugal d'avoir des convoitises sur le Maroc au même titre que les français et les espagnols, d'autant plus que le Portugal prétend avoir des "droits historiques" sur le pays.

A ces deux groupes viennent s'ajouter d'autres voyageurs. Nous examinerons leurs récits de voyage dans le cadre de notre présentation des thèmes abordés dans cette littérature.

La présence des espagnols sur la terre arabe est due, comme on sait, au protectorat espagnol dans la zone nord. Assoiffés d'apprendre et de contempler la réalité du pays, et poussés par un patriotisme qui frôle le paternalisme, ils arrivent au Maroc pour découvrir et admirer le travail civilisateur de l'Espagne dans le pays voisin.

Ces intellectuels arrivent au Maroc pour découvrir et décrire la réalité marocaine, et l'image qu'ils traduisent dans leurs oeuvres, répond à une représentation individuelle et collective.

Il est admis qu'aucun étranger ne perçoit un pays comme le veulent les autochtones, comme il est vrai que tout regard étranger transforme la réalité observée.

Dans la plupart des ouvrages que nous avons étudiés, ressort le caractère mystérieux du Marocain. En effet, la première impression qu'éprouve l'auteur du récit est que la personnalité de l'arabe est difficile à comprendre. Son âme ne s'ouvre à personne. C'est le cas d'Herlandér Ribeiro pour qui l'arabe est un problème et une charade:

L'arabe est un problème, une charade, son âme ne s'ouvre à personne; il naît, lutte, combat, tue et meurt, en cachant toujours son esprit à lui qu'il n'extériorise jamais. La vie intellectuelle que j'essaie de décrire en deux lignes est un mythe et n'a pas de révélations à première vue. (79)

Les secrets et les mystères du Maroc sont une énigme pour les étrangers. Dans *Terras de misterio-Marrocos* Oldemiro Cesar, invité par le pacha de la ville, explique qu'il n'a arrive pas à discerner et à interpréter ou comprendre le sourire énigmatique et mystérieux. Dans ce même sens, Rocha Junior affirme, dans *Terras mouras* qu'il n'a pas réussi à comprendre et à pénétrer la pensée du personnage de Bennouna, ministre des finances du protectorat espagnol. Au cours d'une fête, le personnage de Bennouna sourit, converse, danse, mais l'auteur n'arrive jamais à comprendre le vrai visage et les vraies pensées du *gentleman* marocain envers les espagnols et les portugais. Sa prémonition se confirme, 15 jours plus tard, quand les espagnols réprimeront une rébellion armée aux portes de Tétouan et découvriront que les principaux acteurs faisaient partie du gouvernement arabe de l'époque.

Pour Antonio de Escamilla, l'arabe est un être dissimulé et discret. Son intimité est sacrée; sa femme et ses enfants mènent une vie toujours à l'écart de la curiosité étrangère. Tout contact avec le monde extérieur peut être susceptible du mauvais oeil:

Le maure est dissimulé, discret. Mais soyez sûr que, sans
le savoir, vous avez donné du travail aux imams car tout
de suite après, ils emmèneraient les enfants dans les
mosquées pour les préserver du mauvais oeil. (161)

Urbano Rodrigues insiste sur la difficulté de comprendre l'arabe
comme un obstacle pour comprendre le Maroc. Pour ce voyageur
portugais, l'arabe diffère beaucoup du français, de l'italien et du russe
(Rodrígues 97).

A notre avis, cette apparence mystérieuse que découvrent les
occidentaux, en général, et les ibériques en particulier, est due aux
différences linguistiques et aux spécificités culturelles; à l'ignorance
mutuelle et au traumatisme qu'ont connu les arabes à la suite de
l'expansionnisme européen. L'impact social de l'intervention militaire et
la mise en place d'un système socio-politique complètement étranger ont,
en fait, engendré des séquelles au niveau socio-culturel.

Une autre caractéristique de la société marocaine, soulignée dans
la plupart des textes ibériques est la conciliation entre le caractère
traditionnel et l'apport de la modernité. Morale religieuse et légèreté des
mœurs, civilisation et barbarie, en présence côte à côte, sont une autre
spécificité qui frappe le voyageur ibérique du monde arabe en général et
du Maroc en particulier. La culture marocaine est une culture à base
religieuse. "Saints", "zaouias", "cultes de gins", mosquées, synagogues,
églises, forment la topographie intellectuelle marocaine. Quand l'imam
annonce l'heure de la prière, une mélancolie vague (Ribiero 15-6) envahit
les âmes.

Antonio de Escamilla nous explique comment, en entendant,
pour la première fois, l'appel solennel et troublant de la prière, il sent une
émotion indescriptible:

Je l'avais lu, pittoresquement raconté par des plumes
fidèles sous la dictée d'éminents cerveaux et je vous
déclare avec toute la franchise qui a porté préjudice à ma
vie sociale, que dans son ambiance et en l'écoutant pour
la première fois, l'appel à la prière provoque une émotion
indescriptible. (de Escamilla 93)

Dans la zone du protectorat espagnol, Tétouan apparaît comme la ville la plus religieuse de toute la partie nord du royaume:

> Tétouan, ville sainte, parce que dans chaque quartier il y a une mosquée, dans chaque partie il y a une zaouia, dans chaque coin, un mihrab, car chaque maison appartient à un chérif qui reconnaît Sidi Said comme chef tutélaire. (15-6)

> Quand il y a appel à la prière (Azala), dans les cafés, les guembris se taisent. (94)

Le porugais Cesar Oldemiro met l'accent, depuis le début de son récit, *Terras de misterio-Marrocos* sur l 'importance du facteur religieux. L'écrivain remarque que si l'arabe est de nature fanatique et rebelle, il est, en échange, en matière religieuse, très obéissant:

> Il ne discute pas le pourquoi de cette obéissance et aspire seulement à pénétrer les secrets de sa religion pour se convertir en homme illustre et en marabout respecté. (34)

Les deux voyageurs soulignent l'importance de l'élément religieux dans les pratiques des habitants et ne cachent pas leur fascination devant une telle soumission aux préceptes religieux, d'autant plus que la religion musulmane apparaît comme une arme dangereuse et terrible, pointée constamment vers l'européen:

> Dans tous leurs actes sociaux et jusque même dans leur regard, les maures cachent toute une poésie de reconquête. (35)

Pour les voyageurs ibériques, l'imam et le mendiant, la prière et l'aumône synthétisent durant quelques instants, et avec une éloquence singulière, le crédo musulman (de Escamilla 94).

A coté des lieux du culte et du mysticisme, le voyageur ibérique découvre des zones de distraction, du vice, de la promiscuité et de la prostitution. C'est le cas du "quartier réservé" à Casablanca, pour la vie facile, en référence a la prostitution des femmes et des dancings de type parisien, là où on chante et là où on sert du champagne:

> Des femmes maures, semi-dévêtues, dansent à la manière arabe dans une petite enceinte, pleine de fumée, l'ambiance est lourde, malsaine. (Ribeiro 11)

La ville de Tanger est un autre exemple de profanation. Antón del Olmet nous explique que c'est "la ville la plus vicieuse et la plus anarchique du monde". La corruption, la perversion, le vice et les orgies sont monnaies courantes dans la ville cosmopolite:

> Dans cette ville où l'Afrique commence et où l'Europe se relâche, le péché a cherché son nid pervers et secret. (del Olmet 170)

A Tanger on voit des femmes de toutes les races: juives, arabes, françaises, anglaises, allemandes, toutes audacieuses et assoiffées de liberté. Pour Antón del Olmet, ce sont des femmes mystérieuses et libertines qui:

> parlent toutes les langues, dépensent de l'argent à tort et à travers, chassent, montent à cheval, se baignent en maillot, giflent le satyre inopportun et se ruinent pour un garçon de café. (171)

Le primitivisme est une autre caractéristique de la société marocaine de l'époque du protectorat, aux yeux de ces voyageurs. En effet, les intellectuels espagnols et portugais ne cessent de remarquer la forme des costumes traditionnels et "primitifs". Quelques scènes rappellent à Ricardo Jorge, le grand médecin portugais, certaines images anciennes de l'Egypte du temps de Jésus:

> Quelquefois, j'ai l'impression d'apercevoir la fuite de Jésus, Marie et Joseph vers l'Egypte: mais, ici, Joseph marche à califourchon, Marie marche à pied, son paquet de linge sur la tête et portant son enfant dans un sac sur le dos. (258)

Parallèlement à ce spectacle primitif des habitants des petits villages, l'auteur portugais décrit les voitures qui circulent sur les grandes routes et qui sont conduites par les mêmes indigènes, mais cette fois-ci à la manière occidentale.

Pour sa part, Antón del Olmet souligne le caractère traditionnel de la vie rurale; on cultive la terre comme on l'a toujours fait. Le soir dans les petits villages, résonnent des couplets pleins de "barbarie" et d'exotisme; le marocain préfère la "lebda" (le tapis) à la chaise; les malades se rendent aux sanctuaires pour demander pardon et chercher la bénédiction; les armes sont les uniques institutions et ce que désire un arabe se résume en un fusil, un cheval et une femme (13, 57, 65, 94).

Le marocain est superstitieux et voit le surnaturel dans différents événements qui lui arrivent; les sultans et les riches possèdent des harems; le *Zetat,* classique institution du Maroc, est un garant qui promet de conduire saints et saufs les voyageurs à travers le territoire de sa Kabylie en échange d'une rémunération.

Les Chorfas ou descendants du prophète Mohammed, musulmans vénérés, réussissent à réconcilier les familles, les factions et des communautés entières grâce seulement au rôle bénéfique que représente dans la société marocaine, la mémoire des vieux comme élément de jugement.

Parfois, l'intellectuel voyageur se défait de ses jugements "objectifs" et embrasse le pittoresque et l'exotique de la réalité marocaine. C'est le cas de l'espagnol Antón del Olmet quand il s'enfonce dans les montagnes de Tétouan et découvre dans une somptuosité scénique sublime où se détachent figuiers de barbarie et dromadaires:

L'Afrique! Figuiers de Barbarie et bandes de dromadaires. J'ai vu de grands troupeaux de ces ruminants difformes, paisibles et dociles. . . . Qu'est ce qu'ils sont en harmonie avec le paysage, et quel prestige donnent-ils à la plaine! Ils sont le décor vivant de la scène barbare. Moi, je n'aime l'Afrique ni pour sa fertilité somnolente, ni pour ses abrupts rochers, ni pour ses étranges habitants, ni pour ses mystères et ses légendes. Je l'aime pour ses poétiques dromadaires. (88)

Antonio de Escamilla est un ami passionné du Maroc. Depuis la première à la dernière page de son récit *Marruecos visto y soñado*, l'auteur ne cesse de poétiser le paysage et la réalité marocaine et faire ressortir le pittoresque du pays. Un arôme d'attraction et un parfum de douceur marquent ses notes.

Dans la ville marocaine, le maure est gai "il vend du tabac, du bruit, des éclats de rire et de l'allégresse." L'arabe est hospitalier et noble: "Pour le gagner il suffit de faire appel à son geste spirituel" (del Olmet 46). L'intérieur de sa maison suggère le rêve; sa culture "sui géneris" d'entente et de cœur impose le respect au passager.

Tétouan se conserve pure et simple, pleine de mystère et d'enchantement, ses ruelles sinueuses et sombres, ses magasins "barbares", ses caractéristiques raciales, sa digne humilité, ses "douceurs poétiques" séduisent le voyageur jusqu'à l'extase (de Escamilla 16).

Le dialogue et le métissage des cultures constituent d'autres thèmes importants autour desquels se développent tous les récits de voyage ibériques. Les auteurs que nous avons étudiés illustrent la présence de cet élément leitmotiv dans les composantes de la réalité socio-culturelle marocaine: race, langue, religion, art, tradition.

Dans leur majorité, les personnages qui traversent ces récits de voyage proviennent d'horizons différents et forment une mosaïque raciale originale. A l'intérieur même de ces catégories constituées par les arabes, les européens, les berbères et les noirs, nous pouvons trouver une variété entre latins et anglo-saxons, rifains et soussis, moresques et séfarades.

Comment se présentent cette diversité raciale et culturelle? Rocha Junior nos décrit dans *Terras mouras*, comment à Ceuta, le ministre des finances du protectorat espagnol présente cette ville comme un creuset où reposent les morts des trois grandes races qui l'ont conquise:

Ici et aujourd'hui se réunissent les trois races qui ont conquis Ceuta. Les arabes, les portugais et les espagnols. Cette terre est sacrée pour nous tous, car nous avons tous nos morts ici. (35)

Quant à Herlandér Ribeiro, il décrit la diversité des catégories de travailleurs qui vivent au Maroc. Des travailleurs "maures" cohabitent avec leurs collègues espagnols, français, turcs, juifs, portugais et italiens.

Plus tard, quand il trace un panorama politico-social, l'auteur essaie d'expliquer le caractère audacieux et méfiant du marocain par la mixture des races, des religions et de langues anciennes telles que les carthaginois, les grecs et les romains:

> Comme l'histoire du Maroc remonte à une certaine époque des carthaginois, grecs et romains, caractérisée par un grand mélange de races , de religions et de langues, le musulman marocain d'aujourd'hui continue d'être de nature rusée, audacieuse et méfiante; il est le résultat d'apports divers constituant un héritage atavique caractérisé par tous les défauts et les rares vertues du passé avec plus de défauts que de qualités. (Junior 40)

Dans les terres rifaines de Sidi Moussa, Zegangan, Antón del Olmet admire le spectacle du souk là où trafiquent chrétiens et maures en fraternelle harmonie. A Tétouan, Antonio de Escamilla contemple émerveillé l'hétérogénéité de la réalité tétouanaise. Dans son aspect général, la vie dans la "colombe blanche" est une promiscuité spécifique, une mixture kaléidoscopique de traits, une alternance entre le profond et le superficiel (36).

A Tanger, l'hétérogénéité ethnique explique son cosmopolitisme. La présence de différentes races donne à la topographie de cette ville un aspect syncrétique. Urbano Rodrígues est surpris quand il entend les gens parler en différentes langues: espagnol, français, anglais et portugais en même temps. Dans le commerce, toutes les monnaies circulent de la peseta, du réal, du franc à l'escudo:

> Ici, toutes les monnaies circulent dans le commerce, mais le franc reste l'unique monnaie légale. (21)

Un autre élément qui ressort nettement dans les récits de voyages est la liberté de culte. Il est vrai que la convivialité et la tolérance qui marquent la vie religieuse marocaine ne cessent d'éblouir et d'imposer le respect à tous les intellectuels sans exception . La description de la liberté du culte dans *Uma semana em Marrocos* illustre combien H. Ribeiro est fasciné devant la tolérance et la fraternité entre les trois religions monothéistes:

> Au Maroc il y a aussi beaucoup de juifs, qui possèdent de splendides synagogues, des cimetières et des hôpitaux. Le reste de la colonie est catholique: français, italiens, portugais et maures convertis. Il y a de belles églises, modernes, de formes élégantes et sobres. De la liberté du culte et de la non imposition de n'importe quelle religion ou croyance naît le respect mutuel et la tranquillité de tous. Dans tous les aspects, le Maroc est un modèle pour tous les hitlers d'aujourd'hui. (87)

L'exemple parfait du métissage culturel, on le trouve dans la femme propriétaire du Restaurant *Coq d'Or*. En effet, comme nous la décrit le portugais H. Ribeiro, c'est le prototype de la femme acculturée et métisse. Arabe, elle est mariée à un français, elle parle le français et veut lire *Os lusíadas* de Camões. La cuisine qu'elle prépare est une synthèse de plats universels:

> Tous les plats se font à la manière arabe, même le tournis
> à la française et la langouste à l'américaine. (74)

Il est vrai que l'image du Maroc à travers les récits de voyage espagnols et portugais correspond à un univers où différents groupes ethniques entrent en contact direct et continu aboutissant à une culture complètement métisse. En vertu de ce contact, le Maroc apparaît comme un croisement de cultures et de communautés qui s'entremêlent et se superposent débouchant sur une culture originale.

Les deux dates historiques 711 et 1578 continuent à nos jours à conditionner la conception du Maroc dans les récits de voyage espagnols et portugais. La première date correspond à l'invasion arabe de la péninsule ibérique et instaure un long processus – plus de 8 siècles de présence arabe dans cette partie de la péninsule appelée "Andalousie". Si tous les intellectuels espagnols se souviennent de l'apport bénéfique de la civilisation arabe en Espagne, certains voient dans l'intervention espagnole au Nord de l'Afrique une espèce de revanche historique contre l'arabe et un accomplissement du Testament d'Isabelle de Castille.

Ainsi, dans son récit sur le Maroc, Antón del Olmet ne cesse d'admirer le travail civilisateur de L'Espagne dans la zone du Nord. L'Espagne est en train de réaliser un effort "titanique" au Maroc. On investit des milliards; des généraux, des officiers et des soldats tombent dans les champs de bataille; les élèves chantent l'hymne national espagnol en classe et reconnaissent "le salut d l'Espagne"; il y a des "petits juifs" cireurs et "maures" qui vendent du tabac; une goutte de sang espagnol vaut toute la zone marocaine (15, 67, 48, 22).

Dans ses notes il décrit avec exotisme, passant par un patriotisme aveugle et un impérialisme déterminé pour terminer dans le racisme et la xénophobie (79, 80, 90). Il n'est pas nécessaire de faire ici un procès au voyageur Antón del Olmet pour les mensonges, la grossièreté, les énormités dues à l'ignorance de l'histoire et à un patriotisme aveugle, car beaucoup de ses contemporains prouvent le contraire de ses fantaisies délirantes. De telles opinions sont dues, à notre avis, au traumatisme lointain de la période andalouse qui continue à être mal acceptée par un certain nombre d'auteurs, et surtout à la frustration causée par les défaites subies par l'Espagne face à l'expansion américaine à la fin du XIX siècle. En 1898, l'Espagne avait, en effet, perdu deux dernières colonies, à savoir Cuba et les Philippines. Ainsi, après plus de trois siècles durant lesquels l'Espagne avait découvert, conquis et colonisé presque toute l'Amérique Latine; après la gloire de l'ancien empire, elle se retrouve reléguée au second plan sur la scène internationale. Le Maroc est l'équivalent, donc, d'une terre promise dans laquelle l'espagnol aspire à *corriger* les erreurs et les déroutes antérieures et récupèrer le temps perdu dans une aventure digne de Don Quichotte.

La deuxième date 1578 correspond pour les portugais au traumatisme de Ksar El Kébir. Il s'agit de la bataille connue sous le nom de *La Bataille des Trois Rois* ou de *La Bataille d'Oued el Majazen* en référence au lieu sur lequel se déroula la confrontation. Le roi du Portugal Sebastião et les deux rois du Maroc Abdelmalek et el Moutaouakkil sont tombés morts dans cette Bataille. Les conséquences furent désastreuses pour le Portugal qui a perdu son indépendance au profit de l'Espagne.

Dans *Viagens de Portugal a Espanha e Marrocos e volta*, Laudelino Miranda de Melo décrit le choc psychologique qu'il a senti en passant par la petite ville de Ksar El Kébir:

> Ainsi, après avoir traversé les stations de Cuesta Colorado, Arcila, Gortazar, Mtaran Mehacen... surgit brusquement Ksar el Kébir. Devant ce nom, j'ai eu des souvenirs de certaines pages tristes de notre histoire. J'ai eu l'impression de voir les armées en lutte en train de combattre désespérément. Des voix de commandements. Des cris de guerre. Des chevaux hennissant avec nervosité. Leurs pattes avant bien droites. Des chevaliers furieux s'emportent ensanglantés. L'honneur et la noblesse du Portugal sont tombés par terre dans la poursuite désespérée d'une cause caressée par le rêve du Roi Sebastião! Le désiré. . . . Et profitant du moment d'arrêt du train, je descendis. . . . Et en supposant que cette vaste terre (sur laquelle pâturaient quelques ânes) était la terre que les guerriers portugais avaient laissée tâchée de sang (et en vérité c'était une terre rougeâtre), je m'inclinai et je ramassai un petit bout de terre dans la main et j'observai, de manière protocolaire, un moment de silence. (18-9)

La citation est assez longue; mais elle est indispensable pour une compréhension des séquelles de cette fameuse *Bataille des Trois Rois* toujours présente dans la mémoire et la conscience collectives portugaises. L'auteur nous explique comment en écoutant le nom de Ksar el Kébir toute une page triste de l'histoire portugaise surgit de sa mémoire pour lui rappeler qu'il était sur le même terrain qui a vu succomber ses proches dans la défense d'une cause que le rêve de Dom Sebastião avait caressée. L'émotion que ressent L.M. de Melo n'est pas un cas exceptionnel. En effet, tous les intellectuels portugais qui sont venus vivre ou visiter le Maroc ne cessent d'exprimer leur nostalgie et leur tristesse devant un événement déterminant du XVI siècle. A notre avis, une grande partie de l'attachement porté au Maroc doublé d'une méconnaissance du pays, est due à ce complexe historique de 1578 qui n'a cessé de conditionner les rapports des portugais avec le Maroc.

Dans son apologie de la Diaspora, José de Esaguy nous rappelle dans son livre intitulé *Marrocos* que dans son projet expansionniste, le jeune Roi portugais Don Sebastião avait promis à ses disciples qu'il convertirait les juifs de Tanger au christianisme. Par conséquent, l'appui retiré au souverain lusitain et l'influence des juifs s'est faite sentir chez les empereurs marocains. Rappelons à ce propos que l'élément juif constituait une composante essentielle de l'appareil gouvernemental marocain tout au long des siècles antérieurs.

Ricardo Jorge, lui, découvre, avec surprise, à Safi, le nom de "Sebastianus Rex" gravé sur un canon de l'artillerie portugaise du temps de la bataille des Trois Rois et éprouve une nostalgie et une tristesse en évoquant l'empire et la splendeur du Portugal. L'auteur de *De Ceca e Meca* puise dans sa fantaisie délirante et commence, sous forme d'un dialogue avec, "Le désiré".

Le lecteur attentif découvrirait que l'amour profond que voue le voyageur portugais au Maroc est dû surtout à une nostalgie des siècles écoulés et à un désir inconscient de récupérer l'empire et la gloire de jadis. Les ruines historiques qui datent du passé colonial portugais et l'architecture de style "manuélin" dans les villes côtières réveillent chez le lusitain des sentiments de gloire passée et du déclin qui a suivi.

U. Rodrigues nous explique qu'une excursion au nord de l'Afrique ne constitue pas un pas quelconque. Pour lui, visiter le Nord de l'Afrique constitue un pèlerinage à l'un des lieux saints du patrimoine portugais, et contribuera à enflammer l'amour patriotique et à fortifier l'âme (9-10).

Pour conclure, disons que les récits de voyage portugais et espagnols constituent une représentation individuelle et collective dans laquelle entrent plusieurs éléments intellectuels, affectifs, objectifs et subjectifs. Ces récits jouent d'une ambivalence descriptive et émotionnelle. Hommes mandatés officiellement, explorateurs solitaires espagnols et portugais aboutissent à une reconnaissance du territoire et à l'introspection des ressorts de la société marocaine. L'exotisme colore le récit de l'expérience personnelle du dépaysement; le topos du passé, la poétique des ruines, l'orientalisme (le thème exotique des mille et une nuits) et le pittoresque sont des thèmes qui ne cessent d'être exploités par un grand nombre de voyageurs et de touristes débouchant sur une vision transfigurée de la réalité.

Les écrits espagnols sont écrits avec un point de mire artistique et un dessein patriotique parce que leurs auteurs voulurent concilier le réel avec l'utopique. Dans certaines notes, nous sentons un arôme pénétrant d'attraction, de fraternité; dans d'autres, le patriotisme aveugle conduit à un subjectivisme dédaigneux. Dans les récits portugais, nous trouvons la nostalgie de la splendeur du Portugal, l'orgueil des fortifications historiques et surtout un sentiment de fraternité, d'amitié, d'amour et d'identification. Le voyageur portugais paraît effectuer un retour aux sources en remontant vers les origines des maures de Lisbonne.

Sans pour autant nous faire oublier les transformations et les exagérations de la réalité signalées plus haut, la perception de notre pays à travers ces récits de voyage reste une illustration éloquente d'une vision très particulière qui mérite notre attention.

Works Cited

Cesar, Oldemiro. *Terras de misterio-Marrocos*. Lisboa: Diario de notícías, 1925.

de Esaguy, José. *Marrocos*. Lisboa: Edição de Europa, 1933.

de Escamilla, Antonio. *Marruecos visto y soñado*. Barcelona: Artes gráficas Carlos Sabadell, n. d.

de Melo, Laudelino Miranda. *Viagens de Portugal a Espanha e Marrocos e volta*. N.p.: n.p, n.d.

del Olmet, Juan Antón. *Marruecos: de Melilla a Tánger*. Madrid: Imprenta de Juan Pueyo, 1916.

Jorge, Ricardo. *De ceca e meca*. Lisboa: Edição Minerva, n. d.

Junior, Rocha. *Terras mouras*. Lisboa: Portugália Editora, 1925.

Ribeiro, Herlander. *Uma semana em Marrocos*. Lisboa: Edição do autor, 1933.

Rodrígues, Urbano. *Passeio em Marrocos*. Lisboa: Edição da Empresa Nacional de Publicidade, 1935.

Death in Africa in Muammar Qaddafi's "Death" and Ernest Hemingway's "The Snows of Kilimanjaro"

Gudrun M. Grabher

Hemingway's famous short story "The Snows of Kilimanjaro" (first published in *Esquire*, August 1936), belongs to the works of his middle period and illustrates, in J. Bakker's words, "the way in which his discovery of courage as a moral force and professional skill as a means of warding off the threat of emptiness begin to affect the particular cause his fiction was to take" (61). It is a story about death and the (human) fate of mortality. It is, as I will try to show, in this essay, not a story about the failure of a writer (Harry) to write about the things of life, but the great achievement of a writer (Hemingway) to write about the ultimate theme of death.

"[T]he Hemingway hero is always concerned with the problem of death," remarks Joseph DeFalco (DeFalco 195) and continues to argue that the main issue is not so much the inevitability of death as the *way* in which death manifests itself. "The thematic vehicle rests [for him] on a question: 'What is the nature of death?' As it turns out, death comes in many guises, and the symbols which depict it are a catalogue of the central character's life: buzzard, hyena, women, and money. The final approach to death, however, relates to none of these, for it comes in the form of 'Old Compie,' the pilot who 'saves' Harry at the end of the story. It is Harry's ascendance into death in an almost ironic fashion upon which the story hinges" (DeFalco 208). In my interpretation of the story, however, I do not share with DeFalco his ironic reading of "Harry's ascendance into death." Rather, I think that Hemingway is "dead serious" with his way of thematizing death.

The main protagonist Harry, from whose perspective the story is being told, is dying of gangrene, "the local death of soft tissues due to the loss of blood supply; the death of one part of the body while the rest is still alive" (Young 224). What is alive is, above all, his mind, which through reminiscences and visions tries to come to terms with the meaning of his existence while fully aware that it is approaching its inevitable end. Puzzled by the epigraph about the carcass of the leopard that was found high up in the eternal snows of "the House of God," scholars have been tossed about between various interpretations: "The Snows of Kilimanjaro" has been read as the story of a life wasted and of stories unwritten; of the gifted man succumbing to idleness, money, alcohol, women, and mendacity and thus sacrificing both his talents and his duties; of the fallen man redeemed, or not redeemed, through his final moral self-realization; of a man trading "for security his integrity as a writer" (Evans 601); of a man incapable of loving; of an ego's encounter with its alter ego à la Henry James; of an idealist turned materialist and eventually reconciled with his idealism.

I would prefer to argue in none of these directions but rather in the following one. Let me start with Africa, which Oliver Evans explains in its symbolical meaning as follows: "As for the symbols, there is, first of all, Africa itself, the Dark Continent, which stands in the story for the mysterious nature out of which man comes and into which man returns at last" (Evans 602). I would like to identify the Dark Continent with the concrete human existence, the leopard with the abstract framework of existence. Their goal is identical though it remains unknown what the nature of that goal is: death. Of the leopard it says in the epigraph that "No one has explained what [he] was seeking at that altitude" (Hemingway 52). And Harry, approaching the same summit and altitude, realizes "that there was where he was going" (Hemingway 76). Human existence has been described by Existentialist philosophers as a being thrown into the world (cf. e.g. Heidegger). From his first breath man is approaching death, is doomed to die; death is where he is inevitably going. The whiteness of the snows of Kilimanjaro as the symbol of death contrasts with the Dark Continent of his life but also suggests the light of insight. Oliver Evans has rightly featured Hemingway in the company of Hawthorne and Melville—"Hemingway has less in common with Dreiser than with Hawthorne and Melville—the men, as Cowley puts it,

'who dealt in images that were symbols of an inner world'" (Evans 607),
Melville having introduced the lasting metaphysical implications of
whiteness as the absence of color and the simultaneous manifestation of
all colors. Since the plot of the story takes place in Africa, where white
is regarded as the color of death and mourning, the color white is even
more appropriate in its symbolical significance. However, white as
opposed to dark suggests positive connotations. Death as the end of
earthly existence may then be regarded as the light at the end of the long
dark tunnel called life. This life being ultimately meant for death, is
characterized by death from the very start. This is symbolized by the fact
that Harry's leg has been infected (in the Dark Continent) as the result
of a scratch that has not been taken care of. In fact, there is no way to
take care of the sting of death; it even goes unnoticed, at first. On the
other hand, it is the beginning of the rotting process of the body, that
gradually "eats up"[1] the human being and also gradually makes itself
noticed through its growing smell or stink. The fact that it is Harry's leg
rather than any other part of the body that has been infected is no
coincidental detail either. Legs are used for walking, and the human being
walks, or moves, through life. Harry is incapable of walking or moving
because of his infected leg, which suggests that the motion of his life has
come to an end. The rotten leg, by the way, is also strongly reminiscent
of Melville's *Moby-Dick*. Captain Ahab's wooden leg has not only
incapacitated the old man; when his awe-stricken crew is listening to his
nightly wanderings up and down the deck, his healthy and his artificial
leg making different sounds, they reflect: "On life and death this old man
walked" (Melville 335). All the other symbols of Hemingway's
story—such as the hyena, the vultures or buzzards in particular—have
unanimously been seen as representing death, especially so because they
live on carrion. But I would like to go even a step further in arguing that
the hyena and the vulture also represent parts of this particular human
being's character that is moving towards death. The hyena is
characterized as a stinking, grim, cowardly, insatiable, greedy animal that
is generally not inclined to attacking human beings, but patiently waits
for carrion and even likes to dig up corpses. All of these characteristics fit
Harry perfectly: his insatiable voracity (regarding the materialistic luxury
of his life-style as well as his sexual appetites), his grim mood (reflected in
particular in his ways of treating his wife Helen), his stinking, rotting leg,

his cowardice, and his patient expectance of ultimate death. The buzzard or vulture, in addition to his stinking, is described as mean and idle, both characteristics which fit Harry as well. He diagnoses himself as getting bored with everything, even with death: "I'm getting as bored with lying as with everything else, he thought" (Hemingway 73). What is of particular interest in regard to the vulture is that legend has it that there is a so-called holy vulture that is described as being white with black wings, in ancient times even as completely white. As a black-and-white being it would then represent the two sides of death—the one manifest in the earthly existence from the very first moment (black), the other pointing to the whiteness of ultimate death. As the all-white being it would anticipate the snows of the mountain. The vulture being a bird (a bird of prey at that) could also signify Harry's characteristic of being a writer/artist, wings symbolizing his living in imagination, the bird of prey, however, also suggesting that the power of those wings parasitically draws blood from its prey.

If all these symbols are exterior manifestations of Harry's character, that is his interior qualities signifying his death marks, then what aspect of him does his wife Helen symbolize, if she is to be interpreted as an interior aspect of his character and his motion towards death? Along with Evans' allusion to the Jamesian theme of the ego's confrontation with its alter ego, one might argue that Helen represents the female other of his being, the anima against the animus. His relationship to this alter ego or anima is characterized by lying. The untrue, false, mendacious relationship to his other self accounts for a disharmony within his personality that leads to death, especially so as this other is being described as "fine" and "kind" and well-meaning. It is therefore not the female principle as such that stands for death but Harry's not being honest and open with this other side of him and especially his being unable to love her/it that has to be identified with the death principle in himself.

What about the leopard, then? It is the carcass of the leopard that has been found at the unusual altitude, white bones preserved in the whiteness of the snows of Kilimanjaro. Identifying the leopard with Harry one could argue that the skeleton represents the framework of the human existence, which has taken mortal shape on the Dark Continent. The leopard is described as a beautiful animal, enemy of all animals, bold, clever, cunning, and adroit. What's more, it is supposed to be endowed with sharp vision. On the top of the mountain it has seen and recognized death, the impenetrable whiteness, meaning all and nothing. The skeleton having been preserved up there refers to the eternal abstract being as opposed to the concrete, dark mortal existence that is meant to resolve itself in this nothingness of whiteness. Nothingness, as we know from Hemingway's story "A Clean, Well-Lighted Place," is the author's contents of his prayer—nada—fitting well into the "House of God." The top of Kilimanjaro is, indeed, a clean, well-lighted place, with its eternal, impeccable, illuminated and illuminating whiteness which cannot be grasped in its essence. And yet it is there, unmeltable at those altitudes, freezing the everlasting possibility of being. Being and nothingness then become one, such as the carcass/skeleton and the snow become one in their whiteness, hardly discernible from each other.

Hemingway's Kilimanjaro story is a masterpiece of literary reflection about the meaning of the human fate of death, its ungraspable essence in spite of its clean and clear visibility as the ever-puzzling whiteness.

One might feel tempted to create a daring bridge from Hemingway's story to that of Qaddafi by reflecting on the literal meaning of Islam as "total devotion to God" and linking it to the Kilimanjaro as referred to as the "House of God"—death—to which Harry, and the whole story, are devoted. However, there are other parallels to thrive upon.

As is well known, Qaddafi is a literary writer and inclined towards philosophical reflection. Such as Hemingway seems to identify earthly existence with Africa, the Dark Continent, so does Qaddafi interpret life as a battleground, or identify it with the desert. Interestingly enough, both Africa for Hemingway and the desert for Qaddafi are symbols charged with highly positive connotations.

"Is death male or female?" (Qaddafi 81). With this question Qaddafi begins his story "Death," contained in his volume *Escape to Hell and Other Stories*, which was first published in French by Les Editions Favre, Switzerland, in 1996, and in English by Stanké, New York, in 1998. Both the French and the English edition were published with an introduction by Pierre Salinger and were, of course, translated from the original in Arabic.

The book is divided up into two parts, the first of which contains literary pieces, the second one essays on political reflections. As to my knowledge, there is as yet no secondary material available, unless, perhaps, in Arabic, which I am not capable of reading, which is why I will have to content myself with a close reading of the text at hand from my Western/European point of view. Two days before I left for Morocco, however, my attention was drawn to a comment on Qaddafi's literary work which refers to a review in *The Daily Telegraph* published in February 1999. This comment reads as follows:

> The innovativeness, creativity and ideas of the Leader, Muammar Al Qathafi, have been the subject of deliberations by literarians and intellectuals throughout the world. The Leader's works have also been highlighted in the Arab and international press. *The Daily Telegraph* published a detailed analysis of *Escape to Hell* which was reviewed by John Simpson who stressed his admiration and appreciation of the Leader's literary works. He said: "I know Muammar Al Qathafi as a political leader, but now I know him as a novelist as well." Simpson described *Escape to Hell* as a catalogue of humanitarian contemplations about the vicious state of the world. The reality of life, especially human suffering, is described with an unusual fairness. (JANA News Bulletin)

Whether death is male or female God only knows, says Qaddafi in his story "Death," yet continues to argue that the human being wants to, needs to know and that for centuries writers have reflected on this question. Some have identified death as male, others as female. In Jean Cocteau's film, *Orphée*, for example, death is clearly identified as a woman and referred to as "the Princess of Death."

For Qaddafi death is both male and female in the following manner. He says, "If it is male, then we must combat it to the last breath, and if it [is] female, then we should surrender to it in the end" (Qaddafi 81f.). Qaddafi goes on to describe death in a diction strikingly similar to that of Hemingway. He describes death as "fierce and bold, cunning and cowardly sometimes, . . . with unlimited patience" (82). These are exactly the attributes of the hyena and the buzzards which were identified as death symbols in the Hemingway story. And conjuring up the image of Harry's gangrenous leg, Qaddafi argues that the power of death lies "in his evil appetite for sucking the blood from the wounds of his victims, transforming it into his fiery fighting energy, which inevitably leads to his opponent's defeat" (83). Death, according to Qaddafi, "is truly a determined adversary, who never gives up" (82), "maneuvers and changes color like a chameleon" (83), "is a sly fox . . ., capable of taking on different personalities and forms to suit his whim. He may appear as a knight on a white horse" (83). After such general abstract reflections Qaddafi begins to illustrate his arguments by means of recounting several incidents in his father's life where he fought death successfully: he escaped the deadly wounds of nine bullets and the mortal weapons of his enemies in the Italian war; through his will-power and the remedy of strong black tea without sugar he successfully fought the bite of a poisonous snake; he escaped the snake's venomous bite a second time because repeated snake bites had immunized him. "As my father lived on, death retained its ambition; as my father remained stubborn, death continued to try to fell him" (91).

From these incidents Qaddafi draws an interesting conclusion, which has to be understood on the background of his cultural and personal framework. Every threat to man's existence, he argues, is to be interpreted as male, as long as he does not surrender to death. But when the human being eventually gives in to death, then death is to be seen as female. Qaddafi bases his interpretation on a quote from the Quran: "And they make the angels who are the servants of God of Mercy, females" (Sura 43, verse 18; Qaddafi 92). It would also be justified to regard Qaddafi's vision of death as female as the human being's return to the mother's womb, all the more so since Qaddafi, as we know from Mirella Bianco's biography of Qaddafi, always felt very close to his own mother and highly respected her.

In his story on death, Qaddafi intensifies his female image of death by conjuring up the famous Egyptian singer Um Kalthoum:

The drums of death, which got louder, are nothing more
than a hypnotizing song of Um Kalthoum. The nearer

that death approached, the drumbeats became heavier
and more annoying. My father relaxed in his bed, smiling
as innocently as a baby in a cradle. He became more
relaxed and content, until it seemed to us that the noisy
accompaniment of death's chariot, which would frighten
healthy people, was to the sick like a hypnotizing song
by a famous Egyptian singer. (Qaddafi 92)

Both Hemingway and Qaddafi share the belief that death appears
in many guises. The human being is accompanied by death from the very
beginning of his life. The bites of the snake and the wounds inflicted by
the warriors are symbolical reflections of death's constant presence in
Qaddafi's story, such as Harry's gangrenous wound is in Hemingway's.
Qaddafi suggests that in the end man is to give in to death without
fighting back. Of Harry, it is said, towards the end of Hemingway's
story, that "Now he would not care for death" (Hemingway 72). But
while for Hemingway/Harry death finally "has no shape any more" (74),
for Qaddafi death takes shape as a woman, "entering quietly and
enticingly until we feel her in every part of our bodies" (Qaddafi 96).

And there is no escape. "Wherever ye be, death will overtake
you—although ye be in lofty towers!", Qaddafi quotes from the Quran;
not even the lofty towers of the Kilimanjaro, as Hemingway might add.

Works Cited

Bakker, J. *Fiction as Survival Strategy. A Comparative Study of the Major Works of Ernest Hemingway and Saul Bellow*. Amsterdam: Editions Rodopi B.V., 1983.

Bianco, Mirella. *Kadhafi. Messager du désert. Biographie et entretiens*. Paris: Editions Stock, 1974.

Cocteau, Jean. *Orphée*. 1949.

DeFalco, Joseph. *The Hero in Hemingway's Short Stories*. Pittsburgh: University of Pittsburgh Press, 1963.

Evans, Oliver. "'The Snows of Kilimanjaro': A Revaluation." *PMLA* 76 (1961): 601-7.

Hemingway, Ernest. "The Snows of Kilimanjaro." *The Short Stories of Ernest Hemingway*. New York: Charles Scribner's Sons, 1953. 52-77.

JANA News Bulletin. 9 February 1999.

Melville, Herman. *Moby-Dick; or, The Whale*. Harmondsworth: Penguin English Library, 1972.

Qaddafi, Muammar. "Death." *Escape to Hell and Other Stories*. Montréal and New York: Stanké, 1998. 81-96.

Young, Philip. *Ernest Hemingway. A Reconsideration*. New York: Harcourt, Brace & World, Inc., 1966 (1952).

Ancient North-South Links of Language and Culture in Africa

Aidan Southall

There are innumerable north-south and also east-west cultural links, especially in language and oral culture. They are widespread and long term. The links in other aspects of culture behavior may be equally numerous, but are harder to define and compare with precision. They decisively challenge the still prevalent and formerly dominant picture of Africa as a fragmented and atomistic patchwork of totally separate distinctive tribes. The whole concept of the tribe is increasingly coming to be seen as fallacious and untenable (Southall 1970, 1996). Much of the evidence for these links lies in the oral literature, the objections to which are similar to those against oral tradition, long ago disposed of by Vansina (1961).

Many scholars are partially aware of these links, but few have been able to overcome the serious difficulties in the way of achieving any thorough study of these links which does not wander into fantasy.

There are many cases in which items of language and culture, sometimes linked in clusters, passed from group to group over large areas, undergoing modification and transformation, splitting and accretion, as they went. Full documentation is difficult, as some linguistic knowledge is required of languages which may have been in contact, yet belong to quite different language families. The cultural context of the process must also be known, as it can only be by intensive, long term anthropological fieldwork. This is rarely possible and rarely achieved, so that the linguistic and cultural context of these processes is rarely sufficiently studied, and consequently most examples can only be documented in a fragmentary way.

I lived and worked in Buganda for some years, but did fieldwork in the Nilotic area further north, in Uganda, Congo and Sudan, so that I acquired some background knowledge of the context of Bantu and also Nilotic and other neighboring languages. Uganda itself is a great linguistic crossroads.

Some political and ritual concepts provide striking examples. Jok Rubanga is symbolic of the marriage of Bantu and Nilotic culture, with many more far reaching tendrils as well. Jok is the widespread Nilotic term for spirit and deity, circumstantially varying from benign to vengeful.

Kenya	Uganda			Sudan			
WN	WN	WN	EN	WN	WN	EN	WN
Luo	Acoli	Alur	Teso	Dinka	Shilluk	Lotuko	Nuer
Juok	Jok	Jok	Ajokit	Jok	Jok	Ajyok	Joagh
Juogi*	Juogi*	Jogi*		Jaak*			
chien	ceen	Cien		Cien			"ghost"
Jachien	behind	behind		behind			behind
"devil"	venge-ful ghost	ghost		ghost			

* = Plural; WN = West Nilotic; EN = East Nilotic

Rubanga is a more specific, yet ambiguous entity. Although it might seem Bantu in general appearance, yet it relates to a number of Nilotic terms and concepts also. The phonetic value of the term changes (like Jok) in passage from language to language. In none of these cases is any temporal relationship implied.

Nyoro	rubanga	the omu-cwezi of twins
Luganda	lubanga	a god (cf. Lubaale), thwart or seat of canoe (mortised)
Nyoro	ruhanga	cl. I supreme, otiose deity
Nyoro	ruhanga	cl. VI skull
Nyoro	hanga	v.i. to shine at midday (sun)
Nyoro	hanga	v.t. to create, fix in handle, mortise, dig deep, plough

Ganda	wanga	v. tr. injure, fix in handle, mortise, treat badly
Ganda	wanga	n. the oldest of the gods
Ganda	banga	v.tr. found (city), cut notch, mortise, begin at
Nyoro	banga	v.tr. cut notch, mortise
Nyoro	hangahanga	v.tr. to invent
Nyoro	wanga	v. i. to be sharp (knife), strong (sunbeams)

Acoli	bang'i	twins
Teso	ibangin	twins
Madi	rabanga	the Earth, God
Madi	rubangi	God
Ganda	lubaale (pl. baluubaale)	god, deity, spirit (not lu-class)

We see from the above examples how Jok, in its typical western Nilotic monosyllabic form, picks up eastern Nilotic prefixes and suffixes in Teso and Lotuko. Among the distant Nuer, the abstract Jok reveals its concrete correlative "behind," which always carries an inauspicious note among the western Nilotes, highly appropriate to its immaterial significance of "ghost." The other western Nilotes, Luo, Acoli, Alur and Dinka, have variations of the term "cien" for "behind," which as in Nuer, carries with it, the significance of "ghost," even "vengeful ghost" or "devil."

Rubanga calls forth a wide range of overlapping phonemes and meanings. The phonetic equivalents h-b in Nyoro and b-w in Ganda seem to overlap in semantics as well as in sound change. The notions of mortise, notch, handle, are frequently found as symbols of divine creativity. Rubanga and Ruhanga seem quite distinct in meaning and function as well as potentially in phonetics, but further exploration of the relevant roots suggest the surprising conclusion that Rubanga and Ruhanga may be structurally the same. Yet, Ruhanga as otiose creator is quite separate from Rubanga with its specific attributes as God of twins in his membership of the group of legendary deified kings of Bunyoro-Kitara.

Outside Bunyoro, the emphasis changes, as twinship in its potent, mystical fertility aspects, becomes the supreme attribute of kings and of God himself. Rubanga is here the supreme manifestation of Jok in kingship, with an inevitable aura of creative divinity.

With the eastern Nilotic Teso, Rubanga is left behind, but twins are still "ibangin." For the Acoli, twins are also "bang'i," still with the implied Rubanga derivation, whereas for the very closely related Alur, twins are "rut." But according to others, Acoli twins are also "rut."

These exchanges occurred within an area approximately one thousand kilometers from north to south and five hundred from east to west.

More remarkably, Rubanga has also penetrated the theology of the Sudanic speaking Madi and Lugbara, in the forms, respectively, Rabanga (earth, as general creator and god among the Madi), and Orobangi (a shrine, among the Lugbara). It may be assumed that these names were borrowed from the neighboring Nilotes, since they do not have any other phonetic, grammatical or conceptual links with these Sudanic languages. Lubaale is the general name for deities in Buganda, including many that are local and of limited range, but also Nalubaale, the mother of Gods, which is the Ganda name for Lake Victoria. Lubaale appears in Nyoro as rubaale, meaning "a red bull with tiny white spots." In both Nyoro and Ganda, the term appears phonetically to belong to the ru-(lu) class, but in fact grammatically, it does not. In Nyoro, "omuiru lubaale" means a bondslave, while in Ganda "kaddu lubaale" was the title of the king's chief wife. Despite appearances, these two terms have the same structural base. "Omuiru" (s) = slave; "baddu" (pl.) slaves; "iru" after a vowel "a" becomes "-addu," as in the Ganda "kaddulubaale." The "ka" class of nouns is ordinarily diminutive, but in relation to a few concepts of superior importance in the culture, its force is reversed into magnification, viz. Kabaka (king), Katikiro (chief minister), Kaggo (senior county chief), Kawumpuli (plague, deity) and so on. So it is not surprising that the Ganda generated their term for creator god by applying this prefix to the verb stem "to create" (tonda) thus Katonda. Other prefixes change the meaning of the root "baale." Kibaale is the shrine of the deity and Mbaale is a place with important shrines of deities.

Striking linguistic borrowing and transformation took place along the fuzzy and changing border between Bantu and Eastern Nilotes in southern Uganda and western Kenya. I have studies mainly with a focus on the Gisu people of southwestern Mount Elgon. The earliest Europeans called them Masaba, but the colonial regime in ignorance changed this to Gisu, which was the name of one of the many Gisu localized maximal lineages. The Gisu as a whole had little awareness of overall unity, except the realization that they all participated every few years in elaborate circumcision ceremonies. There was no overall organization of all groups concerned, but the rituals passed from group to group in a regular sequence, following a known path. This imparted a flexible degree of cultural unity and social coordination. The Gisu and their neighbors recognized the existence of Masaba, as they lived on part of it. But the name Masaba derives from Masopyisiek, meaning "the people of the top" in the eastern Nilotic language of the Sebei. Masaba therefore properly referred to the top, rather than to the whole mountain. Gisu tradition attributed circumcision to borrowing from the Sebei. The Sebei circumcised boys, and subjected girls to clitoridectomy. The Gisu only circumcised boys, but the operation was very extensive and severe, far more painful than that of the Sebei. But in the passage of circumcision celebrations along the spatial chain, the operation itself was mild as it took off from the Sebei, but became progressively more and more severe at the further end of the cycle. Beyond the Gisu, the Sebei and their immediate neighbors were the Uasin Gishu Masai on the plateau of the same name. Gisu or Gishu in fact means cattle in the languages of the Sebei and Masai. These two latter were pastoralists, whereas the Gishu and their Bantu neighbors were sedentaary cultivators, but kept some cattle.

Gishu was a major ancestral name for the Gisu. Their neighbors, the Vugusu, who also participated in the circumcision cycle, appear also to be called after the Masai cattle, variably gusu, gushu, kusu. Why this should be so has never been explained, although the Masai were a very powerful and dominant, though not a fully united people, occupying an exceedingly large area as nomadic cattle keepers.

In a prevalent myth, the primal ancestor of Gishu (Masaba), meets Nabarwa, a Masai girl, and asks her to marry him. She says she cannot do so unless Masaba is circumcised. He agrees, so she takes him home and he is circumcised, healed and fulfills all the obligations, then returns home with Nabarwa to marry her. They produce the ancestors of the major sub-divisions of the people. Is this a sufficiently profound involvement with the eastern Nilotes to account for the name Gishu? It is a myth, but there is nothing unlikely in Nabarwa having conferred the Gishu cattle name on her offspring, and variants of it on others. The Gishu continued to take their cyclical age class names from the Sebei and their Kalenjin neighbors.

Some two hundred miles south of the Gishu, across the Kavirondo Gulf, live the Gusii. Their ethnic name thus falls well within the range of variation of the Masai cattle name. Stranger still, the Gusii recognize a major division among them, between those having foreign ancestry and the "real Gusii" whom they call Masaba. Gusii oral tradition suggests that they moved south to their present homeland from the Elgon (Masaba) area in the north a number of centuries ago. Thus, these various groups, over the centuries, rang the changes on gishu gisu, gesa, gushu, gusu, gusii, kichu, kusu, kushu.

The analysis of tranformations within a single language group such as Bantu is less remarkable from the point of view of transcending boundaries, but the most beautiful and poetic analysis of the transformations of mythical ideas in Africa is that of Luc De Heusch, who has "completely transformed our understanding of the thought–world of a vast aggolmeration of Central Africa peoples" (viii).

Works Cited

De Heusch, Luc. *The Drunken King, or, the Origin of the State*. Trans. Roy Willis. Bloomington: Indiana University Press, 1982.

Southall, A.W. "Cross Cultural Meanings and Multilingualism." *Language Use and Social Change*. Ed. W.H. Whitely. Oxford: Oxford University Press for the International African Institute, 1971. 376-96.

____. "Getting your Own Spear Back: Alur Society and the Birth of Tragedy." *African and African-American Sensibility*. Ed. M. Coy and L. Plotinicov. Ethnology Monographs 15. Pittsburgh: Department of Anthropology, University of Pittsburgh, 1995. 55-65.

Vansina, Jan. "De la tradition orale: essai de méthode historique." *Annales du Musée Royal de l'Afrique Centrale, Sciences humaines* 36. Tervuren: Musée Royal, 1961.

Classical Swahili Poetry and its Linkage with the Arabic "North"

Elena Bertoncini

Almost all Swahili poetry of the past is deeply religious and rooted in the Arabic world. Hymns, exhortations and versified theological treatises are mostly translations, often considerably abridged, of existing classical Arabic poems.

Most of the Arabic models for Swahili poetry come from the Middle East, but there are also deep-rooted cultural links with Egypt. Thus the oldest surviving Swahili text, the hymn *Hamziya*, dated AH 1062, i.e. AD 1652 (Knappert, *Four Centuries* 104) by Saiyid Aidarus, is a translation of an Arabic poem in the classical style (called *Al-Hamziya* because of its verses rhyming in 'hamza') by the Egyptian poet Sharafu'd-Dini Al-Būsīri (1212-1296). Among the praises of the Prophet is interwoven a romantic story, or rather a legend, of Hadija, who would later become Muhammad's wife, when she saw the Prophet for the first time, riding in the desert with two angels flying above him to protect him from the sunshine. The poem is written in the archaic Swahili, extremely difficult to translate.

Al-Būsīri is known above all as the author of the "Poem of the Mantle" (*Burda*)—a panegyric poem in honor of Muhammad—which has been also translated into Swahili. Both the Arabic and the Swahili version of the *Burda* are recited when a person wants to pray for protection from the evils of this world and from condemnation at the Doomsday. According to Knappert (*Swahili Islamic Poetry* 2: 166), the Swahili version is from the artistic point of view in many ways superior to the Arabic original: the language is simpler, the imagery more direct; the rhythm too is smoother and flows better.

The Maulid, or Muhammad's birthday, is celebrated in most parts of the Islamic world, and during the celebrations, prose and poetic accounts of the Prophet's birth are recited. A very popular Maulid text translated into Swahili was written by another Egyptian poet, Sheikh Muhammad al-'Azbiyy (or al-'Azabī). In Swahili, there are no fewer than three translations of his *Maulidi ya Dāli*—Maulid in verses rhyming in *dā*.

The finest example of homiletic poetry in Swahili is the poem *Al-Inkishafi* by Sayyid Abdallah bin Nassir (1720-1820), an outstanding poet and scholar from Pate. *Al-Inkishafi* ("enquiry, research" in Arabic) is a didactic composition in which the poet exhorts his soul to abandon the foolishness of mortal life; he enlivens his homily with similes drawn from African experiences, like the perils of the sea or the rage of fire in a dry bush. In the climax of the poem he vividly depicts the past glories of the great sultanate of Pate, now reduced to ruin, illustrating with its downfall the futility of mortal aspiration.[1]

As it has been said above, the eulogistic Swahili poetry is close to the sphere of the classical Arabic tradition. On the other hand, there is no epic in classical Arabic poetry, whereas a typical genre of old Swahili literature are the long epic poems called *tendi* or *tenzi* (sing. *utendi/utenzi*). They are, however, mostly rooted in Arabic history or in Islamic mythology, and deal often with the early Muslim wars, or with some episode in the life of the Prophet Muhammad, of his relatives and friends.

The creator of the great epic tradition in Swahili is Bwana Mwengo bin Athumani who lived in Pate in the first half of the 18th century or earlier. The oldest manuscript of his masterpiece *Chuo cha Herekali* ("The epic of Heraklios") was written in AD 1728 and hence possibly the epic was composed at an earlier date. It is the history of the Arab conquest of Syria, reshaped for the needs of the Islamic society that could only explain the incredible successes of the Arab armies against the much stronger troops of the Byzantine emperor Heraklios by the presence of the Holy Prophet. Thus Muhammad, who was already dead when the great battles took place, and his son-in-law Ali replace in the Arabic legends, the historical figures of the generals Khalid ibn al-Walid and Amr ibn al-As. *Chuo cha Herekali* is a true epic poem comparable to European epics. It is a well organized, highly structured poem of 4,600 strophes, exceptional for its originality: there are several Arabic stories in prose on this subject, but not in verse, hence no direct Arabic model for Bwana Mwengo's poem exists. Moreover, the Swahili epic is much longer and more varied than the Arabic stories.

As we know, originality is not a virtue in traditional literature, be it Oriental or African. All over the Islamic world we find the same subjects, the same heroes (taken from the Koran or from the *hadith*) and the same motifs. The most popular character, besides Muhammad, is Ali called "the lion" or "the sword of Islam," a great warrior who wins all the battles. Ali, like Muhammad, has divine qualities. Thus in the poem *Utendi wa Katirifu*[2] by the son of Bwana Mwengo (the author of *Chuo cha Herekali*), Abu Bakari bin Bwana Mwengo, written around the year 1750, Ali alone puts to flight the enemy that the whole Muslim army could not defeat.

I quote from Knappert's translation the episode where Ali with his wife Fatima and their two sons reach miraculously the battlefield.

308.   When they had raised their hands,
        when they had prayed to God,
        they saw how there arose a wind,
        which caused the camel to fly.

309.   In the time needed to close the eyes,
        And before they could be opened again,
        They saw their camel
        standing near the army.

310.   Sheikh Ali told Fatuma the Flower,
        to dismount first,
        to be greeted by the Prophet
        and his companions.

317.   In the middle of the talking,
        of bringing greetings,
        she saw a dark fog,
        dust spread over the plain.

318.　It was the dustcloud of Ali
　　　fighting for the Prophet,
　　　(It was as if he were) drowning them in water,
　　　those who do not adore the Compeller.

319.　He pressed the murderers hard,
　　　and decided the battle,
　　　his hand (with the grip like) a lock,
　　　held Dhu l'Fikar. [his magic sword]

320.　His rage was enormous,
　　　he even wounded them with his teeth,
　　　whomsoever his hand seized,
　　　found himself on the point of the sabre.

321.　He would lift him up entirely,
　　　and crash him against the ground,
　　　his breathing would soon end,
　　　in the innermost part of his breast.

322.　If he saw someone standing,
　　　he would face him,
　　　and take away his life,
　　　while (the victim) would still be looking, wide-eyed.

325.　It was an unspeakable chaos
　　　with shouting and braying,
　　　the heathens running away,
　　　the Medinese pursuing them.

Such poems are called *māghazī* ("raid" in Arabic). The *māghazī* genre in Arabic literature comprises legendary depictions of the Prophet Muhammad's "holy" wars after the hegira; they are mostly written in rhymed prose. In Swahili, on the other hand, they are written in verse of the *utendi* type. These stories are all of the same pattern: in the introduction the poet calls a scribe or asks for writing materials, then he invokes God's help and praises Him and his Prophet. The story opens usually in Medina, with Muhammad and his companions praying in the mosque when a messenger brings them some news that compels them to set forth and fight the infidels. Seldom the Prophet himself takes part in the battle, usually he just prays, or fights symbolically, but his every act is highly effective. Thus in *Utenzi wa Uhud* he just pricks with a small dagger the Kureish who challenged him to a duel, but after a few minutes the enemy dies.

431.   The Chosen One took
a small dagger.
The Prophet armed himself
with the most suitable accoutrement.

433.   He adorned himself in elegance;
he never dressed like that
except when there was mischief
and he had to go to war.

439.   The Prophet was alone
waiting for his adversary
to approach him
so that he could engage him.

440.   The Prophet was standing aloof
and the Kureish was making ready
to close in on the Prophet
and he turned to face him.

441.   At once the Prophet
pushed against him
and his dagger
pricked his body.

442.   He struck him according to plan,
not in the trunk
but in the neck,
which was the best place,

443.   For he had covered himself
all over except at the neck,
that is, near the backbone
of his body.

444.   He has not covered his neck
with armour completely;
otherwise he was fully covered
and had left no part unprotected.

446.   When he was stabbed with the dagger
the Kureish did not stay to endure it;
he immediately
turned his horse.

447.   The Kureish had had enough;
he turned his animal
to go back to his friends.
He could not bear to stay.

448.   He turned his horse
and galloped off in haste
going quickly;
he did not know what had happened to him.

450.   Because of the pain
he was giddy and weak;
he rode like a novice
(being on his horse).

451.   He reached the group
where his friends were waiting;
he was panting and breathing
with difficulty.

453.   The Kureish started talking
before he had reached them;

he continued saying,
"The Prophet has killed me".

457.   When he had finished
speaking to explain what had happened to him,
his companions laughed
heartily at him.

458.   They mocked him
when they thought he had no good reason,
then they spoke
in answer to his words.

466.   "There was never a day
when you left the battle,
but always you went on
fighting as fiercely as before.

467.   "Today you have no wound
other than that slight abrasion,
yet you come with lamentations
and doing nothing but talk."

471.   The champion Ubayyi told them:
"That is no use,
because you do not know him
nor understand my state.

474.   "I am filled with bitterness
and all confused;
moreover the Prophet's dagger
is very painful.

478.   "If everyone had got it,
all the people on earth,
after getting it,
would have passed over (to the next world).

479. "And Muhammad promised me,
      (he told me)
      that he would harm me
      and that he would kill me."

482. And indeed that Kureish,
      returning home to Mecca,
      died on the road
      before he had arrived.

483. He did not reach his home;
      while on his way back
      he died on the road
      and did not enter Mecca.

Utenzi wa vita vya Uhud is a poem of Arabic origin written probably during the lifetime of the Prophet; the name of the Arabic poet is no longer remembered. The author of the Swahili version is also unknown; it passed on orally from generation to generation until it was collected and written down by the Zanzibari scholar Haji Chum in 1949.[3] The theme of the poem is the historical battle of Uhud against the inhabitants of Mecca, the second battle fought by the Prophet and his followers after they moved to Medina, in which the Muhammad's army suffered severe defeat.

It is most unusual that a *māghazī* poem ends with a defeat of the Muslim army. Even if the poet does take sides with the Muslims, his characters are less schematic than it is normally the case. Usually, in fact, the Islamic heroes are perfect; in the epic they never lose a battle and never die. Analogous to the Western mediaeval poems about the wars against the Infidel, the enemies in the *tendi* are all villain, for they are the enemies of the one God (Knappert, *Epic Poetry* 56).

Other characters of Swahili epic poems are Ali's pious wife (and Muhammad's daughter) Fatima, their martyr son Hussein, Muhammad's companions, friends and other great warriors of his time. The Biblical prophets like Adam, Moses, Job and Joseph the Egyptian are also presented as pious Muslims. A well-known poem, for instance, is *Utenzi wa Ayubu* ("The epic of Job") by an anonymous poet of the 18th century.

Job's vicissitudes are like those narrated in the Bible—a rich and happy man loses his goods, his children and his health, but he does not lose his piety—but there are two differences: the Muslim Job never rebels against God, and his wife remains faithful to him in his misfortune. In fact, this woman, Rehema (i.e. Pity), has a prominent role in the poem; it is one of the few positive woman characters of Swahili poetry.

The *Utendi wa Shufaka* ("The poem of compassion")[4] by Hasan bin Ali from Lamu narrates in 295 stanzas how two pious parents willingly sacrifice their only remaining son in order to save the life of a complete stranger. It is a trial required by the archangels Gabriel and Michael who are arguing whether there is still compassion in the world. At the end not only the sacrificed boy comes to life again, but also all his brothers who had died before. (The moral is very far from the modern Western values, but on the other hand, it reminds us of the Biblical Isaac's sacrifice.) The poem is written in the Lamu dialect with many archaic features. But particularly striking are the large number of Arabic phrases and whole sentences, to the extent that we may perhaps speak of a sort of code-switching.

Even some animals are converted to Islam in the Swahili Islamic narratives, and to it also we may find parallels in other Oriental literatures, as well as in mediaeval Christian hagiographies. Thus in *Utenzi wa Ngamia na Paa* ("The poem of the camel and the gazelle")[5] the two animals of the title, ill-treated by their pagan owners, profess Islam and so convert even their respective masters.

A popular theme is the perfidy of women. Women in the Islamic tradition, beginning with the Biblical Eve, try every means to get men into perdition. There are several Swahili poems illustrating it. The best examples of this kind are the poems by Saidi bin Abdallah Al-Buhry and by his grandson Hemedi from Tanga: *Utenzi wa Barasisi*—the story of a monk who was tempted by the Devil in the shape of a beautiful woman, *Utenzi wa Mwana Hasina na Rashidi Walii*—another story of temptation in which, however, the pious hermit Rashidi resists the schemes of the wicked princess Hasina (both by Said Al-Buhry), and finally a refined erotic and moralistic story of temptation (*Utenzi wa Kadhi Kasim bin Jaafari* by Hemedi Al-Buhry) in which the righteous judge Kasim, persuaded by a beautiful young woman to commit the worst crimes, will be pardoned by the caliph, who puts all the blame on the women.

For more than two hundred years Swahili poetry, of which only a few masterpieces have been mentioned, was religious in content and in form. All longer poems contained the invocation of God's help and praises of His name at the beginning and a brief prayer at the end. Even the poems by the great secular poet Muyaka bin Hajji (1776-1837) of Mombasa, although not ostensibly religious, are embedded in an entirely Islamic sphere of life.

It is important to bear in mind that the formal pattern of the *tendi* is more important than the content. So in the end (rhyme) position a word may undergo changes in order to fit the rhyme scheme, e.g. *Jalali* becomes *Jalia, Shetani > Sheta, fahamu > fahama*, etc. Besides, the poets fill the lines with unnecessary (void) words like "indeed," "hear" or "understand" to get the required eight syllables in a line. On the other hand they are often cryptic, as they leave out important information like who is speaking.

What has a Swahili *utendi* to tell us today? For a Western reader the stories are remote and, besides, they seem to be too repetitive. In fact, the poets would tell the same thing two or more times (see, e.g. the second excerpt, although it has been shortened). However, it is interesting to compare them with European mediaeval and Renaissance epics. In East Africa, on the other hand, the *tendi* are still appreciated and even composed, especially in the coastal area (which is the cradle of the Swahili culture), even if a modern epic form in free verse has been developed in the last decades.

Notes

1. The poem has been edited and published, with an English translation, in 1939.
2. The manuscript was discovered and published by Jan Knappert as "The Utenzi wa Katirifu or Ghaswa ya Sesebani."
3. It was published by East African Literary Bureau in 1962, edited, translated and with notes by H.E. Lambert.
4. The only extant manuscript with the title *Chuo cha Utenzi* was brought to Germany in 1854 by Ludwig Krapf and is kept in the Library of the Orientalistic Society in Halle. It was translated by Carl Büttner and published in his *Anthologie aus der Suaheli-Literatur*.

318 *Elena Bertoncini*

5. It was published by E. Dammann in *Dichtungen in der Lamu-Mundart des Suaheli* and later by J.W.T.Allen in *Tendi. Six Examples of a Swahili Classical Verse Form.*

Works Cited

Allen, J.W.T. *Tendi: Six Examples of a Swahili Classical Verse Form.* London: Heinemann, 1971.

Büttner, C. *Anthologie aus der Suaheli-Literatur.* Berlin: E. Felber, 1894.

Dammann, E. *Dichtungen aus der Lamu-Mundart des Suaheli.* Hamburg: Friederichsen, DeGruyter & Co., 1940.

Hichens, W. *Al-Inkishafi. The Soul's Awakening.* London: S.P.C.K.

Knappert, J. "Utenzi wa Shufaka." *Swahili* 37.2 (1967): 133-65.

____. "The Utenzi wa Katirifu or Ghazwa ya Sesebani." *Afrika und Übersee* 52.3/4 (1969): 81-104, 264-313.

____. *Swahili Islamic Poetry.* 3 vols. Leiden: E.J. Brill, 1971.

____. *Four Centuries of Swahili Verse.* Nairobi, Lusaka, and Ibadan: Heinemann, 1979.

____. *Epic Poetry in Swahili and Other African Languages.* Leiden: E.J. Brill, 1983.

Lambert, H.E., ed. *Utendi wa Vita vya Uhud.* Johari za Kiswahili 3. Dar es Salaam: East African Literature Bureau, 1962.

Black Heroes:
Images of Africa and the Diaspora in the
Spy Novels of Asse Guèye

Debra Boyd-Buggs

Detective fiction invaded the Senegalese book market over 60 years ago and even today many Senegalese enjoy reading detective stories. Asse Guèye published the first spy novel written by a Senegalese in 1986. One of Guèye's concerns when he started writing in this genre was the fact that, in general, detective and spy novels propagated minimizing and degrading images of Africans and peoples from other continents, while in these same texts Europeans were valorized. Guèye's novels manifest a reaction against racist ideology in detective fiction and reflects an attempt by an African to occupy a part of the market.

Most importantly, Guèye understood that spy fiction opens the door for the creation of Black heroes in African literature that resemble and even supersede John Ball's character Virgil Tibbs of television series *In the Heat of the Night* fame. Africans and peoples of color need more heroes who are representative of what a Black man should or could be, someone who imposes himself on all levels. The black man who, as soon as he appears on the scene, asserts himself by his intelligence, by his courage and even by his physique. Literary works that depict traditional society introduce ancient heroes such as Soundiata, Lat Dior, Oumar Tall and others. Still it is important for African peoples collectively to be able to identify with contemporary characters such as Virgil Tibbs and those that we find in Guèye's novels, personalities that forge possibilities for more heroes in the realm of visual production.

The world of Asse Guèye's spy novels *No Woman No Cry* and *Negerkuss, échec et meurtres* is one of international politics and intrigue, of multinational economic organizations. It is no accident that the spy thriller as a literary genre first appears at the beginning of the 20th century, in the imperialist stage of capitalism when the existence of rival imperialist states and a capitalist world system made it increasingly difficult to envision the total of social relations as embodied in any single "knowable community." The novel of espionage or spy story is the tale of the boundary between nations and cultures and the spy acts as a defender or subverter of the nation in the face of the other, the alien. It pretends to take us behind the scenes of world events as they are seen in newspapers or history books. It shows us secret conspiracies which apparently determine the fate of nations and a paranoiac aura typically tints the tale (Cawelti and Rosenberg 55).

In addition to its background of international conspiracy, the secret agent formula usually centers around a particular military or technological secret. According to Alfred Hitchcock: "It's the device, the gimmick, if you will, or the papers the spies are after" (Truffaut and Scott 98). This type of plot is basic to Guèye's two novels. Although it is usually based on current historical situations, the background of the spy story is nonetheless a landscape of the mind. The secret agent's fictional milieu with its omnipresent hidden secrets and conspiracies presents a picture of the world which is probably half reality and half extension to the international scene of the gothic caste with its hidden passages, secret panels and lurking conspirators.

Guèye's principal first-person narrator is Jacques de Camuet, a white Frenchman, an aging intelligence agent looking forward to retirement who wants to give it one more try. He relates the events as they happen, giving the reader not a balanced and measured tale, but a series of incidents whose internal coherence is never entirely clear. The author also infiltrates other first person narrators to introduce the reader to the superhero, a supervillain perceived in Western literature to be "colorful and exotic." What is unique is that Guèye adopts the first person point of view by way of a European to valorize the main character who is an African. Notable also is that the supervillain is more interesting to the reader than his would-be-heroic opponent. An African hero becomes more firmly implanted in the reader's imagination than his austere and colorless nemesis. He remains elusive and calls to mind Bakayoko of Sembène Ousmane's *Les Bouts de bois de Dieu*. All events in the story are linked to him although he is never physically present with the main narrator and the reader, until the novel's dramatic conclusion. A mystical hero, he takes on greater and greater proportions as the story unfolds.

The title *No Woman No Cry* is taken from a song by renowned reggae artist, the late Bob Marley, and constitutes a refrain that is repeated continually throughout the structure of the novel. The oppressed woman serves as a metaphor that symbolizes the African struggle for liberation on the continent and in the diaspora. On one level, the title designates an international underground resistance movement against apartheid, orchestrated and led by a brilliant Senegalese scientist and the subsequent attempts by the CIA and its European counterparts to assassinate the hero and destroy the organization. On other levels Guèye addresses the various facets of liberation struggle and the corruption of international politics.

Most of the action in *No Woman No Cry* takes place in Senegal but, typical of the spy thriller, the hero and members of his group relocate frequently. There are scenes in South Africa, the United States, Jamaica and Japan. An authentic African hero goes to and leaves an indelible mark on all of these geographical locations.

The hero, Bassirou "Bass" Bèye, is the son of a Senegalese film-maker of South African origin and a well-known Senegalese dance artist. Born a genius, details of his exceptional gifts are provided throughout the narrative. Not to be ignored are his physical traits; women are attracted to him. Because of Bèye's commitment to the redemption of oppressed peoples he becomes public enemy number one to forces in the West who label him a terrorist. A type of Christ figure, he is a man who fortifies his rhetoric with definitive action. Through flashbacks provided by his father, Mantu Bèye, and the CIA confession obtained from his friend, Mahuto, a chemist with whom he worked for Hitachi in Japan, the reader witnesses the evolution of an African hero whose commitment to Black people reaches into the diaspora, although it manifests itself most violently against apartheid and political oppression in all of southern Africa.

Bèye has a commanding presence:

> Le jour se levait et apportait dans la pièce où
> nous étions une luminosité d'une tendresse
> exceptionnelle. Cela contrastait violemment avec le flot
> de paroles qui continuait de jaillir de la bouche de mon
> ami. Plus il parlait plus il drainait toute ma sympathie
> vers la cause de ses frères africains dont j'avais ignoré le
> calvaire. Comment cela était-il possible en cette fin de
> vingtième siècle? Comment a-t-on pu faire un tel silence
> sur les souffrances qu'endurent depuis longtemps ces
> millions d'Africains?
>   J'en étais à ces pensées quand Bass me tendit la
> bouteille de saké à moitié vide et tout en poursuivant son
> exposé. Il transpirait légèrement car le climatiseur de son
> bureau n'était pas en marche. Le jour qui entrait de plus
> belle dans la pièce, posait doucement ses reflets sur sa
> peau noire. Son corps était parfaitement sculpté et il se
> tenait là, majestueux, parlant doucement. On aurait dit
> en le voyant que Dieu était Noir. En tout cas, si ce
> dernier existe, il a sûrement fait Bass à son image.
> (Guèye, *Woman* 57)

Bèye is almost a god in the eyes of his intellectual soulmate Mahuto. The hero's resistance organization is comprised of a sophisticated Black and international elite. Characteristic of the hero of the spy thriller, he is able to do what seems to be impossible for the ordinary man. He develops a "scientific" solution to apartheid which favors people of color. It is a chemical agent that will make nature rebel against white skin causing the whites to leave southern Africa; it kills Whites but leaves Blacks immune. Bèye and his company successfully wipe out Johannesburg. He subsequently outsmarts the CIA and its allies who are unable to catch him nor do they ever discover his secret viral formula for the massive genetic destruction of whites who would oppress southern Africans.

Negerkuss échec et meurtres, Guèye's second novel, parallels *No Woman No Cry*. The action takes place entirely in Germany. A young Senegalese professor who studied in Germany ten years earlier is invited to return for a seminar on human rights. He is another example of a typical hero of spy fiction, the educator who is traveling for business or pleasure, looks up old friends and accidently gets caught up in a low and sinister game of spies, informers, thugs and terrorists. The hero is innocent, both in the sense of not being guilty and in the sense of being naive. He is an inexperienced amateur in a world of professionals but again whose courage, intelligence and forceful presence leads to a victory in the realm of human encounters.

The author specifically addresses two issues. The first concerns the African who travels in Europe and who suffers the racial prejudices that being black entails. Guèye also speaks to the problem of German terrorism. In the novel, there is a message that the centers of democracy preach human rights and respect for individual freedom. However, the anti-terrorist struggle as it was executed in Germany showed no respect for the beliefs that Western societies emphatically claim to embrace.

Guèye's deep concern for South Africa resurfaces. In *Negerkuss*, Senegalese air pirates hijack a plane full of Afrikaners and threaten to kill them if their demands are not met. He also incorporates messages to the African diaspora.

The author employs the spy novel format to diminish the power of racial epithets. The main character, Baldé, and his German friends hurl racial slurs at one another without such activity negatively affecting their relationships. Whereas the Harlem Renaissance writers reacted violently to the term "nigger" and the negritude writers revalorized the word "nègre," Guèye disempowers these terms in his fictional universe:

> - Au fait, Prof., est-ce que tu connais celle du Noir-Américain qui monte au ciel?
> - Causes toujours.
> -Alors, il arrive au ciel et se pointe à l'entrée du paradis. Sic. Il tombe sur le Bon Dieu qui lui dit: "Dégages." Et le Noir qui essaie de s'expliquer. Mais le Dabe ne veut rien entendre. "Dégages te dis." Et le Noir au Barbu: "Mais vous êtes en retard vous! Il y a eu de l'évolution. Même qu'au Texas, on prend les mêmes bus que les Blancs, on mange dans les mêmes restaurants. Même que le Maire Huston est un Noir."

"M'en fous, dégages, je te dis."

Mais le Noir insiste.

"Mais puisque je te dis que même au Texas...

Tenez, une seconde avant de venir ici, j'étais en train de demander au Shérif la main de sa fille."

Voilà donc le genre d'individus auquel je suis en train de téléphoner de la cabine où je viens de m'engouffrer.

Sa secrétaire me le passe.

- Salut, sale Juif.

- Salut, sale Nègre. (Guèye, *Negerkuss* 114-5)

When certain passages are deconstructed however, the white man is still portrayed as the master of the discourse of bigotry.

In his disposition for political polarization, Guèye propagates a message of unification for peoples of color and particularly all who have been oppressed in some way by "the Other," the European. He makes reference to the fact that during the USA-Iran conflict, Iranian terrorists released Black hostages as a sign of solidarity. In *No Woman No Cry*, the Japanese Mahuto sets himself aflame in front of the South African Embassy in Washington to protest apartheid. This he does after serious reflection upon the events in Hiroshima during World War II combined with his witnessing, via television news, the vicious and senseless murder of a South African woman and her child during the Soweto uprising.

Female characters play a significant role in spy fiction. In the case of Ian Fleming's James Bond, for example, that Bond should encounter a girl in the course of his mission is a foreordained necessity of the formula. It is, moreover, always a girl he encounters, never a woman, and when not directly present, she is invariably referred to, in the exchanges between Bond and the villain, Bond and M., or Bond and his helpers, as "the girl." In Bond fiction, the girl furnishes a source of narrative tension and constitutes a problem of knowledge, a troubling enigma which Bond must resolve. This enigma takes the form of a disturbing "out-of-placeness" in the respect that, to varying degrees, and in different ways, "the girl" departs from the requirements of femininity as specified by patriarchal ideology. The "place' which "the Bond girls" are "out of" so to speak, is that allotted to them—that which ideologically, they should occupy—in a patriarchal order, defined socially and sexually in relation to men (Bennett and Woollacott 115). Guèye's female protagonists move us away from the realm of Ian Fleming into a domain where the girls of the spy thriller become "women" who are side by side with men in the liberation process.

The introduction of the character Suzanna Maskela in *No Woman No Cry* calls our attention to the problems of women in South Africa and to the oppression of women in general. In *Negerkuss*, Guèye re-addresses this theme as it pertains to Arab women. The reader is introduced to Suzy through the first person account of the Japanese Mahuto after he has been sent to Madagascar by Bèye. Like most of her black compatriots, Suzy led a miserable existence in the South African homelands. Yet she is an African woman who struggles to preserve her dignity and is subsequently arrested for her refusal to submit to the authorities who tried to block her from visiting her husband. Her husband dies in the mines and later she loses her only child to malnutrition. To survive, she hires herself out to care for a white man who eventually abuses her sexually. Guèye portrays Suzy as a Black heroine who responds to this adversity with a violent anger that leads her to join the resistance movement:

> Tu vois Mahuto, pour moi le plus difficile était fait. Oui, le plus difficile, c'est de tuer le premier Blanc, après, c'est facile. J'avais une envie irrésistible de continuer. C'est ainsi que je rejoignis l'A.N.C., puis la lutte armée. (Guèye, *Woman* 144)

Suzy ceases to be a passive victim. Asse Guèye's novels are full of women and persons of color who are depicted in non-traditional roles.

Afro-America is another locale where Guèye's superheroes are born. In *No Woman No Cry* the superheroine is an African-American female, double agent Barbara Jackson. Her assignment is to help the CIA capture Bèye by obtaining information as to his whereabouts from Bèye's father. In accordance with basic plot structure, the spy of fiction generally does not operate without a certain invisibility. Everything about Barbara Jackson, her job, her leisure time, her actual thoughts, her personal life, are clandestine and disguised. She remains an enigma throughout the narrative and the reader is never quite sure of her true identity until the end of the novel.

She appears on the scene disguised as a dancer. A CIA instrument on the surface, she is clandestinely a facilitator of the struggle. Her execution is so precise that her colleagues believe in her unquestionable loyalty to the United States. She appears and disappears without leaving a trace.

> Vous devez comprendre, Monsieur Jacques de Camuet, que Miss Jackson nous a souvent aidés à remporter d'importantes victoires sur les éléments de l'A.N.C. et de la S.W.A.P.O. Le fait qu'elle soit Noire ne l'a jamais empêchée de ne voir dans son action que l'intérêt des Etats-Unis. Ce qui est bon pour les Etats-Unis d'Amérique est aussi bon pour les vingt-cinq millions de Noirs qui y vivent. Et croyez-moi, pour Miss Jackson, l'intérêt de ses frères Américains passent de loin avant ceux de ses frères Africains. Elle bénéficie à cet égard d'une telle confiance de la part de nos autorités qu'il lui arrive souvent de recevoir directement ses instructions d'un Zbignew Brezinski, ou d'un Henry Kissinger pour des missions ultra-secrètes. Et cela au nez et à la barbe des grands manitous de "l'Agence" qui ne sont mis au courant qu'après coup. Vous devrez donc comprendre que pour la mission qui nous concerne, nous pouvons compter sur sa détermination quasi légendaire, n'est-ce pas? (Guèye, *Woman* 27)

Guèye's use of irony through these words spoken by a white American male is clear. As far as whites are concerned, the Black American intelligentsia that they have trained for their purposes would never jeopardize its position in the name of Africa. However the true African superhero/superheroine does not limit himself/herself to the demise of oppression in one geographical location. In his/her ethos, people are always more important than things, including jobs lent by the European.

Bèye meets and loses Barbara during a mission in Angola. From that point on, the driving force in his existence becomes his desire to somehow find her again. According to him, Barbara is "la femme la plus courageuse, la plus intelligente et aussi la plus belle qu'on puisse trouver sur cette terre" (Guèye, *Woman* 136). The superhero thus provides the reader with a simple description of the superheroine.

In spy thrillers there are rarely any true love stories. But melodrama prevails in the fictional universe created by Guèye. Mahuto's friendship with Suzy Maskela results in the conception of an Africasian child who symbolizes the union of the two continents. Just before his suicidal death, Mahuto's final written message is for Suzy: "No woman no cry." Interracial couples are a frequent theme with Guèye. However, his "couple par excellence" is the uniting of the superheroes Bassirou Bèye and Barbara Jackson, two children of Africa.

Afro-America is appreciated for her music which figures in both novels. Guèye mentions the vocalists Tina Turner, Nina Simone and Chuck Berry. He also alludes to significant moments in contemporary African-American history such as the assassination of Dr. Martin Luther King, Jr., an event which has a revolutionizing effect on the life of the hero, Bèye. In one episode of *No Woman No Cry*, Bèye goes to New York City to meet with anti-apartheid leaders as well as his friends in the Black Panther Party and the Black Muslims. In *Negerkuss* the narrator refers to Angela Davis and the Soledad Brothers to whom the character Baldé compares himself when he realizes that two of his friends have been murdered for terrorism in Germany.

The West Indies produced a musical giant in the late Bob Marley and the magnitude of his influence is still being assessed today. In *No Woman No Cry*, Marley's music is considered to be subversive to the white American agent Morrecone, a type of James Bond figure, who feared Marley's capacity to motivate throngs of young people. Marley is said to have been a friend of the hero, Bass Bèye and it is Marley's funeral in Kingston, Jamaica that brings the novel to its shocking but exciting climax. It is the point of unification and peace. The jubilant celebration of Marley's life stands in sharp contrast to the solemn manner in which the West celebrates its departed heroes.

Guèye also employs the theme of rasta. The idea of rasta is attached to the notion of intellectual superiority, courage, physical beauty and physical strength. It also suggests the embracing of African cultures and ideology. In *No Woman No Cry* both the superhero and his main satellite or circulating agent wear dreadlocks, the preferred hairstyle of the rasta. Baldé, the hero of *Negerkuss* also wears dreadlocks and is called the "rastaman" by other characters in the story.

Espionage fiction is not alone in allowing the reader to concretize repressed conflicts into literary symbols so that they can be dealt with safely. But it is the route chosen by Asse Guèye. Guèye's spy novels allow us to pierce deeply into ourselves, where the possibilities are infinite and where the Black hero is not only authentic, but a reflection of reality that Black people in the diaspora and on the continent are familiar with. In a non-classical manner, Asse Guèye clearly indicates his political and artistic preoccupation with the concerns of peoples of color in Africa and in the world.

Works Cited

Bennett, Tony and Janet Woollacott. *Bond and Beyond: the Political Career of a Political Hero*. New York: Methuen, Inc., 1987.

Cawelti, John G. and Bruce A. Rosenberg. *The Spy Story*. Chicago: University of Chicago Press, 1987.

Guèye, Asse. *Negerkuss échec et meurtres*. Dakar: Nouvelles Editions Africaines, 1988.

____. *No Woman No Cry*. Paris: L'Harmattan, 1986.

Truffant, François and Helen G. Scott. *Hitchcock*. New York: Simon and Schuster, 1967.

Intertextuality in *A Deafening Silence* by John Miles

H.P. van Coller

John Miles' Afrikaans novel, *A Deafening Silence* (1991)—originally published as *Kroniek uit die doofpot*—has already been the subject of a number of studies, and has been awarded numerous prestigious literary prizes, among others, the M-Net and Helgaard Steyn Prize. In the novel, Miles creates two alter egos of himself as the real author: the fictional author who assumes the role of text-internal conductor, and the main character, Thumelo John Moleko, whose names are (almost) similar to those of the real author, John Miles.

A Deafening Silence exploits the genre of the chronicle in most original ways—in this literary text the complex process of reconstructing historical "facts" is explored, and by shocking the reader into involvement through the use of alienation techniques a pragmatic orientation is adopted. Moreover, throughout the text, ethical issues are posed in the form of questions. One of these nagging questions deals with the responsibilities of an author within an unjust and dehumanizing political system (as indeed the South African political system was in the 1980s). A variant of this question, posed in the text, considers the value of the folk-tale (and therefore literature) for modern man.

The fictional author, a character in the text, attempts to reconstruct the life history of Thumelo John Moleko using documents, interviews and even police reports, and through this attempt generates a written record of his own role in a violence-ridden South Africa, a record that reflects, even if only at the level of the imagination, the real author's experience in the writing of the novel. That the fictional author in writing his own account seeks to identify himself with the main character is made explicit: "if I have to turn this into a book, then he and I are involved in the process: the policeman and the author, both a black and a white man ... [h]is history is my story ..." (16). This process is similar to the one followed by the historian. Relations are drawn meticulously, verified on the basis of documents and other reliable sources of information, and eventually all unrelated events are re-arranged into a causal whole.

Miles' black main character, Thumelo John Moleko decides, as early as 1961 at the age of nine, that some day he wants to become a policeman. The date itself is not without significance because the early Sixties is seen as the era of violent resistance to Apartheid when unrest occurred across the country—and few of these incidents are more well-known than the notorious Sharpeville uprising. In Thumelo John's period of training some years later, Apartheid is still in full swing in South Africa, and for a black person to make progress in a traditionally white career is an uphill struggle. Nonetheless, Thumelo John makes good progress, later he owns a house and a motor-car, and he and his family "live like white people in town" (59).

Without the intervention of what is known as Fate, his existence beyond this point would probably have been uneventful. On a day in September 1984, however, his life changes dramatically. As a young policeman, he is struck against the head by a senior white officer; his eardrum bursts and his journey into hell commences. Moleko's journey of suffering takes on various facets: physically, he is broken down, and undergoes various operations before eventually going entirely deaf. He enters a spiritual purgatory: he struggles in vain for justice and for recognition of his human dignity. The police officer refuses to admit guilt (which would result in the payment of compensation to Moleko), and the South African police service ignores (turns a deaf ear if you want to pun) all his claims and allegations.

Moleko now learns of the other side of the police force; that of a ruthless machine serving a racist government intent on eradicating all opposition. And parallel to this disillusionment is his private progress back to his roots as a man-of-Africa. His tragic end is predictable in the tradition of the *anti-märchen*: he and his wife are murdered by colleagues, and the investigation is terminated without the guilty parties being brought to book. His only apparent legacy consists of a collection of documents in a yellow plastic bag. It is the fictional author who unearths and narrates this history of a small person, this chronicle of "a deafening silence."

Miles' novel follows the well-known pattern and structure of the fairy-tale, and for this reason shows note-worthy similarities to one of the most well-known poetical and canonized short stories in Afrikaans writing, Eugène Marais' story, "Klein-riet-alleen-in-die-roerkuil" ("Little-reed-alone in the whirlpool"). In this typical African folk-tale the main character dies tragically because he fails to heed warnings (or is "deaf"). By alluding to this text, Miles signals a warning to his Afrikaans reader: namely that Thumelo John's own quest (for justice) will end tragically.

But there are, in addition, three texts written in Dutch (and firmly entrenched in the Dutch literary canon), that serve as intertexts to Miles' novel, to which through the textual links, he pays a form of tribute: *Max Havelaar* by Multatuli, *Terug naar Oegstgeest* [*Back to Oegstgeest*] by Jan Wolkers, and *De bende van Jan de Lichte* [*Jan de Lichte's Gang*] by Louis Paul Boon.

All three Dutch novels flirt with genre expectations, with those associated with "objective reportage" (Multatuli); autobiography (Wolkers), and folktale and the picaresque novel (Boon). Miles' "police novel," too, in a similar fashion, flaunts one's expectations, with the police being the criminals instead of those who catch the criminals.

The influence on Miles of this treatment of genre can be pursued still further: the early pages of Boon's novel are written in chronicle form; from Boon's novel, too, come the Brechtian alienation techniques related to the narrator's conduct, and even more directly the narrator's treatment of history, especially in the way he is both passive recorder but also active creator of history (cf. Rossouw 141). In contrast to Rossouw's view (142), one may argue that Miles' tone is not always deadly serious, and the futile attempts by both the picaresque main character and the fictional author to make sense of a chaotic world are presented in a lightly-ironic and relativizing mode. On this point, W.F. Hermans' *De donkere kamer van Damokles* [*The Dark Room of Darkness*], adds further insight, and it is worth noting that Miles himself wrote the introduction to the South African edition of Hermans' masterpiece.

Miles borrowed the structure of his work from Wolkers' novel. The chapter demarcations, with alternating chapters that broadly place past and present, as well as fiction and fact in opposition, remind the reader of *Back to Oegsgeest*. Like Wolkers' scarred main character, Jan, Miles' is also a "marked" person whose outer scars express the inner trauma. Wolkers' novel is also a quest: a middle aged man suffering from a psychological disorder tries to recapture his youth. In Wolkers' novel, the past is gradually obliterated and everything seems to be in a state of decay. In Miles, it is Thumelo John in particular who is gradually destroyed until he dies. Like Wolkers, who uses a plethora of symbols (the dried plant; the ineffective wipers; the brother's coat), Miles also exploits various exegetical symbols (the clay-pot remains; the image from Zimbabwe; the increasing deafness of both the main character and the police authorities).

Furthermore, all three Dutch novels struggle with presenting an objective account of the past, and with the difficulty of writing factual history at all. Multatuli uses his own biography as a model, turning it into a literary fiction. Boon's account of the life of Jan de Lichte has also been referred to as an "alternative" history, built up by Boon's interpretations. De Wispelaere emphasizes indirectly by implication the determining force of history in which the characters merely act out their roles without, in the words of Boon, being able to precipitate the smallest of changes in the course of history ("Over Jan de Lichte's gang" 81). In addition all of the main characters, Droogstoppel, Jan, Thumelo John and Jan de Lichte, are instances who, as the "splitting offs" of their authors, project their authors' impotence to change history (de Wispelaere, "Aantekeningen" 86).

Miles echoes this sentiment when his main character realizes that a system has actually determined his own personal history (322) and it is suggested that man is doomed to failure if he tries to fight on his own against a system of power. In this way, a tragi-comic, almost picaresque life history eventually emerges from the woodwork. Thumelo John Moleko is the typical "everyman," "the proverbial ordinary man" (15) with his own small ideals, who desires to become a policeman, to work on the side of peace, to be happily married, and to provide for his family's needs. The main figures too of Multatuli, Wolkers and Boon (especially Jan de Lichte) are ordinary people and if man is doomed forever to be defeated, then it is not only the superior force of the oppressor that is to blame, but also man's insignificance (de Wispelaere,

"Over Jan de Lichte's gang" 82). Weisgerber too labels the history of Jan de Lichte as "the history of the insignificance of man resounding through all times" (220).

In this way, a link is established with postmodernism, where master discourses are replaced by the *petites histoires* of ordinary people. "Great narratives" are indeed suspected to be narrated by people with totalitarian, oppressive, repressive and even terrorizing tendencies (Janssens 18).

Ena Jansen engages in a meticulous analysis of the interplay of fact and fiction in Multatuli's *Max Havelaar*, and points out the irony that both Multatuli's and Miles' novels indeed expose reality through fiction. Jan Wolkers' "autobiography" is again an idiosyncratic account of the past, and he concedes that he has established links among these events, thus rewriting his own unstructured past as a coherent narrative. On these grounds, Fens and ven Boef, among others, conclude that Wolkers' work is not an autobiography, but a novel-based version of the past. Van't Hof (1979) also indicates how Boon, in spite of the comprehensive use of sources, eventually provides his own vision of the history of Jan de Lichte, and sides with the gang.

Miles too combines fiction with fact without forfeiting one's sense of authenticity, and his fictitious author makes it clear that the history of Thumelo John Moleko, because of the lacunae, is largely imaginary.

Miles' fictional author in fact continually engages in a metafictional commentary on history writing (cf. 243) and problematizes the process. In this way, he shows an affinity for the modern thinking of writers such as Carr (1991), Ankersmit (*Denken* and *De Navel*) and Hayden White (1986). In these terms, history writing is related to literature because the genre is also a narrative construction. Each author of history texts decides on the narrative structure (the plot); the style, etcetera. Within this thinking, even "facts" are problematized because these "facts" only achieve this status within a particular narrative coherence.

In a lecture, Marcel Janssens ridiculed a critic's definition of Multatuli's novel as "post-modern" (93). However, it is unquestionable that all three of the above-mentioned Dutch novels display characteristics that are currently assigned to post-modern novels. The narrative undermining that occurs in each of these Dutch novels cannot be divorced from a (philosophical) vision of reality, nor from the role of writing and the author within this vision.

It is indeed this narrative *procédé*, followed in all the above-mentioned novels, that serves as an example of a deep scepticism with regard to the author's divine role as a "maker." In *Max Havelaar*, the author indeed enters into the fictional system to subvert it, but ironically remains an actor under the control of the organizing and determining element in the text. Jan Wolkers' narrator realizes, at last, that the past is subject to degeneration, that everything yellows, decays and disappears, and that narratives are not constant. Boon's narrator is assigned absolute narrative mobility within the text, but as an authorial narrator finds himself "at the same time in the closed time dimensions of the futile and failed revolution" (de Wispelaere, "Over Jan de Lichte's gang" 84) and for this reason, is powerless against the reality of history. Weisgerber contends that Boon writes from a sense of duty and love of man, "writing that is intended to hold back the world from the chasm" (226).

A personal anecdote is probably justifiable at this juncture. During my period of study at the University of the Witwatersrand, John Miles lectured on Dutch prose as part of his responsibilities. In the early 1970s, these three novels appeared regularly on his list of prescribed works. However, Miles' novel is not merely a tribute to the above-mentioned texts. It enters into a fascinating discourse with them. Miles' text too is fraught with epistemological and ontological scepticism. Nonetheless, his faith in the role of the author remains unaffected. His conclusion is not that a literary response to a political situation is an absurd attempt to change reality and thus futile. In essence the writing of history is never about the past but deals with the future. A Dutch author, Nelleke Noordervliet (1995: 71) phrased it in the following words: "The relationship with the past has no other and higher objective than determining our own present position. . . . Not the past is given its coordinates but the future."

When the fictional author accepts the responsibility to reconstruct Thumelo John's life on the basis of the documents in the yellow plastic bag, he takes over the role of Thumelo John's grandfather who always assumed an ever-active narrative guiding role. In the African tradition, he climbs into the moccasins of the oral narrator who, within a community, keeps the collective memory and history alive through narrative accounts. It is in this domain, this novel contends, that one encounters the eventual meaning of authorship: "ultimately all stories are without an end, of which we can only remind one another" (354). The fictional narrator (as well as the real author, John Miles) suggests in this way that Thumelo John's legacy is nonetheless valuable: it is a story with no end, and will continue to remind the reader of injustice. In this way, the cyclical course of events is completed: all stories are fiction, but when the narrator begins to speak everything becomes true. Then heroes live again on their fiery steeds, and the past becomes whole, and the dry document catches breath.

Works Cited

Ankersmit, F.R. *Denken over geschiedenis. Een overzicht van moderne geschiedfilosofische opvattingen.* Groningen: Wolters-Noordhoff, 1984.

_____. *De navel van de geschiedenis. Over interpretatie, representatie en historische realiteit.* Groningen: Historische Uitgeverij, 1990.

Boon, Louis Paul. *De bende van Jan de Lichte.* Amsterdam: De Arbeiderspers, 1977.

Carr, D. *Time, Narrative, and History.* Bloomington/Indianapolis: Indiana University Press, 1991.

de Wispelaere, P. "Aantekeningen met betrekking tot Jan de Lichte." *Maatstaf* 28.5 (1980): 80-92.

_____. "Over Jan de Lichte's gang van Louis Paul Boon." *Over verhalen gesproken.* Ed. M.H. Schenkeveld et al. Groningen: Wolters-Noordhoff, 1982. 77-95.

den Boef, A.H. "Jan Wolkers: *Terug naar Oegstgeest.*" *Lexicon van Literaire Werken.* Volume V. Ed. A.G.H. Van der Meijden, J. Goedegebuure and M. Janssens. Groningen: Wolters-Noordhoff, 1990. 1-13.

Hermans, W.F. *De donkere kamer van Damokles.* Amsterdam: G.A. van Oorschot, 1963.

Jansen, E. "Miles's Moleko and Multatuli's Max." *Tydskrif vir letterkunde* 31.1 (1993): 22-42.

Janssens, M. "De postmoderne mixing van hoog- en laagcultureel." *Een nieuw wereldbeeld voor een nieuwe mens? Lessen voor de eenentwintigste eeuw*. Leuven: Universitaire Pers Leuven/Davidsfonds, 1996. 89-121.

Multatuli. *Max Havelaar, of De koffieveilingen der Nederlandsche handelsmaatschappy*. 1860. Amsterdam: Querido, 1993.

Noordervliet, Nelleke. *Geschiedenis verzinnen. Nederlands in culturele context. Handelingen Twaalfde Colloquium Neerlandicum*. Antwerpen: Internationale Vereniging voor Neerlandistiek, 1995. 63-75.

Rossouw, C. "Die ondermyningstrategieë in "Kroniek uit die doofpot" van John Miles." M.A. Thesis. University of the Orange Free State, 1997.

van't Hof, W. "De visie van L.P. Boon on the history of Jan de Lichte's gang." *Ons Erfdeel* 22.3 (1979): 325-39.

Weisberger, J. *Aspecten van de Vlaamse roman 1927-1960*. Amsterdam: Athenaeum/Polak & Van Gennep, 1978.

White, H. *The Content of the Form. Narrative and Historical Representation*. Baltimore & London: The Johns Hopkins University Press, 1987.

Wolkers, Jan. *Terug naar Oestgeest*. Amsterdam: Meulenhoff, 1965.

L'espace nigéro-méditerranéen et le Maghreb africain dans l'histoire

Pathé Diagne

L'histoire de l'espace nigéro-méditerranéen (*Nyagura-Maratarana*) concerne la région géographique qui va de l'Atlantique à la Vallée du Nil, et du bassin nigéro-tchadien au pourtour de la Méditerranée afro-européenne ou afro-eurasienne.

Elle a été façonnée, par des populations qui inventent, à l'époque du Sahara fertile, une civilisation agraire et urbaine (*Tagati-Tichit, Sengati-Chinguit, Warata, Walata*, etc.) dont témoignent l'art rupestre des femmes de *Jubbaren*, les bovidés et chasseurs du Tassili, les cervidés d'Altamira ou les mammouths de Rouffignac de la Dordogne ; l'architecture mégalithique ou *maratana* angulaire de Walata. L'espace nigéro-méditerranéen développe une révolution spirituelle *ramakushi* avec des cultes kushiques ou bachiques de fécondité (*Kas, Kus, Bacchus, Marakush, Kuli, Kulikuli, Kelukas, Nama, Saasum, Sumun*, etc.) et des cultes rahmaniques et monothéistes du Dieu *Ra* ou *Yaa* Infini, *Ba* ou *Raba* Suprême, *Senn* ou *Marogsen* Unique.

Il y a ainsi une géographie culturelle et spirituelle très ancienne, commune à l'espace nigéro-méditerranéen. Elle explique l'onomastique de tous les noms de métropoles, de terroirs, de communautés et de populations. Cette onomastique de métropoles religieuses porte la marque des divinités tutélaires. Pour décrypter le sens donné au nom d'une métropole de culte ou d'un nom de communautés, il faut utiliser toute la grille de lecture appropriée, mise à jour, en 1992, dans *Tara Para*. Cette grille combine le nom du Dieu rahmanique (*Ra, Ya, Ba, Genn, Senn, Aat,*

etc.), le nom des divinités kushiques de fécondité(*Kus, Kas, Bacchus, Kuli,
Kulikuli, Kukulkan, Nama,* etc.) associées à des locatifs (*Ta, Tana Tan,*
etc.) et des dérivatifs d'appartenance (*Ma, Wa, Ka, Sa,* etc.) désignant un
adepte ou un prêtre.

On sait ainsi que *Tara* signifie la terre, *Ta* de *Ra. Maratarana* ou
Maratana désigne la côte *Tana* des *Mara,* adeptes *Ma* du Dieu *Ra,* d'où la
Mer Méditerranée et sa côte appelée *Maratana* ou *Mauretania.* Namata ou
Namatara désigne la Numidie et le *Namadir,* pays du *Nama. Sakasra* a
donné Sahara, pays des adeptes *Sa* de *Kas* et de *Ra. Sakuli, Sakeli, Saheli* ou
Sahel désigne le pays des adeptes *Sa* du *Kuli.* Le *Magalraba* désigne les
populations qui célèbrent *Magal Ra* Dieu *Ba* Suprême. La forme a donné
Magreb. *Makasrakas* qui désigne des adeptes *Ma* de *Kas* a donné Machrek.
Les *Marogsenn,* adeptes *Ma* de *Rog* Dieu *Senn* l'Unique ont donne le
Maroc. *Sennkas,* qui a donné *Zanaga* et Sénégal, désigne des adeptes de *Kas*
et de *Senn* l'Unique. *Nyaka,* qui signifie limite *Nyaka* du domaine de *Ra,*
a donné Nigeria et Niger.

Lébuta terre *Ta* des Lébu a donne *Lebiya* ou *Leptis. Tabarikas* qui
a donné *Tafrikas* Afrika signifie terre *Ta* de *Ra* Dieu *Ba* Suprême et de
Kas. Gebbta terre *Ta* du Dieu *Gebb* (piocher) a donné *Egyptos* et Égypte.
Baragwata signifie Royaume *Ta* du *Barag* monarque du *Waalo* ou du
Marog. Genna pays des adeptes de *Genn* l'Unique a donné Ghana.

Mara-Moro a donné maure et signifie adepte *Ma* de *Ra. Marakus* ou
Marrakech, désigne des adeptes ou prêtres *Ma* du Dieu *Ra* et de la divinité
Kus. Rabata-Rabat est la métropole *Ta* de *Ra* Dieu *Ba* Suprême.

Les entités politiques les plus anciennes se sont édifiées du sud au
nord avec les routes transsahariennes malgré la désertification devenue
effective à partir de 2000 av. J.C. On citera sur cette carte politique de
l'ouest vers l'est : le *Baragwata* entre le bassin du Sénégal et le Maroc; le
Namata numidien ou *Namandirou* sur l'axe *Walata, Sigilmaissa,
Taratakas,* Carthage et l'Ifrikiya tunisien; le *Ghanna* sur le même axe ; le
Lébuta ou pays libyen en contact avec le bassin tchadien et le Kanem
Bornu; le *Gabbta* ou le pays nubo-égyptien, le long de la vallée du Nil ou
Nyul.

.   Ces axes ont continué à dessiner la géopolitique de l'espace
nigéro-méditerranéen, par delà l'expansion eurasienne des Mèdes, des
Perses, des phéniciens, des grecs, des romains, des vandales, des arabes et
des Turcs. Il faut avoir, à l'esprit, l'avènement majeur de la géopolitique

islamo-orientale à partir du VIIè siècle et le rôle du Ghana fatimide, du Tekrour et du *Ghanata-Zanata* almoravides. Cela implique du reste que l'on garde en mémoire l'influence ancienne du judéo-christianisme antérieur (Ben, Douna, etc.) à celle de l'islam. Il faut sur ce plan mettre à niveau et à jour l'historiographie.

Objectifs

Cette communication constitue une tentative d'historiographie critique. Elle n'associe pas par hasard des travaux consacrés à la région de confluence des peuples d'Afrique et d'Eurasie qu'est l'espace nigéro-méditerranéen en l'occurrence, avec un projet de politique linguistique et de promotion de l'Africophonie à la veille du deuxième millénaire chrétien.

L'intégration politique, économique, linguistique et culturelle continentale, doit être la composante préalable principale à la mondialisation plurielle qui réunifierait à nouveau la terre. Celle-ci a été unifiée une première fois avec les révolutions techniques, spirituelles, artistiques et intellectuelles de la Préhistoire, une seconde fois à l'avènement de l'islam initiateur de la Renaissance à partir du VIIè siècle. Le voyage transatlantique de Bakari II, en 1312, et le périple de Christophe Colomb, en 1492, ont ouvert la voie à l'expansion eurochrétienne fondatrice du Monde Moderne. Ce millénaire des nouvelles technologies de la communication sera, disons, «post-moderniste».

Au moment où il faut forger des langages de communication et des cultures plurielles pour le millénaire nouveau, il était nécessaire de rompre avec les discours et les littératures mal informés ou hégémoniques sur l'Afrique, ses régions historiques et ses civilisations stratégiques.

L'espace nigéro-méditerranéen reconstitue, sur la base de faits dûment établis, l'histoire régionale comme facteur d'unification dans une zone stratégique où s'affrontent encore des exclusivismes, alors même que la révolution des communications terrestres et aériennes va vers d'inévitables rencontres.

Des données

On connaît très peu l'histoire et les rôles des populations nigéro-méditerranéenes.

Les populations de *géti mool* mariniers, qui se disent *Raba, Rébu, Lébu, Libya* ou *Lébu Lamtuna*, adeptes du Dieu *Ra, Ro ou Re, Ba* suprême, sont parmi les premiers occupants des côtes de la Méditerranée et de l'Ouest-Atlantique. Leur terroir englobe, du sud-ouest atlantique au nord-ouest nilotique, un espace parfaitement identifié. Il comprend le *Lébugi* des *Lébu* de *Jandeer*, au sud du Bassin du Sénégal, qui ont fondé les ports de *Tengu geej* ou *Tingita* (la mer jument houleuse), de *Bay Kasum*, près de Soumbédioune, dans la Médina de Dakar, de *Bay Saasum* ou *Bay Soogi*, derrière le Palais de la République, à Dakar. On leur doit, en remontant vers le Nord et le Sahara fertile d'où ils viennent, la ville de *Ndeer Geej* ou Saint-Louis sur mer, celles de *Mout* ou Mouit, de *Tennujuk* ou Port Tendick, du *Taragin-Argin* des Imragen du Sahara occidental, de *Kusta*, terre *Ta* de *Kus* ou Ceuta sur les côtes rocheuses et houleuses des *Marogsenn*, des *Magalraba Kasum* et des *Magalraba Saasum*. Le terroir lybien englobe, le long de la Méditerranée, d'ouest en est, le *Talamsenn* des *Magalrakus* du Machreg algérien, le *Lébuta, Lebta, Lybia* devenu la Lybie. Il s'étend de *Tarabukus, Tarabulus, Tarabuli* ou Tripoli jusqu'à *Mennfari*, Memphis dans le *Gebbta*, terre *Ta* du Dieu agraire *Gabb*, divinité éponyme qui a donné son nom à l'*Égypte* ancienne. Ces populations de *géti mool* mariniers, familiers de l'Atlantique et de la Méditerranée, ont donné, à l'Ouest atlantique africain, le nom d'*Ataranta, Atalanta*, ou Atlantique. Ils ont donné, à la mer Méditerranée, le nom de *Maratarana-Meriterane*, terre ou mer *Tana* des adeptes *Ma* de *Ra*.

Les populations de langues mandeng, adeptes de *Nama*, divinité bachique de bonne ou mauvaise fortune, se disent *Namara, Narmara* ou *Narmer*, adeptes de *Ra* et du *Nama, Bamenna* ou *Bamana* adeptes de *Menn* l'Unique, *Suminké* ou *Soninké* adeptes de *Sus Sum* ou *Saman*, le python royal, et de *Kas*, le Nain Divin. Elles ont fondé le *Namata, Namada* ou la Numidie, terre *Ta* du *Nama* des auteurs grecs et romains. On leur doit également le *Namatara-Namandir* ou le pays biblique de Nimrod.

Les *Masasum-Masaesyles*, Numides de l'Ouest et les *Masila*, Numides de l'Est qui interviennent dans les guerres puniques contre l'expansion grecque et romaine sont, comme Tabarka-Caharka, Amin

Karsa ou Amilcar (290-299), Kartaraba-Hasdrubal (247-183), Tannabara-Hannibal, Masaani Siise-Masinisa (238-148) qui ont gouverné le *Namata* ou la Numidie. Ils sont considérés comme fondateurs de l'Empire Ghanawa du Ghana de *Jeg Warata*-Jugurtha (160-104). Ils appartiennent certainement au même univers mandeng-suminké. Celui-ci domine l'Empire ouest-africain, durant la Basse Antiquité et le long Moyen-Age, entre le Vè siècle avant J.C. et le Xè siècle. Ce sont les *Masasum* ou *Masasi* et les *Masila* qui fondent le Tassili, au cœur du Sahara fertile, le *Torosila* et le *Gatimara-Gidimaha* sur la vallée du fleuve Sénégal. Ce sont les *Torogalle-Turaani* ou *Fulani Pël, lamido aal pulaaren* qui, à l'époque du Sahara fertile, ont donné leurs noms à *Waragale-Wargla*, terroir de l'Algérie actuelle et au *Lam Tara Ma Isa* ou *Lam Termes*. Les *Kas Bara, Kabara*, adeptes de *Ra* Dieu *Ba* suprême et de *Kus* ou *Kas*, divinité agraire, ont donné leur nom aux Kabyles et à la Kabylie. L'Est nigéro-méditerranéen *des Magalrakas* ou Machreg couvre une géopolitique qui va de *Tabarikas*, terre *Ta* des adeptes de *Ra* et de *Kas* d'où l'Ifrikiya tunisien, au bassin nigéro-tchadien. Le *Taghawa* a Gao comme métropole. Le *Zaghawa* est formé par le pays Hausa-Zarma, Bornu-Kanembu ; sa géopolitique, se développe parallèlement à celles de l'Ouest *Lébu lamtuna, Ghanawa* et au bassin nilotique nubo-égyptien.

Contrairement à une opinion courante, la géopolitique comme la géographie culturelle nigéro-méditerranéenne qui a rayonné du Sud au Nord sur l'Eurasie occidentale, ibéro-*basakum* basque, *baratana*-bretonne, tyro-phénicienne, a su maintenir sa permanence de l'Antiquité à l'époque moderne. Malgré la désertification, ses pouvoirs ont su contrôler, du Sud vers le Nord, les voies transsahariennes de communication, voire une certaine activité maritime sur l'Atlantique.

La prééminence démographique, militaire et économique de l'État et de l'Empire Sud-Ouest africain, nigéro-sénégalais nigéro-tchadien ayant contrôle sur l'or du Soudan et du monde de l'époque, lui a même assuré une prédominance géopolitique. L'État Taratakas Kartagas ou carthaginois de *Tannabar*-Hannibal et l'Empire *soninké numido ghanawa* de *Masani Siisé* alias Masinisa, s'opposent aux conquêtes gréco-romaines. Ce sont les *Lébu-lamtuna* de *Taragenn* alias *Tarig*, convertis à l'islam qui fondent l'Espagne, Andora-Andalouse. Le Ghana de *Njawar Jaagiliba* fonde le califat fatimide. Le chef de guerre soninké conquiert l'Afrique méditerranéenne et le Proche Orient au Xè siècle. Il se déclare protecteur des trois villes saintes : Jérusalem, la Mecque et Médine. Il est le fondateur du Caire et d'El Azhar. Il fera de Muhiz, le premier calife fatimide. Une autre hégémonie *Ghanawa Zannata*, celle de *Toumer*, fondateur de la dynastie almohade des *Muwaahidun*, viendra du Sud. La prééminence du Mali des *Mansa* sur les routes transsahariennes du centre et de l'est durera jusqu'à l'avènement du négoce euro-ouest africain atlantique (1450) et transatlantique (1492), après le voyage Outre-Atlantique de Bakari II an 1312 et le périple de Christophe Colomb en 1492.

La civilisation et les cultures qui font entrer l'espace nigéro-méditerranéen tôt dans la Préhistoire et l'histoire, ont certainement vu le jour d'abord dans le Sahara fertile des *Sakasra* adeptes *Sa* du Dieu *Ra* et de *Kas*. Le Sahara fertile naît au Nord du *Sakuli* des *Sakili*, adeptes *Sa* du *Kuli* qui ont donné leur nom au Sahel. Le Sahara fertile est le témoin des techniques de la pierre et des métaux, de l'art rupestre, de l'architecture mégalithique et *marata* angulaire, de l'agriculture, de l'élevage, des métropoles urbaines politiques et religieuses, vecteurs de la spiritualité *ramakushi*, bachique et monothéiste (*Tagati, Tichit, Wadd Gati-Awadaghost, Senn Gati-Chingthi, Warata, Kumbi*, etc.).

Le fonds négro-beydaane africain indigène dominant des rives de la Méditerranée au Sahel des *Sakuli*, adeptes du *Kuli* et du culte du Python royal aux écailles d'or, a brassé assez tôt, des populations noires et blanches constitutives du fonds négro-africain et beydano-africain. C'est cette coexistence qui, dès la préhistoire et l'Antiquité, a amené les Lébu à distinguer, du Delta du Nil méditerranéen au *Jandeer* atlantique sénégalais, entre *Lébu nuul nopp* ou *bopp*, c'est à dire des Lébu à tête ou oreilles noires d'une part, des *Lébu honh nopp* ou *bopp* à tête ou oreilles rouges.

L'expansion phénicienne, grecque, romaine, waragati-wisigoth ou vandale, arabe et turque a contribué, sur le tard, à métisser fortement l'Afrique méditerranéenne et sahélienne. On comprend qu'il y ait non seulement des îlots blancs (beydaan-africains) et noirs (nigéro-africains), mais une population dominante négro-beydaane, mulâtre au nord du Sahara, mais également de métis au Sud. Cette population négro-beydaane sédentaire et nomade a produit une culture métissée dite maure ou berbère, pour parler comme Moulay Ismaël Keïta chercheur mauritanien. Les Toubou, les Touareg, les Takuli, Tachleu ou les Kasbara Kabila Kabyles, sont des natifs indigènes du même espace à l'instar des Beydaanoafricains et Négro-africains marocains, algériens, tunisiens, libyens, égyptiens, soudaniens, éthiopiens, maliens, nigériens ou mauritaniens. Ils ont façonné et continuent de façonner le peuple arc-en-ciel de l'espace nigéro-méditerranéen. Cette sociologie complexe, a fait problème et continue à déranger les idéologues qui réinventent l'histoire ou qui théorisent de nos jours l'état d'ethnie ou de race.

L'historiographie coloniale raciste a beaucoup contribué à «blanchir» un espace nigéro-méditerranéen que l'islam et l'historiographie arabophone avaient unifié d'une certaine manière, malgré les dissonances surprenantes d'Ibn Khaldoun et de l'Orientalisme. Le panarabisme contemporain théoricien d'un Maghreb ou d'un Machreg africain négro-berbère, négro-beydaane, kabyle ou tamasheq, touareg ou toubou que l'on cherche à convertir en Magreb ou Machreg arabe exclusif, est venu ajouter à la confusion.

Tahar Ben Jelloun, écrivain marocain francophone assimilé, s'étonne d'avoir des parents mulâtres. On eut, à la réunion de l'*African Literature Association*, l'occasion d'entendre quelques thèses fantaisistes dans l'esprit sudiste américain. Un chercheur, qui se dit spécialiste de l'art musical mandeng, faisait venir du «Portugal» les *Jali Ghanawa* soninké, les *Gewël* wolof, les *Igwan* berbères et les *Gawlo* aal pulaaren. Or les étymologies sont claires. *Gewël* désigne le maître de la scène ou *Geew*, celui pour qui ont fait cercle, que l'on entoure d'où *Gewël*. *Gewël* a donné le *Greo* ou griot tekrourien, almoravide et andalou. Les *Gewël* auraient, selon ce collègue musicologue, atterri en Ibérie, non pas avec les Almoravides conquérants de la presqu'île ibérique, mais comme «esclaves», avant d'être embarqués vers le Maroc (*shipped for Marocco*). Les Marocains les auraient exportés sur les rives du Sénégal Niger. L'argumentation est compliquée et tortueuse. Elle est surtout révélatrice des préoccupations obscures et anti-scientifiques que quelques entrepreneurs peuvent promouvoir pour mobiliser des fonds considérables, perdus pour la recherche véritable au profit de personnages simplement malhonnêtes. Il est vrai que El Fassi, intellectuel marocain, l'un des responsables du volume III de *L'Histoire Générale de l'Afrique*, éditée par l'UNESCO, faisait de Njawar Jagiliba, fondateur *ghanawa* du califat fatimide, un «esclave russe». Le terme mandeng *Sakuliba*, adepte *Sa* du culte du *Kuli* le serpent, *Ba* très grand qui a donné *Sakali*, se serait ainsi mué en racine «slave»-esclave, loin de Kumbi, capitale des *Tunka* du

Ghana. On peut, dans la même foulée, se demander comment Fernand Braudel qui s'est intéressé à l'or du Soudan, n'a pas compris, comme Idrissa Youssoufou et Yves Lacoste, la permanence des relations transsahariennes, ni le rôle de pôle dominant de l'Empire ouest-africain, de la Basse Antiquité à l'époque moderne. Historien éminent de la Méditerranée, s'il en fut, il soutiendra néanmoins que «le désert et l'œcoumène ont été des frontières infranchissables pour les nègres».

Fernand Braudel fera école avec Théodore Monod, Mauny, voire Yves Person et les jeunes universitaires africains de l'École dite de Dakar. La teneur du débat initié par ce groupe, lors du Colloque sur l'Afrique noire et le monde méditerranéen dans l'Antiquité, (Dakar, 1976), aura été symptomatique sur ce plan. On n'a certainement plus besoin «d'inventer une Afrique pannégriste», pas même pour répondre ou réviser les universitaires allemands de l'École de Gottingen qui, le comme le reprochaient Cheikh Anta Diop, dans *Antériorité des Civilisations nègres*, et Martin Bernal dans *Black Athena*, fantasmaient sur l'existence d'un modèle ancien aryen indo-européen ou occidental ou encore d'une Grèce, mère des sciences. Ceci dit, cette rencontre de l'*African Literature Association* aura donné l'occasion de remettre les pendules à l'heure pour une science rigoureuse ouverte qui distingue et sépare l'idéologisme du vrai. C'est en ce sens que ce texte a été conçu et présenté à Fez. Il a pour fonction, de montrer comment, dans ce cas précis, l'on peut procéder à une révision et une relecture du discours historique culturel ou linguistique manipulé par des idéologues incorrigibles. «L'espace nigéro-méditerranéen» est un exercice. Il illustre un type de réflexion qu'il va falloir promouvoir sans parti pris ou frontière, sur une vaste échelle, à la fin du deuxième millénaire chrétien marqué par un nouveau processus de mondialisation du savoir.

De l'historiographie revisitée

L'espace nigéro-méditerranéen superpose, à travers ses historiens de diverses époques et origines, trois formes et types d'historiographie et de discours sur une même région et les mêmes réalités. Tout dépend des sources que l'on utilise et de l'attitude que l'historien prend à l'égard des faits.

Sur ce plan il y a les données de l'archéologie matérielle fournies par les industries de la pierre, de la céramique ou des métaux, de l'art rupestre, de l'architecture mégalithique ou *marata* angulaire, typique de Sahara fertile. Il y a les contributions de l'archéologie culturelle, spirituelle et intellectuelle fournies par l'onomastique encore bien vivante des noms de lieux de métropoles religieuses, politiques ou économiques, de communautés, de populations ou de pays. Il y a enfin les dépositions écrites et les chroniques orales fixées qui remontent à la Haute Antiquité. Elles sont fixées dans des textes nubo-égyptiens, grecs, romains. La destruction des bibliothèques anciennes à Alexandrie et à Carthage prive l'humanité des principales sources écrites sur l'Antiquité et sur l'Afrique. Les données dont on dispose ne sont toutefois pas négligeables. Il suffit ici d'éviter les partis pris. Les textes pharaoniques nubo-égyptiens peuvent et doivent être sollicités de même que les témoignages fixés en langues et écritures *khat* ou *tifinag*, grecques ou romaines, les sources arabophones africaines ou étrangères, les œuvres en langues africaines transcrites en lettres arabes (*ajami, walafal,* etc.), voire en graphies européennes.

La plupart des historiens de langue européenne négligent, en général, de recourir à des textes autres que ceux légués par l'historiographie gréco-romaine. C'est la tendance dominante dans les travaux qui furent présentés à Dakar, en 1976, lors du Colloque sur l'Afrique noire et le monde méditerranéen dans l'Antiquité. On négligea même les premières sources arabes, alors qu'elles apportaient sur le terrain, des indications précieuses, sur des sociétés, non encore sous influence islamo-orientale, et qu'évoquaient les auteurs gréco-romains ou chrétiens. L'historiographie arabophone, qui se développe ici, à partir du VIIIè siècle, dans la foulée de la renaissance géopolitique et scientifique mondiale, se sera énormément enrichie. Elle reprenait à son compte les textes grecs de *Path Ramenn*, alias Ptolémée d'Alexandrie en particulier. Ces données fournies par ces textes seront corrigées progressivement par l'expérience directe des historiens voyageurs.

Les percées de l'archéologie culturelle et linguistique en cours, ajoutées au recours des textes écrits (hiéroglyphes, picto-idéographie *khat, wolafal, ajami,* etc.) permettent, aujourd'hui, de s'enrichir à toutes les sources. Elles habilitent à mettre en parallèle et en perspective pour les confirmer ou les réviser, les thèses, les littératures et les discours qui s'écrivent sur l'Afrique, la Méditerranée ou l'espace nigéro-méditerranéen qui nous intéresse ici. Dans *Pouvoir politique en Afrique Occidentale* (1967) et, plus récemment, dans *Bakari II 1312* et *Christophe Colomb 1492 à la rencontre de l'Amérique* (1992), nous avions entrepris d'explorer en profondeur, pour la première fois, les possibilités d'une reconstitution de l'histoire ouest-africaine en mobilisant de manière critique et simultanément, les sources gréco-romaines, europhones, arabophones et africophones sans frontières et en sollicitant l'éclairage de l'archéologie linguistique et culturelle.

Cette communication illustre, en elle-même, un cadre méthodologique. Quand il s'agit de littératures et discours historiques, nous prenons, comme base de référence, la géographie culturelle de la région. Elle fournit un vocabulaire originel, constitutif d'une littérature et d'un discours historique africophone de première main ; avec son onomastique des noms de cultes, de divinités, de lieux, de communautés, de confréries, de populations, d'ethnies, de nome, de terroirs, de métropoles spirituelles et politiques.

Une fois ce corpus établi, les données sont comparées avec celles de même nature livrées par les sources non africophones, qu'elles soient étrangères ou locales. Ce dialogue contradictoire intertextuel permet ainsi de réviser, sur l'espace nigéro-méditerranéen, non seulement la chronique de Manéthon ou le Timée de Platon, mais Strabon, Pline, Salluste, Mutannabi, Marakondir, Cheikh Dounkali, Es Saadi, Ibn Khaldoun ou les égyptologues linguistes, géographes, et, historiens, contemporains, prisonniers de lectures parfois non informées, parfois erronées.

Le corpus que livre, comme données des littératures et discours historiques, le vocabulaire de la géographie culturelle est celui de langues africaines à classes de type *mennfarite* (lébu, bantu) ou sans classe de type thébain (mandeng, yoruba, etc.) ou à deux ou trois classes de type thinite (hausa, tamasheq, etc.). Le contenu de ce vocabulaire géographique, culturel et historique, appartient au faciès africain nigéro-méditerranéen et même afro-asien occidental d'une révolution spirituelle *ramakushi* de cultes bachiques de bonne fortune et de fécondité associés à un monothéisme pluraliste.

La géographie du faciès nigéro-méditerranéen comme celle du faciès afro-méditerranéen à l'intérieur duquel il s'insère, peut être mise en évidence, par la même grille *ramakushi* à quatre composantes déjà évoquée. Cette grille permet de reconstituer la géographie culturelle d'une

Méditerranée afro-eurasienne où les spéculations ont naturalisé bien des littératures et discours historiques plus ou moins fantaisistes. Il est vrai que la tentation était forte, étant donné la similitude, voire l'identité de fonction des toponymes et noms de communautés et de cités, de faire de Tyr ou *Tara* en Phénicie, de *Tanisa* ou Tunis, de *Teritaram* ou Jérusalem, de *Tayba* ou Thèbes, des métropoles tantôt égyptiennes, tantôt phéniciennes tantôt grecques. En reconstituant, grâce à l'archéologie linguistique, la cartographie et la géographie culturelle nigéro-méditerranéenne africophone originelle encore vivante, on met en évidence le corpus et les vocabulaires qui vont permettre, de réviser les littératures et les discours historiques dus, sur cette partie de l'Afrique, aux auteurs de langues étrangères, grecque, latine et arabe en particulier. Les données linguistiques et les textes en langues africaines écrites ou orales transcrites alimentent ce travail préalable.

Relecture des sources

Les sources anciennes non africophones sont précieuses. Il faut toutefois les réviser en les soumettant à la grille africophone de lecture. Les sources arabophones parce qu'elles sont plus massives, plus récentes et de première main sont généralement meilleures que les sources europhones gréco-romaines souvent tributaires, chez Platon ou Hérodote, Diodore de Sicile, Salluste ou Pline l'Ancien, de simples ouïes-dire ou de témoignages. Cette différence est sensible dans le lexique comparé qui est proposé ci-dessous. Les premiers historiens arabophones dont Wahab Ibn Munabbih (8è siècle) repris par Ibn Qutayaba (889) ou Yakubi, couvrent à leur époque, entre la Méditerranée et le bassin nigéro-sénégalais, un nombre considérable de populations et de pays peu connus, même des auteurs de l'époque romaine. Ces derniers s'en tiennent après les «Nasamans» et les «Éthiopiens» des Grecs aux noms des régions côtières où ils se sont installés.

Les sources gréco-romaines sont celles qui, jusqu'ici, auront servi aux historiens européens à reconstruire l'histoire nigéro-méditerranéenne, selon leurs perspectives propres. Citons *L'Algérie, histoire des guerres des Romains, des Byzantins et des Vandales* de Dureau de la Malle (1852), les textes relatifs à l'histoire de l'Afrique du Nord avec Saint Gsell, auteur de *Hérodote* (1916), *La Lybia Negli Seritti Degli Antichi Rome de* Fantoli

(1933), les travaux de Braudel présentés au Colloque sur *l'Afrique noire et le monde méditerranéen dans l'Antiquité*, organisée par l'Université de Dakar, en 1976, à l'instigation du Président sénégalais Léopold Sédar Senghor. Cette historiographie ignore totalement les sources africophones et même arabophones.

En ce qui concerne la littérature arabophone, *Pouvoir politique* et *Afrique traditionnelle* et *Bakari II 1312, Christophe Colomb 1492, à la rencontre de l'Amérique* discutent des principaux auteurs, qu'ils soient orientaux, africains ou euro-andalous. Les sources arabophones prennent forme et contenu avec les premières œuvres des historiens d'Orient. Elles vont collecter de plus en plus de termes de lieux et de peuples. Lecoq a donné une synthèse de ces œuvres. Ces sources ne seront même pas évoquées, lors du Colloque de Dakar, sur *l'Afrique noire et le monde méditerranéen dans l'Antiquité*, alors que son livre est préfacé par Mauny présent à cette rencontre. Cette littérature, qui évoque les mêmes sociétés ramakushiques que les Grecs et Romains, améliore progressivement le discours historique, même si les transcriptions ne sont pas toujours heureuses. Parmi les auteurs arabophones, on peut citer Wahah Ben Munabih (728), Al Fazari (1068), Muhammaat Ben Khawarizmi (*Kitaab al Buldaan*), Masadi (*Hurri al Dhahab* et *Tanbih*, 956). On sera plus proche des réalités par la suite, avec les auteurs ibéro-africains et maghrébo-nigériens dont El Bekri (*Kitaab Bast*), Ibn Idhari Al Marrakush (*Kitaab al Bayaan*), Abi Zahr Al Fasi (1320), Abul Fida Tawkim, Al Omari (1301), Cheikh Dounkali, Ibn Khaldoun Mukaddima, Said Tariq, etc. Cette lecture arabophone ou arabisé est on ne peut plus précieuse, malgré les réserves exprimées, plus haut, concernant les transcriptions linguistiques.

Reconstruction historique

On peut reconstruire l'histoire de cet espace avec une certaine cohérence en remaniant, eu égard à l'archéologie et à la géographie historique réelle, les données relatives aux faits politiques, culturels et géopolitiques.

Le pouvoir s'est inscrit ici sur la titulature et les noms des détenteurs qui l'exercent sur un territoire physique ou un espace qui évolue. Le pouvoir de tradition ramakushi, qui naît ici, organise des sociétés de chasse, de pêche, d'élevage, d'agriculture et d'artisanat acquises aux cultes de bonne fortune de fécondité et de fertilité. Elles ne choisissent pas au hasard leurs symboles du pouvoir. Le *Kuli*, le *Kas*, le *Sus*, le *Sas* ou le *Ngoy* prennent, comme divinité tutélaires des territoires, figure de chasseur, pêcheur ou éleveur. Kus (*kelukus*) est lesté de sa corne d'abondance, de son javelot, de sa calebasse céréalière (*kelubashi*), du bâton de conducteur de troupeaux. Il est accompagné *Sus* ou *Samaan* le Python royal, symbole de *Sukumun* (vent de sable). Le pouvoir ramakushi ainsi symbolisé s'exercera spirituellement sur un territoire, à travers des prêtres détenteurs qui ont droit d'usage et non de propriété. C'est ce caractère métaphysique et territorial du pouvoir, qui fait que les titres les plus anciens, les plus respectés et les plus universalisés sont de nature foncière. Ici la toponymie territoriale et politique se confond, d'où la prolifération à l'échelle régionale, du locatif *Ta, Tan, Tin, Tana*, pour désigner le territoire et le pouvoir foncier : *Tin Bukutu, Lam Tana, Barutan, Tan Ise, Sustan, Kustan, Gebb Ta, Lebta, Tasali, Tabarta, Tangita, Ta, Ghaza, Tin Buktu, Ten Bawal*. Le *Goygoytara* est maître de terre, le *Gaymool-Gaymas* maître de l'eau, le *Gaynakus* maître des pâturages. L'unification des territoires-nomes confédérant des pouvoirs spirituels et fonciers, donnera naissance à l'espace et au pouvoir politique proprement dit et à son exercice au sein des catégories, classes et castes des sociétés. La confusion entre prêtres des divinités de territoire ou d'espace et autorités politiques (chef, monarque, empereur, éponymes) s'est universalisée ici.

Le culturel comme donnée s'inscrit sur une toponymie qui conjugue territoire physique, spirituel et politique. On peut illustrer cette caractéristique à travers quelques exemples.

Le terme de *lam, lamaan, lamsenn, lamido ou lamtuna*, né à l'époque du Sahara fertile où il prospère, est certainement le titre le plus universalisé dans l'espace nigéro-méditerannéen. Il peut magnifier le maître de territoire ou le prêtre maître de culte. Il est présent au sud du bassin de la Sénégambie : *Lamjafaj, Lambaay Seen* du Sine, *Lamtuna* des *Baruten* du Sahara occidental, *Lam Tana* des *Marogsen* du Maroc, *Talamsen* algérien, *Ta Lam Ghernta* tuniso-lybien. *Lam Ta* au Sud de *Gebb Ta*, l'Égypte, au nord-ouest du *Tabesti* du *Napata*. *Lam Baay Isi*, maître *lam*, prêtre *bay* du culte d'Isis, d'où *Lambaay Ise, Lambesis* ; *Lambaay Geej*, *Lambayeg*, prêtre de la Mer d'où Lambaay sur mer.

Le terme de *Ngoy* ou *Ngoy Ngoy* que l'on trouve dans *Ngoy Leydi*, *Ngoy-Ngoytara* ou *Goygoychea*, maître de l'eau, a servi à désigner les monarques du *Masila* et du *Masasi*, du *Tasili* et du *Ngoy* soninké. On le retrouve avec le toponyme de *Ghanata*, sur la presqu'île ibérique et basque des *Goygoychea*.

Le terme de *Tin, Tan, Ta*, locatif utilisé comme dérivatif, s'est universalisé ici entre l'Atlantique et la vallée du Nil, le Sud du bassin nigéro-sénégalais et l'Eurasie méditerranéenne : *Tin* des *Safeen*, du *Zafunu*, *Teen* du Baol, *Tin Barutan* du *Lamtuna* maghrébin, *Tin Juuf* dans le Tindouf algérien, *Tin Deni* ou *Taw Deni* et *Tin Bukutu* ou Tombouctou sur la boucle du Niger.

Le terme mandeng de *Ma Isa* ou *Mansa* signifie celui d'Isis. Il a donné *Mansa*, alias Menes, porté par le *Mansa Naramara* ou *Menes Narmer*. On le retrouve au Sahara, sous la forme de *Maysa huud* ou est peut-être même moins ancien ou pour le moins contemporain de *Mër Isë* qui en lébu ou wolof, signifie le Champion d'Isis. C'est *Mbër Isë* qui a donné *Berissa* et même *Beeco*, titres des monarques du Delta du Sénégal. *Mbër* a donné le titre de *Buur* que portent les monarques wolofs. *Buurba Jolof* signifie empereur du Jolof.

Le terme de *Baragen-Barag* ou *Brak* désigne des monothéistes adeptes de *Ragen*, Dieu Unique et *Ba* Suprême. C'est le titre des monarques du *Baragwata* qui exercent le pouvoir, le long de l'Atlantique, entre la Méditerranée des *Marogsenn* et la Sénégambie des *Margin*, des *Marowaaro* ou *Waalo-Waalo* et des *Rogseen-Sereer*.

Tunka est le titre soninké que porte *Masaani Siise*, alias Masanissa, Empereur du Ghana et des *Masila* qui s'opposent, vers 230, à la conquête romaine. On retrouve le titre du *Tunka* dans tous les États masila-soninké du Tasili saharien, du *Gatimara, Gidimakha, Guatemal*, du *Toro-Sila-Peru-Chili* sénégambien ou ultramarin. *Tunka* a donné *Inca*, titre des monarques du Ghanahusto mexicain.

Ce sont les adeptes du cycle osirien qui ont donné à leurs métropoles, à leurs ports et pays de la Méditerranée afro-eurasienne, le nom d'Ise alias Isis (*Tan Ise, Tunis, Tanit, Tara Isis, Taris*, Paris, etc.) et de *Masire* alias Osiris (*Masasila, Marsila, Marseille, Sila, Tasili, Toro-Sila*, Peru-Chili, etc.). Cette géographie culturelle a dessiné ses espaces politiques afro-eurasiens autour de la Méditerranée et de ses terres intérieures.

La géopolitique comme dynamique de la géographie culturelle, économique et politique évolue ici du lamana ou du pouvoir foncier et religieux des laman-monarques maîtres de territoires-nome ou de métropoles religieuses et politiques, à l'État et à l'Empire confédéral unificateur de royaumes ou de couronnes.

L'ibéro-maurussien des archéologues, pris au sens large, n'est pas seulement un phénomène de révolution technique, artistique ou spirituelle qui diffuse le rupestre, les mégalithes, les outils du lithique et de l'âge des métaux. Il fait partie d'une géopolitique. Celle-ci a uni, à une époque ou une autre, dans une même mouvance, le *Maratana* qui donne son nom à la *Mauretania*, le *Namata* numidien, le *Tabarikus-Ifrikiya*, le *Lébuta* lybique ou le *Gabbta* nubo-égyptien. Elle a pu étendre son influence vers le *Tabara* ibérique, le *Kasrawa* gaulois où *Barasentareg*, alias Vercingétorix affrontera César. Ce dernier venait de *Rama* ou Rome et du *Tara-Italia* des *Tarasakum* étrusques, des *Sakuli* de la Sicile, des *Taratana* de la Sardaigne. Les Grecs, Crétois du *Kusrata-Kretia* et les Corinthiens du *Taranta-Torentien* accusent les effets de son rayonnement.

Cette géopolitique ancienne peut être reconstituée avec d'autant plus de cohérence que l'on améliore l'historiographie de sources nubo-égyptienne et gréco-romaine, par celle très précieuse des auteurs arabophones et qu'on les révise toutes, avec les données de l'archéologie culturelle et historique.

Le rôle central du Sahara, de la Méditerranée et celui des axes de communication par terre et par mer dans la constitution et la permanence de cette géographie politique, légitiment l'utilisation dans un sens précis des notions d'empire et de pouvoir saharien ou transsaharien, maritime ou transmaritime.

L'espace nigéro-méditerranéen opère ses premières révolutions, au Sahara fertile, des millénaires avant l'avènement de l'Égypte pharaonique et de la Mésopotamie suméro-kouchite et harrapéenne. C'est la désertification amorcée définitivement à partir de l'an 2000 av. JC qui va ensevelir la civilisation, l'État et l'Empire sahariens pour repousser ses forces vives vers le bassin nigéro-sénégalais et tchadien, la Méditerranée, la Vallée du Nil et l'Atlantique. Le mythe pharaonique de l'Atlantide, repris par le Platon du *Timée*, renvoie certainement autant aux milliers de cités enfouies sous les sables du Sahara qu'aux terres de l'Outre-Atlantique. Il reste que les grandes puissances politiques que l'on y reconnaît ne perdront jamais ni pied, ni contact, singulièrement avec la Méditerranée et le Bassin nigéro-sénégalais, même à la Basse Antiquité avec l'expansion eurasienne mède, perse, grecque, romaine ou visigothe.

Une information importante existe sur ce plan, grâce à l'Égypte pharaonique. Celle-ci joue un rôle de premier plan avec ses navigateurs. Ils sillonnent la Méditerranée et l'Océan indien, des millénaires avant l'avènement de la navigation phénicienne Palestine, grecque ou romaine. Sur ce plan, les historiens s'abusent qui identifient les colonies afro-méditerranéennes *comme des «colonies phéniciennes ou grecques».* On parle ainsi de Marsilla ou Marseille la phocéenne, voire plus grave, de Carthage Taratagena la ville neuve phénicienne. En fait, c'est Tanisa, terre d'Isis qui a donné son nom à Phénicia, Phénicie et aux nombreuses métropoles maritimes ou terrestres d'un espace méditerranéen afro-eurasien qui avait universalisé la tradition rahmanique corrigée par le cycle osirien. La prééminence de la navigation nubo-égyptienne, a certainement prévalu jusqu'à la Basse Antiquité. Celle-ci voit affluer, vers toute la Méditerranée afro-asienne, des populations venant du nord, bousculées par les mouvements de peuples et les hégémonies mitanienne, hittite, mede et perse.

La richesse des économies africaines devait du reste attirer de fortes colonies eurasiennes comme celles des Grecs, des Phéniciens, Syriens ou Philistins qui immigraient dans toutes les grandes villes nubo-égyptiennes. Elles prennent des places importantes, comme les Pakistanais, les Chinois, les Grecs et les Européens en Afrique orientale contemporaine, dans l'activité des cités cosmopolites de la Méditerranée africaine.

L'avènement de l'islam redonnera du reste son essor à uns géographie politique transsaharienne qui avait décliné à la Basse Antiquité. La présence maritime africaine nigéro-méditerranéenne en Eurasie Occidentale et Outre-Atlantique est une donnée qui renouvelle l'histoire. On connaît les voies terrestres qui ont assuré en permanence le trafic transsaharien. La route occidentale mène par *Tadd Makka* et *Gadd Ma Isa* aux ports de *Tabarata* ou *Sabartha*, *Gabb Isa* et *Tarabulu-Tripoli*. La route occidentale mène de Tombouctou à *Ta Ghaza* pour bifurquer, soit vers *Ta Mentit Waragala* et les ports de *Tanis*, soit de *Taghaza* à Sigil Maisa, *Ta Lam Sen* et les ports *Marogsen* de *Taratana-Cartenae*, de *Tingita-*Tanger, et *Gad Ise*-Cadix, en Espagne. Cet axe est celui de l'État et de l'Empire transsaharien numide ou *Namata*, *Namatara Namandiir* ou *Nimrod*, *Ghanwa*, *Ghanata*, *Taghana* ou Dagana.

L'axe occidental transsaharien ouest-atlantique mène du delta et du bassin nigéro-sénégalais, riche de l'or du Ngalam, vers *Sigilmaïsa, Talamsen*. Il a pu être doublé par une route maritime dont les principaux ports sont *Tengiij* dans le *Jandeer*, au sud du delta du Sénégal, *Mouit, Ndeer Geej, Port Tennujukk, Taragin, Takasmin* alias *Tchommin* ou *Lixu, Tingita* ou Tanger, *Kusta* ou Ceuta, *Gad Ise* ou Cadix en Espagne. Cet axe est celui du *Baragwata-maratana*. Il a une activité transatlantique considérable avec ses Lébu mool mariniers qui drainent, en Amérique du Centre, du Nord et du Sud et le long du Pacifique, les migrations sénégambiennes qui seront les plus importantes avec celles des deltas du Niger et de la Volta.

Le rayonnement ultramarin de l'activité des populations de *géti mool* mariniers de l'espace nigéro-méditerranéen crée tôt, sur le pourtour de la mer intérieure, toute une économie maritime et portuaire. On trouve la marque des *mool* mariniers africains dans la toponymie des métropoles kushito-osiriennes ou rahmaniques que sont *Baay Kusum, Baay Saasum, Mouit, Taragin-Takurunkum (Lixus), Tingita* Tanger, *Kusta* Ceuta, etc. Ce système portuaire afro-asien naît tôt sous l'impulsion des *mool* mariniers *lébu lamtuna* qui peuplent les côtes méditerannéennes et l'Atlantique auxquelles ils donnent les noms respectifs de *Maratarana Meritaranée* et *Taratana Ataranta*. L'intérieur africain apporte l'or, l'intérieur eurasien ibérique apporte l'argent et l'étain. L'Eurasie orientale proche ou lointaine fournit surtout des épices et des artisanats.

La géographie politique nigéro-méditerranéenne s'est construite, pour des raisons économiques, démographiques et historiques, dans le sens sud-nord, contrairement à l'opinion courante. C'est l'or du Sud et sa puissance militaire (infanterie, cavalerie de chevaux et de chameaux, etc.) qui a assuré la permanence de cette prééminence. C'est du reste cette donnée qui impose une géographie. L'axe nilotique et fluvial a uni, à la Méditerranée, l'Afrique orientale, la Nubie, l'Éthiopie ou le Suten au Sud, à Kusta, le Nord et à Gebbta, l'Égypte. L'empire nubo-égyptien puise une part importante de sa richesse dans ce sud, mais aussi en Arabie. Cet axe voit se développer, le long du Nil, un grand nombre de métropoles portuaires entre les cataractes et au-delà (*Meroe, Napata, Kerma, Senne, Elephantine, T hèbes, Mennfari, Tanis*). Il invente tôt une navigation maritime sur l'Océan indien, vers l'Éthiopie, Punt ou l'Arabie, les côtes de l'Afrique orientale et australe vers le Sud-Est asiatique.

L'axe transsaharien oriental du bassin tchadien (Kanembu, Bornu, Hausa, Zarma Kawara, Sonrhai) va vers la Méditerranée centrale des *Tabarakas* de l'*Ifrikiya* et des *Lébudu* du *Lebta* libyen (par *Nijimi, Zawila, Sohna, Gabb Ise, Tarabulu,* etc.) et la Méditerranée orientale (par *Nijimi Ain Farah, Dongola Asynt, Gebbta,* Égypte). Cet axe qui est celui de l'Empire transsaharien du *Zaghawa* débouche sur le système portuaire méditerranéen oriental (*Tanis, Taratakas, Sabrata, Lepta*). L'axe transsaharien central et occidental part du bassin nigéro-sénégalais qui reçoit l'or des riches gisements de la Côte d'or du Ngalam et du Boure. Il englobe les salines du delta du Sénégal et les riches gisements de sel du Sahara. Il comporte trois itinéraires qui interfèrent au Sud et au Nord. Il sera organisé géopolitiquement par une succession d'empires: Ghana, Tekrour, Mali, Jolof et Sonrhaï.

Writing Over, Overwriting History: Politics and Language in Gisèle Pineau's *L'Exil selon Julia* and *Femmes des Antilles*

Dayna L. Oscherwitz

In a recent episode of a French television series entitled "L'Instit," M. Novak, the elementary school teacher who is the central character, goes to Martinique to fill-in for a colleague.[1] This episode caught my attention for two reasons: first, because the classroom scenes in the episode involve the teaching of history, and secondly because the history in question is that of the island of Martinique from slavery to departmentalization. The discourse on history "imparted" (one might say "imported") by M. Novak comes very close to what Edouard Glissant calls colonial history—a monolithic history which functions to impose on the peoples of the Caribbean both a version of the past, what George Lamming calls "memory" and a version of the present, what he calls "the colonial relation." Specifically, it represents the Caribbean subject as an object of European history, with no existence prior to or beyond the relationship with Europe. Briefly, Mr. Novak's lesson to his students is this: France brought your ancestors from Africa to the Antilles; your ancestors worked as slaves on the islands; France abolished slavery; now you are French. And while he does acknowledge the injustice and cruelty of slavery as an institution, Mr. Novak does nothing to interrogate the experience of the people of Martinique beyond these specific events.

Mr. Novak's version of history, which is French history in general, presents departmentalization as the logical conclusion of a trajectory begun with the slave trade. It functions to legitimize the

356   *Dayna L. Oscherwitz*

present political relationship which exists between France and the DOMs (overseas departments) of Martinique and Guadeloupe, by suggesting that the French citizenship conferred with departmentalization "corrects" the temporal and historical dislocation effected by the abduction from Africa through the imposition of a new historical identity—that of France.

It is in opposition to monolithic history and its legitimization of the French claim to the Antilles that Gisèle Pineau writes. Two of Pineau's texts in particular, *L'Exil selon Julia* (1996) and *Femmes des Antilles* (1998), undermine French historical meaning by questioning France's political assertion that the people of Martinique and Guadeloupe are French and by challenging the form and structure of history as such. Thematically, both texts affirm *créolité* (Creoleness) as an identity radically separate from *francité* (Frenchness); structurally, each is an unraveling of colonial history—an unraveling of the possibility of a unified, chronological representation of the past.

L'Exil selon Julia, the earlier of the two works, is the story of a young girl from Paris, and of her grandmother, Julia, who is from Guadeloupe. The narrative centers on the period during which Julia comes to live in Paris (the period of exile evoked in the title). Through its presentation of Julia's isolation and dislocation in France, *L'Exil selon Julia* points to the uniqueness and specificity of Creole experience. And through its exploration of the racism and rejection experienced by both Julia and her granddaughter, the text suggests that the French nationality of the people of the DOMs is little more than a political fallacy, which even the French themselves reject.

Although it is clear that *L'Exil selon Julia* is an autobiographical text, I wish to assert that it cannot be seen to be autobiography as such. Autobiography, according to Philippe Lejeune, is founded on an implied pact between the author and the reader in which the central character in the text is seen to be and represented as the author herself. As Lejeune explains, "autobiography (a story recounting the life of its author) presupposes the existence of an identification of the name between the author (as he appears, by his name, on the cover), the narrator, and the character about whom he speaks" (23-4).[2] Lejeune goes on to note that this identification between author and central narrator (as well as central character) is essential if the reader is to be certain that the text he/she is reading is a narration of the self. Pineau blocks this identification in

L'Exil selon Julia, and her purpose in doing so is to block precisely the identification of her text as the narration of an individual self. In so doing, Pineau allows the text to function as a more thematically and symbolically resonant fiction, asserting not her individuality, but rather her ties to a collective.

On a purely factual level, the text corresponds quite closely to what is known of Pineau's own childhood. She is the daughter of a man from Guadeloupe who was in the French army. She was born and spent the majority of her childhood in Paris, and there was a period during which her grandmother, Julia, came to live with her family. Furthermore, Julia or Man Ya's impact on the young girl within the narrative is much the same as the impact that Pineau asserts that her grandmother had on her. Why, then, can this not be seen to be autobiography? The first, and perhaps most obvious answer to this question is offered in Pineau's characterization of *L'Exil* as a "récit" or "story." This classification of the text is a deliberate backing away from autobiography—an insistence that at least part of what is recounted is fiction. Pineau compounds this initial act of distancing with her epigraph to the text, in which she writes "Chance of memory, invention? All is true and false, emotion. Here the essential borders adventitious memories" (6). Thus Pineau refuses to allow the text to be read as her recounting of her own, individual experience, because she refuses to allow the reader to distinguish between what is her own experience, and what she has invented.

This inability to distinguish fact from fiction within the text is compounded by yet another strategy used to prevent the reader from identifying the story Pineau recounts as the experience of her own life—her refusal to name the young girl in the story. Although the back cover of the novel identifies the young girl as "Gisèle," the name is never given with the text itself. This refusal to name the protagonist goes beyond a simple blocking of the identification of the text as autobiography—it also functions to generalize the experiences contained within the novel. If the child is not named, then circumstances and events ascribed to her become not only hers, but those of a larger group; and as Pineau has elsewhere stated, this larger group is the Antillean people.

L'Exil selon Julia functions narratively to expand the act of generalization begun with this refusal to name the little girl in the text. Through its presentation of Julia's isolation and dislocation in France, the novel points to the uniqueness and specificity of Creole experience. And through its exploration of the racism and rejection experienced by both Julia and her granddaughter, *L'Exil selon Julia* suggests that the French nationality of the people of the Antilles is little more than a political fallacy, which even the French, themselves, reject.

Beginning with the title, Pineau's narrative aligns itself with the *Créolité* movement of Patrick Chamoiseau and Raphaël Confiant by calling the discourse of *francité* or "Frenchness" into question. Chamoiseau and Confiant have argued for the distinction between the people of the Antilles and all other people, and have called for a literature which celebrates this distinction. Pineau's text seems to respond to that call, affirming, even in the title, the fundamental difference between Frenchness and Creoleness.

In the title of the novel, the period Julia spends in France is referred to as a period of exile. Typically, exile refers to a separation from one's own country; Julia, who is from Guadeloupe and is, therefore, technically French, would not normally be seen to be in exile in France. This paradox of identity has only one of two possible solutions: either Julia is not in exile, or she is not French. It is this second hypothesis which Pineau's narrative explores and affirms. For, it is clear from the beginning that Julia *is* a foreigner in France. Brought there by her son, she feels completely displaced, and wishes desperately to return to Guadeloupe. She is completely unfamiliar with Paris and with urban life. She can not speak French; she can neither read nor write, and is thus forced into near imprisonment in the family's apartment. Against these images of the helpless Julia of France, Pineau's text offers images of the very different Julia of Guadeloupe: a masterful gardener, a capable mother, interpreter of the mysteries of the island. Through juxtaposition, Pineau makes it clear that Julia's handicap is that she is out of her element; France is not her home.

What is more, it becomes clear that France rejects Julia as much as she rejects France. Pineau writes that the family's French neighbors look at Julia "without seeing her" because to them "she represents an ancient state, the bygone era when the city was yet unknown" (114). Because of the color of her skin, Julia represents all of the stereotypes of the primitivism of Africa and by extension the Caribbean, a fact which causes the French neighbors to see her as incompatible with modernity and with France.

The assumption that dark skin is a mark of primitivism and foreignness is generalized and represented as part of a larger French cultural mentality, and it is made manifest in the text by an episode during which Julia is arrested for contempt for France because she walks down the street wearing an army helmet and coat. Pineau sets the episode up very clearly as an example of cultural conflict. Julia, a Creole, characterized by her creole practicality, decides to wear her son's helmet and coat in order to meet her grandchildren after school and prevent them from getting wet. As Pineau describes it, Man Ya's only concern is her grandchildren. Determined to keep them dry, she chooses the coat and hat for purely practical reasons. However, this gesture is read in a completely different manner by the French she encounters on the street. At the sight of an old Creole woman in an army uniform, the police and the people on the street look "as if France has just been invaded by one of its mortal enemies, as if the honor of the fatherland were being trampled, there, before their eyes" (97). The reaction of the bystanders makes it clear that Julia's act of "contempt" is simply to have dared, as a black woman, to have put on the uniform of the French army—another indication that, to the French, Julia's black skin marks her as foreign, as not French, and therefore, when she wears something which represents France, it is seen as an act of derision, as the act of a foreigner who wishes to ridicule the honor of France.

Beyond the obvious racism revealed in this passage, there is another point which Pineau wishes to make. The fact that the uniform which Julia wears belongs to her son is completely lost upon the white Parisians who react with such contempt. In other words, this uniform belongs to a black man, a black man who has fought and dedicated his life to France. This is completely overlooked by the police, who wish to arrest Julia, and the people on the street, and Pineau uses this passage to suggest the degree to which there is an unbridgeable gap between blackness and Frenchness in the minds of both the French people, represented by the bystanders, and the French state, represented by the police.

The separation between blackness and Frenchness in the French cultural unconscious is emphasized by the fact that Julia is not the only member of her family to feel like an outsider in France. Man Ya's granddaughter, who was born in Paris, and who spends nearly all of her life there, feels equally out of place. She, too, experiences racism on a daily basis. Her classmates call her names like "Bamboula" and "Négresse." They see her black skin as an indication that she is not French, and tell her to "go back to her own country." Her teacher calls her "the black" and as a result singles her out and forces her to sit under her desk. These experiences cause the granddaughter to identify much more closely with the Guadeloupe of Julia's stories than with the France she has known all of her life. Ultimately she, like Julia, longs for a "return" to a Guadeloupe she barely knows.

In reaction to the double-bind of identity experienced by both Julia and her granddaughter, caught between being French and not French, Pineau offers a solution. Because Julia is so obviously alienated by her linguistic difference, her grandchildren attempt to teach Julia French. This transmission of language is particularly important in the text, given the place language occupies in the writing of the Créolists. Bernabé, Chamoiseau and Confiant have argued that the French language is a blow to the Creole imagination, and they go on to assert that the acceptance of French is, for a Creole, tantamount to having no identity at all. Thus, the children's attempt to teach their grandmother French is their own re-enactment of France's efforts to erase Creole identity through assimilation. For this reason, Julia's response to the children's efforts is extremely revealing. Instead of simply refusing to learn French, Julia waits until the children are away at school, and washes all of the French out of their notebook, "flipping the pages of the notebook under the stream of chlorinated water, which unravels the letters of the alphabet [. . .] feeling the unstitched words, the grammar rules, the adjectives, the proper nouns and the spelling mistakes flow between her fingers" (165-6). With this simple gesture, Julia is able to demonstrate to her grandchildren the mutability of the French language (and by extension identity), which they have been conditioned to regard as concrete. Instead of being coaxed into abandoning her Creole for French, Julia simply washes away the French and leaves her Creole in its place. Perhaps more revealing is the use that is made of these blank pages, as Élie, the youngest of the grandchildren uses these "washed" notebooks as the material for "his most beautiful drawings: the suns and shacks of Guadeloupe that he had seen through the eyes of Man Ya" (166). In other words, at this moment, Man Ya works with her grandchildren to participate in an act of cultural overwriting: they participate together to substitute a Creole identity for the French identity for that the children have been taught. What is more, the substitution does not occur term for term; Frenchness is seen as a product of written language, whereas Creoleness is presented through pictures, which are themselves linked to oral language (Julia's description). Apart from granting Creoleness a dynamism and duality that Frenchness is here denied, this passage also serves to echo Edouard Glissant.

Glissant reads western (and particularly French) History as a "highly functional fantasy of the West originating at precisely the time when it alone 'made' the history of the World" (64). Glissant, then, points to History (by which he means written History) as the master discourse by which and through which Europe both accomplished and legitimizes its dominance over the rest of the world. He goes on to note that in the case of the Martinique and Guadeloupe, the function of History has been such as to cause "a visible abandonment of the *collective spirit*, of the common will that alone allows a people to survive as a people" (5). Furthermore, Glissant locates this struggle for community as the struggle against written French: "It is against this double hegemony of a History with a capital H and Literature consecrated by the absolute power of the written sign that the peoples who until now inhabited the hidden side of the earth fought, at the same time they were fighting for food and freedom" (76). Given this theoretical context, it could be argued that, with the washing out of the notebooks and the overwriting with drawings of Guadeloupe, Pineau is herself proposing an alternative to the sign-centered French identity imposed upon Julia and her grandchildren. Furthermore, since this act is, itself, communal (it requires the participation of Julia, through the act of washing and storytelling) and of the grandchildren (who draw what they have heard) it could be read that this oral transmission and re-inscription is a realization of that communal identity and spirit of which Glissant speaks—a fact rendered obvious in the text by the identification of the children with their grandmother, and the narrator's subsequent longing for a "return."

This reading of Julia as a model for Creoleness as distinct and different from Frenchness is also evident in the structuring of Pineau's text. For example, the second section of the récit, entitled "The Five Ministries of Man Ya" seems to propose Julia as a nation unto herself, and one which stands in opposition to the nation of France. The final of these "ministries" or governmental departments is "Medicine," and the medicine which Man Ya represents here is the return to Guadeloupe. More importantly, at the end of the text, after the entire family finally does "return" to Guadeloupe, the grand daughter makes Julia's role in the text absolutely unmistakable. She states that what Man Ya really brought to her grandchildren was "cleared footpaths of her Creole tongue [. . .] words, vision, rays of sunshine and patience in existence. She designated to us the three sentinels, past, present, future, which hold the threads of time . . . she had woven them to create, day after day, a solid bridge between over there and our country" (304). In Pineau's own words, Julia is not only an embodiment of Guadeloupe; her presence in the lives of her family created for them, even for those born in France, a bridge upon which to return. Pineau's designation of the geography at play here is also revealing. Instead of using "our country" to refer to France, where the children were born, Pineau uses it to designate Guadeloupe. Also, instead of designating France as the point of origin, she calls it "over there," suggesting again, that it is Guadeloupe to which not only Julia, but her grandchildren belong.

Thus *L'Exil selon Julia* rejects the French political position that Martinique and Guadeloupe are France, in that for Julia and for her family, it is not their country, but a country of exile. Furthermore, she suggests that the people on these islands are not French, through her presentation of a racism which regards blackness and Frenchness as mutually exclusive. Beyond this, however, *L'Exil selon Julia* calls into question the validity of French history. That Pineau is implicating history in the text is evident, albeit subtly, in her inclusion of details which "official" history tends to omit. In the course of the text, for example, Gisèle tells the story of Sylvette Cabrisseau, France's first black television announcer, who was fired because viewers claimed that she was corrupting the French language and that her black face frightened French children. She describes viewer objection to Cabrisseau as grounded in her "foreignness" and she subsequently records the rejection of Cabrisseau not as personal, but as a further rejection of the Frenchness of the Antilles (142).

Like Julia in uniform, Sylvette Cabrisseau on French television is seen as an affront to national pride, as a threat to the purity of French. Thus, like Julia and like her grandchildren, Sylvette is read as a foreigner by enough people in France so as to have her removed from the screen. In this way, Pineau further generalizes the experiences of Julia and her granddaughter so that they now apply to all of those coming from the Antilles. This generalization functions to create the alternate Creole community already suggested in Julia's designation as nation. Furthermore, by including this "forgotten" aspect of the past, Pineau represents her own text as a counter-history to History—inscribing events and aspects which official French history omits.

L'Exil selon Julia, then, takes on history, but does so as a means of questioning the political claims of France on Martinique and Guadeloupe. Pineau's more recent work, Femmes des Antilles, however, takes on history itself. Written to commemorate the 150th anniversary of the abolition of slavery, and co-authored with journalist Marie Abraham, Femmes des Antilles is a much more overtly historical work than L'Exil selon Julia. In her introduction to the text, Pineau explains the work as an attempt to record the experience of female slaves, to "watch them exit, one after the other, from the jail of forgetting where history had entombed them" (10-1). In her own words, history is a force which has been used to contain the black woman, and, as the text illustrates, much of Creole experience in general.

It is not, however, this simple assertion of intent which places Femmes des Antilles in opposition to official history, it is also the structure and the content of the text. Structurally, Femmes des Antilles is quite complex; each of the thirteen sections of the work consists of a primary text which presents a particular aspect or experience of slavery in the Antilles, and several secondary texts which interpret the primary text. All of the primary, or "event" narratives were written by Marie Abraham. They are largely factual and statistical in nature, and are accompanied by etchings and paintings from the colonial period.

The interpretive texts which follow were written by Pineau. These are nearly all first person narratives which present the testimonies of various women whether past or present, real or imagined. These texts, in and of themselves, challenge the authority of history, not only by interpreting the "real" historical events described in Marie Abraham's sections, but by blurring the distinction between real and fictional women. Pineau writes the voices of Solitude the Mulatresse, or Emma the slave as realistically as she writes Firmine Richard, the actress, or Jocelyne Béroard, the musician. Thus it becomes difficult to differentiate Pineau's voice from those of the real women she represents, and the real women from those she has invented.

Furthermore, the structure and composition of the sections of *Femmes des Antilles* openly challenge the accuracy of colonial history. The first of the sections is entitled "Land of Ebony" and recounts life in Africa before the abduction, and the last is "Abolition"; in this respect the text evokes such colonial history, which inscribes Caribbean experience between these two very moments. Through the in-between sections, however, which include "La Loi–Le Code Noir" and "Les Resistances et les révoltes," *Femmes des Antilles* draws attention to events or details overlooked by French history itself. Ultimately, this alternation between what is remembered and what has been forgotten, between past and present, between real and fiction, when combined with the thematic, rather than chronological sectioning of the text, functions in absolute opposition to formal history and explodes any possibility of a closed historical trajectory which begins with abduction and ends with abolition.

In addition to challenging history, *Femmes des Antilles* addresses many of the political issues addressed in *L'Exil selon Julia.* Several of the narratives speak of the racism and exclusion suffered by those who go to the metropole to improve their situation. These narratives attest not only to the degree of racism in France, but to the French inability to accept Creoles as French. Even more than this, however, they point to a fundamental flaw in the relationship between the DOM's and France. By contrasting the economic hardship found in the DOM's with the prosperity of metropolitan France, Pineau's text emphasizes that, despite the legal reality and the political rhetoric, the DOMs are held at arms length by France—they lack the real equality, the economic and educational equality, that departmentalization should bring. Other voices in the text draw attention to the fact that departmentalization, as a continuation of colonial domination, has done fundamental damage to Creole identity. Colette, a young woman who went to Paris to complete her studies, speaks of the way in which the people of Guadeloupe replicate French racism in their dealings with their Caribbean neighbors. She speaks of how Haitians and Dominicans are often looked down upon, and seen as inferior, and she asserts that the people of Guadeloupe tend to forget that all the people of the Caribbean share a common history, that, in her words, "perhaps we even shared the same slave ship. We forget that before we were French from overseas, Domiens, the Departmentalized, we are, for the most part, the descendants of those naked blacks taken from Africa" (54). Through the voice of Colette, Pineau suggests that the inequality and poverty found in Guadeloupe is not simply economic; it is also cultural. It is the result of the politics of *francité*, which leads Creoles to think of themselves as French, but as imperfect French, the "Français d'outre mer" and, therefore, to conceive of themselves as subaltern.

Ultimately, *Femmes des Antilles*, like *L'Exil selon Julia*, functions as a counter-discourse to history as such, and particularly to French history. Thematically, as well as structurally, both texts cast doubt on the substance and meaning of French history, existing in the tension between events and voices which are remembered by France, and those "events" which are ignored and suppressed. They draw attention to the ways in which history functions to bind the islands of Martinique and Guadeloupe to France in an impossible relationship of present/absence. The effect of French history and national politics, according to Pineau's texts, is to estrange Creole people from themselves. In this light, the exile alluded to in the title of *L'Exil selon Julia* is shown to be not only Julia's exile from Guadeloupe, but Guadeloupe's exile from its own past and identity. The solution she offers to this imposed exile is an unwriting and a rewriting of history. Gisèle Pineau, in effect, points us back to Julia. In the same way that Julia washes the children's notebooks to have the written French replaced with pictures of Guadeloupe, Pineau is attempting to wash away the imposed *francité* of the Antilles and to inscribe *créolité* in its place.

Notes

1. This episode of "L'Instit" entitled "Le trésor" aired on France 2 on Wednesday, January 13 at 9pm. According to France 2, "L'Instit," which has been running since 1993, "has always received excellent ratings,

among the network's best . . . approximately 42% of the prime time viewing audience." Clearly, it is a television program aimed at the general public (in France).

2. All translations of Lejeune and Pineau are my own.

Works Cited

Bernabé, Jean, Patrick Chamoiseau and Raphaël Confiant. *Éloge de la Créolité/In Praise of Creoleness*. Trans. M. B. Taleb-Khyar. Paris: Gallimard, 1993.

Glissant, Edouard. *Caribbean Discourse: Selected Essays*. Trans. J. Michael Dash. Charlottesville: University of Virginia Press, 1989.

Lamming, George. *The Pleasures of Exile*. London: Allison and Busby, 1984.

Lejeune, Philippe. *Le Pacte autobiographique*. Paris: Seuil, 1980.

Pineau, Gisèle. *L'Exil selon Julia*. Paris: Stock, 1996.

Pineau, Gisèle and Marie Abraham. *Femmes des Antilles*. Paris: Stock, 1998.

Africa's Word to the World

Okello Oculi

Rejecting withdrawal, renunciation,
or devaluing currency of life here
under Sun, Moonlight,
Rain and Dry seasons,
(for fear of breaking stools and heads),
        we have chosen to fight and bleed:
        Demanding our world within worlds;
        Rejecting mud as perfume on eyes
        of herdsmen, hoemen, fishermen, miners
        for breeding flowers over silence.

Our Nirvana is sap rising in dancing spines:
capacity with arrows are kalashnikovs blue flames in voices
of our women smithing mind and eye ball to courage
in all; rejecting greedy claws of wizards;
Teaching others how to shake the world in milk
gourds, cleansing silted pus from buttocks of their
traditions.

We chose to grow with action;
Breaking twigs;
trampling swamps as midnight snored,
fireflies flirted crickets cheering;
denouncing contemplation as swimming pools
for our pains; Talking and talking and talking
till we enraged an eyebrow, a village market, a
people to cobwebs;
roasting inertia to feed nocturnal commandos,
on prowl, or blaze;
Walking,
        stalking,
                running in charges,
                    retreating;
churning will of motion;

performing History's duty in farming dignity of Man.

Will the dyes on our duties fade,
spreading despair?
Or will the march of ozone sprout new voices
to war, not preludes to hereafters?
Today Mobutu Sese Seko shot people chanting
vote for Zaire, standing on his neck;
Tomorrow they will shoot him,
standing on neck of his Zaire;
actualizing potentiality of small fishes eating
sharks in our sea;
keeping their word, drink of fire,
thunder.

From *Song for the Sun in Us* (Nairobi: East African Educational
Publishers, 2000).

IV. Literary and Political Developments

Counting Caliban's Curses:
A Statistical Inventory

Bernth Lindfors

Once upon a time, during a stormy season in human history, a band of seafarers found themselves shipwrecked on the coast of a tropical island inhabited by several peoples they had never before encountered. Accustomed to misadventures in foreign lands, the mariners quickly set up camp, made themselves at home, and sent out small parties to explore the island and establish commerce with the natives. Thus was communication initiated between heterogenous language communities, one globally expansive, the others relatively fixed and stationary. As in other parts of the world, the mobile language community penetrated, occupied and colonized the immobile language communities, extending communicative hegemony over numerous widely scattered peoples by implanting its own tongue in the mouths of all it met. English, already an international lingua franca, proved an expeditious vehicle for this ambitious networking enterprise. The British—for so these sea dogs were called—soon were in control of much of the import-export trade, for their voices carried farther than anyone else's. They came, they communicated, and they conquered, forging linguistic links not only directly between themselves and their many hosts but also laterally between all those hosts with whom they had established productive parasitic intercourse. Their empire was a vast, worldwide internet connected by a single operational code. Anglophonia ruled the waves.

This alien code did not always work to the disadvantage of those who adopted it or adapted to it. At first a disgruntled, inarticulate Caliban might complain to Prospero and Miranda that "You taught me language, and my profit on't/Is, I know how to curse," but once he had achieved a fuller fluency and learned how to read and write, Caliban discovered himself in command of an expressive power that went well beyond impotent imprecations. English became for him an instrument of self-assertion, a tool of liberation, a means to desirable counter-hegemonic ends. He could now talk back to those who had stolen his island and could make his grievances known to an international tribunal. He was hooked up and plugged into a global information superhighway, a brave new world of intelligible interactive discourse.

But to gain access to this larger universe he had to pay a heavy price. Taking the leap from the past to the future required years of schooling, including faithful adherence to a grueling gymnastic regimen that bent him out of his original shape. By the time he mastered all the necessary moves, he had become a different person—acculturated, assimilated, melded, hybridized. He was now a man of two worlds, no longer at ease in the old dispensation yet not entirely at home in the new. And he was far more conspicuous, far more vulnerable, than before, for whatever he wrote could be read and evaluated not only by others like himself but also by countless strangers abroad who operated in the same metropolitan register. His international idiom had made him an islander no more.

This tempestuous little allegory may serve as a useful cautionary tale for those of us considering problems of scholarly authority and intellectual production in African literature studies today, for it may alert us to some of the lingering geographical, political, racial and linguistic tensions that have produced peculiar distortions in postcolonial literary studies throughout the Third World. The complaint everywhere seems to be that there are still too many Prosperos and Mirandas calling the critical shots, that the little islanders are being crowded out of their own domain by uncouth continentals, that careerist Northerners with easier access to money, machines and magazines are monopolizing discussion of literary works by Southerners, that First Worlders and Third Worlders are not engaged in any sort of dialogue but are speaking only to their own kind, the First Worlders through electronically amplified megaphones, the Third Worlders through baffles and mufflers. Furthermore, in the West the language of literary criticism has itself changed, moving toward higher and higher levels of abstraction and self-reflexivity, leaving many non-Westerners speaking in a quaint, old-fashioned hermeneutic dialect, if they are allowed to speak at all. In short, Africa, a silent partner in its own intellectual marginalization, may be losing control of its own Anglophone literature.

To test these explosive charges, it may be helpful to examine a few statistical charts that reveal in plain, stark numbers where the greatest imbalances in African and non-African production of literary scholarship have existed and continue to exist today. The following data have been gleaned from four consecutive volumes of *Black African Literature in English*, a bibliography listing more than twenty thousand books and articles on Anglophone black African literature published between 1936 and 1991. The first of these volumes, covering forty-one years of scholarly activity, ran to 3305 items; the latest five-year update, covering only 1987 to 1991, contains 8772 entries, almost a threefold increase over the original compilation. This sharp upsurge in scholarly productivity reveals that literary criticism has been a major growth industry in African studies in recent years.

To reduce these charts to manageable proportions I have listed the relevant figures for only the top three writers in Anglophone Africa: Wole Soyinka, Chinua Achebe and Ngugi wa Thiong'o. More has been written about these authors than about any others, so together they provide a sufficiently large sample for statistical analysis. But I have narrowed the database a bit by concentrating exclusively on literary criticism and eliminating from the count all other forms of scholarship—e.g., bibliographies, biographical books and articles, and published interviews. I have also excluded all works that deal with more than a single author, for they would have complicated the scoring system considerably. So the numbers on these tables represent only those scholarly studies that are devoted to one of the big three: Soyinka, Achebe, or Ngugi. And I have subdivided the data into six categories—books, study guides, book chapters, articles, doctoral dissertations, master's theses—each of which may tell us something different about the authors and critics concerned.

In order to get a sense of how the chart works, let us start with the smallest category: books published on a single author (chart 1). BALE is an acronym for *Black African Literature in English*, each volume of which is represented by a roman numeral. To bring the record further up to date, a fifth column covering book production in 1992-95 has been

Bernth Lindfors

added. NI stands for Nigerian, OA for Other African, NA for Non-African, KE (under Ngugi) for Kenyan, IN (under Grand Totals) for Indigene, T for Total, SGT for Super Grand Total, and GTSGT for Grand Total of Super Grand Totals. The horizontal plane represents the place of publication, and the vertical plane indicates the nationality of the scholar. If, for example, we look at the first combinations of figures listed in column I, we see that between 1936 (actually 1965) and 1976 there were a total of four books published on Soyinka, three on Achebe, and none on Ngugi. One of the books on Soyinka was by a Nigerian and was published in Nigeria, one was by a scholar from another part of Africa and was published outside Africa, and two were by non-African scholars and were published outside Africa. Similarly, all three of the books on Achebe were published outside Africa, one by a scholar from another part of Africa, the other two by non-Africans. So from this slice of the chart we may draw the conclusion that most of the earliest book-length scholarship on these two authors was published outside Africa (as it happens, in London, Paris and New York), and nearly all of it was produced by non-Nigerian critics. As can be seen from the figures listed in columns II and III, this pattern in scholarly production continued through the next decade, but began to change between 1987 and 1995, when Nigerian scholars started to assert themselves more vigorously and turn to writing and publishing books at home on Soyinka and Achebe. But if one examines the Grand Totals for each author as well as the Super Grand Total that combines the numbers for all three authors, one cannot fail to notice that the majority of the seventy books on Soyinka, Achebe and Ngugi have been produced by non-Africans and that an even greater majority, including some books by Nigerians and other Africans, have been published outside Africa.

One may refine these generalizations still further by taking into account the nationalities of the scholars who produced the books, noting the languages in which they wrote. Achebephiles have the widest geographical distribution, hailing from five African countries (Nigeria -7, Cameroon -1, Ghana -1 , Kenya -1, Zaïre -1) and eleven non-African countries (USA -3.5, UK -2.5, Canada -1, Germany -1, France -1, Sweden -1, Italy -1, Russia -1, India -1, Australia -.5, and Denmark -.5). Most of them wrote in English, but two published books in French, one in Italian, and one in Russian. The Soyinkaphiles have a similar broad distribution, coming from four African nations (Nigeria -12, Sierra Leone -1, Ivory Coast -1, Swaziland -1) and eight non-African nations (France - 4, UK -3.5, India -3, Sweden -2, USA -1.5, Germany -1, Russia -1, Australia -1). Most wrote in English, except for five who chose to publish in French, one in German, and one in Russian. Ngugiphiles are from three African countries (Nigeria -1.5, Kenya -1, Senegal -1) and seven non-African counties (Canada -2, Germany -2, UK -1.5, France -1, Sweden -1, Italy -1, India -1). Ten of them expressed themselves in English, one in German, one in French, and one in Swedish. Significantly, no book has been written on Soyinka, Achebe or Ngugi in an African language. All three authors are well known abroad, even in non-English-speaking parts of the world, but they have not yet been introduced to other language communities in their own countries.

Study guides (chart 2)—booklets prepared as aids to students—reveal which of these authors are being read most regularly in high schools. As might be expected, Achebe is the clear leader in this category, especially in Nigeria, where his books often have been prescribed for School Certificate examinations. But he also scores well in other parts of Africa and overseas. Ngugi is a distant runner-up, yet he too is studied with some frequency in other parts of Africa (particularly Nigeria), and his books were educational staples in Kenya until he fell afoul of the Kenyatta and Moi regimes, at which point they were removed from the high school syllabus. No study guide on any of Ngugi's works has been published in Kenya since 1985. Many of Soyinka's books are considered too difficult for high school students to deal with, so they seldom are assigned at the secondary level. This may explain why there are so few study guides published in Africa on his work; those published in Europe appear to be aimed at university students.

Book chapters (chart 3) tell a different story. Here the overwhelming majority of studies have been written by non-African scholars for books published outside Africa. This may reflect a significant difference in indigenous and foreign publishing practice—African presses seldom bring out edited collections of essays on literary topics, but Western presses are not reluctant to do so. The sudden increase after 1987 in indigenous collections in which essays on Soyinka and Achebe appeared may be attributed to two extraordinary events, both of them significant milestones: Soyinka's winning of the Nobel Prize in December of 1986, and Achebe's sixtieth birthday celebration in February of 1990. Nearly all the fourscore and more essays recorded in Achebe's Nigerian column were abstracts of papers delivered at an academic symposium held as part of the birthday commemoration festivities, most of which were published in 1996. Discounting these volumes that were brought out in Nigeria to celebrate the achievements of its two greatest writers, the statistics present us with a striking instance of imbalance in scholarly production. Since 1975 (the date of the first contribution of this kind), Nigerians have produced only 14 book chapters on Wole Soyinka, 10 of them for edited volumes published outside Africa. Since 1968 Nigerians have produced only 22 book chapters on Achebe, 14 of them for edited volumes published outside Africa. Since 1973, Kenyans have produced only 6 book chapters on Ngugi, 4 of them for edited volumes published outside Africa. Non-African critics in the meantime have produced 112 book chapters on Soyinka, 97 book chapters on Achebe, and 68 book chapters on Ngugi, publishing all but a handful of them outside Africa. They have produced only two chapters—one on Soyinka and one on Achebe—for books published in Nigeria, and only one chapter on Ngugi for a book published in Kenya. And they have produced only two chapters—one on Soyinka and one on Ngugi—for books published elsewhere in Africa. So in this form of scholarship we have very clear evidence not only of underproduction in Africa and overproduction in the West but also of a disturbing lack of intellectual reciprocity between African and non-African critics. At this level there is hardly any contact, much less exchange, between the two groups, and there is no evidence that the situation has been improving over time. Since books published in the West are too expensive for most scholars based in Africa to buy, and since their financially strapped university libraries may not be able to afford to acquire many of them either, communication via such vehicles has been moving almost entirely in one direction. Westerners have been talking to Westerners, and a few Africans have been talking to Westerners, but hardly anyone has been talking to Africans.

A similar pattern can be discerned in the statistics on articles that have appeared in serial publications (chart 4), but here there is one noteworthy difference. Non-African critics continue to write largely for non-African media; 88% of their essays on Soyinka, 92% of their essays on Achebe, and 87% of their essays on Ngugi have appeared in journals and magazines published outside Africa. African critics, on the other hand, have shown a marked preference for writing for their own media, especially in recent years. This tendency has been most pronounced in Nigeria, but it also prevails in all other parts of Africa except Kenya, where there has actually been a marked decline in interest in Ngugi since 1987. This of course may be connected with his status as persona non grata in his motherland. Elsewhere in Africa, with the understandable exception of Nigeria, Ngugi is a more popular subject among literary critics than Soyinka and Achebe are.

The recent spurt in Nigerian interest in its two favorite literary sons may be attributed in part to the historic events mentioned earlier—the Nobel Prize and the birthday party—but it may also be seen as a natural consequence of the proliferation of indigenous media—particularly newspapers—that carry literary criticism. The cultural columns in the Nigerian press have literally democratized literary debate in that country, moving it from university ivory towers directly to the streets. Nowhere else in Africa has this happened on the same scale. Unfortunately, however, the energy expended in these palavers does not resonate far abroad, for the papers that have promoted such dialogue—mainly *The Guardian*, *National Concord*, *Daily Times* and *Vanguard*, the first two of which have on occasion been banned for political reasons—do not circulate widely outside Nigeria. So Nigerians may be talking productively to one another but what they are saying cannot easily be heard beyond their national borders. Their arguments are internal domestic affairs, not international media events.

If we turn now to doctoral dissertations (chart 5), a similar tendency toward indigenization can be detected, but at this point it is only an incipient tendency. Before 1987 Nigerians and other Africans who wrote doctoral dissertations on Soyinka or Achebe did so at institutions outside Africa, but in recent years about fifty percent of the Nigerians have been writing such dissertations at their own national institutions. Most other Africans, notably those from Francophone countries, have continued to do their Ph.D.s on these Anglophone writers at non-African universities, but since 1987, at least two Algerians and two Nigerians chose to write dissertations on Ngugi at institutions at home rather than abroad. The non-African doctoral students working on African literature, on the other hand, have overwhelmingly elected to earn their degrees at non-African universities, the sole exception to date being an Indian woman who completed her doctorate on Soyinka in 1985 at the University of Ife (now called Obafemi Awolowo University) where Soyinka himself was then teaching. What is perhaps most encouraging about the figures on this chart is that they show that more African scholars have written doctoral dissertations on Soyinka, Achebe and Ngugi than non-African scholars have. A majority of the real experts on these writers, in other words, are African-born, though not necessarily African-trained. But this fact contrasts sharply with the data we have already seen on scholarly production of books, book chapters and articles. Western-trained non-Africans, many of whom have not studied Soyinka, Achebe or Ngugi as deeply as the African dissertation writers, are nonetheless producing the bulk of the scholarship on them. Is this a case of opportunistic foreigners rushing in where abler Africans fear to tread, or is it an infrastructural problem that gives a real edge and incentive to energetic interlopers who are under disciplinary pressure to publish or perish and who possess the means and media to do so? Why should so much of the discourse be dominated by the untrained and self-taught, many of whom have never set foot in Africa?

The incipient tendency toward indigenization perceptible in the doctoral dissertations chart becomes more pronounced on the chart devoted to master's theses (chart 6). Here we can see a real move on the part of young Nigerian academics to claim Soyinka and Achebe as their own intellectual property. Whereas initially they tended to write their theses abroad, most of them writing on these authors since 1982 have been doing their work at home. They have also claimed Ngugi as one of their own. The great majority of theses done on Ngugi by African students at universities outside Kenya have been produced by Nigerians, mostly at Nigerian institutions. Non-Africans, unsurprisingly, have written most of their master's theses on African literature at non-African universities, although lately a few have ventured as far afield as Nigeria and Kenya to write on Soyinka, and Tanzania to write on Ngugi. Again, the exceptions tend to prove the rule: Africans are now increasingly being educated in Africa, while non-Africans, as before, are being educated almost exclusively outside Africa. Perhaps this is nothing to worry about; indeed, it may be what we should expect to happen at the lower postgraduate level. The Nigerian hijacking of Ngugi may also be normal and natural, given the number of Nigerian universities that are now offering graduate degrees.

If we look now at the final set of figures—the Grand Totals and the Super Grand Totals (chart 7)—there are some interesting patterns that emerge. First, up to 1976, non-Africans had produced approximately 60% of the scholarship on Soyinka, Achebe and Ngugi. Nowadays their share of the total output has dropped to about 51%, so it is clear that African critics, particularly Nigerians, have been making gradual gains in the last twenty years. Non-African critics used to produce 59% of the commentary on Soyinka, but now they account for no more than 54% of the total. They also used to produce 63% of the scholarship on Achebe, but today their portion of the total critical corpus has dropped to only 46%. With Ngugi the picture is a little different, with non-Africans, formerly producers of 50% of the criticism, now weighing in slightly higher, at 53%. Yet the drift toward Africanization of the critical industry is unmistakable. Far from losing control of their own Anglophone literature, African critics are slowly taking it back. If this trend continues, they may be able to claim more than 50% of the critical enterprise before the end of this century. This is real progress.

Yet if one examines the bottom line—the places of publication—one finds that a majority of the studies of Soyinka, Achebe and Ngugi are still being published outside Africa. In 1976 the figure stood at roughly 61%; today it stands at almost 63%. But even here the news is not all bad, for 66% of all the Nigerians who have written on Soyinka, 70% of all the Nigerians who have written on Achebe, and 67% of all the Kenyans who have written about Ngugi have published their works at home. But offsetting this promising homeward-looking orientation among the Africans is a far more chauvinistic attitude among the Westerners. 90% of the non-African scholars who have written about Soyinka or Ngugi and 92% of the non-African scholars who have written about Achebe have published their works outside Africa. This is where the greatest inequity (not to mention iniquity) lies. Non-African scholars appear to have little desire to exchange ideas with African scholars. They are eager to publish on African literature but not in African media. They are interested in African writers but not in African readers. These modern-day Prosperos and Mirandas would rather sit in armchairs at home making magisterial theoretical pronouncements in antiseptic isolation than risk getting their feet a little muddy on Caliban's island.

Unfortunately, they are not the only ones with this kind of phobia. A good number of African critics betray some of the same pathological symptoms. These reluctant travelers might be prepared to publish occasionally in Prospero and Miranda's distant kingdom, but they do not appear to be keen to address their own neighbors next door. Of the 321 books, study guides, essays, dissertations and theses that Nigerians have written about Soyinka, only 21 (6.5%) have seen print in other African nations. Of the 339 contributions Nigerians have made to the critical literature on Achebe, only 15 (4.4%) have been placed in non-Nigerian African media. Of the 55 scholarly works Kenyans have published on Ngugi, not one (0%) has been published elsewhere in Africa. And when scholars from other parts of Africa write about Soyinka, only 4.5% of what they write reaches print in Nigeria. When they write about Achebe, fewer than1% of their books, booklets, articles, dissertations and theses get placed in Nigeria. And when they write about Ngugi, less than 1.8% of their scholarship sees the light of day in Kenya. So the absence of transnational, cross-cultural communication is a striking phenomenon within Africa too. Nigerians may talk to Nigerians, Kenyans may talk to Kenyans, and both Nigerians and Kenyans do talk to Westerners with some regularity, but there is hardly any intramural transcontinental dialogue going on among Anglophone Africans. The little islanders don't mind mixing and mingling with big islanders far away, but they prefer to avoid having close contact with nearby little islanders like themselves. They appear to be suffering from an interiority complex.

The statistics on these charts suggest that scholars of Anglophone African literature, wherever in the world they happen to be placed, need to broaden their cultural horizons by exposing themselves to more give and take with their African colleagues. They need to find ways to communicate more effectively with critics, teachers and readers all over the African continent, reaching out to make contact even with those in remote hinterlands who have been routinely cut off from the stimulation of literary debates. Only by thereby Africanizing their own intellectual production will they be able to achieve any measure of true scholarly authority. For if they continue to sail on, oblivious of indigenous conditions and deaf to local alarms, they will surely be blown off course, experience more calamitous shipwrecks, and suffer greater insularity. And for ignorantly visiting such avoidable catastrophes upon themselves and others, they will certainly deserve all of Caliban's curses.

Chart 1: BOOKS

SOYINKA

	BALE I (1936-76)				BALE II (1977-81)				BALE III (1982-86)				BALE IV (1987-91)				(1992-1995)				Grand Totals			
	NI	OA	NA	T	NI	OA	NA	T	NI	OA	NA	T	NI	OA	NA	T	NI	OA	NA	T	NI	OA	NA	T
NI	1			1									5			5	4			4	10			10
OA			1	1										1		1						1	1	2
NA			2	2			3	3	1		4	5			6	6	1	1	2	4	2	1	17	20
T	1		3	4			3	3	1		4	5	5	1	6	12	5	1	2	8	12	2	18	32

ACHEBE

	BALE I (1936-76)				BALE II (1977-81)				BALE III (1982-86)				BALE IV (1987-91)				(1992-1995)				Grand Totals			
	NI	OA	NA	T	NI	OA	NA	T	NI	OA	NA	T	NI	OA	NA	T	NI	OA	NA	T	NI	OA	NA	T
NI					1			1			1	1	2		1	3			2	2	3		4	7
OA			1	1									1		1	2			1	1	1		3	4
NA			2	2			2	2			1	1			7	7			2	2			14	14
T			3	3	1		2	3			2	2	3		9	12			5	5	4		21	25

NGUGI

	BALE I (1936-76)				BALE II (1977-81)				BALE III (1982-86)				BALE IV (1987-91)				(1992-1995)				Grand Totals			
	KE	OA	NA	T	KE	OA	NA	T	KE	OA	NA	T	KE	OA	NA	T	KE	OA	NA	T	KE	OA	NA	T
KE					1			1													1			1
OA																		1		1		1		1
NA						3	3		.5	1.5	2			1	4	5			1	1		1.5	9.5	11
T						3	3	1	.5	1.5	3			1	4	5		1	1	2	1	2.5	9.5	13

GRAND TOTALS

	BALE I (1936-76)				BALE II (1977-81)				BALE III (1982-86)				BALE IV (1987-91)				(1992-1995)				Super Grand Totals			
	IN	OA	NA	T	IN	OA	NA	T	IN	OA	NA	T	IN	OA	NA	T	IN	OA	NA	T	IN	OA	NA	T
IN	1			1	1			1	1		1	2	7		1	8	4		2	6	14		4	18
OA			2	2									1	1	1	3		1	1	2	1	2	4	7
NA			4	4			8	8	1	.5	6.5	8		1	17	18	1	1	5	7	2	2.5	40.5	45
T	1		6	7	1		8	9	2	.5	7.5	10	8	2	19	29	5	2	8	15	17	4.5	48.5	70

Chart 2: Study Guides

SOYINKA

	BALE I (1936-76)				BALE II (1977-81)				BALE III (1982-86)				BALE IV (1987-91)				Grand Totals			
	NI	OA	NA	T	NI	OA	NA	T	NI	OA	NA	T	NI	OA	NA	T	NI	OA	NA	T
NI	2			2	2			2	2			2					6			6
OA		1	1	2		1	3			1	3			2	1			5		
NA			1	1			3	3			3	3			2	2			9	9
T	2	1	2	5	2	1	3	6	2	1	3	6		2	1	6	6	5	9	20

ACHEBE

	BALE I (1936-76)				BALE II (1977-81)				BALE III (1982-86)				BALE IV (1987-91)				Grand Totals			
	NI	OA	NA	T	NI	OA	NA	T	NI	OA	NA	T	NI	OA	NA	T	NI	OA	NA	T
NI	3			3																
OA	1		2	3		3	1			1				5						
NA	1		3	5		3	4			8	2			8	5			8	14	
T	1	6	10			5	4	13	7	2	5	14	8	5	1	14	23	1	14	24

NGUGI

	BALE I (1936-76)				BALE II (1977-81)				BALE III (1982-86)				BALE IV (1987-91)				Grand Totals			
	KE	OA	NA	T	KE	OA	NA	T	KE	OA	NA	T	KE	OA	NA	T	KE	OA	NA	T
KE	1			1	2			2		1		1					4			4
OA		3		3		1	1			9		9		1			14			14
NA	1		1			1	1							1	1			14	4	
T	1	3	1	5	2		1	4	1	9	1	11		1	1	2	4	14	4	22

GRAND TOTALS

	BALE I (1936-76)				BALE II (1977-81)				BALE III (1982-86)				BALE IV (1987-91)				Super Grand Totals			
	IN	OA	NA	T	IN	OA	NA	T	IN	OA	NA	T	IN	OA	NA	T	IN	OA	NA	T
IN	6			6	10			10	11			11	7			7	34			34
OA		5	2	7		7	1			12	1			10			33			33
NA		7	7			5	8	8		8	8			8	3		29		26	
T	6	5	9	20	10	7	9	20	11	12	8	31	7	10	8	22	34	29	30	93

Chart 3: Book Chapters

Soyinka

	B.A.L.E. I (1936-76)				B.A.L.E. II (1977-81)				B.A.L.E. III (1982-86)				B.A.L.E. IV (1987-91)				Grand Totals			
	NI	OA	NA	T	NI	OA	NA	T	NI	OA	NA	T	NI	OA	NA	T	NI	OA	NA	T
NI	1	1		2		1		1	2			3	18	4		22	22	4		32
OA	1	2	4	7		1	2	2		1	6	6	3	4	8	14			10	32
NA		2	11	11	1		16	17		1	21	21	3	1	62	66	4	1	110	115
T	2	2	16	20	1	3	20	24	1	1	23	25	22	1	69	92	28	5	128	161

Achebe

	B.A.L.E. I (1936-76)				B.A.L.E. II (1977-81)				B.A.L.E. III (1982-86)				B.A.L.E. IV (1987-91)				Grand Totals			
	NI	OA	NA	T	NI	OA	NA	T	NI	OA	NA	T	NI	OA	NA	T	NI	OA	NA	T
NI	2	1	3		1	1	2		1	6	6		76	1	10	87	84	1	10	98
OA	4	1	5		1	1	2		1	3	4		1	3	4		1	3	9	2
NA	1	17	18		16	16		1	19	19		3	44	54		4	54	107		
T	3	4	19	26	1	5	18	24	5	1	20	26	76	3	44	144	95	11	10	216

Ngũgĩ

	B.A.L.E. I (1936-76)				B.A.L.E. II (1977-81)				B.A.L.E. III (1982-86)				B.A.L.E. IV (1987-91)				Grand Totals			
	KE	OA	NA	T	KE	OA	NA	T	KE	OA	NA	T	KE	OA	NA	T	KE	OA	NA	T
KE	1	1		1	1		2	2			2	94	1	15	110		1		4	4
OA	1	2		1	7	8		1	3	4		2	37	37		1	4		66	68
NA	5	5		8	10		1	18	20		1	17	18	1	37	37		5		74	83
T	1	5	8		1	8	10		2	22	24	94	1	15	110	108	13	1	143	157

Grand Totals

	B.A.L.E. I (1936-70)				B.A.L.E. II (1977-81)				B.A.L.E. III (1982-86)				B.A.L.E. IV (1987-91)				Super Grand Totals			
	IN	OA	NA	T	IN	OA	NA	T	IN	OA	NA	T	IN	OA	NA	T	IN	OA	NA	T
IN	4	2	1	7	4			7	6		4	6	94	1	15	110	108	4	4	136
OA	2	6	5	14	5	9	2	2	2	2	2	2	39	39		3	16	17	14	34
NA	1	6	34		2	39	41		1	57	58		1	143	157		2	272	290	
T	7	7	40	54	4	2	46	54	6	4	65	75	108	7	162	277	127	20	313	460

Chart 4: Articles

SOYINKA

	BALE I (1936-76)				BALE II (1977-81)				BALE III (1982-86)				BALE IV (1987-91)				Grand Totals			
	NI	OA	NA	T	NI	OA	NA	T	NI	OA	NA	T	NI	OA	NA	T	NI	OA	NA	T
NI	17	4	2	23	14	3	10	27	41	4	21	67	72	9	25	106	144	21	58	223
OA	2	10	4	16	3	4	6	10	15	8	23		1	17	8	36	3	46	26	75
NA	6	13	42	61	3	32	40		71	143	152		6	145	152		14	24	290	328
T	25	27	48	100	43	25	100		165				32	178	284		161	91	374	626

ACHEBE

	BALE I (1936-76)				BALE II (1977-81)				BALE III (1982-86)				BALE IV (1987-91)				Grand Totals			
	NI	OA	NA	T	NI	OA	NA	T	NI	OA	NA	T	NI	OA	NA	T	NI	OA	NA	T
NI	6	11	28		9	1	24	34	29	4	7	40	64	2	21	87	113	13	63	189
OA	10	4	14		7	12	9		10	6	26		10	7	17		37	29	66	
NA	7	57	69		4	56	60		37	39			56	67			12	7	236	235
T	23	72	111		13	92	113		50	95			12	94	171		308	236	490	

NGUGI

	BALE I (1936-76)				BALE II (1977-81)				BALE III (1982-86)				BALE IV (1987-91)				Grand Totals			
	KE	OA	NA	T	KE	OA	NA	T	KE	OA	NA	T	KE	OA	NA	T	KE	OA	NA	T
KE	3				8				13				2				26	10		36
OA	1	7	9		2	9			16	17			19	17	37		2	37	57	96
NA	2	8	12		4	15	20		34	40			4	70	74		4	15	127	146
T	6	9	24		14	21	47		53	88			23	93	119		32	57	180	278

GRAND TOTALS

	BALE I (1936-76)				BALE II (1977-81)				BALE III (1982-86)				BALE IV (1987-91)				Super Grand Totals			
	IN	OA	NA	T	IN	OA	NA	T	IN	OA	NA	T	IN	OA	NA	T	IN	OA	NA	T
IN	31	11	34	7	83	9	30	122	138	19	52	201	26	6	8		318	34	131	448
OA	1	10	34		8	36	71		2	46	32	80	2	51	43	96	5	283	98	217
NA	22	9	39		20	26	46		10	31	72		4	15	66	180	35	114	633	769
T	47	59	129	235	31	65	103	120	2	142	154		67	281	293		318	214	862	1394

Chart 5: Doctoral Dissertations

SOYINKA

	BALE I (1936-76)				BALE II (1977-81)				BALE III (1982-86)				BALE IV (1987-91)				Grand Totals			
	NI	OA	NA	T	NI	OA	NA	T	NI	OA	NA	T	NI	OA	NA	T	NI	OA	NA	T
NI						3		3		7	3	3		3	7		4	13	17	
OA										3	3			4	4			7	7	
NA							3	3		7	8			9	9			19	20	
T						6	6			17	18			16	20	1	5	39	44	

ACHEBE

	BALE I (1936-76)				BALE II (1977-81)				BALE III (1982-86)				BALE IV (1987-91)				Grand Totals			
	NI	OA	NA	T	NI	OA	NA	T	NI	OA	NA	T	NI	OA	NA	T	NI	OA	NA	T
NI						1		1		3	3		2	2	4		2	6	8	
OA		2	2			5	5			7	7			8	8			22	22	
NA		3	3			2	2			5	5			8	8			18	18	
T		5	5			8	8			14	15		2	18	20		2	46	48	

NGUGI

	BALE I (1936-76)				BALE II (1977-81)				BALE III (1982-86)				BALE IV (1987-91)				Grand Totals			
	KE	OA	NA	T	KE	OA	NA	T	KE	OA	NA	T	KE	OA	NA	T	KE	OA	NA	T
KE						1		1		4	4			3	3			8	8	
OA										1	1			9	14		1	13	19	
NA										1	1			4		1	1	5	3	
T						1	1			5	5		1	5	15	21	6	20	27	

GRAND TOTALS

	BALE I (1936-76)				BALE II (1977-81)				BALE III (1982-86)				BALE IV (1987-91)				Grand Totals			
	IN	OA	NA	T	IN	OA	NA	T	IN	OA	NA	T	IN	OA	NA	T	IN	OA	NA	T
IN									6	10			14	1		6		22	28	
OA		2	2			4	4			14	14			21	26	1	5	42	48	
NA		3	3			5	6			13	14			20	21	1	1	41	43	
T		5	5	1		14	15	1		37	38	1	7	49	61	8	6	105	119	

Chart 6: M.A. THESES

SOYINKA

	BALE I (1936-76)				BALE II (1977-81)				BALE III (1982-86)				BALE IV (1987-91)				Grand Totals			
	NI	OA	NA	T	NI	OA	NA	T	NI	OA	NA	T	NI	OA	NA	T	NI	OA	NA	T
NI			2	2			1	1	10		1	11	17		2	19	27		6	33
OA		1	2	3			2	2		2		2		1		1		4	4	8
NA			9	9			4	4			2	2	1	1	4	6	1	1	19	21
T		1	13	14			7	7	10	2	3	15	18	2	6	26	28	5	29	62

ACHEBE

	BALE I (1936-76)				BALE II (1977-81)				BALE III (1982-86)				BALE IV (1987-91)				Grand Totals			
	NI	OA	NA	T	NI	OA	NA	T	NI	OA	NA	T	NI	OA	NA	T	NI	OA	NA	T
NI		1	1	2					7			7	4			4	11	1	1	13
OA						1		1		1	1	2		1		1		3	1	4
NA			4	4							4	4			2	2			10	10
T		1	5	6		1		1	7	1	5	13	4	1	2	7	11	4	12	27

NGUGI

	BALE I (1936-76)				BALE II (1977-81)				BALE III (1982-86)				BALE IV (1987-91)				Grand Totals			
	KE	OA	NA	T	KE	OA	NA	T	KE	OA	NA	T	KE	OA	NA	T	KE	OA	NA	T
KE									1			1	2		1	3	3		1	4
OA										7	2	9		13	7	20		20	9	29
NA			1	1			2	2						1	8	9		1	11	12
T			1	1			2	2	1	7	2	10	2	14	16	32	3	21	21	45

GRAND TOTALS

	BALE I (1936-76)				BALE II (1977-81)				BALE III (1982-86)				BALE IV (1987-91)				Grand Totals			
	IN	OA	NA	T	IN	OA	NA	T	IN	OA	NA	T	IN	OA	NA	T	IN	OA	NA	T
IN		1	3	4			1	1	18		1	19	23		3	26	41	1	8	50
OA		1	2	3		1	2	3		10	3	13		15	7	22		27	14	41
NA			14	14			6	6			6	6	1	2	14	17	1	2	40	43
T		2	19	21		1	9	10	18	10	10	38	24	17	24	65	42	30	62	134

Chart 7: Grand Totals

Soyinka

	BALE I (1936-76)				BALE II (1977-81)				BALE III (1982-86)				BALE IV (1987-91)				(1992-1995)				Grand Totals			
	NI	OA	NA	T	NI	OA	NA	T	NI	OA	NA	T	NI	OA	NA	T	NI	OA	NA	T	NI	OA	NA	T
NI	21	4	5	30	16	5	17	56	90	31	40	161	213	21	87	321	4			4				
OA	3	14	12	29		5	9	14	2	21	15	38	5	59	46	110		2	2					
NA	6	13	65	84	6	3	61	70	6	8	227	241	23	28	463	514		2	2					
T	33	31	82	143	22	6	87	120	126	38	276	440	241	108	596	945	5							

Achebe

	BALE I (1936-76)				BALE II (1977-81)				BALE III (1982-86)				BALE IV (1987-91)				(1992 1995)				Grand Totals			
	NI	OA	NA	T	NI	OA	NA	T	NI	OA	NA	T	NI	OA	NA	T	NI	OA	NA	T	NI	OA	NA	T
NI	15	7	13	36	16	1	26	43	48	4	11	63	196	3	38	198		2	2		236	15	88	389
OA	13	15	12	24		12	19	31		14	14	28	19	15	36			1	1			59	59	120
NA	6	7	88	101	4		89	84	11		79	72		30	123	139		2	2		50	7	368	398
T	22	29	110	161	20	13	125	158	1x	97	141		11	22	178	368		5	5		266	52	515	857

Ngugi

	BALE I (1936-76)				BALE II (1977-81)				BALE III (1982-86)				BALE IV (1987-91)				(1992-1995)				Grand Totals			
	KE	OA	NA	T	KE	OA	NA	T	KE	OA	NA	T	KE	OA	NA	T	KE	OA	NA	T	KE	OA	NA	T
KE	5		5		11	3	14	16	33	26	59	37					37				486	15	389	
OA	2	11				8	19	4		143	62	1	30	34	74						3	95	69	167
NA	2	15	10		11	4	28	34	65				7	123	130			1	1		19.3	221.5	245	
T	9	13	16	38	2	15	79	67	39.5				46	168	229		1	2			114.5	108.5	468	

Grand Totals

	BALE I (1936-76)				BALE II (1977-81)				BALE III (1982-86)				BALE IV (1987-91)				(1992-1995)				Grand Totals			
	IN	OA	NA	T	IN	OA	NA	T	IN	OA	NA	T	IN	OA	NA	T	IN	OA	NA	T	IN	OA	NA	T
IN	41	11	18	71	43	4	46	93	175	48			279	12	79	370	4	2	2		486	76	193	715
OA	5	46	22	67	1	28	16	64	66	41	117		4	90	65	148		1	2		9	214	174	397
NA	14	22	168	204	8	7	168	188	7	x4	232.5	248	17	14	479	410		5	3		51	44.5	1652.5	1158
T	61	79	208	342	79	7	251	344	133	83.5	311.5	480	390	106	622	1028	5	7	15		540	844.5	2419.5	2275

Works Cited

Lindfors, Bernth. *Black African Literature in English: A Guide to Information Sources*. Detroit: Gale Research Co., 1979.

____. *Black African Literature in English, 1977-1981, Supplement*. New York: Africana Publishing Co., 1986.

____. *Black African Literature in English, 1982-1986*. London: Hans Zell Publishers, 1989.

____. *Black African Literature in English, 1987-1991*. Oxford: Hans Zell Publishers, 1995.

Gender, Education, and Literary Output in Francophone Africa

Claire Griffiths

Why is so little of the literature produced in Francophone West Africa written by women? This question emerged in the course of recent fieldwork in Senegal on social development and gender in Francophone Africa, a project which examines trends in access to formal education and considers some of the outcomes attributed to the increase in educational access for girls.

Among the many factors which influence the access women have to a public literary voice in society are educational variables which operate within a network of cultural/religious, political, legal and economic structures which formalize gender distinctions in society and are contained and sustained within a dominant political culture. This paper will focus particularly on the degree to which educational access and political culture might be instrumental in creating a gender imbalance in the production of literature in Francophone Africa. To contextualize the broadly quantitative investigation of educational trends, the importance of education and the prevalent political culture in women's literary output was explored in interviews with a number of prominent women writers in Senegal, including Aminata Sow Fall, Aminata Maïga Ka and Fatou Ndiaye Sow.[1] What follows constitutes an initial exploration of this question.

In her illuminating overview of women's literature in Francophone Africa, "La percée des femmes dans le roman de moeurs africain," Lilyan Kesteloot stresses the impact of what has been referred to as the *analphabétisme programmé*, the policy of keeping colonized women in a state of illiteracy, which prevailed in the colonial era and appears to have persisted into the post-colonial period.

The lack of education in the dominant literary language, in this case French, has played a significant role in producing a situation whereby women were largely excluded from the Francophone African literary system between 1920, when the first literary text by an African writer was published, Ahmadou Mapaté Diagne's *Les trois volontés de Malic*, and 1976, when Aminata Sow Fall published her first novel. The latter was rather later than Fall had expected as she explained in a recent interview:

> I submitted my first novel "Le Revenant" to NEA (Nouvelles Editions Africaines) in 1973. The editor at that time accepted it and then sat on it for three years. But that was because of the content—he said that Europeans wouldn't be interested in a strictly Senegalese story. As if we have to write for a European readership! I told him we shouldn't be making pale copies of what they do over there. So, he published it in 1976. (Personal interview)

The reasons for the long delay in the publication of literary works in French by African female authors could be explained in purely educational terms as the following discussion on educational provision in the colonial and postcolonial eras will demonstrate. However, to do so would ignore the context in which such gender imbalances can be produced and sustained. In her article "Les Africaines prirent la plume–histoire d' une conquête," Angèle Bassolé Ouédraogo focuses on the political context in which a woman enters the literary world. As she puts it, writing can become an act of rebellion if the dominant political culture is one which silences women and keeps them on the margins of public life, beyond the arena of discussion and decision. The additional impact of European political culture is underlined in other analyses of the development of francophone African women's writing: "For a [francophone] woman writer . . . the act of writing in French is, of necessity, an attempt to make a place for herself in that elite, male-dominated, European literary tradition" (n.p., my translation). This points to the multi-layered political context in which a culture can encourage males rather than females to participate in public cultural activity.

Though it is difficult to quantify the influence exerted by political, economic, cultural and religious institutions, it is possible to explore these factors through the experience of women authors who have negotiated a path around any cultural constraints and into print. We can also look at the manner and subject of the writing, and the ease of access into the literary system these authors have experienced. It is these two factors, the provision of formal education for girls and political and cultural context in which this education is delivered, which provide the focus of this paper.

Trends in girls' access to the formal education system is explored in two countries, Gabon and Senegal, which represent the wide variations in economic situation and cultural history which exist within the sub-region of Francophone West Africa. The trends identified in these countries are presented in terms of gender differences and are then located within a discussion of the political and cultural context of female authorship.

It would be unfair and unwise to present a gender analysis of access to education in present-day Francophone Africa without reference to the past, so I shall start by summarizing the situation African governments inherited in 1960.

The extent to which the colonial powers provided formal education in West Africa varied as did the degree of gender discrimination operating in the early education systems. In the French colonies the lack of facilities for girls during the inter-war era when European education systems were being established in sub-Saharan Africa was particularly notable, reflecting a variation in gender discrimination experienced in the colonial metropoles. To take the case of Gabon, officially colonised in 1886 and becoming in 1908 one of the four territories which made up *l'Afrique Equatoriale Française*, there were just under two thousand eight hundred children registered at schools at the outbreak of World War I in 1914, and out of every ten of these children, eight were boys (Nzigou 322). The degree to which formal educational provision for African girls was being neglected in the colonies was raised as an issue for concern by French colonial administrators at the Brazzaville conference of French

African territories in 1944. These administrators were successful in effecting immediate change. In Gabon for instance, the number of girls registered in state-funded schools tripled between 1945 and independence in 1960.[2]

Despite these changes, the numbers of girls receiving an academic education under the colonial administration remained minute. Lack of access to formal education and hence literacy in the colonial language created barriers to women gaining access to new sources of power and influence within the changing economy. African women living in lands taken over by the French found that being illiterate in the coloniser's language meant they could not register claims to land, inheritance rights, and other traditional sources of personal wealth and security with the new colonial authorities. Furthermore, as all women, irrespective of race, had fewer legal rights than men under French law,[3] African women, and particularly heads of households, faced numerous legal barriers to women's economic independence. Consequently, as the legal and political culture of the metropole became more firmly established through the development of the colony, women became increasingly marginalized.

On the eve of independence in French Equatorial Africa, less than one Gabonese woman in ten could speak French, never mind read or write it, a particularly disadvantageous situation in a country which numbers over 50 national languages and where French became the only official language. This literacy level in the colonial language was typical of the situation throughout West Africa. Though in Ghana and Nigeria 25% of the population had been educated in basic literacy by 1960, the norm in the other West African Anglophone states and in the Francophone African countries was an illiteracy rate of over 90% (Quist 128).

Table 1 - Percentage of Gabonese literate in French in 1994 by age and gender

AGE	WOMEN	MEN	WOMEN + MEN
65+	4.9	19.2	11.0
60-64	6.3	33.9	18.3
55-59	11.4	49.7	28.7
50-54	19.6	62.1	39.5
45-49	37.4	76.9	57.8
40-44	62.5	83.2	74.0
35-39	79.0	87.5	83.6
30-34	85.6	88.4	87.1
25-29	88.2	89.5	88.8
20-24	91.1	93.1	92.1
15-19	93.0	95.5	94.2
TOTAL	65.7	79.1	72.4

Source: Principaux Résultats - recensement général de la population et de l'habitat (Bureau Central du Recensement, Ministère de la Planification et de l'Aménagement du Territoire, République Gabonaise, 1994) p.23

The largely unpublished results of the 1993-94 census in Gabon provide a clear example of the huge impact some post-independence governments had on the educational careers of generations of schoolchildren.

Table 1 shows literacy in French in the Gabonese adult population by age-group in the academic year 1993/94. Though illiteracy has been almost eradicated in Gabon among young people under 25, it should still be recognized that the vast majority of older women have remained illiterate in the official national language.

The quality and quantity of data available from other countries in the Francophone African region is very variable. Information that does exist points to the same underlying trend.

Table 2 - Percentage of children of primary school-age registered in primary school in sub-Saharan Africa in 1995 according to UNESCO world report 1998

COUNTRY	GIRLS	BOYS
Benin	52	92
Cameroon	84	93
Congo	109	119
Cote D'ivoire	58	79
Dem Rep of Congo	59	86
Mauritania	72	85
Senegal	57	72
Togo	97	140

Source: UNESCO World Report 1998 (New York, United Nations 1998)

Table 2 provides an indication of how the situation has developed across the central and west African Francophone regions almost forty years after Independence when less than 10% of children were attending schools. Though the picture is varied there has been at least a five-fold increase in primary school attendance throughout the region.

The growth in secondary education, illustrated in table 3, has been far slower. What comes through clearly from both table 2 and table 3 is that in this region of Africa the privileged access to formal education created for boys by the colonial regimes has remained throughout the postcolonial era, and it should be noted that this not the case at primary level throughout the continent as a whole. Boys and men do continue to enjoy privileged access to secondary and tertiary education throughout the continent, except in some countries of southern Africa, for example in Botswana and Lesotho, where more girls than boys attend secondary school.

Table 3 - Percentage of children of secondary school-age registered in secondary school in sub-Saharan Africa in 1995 according to UNESCO World Report 1998

COUNTRY	GIRLS	BOYS
Benin	10	23
Cameroon	22	32
Congo	45	62
Cote D'Ivoire	15	30
Dem Rep of Congo	19	32
Mauritania	11	16
Senegal	12	20
Togo	14	41

Source: UNESCO World Report 1998 (New York, United Nations 1998)

However, Gabon, which could not be included in tables 2 and 3 for reasons noted below, is somewhat exceptional in the Francophone African world in that there are roughly the same proportion of girls as boys entering secondary education.[4]

There occurs a dramatic drop in the number of girls attending secondary schools in Gabon after the age of 14 which does not correlate with evidence of academic performance at this stage. Official reports from international agencies and government departments give the main reason for girls dropping out of school as early pregnancy, a trend, it is claimed, that is sustained by a lack of sex education in schools and the breakdown of extended family units in the urban environment. These conditions occur in other Francophone West African countries in the study but have not provoked a similar incidence of teenage pregnancy. In Gabon this phenomenon appears to be causing a conflictual situation whereby punishment is meted out to the teenage mother through expulsion from school. It has been suggested in some quarters that during the pre-colonial era young girls of the Ogooué-Maritime area in southern Gabon were highly prized if they proved their fertility before being proposed for marriage (Coquéry-Vidrovitch 18-9). However, lack of qualitative sociological research in this area makes it impossible to go beyond mere speculation on the causes of this phenomenon. The fact that Gabon is a predominantly Catholic country, that it has no social services designed to sustain single-parenting, that various possibilities of birth control are not officially sanctioned, would all require further investigation before conclusions were drawn. The issue, as far as this paper is concerned, is the outcome, namely that a lower proportion of girls than boys are completing secondary education in Gabon.

The same is true in Senegal, but in this case progression beyond primary education is conditioned less by gender-discriminatory behaviour (such as expelling schoolgirl mothers-to-be in Gabon while schoolboy fathers-to-be are allowed to remain at school) than by a very low level of entry into secondary education. Despite the drop-out rate discussed above, there are still 40% of 19 year-old Gabonese girls attending secondary school whereas only an average of 14% of girls of secondary school-age in Senegal are reaching the end of their secondary education (estimates vary between 12 and 14% for the mid-1990s).

Table 4 - Educational attainment of Senegalese women in 1997

AGE IN 1997	No formal education at all	Completed primary school	Completed secondary school
15-19	55.1	31	13.9
20-24	60.4	25.5	14.2
25-29	67.8	18.5	13.7
30-34	69.3	17.6	13
35-39	74.6	14.8	10.6
40-44	78.2	13.1	8.7
45-49	85.4	7.1	7.5

Source: EDS-111 (Direction de la Statistique, Ministère du Plan, Gouvernement du Sénégal 1997)

Table 4 illustrates this situation. It indicates the level of education achieved in the current female adult population of Senegal. The trend in primary and secondary access is evidently upward though very slow at secondary level compared with some other countries in the region. Comparisons with Gabon must take into account economic and cultural differences between these two countries. Per capita income in Gabon was $3766 in 1998, over twice that of Senegal at $1815 (*Human Development Report* 129-30). In both cases the governments publicly espouse the principal of equal access to education and the elimination of all forms of discrimination against women. Gabon is a predominantly Catholic country and Senegal predominantly Muslim.

The trends illustrated in tables 1 to 4 reveal a significant increase in French language literacy throughout the Francophone region particularly among boys but also among girls. It can therefore be concluded that the potential reading public for African literature in the French language would also have grown dramatically during the past twenty years. The tables have illustrated how the level of expansion in primary education is not being sustained through secondary level education and it therefore seems reasonable to suggest from this that lack of progression beyond the middle levels of the formal education system is one of the factors holding back literary output from women in this part of Africa.

In the case of Senegal, there are two obvious connections between the development of educational opportunities in the postcolonial era and the development of women's writing. Firstly there was almost no literature being produced by women in Senegal for the first 20 years after Independence. Secondly, women writers in Senegal who have been published, are educated at least to *Ecole Normale* (teacher training) level, and the most well-known to well beyond this level. For example, following her education in Senegal, Aminata Sow Fall, probably the most internationally-recognized of today's generation of Senegalese writers after Ousmane Sembène, was educated at Université de Paris IV (the Sorbonne). The most prominent women authors in the Francophone African world are educated to an exceptionally high level, many are academics. Some such as Khady Fall, Véronique Tadjo, Tanella Boni, are university professors. When asked whether she considers access to a university education as crucial to becoming a writer, Aminata Sow Fall says she personally would have become a writer of some sort without a university education, but she feels she would not have produced the kind of work which has gained her international recognition without her university education (Personal interview). At age 27, Fama Diagne Sène, the youngest woman author to win Senegal's major literary prize in 1997 for her novel *Le chant des ténèbres*, was also educated at university level, in her case at the *Institut Universitaire de Formation des Maîtres* in France. Further examples of successful women novelists include high school teachers, educated to post-secondary level, such as the late Mariama Bâ, the recently retired Aminata Maïga Ka, and Mame Younousse Dieng.

From this most cursory overview, it would appear that progression through formal education to the highest level is a salient factor. Consequently, levels of access to higher education in the region need to be analysed. It is not possible to give a comprehensive account of trends in higher education throughout Francophone Africa due to the absence of data in the public domain. The gender dimension of access to higher education is illustrated in table 5 using a set of student registration data from one of the foremost universities of the region, Université Cheikh Anta Diop de Dakar.[5]

The trends indicated in table 5 show firstly that the level of female participation in higher education is rising. Secondly, though the trend is upward, it is also for the moment extremely slow.

Extrapolation of these data suggests that Senegal may achieve gender equity in higher education but the earliest this may happen, at current rates, is the middle of the 21st century, in 2047.

Simple extrapolations are not sensitive to changes in the political culture or to more immediate changes in university policy. Currently the University of Cheickh Anta Diop in Dakar, in keeping with official government policy, espouses the principle of equal opportunities. The fact that it produces disaggregated admissions data and provides these data for academic research is testimony to its position on this issue.

Nevertheless, the University is not required to formulate and implement an active policy to promote female participation in higher education. This has been true in countries throughout the world such as the UK where some early proposals to correct gender imbalances in higher education were deemed in some quarters unfair to men. However, more recent policies in the UK have been effectively focusing on removing disincentives which have been stopping girls from entering, in this case, science and technology degree courses. Such interventions promote fairness and are consequently now being welcomed in most quarters of UK higher education.

Apart from the possibility of similar pressure from above accelerating the trend in female participation in Senegal, there may also emerge a greater pressure from below for more provision of higher education for girls. The proportion of girls in the total number of young people finishing secondary education in Senegal is rising. In 1993, 32% of high school graduates were girls, by 1998 this had risen to 37% (*Statistiques 1992-93* 80; *Statistiques 1997-98* 109). If this rate were to remain constant, i.e. a rise of 10 points per decade, the same number of girls would be graduating from high school as boys in Senegal by the year 2010. Theoretically this should increase demand for higher education.

One further somewhat tentative observation could be made from these data. The correlation between the percentage of women progressing through the education system and the percentage of published literature by women is similar but there appears to be a higher degree of entry into higher education than into print. This area needs much deeper analysis than is possible here, but it could be assumed that the influence of cultural and structural factors is contributing to this disparity. This question was explored with members of the present generation of women writers in Senegal whose views are included in this concluding section of the paper.

Political climate can operate positively or negatively on trends in girls' education depending on how gender equity is perceived and acted upon by the political classes. A hostile political culture can halt the progress of equity, operating, for example, through oppressive regimes. Such was the case in Afghanistan where the fundamentalist regime expelled all women academics from their university posts, and where almost all professional women were subjected to draconian restrictions on their freedom. It is commonly believed that progress towards gender equity is inevitable nowadays, but Afghanistan serves to exemplify how wary one should be in taking such progress for granted. It also suggests that closely monitoring social and cultural change from a gender perspective is not only intellectually but also politically desirable.

On numerous grounds it seems reasonable to address the question of literary output from a gender perspective. However, it is argued in some quarters that women should not be considered a separate category of writers, that such distinctions are in essence sexist. If categorization is made in the absence of any gender analysis, as in the case of the recent press reviews of Senegalese literature ("Supplément"), then criticism might indeed be considered warranted. However, where women's writing is being explored in terms of structural and cultural constraints which, as it is being argued here, are triggered by gender, it is imperative to examine literary output within a consistent framework.

The question of whether Francophone African women's writing constitutes a definable category was put to a number Senegalese women writers, all of whom prefaced their remarks by stressing that there was no qualitative difference between male and female writing in Senegal. As Fatou Ndiaye Sow observed, French remains "intrinsically foreign to all Senegalese writers irrespective of gender" (Personal interview); it is the alien nature of the literary language and not gender which is of primary linguistic importance.

Once the qualitative observations on the use of language had been made, differences were identified in terms of content. It was noted that women's writing in Senegal and the Francophone African region in general, was characterised by a socio-political critique of the advantages accorded to boys and men on the basis of gender as opposed to merit. This critique of what some refer to as male gender supremacy may well appear in what a sociologist might consider a partial or inconsistent form, as in Mariama Bâ's *Une si longue lettre*. But whatever the form or the social scientific validity of the critique, it is present to an extent not witnessed in literature written by men. This is not to say, however, that the most stinging criticism comes from the pens of women. The novelist and former high school teacher of English, Aminata Maïga Ka, who is often cited as the most overtly feminist of Senegal's women writers, identifies herself as a feminist. However, she qualified this statement by saying that "adversarial feminism," which she takes as the western model of feminism, is inappropriate in her culture. "Nous sommes une société de consensus," she said. "Il faut aborder ces choses avec tacte. Moi je présente ce que je considère comme un problème dans notre société, mais je ne juge pas pour les gens—les lecteurs peuvent en tirer leurs conclusions" (Personal interview). The evidence required for a critique of gender discrimination is assembled in her novels. Her first work, *La voie du salut*, published in 1985, dealt with infanticide. Her second piece, *Le miroir de la vie*, also published in 1985, is the only novel to have discussed both the practice of cutting off parts of the external genital area of female children and the trauma experienced by some Senegalese girls required to submit to forced marriages. She addressed problems facing women within marriage in her third novel *A votre nom et au mien*, published in 1989, and the storyline of her most recent novel, *Brisures de vies* published December 1998, revolves around a rape. In her view the violence that can be committed against women and their dignity in the form of polygamy and rape are subjects that define women's writing. In this sense it could be said that Francophone African women's writing is a form of resistance to situations they consider oppressive. However, women's writing in this part of the world cannot be defined simply in these terms.

The most famous writer of this generation, Aminata Sow Fall, protests against accusations of anti-feminism by pointing out that she is not a social scientist: "je ne cherches pas des explications politiques ou sociologiques, j'ai ma vision de romancière" (Personal interview).

In her novel, *Cris et fureurs des femmes*, the Gabonese writer, Angèle Rawiri, offers an explicit political challenge to social norms. *Cris et fureurs des femmes* explores the horrors experienced by an educated professional young woman in a "modern marriage" who is betrayed by her unfaithful husband on the pretext that she is not producing enough children. She suffers the loss of her only daughter and is then expected to tolerate her husband's extra-marital relationship with her secretary, with whom he sets up a parallel household. The heroine, hitherto an attractive young professional woman, sinks into destructive depression and resorts to desperate measures, including allowing herself to be abused by an expatriate "quack" during dubious fertility treatment for what is assumed to be her sterility. She engages in lesbian relationship with her husband's lover, tortures the body which refuses to produce a living child, and passes through a figurative purgatory before re-emerging into a state of dignity having redefined African womanhood in her own image. Having assumed the right to say what *une Africaine digne de ce nom* is, she has overthrown the dominant ideology which equates the value of a woman to that of wife and mother.

Outside the sociological critique which usually characterises women's writing, the absence of the kind of linguistic experimentation discernible in male writing (linked with the critique of cultural colonialism) is scarcely present in women's writing. Aminata Sow Fall insists that as French has been the only written language available to her generation of writers the questions of what language to use and then how to use it do not really arise: "pour moi c'est naturel d'écrire en français. Il y a des choses qu'on ne peut pas exprimer en français, il y a un blocage, à ce moment-là j'utilise une expression en wolof et je l'explique pour le lecteur—sous forme de note—et cela ne pose pas de problèmes" (Personal interview).

The subject matter of women's literary output in Francophone Africa indicates that socio-political environment normally constitutes a highly salient factor in the production of literature by women. From the evidence presented in the earlier discussion, it appears reasonable to conclude that educational access and progression are also very influential. Unsurprisingly, these factors correspond to the preoccupations of women who live and write in this part of the world. The prevailing concern about these issues was summarized by one prominent advocate of women's rights in the following terms: "the key to developing equity in our society is women's participation in education and politics" (Sow, Personal interview), a view voiced frequently in Senegal among men as well as women active in the political debate. Interestingly, it is generally maintained in Dakar that the literary system is as open to women as it is to men and that a woman author has at least an equal chance of having a literary manuscript accepted by the publisher as her male counterpart. The problem resides in getting from the acceptance stage into print and this is a problem affecting all authors. However, it would be inaccurate to conclude that a woman has an equal chance of being in a position to submit a literary manuscript to a publisher. The discussion of access to education as it translates into literacy and literary training clearly indicates that the educational system favours boys.

There are many factors contributing to the creation of new generations of authors and this paper has explored only some aspects of two important factors, education and political culture. The evidence presented in this paper suggests a close correlation between access to higher education, political motivation and women's literary output. More research needs to be done into how the concept of gender equity operates in the political culture, and more specifically in this context, into the variations in the significance of educational and political variables as they affect access to the literary voice for women and for men.

Notes

1. I would like to thank M. Alassane Wele, Director of Arts and Libraries at the Ministry of Culture in Senegal, Meadow Dibble Dieng of Africa Consultants International, and Professor Lilyan Kesteloot of the Institut Fondamental de l'Afrique Noire at the University of Dakar for advice and help in locating sources used in this paper.
2. The numbers involved were very low, rising from 500 to 1,500 in this period (Nzigou 323).
3. Napoleonic legislation in the first decade of the 19th century severely circumscribed French women's rights before the law. Legal discrimination persisted throughout the colonial era.
4. UNESCO does not have any data on Gabon so it cannot be compared with the data presented here. For more educational data on Gabon see Griffiths (22).

Works Cited

Coquéry-Vidrovitch, Catherine. *Les Africaines—Histoire des femmes d'Afrique noire du XIX au XX siècle*. Paris: Desjonquères, 1994.

Sow Fall, Aminata. Personal interview. 22 January 1999.

Green, Mary Jean, et. al., eds. *Postcolonial Subjects—Francophone Women Writers*. Minneapolis/London: University of Minnesota Press, 1996.

Griffiths C.H. *Social Development in Francophone Africa—The Case of Women in Gabon and Morocco*. Working Paper 211. Boston: Boston University African Studies Center, 1998.

Human Development Report 1998. New York: United Nations, 1998.

Ka, Aminata Maïga. Personal interview. 15 January 1999.

Kesteloot, Lilyan. "La Percée des femmes dans le roman de moeurs sénégalais." *Le Soleil* [Dakar] (17 December 1998): 9-10.

Nzigou, Fidèle Ibouli. *Les problèmes posés par l'interférence des systèmes éducatifs au Gabon* . Diss. Université de Lyon, 1986.

Ouédraogo, Angèle Bassolé. "Et les Africaines prirent la plume! Histoire d'une conquête." *Mots pluriels* 8 (October 1998): n.p. http://www.arts.uwa.edu.au/MotsPluriels/MP898abo.html. 12 November 2002.

Quist, Hubert. "Illiteracy, Education and National Development in Postcolonial West Africa." *Africa Development* 30.2 (1994): 127-45.

Sow, Fatou Ndiaye. Personal interview. 20 January 1999.

Statistiques scolaires et universitaires, 1992-93. Dakar: Direction de la Planification et de la Réforme de l'Education, Ministère de l'Education Nationale, République du Sénégal, 1993.

Statistiques scolaires et universitaires, 1997-98. Dakar: Direction de la Planification et de la Réforme de l'Education, Ministère de l'Education Nationale, République du Sénégal, 1998.

"Supplément." *Sud détente* 54/55 (4-11 December 1998).

Sexualité et identité dans Tahar Ben Jelloun

Patricia Reynaud

Penser à Ben Jelloun dans le contexte de la construction identitaire c'est d'abord avoir à l'esprit la violence faite au corps sexué, au corps parfois mutilé, violence nécessaire à cet auteur pour concilier les contraires d'une identité en quête d'elle-même, ou, comme il sera démontré au cours de cet essai, d'une identité problématique de la condition d'émigré à l'échelle plus vaste de la nation.

I. Le corps Tragique

Certaines de mes références dans cette première partie seront empruntées à l'article d'Abbes Maazaoui sur "Le corps tragique" dans *L'enfant de sable* et *La nuit sacrée*, double livre dont je parlerai ici. La violence symbolique[1] est une constante de base, dès la naissance, en territoire musulman si l'on associe au terme "violence" le terme "exclusion" ou dichotomie irrévocable. Les deux sexes sont élevés, socialisés selon deux modes radicalement différents et totalement séparés. Au premier sexe, celui de la virilité exacerbée, revient de droit la parole, faite surtout d'ordres et commandements, la liberté d'aller et venir, la relation à l'économie et aux affaires, l'apprentissage religieux, enfin toute la panoplie que l'on sait des prérogatives revenant aux dominants. A ce niveau de lecture, la violence de Ben Jelloun revient à bouleverser le paradigme immémorial et à accorder ces mêmes droits à une fille déguisée en garçon par la loi du père qui en a décidé ainsi. Au deuxième sexe, l'obéissance servile, la soumission, le devoir, le respect à cette loi soutenue par les décrets coraniques, le corps caché, dissimulé, enfermé dans l'ère de l'économie domestique, muet ou dont les revendications ne comptent pas, enfin le corps tyrannisé par la violence dont le paroxysme est l'effacement du désir sexuel par l'excision.

Se greffe sur cette problématique de la dissociation tranchée et de l'altérité radicale, celle de la vision ou de son contraire, le manque de vision. Tant que l'héroïne, femme faite homme pour les besoins d'héritage, d'honneur et de respectabilité du père accepte ce jeu, sa vision normale est pourrait-on dire, faussée parce qu'elle ne connaît pas encore sa féminité et donc ce qu'elle voit, bien que pris pour le vrai, n'est que la simple projection de ce qui passe pour le vrai, le monde doxique masculin, et ses valeurs d'autorité, d'austérité, de supériorité, tout l'apanage du mensonge et de la violence justifié par des siècles de tradition. L'acceptation de cette doxa: les choses sont dans l'ordre parce qu'elles sont dans l'ordre des choses prend hommes et femmes dans le filet d'une reconnaissance aveugle faite de méconnaissance. Le pouvoir de l'homme est reconnu précisément parce qu'il est méconnu dans sa valeur arbitraire. L'enfant de sable, qui comme son nom l'indique, est une construction dangereusement mouvante[2] ne voit pas, puisqu'elle est aveugle à elle-même et aux autres, son aliénation, ce qui d'ailleurs l'arrange bien tant qu'elle veut rester en position de pouvoir.

Le tournant prend place cependant. La jeune fille se redécouvre ainsi que ses désirs enfouis, son corps négligé revit intensément des émotions enterrées qui ressurgissent alors qu'elle cherche à échapper à la "malédiction" paternelle. La situation d'homme n'était a posteriori guère enviable, puisque basée, enfin le reconnaît-elle, sur l'esclavage des femmes autour d'elle, et sur une solitude immense dès lors que la mère et surtout les sœurs lui rendent la pareille de son indifférence en la détestant. Si, au cours de cette deuxième phase, la vision redevient plus normale, et si l'idéologie patriarcale apparaît enfin pour ce qu'elle est, une vision parmi d'autres, la violence n'a pas encore disparu et il y aura un chemin long et ardu à parcourir pour que l'héroïne se retrouve être ce qu'elle a toujours été, une femme. Chemin semé d'embûches qui plus est. En termes jungiens, on peut lire ces embûches comme des épreuves symboliques placées sur la route de l'héroïne à la recherche d'elle-même.[3] Si elle sort victorieuse, elle aura mérité d'être ce qu'elle prétend être, femme à part entière. L'épreuve du viol, né d'un imaginaire masculin, fait partie, à n'en pas douter, des rites d'initiation. Du moins, est-ce la lecture que nous choisissons ici. Car, c'est moins en termes de violence que de sacrifice offert (il faut le rappeler de sacrifice d'abord offert à Allah, et l'agresseur ne peut que Le remercier d'avoir mis sur sa route une pareille aubaine) que la scène est décrite: "Dans mon esprit, je fus offerte au buisson et à la terre" (Ben Jelloun, *L'enfant de sable* 63). Mon interprétation en termes symboliques ne veut cependant pas masquer le fait qu'il y aurait beaucoup à redire sur cette scène de viol déculpabilisée, déviolentée, presque aseptisée et qui ne laisse que peu de cicatrices physiques ou psychiques chez la victime, mais au contraire, semble la débarrasser d'une virginité par trop encombrante. . . . C'est tout juste si elle n'éprouve pas de plaisir et ce ne serait pas pousser trop loin l'interprétation que de dire qu'elle semble d'ailleurs avoir cherché ce qui lui est arrivé, en s'égarant dans un bois alors qu'elle se savait suivie. . . . La encore la doxa masculine dans la problématique du viol n'est guère remise en question.

Remarquons également, pour jouer sur un autre stéréotype masculin que la violence la plus terrible et la plus recherchée, dans ces deux romans, est le fait des femmes, Oum Abbas, la mère d'Abbas, le patron du cirque forain dans *L'enfant de sable*, qui, avec son fils, représente le couple crapuleux par excellence et, dans *La nuit sacrée*, l'Assise, la terrible sœur du Consul aveugle, ainsi que les propres sœurs de l'héroïne, qui pratiquent sur elle une clitoridectomie sauvage et monstrueuse pour la punir, semble-t-il, des années de souffrance qu'elles ont dû vivre à cause de son usurpation d'identité.

L'on pourrait accuser l'auteur de ces lignes d'être partiale en favorisant une lecture féministe de ces deux livres de Ben Jelloun; aussi il est légitime de faire remarquer que l'homme n'est pas toujours mieux traité par le narrateur, s'il est parfois mieux disculpé. A témoin, cette remarque sans concession tirée de *L'enfant de sable*:

> Je remarquais combien ce peuple est affamé de sexe. Les hommes regardent les femmes en pétrifiant leur corps; chaque regard est un arrachage de djellaba et de robe. Ils soupèsent les fesses et les seins et agitent leur membre derrière leur gandoura. (101-2)

A moins que les violences du récit ben-jellounien ne soient écrites d'un autre point de vue qui s'empêche consciemment de verser dans la morale sociale. Là encore, laissons parler le je-narrateur (l'auteur?):

> Comme vous savez, je hais la psychologie et tout ce qui alimente la culpabilité. Je pensais que la fatalité musulmane (existe-t-elle?) nous épargnerait ce sentiment mesquin, petit et malodorant. . . . La grande, l'immense épreuve que je vis n'a de sens qu'en dehors de ces petits schémas psychologiques qui prétendent savoir et expliquer pourquoi une femme est une femme et un homme un homme. (88-9)[4]

Après une série d'attentats, non à la pudeur qui ne semble pas exister chez l'héroïne mais où la violence est perpétrée, Zahra, ainsi nommée, renaît femme, femme bientôt excisée et en état d'ascèse. La violence subie a donc due être intégrée, métamorphosée en sympathie pour le genre humain, hommes et femmes réunis, pour que la première condition, à savoir la rupture entre les deux sexes, soit résolue dans un compromis durable et positif: Zahra est bien femme mais femme qui a su et pu être homme.

Reste le problème de la vision. Ahmed (le premier nom de l'héroïne lorsqu'elle est "homme"), au début, malgré ses yeux, ne voyait pas, mais il apprend à voir clair, et à ne plus accepter la doxa qu'il finit par comprendre. La problématique du regard ne s'arrête pas là. Le sens de la vue, accaparé par les désirs, est un détournement de la vision véritable vers le social, qui, quant à elle, est opératoire au-delà de la vue proprement dite. A cette problématique nous pouvons greffer toute l'affaire du voile islamique en ce que d'aucuns affirme que le voile protège la femme contre le désir masculin. Confusément, Zahra comprend cette problématique du regard "qui ne permet pas une communication authentique des sexes" (Maawaoui 74). Pour cela encore, c'est un aveugle, le Consul, qui l'éveille à la féminité, lui qui seul peut "voir" ce que les autres ne voient pas. Néanmoins, le regard étant masculin et mutilateur, l'héroïne en comprend le dilemme (ne pas voir, c'est ne pas être tentée) et se "réfugie" dans une obscurité voulue lors de l'épisode de la prison. Ainsi elle est mieux à même d'écrire—la nuit—et de décrire son monde intérieur, sans sollicitations profanes et éphémères. Ce qui, d'ailleurs n'est pas le moindre des paradoxes dans un livre où la sensualité est à fleur de peau et de page, comme si l'auteur, ne pouvant la refouler sous sa plume rebelle, la reléguait à des limites bien circonscrites, de peur qu'elle ne lui échappe. Mais, comme chacun sait, l'inconscient a ses ruses que la raison n'a pas, même pour un détracteur de la psychologie! Lecture somme toute érotico-mystique, qui, dans "La Nuit sacrée," se termine fort à propos sur le chapitre "Le Saint" joué, encore une fois, par le Consul alors que Zahra, libérée de prison après avoir bénéficié d'une réduction de peine, lui rend visite dans le désert, ayant revêtu à nouveau des vêtements d'homme! L'habitus primaire ne lâche pas si facilement prise.

Pour en terminer avec cette relation intrinsèque existant entre violence et exclusion, je ferais mienne la remarque de Jacques Leenhart: "La vue, par opposition au toucher ou à l'odorat, instaure une rupture entre le percevant et le perçu" (Maawaoui 76). Donc, en annihilant la vue, l'altérité radicale a quelque chance de disparaître brisant le cercle de la violence avec elle. C'est peut-être pour cette raison que la dernière entrevue entre Zahra et le Saint (ou son alter-ego) se fait sur le mode du toucher (et de l'ouïe) dans un passage conclusif où la sensualité fonctionne, allais-je dire, jusqu'au bout des doigts:

> Quand je fus en face du Saint, je m'agenouillai, je pris sa main tendue et, au lieu de la baiser, je la léchai, suçant chacun de ses doigts. Le Saint essaya de la retirer mais je la retenais de mes deux mains. L'homme était troublé. Je me levai et lui dit à l'oreille:
> - Cela fait très longtemps qu'un homme ne m'a pas caressé le visage. . . . Allez-y, regardez-moi avec vos doigts, doucement, avec la paume de votre main. Il se pencha sur moi et dit:
> - Enfin, vous voilà! (Ben Jelloun, *La nuit sacrée* 189)[5]

L'attitude la plus avancée face au problème de la violence symbolique semble être la réconciliation des contraires qui nous amène à notre deuxième volet où, du corps tragique, nous allons vers le corps déchiré, corps en fuite de lui-même, conçu selon la dimension élargie du corps social.

Le corps social, corps en lutte

Sans quitter Ben Jelloun, il faut ici se baser sur un autre de ses écrits, *Hospitalité Française*,[6] essai de nature sociologique, qui fonctionne à bien des égards comme doublet du (double) roman étudié précédemment. Reprenons rapidement certains des développements élaborés en détail dans le livre. L'Algérie semble avoir le comportement d'une "mère amnésique"(100) qui, voulant reprendre ses enfants à la France qui les a vus naître et oubliant que ces enfants sont inculturés, exige d'eux de se plier aux lois de sa culture et d'une nouvelle langue, sans compromission aucune. Je voudrais modifier quelque peu les termes utilisés et proposer, pour les besoins de mon argumentation, que l'Algérie est davantage un "père amnésique" puisqu'il fonctionne sur l'autorité et l'obéissance aveugle, valeurs qui caractérisent le domaine de la loi du père. La France ou société d'accueil, euphémisme pour un vocable plus approprié, la société d'installation[7] est qualifiée de "marâtre" (100) envers ces mêmes enfants, elle qui ne les a jamais vraiment accueillis en son sein et qui s'est comportée davantage en terre d'exclusion qu'en terre d'asile.

Parallèlement, l'image du père musulman, en France, est dévalorisée, celui-ci étant vu comme un émigré dont les valeurs éloignent l'enfant du pays de ses origines. Notre concept de rupture/exclusion fonctionne encore à ce niveau des rapports familiaux, puisque l'enfant refuse le destin dégradé des parents sans toutefois parvenir à se créer une nouvelle identité respectable et respectée, si ce n'est, dans le meilleur des cas, par une culture musicale ou une vie associative de quartier.[8] Pour les exclus, reste la violence, la délinquance ou la drogue. Réponses différentes au même mal de vivre, à la déchirure entre les deux cultures qui a façonné ces adolescents. On comprend mieux alors le manque d'alternative des enfants car,

> que vaut la parole d'un père qui se réfère, soit à la tradition qu'il essaie de maintenir en vie dans la maison alors qu'elle n'est qu'un souvenir ou un morceau de vie

en lambeaux, soit à l'autorité parentale qui ne se discute
pas et qui devient la réponse répressive à des questions
qui le dépassent? (Ben Jelloun, *Hospitalité* 104)

Cette dernière citation, question implacable d'un problème sans
issue réconfortante à court terme, montre à nouveau comment le père, en
œuvrant pour la sauvegarde de traditions dépassées est bien amnésique et
insensible, comme l'Algérie, aux besoins nouveaux et au développement
harmonieux de ses enfants. Peut-être faudrait-il aller plus loin et voir avec
D. Shayegan un cas de "schizophrénie culturelle". Il y a selon lui
schizophrénie culturelle chez un être (ou a l'échelle de tout un peuple
comme dans l'Iran révolutionnaire) lorsqu'il y a coexistence ou plus
exactement juxtaposition de paradigmes traditionnels et modernes. Dans
le cours de la vie économique, sociale ou familiale, l'être ne sait plus
comment se situer, deux "représentation du monde" s'affrontent dans sa
conscience.

L'islam, ajoute Ben Jelloun, peut aisément devenir la réponse à
cette identité brisée. Le discours d'autorité du père est parfaitement mis
en valeur dans *L'enfant de sable*. Là, il fonctionne sans contestation
(apparente) car il prend place sur un terreau sympathique, le Maroc et sur
le mode fictionel. Rapprochons ce discours d'un autre texte traitant lui
aussi de l'aliénation subie par un père émigré et transformé en ce qu'il
nomme "La malédiction" où il déconstruit d'autant mieux les mécanismes
de l'exclusion que lui-même est le premier à enserrer (pour des raisons
culturelles certes) sa femme et ses filles dans l'aliénation qu'il leur fait
subir à un niveau encore plus élaboré.[9] Ben Jelloun propose une
explication fort plausible à ce phénomène: les parents, privés de toute
légitimité, confèrent aux traditions de leur pays une importance
démesurée afin de tenter de renverser le processus par lequel leurs propres
enfants leur deviennent totalement étrangers. Qui a lu le roman d'Azouz
Begag *Béni ou le Paradis Privé* peut se forger une idée bien précise du fossé
culturel entre les deux générations et leurs habitus contradictoires.

Les filles réagissent le plus à cette oppression qu'elles subissent
d'ailleurs doublement, en tant qu'individu du sexe féminin et en tant que
fille d'émigrés. Pour cela, la réponse de la propre fille de cet émigré à un
entretien avec Abdelmalek Sayad est instructive.[10] L'alternative posée à
ces jeunes filles est, de toute façon problématique: soit elles acquiescent

aux désirs du père souverain et sont annihilées en qualité d'individus porteurs d'une voix, pour répondre aux nécessités d'un ordre traditionnel, soit elles s'excluent (ou le sont) de leur famille. Nous retrouvons notre paradigme de l'exclusion qui ici, se fait sur le mode de la fugue. Rupture irrémédiable dans ce cas, car, l'honneur étant perdu pour la fugueuse, le père ne se privera pas de la renier, cette fille indigne qui a bafoué l'idéal musulman de "la voie droite, la pureté, la rigueur, l'honnêteté." Deux sociétés aux valeurs antagonistes s'affrontent et il est vrai, comme le note Ben Jelloun (*Hospitalité* 107) que prôner des mœurs sexistes (à nos yeux) revient, pour le père, à s'assurer tant bien que mal quelques bribes de supériorité, le sentiment de l'honneur irréprochable, la seule supériorité qu'il puisse conserver en sa qualité de déraciné humilié. A intolérance, intolérance et demie qui ne devrait pas conduire à alimenter les sources du préjugé racial puisque, sociologiquement, son attitude est une réponse compréhensible à l'exclusion.

Ben Jelloun a realisé un tour de force, sur le mode littéraire, en montrant comment une jeune fille (L'enfant de sable/Ahmed/Zahra) pouvait finalement échapper à l'oppression au sein de sa famille en conciliant les contraires en elle-même: la féminité, la force de caractère et surtout l'imposition de sa voix comme dissidente. Dans la réalité sociologique, l'absence totale de communication entre le père et sa fille et/ou la fille et son frère m'amène à qualifier cette attitude de terrorisme patriarcal, plus dangereux celui-là que le fanatisme intégriste dont font abusément état les médias qui amalgament de surcroît intégrisme et terrorisme. La jeune fille, dominée parmi les dominés, est en rupture avec son milieu, en rupture aussi avec la France raciste qui la classe. Doublement déracinée, elle ne peut trouver sa force (son salut dirait son père) ni dans les traditions rejetées ni dans la libération affichée des femmes françaises qui ne sera jamais pour elle. Si la condition de la femme arabe préoccupe beaucoup les français (au point d'en oublier la condition de femme) ils pratiquent cependant un autre type d'amalgame et semblent confondre les pratiques du dogme islamique (ou interprétations contingentes à propos des femmes) et la Révélation comme vérité incarnée. Certes, "le voile qui protège la musulmane, devient un rideau qui écarte la femme" (Etienne 213) et, même si le "rideau" est né de l'histoire, sa fonction primordiale de protection reste la raison invoquée par les militantes qui choisissent de porter le voile comme un signe légitime de valorisation de soi.[11]

Le fait de naviguer entre le sujet (fictif) et le corps social à partir des différents écrits de Ben Jelloun, nous permet de nous interroger sur le problème de la coexistence entre les deux identités. L'enfant de sable sentait confusément déjà qu'en elle-même coexistait l'autre. Ce qui se traduit, dans *Hospitalité française*, par une remarque plus assertive: "Qu'on le veuille ou non, la différence est ce qui définit l'identité" (88), l'autre du groupe étant celui qui nous révèle le sens de notre propre identité communautaire.

Les religions monothéistes, tout au moins dans leur dimension exotérique et donc socialisée, confèrent infailliblement l'altérité radicale à la femme et toutes lui resérvent la portion congrue. C'est la redéfinition de l'identité féminine que Ben Jelloun a essayé de traiter dans ses romans. Au niveau sociétaire, "la pensée occidentale ne peut penser une expérience hétéronome, celle d'un Autre qui défait l'autorité du sujet" (Etienne 186). De là naît l'impensé islamique qui, en France, refuse la connaissance de l'Autre et entretient des phantasmes hystériques quant à lui. Il n'est qu'à songer au phénomène Le Pen. Un détour par la tradition "démocratique" française n'est pas inutile. Le droit à la différence, dans une France centralisatrisée et jacobine, est un leurre puisque l'assimilation passe par l'annihilation des différences et fait disparaître l'autre en tant qu'altérité. Le modèle républicain, école laïque en tête, ne réussit plus et l'universalité du concept de laïcité semble avoir fait son temps.

La pensée islamique ne considère pas comme fondée l'opposition entre sphère privée et publique si chère au monde occidental. L'existence d'une *Sharia* implique qu'il n'y ait pas de distinctions tranchées entre le sacré et le profane. En droit, tout est sacré, er René Guénon a raison de dire, dans la perspective islamique, que le profane n'est que le symptôme d'une dégénérescence cyclique. Sa culture se veut aussi théocentrique, puisqu'elle insiste plus que le christianisme sur l'idée d'Unité Divine. Dieu ne s'incarne pas et n'assume pas la condition humaine. En gardant ces considérations en mémoire, il convient de remarquer que les textes littéraires de Ben Jelloum entérinent cette confusion entre le spirituel et le temporel, en réitérant que Dieu reconnaît les intentions droites et cela sans perdre de vue la transcendance théologique. A n'en pas douter, ce souci divin du concret et du prosaïque est d'autant plus difficile à assumer pour musulmans français, qu'ils vivent dans un cadre et un rythme profanes. Cependant, pour une minorité de musulmans refusant l'Etat de Droit français, la majorité veut être des musulmans qui se respectent dans le cadre de la législation et des institutions républicaines. "Pour ces musulmans français, il s'agit tout simplement, à partir d'associations culturelles légales d'obtenir le droit d'ouvrir des lieux du culte décents et de pouvoir donner à leurs enfants un enseignement qui soit conforme à leurs convictions" (Etienne 226). Encore une fois, ceci confirme au niveau communautaire, une lecture de Ben Jelloun et montre que pour les communautés migrantes, la religion est le seul moyen de conserver une quelconque identité et que le Coran en lui-même ne représente pas un obstacle à l'intégration. Cet investissement dans le religieux, en s'opposant à la réification capitaliste, remet en question la célèbre et trop galvaudée formule de Marx de la religion comme opium du peuple.

Au dela de l'identité

A cette jonction, l'ouvrage de Khatibi "Maghreb Pluriel" se révèle approprié. L'auteur fait d'une pensée concrète de la différence l'arme d'une décolonisation effective (20).[12] Cette pensée complexe se base sur le traditionalisme qui n'est pas la tradition mais son oubli et se tourne vers le mysticisme qui n'est pas la religion. Laissons parler Khatibi "Ce qu'il faut . . . . c'est élargir notre liberté de penser, introduire dans tout dialogue plusieurs leviers stratégiques: évacuer par exemple du discours les absolus de la théologie et du théocentrisme qui enchaînent le temps, l'espace et l'édifice des sociétés maghrébines. Cela ne suffit pas. Le dialogue avec toute pensée de la différence est monumental. . . . Une pensée-autre est toujours un complot, une conjuration, une révolte soutenue et un risque implacable. . ."(33-4).

Cette pensée-autre, ainsi que Khatibi l'indique également, représente une menace potentielle pour les dominants en ce qu'elle déclare la guerre sur le plan social et politique et pense le Maghreb pour ce qu'il est, un espace géo-politique, lieu ou la pensée théologique est à la fois une force et un poison. La pensée-autre instaure une différence, une rupture avec cet autre impensé (ou survivance idéologique) que constitue le Maghreb aux yeux de la France. La pensée-autre est anti-impérialiste qui décentre le savoir occidental des anciens colonisés, savoir basé sur la logique du même. Subversive, cette pensée donne le pouvoir à la parole et le reprend à la parole du pouvoir comme pratique courante de l'après-colonisation et Mai 68. Le lecteur averti sait combien Khatibi utilise Derrida, non à des fins d'appropriation opportuniste, mais à celles d'emprunt qui, enrichi d'éléments pris à sa propre culture, le fait fructifier. Il fait valoir cette pensée dérridéenne d'une manière particulièrement originale. Le résultat—une pensée savante de la différence—se trouve encore davantage valorisé si l'on y incorpore la réponse de Nancy Fraser à l'article de Seyla Benhabib "The Generalized and the Concrete Other." Fraser démontre judicieusement que, dans nos sociétés occidentales, la communication accapare et donne une voix à ce que l'on pourrait nommer "le point de vue de l'échange" en constituant chaque être comme une entité séparée des autres, une entité raisonnable aussi et dont les actions visent, dans les rapports à autrui, à maximiser l'utilité qu'il attend des transactions qu'il opère. Bien entendu, nous nous référons ici à des transactions verbales structurées sur le mode de l'efficacité économique capitaliste. Ce point de vue, passant pour universel, est articulé selon un vocabulaire moral et politique qui ne sait, ni ne peut prendre en compte les expériences autres, les réseaux de relations et les interdépendances qui lient par exemple la mère et l'enfant dans l'espace de la famille restreinte. Ce vocabulaire est inapte à donner une voix aux dominés par le sexe, l'ethnie ou le statut économique. Jusque là, rien d'original et l'on sait depuis fort longtemps que le droit à la parole des dominés subit l'oppression. Fraser va pourtant plus loin que ce constat d'échec: le fait qu'ils ne soient pas entendus (ou la surdité[13] dont ils font l'objet) est produit par les moyens socio-culturels d'interprétation et de communication qui sont biaisés dès le départ. Sans contrôle sur ces moyens d'interprétation, les dominés n'ont que deux choix:

> they could either adopt the dominant point of view and see their own experiences repressed and distorted; or they could develop idiolects capable of voicing their experience and see these marginalized, disqualified and excluded from the central discursive institutions and arenas of society. Or they could do both at once. (426)

La première alternative est la solution pourrait-on dire classique du dominé exclu en ce qu'il s'exclut lui-même, ne se sentant pas à la hauteur, faisant "de nécessité vertu" selon l'expression de Pierre Bourdieu. La deuxième, corrobore ce dont il a déjà été fait mention par la référence aux îlots de culture ayant pour base la vie de quartiers, cultures locales qui sauvent certains émigrés d'une aliénation totale à la culture étrangère qui les entoure.

Seyla Benhabib cherchait encore à définir les conséquences "d'un concept non répressif d'autonomie morale et individuelle" (Fraser 426).[14] Fraser poursuit plus avant cette recherche d'un modèle identitaire nouveau "relationnel et interactif" (427) en prenant en considération les interdépendances entre les besoins de l'individu et l'histoire collective qui donne voix à ces besoins. Ainsi, elle opère un saut qualitatif de l'identité individuelle à l'identité collective qui articule cette individualité, ce qu'elle nomme "le point de vue de l'autre concret et collectif" (428). Cet effort d'envisager l'autre comme entité concrète la rapproche de Khatibi et de Ben Jelloun. Ce dernier posait le problème de l'identité selon un mythe archétypique, celui de l'androgyne, présenté concrètement par une enfant ayant incorporé les deux composantes, s'étant joué, pourrait-on dire, de la différence entre les sexes. Fraser parvient à poser le problème non plus en termes d'autonomie et d'unicité de l'individu, cette fiction qui a fait son temps, mais selon l'optique que le point de vue univoque du dominant a perdu son exclusivité car il est désormais battu en brèche par d'autres discours pratiques et solidarités vécues, tous aussi respectables même s'ils ne jouissent pas de l'aura de l'universalité:

> There is a dialogic interaction with actual others, although these are encountered less as unique identities, solidarities and forms of life. In short, the standpoint of the collective concrete other is contextual and hermeneutical, not formal universalist. It is flexible and nonrepressive with respect to emotions. And it acknowledges connectedness to specific human groups, though these are not restricted to intimate ones comprising family, lovers and friends. (428)

L'émergence de ce nouvel individu responsable la conduit à proposer "une éthique de la solidarité" sur le plan social qui implique un contrôle collectif sur les moyens de communication et d'interprétation . Son modèle renverse la subordination pour faire place à une participation effective. Il permet aussi de dépasser l'alternative stérile entre sphère privée (maternelle, celle des soins attentifs) et les institutions (comme système de droits et de récompenses). Si la solidarité doit conduire à l'autonomie du dominé, on a su voir ce processus d'autonomisation à l'œuvre dans *L'enfant de sable* qui apprend en parlant et en étant entendue, en disant et en redisant son histoire de sa propre voix et de celle des conteurs interposés. Cette solidarité me semble particulièrement probante lorsque appliquée à un exemple concret, la situation de la femme musulmane. Dans l'affaire du foulard, l'impasse était complète, par manque d'un concept opératoire, tel que celui de Fraser. Les partisans du voile défendaient leur prise de position au nom des droits individuels qui sont là pour tolérer et respecter les conduites des individus et les détracteurs du "hijab" de leur opposer la conception occidentale de l'individu autonome qui prend pour base les valeurs abstraites et universelles, comme le respect de la laïcité, concept qui essaie d'opérer une impossible médiation entre les droits universels et individuels. Le port du voile conduit alors à la tyrannie du groupe sur l'individu. Dialogue de sourds qui ne s'accorde que sur l'essentiel: le discours dominant masculin a monopolisé le débat sur la légitimité ou l'illégitimité de ce que les femmes doivent porter en France. Le problème a été commenté et médiatisé d'abord et surtout en sa qualité de violation d'une institution républicaine et non comme une réaction au voile en tant que tel.[15] Il n'est aucun exemple plus parlant pour expliciter le danger des universaux aux mains des dominants, concepts commodes dont ils se servent pour statuer sur le sort des opprimés sans même leur laisser le droit de réponse. (Dans l'affaire du foulard, bien peu de jeunes filles ont, librement, pris position.) Il y a donc beaucoup à espérer de cette logique de la solidarité comme concept opérationnel à usage pratique. Le véritable problème de l'affaire des foulards revient à celui de l'autonomie des femmes maghrébines dont la voix est digne d'être écoutée et entendue.[16]

En guise de conclusion, la solidarité dont fait état Fraser ramène, après bien des détours productifs—on voudrait le croire—à l'hospitalité dont parlait Ben Jelloun sur le mode de l'ironie. Rappelons ce qu'il écrit sur cette notion dans son livre *A l'insu du souvenir*: "Dans mon pays/on ne prête pas/on partage./Un plat rendu n'est jamais vide;/du pain/ quelques fèves/ ou une pincée de sel" (40). Si, alors, l'hospitalité existe, "naturellement" chez les musulmans, ils seraient plus proches du modèle solidaire désiré pour l'avenir de l'intégration des deux communautés. Leur tâche est donc de faire valoir cet atout, de le faire accepter dans le contexte français pour en imprégner une population autochtone jusque-là fort réticente. L'hospitalité entendue comme solidarité est alors l'avenir de la France comme d'autres ont chanté que la femme était l'avenir de l'homme. Mais les deux problématiques ne sont-elles pas, pour ce qui touche à l'intégration, fondamentalement liées?

Notes

1. J'emprunte ce concept au sociologue Pierre Bourdieu. Il rend compte de la force cachée qui assure la cohésion et la reproduction d'un ordre basé sur l'exclusion, dans notre cas sur l'exclusion de la femme. C'est une manière douce, une sorte de séduction, qui revient à ce que les victimes n'aient d'autres choix que d'opter pour leur propre soumission. Cette violence, larvée, puisque, nul n'est besoin de recours à la force brute pour qu'elle soit efficace, opère par manipulation de la réalité des rapports sociaux. Elle agit sur l'esprit, c'est une violence psychique, qui légitime, est une façon commode pour les dominants, les hommes dans notre cas de figure, de donner corps à leur domination en auto-culpabilisant les exclus.

2. Je ne parle pas de sables mouvants mais plutôt de cette qualité émouvante de cet(te) enfant, qui n'est jamais véritablement enfant, et qui, jusqu'au réveil de l'adolescence subit de plein fouet la violence car elle est en rupture totale avec le monde, les émotions, sa famille, îlot isolé dans un océan d'indifférence qu'elle s'est elle même créée, une fiction culturelle, un "détournement social," une erreur du destin.

3. Ces épreuves sont formellement inscrites dans un texte labyrinthique et, comme Mircea Eliade l'a écrit, "Cette construction est la défense, parfois magique, d'un centre" (211).

4. Cet autre point de vue pourrait être la "pensée-autre" dont le modèle est développé dans le livre de Khatibi, *Maghreb Pluriel* . Sa pensée fera l'objet de développements ultérieurs. Mais aussi, cette citation qui ramène

à la constitution féminine ou masculine de l'être sans utiliser les outils (et présupposés) constitutifs de la psychologie, semble à nouveau évoquer une autre quête archétypique, celle de l'androgyne comme symbole de la perfection spirituelle. Etre homme et femme "à la fois" c'est opérer un total renversement des valeurs constitutives de toute société et cela dépasse l'analyse purement sociale pour retourner à un temps révolu, avant l'histoire, avant la chute. Le paradis perdu devait être ce monde où les contraires coexistaient sans conflit, comme représentatifs de l'unité divine. Ainsi donc, l'exposé de Ben Jelloun (où l'androgynie fait place à la trilogie femme-homme-femme) ne serait qu'une version édulcorée de notre tentative impossible d'atteindre à l'unité dans une société inscrite dans l'histoire et la temporalité. Nous savons gré à l'écrivain marocain d'avoir essayé, comme beaucoup d'autres d'ailleurs qui se sont tournés vers la problématique de la résolution des contraires. L'enfant de sable (comme son nom l'indique) est donc orientée sur un parcours initiatique qui n'est autre que "la traversée du désert" et les épreuves qu'elle encourt l'éveillent à la vision, à la perception et aux émotions.

5. Je suis partiellement d'accord avec la remarque suivante d'Abbes Maawaoui: "Ce déplacement sensoriel du visuel au toucher n'est pas ici une banale synesthésie. Il représente une disqualification de la vue et constitue un hommage au sens tactile, hommage qui sera d'ailleurs repris dans les différents points stratégiques du roman" (74). Partiellement parce que, comme je l'ai expliqué, seule la vision "normale" est discréditée. La vision au-delà, qui caractérise l'aveugle, est au contraire mise en exergue puisque c'est lui-même, bien que privé de la vue, qui devient le Saint.

6. Le titre de l'ouvrage revêt un intérêt particulier dans le concept de la discussion sur l'orientalisme et sur ce qui le caractérise comme désir fondamental de noblesse, concept qui n'a rien à voir avec la définition occidentale qui attribue cette aristocratie au fait d'être né dans la catégorie sociale appropriée. Or cette noblesse du monde arabe comporte, pour exister, la reconnaissance des lois propres à l'hospitalité qui précisément engagent tout l'être musulman. D'autre part, comme cette hospitalité est une des dernières qualités à être valorisée en France (nombre d'étrangers, immigrés non compris, sont d'accord pour déplorer cet état de choses), il y aurait beaucoup à dire sur l'ironie à la fois mordante et triste de ce titre en forme d'oxymore.

7. On sait comment les parents de ces enfants français ont vécu la condition d'immigré et comment la majorité d'entre eux, d'installation provisoire en installation provisoire, passe leur vie à chercher à s'installer de façon moins précaire. Ils semblent camper dans la société où ils sont exilés, reproduisant ainsi une forme de nomadisme prolétaroïde, condition qui a tout à envier au nomadisme de leurs origines.

8. Bruno Etienne dans son excellent ouvrage, *La France et l'islam* donne un tour intéressant à cette identité en voie de constitution. Pour lui, ces enfants seraient à la fois pris dans la culture mondiale et liés à leur quartier où ils reconstituent une vie tribale. De fait, ils éludent donc le douloureux problème, double lui encore, de la nationalité et de la citoyenneté. Sa conclusion est plus optimiste que Ben Jelloun, peut être parce que quelques cinq années se sont passées entre la parution des deux ouvrages, années qui auraient élargi la base de la vie associative/musicale en intégrant un nombre croissant de jeunes. Etienne d'écrire: "La jonction entre l'amont et l'aval, le particulier et le général, le village-quartier et le village-monde, la tradition et la modernité produit un type de pratiques, un croisement entre l'Occident et l'Orient à domicile en particulier à travers la musique: ce vecteur-média 'moderne' qu'est le raï" (261-2). Si le quartier devient donc le passage obligé par lequel le tissu associatif se constitue, Etienne le voit comme "une zone de participation aux associations volontaires de caractère non directement politique, [qui] constitue un réservoir de citoyenneté" (270). L'évolution est certes encourageante même si "La plupart des Etats modernes ne conçoivent pas (encore) la citoyenneté détachée de la nationalité" (270).

9. Nous nous référons ici au livre de Pierre Bourdieu, *La misère du monde* et à l'entretien d'Abdelmalek Sayad avec un travailleur immigré aux pages 823 à 844.

10. Notons que le livre de Bourdieu n'indique pas qu'il s'agit de la fille du travailleur immigré qui avait parlé de la "malédiction" de sa condition. Mais tous les recoupements portent à croire qu'il s'agit bien de la même famille, ce qui rend le rapprochement des deux textes encore plus intéressant, puisque le père est un homme cultivé. Cet essai s'intitule "L'émancipation" et se trouve aux pages 859 à 859 du livre de Bourdieu auquel il vient d'être fait référence.

11. L'article de Susan Slyomovics "Women and Public Space in Algeria" mérite une attention particulière. L'auteur note en effet que le voile peut,

paradoxalement, ramener la femme dans la sphère publique d'où elle est exclue si elle ne le porte pas. Mais cette mise en liberté surveillée est surtout le fait de l'élite intellectuelle féminine qui est le mieux à même de détourner la signification du voile et de s'en servir à son avantage, manipulant ainsi les rapports de force symboliques entre les sexes: "Today, many women . . . profess fervent Muslim faith but reinterpret Islam's idea of women. It is precisely the protected status symbolized by the veil that encourages them to believe that they will be able to compete in the male public world. But these new and supposedly Islamic conceptions of women's roles are not supported by the FIS. More remarkably, the Islamist leadership's attitudes conform to legislation put in place after independence by the FLN. In other words, the factions now struggling for power in Algeria are in fundamental ideological agreement that women's social freedom must be severely restricted" (13).

12. Le terme "concret" signifie une action programmatique. Il m'intéresse en ce que l'auteur, comme d'ailleurs les autres cités (Etienne, Bourdieu et Fraser) condamne sans appel les relations abstraites fournissant au discours des concepts universalisés donc problématiques tels l'Etat, la Nation, la Laïcité, concepts qui, au lieu de résoudre les problèmes de communication entre les deux cultures, les aliènent l'une contre l'autre dans une fracture irrécupérable. Selon l'évidence, la participation au sein d'une quelconque société n'est pas partagée également par tous ses membres et la liberté du Citoyen (a-sexué mais certes pas androgyne) est souvent édifiée pour mieux masquer la position de fragilité des dominés.

13. Nous avons, dans la note 7, abordé le problème des sens (et du sens). Le sens de l'ouïe faisait encore défaut. Le voilà réhabilité. Le sens de l'ouïe se devait d'être mobilisé si l'on veut parler de cette expérience globale et concrète à laquelle Khatibi fait allusion.

14. La traduction est mienne.

15. On pourrait bien sûr penser que le débat qui aurait porté sur le voile en tant que tel était perdu d'avance pour les français car il n'y avait aucun fondement, sinon d'ordre éthique, à l'interdire dans les écoles. Il semble que récupéré et posé autrement, à travers la violation du concept de Laïcité, ait été la seule façon pour la République de sauver la face (en ne s'avouant pas vaincue) et pour les maghrébins (en campant sur leur position) de sauver l'Honneur, encore une fois en se servant d'une médiation, plus concrète celle-là, la femme-étendard, porte-foulard. Dans

tous les cas, il s'agit d'une mascarade de discours sur des universaux qui ne s'avouent pas pour ce qu'ils sont, et dont la femme masquée fait seule les frais. Je suggérerais ironiquementà ces femmes de porter en guise de foulard le drapeau républicain. Symbole de la laïcité, ce geste devrait faire taire les opposants au foulard qui y verraient peut-être une concession faite aux valeurs démocratiques, tout en calmant les partisans de cette parure. Les hommes, finalement, y retrouveraient leur mise idéologique et les femmes consentantes ne seraient plus stigmatisées.

16. Nous renvoyons ici à l'excellent article de Rachel A.D. Bloul, dont nous nous sommes servie au cours de cette discussion: "Veiled Objects of Post-Colonial Desire: Forbidden Women Disrupt the Republican Fraternal Space."

Works Cited

Begag, Azouz. *Béni ou le paradis privé*. Paris: Seuil, 1989.

Benhabib, Seyla. "The Generalized and the Concrete Other. The Kohlberg-Gilligan Controversy and Feminist Theory." *Praxis International* 5.4 (January 1986): 402-24.

Ben Jelloun, Tahar. *La nuit sacrée*. Paris: Seuil, 1987.

____. *L'enfant de sable*. Paris: Seuil, 1985.

____. *Hospitalité française*. Paris: Seuil, 1984.

____. *A l'insu du souvenir*. Paris: Ed. La Découverte, 1987.

Bloul, Rachel A.D. "Veiled Objects of Post-Colonial Desire: Forbidden Women Disrupt the Republican Fraternal Space." *Australian Journal of Anthropology* 5.1/2 (1994): 113-23.

Bourdieu, Pierre. *La misère du monde*. Paris: Seuil, 1993.

Eliade, Mircea. *L'épreuve du labyrinthe*. Paris: Pierre Belfond, 1978.

Etienne, Bruno. *La France et l'Islam*. Paris: Hachette, 1989.

Fraser, Nancy. "Toward a Discourse of Solidarity." *Praxis International* 5.4 (January 1986): 425-9.

Khatibi, Abdelkebir. *Maghreb pluriel*. Paris: Denoël, 1983.

Maawaoui, Abbes. "*L'enfant de sable* et *La nuit sacrée* ou le corps tragique." *The French Review* 1 (October 1995): 68-77.

Shayegan, Daryush. *Le regard mutilé: Schizophrénie culturelle, pays traditionnels face a la modernité*. Paris: Aubin Michel, 1989.

Slyomovics, Susan. "Women and Public Space in Algeria." *Middle East Report* 25.1 (January-February 1995): 8-13.

Cours d'introduction de littérature francophone–quels objectifs?

Jane Alison Hale

Odile Cazenave nous a proposé plusieurs questions pour structurer la discussion aujourd'hui. Ces questions me semblent à la fois pertinentes et familières. Pour chacune, j'ai trouvé plus qu'une réponse valide, et souvent deux ou trois qui se contredisent. Ce qui veut dire que ce sont de bonnes questions! En fait, ce sont les mêmes que tout professeur de littérature—anglaise, française, africaine, russe, comparée—se pose tout le temps en créant ses cours. La riche variété de réponses valables à ces questions, c'est ce qui paie notre salaire–ce qui crée le curriculum d'un département de littérature, ce qui empêche les étudiants de pouvoir suivre un cours de littérature pour dire à la fin: "Bon, voilà, j'ai compris. Maintenant je connais la littérature x, y ou z".

Mais cette variété de réponses est plus problématique pour nous qui enseignons dans des départements de français aux USA où il faut partager le curriculum avec Baudelaire, le Français 1, Louis XIV, le plus-que-parfait du subjonctif, Duras, Ronsard, Truffaut, la phonétique . . . enfin vous connaissez tous la liste infinie et impossible.

Donc, malgré le fait que je n'ai pas de réponses définitives à ces questions, je tâcherai d'y répondre avec des réflexions venant de ma propre pratique:

Quel seuil de compétence?

Dans mon département nous recommandons aux étudiants de finir, en plus de la séquence élémentaire et intermédiaire de la langue, un cours d'introduction à la littérature française avant de s'inscrire dans le cours francophone. Mais j'accepte des étudiants qui ne répondent pas exactement à ces critères. De plus en plus, nos étudiants nous viennent avec des compétences variables, et acquises de façons très diverses: Haïtiens-Américains, Africains, Canadiens, étudiants internationaux qui ont fait des études de-ou en-français. Comme pour tous mes cours, j'essaie donc de viser plusieurs niveaux différents et de noter les étudiants individuellement à la fois sur leur capacité d'analyse littéraire et culturelle et sur leur progrès oral et écrit en français. Pour ce faire, je donne des devoirs écrits courts et fréquents, en demandant aux étudiants de les récrire tous, et de me rendre tous les devoirs dans un dossier séparé chaque fois, pour que je puisse évaluer le progrès individuel.

Quelle répartition géographique? Vise-t-on un survol superficiel ou une étude plus profonde d'un ou deux sujets/thèmes/périodes/ styles/pays/auteurs?

Cette question difficile, et impossible, a nourri plusieurs versions différentes de mon cours d'introduction à la littérature francophone au cours de ces dernières années.

J'ai proposé et enseigné le cours pour la première fois en 1992 sous la forme d'une "Introduction à la littérature francophone d'Afrique et des Antilles". Évidemment, c'était trop ambitieux! Ce cours a attiré bien plus d'étudiants qu'un cours normal de littérature dans notre département, et les étudiants l'ont évalué très positivement. Leur seule plainte, et c'était une plainte universelle, était qu'on avait essayé de trop faire pendant un semestre. Ils ont réclamé deux cours séparés, un sur la littérature africaine et un sur la littérature antillaise, et avec leurs commentaires je n'ai pas eu de difficultés à convaincre le chef de mon département de me permettre de donner ces deux cours en alternance.

Le cours d'introduction à la littérature francophone des Antilles est bien apprécié par les étudiants, mais je m'y sens moins confortable que dans le cours africain, car j'ai eu moins d'expérience vécue dans ces cultures qu'en Afrique. Mais, de plus en plus de nos étudiants viennent des Antilles et peuvent souvent aider à stimuler les échanges interculturels dans la classe.

Le cours d'introduction à la littérature francophone d'Afrique marche bien, mais les critiques des étudiants ne manquent jamais, comme vous le savez. Plusieurs disent qu' "il y a trop de Sénégalais". Mais d'autres disent que le meilleur aspect du cours est le fait que le professeur partage ses expériences personnelles au Sénégal. De façon similaire, il y a des étudiants qui aimeraient qu'on passe plus de temps à analyser le côté strictement "littéraire" des textes, mais d'autres (la vaste majorité, en fait) trouvent le lourd contenu culturel du cours son aspect le plus valable. Je devrais peut-être faire plus attention à la morale d'un des contes que j'enseigne dans le cours africain—"Lan mooy áddina" [ainsi va le monde] et la version française de la Fontaine, "Le meunier, son fils et l'âne": "On ne peut pas plaire à tout le monde et son fils" ou "ainsi va le monde".

Comme les étudiants, et comme tout enseignant, je ne suis jamais tout à fait satisfaite du cours non plus. Il continuera à changer avec le temps, les étudiants, le curriculum et ma propre évolution professionnelle et intellectuelle. Mes recherches actuelles portent sur la représentation littéraire de l'apprentissage de la lecture et de l'écriture. Il se peut donc que je structure un cours de littérature comparée de plusieurs pays très divers autour de cette question. Voilà pourquoi j'aime le fait qu'on ne peut pas répondre définitivement à la question de ce que ce cours—ou n'importe quel cours—devrait être: c'est la recherche acharnée d'une solution inexistante qui nous force à découvrir de nouvelles voies pour la pensée.

En plus du cours d'introduction à la littérature africaine ou antillaise, j'ai construit un cours de langue (troisième semestre du français) autour des "Cultures francophones du monde". Nous lisons des textes littéraires et culturels, nous regardons des films, nous étudions de l'art, de l'histoire, de la sociologie, de la musique de plusieurs pays francophones autour du monde: africains, asiatiques, nord-américains, antillais. Chaque étudiant choisit au début du cours un pays pour un projet de recherches qu'il effectuera au cours du semestre, en rapportant à la classe ses trouvailles. Chaque fois, ce cours est donc différent, selon les étudiants—leur choix, leurs expériences, leurs goûts, leur culture personnelle. Il n'est pas difficile de trouver des textes scolaires pour ce niveau qui traitent des cultures francophones mondiales, mais je préfère construire mon propre curriculum, avec un carnet de lectures, d'images et de cartes photocopiées de sources diverses.

Il y a encore une autre façon de confronter le problème de
l'embarras de choix pour un seul cours: introduire la littérature
francophone dans d'autres cours de français. On pourrait même accepter
parfois des textes français dans nos cours francophones! Car il me semble
que la "Francophonie" devrait inclure la France aussi, comme un pays où
l'on parle français comme ailleurs. L'inclusion des textes francophones
dans des cours de langue, de conversation, de culture et de composition
est relativement facile. Mais j'ai réussi à le faire même avec les cours plus
avancés. Par exemple, ce semestre j'enseigne un cours sur le théâtre
français du 20è siècle, où j'inclus: un texte de Samuel Beckett (français-
irlandais)—*La dernière bande*; d'Abla Farhoud (canadienne-libanaise)—*Les
filles du 5-10-15*; de Simone Schwarz-Bart (guadeloupéenne)—*Ton beau
capitaine*; de S. Corinna Bille (suisse)—*L'inconnue du Haut-Rhone*.

Comment choisir les textes/auteurs spécifiques?

Je répondrai à cette question en décrivant mon texte idéal pour
ce cours qui, bien sûr, n'existe pas. En fait, même si j'arrivais un jour à
trouver un texte qui réponde à cette formule artificielle, je sais que je le
trouverai fade et insatisfaisant, car il essaierait de dire et de faire tout, en
ne disant ni ne faisant rien. Mais voici quand même les critères que j'ai en
tête en choisissant mes textes; et plus un texte s'y rapproche, plus il est
probable que je l'inclurai dans mon cours: environ 200 pages; écrit dans
un français originel mais pas trop difficile; écrit par une femme non-
sénégalaise (c'est un critère personnel, car j'ai trop de textes écrits par des
hommes sénégalais sur mon syllabus!); traitant du passé, du présent et de
l'avenir proche; racontant une expérience individuelle et personnelle dans
un contexte culturel et historique qui soit à la fois quelque chose de très
différent pour les étudiants et quelque chose avec lequel ils peuvent
s'identifier à certains égards; prenant des risques avec la langue et
l'écriture, mais pas jusqu'au point d'aliéner ou de perdre l'étudiant
moyen; intéressant aux types littéraires ainsi qu'aux types anthropologues
qui s'inscrivent dans un tel cours; disponible aux USA et pas trop cher,
etc. etc. etc. etc.

Le semestre dernier j'ai utilisé deux nouveaux romans qui
répondent à plusieurs de ces critères, et les étudiants les ont bien
appréciés: *Rebelle* de Fatou Keïta et *Le cavalier et son ombre* de Boris Diop.

Ni l'un ni l'autre n'est pourtant parfait: celui-là n'a pas plu à tout le monde, surtout à quelques garçons, car il a un côté féministe très prononcé et même militant, et celui-ci est encore un texte par un homme sénégalais! Tous deux étaient trop chers aussi, ce qui s'avère un problème pour la plupart des nouvelles oeuvres, qui n'ont pas encore paru en édition de poche. Pourtant, les étudiants aiment bien le fait de lire des oeuvres qui viennent de sortir.

Qu'est-ce que nous voulons que nos étudiants sachent à la fin du semestre?

C'est-à-dire, quels sont nos objectifs? Pour moi, ils sont grands et je fais exprès de ne pas les rendre trop précis, pour laisser de la liberté aux étudiants de se concentrer sur l'aspect du matériel qui les intéresse le plus. Voici les objectifs que j'écris sur le syllabus pour le cours de français intermédiaire qui pourraient servir, avec quelques légères modifications, au cours d'introduction littéraire aussi:

> Mes objectifs dans ce cours sont: de vous faire apprécier la grande diversité des cultures francophones du monde; de vous donner envie d'en connaître plus, d'y voyager, de rencontrer leurs habitants ici et dans leur pays; d'améliorer votre français oral et écrit; et de vous inspirer à continuer vos études en français. J'espère aussi que ce cours vous obligera à réfléchir au sujet de la langue et de la littérature en général et de leur rôle dans le développement des individus, des groupes et des sociétés.

Hier matin, à l'ouverture du colloque, Edris a cité un proverbe wolof qui résume bien le but principal de tout mon enseignement de littérature et de langues: "Xam sa bop moo gen ñu la koy wax" (Sache qui tu es avant qu'on ne te le dise). Pour moi, l'enseignement du français est un moyen d'aider les étudiants à se connaître, mais à se connaître toujours *en contexte*, comme nous vivons tous, et de plus en plus, dans un contexte international et agrandissant et à devenir le genre de personne qu'*ils* veulent être, et non une copie de leurs parents/professeurs ou, pire, de notre plus grande rivale: l'éducation de consommation conformiste du film et de la télé.

Être immigrant sans galérer:
Les recettes de Dany Laferrière

Ambroise Kom

En 1998, on a fait grand bruit en France du 150è anniversaire de l'abolition de l'esclavage. A peine a-t-on entendu quelques timides voix s'élever pour se demander au nom de quoi les descendants des Négriers pouvaient se permettre de célébrer avec autant de zèle l'abolition de l'horrible traite. Surtout qu'à aucun moment on n'a eu l'idée de mettre véritablement en relief la contribution des esclaves à la lutte qui allait mettre fin au trafic du "bois d'ébène". Mais à y regarder de près, on se rend compte que la commémoration de l'acte de 1848 participe, une fois de plus, d'une logique désormais établie. C'est toujours et encore l'Autre qui fait et qui écrit, à sa manière, l'histoire des peuples noirs. Il en fut ainsi de l'esclavage. Il en a été de même de la colonisation et il en va pareillement aujourd'hui de l'immigration et de nos mésaventures post-coloniales.

Condamné à la galère, soumis à une précarité sans borne, aussi bien dans son pays qu'à l'extérieur, l'Africain et ses descendants semblent avoir du mal à s'approprier l'histoire. Aussi se laissent-ils nommer, étiqueter et manipuler à souhait. Le continent nord-américain, on le sait, est une société multiculturelle, une terre d'immigration où Européens, Asiatiques et divers autres immigrants se sont installés, chacun avec son identité propre. Assez curieusement, les Africains qui, c'est un fait, y sont arrivés, pour la plupart les chaînes aux pieds, semblent s'être maintenus ou sont à tout jamais rejetés dans les marges. Depuis le sud profond des États-Unis jusqu'aux confins des provinces maritimes du Canada en passant par tous les ghettos qui ont rivalisé de célébrité—Harlem, Watts, etc.—le Noir apparaît comme le souffre-douleur de la riche et prospère Amérique.

Haïtien récemment immigré au Canada, Dany Laferrière était sans doute condamné, lui aussi, à vivre d'expédients. Mais en observateur perspicace et en lecteur attentif de l'histoire des peuples noirs, il a élaboré de savoureuses recettes pour échapper à la galère. Il s'est amusé à réunir un certain nombre de stéréotypes coloniaux pour les resservir sous un emballage original à des lecteurs dont il sait que la plupart ont intériorisé nombre de stéréotypes dont sont victimes les peuples noirs. Pascal Blanchard et Nicolas Bancel rappellent très justement à propos des stéréotypes:

> Depuis l'Antiquité, l'Occident a construit son système de valeurs et sa culture en prenant comme miroir négatif l'Autre. Du mythe biblique de la malédiction de Cham, fils de Noé, au "barbare" de l'Empire romain, un certain nombre de mythes fondateurs ont irrigué la pensée occidentale, dessinant son rapport à l'altérité et à l'identité. Dans ce long processus, l'affirmation scientifique du concept de "race", au milieu du XIXè siècle, offrira une "légitimité" idéologique aux conquêtes coloniales. (Blanchard and Bancel 13)

Et ainsi que le souligne Louis Sala-Molins par ailleurs, les Négriers se sont sérieusement interrogés sur la nature même de cet être maudit qu'est le fils de Cham:

> Des Hommes? Des Bêtes? Des hommes assurément, puisqu'ils dérivent de Noé et d'Adam et qu'ils ont, par conséquent, terrées et assoupies au plus profondément inaccessible de leur nature, les conditions du salut.
>
> Des bêtes sans l'ombre d'un doute, puisque l'esclavage est leur lot, leur part dans l'héritage, et que la malédiction liminaire les tient inexorablement éloignés de la vie politique, du droit, du pouvoir, de tout ce qui en bonne théologie scolastique—et déjà en bon augustinisme,

tout comme en bon aristotélisme—arrime, comme l'attribut à la substance, l'humanité à la cité et la cité à l'humanité. (26)

Au fur et à mesure que l'Occident progresse dans la connaissance de l'Autre, les stéréotypes s'épaississent et contribuent à donner entièrement forme à la vision de l'indigène. Timothy Mitchell, dans *Colonizing Egypt*, montre comment l'Europe a profité de l'Exposition Universelle de Paris et de Londres pour représenter l'Autre et même le façonner selon ses propres fantasmes :

> The Egyptian exhibit had been built by the French to represent a winding street of Cairo, made of houses with overhanging upper stores and a mosque like that of Qaitbay. "It was intended", one of the Egyptians wrote, "to resemble the old Cairo". So carefully was this done, he noted, that "even the paint on the buildings was made dirty".
>
> The Egyptian exhibit had also been made carefully chaotic. In contrast to the geometric lines of the rest of the exhibition, the imitation street was laid out in the haphazard manner of the bazaar. The way was crowded with shops and stalls, where Frenchmen dressed as Orientals sold perfumes, pastries, and tarbushes. To complete the effect of the bazaar, th French organizers had imported from Cairo fifty Egyptian donkeys, together with their drivers and the requisite number of grooms, farriers, and saddle-makers. (1)

L'intention est manifeste. Il s'agit d'installer dans l'imaginaire de l'Européen que son univers en est un de référence. De sorte qu'en se rendant à l'étranger, le monde extérieur soit toujours jugé en fonction des "vérités" occidentales considérées comme universelles. On retrouve ici la vieille démarche ethnocentrique des psychiatres qui nous ont appris, écrit Roland Jaccard, à "juger les autres à partir de nos propres systèmes de valeurs" (33). D'ailleurs, le premier roman de Dany Laferrière, *Comment faire l'amour avec un Nègre sans se fatiguer* s'est écrit et devrait même se lire à la lumière de Freud que cite Bouba, protagoniste quelque peu excentrique, à la fois prêtre et psychothérapeute. En réalité, Laferrière invite l'Occident à se mettre d'abord sur le divan avant de songer à étiqueter l'Autre. En quelque sorte, Laferrière remonte le cours de l'histoire, revisite l'Exposition Universelle et renvoie l'Occident à son propre miroir, en mettant en question, de façon allégorique, son modèle et ses fondements.

A ce propos, Mitchell s'interroge à juste titre:

> If Europe was becoming the world-as-exhibition, I am going to ask, what happened to Europeans who left and went abroad? How did they experience a life not yet lived, so to speak, as though the world were a picture of something set up before an observer's gaze? Part of the answer, I will suggest, is that they did not realize they had left the exhibition. How could they, if they took the world itself to be an exhibition? Reality was that which presents itself as exhibit, so nothing else would have been thinkable. Living within a world of signs, they took semiosis to be a universal condition, and set about describing the Orient as though it were an exhibition. (13-4)

Bien évidemment, les voyageurs européens chercheront, partout où ils seront, à retrouver le modèle de référence. La démarche de Dany Laferrière consiste à prendre l'Occident à rebrousse-poil et à lui faire croire que le Nègre assume l'image que l'Autre s'est acharné à lui coller. Mais qu'on ne s'y trompe pas. La démarche de l'écrivain haïtien n'a qu'une lointaine parenté avec celle des tenants de la Négritude qui se sont évertués à produire des oeuvres pour faire mentir le colonisateur qui prétendait que le Noir était sans culture et sans histoire. Laferrière s'amuse à assumer l'hypermasculinité du Nègre et autres préjugés, mais le romancier s'arrange pour entraîner l'Autre dans son jeu. Désormais, son héros ne sera pas seul à subir le regard inquisiteur des héritiers du discours "orientaliste" pour reprendre un terme cher à Edward Said.

Car si le Nègre a été défini pour que chacun garde sa place et joue le rôle qui lui a été dévolu, on peut se demander de quoi l'avenir sera fait une fois que l'Autre aura, lui aussi, pris plaisir à vivre dans le zoo? Nécessairement, il faudra repenser l'ordre des choses. Mitchell explique:

> The techniques of enframing, of fixing an interior and an exterior, and of positioning the observing subject, are what create an appearance of order, an order that works by appearance. The world is set up before an observing subject as though it were the picture of something, appearing and experienced in relationship between the picture and the plan or meaning it represents. It follows that the appearance of order is at the same time an order of appearance, a hierarchy. The world appears to the observer as a relationship between picture and reality, the one present but secondary, a mere representation, the other only represented, but prior, more original, more real. This order of appearance is what might be called the hierarchy of truth. (60)

Ainsi pourraient également se présenter l'ordre des choses et la réalité des relations entre l'Autre et nous, entre le dominant et le dominé. La présente étude voudrait montrer comment l'écriture de Dany Laferrière procède de la dérision et d'un désir profond de subvertir l'ordre traditionnel du discours. L'auteur manie avec virtuosité l'ironie et l'humour pour permettre à l'objet d'hier, le Nègre, de reprendre l'initiative, de redevenir sujet de l'histoire. Car pour Dany Laferrière, l'éternel conquis a les moyens de devenir conquérant. Sous un jour apparemment anodin donc, l'écrivain haïtien tels que nous le révéleront *Comment faire l'amour avec un Nègre sans se fatiguer* et *Cette grenade dans la main du jeune Nègre est-elle une arme ou un fruit* s'inscrit délibérément dans une perspective de lutte de libération, fut-elle psychologique.

Les récits de Dany Laferrière, on l'aura compris, reposent sur deux vecteurs essentiels, les figures de l'altérité et la tyrannie des préjugés. Tout en se refusant à sortir des sentiers battus, l'auteur emprunte une voie qui ne manque pas de singularité. L'objectif consiste à reprendre, du moins dans *Comment faire l'amour avec un Nègre*, deux types d'individus bien connus dans l'histoire des relations interraciales: l'homme noir et la femme blanche, le domestique surmâle et la belle blonde idiote, mais symbole de liberté. Eldridge Cleaver a écrit à ce sujet: "Every time I embrace a black woman I'm embracing slavery, and when I put my arms around a white woman, well, I'm hugging freedom" (160). Mais la comparaison avec Eldridge Cleaver ne va pas bien loin. Et le Noir dont il est question ici ne ressemble pas non plus au spécimen de Frantz Fanon "qui en plein coït avec une blonde incendiaire au moment de l'orgasme, s'écria: "vive Schoelcher!" (51). En effet, même si chez Laferrière les jolies bourgeoises de McGill, Miz Littérature, Miz Sundae, Miz Suicide, Miz Sophisticated Lady, Miz Snob, Miz Mystic, Miz Chat etc. se laissent souvent prendre dans le piège du protagoniste principal et se font envoyer en l'air dans l'antre sordide qui lui tient lieu de chambre, le Nègre, malgré le poids de ses fantasmes, ne perd jamais le sens de ses objectifs. Autant que faire se peut, il exerce son jugement critique, "de manière à s'élever hors de la caverne des préjugés jusqu'au clair royaume du libre jugement" (Taguieff 219).

Bien qu'il assume entièrement l'identité du Nègre naïf, cannibale, dragueur et objet sexuel, il sait qu'il est avant tout un écrivain avec une thèse à défendre:

> dans l'échelle des valeurs occidentales, la Blanche est inférieure au Blanc et supérieure au Nègre. C'est pourquoi elle n'est capable de prendre véritablement son pied qu'avec le Nègre. Ce n'est pas sorcier; avec lui, elle peut aller jusqu'au bout. Il n'y a de véritable relation sexuelle qu'inégale. La Blanche doit faire jouir le Blanc, et le Nègre, la Blanche. D'où le mythe du Nègre grand baiseur. Bon baiseur, oui. Mais pas avec la Nègresse. C'est à la Nègresse à faire jouir le Nègre (Laferrière, *Comment faire* 50).

Alors que hier l'union interraciale était pour le "conjoint coloré une sorte de consécration subjective de l'extermination en lui-même et à ses propres yeux du préjugé de couleur dont il a longtemps souffert" (Fanon 57), Dany Laferrière nous introduit dans un monde où c'est plutôt l'Autre, la Blanche, qui, frustrée et "désespérée de la baise à la petite semaine" (Laferrière, *Comment faire* 18) investit de son propre chef le ghetto, convaincue qu'elle est, que:

Baiser nègre c'est baiser autrement. . . . En tout cas, il a fallu quasiment tirer des dortoirs nègres les filles aux joues roses et aux cheveux blonds. Le Grand Nègre de Harlem baise ainsi à n'en plus finir la fille du roi du Rasoir, la plus blanche, la plus insolente, la plus raciste du campus. Le Grand Nègre de Harlem a le vertige d'enculer la fille du propriétaire de toutes les baraques insalubres de la 125è (son quartier) . . . la forniquant pour l'horrible hiver de l'année dernière qui a emporté son jeune frère tuberculeux. La Jeune Blanche prend aussi pleinement son pied. C'est la première fois qu'on manifeste à son égard une telle qualité de haine. La haine dans l'acte sexuel est plus efficace que l'amour. (18-9)

On l'a souligné. Chez Cleaver, la femme blanche, autant que la noire d'ailleurs est maintenue dans les ténèbres par le pouvoir blanc: "the white man doesn't want the black man, the black woman, or the white woman to have a higher education. Their enlightenment would pose a threat to his omnipotence" (Cleaver 163). Mais bien que la plupart d'entre elles sentent la poudre Bébé Johnson, les belles blondes de Laferrière, étudient pourtant à l'Université McGill, "vénérable institution où la bourgeoisie place ses enfants pour leur apprendre la clarté, l'analyse et le doute scientifique" (Laferrière, *Comment faire* 30). Et Miz Littérature qui prend plaisir à venir faire la vaisselle dans l'appartement crasseux de la rue Saint-Denis a pourtant "une famille importante, un avenir, de la vertu, une solide culture littéraire et féministe à McGill—les Sorcières de McGill—dont les membres s'occupent de remettre en circulation les poétesses injustement oubliées" (42).

Mais comme on l'a vu avec Timothy Mitchell, on est dans une société où le préjugé dicte sa loi et où chacun est enfermé dans un carcan pour qu'il y ait une apparence d'ordre, de hiérarchie. Taguieff écrit très justement à ce propos:

on peut renverser l'évidence idéologique, en privilégiant le processus d'imputation légitimatoire: "ce ne sont pas les caractéristiques des immigrants qui sont cause de l'antipathie à leur égard, mais . . . on leur attribue plutôt des caractéristiques qui justifient en apparence cette antipathie. (268)

Voilà qui explique l'agression caractérisée dont le protagoniste est victime au bureau de poste lorsqu'il fait montre d'une innocente curiosité en s'intéressant au titre du roman que lit un usager dans la file d'attente:

> La plupart des gens de la file se retournent pour voir le Nègre en train d'agresser la Blanche. Une fille, un peu en avant dans la ligne, les cheveux coupés ras, se retourne, la rage au ventre. Elle élève la voix pour dire qu'ils sont tous des maniaques, des psychopathes et des emmerdeurs qui n'arrêtent pas de draguer. "Tu ne les vois jamais en hiver, mais dès l'été, ils sortent, par grappes, de leur trou juste pour emmerder les gens avec leurs foulards, tambours, bracelets et cloches. Mais moi je n'ai rien à voir avec leur folklore. Si au moins il n'y a avait que les Nègres! Mais non, maintenant, il y a les sud-américains avec leurs dizaines de chaînes au cou, leurs pendentifs, bagues, broches, toute cette bimbeloterie qu'ils n'arrêtent pas de proposer dans les cafés. . . . Si c'est pas un bijou. faussement maya, c'est leur corps. Pensent qu'à ça les Latinos" (Laferrière, *Comment faire* 59-60)

Taguieff a certainement raison: "Les préjugés apparaissent ici liés à l'imaginaire collectif ritualisé plutôt qu'aux caractéristiques du réel social: les traits ethniques attribués sont l'effet plutôt que la cause des préjugés" (268). En clair la réputation des immigrants les précède et point n'est besoin de les voir, de les voir vivre pour s'en faire une idée.

Dans la logique interne de *Comment faire l'amour avec un Nègre*, tout se passe comme si c'est l'agression gratuite de la fille aux "cheveux coupés ras" (59) qui donne au protagoniste la rage d'écrire et de s'inscrire dans le sillage de Chester Himes en empruntant une "Remington 22" dont on dit lui avoir appartenu. Évidemment, la référence à Chester Himes n'a rien de fortuit. Victime des effets de la ségrégation raciale aux États-Unis, Himes dut émigrer en Europe où il vécut essentiellement de sa plume. Dans ses écrits et surtout dans ses romans policiers, Himes exploite de manière plutôt cocasse les travers de ses congénères de Harlem. Et Himes fut un écrivain à succès, ce dont rêve le je-narrant dont le leitmotiv est: "Comment réussir un livre qui se vendra bien?" (Laferrière, *Comment faire* 63). Le cheminement de Himes paraît alors exemplaire pour le marginal qui veut se tirer d'affaire. Plutôt que de subir passivement l'adversité ou de se lamenter sur son sort, il vaut mieux trouver une recette appropriée pour mettre fin à la galère.

L'image de la grenade dont il se sert—*Cette grenade dans la main du jeune Nègre est-elle une arme ou un fruit*—est hautement significative à ce égard. La grenade, on le sait, est un engin à retardement. Et il arrive qu'une personne visée ramasse le projectile avant son explosion pour le retourner contre l'agresseur initial. C'est l'arroseur arrosé. Symboliquement, la grenade peut représenter l'ensemble des stéréotypes dont le Nègre est accablé, les injures qui lui sont lancées. Mais lorsque l'auteur les recueille, il les remballe, en fait un fruit équivalent à l'ensemble de sa production littéraire et le retourne au public, à l'agresseur virtuel. On pourrait ainsi démontrer que l'oeuvre entière de Laferrière n'est qu'un compendium de stéréotypes qu'il ressert à sa manière à un consommateur inconscient de la supercherie. Malgré son âme wasp et son origine bourgeoise, Miz Sophisticated Lady, fille de Westmount, se trouve réduite à une fleur au bout de sa "pine nègre" (Laferrière, *Comment faire* 86). Miz Littérature se met à son école de vol à l'étalage (107) mais il ne veut pas du tout de son aide dans la rédaction de son *Paradis du Dragueur Nègre*: "C'est, prétend-il, le genre de truc qu'il faut faire soi-même" (Laferrière, *Comment faire* 103). Il n'attend rien d'elle mais ne fait rien pour l'empêcher de dépendre d'elle ou tout au moins d'épouser quelques uns de ses "vices". De son côté, Bouba a pris Miz Suicide en charge:

> Bouba est son conseiller en matière de suicide.
> Elle ne s'intéresse à rien d'autre. . . . Bouba l'a repêchée
> à la Librairie ésotérique, sur Saint-Denis, en face de la
> Bibliothèque Nationale.
> Assis sur le Divan comme une diva divaguant
> sans arrêt sur les sentences du vieux maître zen, Bouba
> crée sans le savoir une ambiance délirante. Il lit, avec sa
> voix gutturale et mystique, le précieux petit livre du
> poète à barbiche, Li Po, sur la manière de boire le thé:

-Tu dois d'abord apprendre, explique Bouba, à
respirer le thé avant de commencer à le boire.
     Miz Suicide écoute avec le recueillement d'un
véritable bodhisattva. (71-2)

La technique consiste ici à déployer une stratégie de contrôle et
à en vérifier l'efficacité sur des sujets précis. En situation coloniale, Albert
Memmi a montré comment le dominant dicte sa loi en déshumanisant
puis en mystifiant le colonisé: "on peut dire, écrit-il, que la colonisation
fabrique des colonisés comme nous avons vu qu'elle fabriquait des
colonisateurs" (92). Comme on l'a vu dans l'initiation de Miz Littérature
au vol à l'étalage, Laferrière procède par contamination et joue au
dialecticien de charme:

> Nègres et Blancs sont égaux devant la mort et la sexualité:
> Éros et Thanatos. Je pense que le couple Nègre/Blanche
> est pire qu'une bombe. Le Nègre baisant la Nègresse ne
> vaut peut-être pas la corde qui doit le pendre, mais avec
> la Blanche, il y a de fortes chances qu'il se passe quelque
> chose. Pourquoi? Parce que la sexualité est avant tout
> affaire de fantasmes et le fantasme accouplant le Nègre
> avec la Blanche est l'un des plus explosifs qui soient.
> (Laferrière, *Comment faire* 141-2)

De temps à autre dans le récit, la même image est reprise dans des
formulations différentes: "Si vous voulez un aperçu de la guerre nucléaire,
mettez un Nègre et une Blanche dans un lit. . . . Le Nègre était la
dernière bombe sexuelle capable de faire sauter la planète. Et il est mort.
Entre les cuisses d'une Blanche" (19).
     S'amuser à objectiver le Noir tout en prenant la parole comme
Noir sujet au nom du Noir objet fait partie des recettes que Dany
Laferrière a mises au point pour captiver le public et écouler sa
marchandise. Il s'en cache à peine: "je crève de jalousie, je meurs d'envie.
Je veux être riche et célèbre" (104). Et ce stratagème qui n'apparaît qu'en
filigrane, tout à fait vers la fin de *Comment faire l'amour avec un Nègre*
devient pratiquement la matière de *Cette grenade dans la main du jeune
Nègre*. Après le succès remporté par *Comment faire l'amour avec un Nègre*,

l'auteur choisit de continuer dans la voie de l'exploitation littéraire—et commerciale—des stéréotypes sociaux. Décidé à prendre l'Amérique au mot, c'est un peu en journaliste qu'il croque sur le vif les scènes de la vie quotidienne et nous en offre des tableaux irrésistibles. "L'Amérique, dit-il, n'a qu'une exigence: le succès. A n'importe quel prix" (Laferrière, *Cette grenade* 17). Au lieu de faire la fine bouche, autant lui vendre ce que nous avons comme biens: "Toujours les questions raciales et sexuelles. Et leur mélange explosif. L'Amérique aime manger de ce plat. Et je suis prêt à lui en donner pour son argent" (85). Car "ici, c'est pas le secours catholique, ni Oxfam. . . . Tous les coups sont permis" (98). Dans une longue conversation avec un chauffeur de taxi d'origine nigérienne à New York, il conclut en quelque sorte: "La littérature est un métier que je pratique pour vivre. . . . J'écris pour être connu et pour pouvoir bénéficier des privilèges uniquement réservés aux gens célèbres. J'écris surtout pour avoir ces jeunes filles autrefois inaccessibles" (68).

En fait Laferrière dit tout haut ce dont rêvent secrètement nombre d'écrivains. Et son génie consiste à captiver l'attention en choisissant délibérément d'embarrasser le lecteur avec des propos effrontés, totalement inattendus. Mais par-dessus tout, Laferrière surprend du fait que, contrairement à nombre d'immigrants, il refuse de se faire prendre en pitié. Dans une révolte qui ne dit pas son nom, il s'engage passionnément dans la guerre des fantasmes que se livrent colonisateurs et colonisés: "le colonisé, écrit Memmi, revendique et se bat au nom des valeurs mêmes du colonisateur, utilise ses techniques de pensée et ses méthodes de combat" (118). Et Memmi d'ajouter pertinemment: "c'est le seul langage que comprenne le colonisateur" (118). Le succès de librairie dont bénéficie l'oeuvre de Dany Laferrière est une incontestable preuve du bien-fondé de cette assertion.

Ouvrages cités

Blanchard, Pascal and Nicolas Bancel, eds. *De l'indigène à l'immigré.* Paris: Découvertes/Gallimard, 1998.

Cleaver, Eldridge. *Soul on Ice.* New York: Bantam Doubleday Dell Publishing Group, Inc., 1968.

Fanon, Frantz. *Peau noire, masques blancs.* Paris: Seuil, 1952.

Jaccard, Roland. *La Folie.* Paris: PUF, 1979.

Laferrière, Dany. *Cette grenade dans la main du jeune Nègre est-elle une arme ou un fruit*. Montréal: VLB éditeur, 1993.

____. *Comment faire l'amour avec un Nègre sans se fatiguer*. Paris: Belfond, 1989.

Memmi, Albert. *Portrait du colonisé*. Montréal: L'Étincelle, 1972.

Mitchell, Timothy. *Colonizing Egypt*. Berkeley: California University Press, 1991.

Sala-Molins, Louis. *Le Code noir ou le calvaire de Canaan*. Paris: PUF, 1987.

Taguieff, P.A. *La Force du préjugé, essai sur le racisme et ses doubles*. Paris: Gallimard, 1987.

Myriem and the Barbaresques: Politics and the Origins of the Algerian Novel

Seth Graebner

Critics of colonial literature who are not colonialists themselves are often particularly interested in searching for the ways in which pro-colonial discourses break down, or in locating the spaces in which literary acts of resistance to the dominant order take place. Carried out within the genres of literature produced in French Algeria, such a search might disappoint those determined to find pure or absolute resistance, but an examination of a few places likely to harbor aporia in the colonial discourse nonetheless provides lessons for reading resistance in colonial texts. This article will examine works by three of the very earliest Algerian participants in a genre of the 1920s which contemporaries labeled "romans indigènes": novels about or by Arabs and Berbers, the genre in which critics at the time placed the first novelistic productions in French by Algerian writers. We might expect that giving voice to *indigène* protagonists would provide a potential opening for an alternative view of the colonial project. In fact, however, the simple inclusion of non-European main characters did not suffice to do anything of the kind. Considerably more innovation on the level of plots and their ideological investments was necessary to escape a simple justification of the French "civilizing mission." Literary critic Richard Terdiman has identified the task of counter-discourse as a "mapping of the internal incoherence of the seemingly univocal and monumental institution of dominant discourse" (Terdiman 77). What happens, however, when the dominant discourse has the power to recuperate its own "internal incoherence"? What happens in situations like Algeria in the twenties, with a heavier discursive policing than Terdiman's nineteenth-century France, situations in which a counter-discourse can scarcely find the space to exist?[1] In this context, counter-discourses proposed by works by Algerians had to be extremely subtle, and inevitably participated in a panoply of contingent arguments and discursive compromises.

Most accounts of the origins of the Maghribi novel in French place its debut in the political and historical conjunction of the 1950s and the Algerian war of independence. Born amidst the violence and polarization of a war of decolonization, the Francophone Algerian novel necessarily reflected its contestatory and confrontational origins. The arguments attaching Mouloud Feraoun's *Le Fils du pauvre* (1954) or Kateb Yacine's *Nedjma* (1956) to the political and emotional context of the "savage war of peace" have been repeatedly rehearsed to explain certain qualities most readers concur in attributing to the genre.[2] These include a political consciousness of oppression, an ever-present textual and physical violence, and a sense of cultural alienation from those in power, whether French, in early works, or Algerian, in later ones. Compelling arguments trace these elements back to the 1950s in representative novels, and situate there the origins of the genre itself. There exists, however, an earlier set of texts with a prior historical claim to the status of "origins" of the Algerian novel in French.

While authors like Kateb, Feraoun, and Mammeri indeed founded the genre as we know it, they nonetheless had important predecessors. Ahmed Bouri's *Musulmans et Chrétiennes*, possibly the very first novel in French by an Algerian, appeared in serial form in 1912.[3] The first significant crop of novels in French by Algerians appeared between the wars. These novels were few and scattered, perhaps numbering ten altogether; the three I will discuss here, the Caid Ben Cherif's *Ahmed ben Mostapha, Goumier* (1920), Khodja Chukri's *El Euldj, Captif des barbaresques* (1929), and Mohammed Ould Cheikh's *Myriem dans les palmes* (1936) appeared over a period of sixteen years, and to some extent resist grouping.[4] Taken together, however, the obvious political consciousness and concern with cultural alienation shown by these "other" *indigène* novels suggest that the origins of these phenomena in the Algerian novel go back considerably farther than the independence era. These novels, too, enter into dialogue with the discourses of colonialism; however, their positions are considerably more difficult to place than those of their successors.

As Terdiman has argued, writers struggling to change a dominant discourse (in this case, one that excluded them from almost all political participation) discover its capacity to ignore or absorb subversion, but also its contingence and permeability (Terdiman 13). The three writers I will discuss here proceed from this discovery to a highly selective counter-discourse, picking their battles carefully, leaving other issues—even important ones—aside. Under the government's heavy policing of all expressions of dissension, counter-discourses became problematic for very immediate legal reasons. The colonial authorities could and did shut down by decree any newspaper they felt objectionable, and under this pressure, the *indigène* press, both source and outlet for these writers, dwindled from approximately twenty titles before World War I to three or four in the thirties.[5] Selectivity in deciding where to apply discreet pressure on the dominant discourse became both necessary, to get their message across at all, and inevitable, to deal with the complicated political stakes of the period.

All three of these novels quickly fell into relative obscurity; Chukri's, perhaps the most compelling from a stylistic perspective, does not even seem to have been reviewed in any of the Algerian literary journals.[6] The Caid Ben Cherif was a captain in the French army during World War I, thus outranking the protagonist of *Ahmed ben Mostapha*, who joins the army with dreams of glory, and fulfills them fighting Moroccans and proselytizing for the expansion of the French empire among the clans he is sent to subjugate. Page after page details his bravery and devotion, attracting the attention of his captain, a young Arabic-speaking French officer who teaches him the glorious history of Arab military conquest. After a respite at home, spent in picturesque falcon hunting and feasting episodes, Ahmed insists on volunteering to serve in Europe, the moment France enters World War I. The Germans soon capture and intern him with other Algerian troops. Tunisian and Moroccan agents of the Kaiser fail to convince him of the evils of French colonialism, which he defends with very sophisticated political arguments, and his loyalty to France earns him harsh treatment. He falls ill and has the good fortune to be sent to Switzerland, where his charm earns him social success among the spa inhabitants. The climate, however, does not agree with him, and after a series of touching but chaste letters to a French woman he had met in Paris, he dies, far from home, of pneumonia.

Khodja Chukri reaches much further back in history for the setting of *El Euldj, captif des barbaresques*, and chooses the early sixteenth century, the height of the pirate regime of Algiers. The "Barbaresques" capture a French vessel and crew, including the young Bernard Ledieux. He and his comrades suffer many misdeeds and tortures at the hands of Algerians, themselves subject to the arbitrary cruelty of Barbarousse. Years pass; the young man forgets his wife in France and marries his master's daughter, after committing the unthinkable, converting to Islam. He immediately finds himself cut off from his fellow European slaves, and begins to regret his decision, despite his increase in status with his captors. To add to his distress, his son by his new wife grows up to become imam of the Ketchaoua mosque (ironically the same mosque the French would transform into the Cathedral of Algiers three hundred years later). Ledieux grows taciturn and disaffected, becomes convinced he is a traitor, and dies miserable and insane shortly after Charles V's failed conquest of Algiers in 1541.

Finally, Mohammed Ould Cheikh also took his inspiration from more recent history for *Myriem dans les palmes*. Myriem Debussy, a rich heiress from Oran, has a Muslim mother, alive, a French officer father, dead, two suitors, one Arab and worthy, another Russian and scheming, a villa, and an airplane, in which she takes off to visit her brother, an officer in the French army "pacifying" the Tafilalet in southeastern Morocco. After a forced landing, she falls into the hands of Belqacem, leader of the unsubjugated Tafilalet. He of course wishes to include her in his harem, but Ivan Ipateff, an unscrupulous Russian arms dealer (and her former fiancé) challenges Belqacem to a single combat for her. Too cowardly to fight, Ivan hires a dashing cavalier who wins the joust, but carries Myriem off to her brother and the safety of the French army, for he is none other than Ahmed, her worthy Arabic professor and admirer from Oran. Belqacem flees into the desert with his concubines, and Ahmed and Myriem return to civilized marital bliss in the city.

These books at first appear positively to glorify French rule: Arabs are often barbarians, while French people usually look like enlightened gentlefolk. The novels initially seem to present no alternatives to the status quo: they apparently envision no change in

Algeria's colonial status. However, we must realize that the political demands of the *indigènes* would only begin to sound overtly nationalist around 1930; around that time the leaders of the political opposition (the Emir Khaled Ibn al-Hachemi, Cheikh Ben Bādis, and Messali Hadj, for example) began to speak openly of a French withdrawal from Algeria. The Emir Khaled, a former Army captain and grandson of the legendary nineteenth-century Emir Abdelkader, was among the founders of the *Étoile Nord-Africaine*, the first party to demand independence. Cheikh Ben Bādis founded the *Association des Ulémas Algériens*, an explicitly Islamic and pro-Arab opposition group, in May 1931. He also edited a review called *Shihāb*, which strongly advocated resurrecting an "Arab personality" and culture in Algeria. As for Messali Hadj, he would found a succession of highly influential militant nationalist parties until his marginalization during the Algerian War, and the purge of his supporters by the FLN. Messali in particular would radicalize his position in the mid thirties. In the late twenties, the Emir Khaled denounced the irony of *indigène* troops fighting for France, and thereby defending rights they themselves had never enjoyed; at that time, however, he demanded political rights from the French, rather than independence for the colony.[7] The first newspapers in Algeria to support Arab nationalism wholeheartedly, *Ikdām* and *El Ouma*, began publishing between 1928 and 1930.[8] Given the novelty and marginality of radical nationalism at the time, it would be unrealistic to hold works from the twenties and thirties to a standard of radicalism from the fifties.

Before and after *El Ouma*, most significant opposition newspapers in French or Arabic concentrated their attention on other matters, notably pay equity, fair elections, and educational opportunity. Reformist papers with considerable followings among educated Muslims (for example, the *Voix des indigènes* and the *Voix des humbles*, as well as *El Hack*) fought for the abolition of the *régime d'indigénat*, a set of laws prescribing separate legal treatments for *indigènes* and Europeans, and for the extension of citizenship and political representation to at least some of the five million *Français musulmans* who enjoyed neither. These demands, whose radicalism we should not forget, found support in several arguments: the service provided by Arab and Berber soldiers fighting and dying for France in World War I, and the "evolution" and acculturation to French thinking which the editors and readers of opposition journals could easily display. At least until the early 1930s, most of these journals favored political assimilation, in that they demanded equal status within the French nation for Arabs and Berbers. With some notable exceptions, such as Ben Bādis's journal *Shihāb*, they often as well favored cultural assimilation, asserting that the way of progress for all Algerians lay in better education and integration in the French mold.[9]

The contemporary ramifications of some otherwise inexplicable developments in the novels whose plots are outlined above become much clearer to today's readers when interpreted in conjunction with this political rhetoric. While such a reading does not eliminate all political ambiguity, the ideological context of the 1920s and 30s reframes in a much more positive light motivations which might otherwise appear suspect, perhaps even arguably pro-colonial. What can it mean, for example, that Ahmed ben Mostapha shows diehard bravery in supporting the French cause, fighting and humiliating "backward" Moroccans? In the struggle for enfranchisement of the *indigènes*, many proponents of citizenship declared that decorated veterans should be the first so rewarded.[10] Proving one's valor and loyalty thus had extremely concrete political rewards. This was more than mere toadyism; *indigène* army veterans were among the few non-Europeans with the moral authority to address the French on matters regarding treatment of the *Français musulmans*; the early opposition movements frequently placed them in the foreground of their agitations. Readers today may certainly choose to blame Ahmed for his lack of solidarity with other colonized people, but we will not advance far without understanding all that the early political rights movements quite reasonably hoped to gain through demonstrations of loyalty immediately after the First World War.

This would soon change, as it became apparent even to the most sanguine that they had little to hope for from French good will. The 1930 defeat in the Assemblée of the proposal to give political representation to the *Français musulmans* demonstrated how little cooperation the *indigènes* could expect from the French either in the colony or in the metropole, and prepared the way for more overt nationalism.[11] Ben Cherif anticipates this at the very moment his brave Ahmed is haranguing the Moroccans, supposedly about the benefits of belonging to the French empire:

For centuries we have fought for honor, to avenge our
dead, to use pasture land, or to drive the enemy away
from our villages. Today all this is summarized as a single
idea, in one word: "el ouatan."
- "El ouatan"? repeated the Moroccan, amazed.
- Yes, "el ouatan"! It means the cult of the ground in
which our fathers are laid to rest, and love for those who
help us secure it against our enemies, wherever they
may come from; yes, love without limits for the
protectors of our possessions and our religion. (Ben
Cherif 86-7)

Ben Cherif published his novel one year after the Egyptian
revolution of 1919, whose leader Saad Zaghloul had done a great deal to
popularize the word "al-watan," the nation, in modern Arabic. He might
not have appreciated the speedy slippage in Ben Cherif's text toward the
notion of the French as protectors of Islam. However, one of the most
highly charged words in the history of Arab nationalism has nonetheless
"slipped out" and been hammered in by a most un-accidental repetition
in a speech connecting it with love of the homeland, military security,
and private property. Ben Cherif's hero also links the word with the
Arab literary tradition; no situation finds him at a loss for a classical
citation or reference to the canon of heroic poetry.[12] Despite the window-
dressing of casting the French as necessary defenders of the Arabs, Ben
Cherif hardly wins converts to colonialism by sketching a history of
bravery reaching from the sixth century to contemporary Egypt. In 1920,
with the eyes of every educated Arab on Egypt's independence struggle,
the word "al-watan" could scarcely have left anyone as stupefied as it did
Ahmed's Moroccan. The mask of loyalty to France lets Ben Cherif use
the word "nation" a decade before the newspapers supporting the
indigène cause mentioned the term.[13]

Khodja Chukri seems to respond to the growing radicalization of
political demands around 1930 anticipated by Ben Cherif, as democratic
reform began to seem less likely.[14] His tale, like Ben Cherif's, also admits
of several readings: the theme of barbarous pirates causing the physical
and emotional ruin of a young Frenchman has clear pro-colonial echoes,
both optimistic ("thank goodness the French have come to put an end to

this") and pessimistic ("we French make enormous sacrifices here; this country still ruins us to this day").[15] Chukri, however, ensures we read his historical novel as a parable of failed assimilation.

Assimilate is exactly what the protagonist Ledieux cannot do, despite his apostasy. He works hard for his master, learns to speak his language, and marries his daughter, the ultimate assimilation an *indigène* could dream of or a European could revile. In order to do this he must convert to Islam, thus shedding his chains and becoming the slave overseer himself. This earns him the traditional label of "renegade," the ostracism of his former comrades, and the assurance of eternal damnation from the slaves' chaplain. It represents a point of no return: diplomatic convention traditionally barred renegades from inclusion among the slaves ransomed every year by European governments and charities. Wholly cut off from his cultural background, Omar Lediousse, ex-Bernard Ledieux, goes slowly mad. The parallels between the impossible asked of Ledieux, and that asked of any Arab or Berber wishing to assimilate to French colonial society, underscore the warning Chukri sought to convey. Assimilation, he says to his fellow *indigène* intellectuals, is a trap, in which you will lose everything. Other elements of the story complicate this warning, however. With his Algerian wife Zineb, Omar Lediousse has a son Youssef, who becomes an imam preaching and answering questions from the faithful in the mosque. His sixteenth-century questioners seem preoccupied with topics uncannily related to Chukri's time: "what would you say of a Muslim who, without denying his religion, wore a hat, after adopting European dress?" asks one (Chukri 114). Of course the appropriateness of this question to Chukri's time is only apparent: few people in 1929 really needed reassurances about the acceptability of such behavior. In response, Youssouf predicts the fever of "Europeanization" which would strike the Arab world following the French invasion of Egypt, and declares "I like to think that this new life will have a salutary effect on people's minds" (116). Youssef carries the standard of Europeanization and what the French and *indigène* intellectuals liked to call "évolution des moeurs": little by little, through the effects of education and contact with Europeans, the Arab and Berber populations would lose their rough edges and backward ways, without having to lose their cultural identity.

As a kind of compromise with assimilationism, this idea could appeal to people like Chukri who clearly saw the danger of trying to become French. It certainly appealed to Youssef, who as it happens speaks perfect French, having tasted "the fruits of the garden of French rhetoric" (133). Paradoxically, the narrator reveals Youssef's inexplicably unaccented French just after he rescues his re-apostatizing father from an angry crowd of Muslims, which he does with a flourish of rhetoric, presumably in Arabic. As he explains to his surprised father, "God willed that the Muslim son of a father who had returned to Christianity have in him the august mixture of Arab pride and French chivalrous spirit, thanks to which he was able to protect you from the harm that the believers were determined to do you" (133). Some mysterious cultural alchemy is apparently necessary so that overzealous and (to use Chukri's own word) barbarous *indigènes* may restrain themselves from intolerant violence. Although Omar Lediousse's forced assimilation fails miserably, his son's voluntary rapprochement with French culture works wonders. Despite the Algerian critic Abdelkader Djeghloul's effort to characterize Chukri as categorically rejecting assimilation in favor of retaining a "true" Algerian identity, the novel presents a double discourse.[16] Assimilation as then defined might indeed constitute no more than a lure, but Chukri nonetheless tries to change its terms to give it substance and the possibility of becoming a tenable position: "he speaks French, therefore he is French," says Omar/Bernard of his son (Chukri 135). If assimilation were simply a matter of language and cultural knowledge, Chukri might accept the deal; at any rate, he seems somewhat wistfully to propose it. Though Omar/Bernard dies insane and rejected, the flower of French influence lives on unexpectedly in Algiers in the guise of an imam *rhétoriqueur*, transmitting an essential modicum of Frenchness to future generations. For the cosmopolitan Chukri, hoping for a positive and flexible cultural understanding between French and Arab and Berber Algerians, this represents the predestination of a Mediterranean compromise.

Such a double discourse continues to work through Mohammed Ould Cheikh's *Myriem dans les palmes*, the only one of these three novels published in Algeria, and the one most approaching popular melodrama.[17] The contemporary Algerian historian Abdelkader Djeghloul has perspicaciously called Ould Cheikh "a good example of the double tendency of pro-colonial mimicry and affirmation of the Algerian identity" (Djeghloul 34). On the one hand, Ould Cheikh, like Chukri, does seem to push aside the temptation of excessive Europeanization. His heroine safely marries her Arabic teacher, a good Muslim named Ahmed, making her *indigène* mother happy. On the other hand, he also seems to endorse the conquests of the French Army. In the novel, the French safely wipe out the last stronghold of military opposition in North Africa, Morocco's Tafilalet (actually subdued in 1936, the year of *Myriem*'s publication), thus ensuring peace, prosperity, and progress for all. The Algerian critic Ahmed Lanasri makes a cogent argument for a further disjunction between discourse and story: although the narrator ostensibly supports the French conquerors, he describes the pre-colonial Tafilalet region as a prelapsarian paradise. The descriptions Lanasri cites, however, could have been drawn from any of the classic sources of exoticist nostalgia, a descriptive tradition rarely liberating for the countries and peoples it treated (Lanasri 182-4). In other words, the narrative conveys exactly the mixed message *indigène* novelists of the colonial period were so good at sending. Myriem's penchant for aviation and her objections to veiling might simply come as progressive icing on the cake for liberal readers. Progress can coexist with adherence to tradition; her Ahmed, if not an *évolué*, seems like exactly the sort of figure Bén Bādis hoped would advance the Algerian political personality: well educated, certain of his rights, and respectful yet open-minded about the Islamic tradition.

This account of Ould Cheikh's mixed but ultimately unsurprising message leaves out two important problems which complicate it significantly: the political implications of rapprochement, and Myriem's mixed identity in it. First, in the political discourses of the twenties and thirties, where we hear few hints of real separatism, there was as yet little notion among pro-*indigène* activists of the political significance of affirming a separate Arab Algerian cultural identity. In fact, the system of colonial domination depended on keeping such a separation rigidly intact; *indigène* writers typically responded by taking an opposite tack, and basing their claims on political (and if necessary cultural) rapprochement between *indigènes* and *colons*. Rather than "we are different, and demand a country of our own," they tended to say "we are more like you than you think, and demand rights like yours." Generally, those in favor of rapprochement turned out to be progressive-minded *indigène* intellectuals for whom mixing in all its forms, especially the endlessly debated mixed marriage, had great potential political benefits. Those who believed in the radical difference of a definable Arabo-Berber identity fell almost exclusively on the other side, and supported the status quo of a separate and oppressive legal regime for Muslims.[18] Unless we are willing to make the autodidact Mohammed Ould Cheikh into a prophetic figure reversing the political charges of these positions, it is difficult to envision him as a champion of Arabo-Berber identity victorious in the struggle against assimilationism.[19]

Such an argument might prove tenable if Myriem's identity, and therefore her marriage, did not present considerable complications. Her father was a rich French officer who struggled mightily with his Muslim wife over the children's religion; their Muslim identity is merely a name in Myriem's case, and a name and a circumcision in her brother's (Ould Cheikh 22). In fact, the story makes clear, Myriem and her brother "frequent neither Church nor Mosque"; according to their mother "they concern themselves with 'modernism,' which is the enemy of all religion because it corrupts those who abuse it, and often leads them to bad ends" (22). We sense where this might lead: Myriem the aviator literally crashes to earth, realizes her mother is right, and chooses a sensible marriage with a man of her ethnicity and religion.

The story never gets there, however, as the narration cannot decisively specify Myriem's identity. From the beginning, the narrator insists he is presenting the "idyll of two young Algerians of the twentieth century: an Arab *évolué* and a French woman" (cover page). According to Lanasri, "the fiction brings a serious correction to the preliminary words of the author": Myriem studies Arabic, and Ahmed looks more and more like a traditionally-educated Arab than an *évolué* (Lanasri 178). However, every character in the book who refers to her in the third person calls her "the French woman," "the foreigner," or "la roumia," suggesting that in the context of the story, her identity remains foreign; at the very least, she is unreadable to the other characters (Ould Cheikh 196).[20] Further emphasizing the theme of *mixité*, Ahmed declares his love in these terms: "I love you, Myriem; I've loved you for a long time. But there is a problem ahead of us: race!" To which his beloved replies "What are these absurd prejudices to us, if we love each other . . . is my

Seth Graebner

mother not a Muslim? Am I not free to love and marry whomever I please? Do we not share the same commonality of sentiments and habits?" (Ould Cheikh 212). Myriem sounds not like a straying Arab returning to the fold, but a (mixed) French person entering a mixed marriage. These somewhat stilted vows of eternal love hardly plead for the recognition of a "pure" Algerian identity in the way some post-independence criticism would like to see it. Rather than addressing post-independence needs for political affirmation, Ould Cheikh addresses his contemporaries' need for a response to assimilation. The implicit criticism of purist conceptions of identity here applies to the view of assimilation that defined it as the seamless adoption of a pure French identity by all Algerians, and that set it up as the only—and impossible—means of fully joining colonial Algerian society.

This may seem considerably more conservative than Chukri's position, and it is at least possible that Ould Cheikh was; he published articles in the extremely conservative paper *Oran matin*.[21] However, if we believe that he placed an impossible precondition on his cooperation—i.e., modifying the terms of assimilation—we might read his text as a veiled refusal to assimilate. Alternatively, the novel may represent a fairly sophisticated view of the multiple possibilities for Algerian identity, accepting at least the historical fact of French presence, and beginning from the notion of the elusiveness and counter productivity of cultural purity. With this in mind, we should listen closely to the rhetoric of his preface:

> After a century of occupation, Algeria is awakening from its torpor . . . western education having born its fruits, the new generation of Muslims and French, unlike the previous ones which remained for a long time hostile to one another, are beginning to understand and love each other.
>
> This is thanks to education, that cherished light which enlightens men, brings them together, and guides them toward peace, life, and happiness.
>
> However, I do not pretend to have written an ideological book [*livre à thèse*].

On the contrary, I have simply tried to please the
pioneers of the Franco-Muslim rapprochement by
dedicating to them this modest work, to which I have
given a fictionalized style. (Ould Cheikh, preface)

This statement begins with a hymn to French Algeria which
could have come from the pen of any of the colony's many apologists at
the time of the Centenary. However, it manages to undercut its apparent
conservatism in several ways. First, it emphasizes the importance of
education, and thereby aligns the author against the many conservatives
who argued that schools for *indigènes* were a waste of money. Second, in
saying the country is awakening under the influence of Western
education, Ould Cheikh also hints that the formerly acquiescent *indigènes*
are at last rising to demand the rights that their French-style formation
has led them to expect. Finally comes the disavowal at the end,
abandoning the ostensible hymn to French-inspired progress: "but I do
not pretend to have written a livre *à thèse*"—or at least, not a book with
that *thèse*. Instead, Ould Cheikh declares his wish to further the cause of
the pioneers of rapprochement, a goal certainly consistent with the
novel's ending. In a context where rapprochement would have meant
undeniable political progress for the *indigènes*, allowing them effective
opposition, and where a successful mixed marriage overtly threatened
rigid ethnic boundaries, Ould Cheikh's ideological commitment, while
veiled, is not nearly as conservative as it first seems. It represents a
carefully drawn, selective counter-discourse, striving to find an audience
which might hear it.

It is intriguing to ponder whether the recognized founders of the
genre of the Francophone novel in the Maghrib (Dib, Feraoun, Kateb,
etc.) read any of the works of their predecessors. The argument here is
not one of influence in the traditional sense, but of literary interpretation
that devolves upon the reader, who must be aware of principles operative
in the history of decolonization. Reading anti-colonialist commitment in
the colonial novel requires us to consider disavowals, cross-purposes, and
ambivalences of myriad origins. In reading works by colonized authors,
we cannot satisfy ourselves with generalized arguments about political
commitments in the anti-colonialist struggle. To reach real understanding,
we need to ask questions less about global ideological strategy than about

local political tactics. The importance of these novels lies less in their influence, or even in their founding a proto-nationalist movement, than in their lessons for reading the complex counter-discourses of their more famous successors. Examining particular genres and specific historical situations on the periphery of colonial power—and of literary studies—demonstrates the way fictional discourses can intertwine with politics to produce results both more complex and more concrete than critics have imagined.

Notes

1. In a moment, I will outline some of the practical means at the disposal of the colonial administration for preventing counter-discourses from gaining wide audiences.

2. "Savage wars of peace" is Rudyard Kipling's epithet for campaigns of colonial "pacification," recalled by the title of the British historian Alistair Horne's recently revised study of the Algerian war.

3. *Musulmans et Chrétiennes* appeared in the Oran weekly *El Hack* (subtitled "Le Petit Egyptien. Organe de défense des intérêts musulmans"), beginning in April of that year. None of the standard bibliographic tools indicate that this novel ever appeared in volume form. Here and throughout, I have used the standard and familiar French forms of Arabic names and titles, rather than rigorous transcriptions.

4. Caid A. Ben Cherif, *Ahmed ben Mostapha, Goumier* (Paris: Payot, 1920); Khodja Chukri, *El Euldj, captif des barbaresques* (Paris: Editions de la Revue des indépendants, 1929); Mohamed Ould Cheikh, *Myriem dans les palmes* (Oran: Editions Plaza, 1936). Other very early works by Arab or Berber authors included a series of collaborations in the 1920s between the painter Etienne Dinet and Sliman ben Ibrahim Baamer, including a number of short stories published in reviews by Hadj Hamou Abdelkader in the 1920s and 30s. Abdelkader was also the author of a novel, *Zohra la femme d'un mineur* (Paris: Editions du monde moderne, 1925), which has eluded my attempt to locate.

5. The basic reference on the press produced by and for the *indigènes* is Zahir Ihaddaden's thesis from the mid-1980s, "L'Histoire de la presse "indigène" en Algérie, des origines jusqu'en 1930," Thèse de doctorat du 3eme cycle (Université de Paris II, n.d.).

6. It did rate mention in Roland Lebel's landmark study of colonial literature, purely to illustrate the existence of works by Algerian *indigènes*, and with no discussion (*Histoire de la littérature coloniale en France* (Paris: Larose, 1931), 104).

7. "Hundreds of thousands of us died for a country which still considers us subjects. Nevertheless, those who died had to fight to defend rights which they never possessed" (Emir Khaled Ibn al-Hachemi, *La situation des Musulmans d'Algérie: Conférences faites à Paris les 12 et 19 juillet 1924*, 1924 (Algiers: Éditions du Trait d'Union, Victor Spielmann, 1930), 41).

8. *El Ouma*, with the larger circulation, proclaimed its ideal in its title: "The Nation." Both these papers were rapidly suppressed, and copies are rare. Research on the "presse indigène" in Algeria is severely limited by the physical deterioration of a very large number of titles in the Bibliothèque Nationale, the most substantial collection of this material outside Algeria. The collection at the Archives d'Outre Mer is also respectable, but has major gaps as well. Zahir Ihaddaden provides essential references on the subject in "L'Histoire de la presse 'indigène' en Algérie".

9. See, for example, Ait Kaci's article in the *Voix des Humbles*: "The development of the *indigènes* in their own environment and civilization is impossible . . . Western civilization is master of the world, and whoever does not advance in its heart is doomed to immobility, and immobility is death. Assimilation is therefore the only logical policy, and the only one that is possible and viable in French North Africa" ("La Représentation des indigènes au Parlement," *La Voix des humbles* 74 (May 1929): 3. Despite its advocacy of an "Arab personality," Ben Bādis's journal also supported the campaign for political rights within the French nation.

10. "Naturalization in stages is the only kind on which *indigènes* and Europeans are likely to agree. One could begin for example by admitting a minimum number . . . chosen among men and women holding university diplomas, civil servants, elected officials, army officers, those decorated with the Légion d'Honneur, soldiers cited for bravery, and those who enlisted voluntarily during the great war" ("Le Centenaire: revendications politiques," *La Voix indigène*, 21 November 1929). Despite this fairly conservative estimation of who deserved immediate citizenship, the anonymous author of this article declared that it was

"indispensable" that non-citizens be represented in both the Sénat and the Assemblée.

11. "This centenary, our supreme and only hope, has been nothing but an endless parade of parties. . . . We did not need these passing celebrations, but rather something positive: practical accomplishments" (Labiod, "Désillusion et espérance," *La Voix indigène*, 10 July 1930).

12. His favorite references are to the pre-Islamic poets and the Antar cycle. See his citations, pp. 42 and 139.

13. The first paper to adopt the demand for national independence in its platform was *El Ouma*, in 1930. The authorities quickly suppressed it. On the radicalization of 1930, see Abdelkader Djeghloul's chapter on "Les revendication d'indépendance au début du Xxe siècle" in *Eléments d'histoire culturelle algérienne*.

14. The Blum-Violette reform of the status of the *indigènes* in Algeria was definitively pushed aside in 1935; it represented the last serious possibility for reform coming from the government. Most observers trace the birth of an explicitly nationalist opposition to this period.

15. For the first message, compare Henriette Celarié's *Esclave à Alger* (1930), a rosy captivity narrative set just before the 1830 conquest, and ending optimistically with its advent. For the second, see Charles Courtin's *La brousse qui mangea l'homme* (1929), in which a young man loses his fortune and his life in a pointless, doomed, and above all unheroic effort to establish himself as a *colon*.

16. In one of the very few contemporary critical treatment of Chukri's novel, Abdelkader Djeghloul speaks of assimilation as "the deal which no Algerian writer in French would accept" (Djeghloul). No doubt; however, the refusal was not always categorical. Some, like Chukri, tried to modify the terms of the deal. Although Djeghloul seems to wish, at all costs, to document the birth of nationalism in Algeria in Chukri's novel, he is aware of the internal contradictions of texts by Arabs and Berbers from this period.

17. The phrase "double discourse" is Djeghloul's (107).

18. Zenati, the progressive (though not radical) editor first of the *Voix des humbles*, and later of the *Voix indigène*, and Charles-Collomb, the rabid "arabophobe" editor of the *Evolution nord-africaine*, embodied these two positions. Ben Bādis was perhaps the only one among the very early theorists who began to reverse these positions.

19. Djeghloul argues precisely this, probably again because he wishes to see in these writers precursors of the Algerian nationalist struggle. Their status as precursors, however, need not depend on their doubtful affirmation of some sort of essential Arabo-Berber identity.

20. "Roumia" is the feminine of "roumi," literally and originally a person from Rome, but generically (and to this day) any European-looking foreigner in the Maghrib.

21. Djeghloul calls this paper "close to the Fascist millieu of Doriot" (Djeghloul 36).

Works Cited

Ait-Kaci. "La Représentation des indigènes au Parlement." *La Voix des humbles* 74 (May 1929): 3.

Ben Cherif, Caid A. *Ahmed ben Mostapha, goumier.* Paris: Payot, 1920.

"Le Centenaire: revendications politiques." *La Voix indigène*, 21 November 1929: N. pag.

Chukri, Khodja. *El Euldj, captif des barbaresques.* Paris: Editions de la Revue des Indépendants, 1929.

Djeghloul, Abdelkader. *Eléments d'histoire culturelle algérienne.* Algiers: ENAL, 1984.

Horne, Alistair. *A Savage War of Peace: Algeria 1954-1962.* 1977. London: Papermac, 1996.

Ibn al-Hachemi, Emir Khaled. *La situation des Musulmans d'Algérie: Conférences faites à Paris les 12 et 19 juillet 1924.* 1924. Algiers: Editions du Trait d'Union, Victor Spielmann, 1930.

Ihaddaden, Zahir. "L'Histoire de la presse "indigène" en Algérie, des origines jusqu'en 1930." Thèse de doctorat du 3eme cycle. Université de Paris II, n.d.

Labiod. "Désillusion et espérance." *La Voix indigène*, 10 July 1930: N. pag.

Lanasri, Ahmed. *La littérature algérienne de l'entre-deux-guerres: génèse et fonctionnement.* Paris: Publisud, 1995.

Lebel, Roland. *Histoire de la littérature coloniale en France.* Paris: Larose, 1931.

Ould Cheikh, Mohammed. *Myriem dans les palmes.* Oran: Editions Plaza, 1936.

Terdiman, Richard. *Discourse/Counter-Discourse: Theory and Practice of Symbolic Resistance in Nineteenth-Century France*. Ithaca, NY: Cornell University Press, 1985.

Identity Politics in Morocco

Taieb Belghazi

This paper seeks to elucidate some of the problems, paradoxes and blindspots in the recent debates on identity, to consider its relevance in the Moroccan context, and to show how it operates in the context of Moroccan NGOs (Non-Governmental Organizations). The emphasis throughout is on the idea that identity politics is empowering when it is construed in terms of hybridity. The paper is divided into three parts or three moments. In the first part, I discuss the relevance of the notion of identity to Morocco and elaborate on some criticisms directed against it. In the second part, I give an account of the debate on the question of the "différend," between Lyotard and Rorty and indicate the way this debate is a playing out of the particularistic vs. the universalistic lines on identity. In the third part, I concentrate on Moroccan NGOS and show how they open up a new space of empowering politics beyond what Homi Bhabha calls "identikit political idealism" (Bhabha, "Commitment" 117).

A number of scholars who work on Morocco may object to my use of the phrase "identity politics" in the title on the grounds that it represents an unproblematized and a simplistic adoption on my part of a notion that is fashionable in North America, Britain, Australia, and Western Europe where it has a justifiable descriptive force, where it is used as an analytic category in poststructuralist scholarship, and where it operates as a mobilizing and as an empowering slogan among disadvantaged and marginalized groups. But this phrase, my imagined critics would argue, is inadequate in the Moroccan context. For one thing, the word identity (*huwiya*) in Arabic is usually perceived as a problematic (*ichkaliya*) and is associated with culture rather than politics.

With the notable exception of nation (*watan*), a category often coupled with the term cause (*kadiya*), the language pertaining to politics is not deployed in conjunction with the various modes of belonging available to, or struggled over, by Moroccans. The new dynamic of the Moroccan political scene, characterized by the phenomenal rise of new social movements is generally referred to by both political activists and researchers as *siyasa thakafiya al jadida* (a new political culture), a culture where the various parties accept politics as an open democratic game where rules derived from the ethics of political modernists constitute the framework for political action.

For my imagined critics, the use of "identity politics" in connection with Morocco, like the use of "postmodernism" and "poststructuralism" is an imposition, a transposition of a basically European or Western concept into a third world context. Their view, premised on the classical notions of representation and reality where language is marked by transparency, upholds that theoretical categories are rooted in specific places and enjoy a great measure of determinacy, and if they travel at all, they are more likely to lose their explanatory force along the way. To their understanding, there seems to be an automatic fit between theoretical notions and various territories. The latter exist mainly as neutral grids upon which people and their defining characteristics are mapped through a constraining and a determinate interpretative vocabulary.

I think that one crucial consequence of this theoretical territorialisation is to produce an essentialism and a naturalism where a specific theory along with a determinate identity are thought to inhere in a given place. Another is to establish a hierarchical situation where the third world figures as a ghettoized domain that can be easily apprehended by a less "sophisticated" critical battery of terms. In other words, the critic who wants to maintain the grounds of militancy by keeping the first and the third world separate ends up leaving the asymmetrical relation between the two firmly in place: a "sophisticated" theory for one world, concrete language of resistance for the other. What is ignored in this line of thinking is that there is no way around or beyond theory, and that the "untheoretical" and authentic stance it advocates with respect to the third world is very much imbricated with a theory that presents the third world as homogeneous and undifferentiated while it allows the first world to exist as a multiplicity of identities in flux, requiring the attention of an ever changing theory.

This dichotomizing perspective of first world versus third world may be discerned in the writing on Morocco for more than four decades. Indeed, since the 1950s most western scholarship on Morocco in the fields of sociology, history and anthropology, has produced a highly homogenizing discourse which constructs this country as characterized by a rigid social structure hampering its entry into political modernity. Morocco has, thus, been construed as prey to a series of antinomies: tradition vs. modernity, scriptural vs. maraboutic religion, country vs. city, Berber vs. Arab. Such a binary perspective has led to a monolithic and unproblematized image of both society and polity. In this perspective, Morocco presents itself as a neutral space on which a stagnant society and culture are mapped. Moreover, a political stalemate is too easily discerned in workings of the state and in the relationship between the latter and the various opposition and collaboration forces with which it interacts. On this reading, collective political and cultural identities are readily homogenized, essentialized and territorialized. Accordingly, the Berbers' location is the country, their religion is maraboutic, their culture is traditional. By contrast, the Arabs are more urbanized, their religion basically scriptural, and their culture prone to be influenced by modernizing forces. This highly polarized view of Morocco rules out the possibility for identities to cut across tribal divisions, localities, status, gender, ethnicity, etc.

Thus, Moroccan identities have been fixed along clearly demarcated lines which disallow negotiations, ambivalence, or hybridity. On the contrary, the various collective identities analyzed by this literature simply imprisons them into determinate and bounded spaces, and confines them to predictable functions. In this interpretation, the dynamic involving the constituents of Moroccan society and the interaction between the latter and outside influence do not alter the basic structure of Moroccan social culture and polity.

A powerful category— segmentary society—has been used, mainly by anthropologists, to describe the constitutive elements of this society as well as its social culture and political dynamics. As Dale Eckleman points out:

> Under this theory, a society is called "segmentary" if
> ... there is no permanent authority of one person over
> another. Political relations are conceived primarily or
> exclusively in terms of some form of linear descent,
> through which individuals are organised into competing
> groups with various encapsulated levels of inclusiveness.
> These groups are roughly equal in strength and coalesce
> only upon challenge from groups of an equal "level".
> Alldisputes within the "ordered anarchy" of segmentary
> societies are presumably regulated by reciprocal violence
> or by the threat of it among the "balanced " group. (282)

The groups described in this passage are homogeneous and timeless. Both the internal divisions of these units and their historicity are occluded here. What is foregrounded is the image of a pre-modern society where one's identity is fixed: "one was born and died a member of one's tribe or group with one's life trajectory fixed in advance" (Kellner 141)—determined and given, this type of identity is unproblematical and at odds with modern identity which is "more mobile, multiple personal, self-reflexive, and subject to change and innovation" (141). On the reading of the segmentarists, Morocco consists of autonomous units which are basically stagnant and oblivious to outside influence, including that of the state. The latter's role in the societal order is minimized.

This segmentary perspective on Morocco is deployed by John Waterbury in his discussion of the political system in Morocco. He offers an eloquent elaboration on the political stalemate alluded to earlier:

> For centuries Moroccan society has been characterized
> by constant tension and varying degrees of violence, but
> at any given point in history, with a few rare but notable
> exceptions, the most salient product of this tension has
> been stalemate. Moroccan society appears to be ever on
> the verge of an explosion that never occurs. Despite the
> indisputable upheaval in Moroccan social institutions
> caused by forty-four years of the protectorate and eleven
> years of independence, Moroccan society is still
> characterized by stalemate. In the last eleven years, and

probably for some years to come, stalemate has been and will continue to be the dominant trait of Moroccan politics. (Waterbury 61)

For Waterbury, as the passage above illustrates, there is a continuity in Moroccan history guaranteed by the unchanging nature of its social order and the permanence of its collective identities; the latter operates on the model of the tribal system which constitutes the defining characteristic of the segmentary society.

     This idea of a continuous, linear history where hardly any change happens and of a homogeneous and an autonomous society sealed off from outside influence has been challenged by many scholars. However, my point is that what is at stake is not the question of an adequate account of society and history, for the issue of adequacy is highly problematic in view of the current poststructuralist wisdom on the construction of the real and historical. Rather, it is the difficulty of sustaining the perspective that sets up the local as the only valid object of analysis and, then, proceeds to map both a theory and an identity onto it. The consequence of this move is to disallow any travel of theoretical categories. The claim that identity politics is irrelevant to the Moroccan context is premised on this localized view of theory.

     However, I would point out that there is another set of objections to the use of identity politics. This time, the argument centers around the inadequacy of this notion in the American and European contexts where it originated. Its detractors point out the essentialism of identity politics as well as its reductionism. They say that the emphasis on identity as a ground for making political claims negates the multiplicity of subject positions and affirms a singular subjectivity, a singular mode of experience as the only origin and motivation of one's action. Instead of being a question of empowerment, identity can turn into a limiting and a disabling factor. As Todd Gitlin says:

The rise of "identity politics" forms a convergence of a cultural style, a mode of logic, a badge of belonging, and a claim to insurgency. What began as an assertion of dignity, a recovery from exclusion and denigration, and a demand for representation, has also developed a

hardening of its boundaries. The long overdue opening
of initiative to minorities, women, gays, and others of
the traditionally voiceless has developed its own methods
of silencing. (172)

On this reading, identity politics does not take into account more
inclusive solidarities, the possibility of articulating interests across larger
collective identities and the formation of coalitions based on common
goals. Moreover, it is oblivious to the internal divisions within each
collective identity. Kobena Mercer makes a similar argument in her
article "1968: Periodising Politics and Identity." For her:

Insofar as contemporary enthusiasm for "identity"
replays previous debates on what used to be called
"consciousness" in the 1960s or "subjectivity" in the
1970s, the challenge is to go beyond the atomistic and
esentialist logic of "identity politics" in which differences
are dealt with only one-at-a-time and which therefore
ignores the conflicts and contradictions that arise in the
relations within and between the various movements,
agents and actors in contemporary forms of democratic
antagonism. (425)

Now, while I think that criticism of the use of identity politics on
account of its irrelevance is untenable because it is premised on a
simplistic and an essentialized idea of the rootedness of theory, I find the
second set of charges which emphasize the homogenizing thrust of
identity politics more challenging. I think the question that needs to be
asked in light of these more interesting criticisms is the following: is there
a way of conceptualizing the practice of making political claims on the
basis of identity while taking into account the latter's constructions and
ambivalence? I would argue that the category of hybridity could provide
such a way. It is a category that enables the view of identity not as a fixed
essence, tied to a transcendental origin, operating outside history. It also
highlights identity's historicity, its discontinuities as well as its
continuities, and its existence in constant flux. Hybridity also allows us
to understand identity politics as a politics of position "which has no

absolute guarantee in an unproblematic, transcendental law of origin" (Hall 395). This notion of hybridity constitutes a revision of both the traditional view of individual identity as discrete, whole, self-defining and self-knowing, as well as the view of collective identity as homogeneous, stable, and inescapable.

Moreover, hybridity has also come under criticism from a number of scholars engaged in the effort of theorizing postcolonialism. Thus Linda Hutcheon advises us "to put on hold . . . [t]he poststructuralist postmodern challenges to the coherent, autonomous subject . . . in feminist and post-colonial discourses. . . for both must work first to assert and affirm a denied or alienated subjectivity: those radical challenges are in many ways the luxury of the dominant order which can afford to challenge that which it securely possesses?" (51). Other detractors of the notion argue that identity "is constituted theatrically through role playing and image construction"; it is "a function of leisure and is grounded in play, in gamesmanship" (Kellner 153). They also point out that this construction of identity is at odds with the aspirations of oppressed groups that require a more serious and a more committed approach. However, the problem with this criticism is that it construes identity outside the system of representation and away from discursive construction.

Furthermore, there are two more major criticisms that are levelled at the notion of hybridity. The first one is that it lacks both descriptive force and historical specificity. It operates, according to Ella Shohat and Robert Stam, "[a]s a descriptive catchall term. Its users, who lack the critical rigour of committed intellectuals, easily lapse into a facile celebratory tone and fail 'to discriminate' between the diverse modalities of hybridity: colonial imposition, obligatory assimilation, political corporation, cultural mimicry and so forth?" (43). The consequence of this undifferentiated and uncritical adoption of the term, for Shohat and Stam, is to neglect the issue of power. To counter this view, I would like to point out that hybridity has no essence which makes it empowering. It is a contested terrain that has been marked by numerous shifts.

The second charge made against the use of hybridity is that it reflects the concerns of a westernized minority in the third world which finds it difficult to feel at home in their native cultures. On this reading, hybridity reflects the interests of a minority living on the border between two or more cultures and not a pervasive phenomenon marking society as a whole. Thus, Ahmed Boukous in his thought-provoking discussion of Khatibi, and despite his sympathetic reading of the latter's work and, indeed, his espousal of a similar stance concerning hybridity and interculturalism, says, at one point in his discussion of this writer, that interculturalism constitutes a phenomenon which is limited to the minority of intellectuals who write in French and to the urban Bourgeoisie which is open to western culture (178). Boukous is discussing the case of Maghribi intellectuals who write in French, but the same remark can be made about Derrida, Said, and Homi Bhabha. It may be said that these major figures of poststructuralist and postcolonialist thinking partake of a liminal and interstitial position which justifies their advocacy of hybrid theory. Said is a Palestinian exile whose predicament pushes him to argue that "one is always *in* a country, never *of* it." Khatibi describes himself as a "professional foreigner whose stance can only be intercultural, having been brought up in-between languages and cultures" (55). Derrida speaks about his trouble of identity as a Franco-Maghribi, occupying an interstitial space between several cultures. Finally Homi Bhabha speaks of himself as "a middle class Gujarati, an English speaking Parsi; always a minority in the Indian context."[1]

I would like to point out that despite the charge made against these intellectuals which consists in saying that their theorization of hybridity is a reflection on their own predicament and that it is prompted by the desire for self-promotion in Western academe, it is only fair to argue that the border position occupied by intellectuals may constitute the ground for an enabling critical stance that breaks with substantive and essentialist notions of identity. These intellectuals, whom Abdul Jan Mohamed calls "specular border intellectuals" because of their inability to be at home in either their "original" culture or in their "adopted" cultures are "[c]aught between several cultures or groups none of which are deemed sufficiently enabling or productive." As a consequence of this situation, these intellectuals "subject [these different] cultures to analytic scrutiny rather than combining them; [they] ulilis[e] [their] interstitial space[s] as . . . vantage point[s] to define implicitly or explicitly, other utopian possibilities of group formation" ("Worldliness" 97). The political stance of these "specular intellectuals" is neither one of synthesis that reproduces the liberal search for universalism nor one of specificity that is consonant with the particularistic discourse of celebratory postmodernism; instead, it is a hybrid of politics of articulation, of joining and disjoining, of a practice of negotiation where location operates as a site rather than as a place and where radicalism does not come fully inscribed in any given subject position. In other words, it constitutes a movement away from the politics of universalism associated with the liberal humanist position and the politics of particularism found in some writings which advocate incommensurability and the lack of common measure between different cultures.

Thus, on the one hand, the politics of universalism is premised on the liberal humanist perception of identity as an ensemble of characteristics shared by human beings regardless of their specific belonging to class, nation, or gender. This politics "emphasi[zes] the equal dignity of all citizens, and the content of this politics [is] the equalization of rights and entitlements" (Taylor 37). It also demands that institutions treat individuals in a way that is blind to their ethnic, clan, or gender differences. But one major criticism of this view is that in spite of its argument for mutual respect, it obliterates the specific rights of certain social categories and may even represent the perspective of one hegemonic single identity. Moreover, respect loses its character as respect when it is equally divided. On the other hand, the particularistic perspective promotes a politics of difference. It insists that "[e]veryone should be recognised for his or her unique difference" (38). This view as we saw in the first part of this paper can easily lapse into essentialism. Now, of course both views can be construed as having a descriptive force. The particularistic view can justify its insistence on the uniqueness of different struggles by pointing to the loss in influences of universal ideologies that cut across racial and national boundaries and the rise and expansion of movements that do not ground their claim on any legitimizing grand narrative. But the universal view can also corroborate its claim by invoking the fact that, at present, the globe is the essential unit of human activity.

An interesting presentation of these two lines of argument on the question of identity is found in a debate between Richard Rorty and Jean-François Lyotard, and raises a question that is of crucial importance to the issue on hand: "Can we continue today to organize the multitude of events that come to us from the world, both the human and the non-human world, by subsuming them beneath the idea of a universal history of humanity?" (Rorty 559). Lyotard's answer is that we cannot since different cultures are incommensurable and have no common denominator. Their interaction is more likely to result in a differend: "As distinguished from a litigation, a differend [différend] would be a case of conflict between (at least) two parties, that cannot be equitably resolved for a lack of rule of judgement applicable to both arguments" (Lyotard 73). Thus, whereas a litigation can be resolved, a differend is marked by incommensurable stands that can never be reconciled (73). Since the differend seems to be the main mode of cultures' interaction, there can be no understanding between the self and the other, only dissensus and the raising of the stakes are operative in such an interaction. Lyotard's particularistic view is shared by a number of intellectuals involved with both postcolonial and cultural studies and who are keen to undermine the liberal humanist emphasis on the existence of a human nature shared by different peoples. These critics insist that the other is irreducible and that the self can understand the other only by reducing the latter to the same. An instance of this position is provided by Abdul Jan Mohamed in his discussion of the relation between Europe and its other:

> Faced with an incomprehensible and multifaceted alterity, the European theoretically has the option of responding to the Other in terms of identity or difference. If he assumes that he and the other are essentially identical , then he would tend to ignore the significant divergences and to judge the other according to his own cultural values. If, on the other hand, he assumes that the other is irremediably different, then he would have little incentive to adopt the view-point of that alterity. He would again tend to turn to the security of his own cultural perspective. Genuine and thorough comprehension of otherness is possible only if the self can somehow negate or at least severely bracket the values, assumptions, and ideology of his culture. ("Economy" 83)

Rorty takes a different view. For him there is still a basis for communication and common action between human beings who belong to different cultures provided they manage—as human beings to replace force by persuasion, thus increasing the degree of consensus among themselves. It is true that Rorty criticizes "universal principles" and urges us to attach ourselves to empirical narratives and to avoid metanarratives, but this anti-universal stand is undercut by his subscription to what he calls "postmodern bourgeois liberalism," arguing that it is the best option on offer for humanity at present. In other words, Rorty writes universalism back into his argument although he takes a debunking attitude towards it. He defines what he calls "a moderate ethnocentrism" where the standards of value are defined and improved by western intellectuals of Whiggish tendencies who persuade, rather than force other people to adhere to western ways of thought. On this account, colonized people adopt the colonizer's culture and institutions because of the advantages the latter are likely to bring them. Similarly, anthropologists can be seduced by "primitive" cultures and decide to cast off their own European culture and "go indigenous" of their own accord. Rorty agrees with Lyotard that the idea of emancipation is no longer tenable, but he wants to hold onto cosmopolitan narratives that are simply the account given by neopragmatists of different phenomena.

Against both the particularistic and the universalistic views of identity, I would like to argue for a position which posits it as a process of negotiation and translation. As I have argued in the first part of this paper, though it may be justified in some respects, criticism levelled at the use of identity politics does not mean that this concept needs to be discarded. On the contrary, I think, the construction of identity as hybrid can be politically an enabling strategy at a time when globalization requires a reconceptualization of traditional modes of belonging in such a way as to lead to the situation sought by Bhabha, one where there is "less pietistic articulation of political principle (around class and nation); [and] a little more of the principle of political negotiation" (Bhabha, Location 28). To that end, we need to be aware "that every identity is relational and that the affirmation of a difference is a precondition for the existence of any identity" (Mouffe 107). We need also to remember that his relationship, which may become the terrain of a multi-faceted conflict and antagonism between human beings, should constitute an important dimension in conceptualizing hybridity. On this understanding, identity becomes the locus of politics as *polemos*, i.e. as conflict, but also as polis, i.e. "seek[ing] to establish a certain order and to organise human co-existence in conditions that are permanently complicated because they are affected by the political" (Mouffe 107). Neither the politics of universalism advocated by liberal humanism, nor the politics of particularism hastily celebrated by some postcolonial and postmodern intellectuals, but a politics of hybridity, conceived not as a third term that resolves conflicts in a dialectical or synthetic way. Hybridity politics, in this sense, does not refer to a single mode of struggle. It is not a settled terrain, but a multitude of practices.

In Morocco, whose culture consists of Tamazigh, Arab, Islamic, and western elements (Boukous 176), hybridity has a descriptive force. It provides a framework for the apprehension of a multi-faceted identity which is precarious in an ever-changing world. It can also operate as a means to counter the fundamentalist view of identity, which locks it in an unmovable past. The recent development of NGOS may be construed as a way a politics of hybridity, which takes into account both politics and the political, can be played out.

Moroccan NGOS constitute a movement through which different social categories, occupying a variety of identity positions, seek to further their rights in ways that are at odds with traditional modes of experiencing identity. Situated at the intersection between gender, class, and nation, these NGOS reflect an interesting negotiation of identity.[2] Furthermore, as constitutive of a fragile civil society, these movements do not in any way substitute for political society, but fulfil an important function which consists in preserving or bringing about democratic practices via the exertion of influence on decision-makers and the defense of democratization processes. Moroccan NGOS may be divided into three groups: regional NGOS; economic and social NGOS; and political NGOS.

Regional NGOS are organized along regional lines; they reflect the interests of the regional elite, whose declared aim is to achieve a degree of social, economic and cultural development in their regions. Individuals who are close to the Makhzen (the state) run these regional NGOS. The latter may, therefore, be seen as implementing a politics that is hardly oppositional. However, it should be pointed out that some of the members of these organizations come from left-wing parties and seek to further agendas that are in line with left-wing agendas. These individuals take the view that the state is neither monolithic nor homogeneous: it is multi-faceted and multi-functional. While keen to maintain autonomy, they are aware that the latter depends, to a large extent, on the state's active involvement through the adoption and the implementation of adequate legislative texts. Furthermore, because the members of these regional NGOs are situated at the intersection between gender, class, and nation, they reflect an interesting negotiation of identity and constitute collective subjectivities which are both coherent and antagonistic. These NGOS are fractured and experience a measure of internal antagonism, but because these members have a degree of commitment to their region, we can talk about the existence of internal solidarity, fragile though it might be.

It should also be pointed out that although these NGOS are called regional, their work interacts with a politics that is informed by what happens on the regional, the national, and the international levels. Such an interaction between the local, the national and the global is not merely due to the organizations' search for funding from both the central government and the international organizations, but because location can no longer be construed as a unit which is sealed off from both national and international processes.

Economic and social NGOS consist of men and women whose primary aim is to further the interests of some targeted groups in the fields of health, rural development, integration of women in professional life and small companies. Thus, *l'association migration et développement*, which was founded by a Moroccan emigrant who had been dismissed from the factories of Péchiney, seeks to develop the basic electricity and sanitary infrastructure in the area of Taliouine in the region of Taroudant. These NGOS, like the regional NGOS above, do not operate as independent entities, sealed off from the political domain. Nor are their members inactive in society. For instance, ALCS (*Association de lutte contre le sida*) consists of people from various professions, and have a variety of political affiliations. Other organizations consist of individuals who belong to special professional categories : *l'organisation des femmes de carrières libérales et commerciales, l'union des femmes des administrations publiques et semi-publiques, l'association des femmes artistes, le comité des femmes journalistes*, but while these women further their interests as members of these organizations, they negotiate other facets of their subjectivities as wives, sisters, mothers, urban or rural women, etc. Therefore, these women occupy different subject positions that cannot be reduced to one singular identity. Although these organizations are primarily economic and social in character, they may be described as exerting politics as both polemos and politics. One may want to argue that *l'association de solidarité féminine*, which, among other things, supports battered wives, is much more politically oppositional than other NGOS classified as social or economic. I would want to emphasize that oppositional politics is not naturally inscribed in these NGOS.

The third group of NGOS—the political NGOS—operate in three main areas: defense of human rights, the reform of the legal status of women and the promotion of Berber culture. This third group has a much more direct interaction with political parties (especially those which are positioned on the left of the political spectrum). Nevertheless, the relation between these organizations and left-wing parties is not one of straightforward symbiosis. While it is accurate to say that some parties on the left have a passive presence in these organizations, and use various strategies to enlist them in their overall programmatic endeavors, still the various political NGOS consist more of members whose multi-faceted and hybrid subjectivities resist being harnessed to seemingly rigid perspectives. Sometimes a tension arises between these organizations and the political parties with which they are associated because the former's demands exceed the latter's programs which depend on the political context and the balance of powers. A case in point is the criticism leveled by some women's NGOS at the parties to which they are affiliated for not airing women's demands in the memorandum submitted to the King and in which these parties produced their own criticisms of the constitution proposed in 1995. These NGOS wanted a radical revision of the women's statutes and ascribed the parties' moderation to the latter's attempt to appease traditionalists and to avoid alienating the religions fundamentalists. Other examples of the tension between these NGOS and the political parties can be easily provided, especially after the left acceded to government. The main point, however, is that Moroccan NGOS exemplify the emergence of an interesting mode of identity politics and justify the deployment of this notion in the Moroccan context.

In conclusion, I would point out that hybridity is not only operative in NGOS. Left-wing parties have also moved towards a much more fluid and less doctrinaire practice which is organised along lines that are less fixed than they used to be in the past. We witness the emergence of a new oppositional politics which is based on fragile and constantly negotiated rainbow alliances. In this context, the categories of nation and class are still operative, but they are no longer shrouded in the mythical discourse of original and singular allegiances where they are fully formed entities prior to their interaction. "Identities are not simple allegiances to a place, or . . . a property, we ought to realise that they are the stake of power struggle" (Mouffe 10).

Notes

1. Arguments in defense of hybridity suffuse the writings of Said, Khatibi, and Bhabha. But they are best articulated in the following works: Edward Said's *Culture and Imperialism*; Jacques Derrida's *The Monolingualism of the Other or The Prothesis of Origin*; Abdelkebir Khatibi's *Penser le Maghreb*; and Homi Bhabha's *The Location of Culture*.
2. In my discussion of Moroccan NGOS, I have drawn mainly on Guilain Denoeux and Laurent Gateau's work in "L'essor des associations au Maroc: à la recherche de la citoyenneté."

Works Cited

Bhabha, Homi. "The Commitment to Theory." *Questions of Third Cinema*. Eds. Jim Pines and Paul Willenen. London: British Film Institute, 1989. 111-32.

____. *The Location of Culture*. London: Routledge, 1994.

Boukous, Ahmed. *Société, Langues et Cultures au Maroc Enjeux Symboliques*. Rabat: Faculté des Lettres et des Sciences Humaines, 1995.

Denoeux, Guilain and Laurent Gateau. "L'essor des associations au Maroc : à la recherche de la citoyenneté." *Monde Arabe Maghreb Machrek* 150 (Oct-Dec 1995): 19-39.

Derrida, Jacques. *The Monolingualism of the Other or The Prothesis of Origin*. Trans. Patrick Mensah. Stanford, CA: Stanford

University Press, 1998.

Eckleman, Dale. "New Directions in Interpreting North Africa." *Nouveaux Enjeux Culturels au Maghreb*. Ed. Jean-Robert Henry. Paris: CNRS, 1986. 279-89.

Gitlin, Todd. "The Rise of 'Identity Politics'." *Dissent* 40 (Spring 1993): 172-7.

Hall, Stuart. "Cultural Identity and Diaspora." *Colonial Discourse and Postcolonial Theory*. Eds. Patrick Williams and Laura Chrisman. London: Harvester Wheatsheaf, 1993. 392-403.

Hutcheon, Linda. "Circling the Downspout of Empire: 'Postcolonialism and postmodernism'." *Ariel* 20.4 (October 1989): 149-75.

Jan Mohamed, Abdul. "The Economy of Manichean Allegory: The Function of Racial Difference in Colonialist Literature." *Race, Writing, and Difference*. Ed. Henry Louis Gates, Jr. Chicago and London: The University of Chicago Press, 1985. 78-106.

____. "Worldliness Without World, Homeliness As Home: Towards a Definition of the Specular Border Intellectual." *Edward Said A Critical Reader*. Ed. Michael Sprinker. Oxford: Blackwell, 1992. 96-120.

Kellner, Douglas. "Popular Culture and the Construction of Postmodern Identities." *Modernity and Identity*. Eds. Scott Lash and Jonathan Friedman. Oxford: Blackwell, 1992. 141-77.

Khatibi, Abdelkebir. *Penser le Maghreb*. Rabat: Société marocaine des éditeurs réunis, 1993.

Lyotard, Jean-François. *The Differend*. Manchester: Manchester University Press, 1988.

Mercer, Kobena. "1968: Periodising Politics and Identity." *Cultural Studies*. Eds. Lawrence Grossberg, Cary Nelson, and Paula A. Treichler. New York and London: Routledge, 1992. 424-49.

Mouffe, Chantal. "For a Politics of a Nomadic Identity." *Traveller's Narratives of Home and Displacement*. Eds. Robert Roberston, Melinda Mash, Lisa Tichner, Jim Bird, Barry Curtis, and Tim Putman. London: Routledge, 1994. 105-13.

Rorty, Richard. "Histoire Universelle et Différences Culturelles." *Critique* 41.456 (May 1985): 558-68.

Said, Edward. *Culture and Imperialism*. New York: Knopf, 1993.

Shohat, Ella and Robert Stam. *Unthinking Eurocentrism*. London: Routledge, 1994.

Taylor, Charles. "The Politics of Recognition." *Multiculturalism and "The Politics of Recognition"*. Eds. Amy Gutman, et. al. Princeton, NJ: Princeton University Press, 1992. 25-73.

Waterbury, John. *The Commander of the Faithful*. New York: Columbia University Press, 1970.

The Development of the Moroccan Short Story

Jilali El Koudia

Any survey of a literary genre needs to take its departure from an intensive and extensive reading of the primary sources through different periods of production. Necessary is also the collection of information from the biographical background, the historical and social context and the critical opinions of literary scholars. The two procedures offer a descriptive and analytical approach at the same time. The present general view of the Moroccan short story is based on a combination of both procedures as an attempt to arrive at a balanced and comprehensive picture of this genre. The reading of several short stories produced over a period of fifty years, from the early forties to the late nineties, along with a few critical books and articles, and above all through direct discussions and consultations with specialists in the field have contributed positively to this project, the fruit of which has been published in an anthology entitled *Moroccan Short Stories*, including 38 writers represented by one story each.

The intention behind such a brief survey is to draw the attention of the English-speaking audience to the Moroccan short story written in Arabic in particular. As far as I know, two American scholars have pointed out the need of making this kind of literature known in the English-speaking world. In his scholarly book *Desert Songs: Western Images of Morocco and Moroccan Images of the West*, Professor John Maier notes: "In my experience, when Moroccans are asked to name their important authors, they invariably mention Driss Chraibi and Tahar Ben Jelloun. Both write in French and are considered important because they have been recognized by the French. . . . The Arabic language is necessary to understand the society from within" (181).

The other scholar well known for his works on Arabic fiction and translations from Arabic into English is Professor Roger Allen. In recent years, he has shown great interest in the literature of the Maghrib. Like Professor Maier, he makes the same appeal to give some attention to Arabic literature written in these countries. In the *Newsletter of the Moroccan-American Commission for Educational and Cultural Exchange*, he states: "English-speaking scholars have tended to overlook or give scant attention to the Arabic literature of the Maghreb, while French and Spanish scholars have concentrated on the region. This has resulted in an imbalance in scholarly writings in English on modern Arabic literature" (8).

Indeed, within the context of the contemporary history of Morocco, fiction is generally believed to be written largely in French, the predominant colonial language. No doubt, to the Western ear, names like Tahar Ben Jelloun, Driss Chraibi, Ahmed Sefrioui, Mohamed El Berini, Moha Souag, Abdelhak Serhane and others are familiar.[1] Other writers have chosen Spanish, the other colonial language, to express themselves. Some of these are: Mohamed Chakour, Mohamed Temsamani, Abdellatif Khatib, Ahmed Daoudi, Abdelkader Wariachi, Mohamed Bouissef Regab and Mohamed Sibari.[2] Today we can even speak of a few rising voices of English expression: occasionally the British Council in Morocco organizes readings of fiction from university teachers. Two collections of short stories *Graffiti* (1997) and *Between the Lines* (1998) were published by Abdellatif Akbib, and a collection of stories entitled *Stories Under the Sun* was published by Jilali El Koudia in 1999, in addition to a few stories that have been broadcast on BBC World Service or published in various journals.

If such writings in European languages are accessible to the West, the short story written in the mother tongue, Arabic, remains hardly known, except for a very limited number of names that found their way through translation. Indeed, in recent years, foreign scholars have made a few translation attempts. There is no doubt that Paul Bowles has significantly contributed in this field through his translation and rewriting of Moroccan narratives like Larbi Layachi's *Yesterday and Today* (1985) and *Life Full of Holes* (1964). In 1983 Denys Johnson-Davies published a collection of short stories called *Arabic Short Stories* where "Life by Instalment" by Mohamed Berrada and "Flower Crazy" by Mohamed Choukri were included. It is only in 1994 that *An Anthology of Moroccan Short Stories* was compiled and translated by Malcolm Williams and Gavin Watterson and was published by King Fahd of Translation in Tangier. As already indicated, in 1996 John Maier published a scholarly work *Desert Songs: Western Images of Morocco and Moroccan Images of the West* where he analyses Abdelmajid Ben Jelloun's "A Stranger" (1947), Mohamed Berrada's "Life by Instalment" (1979), Mohamed Choukri's "Flower Crazy" (1987) and Leïla Abouzeid's "Divorce" (1983). Very significantly, John Maier observes that "[these writers] have chosen to write in Arabic, when they might well have chosen French"(181). As far as Spanish is concerned, perhaps the book that includes the largest number of Moroccan writers in translation is an anthology called *Literatura Y Pensamiento Marroquies Contemporaneos* published by the Instituto Hispano-Arabe de Cultura, Madrid, 1979.

For all these attempts, the Moroccan short story written in Arabic still calls for more efforts to be made known abroad, surprisingly not only in the English speaking world but also in the Arab countries. If the linguistic obstacle in the former can be understood, it is quite ironic that in the Middle East, where Arabic is the native language, the Moroccan short story is almost completely ignored. In *The Short Story*, Dr. Sayed Hamid An-Nassaj admits that: "As to our knowledge in the Arab East of this art [the short story in the Maghrib] and its trends, it is very limited, if not completely absent" (55). The only justification Dr. An-Nassaj seems to offer for this unfortunate situation is the predominance of French in the Maghrib as a whole, which shows the impact of French colonialism. Nevertheless, the situation is now changing through the constant exchange between Moroccan writers and their counterparts in the Arab world.

Such considerations and the artistry of the Moroccan output in this genre have led me to focus in particular on the short story in Arabic. The procedure I have indicated earlier, that is the combination of primary sources and background references, has enabled me to chart the evolution of this genre through a period of five decades. The division is then made in four major phases as suggested to me by two eminent Moroccan scholars.[3]

The phase delineated above will be illustrated by excerpts from short stories that represent the predominant narrative modes, styles and themes.

Roughly between 1915 and 1935, literary critics like Ahmed El Yabouri and Abderrahime Mouedden talk of tales rather than the short story in its modern form (6), or as Edgar Allan Poe defined it in the early nineteenth century. Only in the early 1940s can we speak of the real beginning of the short story. Ahmed Bennani, Abderrahmane El Fassi and Ahmed Ziyadi are among those who represent this phase.

During the twentieth century, the colonization of Morocco by France in 1912 and Spain has left a great impact on its history and literature. The works of fiction written from the late forties to the fifties, or what we call the middle period, reflect the Moroccan struggle against the colonial powers.

"Uncle Boushnaq" by Abderrahmane El Fassi illustrates very well the predominant narrative aspects of the story written in this period. The general tendency is the employment of traditional narrative techniques such as the omniscient point of view, realistic description of characters and setting and the chronological sequence of events.

"Uncle Boushnaq" deals with an old man who feels nostalgic about the past. He laments the new changes in society and in the behavior of the young generation. The writer offers a minute description of the protagonist and his environment. The following extract sums up the main theme and mood of the story:

> He regretted the past when he used to buy many pounds of sugar for one dirham and five eggs for one franc. When he remembered the old days, he sighed and moaned. He was absolutely sure of his opinion, ready to give a thousand proofs that bliss had vanished from life, that there was no kindness in people any more, and that the end of the world was surely near. Wasn't one of its signs the strutting women in men's gowns? Smoking, cutting hair, shaving beards and moustaches were yet other signs. (My translation)

The emergence of the short story coincides with the rise of nationalism and resistance. In both politics and literature, the main concern was indeed the search for national identity. Thus, the awakening of national consciousness as a reaction to colonization found one of its best expressions in the short story.

In a review of Najib El Oufi's *An Approach to Reality in the Moroccan Short Story*, Abdelhamid Akkar underlines the intimate relationship between story and reality with its various layers; hence the short story parallels the historical and social changes (6). In the same review, Abderrahime Mouedden goes even further as to raise interesting questions about the interaction between story and reality.

The theme that dominates the narratives in this period is obviously the awareness of the threat to national identity and its defense. Other topics are also explored, such as social issues, sacrifice, marriage and traditions. Usually the writer praises and records the heroic deeds of those who resist foreign invasion. The style in which such stories are presented is direct, persuasive, and preaching, relying on local wisdom, proverbs and myths with the purpose of glorifying the Moroccan character; it is generally descriptive and photographic. Therefore, the general mode that characterizes the stories produced during this period is realistic and committed. Some of the writers who represent this period are: Abdelmajid Ben Jelloun, Mohamed Aziz Lahbabi, Mohamed Zniber, Ahmed Abdeslam El Bakkali, Abdelkrim Ghallab and Mohamed Ibrahim Bouallou.

Abdelmajid Ben Jelloun's "The Valley of Blood" explores the central theme that preoccupies most writers of this period: the invasion of Morocco by colonizers and the resistance they faced. The French despot and his assistants arrive in Marrakesh with self-confidence that Morocco is easy to exploit, but soon they realize that the situation is different and are eventually led to their destruction when they vanish in the valley of blood. The writer condemns the invaders and praises the national spirit. The following excerpt embodies the main theme of the narrative:

> He will reach the edge of the red lake and the hands of
> victims he had impoverished, scattered and humiliated,
> will grab him as they had done to the despotic ruler

before. They will always do so to any tyrant in the future. In fact, all the other tax collectors are heading for the valley to join their victims. Those dreadful hands will exact from them the price of the crops they have destroyed and stolen.

We saw them advancing step by step through mud towards the awful valley—the valley that was boiling with the blood of victims, the tears of virgins, the cries of children, the moans of mothers and the wailing of old people. (My translation)

By the sixties the short story has known new developments in both form and content, developments that are in particular marked by influences from Eastern Arabic and Western literatures. Intellectually and artistically, this phase is more important than the previous one.

Thematically, the stories reflect the new reality after independence. The focus has now shifted from nationalist themes to social and economic issues, and so the search for national identity has switched to a search for social identity. The writers experienced disillusionment with the new situation, since only a minority, the bourgeois class, benefitted from independence. The characters are generally depicted as frustrated, living in economic difficulties and fighting against social injustices. This general feeling is summed up by El Oufi as "the mirage of independence" (El Oufi 72). Hence, the struggle between social classes came to the foreground as a recurrent theme, as it has also become the concern of the writers to reflect on the condition of man instead of the nation. In this respect, two major Western philosophies, namely existentialism and Marxism, became popular among the writers in this period, informing them and shaping their visions.

As a literary genre, the short story has become more conscious of its form, its material and critical function. The writer has come to the realization that the old or traditional form is no longer flexible enough to express himself and to respond to the new changes in society. Thus he begins to explore new narrative territories and methods and to experiment with new styles. In *The Language of Childhood and Dream*, Mohamed Berrada argues that in the light of such social and political changes, the classical forms have become inefficient and outmoded;

therefore a new language and new forms have to be introduced. In academic circles, in particular at the University Mohamed V, Rabat, lecturers of Arabic literature began to show their dissatisfaction with the "Tymourian" story with beginning, middle and end, introducing their students to new narrative modes, insisting on disrupting time and capturing the moment. Anton Chekhov, Katherine Mansfield, Virginia Woolf and Edward El Kharrat were the models to learn from (Berrada 6). Indeed, many future young writers of the sixties and after were either teachers or students or both, at the University Mohamed V during this period.

By now the short story has become very popular and was widely written and published in periodicals, newspapers and collections. Through discussions in lecture halls, comments in newspapers and colloquia, professional criticism of the short story announced its real beginning. Some well-known writers who represent this period are: Mohamed Sebbagh, Driss El Khouri, Mubarak Rabii, Mohamed Berrada, Abdeljabbar Sehimi, Khnatha Bennouna, Rafikat Tabiaa (Zeinab Fahmi) and Mohamed Zafzaf.

Mohamed Sebbagh's "A Point of Order" is written in a different style from the previous stories, more poetic and simple in terms of plot. The writer describes the situation of an aristocratic woman who loses her privileges when her husband (an ambassador) dies. It is obvious that the writer is concerned with the changes in Moroccan society after independence. There is a sense of disillusionment with the new class that comes to power after the departure of the colonizers. But once such privileges are gone, the lady is awakened to the reality that no one should be above the law. Hence, in general terms the story illustrates the recurring theme of stories produced in this period, which is no longer the colonial issue but the struggle between social classes. Here is a telling extract selected from the story:

> "The law?" It was a strange word to Lalla Zeineb's ear and, for the first time, she tried to understand its significance.

Only a certain group of people is subject to the
law.

"Why am I confronted by the law this time? My
affairs and those of my family and relatives used to get
through all obstacles and barriers as quickly as a flash of
lightning."

In the name of the law she raised her eyes to
heaven and shouted imploringly: "A point of order!"
(My translation)

The disillusionment of the sixties only deepened more, both on
the national level and on the level of the Arab nation as a whole. While
preoccupied with local problems, the Moroccan writer has always
expressed his deep concern with political developments in the Middle
East.

The narratives tend more toward the subjective, depicting the
main character as the individual in crisis and reflecting the "I" of the
intellectual himself, as El Oufi argued in a colloquium on the Arabic
short story held in Meknes after the Beirut crisis (72). Philosophically,
Marxism and existentialism remain great philosophical influences, to
which other literary movements were added like impressionism, the
nouveau roman, the modern novel, Kafkaism, stream of consciousness
and the theater of the absurd.

Therefore, aesthetically, the form of the short story has become
more sophisticated and refined. While the traditional structure and plot
are rejected, the emphasis is laid more on the process of telling, the
attempt to catch the moment and the disruption of chronological time.

The list of the writers who represent this period is long, of whom
I mention only a few: Mohamed Choukri, Mubarak Dribi, Ahmed
Bouzeffour, Miloudi Cheghmoum, Mohamed Daghmoumi, Mohamed
Azzedine Tazi, Ahmed El Madini, Bachir Jamkar, Mohamed El Harradi,
Bouchta Hadi, Mohamed Gharnat, Mustapha El Mesnaoui, Hassan
Bakkali, Mohamed El Mezdioui, Jamal Boutayeb and Abderrahmane
Mouedden.

Mohamed Choukri's "Forbidden to Talk About Flies" is written
in the interior monologue mode, and therefore the main emphasis is on
the individual character. The first person narrator reveals his present

situation in terms of the fantastic mode of narration, very similar to Kafka. The narrator is condemned to death for writing an article about flies while he wrote about begging. Wherever he goes he feels persecuted and haunted by injustice, and so his life becomes a long nightmare. In fact he is a dead man who returns to this world to tell us about the last moments of his life. The style is economical and the narrative technique depends on a series of associations. Indeed, Choukri's story demonstrates how the Moroccan short story has become refined and sophisticated, making use of new narrative strategies. The following quotation is representative of the story as a whole:

> On the wall at the entrance of the lane was posted a large photograph. It looked like the photograph of an artist as usual: an actor or a singer. Oh, no! What's that? Why, it's my own photograph! That far! The photograph was becoming clearer and clearer. I didn't know how this photograph was taken of me with such clarity and precision, and without my knowing Amarush Tamsamani. Forbidden to deal with this person under any circumstance. Anyone who disobeys this warning shall be punished according to the law issued in this matter. (My translation)

Broadly speaking, the Moroccan short story has known a great evolution in both vision and techniques since its beginning in the early forties. It has shifted its focus from external reality to internal reality, from the object to the subject, and from a general perspective, to a specific one (El Oufi 73). In structure it has been moving from the traditional harmony, or the Aristotelian plot, to the apparent disruption and disharmony.

Today, the Moroccan short story still plays an effective role in both society and literature. Thanks to its condensed form and brevity, it has been able not only to survive but also to challenge the increasing invasion of the mass media, especially audio-visual. Given its flexible nature, it has undergone significant changes in style and form. Although its aesthetic structure is deeply rooted in its Arabic and oral traditions, it has always been open to modern and contemporary innovations in the

West and East. As far as its themes are concerned, and despite its increasing tendency towards the subject, it has remained in close contact with the contemporary social background of its Moroccan context. It has certainly benefitted a great deal from the artistic achievements of the short story in the Eastern and Western worlds, but it has never lost its local flavor, making use of its setting, legends, folk tales and proverbs. Hence, the Moroccan short story writer has never severed his ties with his national and cultural heritage, always preserving his originality, authenticity and identity. The convergence of Eastern and Western cultures in Morocco can only make its literature richer, more varied and colorful, and less shut upon itself. In brief, like other short stories in the world, the Moroccan short story has proved an effective art from, dynamic and ever changing itself to keep pace with the changes of human society.

Notes

1. For information on Moroccan writers in French I am grateful to Dr. Abderrahmane Tanekkoul of the Department of French, Fès.
2. I am thankful to both Dr. Limami and Dr. Bonou of the Department of Spanish, Fès.
3. This division is suggested by Professors Mohamed Serghini and Hassan Lamnii.

Works Cited

Akbib, Abdellatif. *Between the Lines*. Tanger: Slaiki Brothers, 1998.

____. *Graffiti*. Tanger: Slaiki Brothers, 1997.

Akkar, Abdelhamid. "On the Short Story." *Al-Alam Athaqafi* 882 (16 July 1988): 6.

Allen, Roger. "Morocco: A Powerhouse of Arabic Fiction." *Newsletter of the Moroccan-American Commission for Educational and Cultural Exchange* (2000): 8.

An-Nassaj, Sayed Hamid. *The Short Story*. Cairo: Dar Al-Maarif, 1977.

Berrada, Mohamed. *The Language of Childhood and Dreams*. Rabat: The Moroccan Society of United Publishers, 1986.

El Koudia, Jilali, ed. *Moroccan Short Stories*. Fes: I'Media, 1998.

____. *Stories Under the Sun.* Fes: I'Media, 1999.

El Oufi, Najib. *Studies in Arabic Stories.* Beirut: The Institution of Arab Research Publishers, 1987.

Johnson-Davies, Denys, ed. and trans. *Arabic Short Stories.* London: Quartet Books, 1983.

Layachi, Larbi [Driss ben Hamed Charhadi]. *A Life Full of Holes.* Trans. Paul Bowles. New York Grove Press, 1982.

____. *Yesterday and Today.* Santa Barbara, CA: Black Sparrow Press, 1985.

Literatura y pensamiento marroquíes contemporáneos. Madrid: Instituto Hispano-Arabe de Cultura, 1981.

Maier, John. *Desert Songs: Western Images of Morocco and Moroccan Images of the West.* Albany: State University of New York Press, 1996.

Mouedden, Abderrahime. "The Moroccan Short Story." *Al-Alam Athaqafi* 882 (16 July 1988): 6.

Williams, Malcolm and Gavin Watterson, eds. and trans. *An Anthology of Moroccan Short Stories.* Tangier: King Fahd School of Translation, 1995.

Seeing Things:
"Magic Realism" from Tutuola to Okri

Donald Hoffman

Tutuola and Okri are both visual as well as visionary artists. In their varied visions, they see things differently from each other and from what most of us are accustomed to see in ordinary life. While the magic and the realism of their visions bear a similarity to the work of Garcia Marquez and other Latin American writers whose work defines the genre of magic realism, there are differences as well, differences that may sometimes be underestimated through a too easy association of the African with the Latin American writers. While some critics are happy with the term (such as Brenda Cooper in her recent study, *Magical Realism in West African Fiction: Seeing with a Third Eye*), others, such as Robert Elliott Fox argue strongly that the term "is misapplied to African literature – whether it's Tutuola's work or the *abiku* novels of Ben Okri" (206), and he suggests that the novels present "the magic of a *different* realism" (206). That difference lies (in part, at least) in modes of seeing and the nature of what is seen. Even when the Nigerian and the Colombian writers look at a forest, for example, they do not see the same forest, nor do they see the same things in it.

In *The Palm-Wine Drinkard* and his other works, Amos Tutuola virtually invents the African novel in English and an African English suitable for telling narrative which brilliantly combines traditional folklore and myth with wildly imaginative, terrifying, and original comic visions. The very first paragraph of *The Palm-Wine Drinkard* introduces the reader to the ten-year old hero of the novel, who has already adopted his profession, palm-wine drinking. He will soon embark on a quest to find his dead palm-wine tapster, but his quest is located in a specifically defined past with a concomitant sense of loss: "In those days we did not know other money, except COWRIES, so that everything was very cheap, and my father was the richest man in town" (7). It is, however, the spirit quest rather than the cultural context that Tutuola takes pains to root in the real by means of a numerical accuracy that both amazes and authenticates. The numbers are impossible (or perhaps irrelevant) and, therefore, comic; on the other hand, there is a kind of solid, undeniable reality to the precision of numbers that authenticates the drinkard's quest.

> [The farm] was nine miles square and it contained 560,000 palm trees, and this palm-wine tapster was tapping one hundred and fifty kegs of palm-wine every morning, but before 2 o'clock p.m., I would have drunk all of it; after that he would go and tap another 75 kegs in the evening which I would be drinking till morning. (7)

This wildness of the authenticating number grows more comical and more serious, when, after the palm-wine tapster, fifteen years later, falls from a tree and dies, and the hero begins his journey from this world to the next.

Numbers proliferate in the journey to the Dead's Town and beyond. There are, for example, precisely 50 holes in the bodies of the animals pecked by the monstrous birds in the forest just past the "greedy Bush;" there are 30 horns on the frightening huge red fish, and exactly 400 dead babies "singing the song of mourning and marching to Deads' Town at about two o'clock in the midnight" (102). The white tree that encloses the "Faithful Mother in the White Tree" is "about one thousand and fifty feet in length and about two hundred feet in diameter" (65), and houses, among other things, a technicolor dance hall in which 300 people are dancing. More eerily, the narrator has time to measure the bag 150 feet in diameter that can hold 45 persons (and, as we later learn, nine monsters) carried off by the cannibal fisherman.

In addition to this counting, Tutuola grounds his narrative in time, space, and economics. Bizarre as the adventures may be, they occur at precise times. For example, it is at 4:00 in the evening on the fifth day that the headman's daughter meets the Complete Gentleman at the market. Later, when he wishes to escape from the bush, which was very dangerous, "because of the wild animals, and the boa constrictors were uncountable as sand" (40), he turns himself into a big bird and flies for exactly five hours before he lands at 4:00 and treks until 8:00 when he reaches the town where his tapster was. There is, similarly, a random, if precise, indication of distances. It is, for example, forty miles from the town he reaches at 8:00 to the bush he enters on his continuing quest for the tapster.

Above all, however, Tutuola seems obsessed with monetary precision. Even in the course of his fantastic journey everything seems to have its price. The Complete Gentleman, for example, is so beautiful that "if he had been an article or an animal for sale, he would be sold at least for £2000 (two thousand pounds)" (18); when he changes himself into a canoe, so his wife can earn money by paddling travelers across the river on his back, "the fare for adults was 3d (three pence) and half fare for children" (39), and on the first day they earn £7: 5: 3d (39), mounting up to £56: 11: 9d for the first month (40); when they enter the White Tree, they sell their death to somebody at the door for £70: 18: 6d, and their fear at an interest rate of £3: 10: 0 (67); and, as a final example, when he meets the poor man who wants to understand POOR, "he said that he wanted to borrow two thousand cowries (COWRIES), which was equivalent to six-pence (6d) in British money" (86).

As Michael Thelwell suggests in his introduction to the novel, this difference in accounting points to the transition from a traditional to a colonial economy. While the cowries point to an earlier form of exchange and the two thousand implies wealth and opulence, the translation into 6d suggests the creation of a new system of poverty imposed by the alien, colonial culture. The difference between 6d and 2000 cowries is not merely a difference in quantity but a difference in quality, reflecting the forced transition to a colonial culture. This devaluation is something Tutuola rages against in the "Africanism" of his text, although his systems of measuring, counting, and timing lend an implicit priority to the alien culture. Later in life, Tutuola himself had second thoughts about these calculations, pointing out that "Africans had their own concept of time before the Europeans came" (qtd. in Fox 205). It goes (almost) without saying that Africans also had their own economy, before pence replaced cowries.

Whatever conclusions may be drawn from this specificity, it is clear that the effect of these calculations is to ground the "magic" in the "real." But it is the "magic" that reflects the real genius of Tutuola as we move from counting things to seeing things. No one sees monsters with such visual specificity or such infinite variety as Tutuola. There is, for example, the amazing red fish, whose 30 horns we have already noted.

> As a matter of fact, when I saw this red fish, I was greatly terrified. [. . .] At the same time that the red fish appeared out, its head was just like a tortoise's head, but it was as big as an elephant's head and it had over 30 horns and large eyes which surrounded the head. All these horns were spread out as an umbrella. It could not walk but was only gliding on the ground like a snake and its body was just like a bat's body and covered with long red hair like strings. It could only fly to a short distance, and if it shouted a person who was four miles away would hear. All the eyes which surrounded its head were closing and opening at the same time as if a man was pressing a switch on and off. (79-80)

Such a monster is in fact a relatively simple accumulation of parts, a cut-and-paste job on more or less familiar creatures, a process no more complicated, although carried on with several more additions, than that which constructs a mermaid out of a fish and a woman. Tutuola, however, animates the monster, and, even more remarkably, makes it contemporary. In addition to the tortoise and elephant, the snake and the bat, its horns spread out like an umbrella and all its eyes open and close like a switch. The monster, then, is not only a conjunction of disparate animal parts, but a cultural grotesque as well. It is not a simple, ancient African monster, but one that incorporates objects introduced by the British; it not only straddles species, it straddles cultures and time. This monster reverses the impression of a cultural primacy bestowed on the Europeans, for if Tutuola allows Africa to be governed by English time, he turns the products of English culture into a complex and essentially African monster.

This cultural dissonance also deepens the effect of Tutuola's most disturbing grotesque, the drinkard's monstrous son, born at the age of ten from his wife's swollen thumb, and named ZURRJR, a name "which means a son who would change himself into another thing very soon" (32), and whom the village determines to destroy. Frighteningly, however, "the middle of the ashes rose up suddenly and at the same time there appeared a half-bodied baby, he was talking with a lower voice like a telephone" (35).

If the monster composed of umbrellas and switches is richly imaginative and visually exciting, the half-bodied baby with a voice like a telephone is one of the eeriest creatures in literature, as it combines the ghost with the machine in a not easily imaginable, but definitely disturbing way. Like the notorious Television-Handed Ghostess in *My Life in the Bush of Ghosts*, these striking creatures incarnate a culture clash. Tutuola has explained that the television-handed ghostess was created because he first saw television while he was writing that novel, but he has also recanted his creation, arguing that his reference to television, like his references to clocktime were mistakes (Fox 205). This recantation, however, occurred more than twenty years after the writing of the novels and at a very different moment in Nigerian history and a very different time for the author who had moved from being a very unhappy civil servant in "this unsatisfactory job which I am still carrying on at present" (Tutuola, "My Life and Activities" 130) to a distinguished visiting writer at the University of Ife in 1979-80. Tutuola's rejection of his earlier "collaborations" make sense for a writer who now has a sense of his own importance in a nation in the act of constructing itself. Luckily, however, his actual writing occurred at a time when he was not obliged to search for an African "purity" in his narrative and was content to achieve a far richer "authenticity." Rather than being pure, his fictions incorporate colonial innovations within African narrative structures and accomplish an act of appropriation. If occasional references seem to give a priority to colonial imports, like time and television, the structure enclosing them naturalizes and critiques them. Rather than searching for an irrecoverable purity, Tutuola (the artist rather than the critic) tells us what he sees, not what he imagines he was supposed to see. According to Fox, "as he is writing, he starts to get a picture in his mind which he then endeavors to describe" (205). These pictures, these things he sees, are the essence of his art. Significantly, he sees at a moment when two cultures conflict and, even his monsters, participate in this cultural clash, resulting in African monsters with television hands.

Finally, let us return to the Complete Gentleman who would have sold for £2000 had he been an animal or article. This beautiful Complete Gentleman has a secret: his beauty, indeed his entire body, is rented. He returns his left foot, his right foot, and crawls to where he must return his belly, ribs, and chest, then hops like a frog with his head and arms and neck, until he returns everything, including his skin and flesh, and he is reduced to a skull.

Thus, one of the things Tutuola sees is the instability of the body, a reflection of an inability to trust in a coherent body. In so far as the narrative of the Complete Gentleman tells a variant of the story of the recalcitrant maiden who rejects all suitors only to fall in love with the most unsuitable suitor of all, it participates in myth and folktale. It can, however, also be read as a kind of allegory with the £2000 Complete Gentleman an image of apparent colonial wholeness, who is deconstructed into his parts and his essential frightening emptiness. In this reading, the narrator becomes more a symbol of Africanness than he might appear, for it is he who, after revealing that his name means "Father of gods who could do anything in this world" and sacrifices a goat to his juju (25), defeats the Complete Gentleman and marries the haughty maiden.

This separability of body parts, which implies a lack of faith in the stability of the body, also permits the possibility of metamorphosis. The narrator himself is perhaps the most consistent shape-shifter in the narrative, changing himself into a canoe, as we have seen, but also into a "very big bird" (10) who flies to fetch the god's bell from the blacksmith; he changes into a lizard to follow the Skull that was once a Complete Gentleman; into a "big bird like an airplane" (40) to escape the Bush of Ghosts, and to escape from the "hungry creature"; he changes his wife and all his possessions into a wooden doll that he puts in his pocket (108) with unforeseen consequence, when the hungry creature swallows the doll. These metamorphoses and separable body parts imply a vision without boundaries. There seems to be no clear separation between forms and species, no clear boundary to the self. The most remarkable erasure, however, is the erasure of the boundary between the living and the dead.

At the market where we encounter the Complete Gentleman, we are told that "the whole people of that town and from all the villages around the town and also spirits and curious creatures from the various bushes and forests were coming to this market every 5th day to sell or buy articles" (17). Apparently, even spirits need to shop.

There is indeed a healthy quantity of both magic and realism in the work of Tutuola, but there is also a more particularly African quality, which resides essentially in the relation to the spirit world. While the novels of the Latin American authors are certainly haunted by spirits, they are the sprits of the familial dead and the ghosts of those who cleared the forest to build the towns. In Tutuola, it is the forest that seems to give birth to the spirits and they take on appearances that are not at all related to any human ancestor, but are probably derived from the *egungun*, the ritual masks of Yoruba tradition. Parallels can certainly be drawn between African and Latin American authors, but the formal similarities tend to efface the great difference in spirit, a difference that is essentially the difference between a Creole Catholicism and a more ancient system of Yoruba beliefs.

The differences are, perhaps, both subtler and clearer in the work of Ben Okri, a later and more sophisticated writer than Tutuola, as well as an exile from Nigeria. He is also admittedly influenced by Gabriel Garcia Marquez. Okri, nevertheless, despite the disadvantages of exile and education, shares Tutuola's vision of the spirit world.

It is fortuitous, but suggestive, that Tutuola's *Palm-Wine Drinkard* concludes with the end of a famine, while Ben Okri's *The Famished Road* begins with hunger:

> In the beginning there was a river. The river became a
> road and the road branched out to the whole world. And
> because the road was once a river it was always hungry.
> (3)

While hunger and famine may link the two authors, style points to their differences. There is a kind of intellectual striving for mythic effect in Okri that replaces the directness and immediacy of Tutuola's confident inventions. The difference in narrative voice also reflects the difference in the narrators. While Tutuola deals with a young man who determines to visit the land of the Deads to bring back his palm-wine-tapster, Okri's narrator is one of the dead, or, rather, one of the once-dead, for he is one of the *abiku*, "a child in an unending cycle of births, deaths and re-births" (Quayson 122). Thus, while Tutuola tells the story of a man journeying to the Deads, Okri tells of a once dead child's journey into life. Both narratives, however, clearly depend on a belief that the boundary between the living and the dead is a porous one.

When Okri's narrator describes the world before he is born, he may be drawing on Yoruba-inflected beliefs,[1] but he also seems to echo the visions of unborn baby worlds evoked by Western writers from Plato to Spenser.

> In the land of beginnings spirits mingled with the unborn. We could assume numerous forms. Many of us were birds. We knew no boundaries. There was feasting, playing, and sorrowing. We feasted much because of the beautiful terrors of eternity. We played much because we were free. And we sorrowed much because there were always those amongst us who had just returned from the world of the Living. (3)

Okri here shares with Tutuola an awareness of the lack of boundaries between sprits and the (un)born, and introduces the notion of shape-shifting and metamorphoses with a special fondness for birds. But there is a sense that Okri is as aware of Ovid as he is of Tutuola, and not unaware of Cicero in his carefully balanced sentences, "We feasted much...", "We played much...", "We sorrowed much..." The self-conscious artistry predominates in the conclusion of the introduction to the *abiku* world.

> There was not one amongst us who looked forward to being born. We disliked the rigours of existence, the unfulfilled longings, the enshrined injustices of the world, the labyrinths of love, the ignorance of parents, the fact of dying, and the amazing indifference of the Living in the midst of the simple beauties of the universe.

We feared the heartlessness of human beings, all of
whom are born blind, few of whom ever learn to see. (3)

This is by no means bad writing, but it is clearly "literate" writing,
writing that is aware of itself and of a tradition that is clearly Western; it
is writing schooled in Cicero and Garcia Marquez and others in-between.
The cultural conflict between "Africa" and English embedded in the
highly original and consciously constructed language of Amos Tutuola
has here been resolved with English as the undisputed victor.

By contrast, the victory granted to the language is qualified by the
narrative itself which is more overtly political than Tutuola's and deals
with the aftereffects of colonialism, the legacy left by the domination of
the "complete gentlemen" and their chronometric and economic systems.

The village into which Azaro, the *abiku* is born is dominated by
the forest on the edges and the bar in the center. The bar, owned by the
archetypal Mme. Koto, marks the changes from pre- to post-colonialism.
When Azaro first encounters Mme. Koto, she is both accommodating
and frightening, but keeping a negligently benign watch over Azaro.
There are, however, rumors about Mme. Koto.

They said of Madame Koto that she had buried three
husbands and seven children and that she was a witch
who ate her babies when they were still in her womb.
They said she was the real reason why the children in the
area didn't grow, why they were always ill, why the men
never got promotions, and why the women in the area
suffered miscarriages. They said she was a bewitcher of
husbands and a seducer of young boys and a poisoner of
children. They said she had a charmed beard and that she
plucked one hair out every day and dropped it into the
palm-wine she sold and into the peppersoup she made so
that the men would spend all their money in her bar and
not care about their starving families. They said she made
men go insane at night and that she belonged to a secret
society that flies about in the air when the moon is out.
(100-1)

These magical explanations for the effects of poverty on the village are the kind of ancient rumors that tend to surround powerful women, particularly those who do not settle in to the accepted roles of wife and mother. By being an entrepreneur, Mme. Koto automatically sets herself up as an object of jealousy and suspicion.

These ordinary rumors cross over into a nightmarish reality when Azaro's visions begin to accommodate a darker aspect of Mme. Koto's nature. Lost in a terrifying tempest, Azaro feels himself riding an invisible horse through a landscape of masked gold figures.

> The winds blew the army of statues one by one off their horses and they broke into golden fragments. Only Madame Koto, an implacable warrior, stayed on her horse and thudded after me. Just before she fell on me, it began to rain. The water, pouring down, gradually effaced her, beginning with her raised arm and her grim sword. Her arm dissolved into an indigo liquid and poured down her face; and her face dissolved slowly, as if the rain were an acid that ate away flesh and steel. Then her hair fell off and her head became reduced; and then her head rolled off into a ball of red waters and her shoulders melted and eventually her great massive bulk disappeared and all that remained were her two big fierce eyes which throbbed on the ground and stared at me. And then the horse neighed and lifted its front hooves in the air and turned and galloped away, bursting her two eyes with its hind feet. (139)

Okri here borrows from Tutuola a vision of the body reduced to a skull. In addition to the obvious, but interesting change of gender from the Complete Gentleman to the powerful woman, there is a great difference in tone and intent. In Tutuola, the narrative of the skull is grim, but grimly comic, and leads to the narrator's winning a wife. It is a tale, then, that demonstrates the heroism and power of the narrator. In Okri, on the other hand, in part because the narrator is a child, the narrator does not achieve power over the terrifying skull. He may escape, but he does not dominate.

Okri replaces Tutuola's comically direct style with a more ambiguous and sophisticated one. He seems more concerned than Tutuola to ground the magic in the real, so even his nightmarish vision has a certain plausibility. As the increasingly torrential rain blurs his vision and muddles outlines, what the boy sees could be explained as the effects of the rain on sight. As with Tutuola, the border between the real world and the spirit world is porous, but Okri is more concerned with expressing the ambiguity of that boundary. It is not simply that one can cross from one to the other, but that the moment of crossing is unclear and uncertain. We are not always sure when the "alives" are dealing with the "deads." With Okri, however, the theme of shape-shifting effects not only individuals, but society. The cultural conflict in Tutuola becomes explicit in Okri. The forest, the source of visions and the home of the *egungun* and other spirits, is cut down, and the old gods are displaced.

> All around, in the future present, a mirage of houses was
> being built, paths and roads crossed and surrounded the
> forest in tightening circles, unpainted churches and the
> whitewashed walls of mosques sprang up where the
> forest was thickest. . . . The world of trees and wild
> bushes was being thinned. I heard the ghostly wood-
> cutters axing down the titanic irokos, the giant baobabs,
> the rubber trees and obeches. (242)

It is difficult in this case to distinguish metamorphosis from simple destruction. An ecological massacre occurs as the churches and mosques are raised, and the spirits are deprived of a habitation.

A similar sort of transformation effects Mme. Koto, who acquires wealth and the sort of respectability that it brings, even though her wealth is derived from providing prostitutes to the members of the Party of the Rich. Acquiring economic power, Mme. Koto no longer needs the power of the witch and begins her transformation from archetype to entrepreneur. Significantly, her economic transformation is pictured primarily in terms of the redefinition of the road made possible by the construction workers who had destroyed the forest. The road now enables Mme. Koto to (more or less) drive her brand new automobile:

> it most certainly was news for a woman in the area to
> own a car.... We still clung to our disbelief even when
> we saw her hopeless attempts at driving it, which resulted
> in running over an old woman's stall. She promptly had
> the stall rebuilt and gave the woman more money than
> she had possessed in the first place. We watched her
> learning to drive the car. She was much too massive for
> such a small vehicle and at the steering wheel she looked
> as if the car was her shell and she merely the third eye of
> the tortoise. (378)

To a great extent, Mme. Koto is more dangerous as a driver than she was
as a witch. But despite her wealth and power, there is, nevertheless, a
sense of loss here, too. The massiveness of Mme. Koto, which suggests
her archetypal amplitude, is uncomfortably squeezed into the confines of
the foreign car. While she is increasing in the sort of powers granted by
collaboration with the heirs of the colonials, she has also collaborated
with the loss of the power that resided in her own massive, mythic body.
Her collaboration with the Party of the Rich, then, both enriches and
diminishes her.

    An equally dramatic metamorphosis occurs in the character of the
father. Dad, somewhat like Achebe's Okonkwo, but in a period when the
battle with colonialism has already been lost, represents traditional values,
possesses the heart of a warrior, but lives in circumstances that only
rarely allow him to demonstrate these qualities. His first moment of
something like grandeur occurs when he appears in Azaro's spirit vision
cum feverish delusion (a consequence of the rain storm and its visions)
and also after Dad has severed his relationship with Madame Koto. The
roads that are destroying the forest are re-visioned as roads connecting
earth to heaven, connecting, in Tutuola's words, the Alives and the
Deads. At the end of his feverish vision, Azaro sees his father as shaman
and healer fighting heroically with a murderous old spirit woman.

> I saw Dad tower over me, a white hen in one hand, a
> knife of menacing sharpness in the other.... Dad held
> the white hen firmly, wings and feet and head. Blood
> dripped down his arms. There was another figure in the

room, whose shadow expanded the spaces, filled it with
the aroma of wild village shrines, and the solemnity of
rock-faced priests. He danced about the room with a
mighty fan of eagle feathers that threatened to set the
room into flight. His dancing, fervent and insane, with
red amulets and cowries cackling round his neck, became
the whirling torment of the twice-beheaded spirit. (339)

Dad's heroic fight with the spirit continues until it "saw itself separated
from its body, and let out its final scream of horror, cracking the surface
of the river" (339). In this vision of the father, Azaro sees him as
exercising power and performing rituals that are now practiced more
rarely and more privately. It is a moment in which the old ways live again
and prove their efficacy. And it is a moment in which Dad transforms
himself from the somewhat ineffectual man beaten down by the travails
of poverty to a heroic figure able to fight the spirits to save his son.

Dad later fights another significant battle when as Black Tiger he
fights as the champion of the people against Green Leopard, the
champion of Mme. Koto and the Party of the Rich. His great struggle in
this battle leads, however, to Dad's final metamorphosis into a prophetic
madman. Deciding that he himself shall become Head of State, he
becomes increasingly delusional, but at the same time, increasingly
utopian in his vision of the possible, and, in his last vision, increasingly
perceptive in analyzing the corruption of the postcolonial state.

Dad was redreaming the world as he slept. He saw the
scheme of things and didn't like it. He saw the world in
which black people always suffered and he didn't like it.
He saw a world in which human beings suffered so
needlessly from Antipodes to Equator and he didn't like
it either. . . . He saw the divisions in our society, the
lack of unity, he saw the widening pit between those
who have and those who don't, he saw it all very clearly.
(492)

Dad sees a great deal more with equal clarity in the final painful
and prophetic pages of *The Famished Road*, which concludes with the

poignant gnomic utterance, "A dream can be the highest point of a life" (500).

It is as instructive to compare the endings of the two novels, as it was to contrast their beginnings. While Tutuola seems to spend all his time in a dream world of amazing monsters and remarkable feats, the ultimate effect is to accomplish sacrifice and perform the rituals that remove hunger from the world. In other words, detached and fanciful as it seems its intent, which is always the intent of magic, is to affect reality. In contrast, Okri, who seems far more engaged with the politics of contemporary Nigeria, concludes by escaping from the real into a dream world, Dad's powerful visions having a profound rhetorical effect, but changing nothing.

It may seem then that Tutuola and Okri not only see things differently but see different things. The kind of "primary process" immediacy of the spirits and monsters and Television-Handed ghostesses in Tutuola are absent from the more surrealist, literary visions of Okri's *abiku*. Nevertheless, they seem to have more in common with each other than either does with the "magic realists" of Latin America. They do not share the Creole-inflected Catholicism and fatalism of the Western authors. Rather, they live in a world inhabited by spirits and surrounded by a forest, not always benign, but remarkably powerful. And both seem to accept the reality of dream visions, spirit journeys, and shaman visits to the land of the dead. While the Latin authors are full of wonders and frequent hauntings, Tutuola and Okri share a particular awareness of the unreliability of bodies and the fragility of the border between the living and the dead. What we believe is real is very often seen to be merely a transparent cloak veiling the truly real, the magic which informs and gives meaning to the amorphous mass of disconnected incidents we call reality. Tutuola and Okri see monsters and visions and make us see these things, too. As they change our ways of seeing, they shift our perceptions and our construction of the real, so that we learn to see magically. They teach us to see things. And show us how to see things differently.

Note

1. I use this awkward phrase to indicate Quayson's argument that, while Okri is not Yoruba (his parents were Urhobo), his work, nevertheless,

"articulates the same conceptual resource-base," and "aspects of what might be seen as a Yoruba belief system" (Quayson 101).

Works Cited

Cooper, Brenda. *Magical Realism in West African Fiction: Seeing with a Third Eye*. New York: Routledge, 1998.

Fox, Robert Elliot. "Tutuola and the Commitment to Tradition." *Research in African Literatures* 29.3 (Fall 1998): 202-8.

Okri, Ben. *The Famished Road*. New York: Doubleday, 1991.

Quayson, Ato. *Strategic Transformations in Nigerian Writing: Orality and History in the Work of Rev. Samuel Johnson, Amos Tutuola, Wole Soyinka & Ben Okri*. Bloomington: Indiana University Press, 1997.

Tutuola, Amos. *The Palm-Wine Drinkard and His Dead Palm-Wine Tapster in the Dead's Town*. New York: Grove, 1953.

____. "My Life and Activities." *The Palm-Wine Drinkard and His Dead Palm-Wine Tapster in the Dead's Town*. New York: Grove, 1953. 126-30.

____. *My Life in the Bush of Ghosts*. New York: Grove, 1954.

Oral Tradition and Cinematic Point of View in *Fary l'Anesse*

Suzanne H. MacRae

The broad and deep debt African literature owes to African oral traditions is well documented by distinguished critics such as Isidore Okpewho. African film scholars such as Frank Ukadike (cf. esp. ch. 4) and Manthia Diawara (1988) likewise acknowledge African cinema's similar obligation, incorporating oral ingredients such as ceremonial ritual, music, dance, proverbs, and aphorisms. African films also draw on the resources of traditional, authoritative adult tale tellers—whether *griots* or grandmothers—and their malleable themes, supple narrative techniques, and penchant for satire with a didactic pulse. Films such as Ababakar Samb-Makharam's *Jom* (Senegal 1981) and Jean-Pierre Bekolo's *Quartier Mozart* (Cameroon 1992) invest the *griot*'s role in an on-screen or voice-over narrator. Filmmakers such as Sembène exemplify the director himself as *griot* (Diawara, 1987; Pfaff). Some deem the camera a silent *griot* (Diawara, 1988). A few critics have scrutinized in detail the use of oral tradition in a specific film such as *Wend Kuuni* (Diawara, 1987).

Yet one essential aspect of orality in cinema has received less attention than it deserves—the complex point of view created by the intersection of diverse perspectives: (1) the words of a narrative or choric voice; (2) the imagery of the camera; and (3) the aural images of the soundtrack. This meld distinguishes film from written and orally performed literature and creates both challenges and opportunities for filmmakers in that the surreal power of the visual and aural images can subvert or overwhelm both dialogue and narration. Director Mansour Sora Wade has worked for the Senegalese Ministry of Culture to preserve and revitalize oral traditions, and his short 1990 film *Fary l'Anesse* ("Fary the Donkey") offers an excellent test case to explore the artistic and social implications of adapting traditional storytelling materials and techniques into cinema. Despite its brevity—17 minutes—this rich, subtle fable incorporates ceremonial song and dance, folklore, moral edification, choric commentators, and voice-over narration. Its cinematography is compelling and thematic. However, the narration and visual images express divergent points of view and produce multiple, perhaps even contradictory, moral interpretations. The verbal perspective concentrates on a conventional rebuke of the male protagonist's vanity and obsession; the images center on the plight of a beautiful woman victimized by her husband and an entire village.

The kernel story of *Fary* is clearly related to an African folktale "Fari the She-Ass" well known from the version in Birago Diop's *Tales of Amadou Koumba* although the differences between the two tales are more significant than the similarities. The film dramatizes the story of a farmer named Ibra Serigne, who rejects all the attractive, eligible women in his village, insisting that his wife must be absolutely beautiful without flaw. Even a tiny scar on one woman's breast disqualifies her. When a strange, unimpeachably lovely young woman, Fary, walks into the village from out of nowhere, Ibra immediately marries her even though no one knows who she is or where she came from. Her perfect behavior—gentle spirit, sexual tenderness, hard work, and submissiveness—fulfills Ibra's desire beyond his dream of physical perfection. Yet Ibra's marital paradise shatters when he confirms the truth of the mocking rumor spread by the village Moor that Fary turns herself into a donkey. Ibra then humiliates his wife and viciously drives her, in donkey, form away from his household.

The explicit moral drawn from this tale is directed toward Ibra's pride and presumption and emanates from dual sources: two village women and the male narrator. The women, Yama and her friend, form a dramatic chorus to articulate community values and village consensus. They are mortified by Ibra's disdain for the local women no matter how lovely and worthy. These two women themselves entertained hope of becoming Ibra's bride but were rejected. Their insult is aggravated by Ibra's total violation of traditional propriety in marrying Fary without knowing anything of her family, background, character, or identity. Fary is a stranger who suddenly appears with only her beauty and the clothing she wears. Her arrival seems uncanny in its timing—immediately after Ibra has rejected the last local candidate. Furthermore, the marriage is not properly brokered, there is no courtship period, and no dory is given. Wade cuts directly from a shot of Fary entering the village to shots of the wedding.

The women pity Ibra's female cousin, Diatou, who has exhausted herself trying to find the proper match for him, only to have all her efforts insultingly rebuffed. Diatou now must undeservedly share the shame her cousin has reaped from his hasty, ill-advised marriage. They fear that the family may disintegrate as a result of the ignominy.

Yama and her friend speculate on the causes of Ibra's folly: is he impotent, crazy, or "just no good?" They expect only trouble from this marriage and intend to "wait to see his child"—the acid test for an African marriage. Later, when the truth about Fary's donkey self becomes known, the two women confound surprise with righteous indignation and a dash of "I told you so."

Although Yama seems at first to be a cultural touchstone whose moral and social judgment is dependable, she is still biased against Fary for having defeated her in the bridal contest. And at the conclusion of the film she reveals the limits of her ethical perception as she sums up the lesson learned:

> Nowadays, men are strange. By blindness they look for
> the impossible, and they fall on disaster and shame.
> Nobody knows how to behave with a woman who's a
> donkey.

She analyzes Ibra's mistakes as reflections of distinctively contemporary male problems—misguided idealism and failure of rational judgment rather than a vicious character flaw for which he is personally responsible. She also considers that he might be a hapless victim of a malevolent shapeshifter.

The unseen male whose voice-over punctuates the film from time to time executes the role of *griot*-storyteller whose perspective on Ibra's behavior is more detached and less harsh than the views of the village women. Removed in time from the events of the story, he invokes the ancient formula "once upon a time" and narrates in the past tense. Yet at times he becomes emotionally involved with his characters and shifts to the present and the present progressive tenses. Such grammar implies that he along with the film audience is watching the actions unfold in real time. Then during less volatile sequences the storyteller returns to the past tense, reiterating the chronological and emotional distance he first used.

Like an actual storyteller, the narrator also poses rhetorical questions to engage his audience in active thought about the story and to step back from personal judgment on a sensitive issue. At a crucial juncture, when a lecherous villager discovers Fary changing into a donkey, he asks, "What did the Moor see that day?" as if his vision, like that of the viewer, were blocked from seeing Fary's actual metamorphosis taking place behind a large baobab tree. Fary's exclamation indicates that she is being transformed. But there is no "ocular proof," only a juxtaposed full body shot of a white donkey prancing and braying. But, cinematically, the audience believes the Moor's testimony that this is Fary's equine self.

Finally, the narrator pronounces literally the last word of the film in moral summation, expressing a muted, gentler judgment against Ibra than the village women have articulated:

> The man who falls in love with beauty forgets that in woman there are so many other qualities. Since Fary the donkey has time changed?

Here the narrator combines a generic and hypothetical expression, "the man who," with the universal, timeless present tense of an aphorism. Ibra has been replaced by men in general, and the rhetorical question challenges the audience to consider likely parallels throughout history into contemporary life. "Once upon a time" has become "now." Ibra's case rises to generalized sociology, thereby lessening Ibra's personal guilt.

This final, synoptic comment softens earlier criticism of Ibra by charging him only with being so overwhelmed by the natural, forgivable male tendency to pursue beauty—the touchstone of Platonic eroticism—that he loses rational perspective. He has merely "forgotten" his earlier knowledge, another Platonic axiom characterizing all reincarnated souls. The narrator does not condemn Ibra's quest for a mate of supreme beauty but merely denies it dominance in sexual and matrimonial choice. Ibra is not exonerated but is guilty merely of being a man.

But Wade's cinematography—both visual and aural imagery—drives the film in another direction, seducing the viewers through surrealistic persuasion to accept a competing interpretation of the film rather than the conventional, rational moral. Wade undermines and deflects the verbally explicit moral. His cinematic point of view condemns Ibra more strongly than either the village women or the narrator and transposes the charge of obsessive vanity and folly to the more reprehensible crime of selfish, merciless cruelty to innocent women—the beautiful and worthy nubile women Ibra rejects, his long-suffering and diligent cousin Diatou, and, most importantly, Fary, who replaces Ibra as the emotional center of the film.

Many factors elicit viewers' sympathy for Fary. They approve her natural grace and beauty and simple yet elegant dress and coiffure with just the proper addition of jewelry. Fary walks with modesty yet confidence, and her marital behavior is exemplary, at least judged by the criterion of service to her husband. Fary's sweetness, sexual tenderness, hard work, and gracious submission fulfill Ibra's fairy tale dream far beyond mere physical beauty. Like a gift of Fate or grace Fary appears precisely when Ibra has exhausted the local candidates for his bride.

Almost all the shots involving Fary show her performing domestic duties as lover, cook, and the bearer of Ibra's food to the fields who pours cool water over his hands to cleanse them. Her body postures convey subjection: her head is slightly lowered and she crouches or kneels when dealing with Ibra. After she rises from her boiling stew to greet her returning husband as "darling," she bows to him even when he violates basic courtesy and refuses to speak to her or acknowledge her presence.

The exceptions to such domestic scenes occur when she walks alone in the bush near a group of grazing donkeys. On these occasions when she can be her natural self, uncontrolled by Ibra or domestic expectations, she is transformed into a donkey. The film implies that she is unable to control her metamorphosis: "My God, I can't resist," she wails at the first shapeshifting. We assume that her maintenance of human form most of the time derives from strong self-control. In addition, her transformations coincide with perverse male behavior directed toward her. In the first incident a womanizing and rumor-mongering Moor pursues her for sexual conquest, but after spying on her metamorphosis he literally runs to spread the gossip to the village, triggering tragic results. The other instances derive from Ibra's suspicion and then persecution of his wife. Informed of the gossip, Ibra assumes it is true without proof, and that night, without explanation, he coldly rebuffs Fary's affectionate overtures in bed, shoving away her caressing hand.   In order to catch her while changing form, Ibra spies on her from behind a tree, mimicking the Moor's behavior at the same location. The viewers see nothing happening behind the baobab, only Ibra's astonishment as he watches. He becomes, instantly, totally estranged from Fary and never solicits any explanation from her. Her final transformation occurs when Ibra comes home that night after spying on her; he refuses to recognize Fary or respond to her affectionate greeting. Instead he sings a mocking song to humiliate her: "Fary is not a woman; she is a donkey. She is trotting, trotting." Fary weeps and pleads on her knees for him to cease singing.

When Ibra persists, Fary sprouts large white, donkey ears—the first time the camera has actually shown Fary's transformation happening. The visual imagery manipulates audience's pity for Fary. The camera switches back and forth between Ibra and Fary with close-up shots of their heads. His face distorts with anger and vengeance; her face and especially her large, luminous eyes ironically appear even softer, more radiant and compelling when framed with donkey ears. Her expression is plaintive. The darkness of the room dramatizes Fary's face, which seems itself to be the source of light. The setting in the couple's bedroom renders the betrayal of love even more heartbreaking. The next shot shows Ibra, in merciless rage, shouting and waving his arms, violently driving a white donkey from his hut and yard until it disappears in the night.

The satiric song Ibra sings occurred earlier as a non-diegetic sound track for the scene where Ibra spies on Fary. Chanted by a group of women, the song mocks Fary, expressing the village's scorn and attempting to ritually exorcise this alien being from the community. It counterpoints the earlier ritual praise sung by the village women to accompany Fary's wedding procession. Heretofore, communal derision has been directed at Ibra for his so called "perfect marriage." Now Ibra employs the ceremonial chant as a weapon to humiliate, convict, and expunge Fary from his life. His former "love" for her is now exposed as selfish exploitation. In further irony the song itself is what effects Fary's transformation, a self-fulfilling indictment, and confirms her lack of control over the metamorphosis.

Ibra's cruelty is particularly shocking because Fary came to the village in response to his desire for a perfect wife. Without realizing it he really needs Fary less as a beautiful woman than as a virtual donkey, the staple African beast of burden and strong but submissive servant. The concept of woman as "donkey" is a motif throughout the film. A shot from an early scene subtly associates Yama and her friend with donkeys: they sit in the foreground preparing grain while a quiet donkey stands in the background behind the women, who frame it like bookends. This image implies that they, too, are society's asses. With one exception, all the shots of the village women (including Diatou) display women working at physical labor to process, cook, and carry food; draw water; and prepare skins or else performing the social function of marriage broker. In contrast, there is but one brief shot of a male at work, Ibra raking his fields.

Wade also creates sympathy for Fary through her disreputable persecutors. In addition to his status as an ethnic alien no more than tolerated in the village, the Moor is an idle, lecherous voyeur and scandalmonger. His credibility and integrity are questionable. When the Moor runs to tell the first villager he meets about Fary's donkey nature, the man refuses to believe the "crazy" tale, retorting that the Moor clearly deserves his bad reputation, "You're not a Moor for nothing." Ironically, almost comically, this man himself is riding a donkey.

Ibra also, from the first scene of the film, merits no sympathy from the audience. He violates the code of African courtesy and protocol when a young woman is presented to him as a possible bride—a serious breach of the African social etiquette requiring elaborate rituals of greeting. Ibra does not speak to the young woman but only surveys her elegant face, hair, and garments as a customer might examine appealing merchandise. The camera shoots from behind Ibra, who sits in his formal, carved-back chair like a chief in judgment, thus conveying the action from his point of view. But Ibra's behavior voids any genuine moral and social authority. When Ibra's cousin and marriage broker, Diatou, tells him the candidate has a tiny scar on one breast, he refuses to look at the young woman again; she is nullified before she has a chance. We don't even know her name. Ibra leaps from his chair, shakes his finger in Diatou's face to berate her malfeasance in submitting a flawed candidate. He stalks away, insulting both family and prospective wife. Therefore, his later brutal treatment of Fary, who has given only good to him, is no surprise. Ibra's egotism judges himself as victim of others' dereliction or betrayal. The contrast between Wade's version of the story and the folktale as told by Birago Diop in *The Tales of Amadou Koumba* reveals that Wade fundamentally alters the traditional narrative and generates a new interpretation with a strong feminist slant and a fierce indictment of both Ibra and by metaphorical extension African male dominance in general. Koumba's version displays none of these themes.

Koumba's story rebukes Diop's pity for the dead bodies of worn out pack of asses by telling an explanation story (one of the major types of oral narrative) which blames the asses themselves for losing their original Edenic freedom and becoming "slaves of slaves" subject to hard labor, beatings, and general abuse from humans. Fari, Queen of the asses, leads her court ladies away from drought and famine for the more prosperous land of humans. Her strategy for acceptance in this desirable country is to transform to human women, since human males are reluctant to beat women or deny them anything. (Remember that this is a fable.) Fari's beauty leads King Bour to make her his favorite wife and her ladies royal attendants. Despite their luxurious court existence the asses pine for the pleasures of asinine life such as braying, farting, rolling on the ground, and kicking. So they journey to a lake each day at sunset and chant a song similar to one used in the film:

> Fari! hee haw!
> Fari! hee haw!
> Fari is a she-ass.

> Where is Fari the Queen of the asses
> Who left her land and never returned?

As this song triggers their transformation, they frolic in asinine style. A gossipy and loose-tongued Moor (an alien Muslim) tells the king about the donkey-ladies and plots to prove his story by coaching the *griot* to sing their song when the Queen and King share an affectionate moment. Fari begs the griot to stop singing what she calls a funeral song, but she and her ladies metamorphose and are quickly beaten and hobbled. A similar fate traps a search party of asses seeking their lost queen. Thus the destiny of all asses ever since has become harsh labor and subjection to the cruel whims of human masters.

Koumba tarnishes the character of the donkey-women and condemns them and all their descendants without pity, as deserving their enslavement. He fails to credit the fact that the asses acted to save their lives, showed ingenious enterprise, and harmed no one with their donkey games. His counterparts to the film villains are considered good or at least not seriously flawed. The King is a decent man who marries with good intent and at first is a loving husband. This Moor seems faulted more for being Muslim, heir to the imposed, alien religion, than for his talebearing.

Wade takes an adversarial stance toward the moral dynamic of the traditional story. He creates shameful, discredited men who "pile on" to persecute Fary. The behavior of Ibra and the Moor is contemptible. He also elicits sympathy for Fary through her virtuous conduct and modesty. Her attempts to serve Ibra and fit into the community are rewarded only with suspicion, scorn, and abuse. Chosen by Ibra solely for her physical appearance, Fary incarnates the concept of external beauty, yet her genuine loveliness derives from her gentle, loving spirit. Even her donkey self is appealing in its exuberant, natural freedom within a community of her peers. Her metaphorical donkey nature is also positive as she cheerfully performs domestic duties.

Wade intensifies Fary's power through further paradox; he both humanizes and mythologizes her. She is not queen of a donkey constituency whose plot function is merely to rationalize the ruin of a whole class of animals. Rather Fary is a complex individual—a modest, gentle young woman of indescribable beauty and sartorial elegance whose mission is to satisfy Ibra's desire. She attempts to avoid transformation but is overpowered by an inner nature. She strives to maintain privacy for that secret self while seeming to need the natural freedom and happiness it affords and which marriage does not allow.

Yet Fary also radiates something beyond a personal, psychological appeal. She radiates a numinous presence demonstrated in haunting visualizations: first, her sudden appearance walking with deliberate purpose on the shore into the village, born seemingly spontaneously and full grown from the sea, a kind of African Aphrodite; second in the dramatic image of her head sprouting large white donkey ears as Ibra humiliates and torments her.

Another mythic resonance derives from a gender role reversal of the Cupid-Psyche myth. Fary represents Cupid, the power of love itself under a powerful spell; Ibra fills the role of Psyche as violator of privacy, trespasser of taboo, and possessive destroyer of love.

Fary also resembles both Beauty and the Beast of Grimm's fairy tale. Perhaps she is a spell-bound being who can be released from her animal self only when she finds acceptance in love without question. Like Beauty she loves dutifully and completely a truly bestial husband who, unlike Beast, under human guise hides behavior worse than any animal's.

If we consider an alternative view of Fary's nature—a particularly African interpretation—we could see Fary as a *djinn*, a powerful shapeshifting spirit which could prove either malevolent or beneficent to humans. She could visit Ibra as a dream wrapped in a nightmare (or should we say "nightdonkey?") to wreak vengeance on his selfish egotism. Conversely she could offer Ibra the chance for redemption either through love or else a painful, mocking exorcism. Both of these functions would merit praise for Fary's mission.

Certainly Ibra sees in Fary only a demonic force come to persecute and humiliate him without cause. Yet his punishment pales in significance when compared with Fary's suffering. And Ibra certainly fails to become enlightened or redeemed. In fact, we can imagine an aging Ibra with an ever more imperious, swollen ego, milking sympathy for having been so abused by the deceitful creature he honored by marriage. Or he could boast of how he expelled the supranatural *djinn* who tricked and betrayed him. Both strategies would enable him to rationalize more ardently his own perfection and the utter failure of the female sex—human or *djinn*—to measure up to his standards.

If Fary were an avenging agent of spiritual justice, should not the villagers and certainly the narrator praise her virtuous mission? If she were a redemptive force, would she not deserve even greater credit? But she receives no accolades, gratitude, or even recognition from the commentators in the film. At worst, Fary is the forgotten victim; at best, the unacknowledged spiritual power. However, this is the nub of Wade's subtle strategy for cinematic edification of his audience. He opens a range of interpretative options for the eye of the beholder and posits evidence for them all. Those who espouse Ibra's male privilege can experience catharsis of righteous indignation over Fary's female deceit as well as triumph in Ibra's expulsion of Fary. Those who see the film as an implicitly feminist story can rejoice in the hagiographical images for Fary and can also undergo cathexis of rage at Ibra's "victory" and the misperceptions of Fary by the village women and the narrator. The film functions as a litmus test of each viewer's character and philosophy.

The two rhetorical questions posed by the narrator mimic oral performers and challenge the audience to stake out a position. The final question from the narrator—"Since Fary has time changed?"—forces the audience to consider how the story might apply to their own contemporary life.

This brings us back to the question of point of view in films using oral narration. Is *Fary l'Anesse* incoherent or improperly thought out because it expresses disparate interpretations of the events? Do the various points of view conflict, co-exist, or ultimately cohere? I think that Wade, following the tradition of oral tales, believes that the malleability of the material—which can be tailored, sheared, mended, and let out to suit the occasion, the audience, the teller, the musicians, the mood, and the need—is a virtue to be exploited. The oral materials have evolved through a long pedigree of performances, and their sustained value rests on both their ability to articulate the contradiction, paradox, and multiplicity of human experience and also to alter these themes as time and circumstance dictate. Both the pleasure and the edification derive from being able to turn the artistic kaleidoscope.

Since film, once finally edited, cannot spontaneously adapt to its audience in the fashion of a live performance, a director must build in ambiguity, complexity, and plasticity using the distinctive characteristics of the medium. One of the most important cinematic techniques for sustaining the hydra-headed orality is to capitalize on the ability of film to create multiple, colliding points of view through the intersection of visual and aural images with narration and dialogue. Wade has certainly done this in *Fary l'Anesse*.

However, this does not preclude him from expressing his own perspective. Wade sees this story as a feminist fable, indicting and illustrating the disastrous consequences of male control over women based on the assumption that men deserve and can expect women to both execute the bulk of domestic labor and also fulfill the ultimate male sexual fantasy—perfect physical beauty and perfect subordination. If men fail to possess this ideal, they can anticipate public shame and are allowed to wreak vengeance.

A scene near the beginning of *Fary l'Anesse* creates a deft African emblem of Wade's themes and film technique. Under a shade tree two men play checkers involving two kinds of competition: (1) winning the play pieces of the opponent; and (2) winning a debate in which one player will propose an idea in the form of a proverb or aphorism and the other will refute the first with his own counter assertion or fact. Each assertion is stated at the same time the player moves a game piece—the two functions merge. This is their dueling dialogue:

> *Player one:* That which is new is beautiful.
> *Player two:* Except a grave.
> *One:* The stronger in strength the more active one is.
> *Two:* Not watermelons.
> *One:* That which is beautiful is enjoyable.
> *Two:* She is a married one.
> *One:* One expects beauty from a woman.
> *Two:* And when she will have faded?
> *One:* Then look for a donkey that will carry your
> shame. Or exile yourself to the El Dorado. In the
> worse case, you will go crazy. What do you say?

As the men play, in the background and unnoticed by them, Fary walks into the village to encounter her fate. She will become part of a drama exemplifying the issues the players are debating, a drama which will galvanize divergent interpretations. Such a complex, subtle visualization is typical of Wade's cinematic artistry. The men articulate the conventional African male perspective on women while a silent, eloquent witness and victim passes by on the fringe of male power. Wade employs traditional oral techniques to imitate and clarify the inherited value system and mode of thought of his society, but he also drags these concepts into the domain of modern cinematic practice where he expects his audience to ponder and analyze what they see and to be moved by the powerful cinematic images. Like many of his distinguished African colleagues and filmmakers such as Sembène, Cissé, Sissoko, and Mambéty, who all espouse feminist ideals, Wade intends for his art to delight, instruct, and perhaps alter the reality outside the screen.

Works Cited

Cham, Mbye. "Ousmane Sembène and the Aesthetics of African Oral Traditions." *Africana Journal* 13 (1982): 24-40.

Diawara, Manthia. "Oral Literature and African Film: Narratology in *Wend Kuuni*." *Présence Africaine* 142 (1987): 36-49.

___. "Popular Culture and Oral Traditions in African Film." *Film Quarterly* 41, 3 (1988): 6-14. Rpt. in *African Experiences of Cinema*. Ed. Imruh Bakari and Mbye Cham. London: British Film Institute, 1996. 209-18.

Diop, Birago. *Tales of Amadou Koumba*. Trans. Dorothy S. Blair. Harlow, England: Longman, 1985.

Fary l'Anesse. Dir. Mansour Sora Wade. Les films du Baobab; M.P.A. Production. 1990.

Okpewho, Isidore. *African Oral Literature: Backgrounds, Character, and Continuity*. Bloomington and Indianapolis: Indiana University Press, 1992.

Pfaff, Françoise. *The Cinema of Ousmane Sembène*. Westport, CT: Greenwood Press, 1984.

Ukadike, N. Frank. *Black African Cinema*. Berkeley and Los Angeles: California University Press, 1994.

Through a Glass, Darkly: Paradoxes of Post-Colonial Fiction. The Case of Mohammed Berrada

Lucy Stone McNeece

> For now we see as through a glass, darkly;
> but then face to face: now I know in part;
> but then I shall know even as also I am known.
>
> - First Epistle of Paul to the Corinthians, xiii

One of the daunting challenges of literary and cultural study in the post-colonial era has been the question of readership and the difficulty of determining the criteria for interpreting texts emanating from extremely diverse cultural and historical contexts. Colonial discourses were condemned for their myopia, for systematically absorbing the cultural productions of subaltern groups into their existing paradigms. But the demise of those dominant paradigms has left a legacy of relativity that offers slight support for critical objectivity in a post-colonial context. Now that narrowly eurocentric models of interpretation have been found to be relative, i.e. ideologically bound to a certain conception of art and society that prevailed recently in the industrialized West, readers have been obliged to revise their aesthetic norms and to devise modes of reading more relevant to the cultural contexts of a diverse literary production. The tendency towards globalization, or the increasing uniformity of modes of informational and economic exchange, however, has lured readers into assuming that cultural alterity is more and more of an illusion, that the West's hegemony has simplified questions of reception by reducing the variables conditioning both the nature and the function of literature in disparate cultural spaces (e.g. Barber).

Yet we find everywhere evidence that the post-colonial era has brought the world of advanced technology face to face with radically different cultures, in which artistic forms have played and continue to play very different social and aesthetic roles. In North Africa, the disparity between the oral dialects and the written Arabic language, termed "disglossia," is compounded by the imposition of French language and discursive categories dating from the early 19th century. Interpolating between foreign language systems involves moving between different ways of organizing reality, and the failure to do so has contributed to the escalation of violence in social, political and religious spheres. In a contemporary context, the way one conceives of the relation of form to reference, like that of signs and images to things, is symptomatic of one's deepest convictions about the structure of reality and one's place in human history. The double face of the global present, a condition both postmodern and post-colonial, challenges everyone to reflect upon the contingency of their own beliefs but offers few clues for determining objective criteria.

Post-colonial readers are obliged at every moment to reframe their vision according to concrete historical circumstances that differ from their own. They must become "travelers" between contrasting semiological and ethical oceans; in other words, they must become translators adept at reading the foreign language of forms. But aesthetic judgment is complicated by the tendency of Western readers to assimilate even the most radically experimental writing to European categories of thought, as if post-colonial writers' long indenture to European culture made them incapable of any independent literary production.

As Edward Said has amply shown, one of the results of the prolonged separation of Muslim and Christian worlds has been a type of analogical thinking that evaluates Oriental cultures in terms of Western ideals, and in which projections of the "Orient" are used to resolve conflicts within the West.[1] Among the consequences of this for our understanding of foreign literary production has been a polarization of values arranged hierarchically, leading to a world view that places Europe and the West as heroic defenders of civilization against enemies of progress. The academic establishment in the West has also produced facile dichotomies such as the opposition of "science" to "art" or "history" to "myth," categories rooted in the ideology of recent Western industrial development, that have prevented readers' from seeing Arab cultures as different representational systems rather than merely aberrant versions of European civilization.

One underestimates the fact that differences in artistic practice and epistemology may be related to sources of social and political violence, or that hatred, often born of fear, erupts when people feel that their vision of the world is either distorted, disdained or silenced and can find no common code for dialogue. The problem of transcoding information across cultural boundaries is never a purely technical one: the fact that forms and signs operate differently in different cultural contexts has significant implications for what we might call an ethics of post-colonial representation, as much as "ethics" may seem to be an outdated concept in our postmodern culture. Yet this is precisely the terrain on which the debate must be waged: between the culture of postmodern relativism, in which history and tradition, as well as notions of "origin" and "identity," appear increasingly as so many images to be manipulated for consumption in an imaginary, supposedly neutral, space, on the one hand, and on the other, the cultures of peoples emerging from colonial domination for whom suppressed or dormant—sacred—traditions and transcendent values still inform and legitimize daily existence. On the one hand, a culture of arbitrary, deracinated forms, provoking a sense of freedom and/or a sense of confusion and loss; on the other, cultures attached, despite their modernity, to archaic forms and charged with redeeming centuries of dishonor; a weighty historical burden often tainted by oppressive religious and social practices. In both cases, modernity's contradictions have exacerbated the confusion between form and function, between structure and meaning. In the realm of literature, these oppositions have engendered a complex contestation of the terrain of narrative itself, inspiring post-colonial writers to experiment with multiple traditions.

Francophone texts from North Africa have always raised controversy because of the linguistic and cultural variety of the region and the degree to which language became a political tool before and after independence from France. The readership for writers in French involved a minority culture in the Maghreb, despite the dissemination of selected writers by the French press. The debate over the "viability" of francophone literatures of the Maghreb has largely dropped away, at least in Morocco and Tunisia, but the debate over legitimacy continues, particularly in relation to local readership, in part because of the degree of illiteracy. Increased translation of texts into other languages such as English has made writers schooled in Arabic more accessible to Western audiences, but questions surrounding the role of language and culture in regard to national consciousness persist, in spite of the growing number of transnational initiatives shaping the Maghreb's development. Francophone writing has emerged from its former ghetto as more Maghrebi writers (such as the Algerian Rachid Boudjedra and the Moroccans Leila Abouzeid and Mohammed Berrada, to name but a few) now write both in Arabic and French or English. Nonetheless, the politics of literacy in the Maghreb raises questions concerning the accessibility of these texts for the population at large, inviting accusations of hermeticism and elitism with respect to certain writers. Ironically, perhaps, many of these writers are attempting to expose hidden truths, to reveal suppressed or distorted features of their traditions that might aid the culture's passage to modernity.[2]

Reading texts from the Maghreb in any language involves a radical ethical gesture of translation, not merely because some texts have been translated from Arabic or Berber into French and then to English, but because of the myriad ways by which diverse cultural substrata filter into these texts, as does the mother-tongue, the oral dialect, into their use of French. In a recent talk on the occasion of the Salon du Livre in Paris, Mohammed Berrada spoke of this process of "transfiltration" in writing *The Game of Forgetting* (Le Jeu de l'oubli):

> En retournant en arriere pour m'inspirer de mon enfance passée a Fes . . . la langue maternelle . . . est venue me surprendre, jaillissant a mon insu du fin fond de la memoire et de l'inconscient pour s'imposer dans les dialogues et dans la description de certains lieux qui ne peut se passer de termes définis. ("Fes, la matrice")

> Looking back for inspiration to my childhood spent in Fez . . . the mother-tongue . . . came to surprise me,

gushing forth without my realizing it from the depths of
memory and the unconscious to impose itself upon
dialogs and upon the description of certain places that
cannot do without definite terms. (My translation)

The ethical implications for reading texts from the cultures of
North Africa are to be found in our readiness to interpret narrative
elements according to our own epistemological categories and aesthetic
models. These govern our "reading" of metaphors and symbols, but also
our cognitive relation to the structures of the text in general. For
example, Western prejudices lead us occasionally to interpret formal
linguistic "play" in writing as either literary embellishment, escapism, or
solipsism in contrast to realist narratives which are thought to allow the
expression of more substantive, objective information.

Most Maghrebis were educated to read classical French narratives
and quite naturally took these as models at first for their own writing.
While their appropriation of realist conventions was never "literal," and
in many cases involved a conscious choice, European readers and critics
were more at ease—if condescending—with writing produced by the
generation of Maghreb authors preceding independence, than with those
since, with the exception of a writer like Kateb Yacine, a highly poetic
novelist and playwright who early on received high esteem in France.[3]
Writers of recent generations have endured accusations of mimicry with
respect to European modernist and even postmodern literature.

Literary genetics, however, is not an exact science. European
Modernism, often described as a belated development of European
romanticism, reacted against the rising spirit of science and the collapse
of objective values by turning in upon the individual psyche, plumbing
its depths in search of some other form of transcendence. Modernism's
self-conscious experiments with form elevated formal preoccupations to
the status of a refinement, but they remained a sign of a cultural
dissociation. In the late 19th century art became a protected realm of
"action" for many writers who saw it as a refuge from a society in the
throes of rapid modernization. Modernism broke the models that had
thus far dominated European representation in the realms of literature
and the plastic arts, rejecting classical conventions and the serene distance
of the viewer-prince from his object to reveal darker areas of psychic life

such as dream and hallucination. This retreat into subjectivity often took the form of negativity and anguish at an increasingly depersonalized world. Modernism made art its sacred realm, its only salvation in a materialist world bent on technological progress.[4] One forgets the extent to which the inspiration for Modernist art came from outside of Europe, from different colonized regions of the globe: from Africa (Picasso), Tahiti (Gauguin), the Antilles (Breton), the Maghreb (Flaubert, Maupassant, Matisse, Klee), to name only a few of the sources of a movement usually referred to as "European."

Although Modernism became a harbinger of the new culture of Europe and America, entering into "mainstream" culture, its apparently categorical rejection of the rules of representation that had dominated since the Renaissance, as well as its relative inaccessibility to the masses, made its reign an ambiguous one. Seemingly detached from political and social developments, the ludic verbal experimentation and stark abstract forms typical of modernist art eventually came to signify for many a kind of elite dilletantism, despite architecture's claim to "functionalism," and became relegated to the realm of *decor*. It appeared to have little impact on human society except to confirm its distance from political and social life. For many, formalism became the cultural signifier of cultural decadence.[5]

Postmodernism, on the other hand, has made the play of forms the very rhetoric and syntax of its literary and artistic discourse, but these inflated forms are like shades or screens inscribed with citations written in any idiom, from any period. Detached from a psychological entity (the disappearing Subject) these forms operate as floating signifiers unattached to any context except that of the marketplace. We may term these virtual or "profane" forms, not because they are truly transgressive—that would require another type of involvement—but because they have been emptied of their human specificity, drained of any social function.

In North Africa, however, as in many other cultures with strong oral traditions, both narrative and graphic forms have had and continue to have a strong social dimension just as they have always had both a political and cognitive function, expressing ways of apprehending reality. Despite the influence of Western literary models, their literary and artistic forms need to be read as frames and patterns that translate principles of human existence. They must be read "semiotically" rather than "mimetically," as Westerners expect; not as analogs of reality but symbolically, as paradigms of social exchange. In order to understand literary texts from many African writers, even those who appear to be writing according to realist conventions, one must also recognize that the notion of "writing" itself may be broader than purely verbal art: visual patterns in decoration and designs on textiles or pottery, like those of oral narratives and poetry, speak to critical issues such as the individual's place in society, the relevance of the past, the importance of seeing through another's eyes, and even address metaphysical questions such as humanity's place in the cosmos. All these patterns constitute forms of "writing" that operate obliquely, by means of formal enigmas to be deciphered, rather than by anecdotal content or by illustration as in much representation in the West.

Signs are always both images and symbols in the Maghreb, part *signe* and part *scène*, combining symbolic and iconic elements that encode complex principles. This mixture of different signifying mechanisms has its corollary in the ideogram as Sergei Eisenstein theorized it in *Film Form* and *Film Sense*, where he intended to interfere with automatic or conventional responses to the content of the image. In Islamic cultures, the image of writing is present in the art of calligraphy which makes of writing a spectacle, whose dancing, soaring forms "reflect" the subject's spirit (*anima*) and desire. The variety of markings found on artisanal products as well as on women's hands and faces, speak of a love of signs that signify indirectly, suggestively, rather than pointing to explicit meanings. Patterns in decoration and architectural design also reflect this attachment to sensory forms that are rooted in communal history.

The paradox of the systems of representation developed on the northern and southern shores of the Mediterranean may be found in their apparent points of convergence which nonetheless may be tied to very diverse meanings. When Henri Matisse, visiting Morocco in 1911, was inspired by the use of colors and the two-dimensional designs found on tribal carpets, he responded immediately to their aesthetic qualities but was blind to their social function. Similarly, Paul Klee, visiting Tunisia in 1914, was captivated by the abstract play of color in architecture and design as "pure" form, divorced from its social logic. These artists experienced as "new" archaic designs which inspired their creation of a "modern" art, transporting forms without understanding their system of meanings . But they were enraptured by just that "lack"—by the absence of specific social reference—by the sense of mystery it conveyed. We might say that foreigners' fascination with the Islamic world, in the visual arts especially, is drawn to the effects of its own ignorance: forms perceived to be detached from social and ethical reference have enticed them toward visions of pure sensory delight and spiritual transcendence.[6]

These artists introduced a two-dimensional surface into a culture that had relished depth since the Renaissance, just as they introduced a conception of the human subject that differed from that of Western individualism by virtue of its being embedded in a complex fabric of social relations as part of an elaborate web of associations connecting the individual to place and to a collective history. Against both the classic and the romantic notions of individual subjectivity, these artists were excited by what they felt to be new sources of meaning and identity for a culture that they sensed to be on the brink of exhaustion. The divergent relation to signs, at the heart of the darkness that long separated Europe from the Maghreb, became for many artists the hope of liberation, of a cultural rebirth.

The writers coming of age at or after the time of the radical Moroccan review *Souffles*, founded in 1966 by Abdellatif Laâbi and shut down by the government in 1971, all have addressed questions of language and narrative form in their effort to explore the changing role of the writer in a Maghreb emerging into modernity.[7] Sounding the depths of personal memory and public history simultaneously, they sought to reinvent a effective literary poetics from the diverse traditions that form the substratum of their history. Taking different paths, they have produced a variety of texts, some working in several languages and genres, others moving through different phases associated with different genres or styles.[8] In fact, one of the characteristics of post-colonial generations is the degree to which their writing resists classification and moves across all types of categories. Neither Modernist—as much as their work may resemble modernist preoccupations with form—nor "postmodern," however much their work seems to celebrate hybridity, pastiche and citation—these writers' work demands another critical terminology.

The dichotomy between a mimetic use of form and one I have termed "semiotic" will necessarily have consequences for the way foreign readers interpret works produced by these Maghrebi authors. Many of the authors who came of age with independence must be read with a sort of "plural vision" because they deploy a strategy of multiple coding, manipulating several "languages" or cultural codes (in Barthes' sense of the term as well as that of information theory) simultaneously, playing one system of reference against another. They are intent upon reworking their own poetic traditions in a modern context. In so doing, they ask that readers revise their categories of experience as well as the values assigned to them. For example, does personal memory, for all its frailty, preclude an ability to bear witness to a collective history? Are the forms of parable and myth unreliable vehicles of historical truth? Is poetic discourse necessarily "unscientific"?

The Moroccan author, Mohammed Berrada, a literary critic and novelist who writes in Arabic as well as French, is an example of a writer working across linguistic conventions that are tied to different theories of representation.[9] *The Game of Forgetting*, published originally in Arabic in 1987 and then in French in 1993 as *Le Jeu de l'oubli*, provides an example of a post-colonial/postmodern text that is nonetheless replete with archaic elements, but at the level of style and structure rather than plot, and hence challenges readers to reflect upon the assumptions underlying their habits of reading. The text may be termed "meta-fictional" (an exemplary postmodern term) in that its discourse concerns the techniques of its own fictional narration. But we may also refer to it as a type of allegory or parable concerning the relation of writing to reality, as well as that of personal to historical truth. The story engages several entrenched beliefs about modern narrative, such as the presumed difference between "playful" verbal art and "serious" representation, fantasy and verisimilitude. It progressively dismantles the conventional opposition between subjective and objective realms of experience, revealing them to be inextricably bound, indeed, constitutive of one another.

First-person narration, like autobiography, traditionally afforded the European reader the voyeuristic pleasure of imaginative identification, proceeding through the evocation of psychological depth, of a recognizable character in a particular historical moment, conventions eschewed by most postmodern writers.[10] Whereas traditional or classical (realist) narrative posits the possibility of total disclosure of a content, as if writing could only be measured in relation to its capacity to reveal the truth, subjective or "autobiographical" types of narratives, even if "realist," are rarely considered "reliable" sources of information about society because of the danger that the narrating subject may retreat into solipsism and lose contact with the objective world. A notable modernist exception might be Faulkner's *The Sound and the Fury*, which uses several subjective consciousnesses to accuse social injustice in the American South.

Similarly, fiction has often been recognized for its escapist potential, its ability to liberate the reader from the constraints of historical responsibility, a liberation which, in some texts, turns back to reveal its own artifice after the provisional escape. As suggested earlier, fiction that departs from the conventions of realism is frequently accused of producing a distortion of reality that is socially innocent—impotent—that is, generally opposed both to historical reality and to scientific discourse.

In *The Game of Forgetting*, Berrada invites his readers to participate in a revision of such conventional assumptions, asking them to examine their habits of reading and even to question their conception of literature. The author plays with several of the devices of modernist and postmodernist European literary culture, as well as those of his own Moroccan and Arabic traditions to explore the differences in our relation to forms. Berrada's autobiographical chronicle works like a distorting mirror to explore the paradoxical intersection of the West's Godless, postmodern privileging of form over reality with the Andalusian mystic's ecstatic, arduous vision of form as a privileged epistemological instrument. Like a shifting prism, Berrada's incandescent prose moves back and forth between depth and surface, between oblique or "veiled" signification that must be decoded and a supposedly "transparent" use of signs characteristic of postmodern culture in the West.

To modify his readers' expectations of rationality and explicitness, Berrada exploits their desire for the illusion of vicarious "possession" of the novel's *diegesis*, its *peripetaie* and its characters, providing multiple narrators placed in a conflicted field of shifting frames rather than in an orderly hierarchy, thereby forcing readers constantly to adjust their perspective on any given character or event. The opening of the novel occurs in three abortive steps, destabilizing the familiar power relations between author, narrator and protagonist typical of a certain social structure that normally permits us to make comfortable distinctions between a real and a fictional world. Berrada's text announces itself with: "First project of a Beginning: 'From now on, I shall see her no more.'" A few lines later, he shifts from his mother's burial to a "Second Project of a Beginning," in which he tries to speak about his feelings for his mother, comparing her to a shady tree and claiming for her a distinct ontological status akin to that of the sacred. Finally, he announces, "The Beginning became thus: 'It is almost a blind alley, but actually it is a thoroughfare" after which he begins to describe a neighborhood in his native city of Fez (16). It is significant that he shares with the reader several possible beginnings, and that he decides upon one that takes us into the complex space of the old city of his childhood, for the meaning of his experience, identified with his mother, is traced embedded, inscribed—upon the stones, archways and alleys of the medina. His imaginary has the shape—as in a *geshtalt*—of the old city. He begins with a "blind alley" to suggest both the notion of impassible darkness, but admits that it is also a "thoroughfare," a way open to all. Here Berrada suggests that the entire structure of his "novelistic text" is one which flows simultaneously within the narrator's consciousness and through the public spaces of history.

The author plays upon expectations that a first-person narrative will, like conventional autobiography, proceed towards order, coherence and explicitness through the sifting of memory, even if forced to begin with disconnected fragments of experience. Berrada's text, however, operates inversely to undermine the presumed or desired cohesion of experience often seen as indispensable for the forging of identity, revealing experience to be a mercurial process of constant flux and reflux that foregrounds motifs and images rather than events and actions. Like a dream-text, the novel gradually yields its secrets, but they are not those we have come to expect: little by little the novel surrenders its "body," its "unconscious" sensory patterns, its fleeting memories and obsessions, the motifs which mobilize the protagonist's desire. The text's "revelations," however, in no way constitute a cognitive appropriation of the events or of the people in question. Rather, the narration confirms the opaque density of consciousness as an analogue of history, its structure as a palimpsest of its infinitely complex forms and movements.

A meditation on time, the novel is nonetheless orchestrated spatially, returning again and again to its "origins" in Fez, the city of labyrinthine passages, hidden gardens; the place of childhood, affectivity, and magic, but also the locus of pain, violence, and death. Fez, forgotten, becomes the point of eternal return for Hadi, the novel's protagonist. As in Proust, however, the act of "forgetting" is less a lapse or loss than an opening up of otherwise inaccessible regions of experience which surface in unexpected and often contradictory ways. It refers to a type of consciousness that is open to echoes and traces of the past, to fragments of dialogue, voices, glances and gestures never wholly tied to specific acts or events, so that they float, assuming more abstract significance as formative structures of consciousness. Forgetting is etymologically related to "fore" meaning "outside" (as in forum, forain, foreign) so that "forgetting" might be translated as "getting outside oneself" or even moving beyond a certain type of individualized consciousness.[11] Hadi, although accused of self-centeredness and hedonism in the novel, becomes in fact a kind of cipher for other voices who speak through him and converse across him, in contrast to the normally "egocentric" voice of Western autobiographical subjects.

The word "game" in English is linked to "gamble" and to "gambol" (a skipping or dancing movement of the legs). In contrast to memory, which may be considered constructive and rational, "forgetting" may be a kind of psychic "wager" in which the subject surrenders himself to a dance involving the dissemination of volatile associations of his imaginary and his unconscious. Games in Hadi's world may be either friendly or sinister, but they always involve a doubling, a re-presentation or recreation of the real. The novel's title, therefore, suggests a very serious reflexive operation which, paradoxically, aids the narrator in discovering the contradictory truths of his past and present. Yet Hadi's perceptions are always clouded, coming to him at moments between sleep and waking, and signaled in the text by enigmatic titles such as "clair-obscur."

The novel's title plays upon the contrast between ways of knowing that prevail in different cultures. The novel's insights, its historical truths, arrive indirectly through a play of shadowy motifs and figures discerned "darkly," that is, as enigmas which translate the events of time into plastic, spatial forms and sensory qualities. As an example, the question of revolution is never resolved by means of rational debate about what went wrong: its failure is suggested obliquely through references to a loosening, a blurring of perceptual distinctions and a yielding to desires for personal gain among the former radicals. This moral laxity, or exhaustion, is never treated ideologically, but is diffused into Hadi's impressions of his surroundings. Even the suggestion that in "modern" society, idleness is a concomitant of power, is conveyed obliquely, through sensory details instead of anecdotal information. But the "idleness" of corruption and that of Hadi's day-dreams are hardly the same. By refining conventional distinctions, the author manages to cut across stereotypical notions of virtue to demonstrate the deep distortions of cultural prejudice. Hadi's behavior—his indolence, his sensuality, his passivity and lack of worldly objectives—could suggest many of the negative stereotypes historically applied to Arabs by the Westerner.

In contrast to protagonists in most realist fiction, the boundaries of Hadi's subjectivity reveal themselves to be porous and fluid, so that his associations are inextricably woven into those of others who know things he cannot possibly have known. Yet the frames within frames in the novel make it difficult to determine logical sequences and the psychological "center" will not hold, so that Hadi's consciousness effectively merges with those of his family and his community. His relation to society, however, is neither simple nor conventional, as is his brother Taye's, a feverish revolutionary who succumbs to numbness and retreats from life upon viewing the "betrayal" of independence. Hadi's relation to his environment involves instead a constant sifting of material, a process of questioning, prodding, obsessing, dreaming and analyzing, which, instead of yielding a more explicit, thorough truth about particular events, makes him a kind of eclectic conscience of his generation, a person through and by whom others reveal their complexity. Gradually, latent figures and forms of desire emerge, not into daylight, but into a twilight awareness that resists logical analysis. The novel's motifs circulate in and out of times and spaces, slipping across categories to affirm unexpected associations, transforming themselves into different narrative elements. In fact, the conventional categories of narrative fiction, such as character, action, decor, dialogue and description, over which an omniscient narrator often presides, increasingly surrender to a kind of magnetic pressure, dissolving into elements which then seek out others across boundaries of empirical reality, as in a kaleidoscope, where fragments of color dissolve and reunite to form new entities. We might compare this process to the way a tapestry or carpet is made: the face shows a harmonious and "logical" design, while the back, however, reveals the myriad threads cris-crossing the carpet in an apparently arbitrary manner.

Like an arabesque, the novel's "action" moves between two primary symbolic spaces, that of the old city of Fez and the new city of Rabat. Replete with mysterious depths, echoes and age-old customs, and its sense of receding origins and archetypal figures, the old city incarnates a type of representation dramatically opposed to the supposedly "transparent logic" of European culture since the Renaissance. Dark and womb-like, Fez becomes a metaphor for the latent sensory text of Hadi's dreams, his imaginary or his unconscious, for his mother's diffuse but ubiquitous and resonant presence. He says to her, "I interrupt one conversation with you to resume it again, and then associations fall upon me all at once and leave me no opportunity to arrange my thoughts, to control my emotions, to distinguish times and places" (*The Game of Forgetting* 22).

A principle of plenitude and light in the darkness, Laila Ghalyya, as she is called, is the imaginative space in which the protagonist's affective and creative apprenticeship unfolds. "We lose nothing if we do not know our father. . . . As for the mother, she can't be invented: she creates us" (22) Obliged to move from Fez to the coast, to Rabat and Casablanca, in order to watch over her daughter, Hadi's mother also models the necessity of leaving home and all that is familiar (but unknown) in order to re-discover it. She symbolically authorizes Hadi's entry into the double world of writing and of deception, that deception that we might term "fiction," and to that which protects him from death as did Sherazade's stories. Illiterate, Hadi's mother asks him to write letters back to the family in Fez from their new home in Rabat. Writing henceforth becomes a means of contacting the past, the dead, the forgotten, an kind of archeological tool. Hadi's fist experience as a writer, however, demonstrates his cultural and ethical distance from Western conceptions of authorship: it is less a moment of personal expression than a moment that connects him to his society. His role is analogous to that of the medieval scribe or the *écrivain public* who transcribes, translates, the desires and hopes of the community at large.

Like a primal semiotic force, his mother resists the efforts of the protagonist and the narrators to bind the narrative into a predictable form, to establish rational connections among events. Because of her pervasive sensory presence, neither can Hadi's youthful energies be bound to a nationalist agenda or to any other ideological project. Instead, Hadi will become a "rebel without a cause" in a sense, given to transgressions of all types, shuttling between symbolic figures of father and mother, between forces of the law and the forces of the heart, never accepting any permanent identity or ideal but constantly seeking something beyond what he has at any moment. Writing, for Hadi, becomes paradoxically the vehicle of his unlearning, of the dismantling of false knowledge.

The very form of this novel models a mode of reflexive inquiry that treats all realities and ideals as transitory, susceptible to the indenture of particular interests. Contrary to the Enlightenment ideal of knowledge achieved by rational self-possession and material possession of the world, *The Game of Forgetting* suggests a wholly different orientation that echoes the tenets of Buddhism, but which has been present in Islam in Sufist doctrine.[12] For the initiate, the means to the absolute passes invariably through a letting go of worldly contingencies and desires, allowing reality to speak through the self, rather than supporting the self as a speaking, discursive subject, imposing desire upon reality. The Sufist conception of the subject is tied to a notion of time in which temporality is viewed less as a causal chain of logic (progress) than as a series of instances that are ultimately reversible, having seemingly random connections, like the back of our carpet, between a variety of different points. The novel's seemingly erratic temporal and spatial displacements, its resistance to closure, enact a kind of dispossession that corresponds to the Sufi mystic's paradoxical distance and attachment to life. Hadi's quest for knowledge of his past and himself, becomes less an "autobiographical" process of crystallizing his individual character than one that involves his imaginative participation—diffusion, dissemination—into his society as a whole.

In contrast to the Western tradition of the *bildungsroman* or the classical education novel, which create cognitive "thickness" out of the logical accumulation of events, Berrada's text becomes increasingly limpid, almost transparent, but less to suggest that all is vanity or artifice than to indicate that the truth is mercurial and always changing as it moves across the times and spaces of what I will call an "absent" history; Hadi's memory, if we may call it thus, is molten: it refuses to solidify into "meanings" that are valid for everyone or for all time. Yet this same novel that appears to abandon its original project of producing knowledge and coherence, also miraculously brings to light, as might the rubbing of a relief carved upon stone, or the peeling away of a palimpsest, the poetic, sensory motifs and desires that organized the imagination of an entire generation of Moroccans.

Berrada's *The Game of Forgetting* exemplifies the author's conception of writing as a profoundly social and ethical act, one which provides a means of entering history, not for personal distinction, nor mastery, but for discovery of the hidden forces that only occasionally rise to the surface of a culture's existence. *The Game of Forgetting* is less a tale of one individual's life during the tumultuous years leading to Moroccan independence and beyond, than it is a text which testifies to the critical function of the novel as an epistemological tool of liberation, a liberation from a dualistic conception of writing, as of thinking, imposed on the Maghreb for over a century, and one which still limits Western ideas about both narrative fiction and the complex reality of the Islamic world. Neither a mode of rationalistic disclosure, a mirror of human existence, nor an escapist retreat into subjectivity, Berrada's text celebrates narrative fiction as an experiment in forms that becomes an instrument for the awakening of a genuinely social, historical, and ethical consciousness.

Notes

1. In *Orientalism,* Said set forth his now famous theory of the West's creation of several "Orients" which reflect Western interests, desires and anxieties rather than providing any reliable vision of the Arab world.
2. Writers such as Abdelkebir Khatibi (Morocco) and Abdelwahab Meddeb (Tunisia) are among those most often accused of deliberate opacity. Both of these authors, however, are engaged in a serious "archeological" project with respect to cultural history. See especially Khatibi's *Maghreb pluriel*.

3. Jean Dejeux, in his *Littérature maghrébine de langue francaise: introduction générale aux textes et auteurs*, describes the evolution of these narratives in relation to their sociopolitical situation and suggests that stylistic experimentation reflects a certain stage of independence.

4. Interestingly, technology was often the handmaiden of Modernism, as railroad transportation and photography transformed perceptions of reality and hence painting, just as the radio and the airplane would inspire the Surrealists.

5. Nonetheless, Modernism's apparent remove from society and politics veiled a paradoxical complicity with imperialism. The "primitive" worlds of colonial occupation were equated with the dark urges of humanity or treated as effeminate sites of sensuality and indolence. For all its seemingly radical attack on bourgeois culture, modernism failed to revise the profound ideological structures that had legitimized imperialism.

6. I do not mean to suggest that artists and/or writers were "outside" or immune to the influence of imperialist ideology, and merely traveled to seek artistic inspiration. As Said has explained, France's political investments in the Orient filtered into all manner of activity, even into those seemingly divorced from questions of power.

7. The review published articles and creative work in literature and the plastic arts and cinema, from a wide range of national cultures. It's "project" included revising the forms of representation to correspond more closely to the suppressed traditions long under European domination. The review crystallized many writers' and artists' consciousness of the extent to which European ideology had become entrenched in the imaginations of the colonized.

8. Mohammed Dib began writing well before independence, moving from the realism of *La Grande Maison*, *L'Incendie*, and *Le Métier a tisser*, published in Paris by Seuil in the 50's, to the surrealism of *Qui se souvient de la mer*, in 1962, and then to short parables such as those of *La Nuit sauvage*, published by Albin Michel in 1995. In Dib's case, the choice of realism must be seen as part of a decolonization project in which he wished to present Algeria to the French in a non-folklorized manner. Winnifred Woodhull argues convincingly for revising attitudes towards realist aesthetics with respect to anti-imperialist struggles in a paper presented at the 20th century French Studies conference in Chapel Hill in March 1999.

9. Mohammed Berrada, born in 1938, initially wrote in Arabic, was a practicing critic and teacher of Arabic literature, and was also named president of the National Writer's Guild in Morocco.

10. I am referring to the type of autobiography that evolved in the West after the 18ᵗʰ century, guided by the concept of the Subject born with the Romantic movement. The concept of a pact with the reader was most recently theorized by Philippe LeJeune in his *Le pacte autobiographique*.

11. This and subsequent definitions taken from *Origins: An Etymological Dictionary*.

12. Sufism is a movement within Islam which has occasionally been treated as heretical with respect to orthodox Islam, but which seeks primarily an intense and authentic relation to the deity by means of self-renunciation.

Works Cited

Barber, Benjamin. "Culture McWorld contre démocratie: vers une société universelle de consommateurs." *Le Monde diplomatique* (August 1998): 14-5.

Berrada, Mohammed. *The Game of Forgetting*. 1987. Trans. Issa J. Boullata. Austin: University of Texas Press, 1996.

____. "Fes, la matrice." Salon du Livre. Paris, 4 June 1999.

Boudjedra, Rachid. *Peindre l'Orient*. Algiers: ZULMA, 1996.

Dejeux, Jean. *Littérature Maghrébine de langue française: Introduction aux textes et auteurs*. Sherbrooke: A. Naaman, 1980.

Dib, Mohammed. *La Grande Maison*. Paris: Editions du Seuil, 1952.

____. *L'Incendie*. Paris: Editions du Seuil, 1954.

____. *Le Métier à tisser*. Paris: Editions du Seuil, 1957.

____. *Qui se souvient de la mer*. Paris: Editions du Seuil, 1962.

____. *La Nuit sauvage*. Paris: Editions du Seuil, 1995.

Eisenstein, Sergei. *Film Sense*. Trans. Jay Leyda. New York: Harcourt, Brace & Jovanovitz, 1970.

____. *Film Form*. Trans. Jay Leyda. New York: Harcourt, Brace & Jovanovitz, 1975.

Khatibi, Abdelkebir: *Maghreb pluriel*. Paris: Denoel, 1983.

Lejeune, Philippe. *Le pacte autobiographique*. Paris: Seuil, 1975.

Origins: An Etymological Dictionary. New York: Rodale Press, 1975.

Said, Edward. *Orientalism*. New York: Random House (Vintage Books), 1979.

My Mother's Language

Abdellatif Laâbi
(Translated by *Victor Reinking* and *Edris Makward*)

I haven't seen my mother for twenty years
She let herself starve to death for me
They say she removed her scarf each morning
and struck the earth seven times
cursing heaven and the Tyrant
I was in the cave
where the convict reads in the shadows
and paints on the walls the bestiary of the future
I haven't seen my mother for 20 years
She left me a Chinese coffee set
whose cups break one by one
and I don't miss them they are so ugly
But I love the coffee in them all the more
Today, when I am alone
I borrow my mother's voice
or rather she speaks with my mouth
with her curses, her profanities and invectives
the rare rosary of her pet names
all the endangered species of her words
I have not seen my mother for twenty years
but I am the last man alive
who still speaks her language

Index

Ribeiro, Herlander 279, 280, 285, 286-287
Richard, Firmine 364
rites of passage 94, 213-214, 215
Rodrigues, Urbano 279, 281, 286, 290
Romanticism (European) 519
Rorty, Richard 467-468, 469
Roy, Arundarathi 56
Rwanada, genocide 59-60

Saber, Ahmed 1-7, 19
Sadat, Anwar 90, 94, 95
Said, Edward 82-83, 130, 466, 516
Said, Oumar Ibn 26
Salinger, Pierre 296
Samb-Makharam, Ababakar 502
Sample, Maxine 213-225
Sartre, Jean Paul 113
Scarlet Letter, The 254
Sebbagh, Mohamed 482-483
Sebei 305
Sebti, Youssef 124
Sefrioui, Ahmed 477
Sehimi, Abdeljabbar 482
Sembène, Ousmane 267, 272, 275, 321, 396, 502
Sénac, Jean 124
Sène, Fama Diagne 397
Senegal 267-276
Senegal, education in 395-396, 398
Senghor, Léopold Sédar 267, 268, 269, 272, 273
Sereer 272
Sereer (literature) 61
Serhane, Abdelhak 477
sexual harassment 152-153

sexuality, control of 67-68, 94, 109-110
sharia 91
Sheherazade 135-136
Shihab 455, 456
Shilluk 302
short story, development of (Morocco) 479-485
Sibari, Mohamed 477
Sierra Leone 226
Simone, Nina 327
slavery 20, 22, 26, 251, 274, 355, 363
Socé, Ousmane 275
Sofala 22
Sokoto Jihad 158
Soledad Brothers 327
Son of Scheherazade (film) 82
Songhay (empire) 23
Souag, Moha 477
Souffles 522
Sound and the Fury, The 524
Soundiata 319
South Africa 321
Southall, Aidan 5, 301-307
Souto, Myrielles 279
Sow, Charles Cheikh 270
Sow, Fatou Ndiaye 388, 399
Soyinka, Wole 56, 371-378
speech, and silence (voice) 251-255, 256-257, 263-264
Spenser, Edmund 494
Spleth, Janice 5, 78-87
Stevens, Wallace 186
Stewart, Maria W. 140
story-telling 135-138
stream of consciousness 483
Strong-Leek, Linda 140-156
Sufism 529
Susso, Al-Haji Papa 4

Contributors

Elisabeth Bekers is a research and teaching assistant in English literature at the University of Antwerp (Belgium). She is currently preparing a doctoral dissertation on continental and diasporic African creative writing on female genital excision and has published articles on Ngugi wa Thiong'o, Nawal El Saadawi and Alice Walker. She holds a Master of Arts in New Literatures in English from the University of Hull (England) and has been a Fulbright Scholar at Hollins University (United States). She is co-founder of the Postcolonial Literatures Research Group at the University of Antwerp and founding member of the Graduate Student Caucus of the African Literature Association (European liaison since 1998).

Taieb Belghazi is professor of English in the Department of English, University Mohamed V, Rabat and member of the Culture and Development Research Unit. He holds a PhD from the Center for Critical and Cultural Theory, Cardiff, Wales. He has a number of writings in the areas of cultural studies, African studies, and postcolonialism. His most recent publications are a co-edited book on the issue of globalization and a co-authored book on social movements in Morocco.

Elena Bertoncini is Professor of Swahili Language and Literature at the Oriental Institute (Istituto Universitario Orientale), Naples, Italy.

Abdelmouneim Bounou is a professor and head of the Department of Spanish at the University Sidi Mohamed Ben Abdellah, Dhar al-Mahraz campus in Fez, Morocco. He is the author of many scholarly articles published in Morocco and overseas on contemporary Spanish and Portuguese literatures, and of translations from these languages into French and Arabic. He contributed to the 2001 University of Fez volume

Les langues vivantes au service des causes nationales in honor of the late professor Mohammed Abu-Talib.

Fatima Bouzenirh was born in Kénitra, Morocco. She received her primary education at l'école des filles de notables, secondary education at lycée Abdelmalek Assaadi (Kénitra) and lycée Lalla Nouzha (Rabat), and her undergraduate education at Mohamed V University. She completed her graduate studies at the universities of Edinburgh and Sheffield (U.K.) with a Diploma in Stylistics and an MA in Modern African Literature (1973-1975) respectively. She also worked on methodology of writing at Laval University, Québec, Canada. First to introduce the course of African Literature at university level in the early 1970s in Morocco, she presently teaches in the Department of English and leads a seminar on African Women's Writings within the Women's Studies Unit at the graduate level of the Faculté des Lettres et des Sciences Humaines, Université Mohammed V, Rabat, Morocco.

Debra Boyd-Buggs is Associate Professor of French at Winston-Salem State University. She received Fulbright research and teaching awards to Senegal, Niger and Mali. Boyd-Buggs is the author of several articles on Islam in Senegalese fiction, the literary works of Niger, African-American culture and co-editor of a book, *Camel Tracks: Critical Perspectives on Sahelian Literatures*. Dr. Boyd-Buggs is also the producer of a documentary film series about artistic creation in the Sahel.

Pathé Diagne is a linguist and historian of civilizations with a strong interdisciplinary background acquired at the Universities of Dakar in Sengal and the Sorbonne in Paris. He is the co-author with David Dalby of the introductory linguistic chapter of Volume II of *The General History of Africa* published by UNESCO. He is the author of many books on African history, politics and linguistics and has taught at the University of Dakar and at a number of universities in the United States.

Boubacar Boris Diop, born in Dakar, Senegal in 1946, first taught literature and philosophy before devoting most of his time to his work as a writer, journalist and film script writer. His innovative published fiction include *Le temps de Tamango* (1981), *Les tambours de la mémoire* (1990), *Les traces de la meute* (1993), and *Le cavalier et son ombre* (1998). After making a name for himself among the finest Francophone creative writers, and winning several national and international literary accolades, he published—in 2001—a full length novel in his native Wolof: *Doomi golo* (The Ape's Offspring).

Christine Drake is a professor of geography at Old Dominion University in Norfolk, Virginia, with interests in cultural and political geography, world resources, development issues, Africa, and Asia. She has a BA (first class honors) from Oxford University and a PhD from Rutgers. She has written a number of books and numerous articles and book chapters on Indonesia (where she lived for five years in the 1970s and returned on a Fulbright in 1996), Oman, water and other resources, development issues, women in the developing world, etc. She has also published two sets of slides on Cote d'Ivoire and Tanzania. She has been awarded four grants from the National Endowment for the Humanities to run summer institutes for high school French teachers on the literature and geography of the Francophone world, with a focus on West Africa, the latest two including an overseas component in Senegal. She was awarded a university professorship in 1998 and an Outstanding Faculty Award from the State Council for Higher Education in Virginia in 1999.

Jilali El Koudia is Professor of English and American literature at the University Sidi Mohamed Ben Abdellah, Fès. A translator and writer of fiction in Arabic and English, he is a member of the Union of Moroccan Writers and winner of First Prize of the British Council for Moroccan Writers in English 2000 (Fiction Category). He has translated Wolfgang Iser's *The Act of Reading* and *The Fictive and the Imaginary* and Robert Holub's *Reception Theory* into Arabic, and the volume *Moroccan Short Stories* into English. He has also published his own collection, *Stories Under the Sun*, in English.

John Erickson is Professor of French and Francophone Studies at the University of Kentucky. He is founder and editor of *L'Esprit Créateur*. He has co-edited three volumes of critical essays and published three books: *Nommo: African Fiction in French*; *Dada: Performance, Poetry and Art*; and *Islam and Postcolonial Literature*. He has also published numerous essays on comparative literature, modern European literature, and "Third-World" writing.

Gudrun M. Grabher, Professor and Chair of the American Studies Department at the University of Innsbruck, Austria, specializes in the fields of American poetry, literature and philosophy, literature and the other arts, women's studies, and cultural anthropology. He has published two books and is editor of several volumes as well as author of various articles.

Seth Graebner is an assistant professor in Romance Languages and in International and Area Studies at Washington University in St. Louis. His thesis was titled *Out of Time, Out of Place: History, Nostalgia, and the City in French and Algerian Literature since 1830*; his current project, *Modernity in the Shadow of the Minaret: Paris and the Mediterranean City, 1830-1900*, examines the development of *modernité* in urban observation in Paris, Cairo, and Alexandria.

Claire Griffiths is a lecturer in the Department of French at the University of Hull, U.K. She is a member of research groups working on Francophone African Studies in the U.K., Africa and the U.S.A. She has published a number of studies on social development issues in relation to women and development in Morocco, Gabon and Senegal. She is currently writing a book on women's lives in colonial French Africa, and is also working on a monograph on gender identity as manifested in contemporary sociological and literary accounts of women's lives in Francophone Africa.

Jane Hale is associate professor of French and Comparative Literature at Brandeis University. Previous publications include *The Broken Window: Beckett's Dramatic Perspective* (Purdue University Press, 1987) and *The Lyric Encyclopedia of Raymond Queneau* (University of Michigan Press, 1989). She was a Fulbright Scholar in Senegal in 1994.

Donald L. Hoffman is Professor of English at Northeastern Illinois University. He is a Medievalist with a special interest in Arthurian literature and he has published widely in this area. He edited an anthology of essays titled *King Arthur in Popular Culture* (co-edited with Elizabeth Sklar, 2002). He is just beginning to explore his new interest in Caribbean and African literatures.

Eileen M. Ketchun completed her doctorate in French literature at the University of Wisconsin-Madison and is pursuing an interest in the image of women in French literature, particularly Francophone Sub-Saharan African literature. She received both her BA and MA in French from the University of Notre Dame and, after a year teaching English in France, she began her graduate degree at UW-Madison in 1995.

Touria Khannous is a doctoral student in English at Brown University. Her primary interests are African modernism, African women's literature and African cinema. She is currently working on her dissertation in which she examines the way African women writers deploy the techniques of literary modernism to critique both African nationalism and European colonialism.

Ambroise Kom is a graduate of the universities of Yaounde, Pau and the Sorbonne. He has taught African, African American and Caribbean literatures in the United States, Canada, Morocco and Cameroon. As a visiting professor, he has taught in Germany, France, and South Africa. He is the editor of *Présence Francophone*. Presently he is Professor and Eleanor Howard O'Leary Chair in Francophone Studies at the College of the Holy Cross, Worcester, Massachusetts. He is the author of *Le Harlem de Chester Himes* (1978), *George Lamming et le destin des Caraïbes* (1986), *Le Cas Chester Himes* (1994), and *La Malédiction francophone* (2000). He has also edited several volumes including the *Dictionnaire des oeuvres littéraires de langue française ed Afrique au sud du Sahara* (Volume 1, 1983; Volume 2, 1996).

Abdellatif Laâbi, born in Fez, Morocco in 1942, taught French and literature in his native Morocco until his imprisonment by the late King Hassan II for violation of the laws governing the freedom of expression (1972-1981). Laâbi founded the avant-garde literary review *Souffles* in 1966 carrying articles both in French and in English. He is also founder of the Arabic language journal, *Anfas*. He is a prolific poet, passionately committed to freedom and justice for all, and has won many literary accolades, overseas first, and now at home as well. He has been living in Paris since his release from prison, but travels frequently to his native Morocco, and overseas as well. His published works include *L'Oeil et la Nuit* (1969), *Le Règne de barbarie* (1980), *Le Chemin des ordalies* (1982), *Le Spleen de Casablanca* (1996), and *Le fond de la jarre* (2002). A selection of Laâbi's poetry, *The World's Embrace: Selected Poems*, will be published in 2003 by City Lights Publishers.

Hasna Lebbady is a Moroccan professor of English literature at Mohammed V University in Rabat, Morocco. She has taught language courses as well as numerous courses on American, British and other literatures in English. Her areas of interest include women's studies, cultural studies, and, contemporary theory in general.

Bernth Lindfors, a professor of English and African Literatures at the University of Texas at Austin, has written and edited a number of books, including *Africans on Stage: Studies in Ethnological Show Business* (1999) and *Black African Literature in English, 1992-1996* (2000). He is the founding editor of *Research in African Literatures*.

Sharifa Saa-Atma Ma'at, PhD, is associate professor at Georgia Perimeter College, Clarkston, Georgia, and teaches English, African American Literature, and Radio and Television Studies. She is included in *Research and Development in Africa, African American Women's Spirituality*, and has written numerous articles on the African Diaspora. She is producer of the radio program *The African Experience Worldwide* in Atlanta. She is currently working on a development project for Africa.

Suzanne H. MacRae teaches a variety of English world literature and humanities courses at the University of Arkansas including African film and African literature. Her research of African subjects has appeared in such publications as *Research in African Literatures, African-American Review, Worldview, African Arts, Matatu*, and *African Cinema: Feminist and Post-Colonial Readings*. She is currently preparing an edited book of essays on Djibril Diop Mambety.

Florence Martin is an Associate Professor of French at Goucher College, Baltimore, Maryland. Her teaching and research interests include French and francophone cinema, French 20th century literature, francophone literature (West African and Antillean in particular), post-colonial literature, the literature and cultural studies of the African diaspora. Her study, *Bessie Smith* (Paris: Éditions du Limon, 1994; Marseille: Éditions Parenthèses 1996), received the Prix Charles Delauney for the best publication in jazz studies in France in 1994. Her most recent project, *Traces-mémoires et marronnages: de la Guyane au Tout-monde*, written in collaboration with Dr. Isabelle Favre (University of Nevada), is under review. Her publications on music, cinema, literature, have appeared in various journals in the U.S. and elsewhere (e.g. *French Review, Études Francophones, PSA News, Journal of American Music, Europe, Atlantiques, Les Cahiers du Jazz, Cahiers de Recherche de CORHUM, Le Monde*). She is currently working on a book-length study of voice and its various soundings from an interdisciplinary perspective, with special attention to francophone cinema and literature.

Amadou Mahtar M'Bow is the former Director-General of UNESCO (1974-87). He has also twice been a cabinet minister in his native country of Senegal, first as a Minister of Education, Culture, Youth and Sports in the young autonomous *Loi-Cadre* government (1957-58) and as Minister of National Education with Mamadou Dia as Prime Minister (1966-68). He was a staunch student activist in France after his demobilization there at the end of World War II, and then taught history in various establishments in Mauritania and Senegal. He is a member of the Academies of the Kingdom of Morocco, of Athens (Greece) and of Islamic Civilization of Amman (Jordan). He is the author of many articles and books on history, culture and communication including *Le temps des Peuples* (1982) and *Where the Future Begins* (1982).

Lucy Stone McNeece is Associate Professor of French and Francophone Studies at the University of Connecticut where she is also Chair of the Program in Comparative Literary and Cultural Studies. She teaches courses in French literature and film, Caribbean, West African and Magrebian literatures and film, cultural theory, postcolonial theory, women's literature and film and comparative literatures of the developing world. In the realm of African studies, she has published on Sony Lab'ou Tansi and other West African authors, as well as a large number of North African writers (Khatibi, Berrada, Ben Jelloun, Djebar, Mokaddem, Sebbar, Meddeb, etc.). She is currently working on a study of the translation of form across cultural boundaries in writers of the Franco-Arab world.

Anita Mooijman has an MA in English from Leiden University in The Netherlands. Her thesis was on folklore in the work of Zora Neale Hurston and Alice Walker. After working as a translator for a year, she got a PhD in African American Studies from Temple University in Philadelphia. She did her dissertation research in Niger (West Africa). Her dissertation is entitled *Mata masu dubara da asiri suke daga: The Roles of Women and Gender Complementarity in Hausa Folktales* (UMI, March 1999). Dr. Mooijman has presented papers on a number of topics at Temple University, Rutgers University, Leiden University, and at the ALA conference in Morocco (1999). Her publications include articles on Carter G. Woodson and Africalogy (1998); Afrocentricity and the Literary Tradition (2001); The Roles of Women in Hausa Folktales (2000), The Roles of Women in African Epics, and a Dutch translation of the Mwindo Epic with an introduction (both forthcoming). She has taught at Temple University and at Leiden University. She currently teaches at The University of Professional Education in The Hague, The

Netherlands. Her research interests include African and African American literature, oral literature and culture; multicultural issues; women; and curriculum development.

Sally-Ann Murray is an award-winning poet and teacher who lectures in the Programme of English, and in the Programme of Media & Communication at the Durban campus of the Univesity of Natal, South Africa. Her research actively seeks out connections between these two disciplines. Her publications include articles and chapters on African and South African poets, novelists, and consumer culture. She has also edited two poetry anthologies, and an edition of Olive Schreiner's novella *Trooper Peter Halket of Mashonaland*.

Dayna Oscherwitz received her Ph.D. in French and Francophone Studies from the University of Texas at Austin in August of 2001. Her dissertation, "Representing the Nation: Cinema, Literature and the Struggle for National Identity in Late Twentieth-Century France" is a cultural exploration of the discourse on national identity in contemporary France. She is currently working on an expanded, book-length manuscript entitled *Emerging Cultures: Nationality, Post-coloniality, and Collective Identity in Contemporary France* which expands her dissertation research and includes an analysis of the relationship between metropolitan discourses of national identity and the Créolité movement in the Francophone Antilles. Dayna has published articles on Patrick Chamoiseau, Gisèle Pineau, Calixthe Beyala and Paul Smäil, among others. In the Fall of 2002, she joined the Department of Foreign Languages and Linguistics at Southern Methodist University in Dallas, as Assistant Professor of French.

Pushpa Naidu Parekh is currently an Associate Professor in the English Department, Spelman College. She teaches Post-colonial Women's Literature, Women in Non-western Literatures, Contemporary African Literature, African Diaspora and the World, Immigrant Women's Literature, and Victorian and Modern British Literature. She has published several essay chapters and articles on post-colonial writers. She is co-editor of the reference book, *Postcolonial African Writers: A Bio-Bibliographical Critical Sourcebook* (Greenwood Press, 1998) and is the author of a book-length critical study of selected nineteenth and twentieth-century British poets, *Response to Failure* (Peter Lang, 1998).

Patricia Reynaud is a professor at Miami University in Ohio. Dr. Reynaud's interests include the sociology of culture and theories of exclusion and social domination, Maghrebine/Muslim perspectives and gender identity, the intersection between literature and economics/political ideology, and medieval heresies, in particular Catharism. Her book project "La voie mystique au quotidien" explores how the transgressive views of the mystics can be used to expand academic boundaries and how their spirituality can become a model for individual transformation.

Maxine Sample, a former Fulbright Scholar to Kenya (1995-6), is an associate professor of English at Virginia State University, where she teaches African American and African literature and composition. She is a contributor to *African American Authors, 1745-1945* and *Who's Who in Contemporary Women's Writing* and has published articles on African and African American writers in such publications as *The Explicator*, *Modern Fiction Studies*, and *Studies in Short Fiction*. She is currently editing a collection of critical essays on South African writer Bessie Head and studying the works of Kenyan dramatist Francis Imbuga.

Aidan Southall is emeritus professor of Anthropology at the University of Wisconsin-Madison, now living in France. A research pioneer and leading authority on African urbanism, his work with the Alur of Uganda, published as *Alur Society*, is a theoretical starting place for all scholars dealing with the evolution of the centralization of authority. His more recent volume, *The City in Time and Space, from Birth to Apocalypse*, was published by Cambridge University Press (2000).

Janice Spleth is professor of French and African Literature in the Department of Foreign Languages at West Virginia University where she teaches courses on French and Francophone literature. In addition to having published numerous articles on African writers, she is one of the co-editors of *Interdisciplinary Dimensions of African Literature*, the author of *Léopold Sédar Senghor*, and the editor of *Critical Perspectives on Léopold Sédar Senghor*. She is also Assistant Editor for the *West Virginia University Philological Papers*.

Linda Strong-Leek is an Associate Professor of English at Florida International University. A Fulbright Scholar, Dr. Leek has published articles on African women writers, and her monograph, *Excising the Spirit An Analysis of Female Circumcision in the Novels of Flora Nwapa, Ngugi wa*

Thiong'o, and Alice Walker, is under contract with Africa World Press and scheduled for publication in the Fall of 2001. She is also the co-editor with Adele Newson of a volume of essays by Caribbean women writers entitled, *Winds of Change: The Transforming Voices of Caribbean Women Writers and Scholars.*

H.P. (Hendrik Petrus) van Coller was educated at the Witwatersrand University (Johannesburg), Rand Afrikaans University (where he completed his thesis) and the State University of Utrecht where he completed his doctoral studies in theoretical and comparative literature under Douwe Fokkema. He has lectured at various South African and European universities and read papers at various international conferences. At present he is "professor with special merit" and head of the Department of Afrikaans and Dutch, and Modern European Languages at the University of the Free State, Bloemfontein. He has published numerous articles and authored, co-authored and edited eleven books. Prof Van Coller was the editor of *Perspektief en profiel* (*Perspective and Profile*) an Afrikaans literary history published in two parts. In 2000 he was awarded the Gustav Preller Prize for Literary Theory and Literary Criticism by the South African Academy for Arts and Sciences with.

The Editors

Edris Makward is an emeritus professor of African and French Literature at University of Wisconsin-Madison. He is the author of *Contemporary African Literature* (1972) and of many articles and book chapters on African literature and culture. He is also co-editor of *The Growth of African Literature* (Africa World Press, 1998), past president of the West African Research Association (WARA), the African Studies Association (ASA) and the African Literature Association (ALA), and co-convener of two ALA annual conventions in Africa (Dakar, Senegal in 1989 and Fez, Morocco in 1999). He is currently the Acting Vice-Chancellor of the newly established University of the Gambia, his country of birth.

Mark L. Lilleleht is currently completing his dissertation in the Department of African Languages and Literature at the University of Wisconsin-Madison.

Ahmed Saber holds a PhD in comparative literature from the University of Georgia (1985) and a MA (1976) in African-American Studies from Atlanta University. He is currently Professor of Comparative and African and African-American literatures at Sidi Mohamed Ben Abdellah University, Department of English, Faculty of Letters, Dhar Almahraz, Fès, Morocco. Many of his articles on African, African-American literature, education, comparative literature, and the English language have appeared in national and international journals and periodicals. A collection of poems, entitled *Voices From Underground*, is ready for publication. He is a member of several scholarly organizations and associations and a member of the ALA since 1982.